ENCYCLOPEDIA OF AMERICAN LAW AND CRIMINAL JUSTICE

REVISED EDITION

Encyclopedia of American Law and Criminal Justice

Revised Edition

Volume I

David Schultz

Facts On File
An Infobase Learning Company

Encyclopedia of American Law and Criminal Justice, Revised Edition

For information contact:

Facts On File, Inc.
An imprint of Infobase Learning
132 West 31st Street
New York NY 10001

Library of Congress Cataloging-in-Publication Data

Encyclopedia of American law and criminal justice / [edited by] David Schultz. — Rev. ed.
p. cm.
Rev. ed. of: The encyclopedia of American law.
Includes bibliographical references and index.
ISBN 978-0-8160-8145-5 (alk. paper)
1. Law—United States—Encyclopedias. 2. Criminal justice, Administration of—United States—Encyclopedias. I. Schultz, David A. (David Andrew), 1958–II. Encyclopedia of American law.
KF154.B528 2012
349.7303–dc22 2011012487

Facts On File books are available at special discounts when purchased in bulk quantities for businesses, associations, institutions, or sales promotions. Please call our Special Sales Department in New York at (212) 967-8800 or (800) 322-8755

You can find Facts On File on the World Wide Web at http://www.infobaselearning.com

Text design by Cathy Rincon
Composition by Hermitage Publishing Services
Cover printed by Yurchak Printing, Landisville, Pa.
Book printed and bound by Yurchak Printing, Landisville, Pa.
Date printed: March 2012

Printed in the United States of America

10 9 8 7 6 5 4 3 2 1

This book is printed on acid-free paper.

For Dan Kramer, a friend and scholar

CONTENTS

LIST OF ENTRIES

PREFACE

Law and crime fascinate us. From a pop culture perspective, the legal or criminal justice system dominates movies, television shows, books, plays, and a host of other mass-culture venues. Crime dramas have been a staple of television since its early days, and tales about trials and breaking the law go at least as far back in Western culture to Socrates and Antigone, both of whom broke the law and faced accusations that forced them to defend themselves. "Murder most foul," declared in Shakespeare's *Hamlet,* is a staple of almost every crime novel, and the phrase "if it bleeds it leads," in describing what the news reports, captures the powerful and continuing fascination that crime holds for many.

Stories of great crimes, criminals, and trials are woven into the fabric of American culture. The Salem Witch Trials, the Scopes Trial, Sam Sheppard (the inspiration for the 1960s television show and 1990s movie *The Fugitive*), Charles Manson, O. J. Simpson, and even questions pondering the fictional question "Who shot JR?" (from the 1980s television series *Dallas*) all are historical points of reference in the United States. Additionally, great lawyers, such as Clarence Darrow and F. Lee Bailey, are names ingrained in our psyche. More recently, the NBC drama *Law and Order* etched crime dramas into the public's mind by telling viewers: "In the criminal justice system the people are represented by two separate, yet equally important groups: the police who investigate crime and the district attorneys who prosecute the offenders. These are their stories." *NCIS, Dragnet,* and *Hawaii Five-O* are simply other examples of police dramas that have dominated television. Crime, law, and order are compelling subjects.

But law and crime are more than fiction; for Americans they are reality. Every year, millions of crimes are committed; victims are violated; and the accused are acquitted, found guilty, and punished. Police really do read Miranda rights; prisons exist, and guilty parties are condemned to death, sometimes falsely, though occasionally exonerated with DNA evidence. CSI (crime scene investigation) is more than the subject of a television show; it is something that affects actual police investigations and juror deliberations. The criminal justice system is a reality with real stories.

Law and crime are obviously connected. Laws are rules laid down to regulate conduct; breaking them often constitutes a crime. However, the law often tells us what we cannot do—such as steal or kill—but it also enables action. It permits the selling of homes, marriage, adoption, reproductive rights, and a host of other activities. Without the law, society might not be possible, and most human behavior would grind to a halt, lacking the rules needed to regulate behavior.

Despite this real and fictional omnipresence of the law and crime, most people are confused and bewildered by the law. Much like the character Joseph K. in Franz Kafka's novel *The Trial,* many people are confused when it comes to understanding law, crime, and the criminal justice system. Sorting out fact from fiction or myth from reality when it comes to the law can be confusing. Many do not understand their rights when arrested, the stages in a criminal proceeding, or what the Constitution says about the law.

Because of this intense interest and importance that the law and crime have in the lives of Americans, *Encyclopedia of American Law and Criminal Justice* was written for both students and the general public. It explains many critical questions about the law and criminal justice. It provides a readable overview of many of the important concepts, cases, persons, and events that have shaped and defined American law. It blends discussion of criminal justice issues with explanations of other aspects of the legal process that affect everyday lives. The encyclopedia essays, written by leading scholars from around the world, provide clear explanations and overviews to many of the most basic and often times advanced questions about law and crime.

Readers will find this encyclopedia a useful guide on many grounds. It provides answers to basic questions about what police do or what rights those accused of crimes have. It also provides historical essays on changes in the law and the criminal justice system and explores issues such as why crime exists or what punishment is supposed to do. *Encyclopedia of American Law and Criminal Justice* is a reference book and a research tool, as well a collection of articles that are educational and enjoyable to read.

David Schultz
Hamline University
Saint Paul, Minnesota
dschultz@hamline.edu

ACKNOWLEDGMENTS

While I am the editor of *Encyclopedia of American Law and Criminal Justice,* it is more than simply the product of one person. Approximately 200 individuals, including academics, lawyers, and those from government, private industry, and the nonprofit community, have contributed to it. They have lent their expertise to this project, and I thank them all. Truly, these individuals made this project possible, and while I thank all of them for their contributions, I also assume any responsibility if I have failed to give them the credit they are due.

CONTRIBUTORS

Rafael Abramovitz, Breck School, Minneapolis, Minnesota

Ryan Adoor, Westminister College

Mark Allan, RTI International, LGP3—Iraq

Jennifer Allison, Pepperdine University School of Law

Bruce E. Altschuler, State University of New York, Oswego

Deborah Anthony, University of Illinois at Springfield

Stephanie Arrowsmith, Monmouth College

Hugo Ascencio, Auburn University

Mary Welek Atwell, Radford University

Bruce E. Auerbach, Albright College

Gayle Avant, Baylor University

Gordon A. Babst, Chapman University

Thomas E. Baker, University of Scranton

William D. Baker, Arkansas School for Mathematics and Science

Jeremy Ball, Boise State University

Kyle Barbieri, Georgia Perimeter College

Kathleen Barrett, Georgia State University

Michael S. Barton, SUNY Albany

Nancy Winemiller Basinger, University of Georgia

Jesse Beal, Ball State University

Stephen F. Befort, University of Minnesota Law School

Bernard W. Bell, Rutgers Law School, Newark

Sara C. Benesh, University of Wisconsin, Milwaukee

Danton Asher Berube, Yale University

Bradley J. Best, Austin Peay State University

Bruce Bikle, California State University at Sacramento

James M. Binnall, University of California at Irvine

Ryan C. Black, Michigan State University

Michael P. Bobic, West Virginia Wesleyan College

Winston D. Boswell, Boulder County Sheriff Office, Colorado

Lyn Boswell, University of Colorado School of Public Affairs, Denver, Colorado

Michael W. Bowers, University of Nevada, Las Vegas

Scott R. Bowman, California State University, Los Angeles

William E. Brigman, University of Houston–Downtown

Avi Brisman, Emory University

OWEN G. BURNETT. OFFICE OF ATTORNEY GENERAL, State of Tennessee (13th Judicial District)

JAMES V. CALVI, West Texas A&M University

KIMBERLEE CANDELA, California State University, Chico

LORETTA CAPEHEART, Northeastern Illinois University

ROKKI KNEE CARR, Attorney, Stone Ridge, New York

DIANA CARREON, Texas A&M International University

NATHANAEL CAUSEY, United States Military Academy, West Point, New York

JAMES N. G. CAUTHEN, City University of New York

H. LEE CHEEK, Jr., Gainsville State College

HERB E. CIHAK, Pepperdine University

DOUGLAS CLOUATRE, Kennesaw State University

CAROLYN E. COCCA, State University of New York, College at Old Westbury

SUSAN COLEMAN, West Texas A&M University

MEGAN COLLINS, University of Maryland

PETER A. COLLINS, Washington State University

TODD COLLINS, Western Carolina University

VICTORIA COLLINS, Old Dominion University

MARIE COMISKEY, University of Michigan

MICHAEL COMINSKEY, Pennsylvania State University

SCOTT COMPARATO, Southern Illinois University at Carbondale

WILLIAM H. COOGAN, University of Southern Maine

JOCELYN CUFFEE, Western New England College of Law

QUINTIN HOWARD CUSHNER, University of Arizona

ROGER J. CUSICK, Morehouse College

PETER J. DAHL, Northern Arizona University

JOHN KELLY DAMICO, Georgia Perimeter College

DIANA DAVINO, Fairleigh Dickinson University

CAROL A. DAY, District Attorney's Office, Eau Claire County, Wisconsin

MATTHEW DEGARMO, Washington State University

JOANNA DESMITH, Ball State University

MATTHEW DOLLIVER, Northeastern University

JESSICA DREWITZ, Pepperdine University

AMANDA DROST, Western Kentucky University

KATY ELDERS, Western Carolina University

JAMES W. ELY, Jr., Vanderbilt University Law School

JEDON EMENHISER, Humboldt State University

FRANCENE M. ENGEL, University of Michigan

BEN EPSTEIN, CUNY Graduate Center

CAROLINE ETTINGER, Macalester College

MARIE FAILINGER, Hamline University, School of Law

STEFANO FAIT, Fondazione Museo Storico del Trentino, Trento, Italy

ZOLTÁN LEVENTE FEJES, School of Criminal Justice, Michigan State University

NEIL FERRERA, California State University, Chico

JAMES DANIEL FISHER, Edinboro University of Pennsylvania

JAMES C. FOSTER, Oregon State University

MICHELLE L. FOSTER, Kent State University

RICHARD S. FRASE, University of Minnesota, School of Law

Mark A. Fulks, Tennessee State University

Raquel J. Gabriel, City University of New York School of Law

Mary Kathleen Geary, Northwestern University

Bobbi Gentry, City University of New York Graduate Center

Tobias Gibson, Westminister College

Clark Andrew Giles

Collin Glennon, University of Tennessee

J. David Golub, Touro College, New York Institute of Technology, Kean College of New Jersey

Susan F. Goodman, California State University, Chico

Karen Gottlieb, BioLaw, Nederland, Colorado

Stephen E. Gottlieb, Albany Law School

Jon Gould, George Mason University

Stuart P. Green, Louisiana State University

Emily Greenelsh, Western Carolina University

Ellen Grigsby, University of New Mexico

Kevin E. Grisham, California State University, San Bernardino

Martin Gruberg, University of Wisconsin at Oshkosh

Hans J. Hacker, University of Maryland

Michael Hannon, Duke University Law Library

Richard J. Hardy, Western Illinois University

Robin Harper, York College

Roger Hartley, University of Arizona

Frederick Hawley, Western Carolina University

Sharma Hemant University of Tennessee, Knoxville

Craig Hemmens Boise State University

Jim Herring, United States Military Academy, West Point

Rhys Hester, University of South Carolina

Thaddeus Hicks, Ohio Christian University

Jennifer Holsman, Arizona State University

Jennifer Hopper, CUNY Graduate Center

Charlie Howard, Tarleton State University

David I. Hull, St. Anselm College

Charles F. Jacobs, St. Norbert College

Robert Jacobs, Central Washington University

Arthur Jipson, University of Dayton

Timothy R. Johnson, University of Minnesota

James H. Joyner Jr., Troy State University

Lucy E. Juarez, Texas A&M International University

Chad Kahl, Illinois State University, Milner Library

Ronald Kahn, Oberlin College

Naim Kapucu, University of Central Florida

Stacy Kaye, Appelman Law Firm, St. Louis Park, Minnesota

Judith Kilpatrick, University of Arkansas, Fayetteville

Alison Knowles, California State University, Chico

David Thomas Konig, Washington University in St. Louis

Kyle C. Kopko, The Ohio State University

Daniel C. Kramer, College of Staten Island, CUNY

Kyle L. Kreider, Wilkes University

Adam L. Kress, SUNY Albany

ANN C. KRUMMEL, Circuit Court for Columbia County, Kennesaw State University, Wisconsin

ASHLYN K. KUERSTEN, Western Michigan University

JOSEPH B. KUHNS, University of North Carolina, Charlotte

SUSAN M. KUNKLE, Kent State University

PAUL KURITZ, Bates College

DAE-HOON KWAK, Illinois State University

MARTHA M. LAFFERTY, Tennessee Fair Housing Council

MAURY LANDSMAN, University of Minnesota Law School

BARBARA J. LAWRENCE, Guilford College

BYUNG LEE, Michigan State University

GAVIN LEE, University of California at Irvine

PAUL LEHTO, Independent Scholar

MICHAEL LENZA, University of Wisconsin, Oshkosh

OLIVIA KATHLEEN LEONARD, Monmouth College

NANCY LEONG, William and Mary School of Law

DANIEL LEVIN, University of Utah

MICHAEL LEWKOWICZ, Georgia Gwinnett College

STEVEN A. LIGHT, University of North Dakota

PAUL D. LINK, Daniel, Clampett, Powell and Cunningham, Springfield, Missouri

MARY F. LOSS, Bowles Rice McDavid Graff and Love PLLC, Fairmont, West Virginia

ARTHUR J. LURIGO, Loyola University Chicago

ROBERT W. MALMSHEIMER, SUNY College of Environmental Science and Forestry, Syracuse, New York

CHRIS MARKWOOD, University of Central Oklahoma

WENDY L. MARTINEK, SUNY, Binghamton

JOHN H. MATHESON, University of Minnesota Law School

DAVID A. MAY, Eastern Washington University

ERIC MCADAMIS, Michigan State University

ANGELA MCCAFFREY, Hamline University School of Law

MICHAEL A. MCCALL, San Diego State University

WM. OSLER MCCARTHY, Supreme Court of Texas, University of Texas, Austin

MARK MCCLAIN, Central Washington University

MAGGIE MCGRANE, Malsbury

MARIA COLLINS MCGREGOR, University of North Carolina at Wilmington

CHAD J. MCGUIRE, University of Massachusetts, Dartmouth

CASSANDRA L. MCKEOWN, University of South Dakota

JANE CALABRIA MCPEAK, Hamline University

KENNETH MENTOR, University of North Carolina at Pembroke

ROSEMARY L. MESZAROS, Western Kentucky University

SUSAN GLUCK MEZEY, Loyola University, Chicago

JASON C. MILLER, United States Court of Appeals for the 6th Circuit

KAREN S. MILLER, West Virginia Wesleyan College

MARK C. MILLER, Clark University

TYLER MILLSAP, California State University, Chico

VERNON MOGENSEN, Kingsborough Community College, CUNY

MELANIE MORRIS, United States Government

STANLEY M. MORRIS, Attorney, Cortez, Colorado

KEN MULLEN, Appalachian State University

STEPHEN L. MUZZATTI, Ryerson University

WILNEIDA NEGRÓN, CUNY Graduate Center

JEANINE NEHER, California State University, Chico

CARYN E. NEUMANN, Miami University of Ohio

TIMOTHY J. O'NEILL, Southwestern University

MYRA ORLEN, Western New England College of Law

KAREN ORREN, University of California at Los Angeles

ELIZABETH SHARPE OVERMAN, Jackson State University, Jackson, Mississippi

REBECCA E. PADDOCK, William S. Boyd School of Law, University of Nevada–Las Vegas

SUSAN C. PADDOCK, University of Wisconsin–Madison

DEMETRA M. PAPPAS, London School of Economics and Political Science

RAYMOND PATERNOSTER, University of Maryland, College Park

DAVID PEREZ, Yale Law School

PATRICK J. PLATTER, Daniel, Clampett, Powell and Cunningham, Springfield, Missouri

VINCENT KELLY POLLARD, University of Hawaii at Manoa

BRIAN L. PORTO, Vermont Law School

CHAD POSICK, Northeastern University

BYRON E. PRICE, Barbara Jordan Institute, Texas Southern University

NORMAN PROVIZER, University of Louisiana

STEVEN PURO, Saint Louis University

JANE G. RAINEY, Eastern Kentucky University

KATHRYN R. L. RAND, University of North Dakota School of Law

DAVID M. REDDY, Sweet and Reddy, S.C., Elkhorn, Wisconsin

CHRIS RICHARDSON, The University of Western Ontario

PATRICK K. ROBERTS, Daniel, Clampett, Powell and Cunningham, Springfield, Missouri

MICHAEL ROCQUE, Northeastern University

NORMAN L. ROSENBERG, Macalester College

JONATHAN RUSCH, U.S. Department of Justice

GERALD J. RUSSELLO, Covington and Burling, New York

CLAIRE RYAN, Macalester College

MARGARET R. RYNIKER, SUNY, Oswego

LEILA SADEGHI, Center for Executive Leadership in Government, Rutgers University, New Brunswick

ROBERT KENNETH SAMMONS, Northern Arizona University

JOHN M. SCHEB II, University of Tennessee, Knoxville

PATRICK SCHMIDT, Macalester College

DAVID SCHULTZ, Hamline University

MARCUS SCHULZKE, State University of New York at Albany

KATHLEEN SEARLES, Washington State University

DAVID SELLERS, Administrative Office of the U.S. Courts

CELIA A. SGROI, State University of New York, Oswego

VICTORIA S. SHABANIAN, Office of Andrew J. Wistrich, Magistrate Judge, U.S. District Court, Central District of California

ALEX SHALOM, New Jersey City University

HEMANT SHARMA, University of Tennessee, Knoxville

ELSA M. SHARTSIS, Attorney

STEPHEN K. SHAW, Northwestern Nazarene University, Nampa, Idaho

CHRISTOPHER SHORTELL, University of California, San Diego

DAVID S. SIDHU, Georgetown University Law Center

JOSHUA M. SILVERSTEIN, Freeborn and Peters, Chicago

CHARLES ANTHONY SMITH, University of California, San Diego

CHRISTOPHER E. SMITH, Michigan State University

LINDSLEY ARMSTRONG SMITH, Martin and Kieklak Law Firm, Fayetteville, Arkansas

STEPHEN SMITH, University of Arkansas, Fayetteville

ANTHONY SMITH, University of California, San Diego

SHANNON ISHIYAMA SMITHEY, University of Pittsburgh

WILLIAM D. SMOOT, United States Military Academy, West Point

KAMESHA S. SPATES, Colorado State University Pueblo

JERRY E. STEPHENS, U.S. Court of Appeals for the 10th Circuit

KRISTIN L. STEWART, Attorney

ROBIN STEWART, Attorney

EDWARD STILL, Lawyers' Committee for Civil Rights Under Law

NORMAN OTTO STOCKMEYER, Jr., Thomas M. Cooley Law School

RUTH ANN STRICKLAND, Appalachian State University

PHILIPPA STRUM, City University of New York

DIANA L. SUMMERS, Northeastern University

JENNIFER SUMNER, Pennsylvania State University, Harrisburg

ROBERT SWAN, University of South Dakota

RICK SWANSON, University of Louisiana, Lafayette

STEVEN R. SWANSON, Hamline University School of Law

BETH SIMON SWARTZ, Attorney

G. ALAN TARR, Rutgers University, Camden, New Jersey

MARIE-JOSE LOUIS TAYAH, Kent State University

STEVEN L. TAYLOR, Troy State University

KYLE J. THOMAS, University of Maryland–College Park

LOUISE ADAMS TYLER, Philadelphia, Pennsylvania, Independent Scholar

GEORGIA WRALSTAD ULMSCHNEIDER, Indiana University–Purdue University, Fort Wayne

MATTHEW VALASI, University of California, Irvine

ERIC VANDERVORT, Ball State University

JOHN R. VILE, Middle Tennessee State University

MITCH WALKER, Queens University Belfast

MICHAEL H. WALSH, Loyola University, Chicago, Illinois

ARTEMUS WARD, California State University, Chico

MARIA WARREN, University of North Carolina, Wilmington

KIESHA WARREN-GORDON BALL STATE UNIVERSITY

ANDREW J. WASKEY, Dalton State College

MARC D. WEINER, Rutgers University, New Brunswick, New Jersey

PAUL WEIZER, Fitchburg State College

STEPHEN WERMIEL, American University, Washington College of Law

DARREN A. WHEELER, Ball State University

KEITH E. WHITTINGTON, Princeton University

KIMBERLY A. WILLIAMS, California State University, Chico

JOY A. WILLIS, Michigan State University

PHILLIP J. WININGER, University of Kentucky

STEVEN WISE, Center for the Expansion of Fundamental Rights

ANDREW J. WISTRICH, Magistrate Judge, U.S. District Court, Los Angeles, California

JAMES WYER, California State University, Chico

JULIE YINGLING, Michigan State University

LORETTA M. YOUNG, Family Court of State of Delaware

KATHRYN ZAFFT, University of Maryland, College Park

MARVIN ZALMAN, Wayne State University

SUSAN ZINNER, Indiana University Northwest

MARVIN ZOLMAN, Wayne State University

NOTE

When a case has been decided, but not yet published in the case reporter, the citation may note the volume but leave blank the page of the case reporter until it is determined. For example, *Meredith v. Jefferson*, 551 U.S.__(2007).

A

abortion Abortion rights for women were found to be constitutionally protected in the 1973 Supreme Court ruling in *ROE V. WADE*, 410 U.S. 113 (1973). Nevertheless, the Court's ruling in *Roe* did not end the legal controversy surrounding abortion. The federal government and states continued to enact legislation regulating the procedure in specified circumstances, and much of this legislation was constitutionally challenged in the courts over the ensuing decades.

During the 19th century, many states passed criminal statutes that prohibited all abortions except in cases when necessary in order to save the life of the mother. Because abortion was a dangerous medical procedure, many states enacted laws banning abortions in order to protect the public health, safety, and morals of women. However, as medical technologies improved in the 20th century, abortion also became a safer medical procedure, and consequently, a state's interest in prohibiting most abortions began to appear less legitimate. Many of the constitutional questions surrounding abortion were finally examined by the United States Supreme Court in the landmark case of *Roe v. Wade*.

Roe v. Wade considered the legitimacy of a Texas criminal abortion statute, which prohibited all abortions unless they were performed to save the life of the mother. In *Roe*, the Court found the Texas abortion law to be too rigid. Noting that abortion procedures were now "relatively safe," the Supreme Court ruled that states could not regulate abortions during the first trimester of a woman's pregnancy. However, because abortion became more dangerous after the first trimester, the Court ruled that states could regulate abortions during the second trimester of pregnancy if the regulations were created in an effort to promote maternal health and safety. Finally, the Supreme Court explained that during the third trimester of pregnancy, states could prohibit abortions as long as they provided an exception to save the mother's life. The Court argued that during the third trimester, the fetus was viable outside of the mother's womb, and thus, at that point, the states had an important and legitimate interest to protect the potential life of the unborn.

While *Roe* asserted that states could not regulate abortions during the first trimester of pregnancy, questions still arose as to what types of procedural requirements states could impose on women under the ruling. One of the first issues to come before the Court after *Roe* was the question of parental consent for minors. In the 1976 ruling of *Planned Parenthood v. Danforth,* 428 U.S. 52 (1976), the Court ruled that the parental consent provision in this suit lacked sufficient justification and thus was inappropriate. However, in arriving at this conclusion, Justice Harry Andrew Blackmun emphasized that this ruling did "not suggest that every minor, regardless of age or maturity, may give effective consent for termination of her pregnancy." In fact, soon after the *Danforth* ruling, the Supreme Court upheld laws requiring parental consent for minors in cases such as *Belloti v. Baird,* 443 U.S. 622 (1979) and *H. L. v. Matheson,* 450 U.S. 398 (1981). Similarly, in the 1992 ruling of *PLANNED PARENTHOOD V. CASEY,* 505 U.S. 833 (1992), Justice SANDRA DAY O'CONNOR reiterated that states could impose parental consent requirements on minors as long as the juveniles were able to acquire a bypass from a judge in extraordinary circumstances.

The Supreme Court has also upheld state laws that require physicians to inform women of the dangers of abortions, as well as laws that require women to sign informed consent waivers. Likewise, the Court has upheld 24-hour waiting period regulations, which require women who have been informed about the circumstances surrounding abortion to wait at least a 24-hour period after receiving the information before undergoing the procedure. The Court has ruled that these types of restrictions on the abortion process do not cause "an undue burden" on the women seeking the procedure and thus are constitutionally permissible.

The Supreme Court has, however, ruled that spousal notification requirements do place an "undue burden" on women seeking abortions and therefore are invalid. In *Casey,* Justice O'Connor noted that spousal notification requirements would most likely prevent many women from obtaining abortions, especially those women "who fear for their safety" because of abusive husbands. Moreover, although states have often required spousal notification in an effort to protect the father's rights, the Court rejected this justification. O'Connor states: "It is an inescapable biological fact that state regulation with respect to the child a woman is carrying will have a far greater impact on the mother's liberty than on the father's. . . . Inasmuch as it is the woman who physically bears the child and who is the more directly and immediately affected by the pregnancy . . . the balance weighs in her favor."

While the Supreme Court has generally adopted an "undue burden" analysis for testing the validity of most first trimester abortion procedures, many individuals who support abortion rights for women have been critical of the Supreme Court for not recognizing and appreciating the adverse effects and undue burdens some abortions laws have had on poor women. For instance, in 1976, Congress passed a law called the Hyde Amendment, which prohibited the use of Medicaid funds for abortions. The only exceptions were situations in which the procedure was necessary to save the life of the mother or in cases of rape or incest. In the case of *Harris v. McRae,* 448 U.S. 297 (1980), the Court upheld the constitutionality of the Hyde Amendment, explaining that the *Roe v. Wade* decision did not require the federal government to subsidize abortions for poor women electing the procedure. Thus, while first trimester abortions are constitutionally protected, indigent women often have far greater difficulty acquiring the procedure than middle- and upper-class women.

Members of Congress have often proposed a "Right-to-Life" Amendment to the Constitution to overturn the controversial *Roe v. Wade* decision; however, these proposed amendments to the Constitution have never been successful. There also have been times when it has appeared that the Supreme Court itself may actually be close to overturning (or at least modifying) the *Roe v. Wade* decision. In the decision of *Webster v. Reproductive Health Services,* 492 U.S. 490

(1989), four justices on the Supreme Court expressed an interest in retreating from *Roe.*

The holding of *Roe* remains controversial, with a Supreme Court divided over whether to uphold it. In 2000, the Supreme Court in *Stenberg v. Carhart,* 530 U.S. 914 (2000) voided by a 5–4 vote a federal law that banned "partial birth abortions." But in *Gonzales v. Carhart,* 550 U.S. 124 (2007) in another 5–4 the Court upheld another federal law banning partial birth abortions. Changing personnel on the Court seem to affect the status of abortion rights and how it rules. President Clinton's appointment of RUTH BADER GINSBURG and STEPHEN BREYER were both pro-choice, whereas President George Bush's appointments of Chief Justice John Roberts and Samuel Alito were antiabortion. Sonia Sotomayor and Elena Kagan, both appointed by President Obama, are presumed to be pro-choice, and they replaced David Souter and JOHN PAUL STEVENS, both of whom had supported abortion rights. The Court thus remains closely divided on the abortion issue.

For more information

Craig, Barbara Hinkson, and David M. O'Brien. *Abortion and American Politics.* Chatham, N.J.: Chatham House, 1993.

Devins, Neal. *Shaping Constitutional Values: Elected Government, the Supreme Court, and the Abortion Debate.* Baltimore: Johns Hopkins University Press, 1996.

Kazor, Christopher. *The Ethics of Abortion: Women's Rights, Human Life, and the Question of Justice.* New York: Routledge, 2010.

Tushnet, Mark. *Abortion.* New York: Facts On File, 1996.

Francene M. Engel
University of Michigan

Abrams v. United States 250 U.S. 616 (1919) *Abrams v. United States* is most famous for the libertarian dissenting opinion by Justice OLIVER WENDELL HOLMES, JR., penned in favor of political dissidence by an unpopular minority, an opinion that the Supreme Court has since embraced as part of the law of the First Amendment. The 1919 decision affirmed the convictions of five Russian immigrants who had circulated leaflets objecting to the decision of the United States to send troops to Eastern Europe in response to the Russian Revolution. The leaflets were addressed to "Workers of the World" and called on them to "wake up" to the government's foreign intrigues and were signed "Revolutionists." The defendants' speech had nothing to do with World War I or the draft, yet they were convicted and sentenced to 20 years imprisonment for violating the wartime Espionage Acts, which prohibited the encouragement of draft resistance and CONSPIRACIES to urge curtailment of war materials production.

Holmes insisted that the defendants had as much right to publish their leaflets as the government had to publish the CONSTITUTION. Governmental persecution of speech seemed logical to him in the abstract, if the ruling majority is certain what it wants and has reason to feel threatened that the speech of a minority might get in the way. He observed that history teaches that "time has upset many fighting faiths." But "the theory of our Constitution" is based on the "experiment" that "the best test of truth is the power of the thought to get itself accepted in the competition of the market." Thus, we need to be "eternally vigilant" against attempts to interfere with our nation's "wager" of truth.

For Holmes, only a serious and imminent emergency—a clear and present danger—allowed the government to short-circuit public debate. Otherwise, the First Amendment presumption that "Congress shall make no law" obtains. Therefore, speech, even divisive and controversial and unpopular speech, should have its say to see if it will have its way in the marketplace of ideas.

Despite all this heroic rhetoric, however, Holmes was not actually buying the defendants' "poor and puny anonymities." He believed that most dissident speech amounted to foolish, even silly, opinions of zealous but ignorant people, and the most effective way to marginalize them and their message was to let them have their say so others could recognize them for what they were. In a letter explaining his *Abrams* dissent, he wrote, "To show the ardor of the writer is not a sufficient reason for judging him. I regarded my view as simply upholding the right of a donkey to drool. But the usual notion is that you are free to say what you like if you don't shock me. Of course the value of the constitutional right is only when you do shock people. . . ."

Holmes ends his eloquent dissent with the fulsome lament, "I regret that I cannot put into more impressive words" the importance of the FREEDOM OF SPEECH. No other member of the Supreme Court ever has.

For more information

Abrams v. United States, 250 U.S. 616 (1919).

Bezanson, Randall P. *Speech Stories—How Free Can Speech Be?* New York: New York University Press, 1998.

Fish, Stanley. *There's No Such Thing as Free Speech . . . and It's a Good Thing Too.* New York: Oxford University Press, 1994.

Schauer, Frederick. *Free Speech: A Philosophical Enquiry.* Cambridge: Cambridge University Press, 1982.

Smolla, Rodney A. *Free Speech in an Open Society.* New York: Vintage Books, 1993.

Thomas E. Baker
University of Scranton

abstention Abstention is the practice of FEDERAL COURT nonintervention in ongoing state legal proceedings. The practice is grounded in both the desire to prevent federal courts from encroaching on state powers and a reluctance to decide issues on a constitutional basis if they can be resolved on narrower legal grounds. As early as 1793, Congress passed an Anti-Injunction Act to prevent federal courts from enjoining state officials from carrying out state laws. However, with the enhanced power of federal courts to protect the right of citizens under the Fourteenth Amendment, federal court involvement in state actions took on a new dimension. In response, the Supreme Court developed the judicial doctrine of abstention to supplement the legislative mandate.

One of the basic principles of CONSTITUTIONAL LAW in a federal system is that federal courts will not determine the meaning of a state law or constitution but instead rely on the interpretation made by the highest state court to rule on the issue. This presents a dilemma with a newly enacted statute which has not been interpreted by a state court. In early years, it was standard practice of federal courts to try to predict how a newly enacted statute would fare in state courts before it could be evaluated on federal constitutional grounds. However, in a series of cases known as the *Pullman Doctrine (Railroad Commission of Texas v. Pullman Co.,* 312 U.S. 496 [1941]), the Supreme Court ruled that federal courts must decline to hear a case and send it to state court if the state statute contains ambiguities or vague language which requires authoritative interpretation.

As a result of the CIVIL RIGHTS revolution, the Supreme Court seemed to retreat from the *Pullman* doctrine. In the early 1960s, federal court intervention was allowed when the state legal issues were minor or the state law was so flawed that no reinterpretation could make it constitutional. The most important case was *Dombrowski v. Pfister,* 380 U.S. 479 (1965), which held that abstention was inappropriate when state laws on their face abridged free expression or discouraged constitutionally protected activities.

However, in *Younger v. Harris,* 401 U.S. 37 (1971), the Supreme Court returned to a stricter position. It held that federal courts could not enjoin pending state criminal prosecutions except under extraordinary circumstances where the danger of irreparable loss to federally protected rights is both great and immediate. Subsequently, the *Younger* doctrine has been extended to apply to civil cases except where the state statute involved is clearly unconstitutional or the state case was conducted in bad faith. (*Colorado River Water Conservation District v. United States*, 424 U.S. 800 [1976], sets forth tests to be used by federal courts in civil abstention decision making where both federal and state courts have JURISDICTION.)

The most recent major case is *Pennzoil Co. v. Texaco, Inc.*, 481 U.S. 1 (1987), in which a unanimous Supreme Court ruled that a lower federal court could not intervene in an ongoing state civil case, although one of the oil companies contended that the state requirement for posting a $10 billion bond in order to appeal would bankrupt it. Justice Powell ruled that comity, or federal court respect for the rights of state courts, required federal court abstention. In an era of increased Supreme Court deference to states' rights, the abstention doctrine will remain a bulwark of federal jurisprudence.

For more information

Currie, David P. *Federal Jurisdiction in a Nutshell*. 4th ed. St. Paul, Minn.: West, 1999.

Young, Gordon G. "Federal Court Abstention and State Administrative Law from Burford to Ankenbrandt: Fifty Years of Judicial Federalism under *Burford v. Sun Oil* and Kindred Doctrines," *DePaul L. Rev.* 42 (1993): 859.

William E. Brigman
University of Houston—Downtown

academic freedom Academic freedom is a doctrine that protects the right of teachers to be free to research, write, teach, and comment about issues without fear of retribution. The purpose of academic freedom is to preserve the intellectual integrity of persons who research, write, and speak on issues of public interest and who are responsible for educating the young of society. In the United States, a formal, written claim for these rights first appeared in a Declaration of Principles (1915) and a Statement of Principles on Academic Freedom and Tenure (1940) drafted by the American Association of University Professors (AAUP).

The concept has a long history. It was discussed as early as the death of Socrates for teaching ideas not approved by the government. The Declaration and Statement were intended to apply only to teachers in higher education after a national study found that they were in significant danger of having their ideas and speech stifled when they criticized authority (university administrations, local school boards, and local, state, and national governments). This concern about authoritarian repression in the flow of ideas focused on the individual teacher and not on education as a whole. The claims made in the 1915 and 1940 documents have never been wholly accepted by educational institutions or by the courts, although some aspects of each have been incorporated in teacher employment contracts, in teacher evaluation and performance review structures of universities, and in decisions of the U.S. Supreme Court and other courts.

It was not until the late 1940s and 1950s that there was substantial court review of the doctrine. Despite its original focus on teachers in higher education, many of the cases have involved grade school and high school teachers. This came about when proponents attempted to link the concept of academic freedom to the individual rights granted in the First and Fourteenth Amendments to the CONSTITUTION. Before then, the United States Supreme Court had determined that the First and Fourteenth Amendments protected individuals only against actions by state and federal governments and had no authority when it came to the actions of private individuals and institutions. In addition, the Court had held that the state could place "reasonable conditions" on public employment, which was not a right but a privilege. These interpretations prevailed in teachers' claims of interference with academic freedom until the 1952 decision of *Wieman v. Updegraff*, 344 U.S. 183 (1952), in which the Court declared unconstitutional an Oklahoma law that excluded from state employment any person who would not swear that they did not belong to any subversive organizations.

In 1960 the Court struck down an Arkansas statute that required public employees to provide the state with a list of all their organizational memberships in *Shelton v. Tucker,* 364 U.S. 479 (1960). In *Shelton,* Justice Potter Stewart declared "[t]he vigilant protection of constitutional freedoms is nowhere more vital than in the community of American schools." In *Wieman* the plaintiffs were college teachers while in *Shelton* the case involved teachers at all levels of education. The language of these cases seemed to indicate that it was the atmosphere in which education takes place, not only the rights of the individual teacher, that is entitled to First Amendment protection from authoritarian controls. This notion was borne out in *Dixon v. Alabama State Board of Education,* 294 F. 2d 150 (5th Cir.), cert denied, 368 U.S. 930 (1961), where the Court held that students had a right to DUE PROCESS notice and a hearing before they could be expelled for protesting on school grounds. With this opinion, academic freedom was extended to all persons engaged in education.

Although various portions of the concept of academic freedom now have been given some protection through the courts, the extent of that protection has not been clearly defined. In *Pickering v. Board of Education,* 391 U.S. 563 (1968), the Court held that the First Amendment interest of a teacher must be balanced against the school board's interest in efficient operation of the schools. In that case, the Court found no interference in the school's operation as a result of a letter by the teacher criticizing the board and published in a local newspaper. In a later case, the Court held that where there were mixed motives for dismissing a teacher, only one of which involved protected conduct, the employer might prevail if it could show that dismissal would have occurred solely on the basis of the unprotected conduct, *Mt. Healthy City School District Board of Education v. Doyle,* 429 U.S. 274 (1977). In *REGENTS OF THE UNIVERSITY OF CALIFORNIA V. BAKKE,* 438 U.S. 265 (1978), the Court, noting that "[a]cademic freedom, though not a specifically enumerated constitutional right, long has been viewed as a special concern of the First Amendment," defined academic freedom as including "[t]he freedom of the university to make its own judgments as to education." This view was reiterated in *Regents of the University of Michigan v. Ewing,* 474 U.S. 214 (1985), where the Court rejected claims that the school had acted arbitrarily and refused to interfere with the decision to dismiss a student, stating that it was a "genuinely academic decision."

For more information

Hofstadter, Richard, and William Metzger. *The Development of Academic Freedom in the United States.* New York: Columbia University Press, 1955.

Pincoffs, E., ed. *The Concept of Academic Freedom.* Austin: University of Texas Press, 1975.

Judith Kilpatrick
University of Arkansas
Fayetteville

accessory Accessory describes one who assists another in the commission of a crime. The word is originally derived from the Latin word *accessio,* meaning something that accompanies or supplements something else. In Roman law, accessory came to mean a mode of acquiring additional property as an outgrowth of or addition to property already owned. This older usage still survives in some contexts. For example, an accessory CONTRACT is an agreement entered into between parties to effectuate or bring about the terms of another contract that is more central to the parties' relationship. However, its primary meaning is in the criminal law.

In criminal law, the original distinction between an accessory and a *principal* or main actor was whether the person was present at the scene of the crime. The principals were present at the scene of the crime and either committed the crime themselves or assisted others to do it. The accessory, on the other hand, was not actually present during the commission of the crime but assisted the principal(s) "before the fact" or "after the fact." For example, someone who provided the principal with a weapon or other assistance before the crime could be considered an accessory "before the fact," while someone assisting the principal in escaping from the authorities after the crime was committed would be considered an accessory "after the fact." At common law, the latter crime was called "misprision of FELONY" but was generally limited to those who failed to disclose or actively concealed the commission of a felony.

An accessory is similar to an *accomplice,* in that both assist the principal in the commission of a crime, and in some states there is little distinction between them. However, an accomplice is usually a greater participant in the crime than an accessory, often being defined as a witness to a criminal action who is determined to have participated in the crime itself. In some states, such as New York, an accessory, even one after the fact, may be found guilty to an equal degree as the actual perpetrator of the crime, so long as the indictment of the accomplice provides enough information as to the crimes charged to prepare a defense.

Contemporary criminal law has generally eliminated the difference between a principal and an "accessory before the fact," and accords them both the same level of culpability. However, most states still accord a lesser degree of culpability to those accessories who did not know of the crime before its commission but offered aid or assistance to the principals "after the fact." Most states require that an accessory after the fact take some intentional action to conceal the crime or aid the principals to escape rather than mere inaction. While at common law an accessory could not be tried or convicted before the principal, the criminal law of most states has now eliminated that requirement and an accessory can be tried and convicted regardless of whether or not the principal of the crime is tried and convicted.

For more information

Kaplan, John, and Robert Weisberg. *Criminal Law: Cases and Materials.* Boston: Little, Brown, 1986, pp. 580–612.

Black's Law Dictionary. 6th ed. St. Paul, Minn.: West, 1990, p. 14.

Gerald J. Russello
Covington and Burling, New York

acquittal Acquittal is the legal term that denotes being found not guilty of the charges upon which a defendant has been tried. An acquittal decision is important both because it means a defendant has been found not guilty for the crimes charged, but also because it triggers the constitutional protections against DOUBLE JEOPARDY.

The application of double jeopardy means a person cannot be tried again on the same charges upon which he or she has already been acquitted, per the clause of the Fifth Amendment that reads, ". . . nor shall any person be subject for the same offense to be twice put in jeopardy of life or limb . . ." The one exception to this is if bribery of a judge resulting in an acquittal can be proven, as was the case in *Aleman v. Judges,* 183 F.3d 302 (1998), else the government cannot at any level seek to retry a defendant on the same charges.

Acquittal can be issued by a JURY or a JUDGE in cases where the law does not require one be empaneled, and such a decision removes any legal culpability of the defendant. Should an attempt be made to retry a defendant on similar grounds an "autrefois acquit" (from the French meaning "previously acquitted"), plea may be filed at bar in an effort to forestall proceedings before they commence. This pretrial plea means that the record clearly shows the defendant has already been tried and acquitted for the stated offenses and therefore proceedings should cease.

Related to this is the 1986 decision in *Smalis v. Pennsylvania,* 476 U.S. 140 (1985), which held that "subjecting the defendant to post-acquittal fact-finding proceedings going to guilt or innocence violates the Double Jeopardy clause." However, a decision of the court must be final to trigger double jeopardy protections. If no final decision is reached, such as in the case of a mistrial, this will not be treated the same as an acquittal, and the defendant may be retried. Furthermore, this constitutional protection does not prevent individual citizens from bringing civil claims against the defendant in a criminal case on grounds that are related to a criminal case. The O. J. SIMPSON case has become the most notable example; while Simpson was acquitted in a criminal trial for the murders of Nicole Brown Simpson and Ronald Goldman, he was subsequently taken to civil court for his supposed role in their wrongful deaths. Then on February 5, 1997, some two years after his criminal trail absolved him of criminal guilt, Simpson was found liable for the wrongful death and battery of Ronald Goldman and the battery of Nicole Brown Simpson. Subsequently, the case has continued to make the news as a related proceeding has been repeatedly initiated by the families in a continued effort to collect the remaining portion of the large civil judgment they are still owed. Hence, this underscores that while acquittal is an absolute end in criminal law, related claims in different venues may go forward, as did the civil suit in this case.

For more information

LaFave, Wayne, Jerold Isreal, Nancy King, and Orin Kerr. *Criminal Procedure.* 5th ed. Eagan, Minn.: West, 2009.

Adam L. Kress
SUNY Albany

actual innocence In criminal law cases, a finding of "actual innocence" occurs when the defense is able to raise REASONABLE DOUBT that either no crime was committed or that the acts committed by the defendant do not equate to the alleged criminal act. This differs from a finding of innocence that occurs when the prosecution fails to establish "beyond a reasonable doubt" that a criminal act was committed. Typical actual innocence defenses may include alibis, arguments for mistaken identity, or that the accused has been framed, questioning the credibility of witnesses, and more recently scientific EVIDENCE such as DNA TESTING.

Recent court cases have highlighted the complexities of findings of actual innocence, especially the limits of when a convicted person has exhausted all review of convictions. In *HERRERA V. COLLINS,* 506 U.S. 390 (1993), the defendant, Leonel Torres Herrera, was found guilty of murdering two Texas police officers and sentenced to death. Throughout the case Herrera maintained his innocence. After his conviction, the defense was able to acquire four affidavits declaring that his brother, Raul Herrera, was the real killer. Despite this new evidence, the defense was not able to find relief in state courts. Eventually, the case reached the Supreme Court in 1992. The Supreme Court affirmed that a claim of actual innocence was not enough to bar him from execution. CHIEF JUSTICE REHNQUIST declared that the EIGHTH AMENDMENT ban on CRUEL AND UNUSUAL PUNISHMENT would not be violated by executing a person who may be able to show actual innocence but had exhausted all possible reviews of their conviction. Justice Blackmun issued the dissenting argument by affirming that the execution of a person who may be able to show his innocence is very close to MURDER. Despite the controversy of this finding and public outcry, in *Ex parte Elizondo,* 947 S.W.2d 202, 205 (Tex. Cr. App. 1996), the Supreme Court upheld this legal PRECEDENT and declared that even if one could prove actual innocence, a defendant may still be barred from further review.

In the CAPITAL PUNISHMENT setting, actual innocence may serve as an exception to the cause-and-prejudice rule and can result in a successful challenge to the death sentence. As a result, a petitioner who has committed a crime may still be "actually innocent" of the death penalty. In the case *Sawyer v. Whitley,* 505 U.S. 333 (1992), the Supreme Court first exemplified the traditional definition of actual innocence by declaring that in order to demonstrate "actual innocence" one must show by clear and convincing evidence that but for a constitutional error, no reasonable juror would have found the petitioner eligible for the death penalty under the applicable state law. A defendant's ability to have his or her case reopened pending new evidence of innocence was further expanded in *Schlup v. Delo,* 513 U.S. 298 (1995), in which the Supreme Court declared that actual innocence could be found if it is more likely than not that no reasonable juror would have found the defendant guilty beyond a reasonable doubt.

For more information

"Actual Innocence awareness database" maintained by Tarlton Law Library at the University of Texas at Austin. This database contains resources related to wrongful convictions.

Dwyer, Jim, Peter Neufeld, and Barry Scheck. *Actual Innocence: Five Days to Execution and Other Dispatches from the Wrongly Convicted.* New York: Doubleday, 2000.

Wilneida Negrón
CUNY Graduate Center

actus reus Actus reus is a Latin phrase, which, when translated, means "guilty act" and serves as one element of several that helps to establish that a crime has occurred.

A crime is committed only when there is EVIDENCE of a voluntary physical act that is regulated in some manner by LAW. Although actus reus is typically associated with commissions—the perpetration of some act—guilty acts may also be defined as omissions—the failure to act to accomplish an obligation created by law. The act itself, however, may not be criminal if it is not linked to a second element known as MENS REA, or the "guilty mind." Mens rea is the mental component of the guilty act that demonstrates intentionality on the part of the criminal actor. The causal relationship between the guilty act and the guilty mind is what determines whether or not a crime has been committed, and it is a necessity of the common law to demonstrate criminal responsibility. A number of justifications and excuses can be used to break the causal relationship between the guilty act and the guilty mind to relieve an individual of liability for a particular behavior. Excuses for criminal conduct include duress, intoxication, mistake, INSANITY, infancy and ENTRAPMENT. SELF-DEFENSE, public duty, necessity, and consent are examples of justification under law.

For more information

Katz, Leo. *Bad Acts and Guilty Minds: Conundrums of the Criminal Law.* Chicago: University of Chicago Press, 1987.

Schubert, Frank A. *Introduction to Law and the Legal System.* 9th ed. Boston: Houghton Mifflin, 2007.

Charles F. Jacobs
St. Norbert College

Adamson v. California 332 U.S. 46 (1947) *Adamson v. California* reopened the great dispute over the "fundamental rights" interpretation of the DUE PROCESS clause of the Fourteenth Amendment and whether the BILL OF RIGHTS applies to state governments. A widely noted dissent by Justice HUGO BLACK argued that the clause should be read to INCORPORATE all of the Bill of Rights guarantees against encroachment by state governments. The majority's position was that only rights which the justices think are "fundamental" should be included.

Admiral Dewey Adamson was convicted of MURDER in the first degree in California in 1946 and was condemned to death. California's criminal procedure at that time authorized the JUDGE and PROSECUTOR to comment on the defendant's refusal to testify. Adamson had committed earlier offenses which would have been revealed to the JURY on cross examination had he testified in his own defense. In his closing argument, the prosecutor pointed out Adamson's refusal to take the stand. After his conviction, Adamson APPEALED on the ground that the California procedure violated his privilege against SELF-INCRIMINATION under the due process clause of the Fourteenth Amendment.

The Supreme Court decided the case on June 23, 1947. Justice Stanley Reed, writing for a majority of five, held that the privilege against self-incrimination is not part of the right to a fair trial protected by the due process clause of the Fourteenth Amendment. Reed argued that "the purpose of due process is not to protect a defendant against a proper conviction but against an unfair conviction. When EVIDENCE is before a jury that threatens conviction, it does not seem unfair to require him to choose between leaving the adverse evidence unexplained and subjecting himself to IMPEACHMENT through disclosure of former crimes. In short, California's procedure was not "fundamentally unfair."

Justice FELIX FRANKFURTER concurred, arguing that the due process clause of the Fourteenth Amendment was not meant by its framers to include the whole Bill of Rights: "It would be extraordinarily strange for a Constitution to convey such specific commands in such a roundabout and inexplicit way . . ." as the due process clause.

Justice Hugo Black's dissenting opinion argued that inclusion of the entire Bill of Rights in the Fourteenth Amendment had been the intention of its framers. He attached to his opinion a long historical appendix citing many of the speeches of Congressman Jonathan Bingham and other influential members of Congress who had participated in the drafting and ratification of the Fourteenth Amendment. Black argued further that the "fundamental fairness" rule was too open-ended; it gives too much power to judges to include and exclude rights according to their personal wishes rather than on the basis of principled constitutional analysis.

Frankfurter's position prevailed in theory and Black's in practice. By 1970 nearly the entire Bill of Rights had been incorporated in the Fourteenth Amendment. The major exceptions are the Second Amendment's right to keep and bear arms, and the Fifth Amendment's command that criminal defendants are entitled to indictment by GRAND JURY. The Court's specific decision in *Adamson* was changed in 1964 in *Malloy v. Hogan;* state prosecutors may no longer comment to the jury on the defendant's refusal to testify.

The open-ended character of the due process clause of the Fourteenth Amendment permitted later courts to expand personal liberty and privacy rights. *GRISWOLD V. CONNECTICUT* and *EISENSTADT V. BAIRD* established constitutional rights to receive and use birth control devices and information; *ROE V. WADE* established a constitutional right to an ABORTION in the first trimester of pregnancy. Had the Supreme Court accepted Justice Black's interpretation of the Fourteenth Amendment, these expansions of individual autonomy would have been much more difficult to achieve.

For more information

Fairman, Charles, and Stanley Morrison. *The Fourteenth Amendment and the Bill of Rights: The Incorporation Theory.* New York: Da Capo Press, 1970.

Silverstein, Mark. *Constitutional Faiths: Felix Frankfurter, Hugo Black, and the Process of Judicial Decision Making.* Ithaca, N.Y.: Cornell University Press, 1984.

Robert Jacobs
Central Washington University

administrative discretion Administrative discretion describes the freedom of public administrators to make choices, within the limits of their authority, among possible courses of action. Administrative discretion is not necessarily limited to substantive policy decisions. It extends to decisions as to timing of action and the procedures used.

When government officials seek to achieve public goals in legally permissible ways, those officials and the government are exempt from damage claims from those hurt by the government's action. "Administrative discretion" is also sometimes termed the "discretionary function exemption." This exemption gives officials room to make judgment calls and carry them out without fear of being sued, even if their decisions prove to be bad. For example, FBI law enforcement action in 1993 at the Davidian complex outside Waco, Texas, led to the death of 74 members of that religious sect, including many children. A federal district court held that the FBI agents as individuals and the FBI as a federal agency acted within the discretion permitted by law.

Administrative discretion also grants government agencies broad authority to interpret laws passed by Congress. In *Chevron v. Natural Resources Defense Council*, 467 U.S. 837 (1984), the Supreme Court ruled that in general they would defer to interpretations of congressional acts if they were unclear and if interpretation they offered was reasonable and within their expertise. While the Court has slightly modified the *Chevron* ruling since, the basic holding remains that federal agencies are given significant leeway to interpret the law and make decisions, subject to limits imposed by the CONSTITUTION and law, such as the ADMINISTRATIVE PROCEDURES ACT. State and local administrative is similarly limited.

"Prosecutorial discretion," a related concept, describes the range of alternatives available to a PROSECUTOR in criminal cases. Alternatives include (1) whether or not to prosecute, (2) the specific charges to be brought, (3) the timing and modes of bargaining with defendant's counsel, and (4) the substance of sentencing recommendations. For example, it is an act of prosecutorial discretion when a district attorney offers to reduce charges against a drug dealer if he will testify against his supplier.

For more information

Davis, Kenneth Culp. *Discretionary Justice.* Baton Rouge: Louisiana State University Press, 1969; Reprint, Greenwood Press, 1999.

Froomkin, Michael. "In Defense of Administrative Agency Autonomy," *Yale Law Journal* 96 (March 1987): 798.

Gayle Avant
Baylor University

Administrative Procedures Act The Administrative Procedures Act regulates the procedures by which federal government agencies conduct their business. There are many diverse agencies, departments, and commissions of the U.S. government. The duty of each of these administrative units is to oversee and regulate a particular policy area such as communications, transportation, or the environment. Although the substantive area of their expertise differs, most federal agencies follow the same law regulating the procedures by which they operate. That law is called the Administrative Procedures Act (APA). The APA was enacted by Congress in 1946 in order to standardize the procedures by which agencies enact regulation and conduct hearings. The three overall goals of the APA were public information, public participation, and public accountability. The APA standardized and simplified administrative law, making it easier for courts, agencies, and the public to understand the procedures. The APA also was designed to allow more involvement by the public in the way agencies conduct their business, as well as judicial review of agency actions to ensure that the agencies were following the law.

The APA has numerous features. One of the most important requirements of the APA is the rulemaking procedure found in chapter 5 of the *U.S. Code,* section 553. This section requires that agencies wishing to adopt a generally applicable regulation must publicize their intent to do so and then allow a period for public commentary on the agency's proposed regulation. Specifically, although the APA allows for certain exceptions, in most cases the agency must first publish their proposed rule (the actual text or a description of the rule) in the *Federal Register,* along with the time and place of a hearing in which the agency will listen to public comments and debate about the proposed rule. Interested persons may either speak at the hearing or submit written opinions containing data and opinions, as well as legal and policy arguments. After the period of public comment is over, the agency will then announce the final version of the rule along with its basic purpose. Interested persons also have the right to petition for the issuance, amendment, or repeal of a rule.

Another one of the most important elements of the APA is found in section 554. This section requires that when an agency is about to adjudicate a decision that involves the interests of one or more specific individuals or businesses, those parties must be given notice of the intended agency action as well as an opportunity to present their own viewpoints. The requirements are similar to those for rule making described above. The affected party must first be notified of the specific time and place of the hearing along with the specific facts or laws that are being asserted by the agency. Then, at the hearing, the affected party must be given the opportunity to present facts and arguments in favor of or against the specific action the agency wishes to take.

Sections 701 through 706 of chapter 7 of the *U.S. Code* lay out the APA's guidelines for JUDICIAL REVIEW of agency actions. This review includes both the substance and procedure of an agency's final action. If a party challenges an agency's action in court, the action can be overturned on several grounds. These reasons include instances in which the agency action violated any constitution, statute, administrative regulation, or other law. As another example, a court will reverse an agency's action if the substance of its decision was unsupported by substantial EVIDENCE, or was reached in an arbitrary or capricious manner.

The APA is not without its critics. Some believe the APA places too many procedural obstacles in the way of agencies, making it more difficult for them to enact important regulations to protect people's health, safety, or the environment. Others, on the other hand, believe the APA gives too much power to agencies to regulate minute details of behavior, and that compliance with excessive, costly, and confusing regulations ends up choking the private business sector. Either way, the APA's basic elements have probably become a permanent fixture on our legal landscape.

For more information

Aman, Alfred C., and William T. Mayton. *Administrative Law.* St. Paul, Minn.: West, 1998.

The Administrative Procedures Act, 5 U.S.C. §§ 551–59, 701–06, 1305, 3105, 3344, 5372, 7521.

Rick Swanson
University of Louisiana

administrative searches An administrative search is one that is conducted according to a predetermined statutory scheme. Searches undertaken for administrative reasons stand in contrast to criminal searches.

Common examples of administrative searches include fire inspections, health and safety inspections, and environmental inspections. Administrative searches are conducted to ensure compliance with established governmental codes that regulate health, safety, and morals. Unlike searches that are conducted in order to uncover EVIDENCE of criminal wrongdoing, administrative searches tend to be performed for corrective purposes rather than for punitive purposes. For example, an inspection to detect faulty electrical wiring is not designed to punish the responsible party as much as it is to point out the potential danger so that the property owner may take corrective measures. In most cases the property owner will be directed to make the necessary corrections, and only if the person fails to comply will civil or criminal penalties be imposed.

Administrative searches present a special problem for CONSTITUTIONAL LAW. The FOURTH AMENDMENT prohibits searches without either PROBABLE CAUSE or a warrant. In most cases, an electrician checking for faulty wiring will not be able to tell from outside the dwelling whether that particular dwelling has faulty interior wiring. Therefore, it is almost impossible to establish sufficient probable cause to obtain a warrant to inspect a particular dwelling. As a result, the Supreme Court has ruled that a standard that requires less than probable cause is permissible. The Court held that because administrative searches are corrective rather than punitive in nature a lesser standard is justified. In addition, public safety justifies a lower standard than probable cause. For these reasons, administrative searches are not "unreasonable" within the meaning of the Fourth Amendment.

Administrative searches take different forms with varying degrees of constitutional protection. One category of administrative search involves routine searches of private homes and businesses. In this type of search, if the property owner refuses to consent to the search, a warrant must be obtained. However, the warrant need not meet the strict standard of probable cause required in criminal cases. All that must be shown is that the particular house or business was selected according to an existing statutory scheme that eliminates arbitrary selection. The second type of administrative search involves "historically and heavily regulated industries." For example, the firearms and liquor industries qualify as historically and heavily regulated industries. Because these industries require state or federal licenses, the owners are aware from the outset that they are engaged in a business subject to periodic inspection. A third category of administrative searches are inventory searches. A typical example is the search of an impounded automobile. To protect the impounding authority from charges that items were stolen from the impounded car, a list is made of items found in the car.

For more information

Camara v. Municipal Court, 387 U.S. 523 (1967).

Scheb, John M., and John M. Scheb II. *Law and the Administrative Process.* Belmont, Calif.: Thomson Wadsworth, 2005.

Warren, Kenneth F. *Administrative Law in the Political System.* 3rd ed. Upper Saddle River, N.J.: Prentice Hall, 1997.

James V. Calvi
West Texas A&M University

admiralty law Admiralty law or maritime law is the unique set of substantive and procedural legal rules generally applicable to activities on navigable waterways. The core policy goal is to provide a uniform and predictable legal system that encourages waterborne commerce. Significant substantive coverage areas include ship collisions, personal injury, carriage of goods, maritime liens and ship mortgages, charter agreements, towing, pilotage, limitation of liability, salvage, marine pollution, maritime insurance, and recreational uses.

Admiralty's history extends back to ancient Babylonian, Roman, and Greek law. By the end of the first millennium A.D., maritime trade had expanded to create centralized maritime rules often named for the seaport in which they arose. Of greatest interest to American lawyers was the French island Olíron's sea code, which traveled to England in the 11th century. At this point, continental and English maritime practice took different paths. In most civil law countries, admiralty was incorporated into national codes; while in England, court decisions developed maritime law.

In medieval times, English ports had their own admiralty courts, but as the English government became more centralized, the king gave the lord high admiral the right to create a system of admiralty courts, leading to jurisdictional disputes with local courts. By the 1500s the growth of English shipping had increased the significance of admiralty courts, which commercial interests preferred because substantive admiralty law applied, the process was quicker, the court generally accepted written testimony, and no JURY was required. These same benefits threatened the English common law courts, which attempted to take exclusive JURISDICTION over many traditional admiralty claims. Ultimately, admiralty and common law courts acted to prohibit each other's jurisdiction. In the 1600s, the common law courts won this battle, severely limiting the admiralty courts' ability to hear commercial cases or any cases that arose on British internal waters or land.

Prior to the CONSTITUTION's adoption, the newly independent states of the United States followed English law and created their own admiralty courts. The need for uniform and predictable trade rules and dissatisfaction with the states' decentralized regimes led to the creation of admiralty jurisdiction in the federal courts in Article III, section 2 of the Constitution, which provides, "[t]he judicial Power shall extend . . . to all Cases of admiralty and maritime Jurisdiction. . . ." Congress furthered national uniformity in section 9 of the Judiciary Act of 1789, which provided: ". . . the district courts . . . shall also have exclusive original cognizance of all civil causes of admiralty and maritime jurisdiction . . . saving to suitors, in all cases, the right of the common law remedy, where the common law is competent to give it . . ." Unlike England, where special admiralty courts were used, the United States allowed regular federal courts to decide maritime disputes, although applying different laws and using different procedures.

The Constitution and the Judiciary Act fail to define "admiralty and maritime jurisdiction," leaving it to judicial determination. Over the years this has led to disputes over exclusive application of federal admiralty law over state law. The strongest statement of federal admiralty supremacy came in the Supreme Court's 1917 decision in *Southern Pacific Co. v. Jensen,* 244 U.S. 205 (1917), which struck down the application of a state workers compensation award to a maritime worker. The Court found that the need for maritime uniformity rendered the state law unconstitutional if it "contravenes the essential purpose expressed by an act of Congress or works material prejudice to the characteristic features of the general maritime law or interferes with the proper harmony and uniformity of that law in its international and interstate relations."

Despite this strong statement, the courts have not provided clear guidance on this important FEDERALISM issue. The case-by-case determinations make little attempt to provide a unifying theory, and recent Supreme Court decisions have added to the confusion. For example, in *American Dredging v. Miller,* 510 U.S. 443 (1994), the Court refused to require that the state of Louisiana apply the maritime law's traditional doctrine of *forum non conveniens* because the rule did not originate in admiralty or find its exclusive home in maritime law. Although that case acknowledged the *Jensen* standard, it seemed to create an entirely new approach. In another important case, *Yamaha Motor Corp. v. Calhoun,* 516 U.S. 199 (1996), the Court refused to find that a general maritime remedy preempted a state wrongful death statute for a death that occurred within U.S. territorial waters. Such cases misunderstand the important maritime policies of uniformity and predictability. Similarly, recent congressional enactments have not respected these goals. For example, the Oil Pollution Act of 1990 allows each state to create an unlimited liability regime for oil spills occurring in its territory.

For more information

Benedict on Admiralty. 8th ed. New York: Mathew Bender.

Schoenbaum, Thomas J. *Admiralty and Maritime Law.* 2nd ed. St. Paul, Minn.: West, 1994.

Swanson, Steven R. "Federalism, the Admiralty, and Oil Spills," *Journal of Maritime Law and Commerce* 27 (1996): 379.

Steven R. Swanson
Hamline University School of Law

adversarial process The U.S. system of law is based on an adversarial process. The adversarial process is similar to a game or contest in which both parties are trying to win and a neutral umpire is present to make sure the parties play fair. The belief is that competition between the two parties is the best way to uncover the truth. This is fundamentally different from the inquisitorial system that holds judicial control of the investigative process is the best way to uncover the truth.

For both civil and criminal proceedings, there are rules of procedure to ensure both parties play fairly. In general, the rules balance the constitutional right of an individual to have his/her rights adjudicated with society's interest in having an efficient and effective way to ensure justice. For example, both civil and criminal procedures have rules limiting the amount of time an individual has to APPEAL his verdict. These rules serve to protect the individual's right to an appeal while also ensuring that the adjudicative process is efficient and that there is some finality to it.

Additionally, in response to abuses of citizens by the government, the United States has implemented various constitutional procedural safeguards for individuals. These include the right to an attorney, the right to remain silent, the right to be free of unwarranted searches and ARRESTS, the right to compel witnesses to appear for the defense, the right to confront one's accuser, and the right to appeal the decision made by the court or JURY. The extent of these procedural safeguards differs depending on whether the proceeding is civil or criminal. In criminal proceedings, because the individual is facing a deprivation of liberty, versus economic deprivation in a civil proceeding, the procedural safeguards are often more reaching. For example, an individual's right to remain silent applies only to criminal proceedings; however, an individual has the right against SELF-INCRIMINATION in both civil and criminal proceedings.

Along with the procedural rules and constitutional safeguards, the U.S. adversarial process implements certain ethical duties to ensure the parties play fairly. With respect to civil proceedings, the ethical duties are the same for both sides. However, with respect to criminal proceedings, the prosecution has an added ethical duty. In a criminal proceeding, the prosecution represents the state and, as such, its ethical duty is that justice shall be done, not that it necessarily should win the case. Consequently, during the investigative process, the prosecution has a much broader duty to turn over to the defense any material EVIDENCE that may prove the defendant's innocence. This duty is primarily a result of our justice system being built on a presumption of innocence until proven guilty. As for the defense, its duty is to be a zealous advocate for its client and to ensure that the defendant's constitutional rights are protected. As such, the defense may, and in most cases has a duty to, continue to represent the defendant even if the attorney knows the defendant is guilty. This duty is primarily to ensure a fair trial, which is a constitutionally protected right provided to all citizens regardless of guilt or innocence.

The adversarial process is fundamental to the U.S. practice of justice and the rules and procedures implemented help to ensure the process is fair.

For more information

Fairchild, Erika, and Harry R. Dammer. *Comparative Criminal Justice Systems*. Stanford, Conn.: Thomson Learning, 2001.

Rebecca E. Paddock
William S. Boyd School of Law, University of Nevada–Las Vegas

advisory opinion An advisory opinion is a judicial interpretation of the law that has no binding effect because it does not occur in response to an actual dispute in which the parties have adverse interests. In other words, a court issues an advisory opinion in a "dispute" that is hypothetical, not real. The supreme courts of 12 states have authority to issue advisory opinions, but the courts of most states, and the federal courts, do not.

Federal courts cannot issue advisory opinions because Article III of the CONSTITUTION prohibits them from doing so. The United States Supreme Court reached that conclusion in 1793, after President George Washington sought the Court's advice about legal questions that resulted from America's neutrality in the war then in progress between England and France. The Court declined to give President Washington the advice he sought. CHIEF JUSTICE JOHN JAY replied to the president that Article III restricted courts to deciding "cases" or "controversies," which Jay and his fellow justices interpreted to be actual disputes between adverse parties, in which court decisions could resolve matters. He added that the Constitution allowed the president to seek advice only from the heads of executive departments (i.e., members of the cabinet), not from the Supreme Court.

That reasoning is still good law today. Indeed, ever since 1793, the Supreme Court has held that requests for advisory opinions present "nonjusticiable" issues, in other words, issues that the Constitution does not permit the Court to decide or even to consider. The Court provided a formal statement of its views on advisory opinions in *Muskrat v. United States,* 219 U.S. 346 (1911). Congress had authorized certain Indians to file suit to determine whether a particular law was constitutional and had given the Indians a right of APPEAL to the Supreme Court. The Court concluded that even though Congress had authorized it, the lawsuit did not present a case or a controversy between adverse parties but instead sought to obtain advisory opinions from the Court about whether certain federal laws were constitutional. The Court stated in *Muskrat* that it was inappropriate for courts "to give opinions in the nature of advice concerning legislative action, a function never conferred upon it by the Constitution and against the exercise of which this Court has steadily set its face from the beginning."

There are two sound reasons why the Constitution limits the power of federal courts to actual disputes between adverse parties. The first reason is a practical one. JUDGES' training and professional experience qualify them to resolve live controversies between parties with adverse interests but not to decide abstract or hypothetical issues. The second reason is a more formal one that concerns the governmental structure that the Constitution established. When courts decide abstract or hypothetical questions, outside the boundaries of lawsuits, they violate the "separation of powers" principle that underlies our governmental structure and thus invade the domain of Congress and the president. The constitutional prohibition against the issuance of advisory opinions by federal courts honors the separation-of-powers principle by limiting the exercise of judicial power to matters in which it is appropriate, indeed, necessary.

The state courts of 38 states honor the same prohibition on advisory opinions. In the other 12 states, the state supreme court has the authority, under either the state constitution or a law enacted by the state legislature, to issue advisory opinions about proposed actions in response to formal requests by the governor or the legislature. For example, the New Hampshire Constitution permits the governor or either house of the state legislature to seek advisory opinions from the New Hampshire Supreme Court. In 1998 the state senate asked that court for its opinion regarding the likely constitutionality of the governor's plan to reform the way in which New Hampshire finances its public schools. The court advised the senate that the governor's plan would violate the state constitution, which forced the governor and the legislature to search for an alternative solution. Thus, where permitted, advisory opinions can influence public policy in important ways.

For more information

Fisher, Louis. *American Constitutional Law.* 3d ed. Durham, N.C.: Carolina Academic Press, 1999.

Porto, Brian L. *May It Please the Court: Judicial Processes and Politics in America.* New York: Addison Wesley Longman, 2000.

Brain L. Porto
Vermont Law School

affirmative action Affirmative action policy seeks to overcome past and continuing racial, ethnic, or gender discrimination by increasing educational or employment opportunities through the preferential treatment of targeted groups. Preferential treatment may entail efforts to enlarge the pool of applicants for positions through advertising or other forms of publicity. However, the public and legal dispute over affirmative action centers on programs that provide bonus points for minority or women applicants to improve their chances for selection or that set firm quotas for qualified minority or women applicants.

The conviction that a color-blind policy would overcome the effects of racial discrimination animated the early CIVIL RIGHTS MOVEMENT. The theory was that if the stigma of public racism were removed, then the plight of blacks and other minorities would disappear. The passage of the 1964 Civil Rights Act and the 1965 VOTING RIGHTS ACT seemed to accomplish this aim. By the late '60s, however, it became clear that racially neutral programs of nondiscrimination failed either to guarantee equal opportunity in employment and higher education or to overcome inequalities in income among racial and ethnic groups. Executive orders issued by the Kennedy and Johnson administrations encouraging efforts to recruit and promote minorities in federally funded programs were unsuccessful. In 1969 President Richard Nixon stiffened existing programs with the implementation of the Philadelphia Plan, a program establishing specific goals and timetables for minority recruitment in the Philadelphia building trades.

By the 1970s affirmative action programs were common in higher education and in employment markets. Legal suits challenging such programs as "reverse discrimination" were also common. The Supreme Court first ruled on the legality of affirmative action in *REGENTS OF THE UNIVERSITY OF CALIFORNIA V. BAKKE* (1978). A divided Court rejected a University of California, Davis Medical School program because of inflexible quotas but indicated that other forms of affirmative action were permissible. Later cases upheld affirmative action in private (*UNITED STEELWORKERS V. WEBER* [1979], relying on Title VII of the 1964 Civil Rights Act) and public (*Johnson v. Transportation Agency, Santa Clara, California* [1987]) employment and in federal construction contracts (*Fullilove v. Klutznick* [1980], citing Congress's grant of the spending power under Article I of the Constitution). More recent cases such as *City of Richmond v. J. A. Croson* (1989) and *Adarand Constructors, Inc. v. Pena* (1995) suggest that the Supreme Court will approve voluntary affirmative action by governments only when the program passes "strict scrutiny." This test, traditionally applied to government actions affecting "suspect classes" such as race or ethnicity, requires that the state demonstrate that the means it has selected to accomplish its compelling interest are least intrusive on individual rights. Some lower courts have rejected affirmative action outright (*Hopwood v. Texas, 999 F. Supp. 872* [1998]). Voters in California and Washington state banned state and local affirmative action programs during the late 1990s.

Opponents of preferential treatment rely either on the Fourteenth Amendment or Titles VI and VII of the 1964 Civil Rights Act as the legal bases to their challenge. They assert that the Fourteenth Amendment's guarantee of equal protection is unequivocal. The declaration that "No State shall . . . deny to any person within its jurisdiction the equal protection of the laws" rejects racial or ethnic ancestry as a relevant basis for awarding a government benefit. Moreover, they argue, the 1964 Civil Rights Act requires that individual, not group-based, attributes be the only permissible factor when governmental or private goods or opportunities are dispersed. Opponents also invoke policy arguments. Preferences tend to reward the most advantaged members of the targeted groups while hurting the least advantaged members of the non-preferred groups, creating an unjust form of compensation. Preferences also stigmatize minorities as inferior since they may be seen to succeed not through merit but through gift. Finally, opponents fear that preferences encourage racial and ethnic identities as a means to win social goods and services, "balkanizing" rather than uniting the nation.

Supporters of affirmative action appeal to a mixture of policy and legal considerations. The Fourteenth Amendment and the Civil Rights Act permit carefully tailored programs designed to overcome systemic discrimination against minorities and women. They further argue that preferential treatment produces significant social benefits that outweigh the harm inflicted on the supposed victims of reverse discrimination. It preserves social peace by establishing society's sensitivity to the plight of its minority citizens. It stimulates social mobility by providing role models who will inspire minority youths. It improves access to professional services such as medical and legal care by training minorities to serve traditionally underserved communities. It enriches the marketplaces of goods and of ideas with a diversity of viewpoints, experiences, and interests. And it responds to the remedial spirit of the RECONSTRUCTION amendments, allowing government and private redress for past social wrongs.

The controversy over affirmative action seems to pose a choice between two unpalatable alternatives. Endorsing race- or ethnic-conscious programs may further legitimize these characteristics as means to apportion benefits and burdens in American society. Rejecting such programs on a "color-blind" principle may condemn minorities to a continued status as an underclass.

Affirmative action remains controversial. In *Gratz v. Bollinger,* 539 U.S. 244 (2003), the Court ruled 5-4 that an undergraduate admissions policy that gave automatic points to students of different ethic groups was unconstitutional. But in *Grutter v. Bollinger,* 539 U.S. 306 (2003), a closely divided Supreme Court (5–4) upheld a law school admissions policy that considered race along with grades and test scores for admission. Here the Court asserted that efforts to create an educationally diverse student body permitted this type of admissions policy. Moreover, in writing for the Court, Justice SANDRA DAY O'CONNOR indicated that she hoped in 25 years schools would no longer need to consider race in order to achieve diversity. In *Parents Involved in Community Schools v. Seattle School District No. 1,* 551 U.S. 701 (2007), the Court struck down as unconstitutional a school district assignment plan that used race to determine which public schools children could attend. The purpose of the use of race was to achieve a racial balance in schools in order to promote integration. This decision seemed to suggest that the Roberts Court was merging debates about affirmative action with those on racial integration.

Whether affirmative action works is further part of the debate. In 1974 the unemployment rate among African Americans was double that of non-Latino whites. In 1999, the rate was still double. In the late 1960s, the proportion of families with incomes below the poverty line was four times greater among blacks than whites. It is still four times greater. There has been some rise in the numbers of minorities in higher education and the professions, but with the exception of women, most groups have not seen appreciable improvement since the mid-1970s, with an actual decline among African-American males entering college.

For more information

Anderson, Terry H. *The Pursuit of Fairness: A History of Affirmative Action.* New York: Oxford University Press, 2005.

Sindler, Allan P. *Bakke, Defunis, and Minority Admissions.* New York: Longman, 1978.

Skrentny, John David. *The Ironies of Affirmative Action: Politics, Culture, and Justice in America.* Chicago: University of Chicago Press, 1996.

Timothy J. O'Neill
Southwestern University

age and crime debate The age and crime debate refers to the issue of whether the commission of crimes is related to age, especially those who are teenagers and young adults.

The age and crime debate has been an issue for decades. What is it about a person's age that can contribute to an increase or decrease in criminal activity? An examination of individuals' offending patterns over time reveals a decline in activity as persons progress in age. In contrast, persons in their late teens and early twenties have a greater propensity to commit crimes.

If negative behaviors are reinforced at the age of onset of criminal activity, it is likely the behavior will continue. The onset of criminal activity varies by type of offense and includes, for example, SHOPLIFTING, which occurs around age 10, and drug offenses, which occur around the age of 19. Criminal tendencies can be reinforced if the juveniles form friendships around criminal activity. How juveniles develop and form social bonds tends to affect how likely they are to develop criminal tendencies. Travis Hirschi's social bond theory, which was modified twice to include more developed aspects of self-control, is considered a prominent theory for understanding delinquency and future criminal behavior. Positive social bonds help prevent delinquency. Social bonds that are beneficial include such factors as attachments to parents, teachers, and other positive role models; commitments to follow rules and realize consequences; involvement in positive extracurricular activities; and the belief in following laws. When positive bonds such as these are broken, the tendency toward participating in delinquent behaviors rises.

Further, problems with self-control are especially pronounced for juveniles because they are developing their own self-image and relationships with others. Low levels of self-control are exhibited in forms of impulsivity, insensitivity, short-sighted and risk-taking tendencies. Of course, not every juvenile who has low self-control will develop criminal behaviors, but negative behaviors contribute to the tendency. Hirschi's enhanced theory of self-control notes that it is the recognition of the consequences of acts that is key to whether or not juvenile delinquents will continue committing crimes or cease in adulthood. If juveniles do not develop self-control mechanisms, criminal activity will persist. Criminal activity generally peaks around the age of 18 to 19 and declines rapidly around the age of 22. As persons continue to age, the likelihood for committing a crime then continues to decline through the age of 30, 40, etc. This process is known as "aging-out." Typically, a desistance or stopping point occurs wherein offenders no longer commit crimes.

When individuals move into adulthood, they are no longer under the authority and direction of their parents. They have to make their own decisions about where to reside, their education, their career, etc. About this time, persons usually realize they are adults and decisions have consequences.

One explanation for why there is a termination in criminal activity by repeat offenders is the idea that offenders eventually grow out of the need or desire to offend due to the realization about their adulthood. The dangerous lifestyle becomes threatening and is no longer a thrill. Maturation and life-course changes are important to encouraging desistance. As persons age, they typically start thinking about usual life-course events that include moving out of the family home, employment, marriage, children, etc.

As responsibilities are learned and gained, the offenders may come to enjoy a life that does not involve crime. There may be a desire to hold onto their achievements. These desires may help reinforce a law-abiding lifestyle. For those ex-offenders, motivation may be the key to success in work programs, and thus, a reduction in repeat offending. Marriage may mean to the offender that the next step is to be financially responsible and a good provider. Children may also help decrease the likelihood previous offenders may participate in risky behavior. They do not want their children exposed to former friends who may have encouraged the criminal lifestyle. Breaking ties with other co-offenders and persons with addictive personalities also helps prevent reoffending as well. Breaking away from negative influences and establishing positive ones enforces law-abiding behavior.

Further, taking advantage of developing positive social bonds can prevent possible returns to criminal behavior. These life-course changes, which occur with age, are considered to be connections to a termination in crime. When offenders are not subjected to the strains of poverty and develop support networks, the likelihood of reoffending is reduced and may even come to an end.

In summary, a positive resolve from illegal to law-abiding activity appears to be possible for offenders as they age-out of offending behaviors. However, prevention by the establishment and enforcement of positive social bonds may prevent criminal behavior altogether. These positive activities are where resources should be directed.

For more information

Mortimer, Jeylan T., and Michael J. Shanahan, eds. *Handbook of the Life Course*. New York: Kluwer Academic/Plenum, 2003.

Soothill, Keith, Claire Fitzpatrick, and Brian Francis. *Understanding Criminal Careers*. Portland, Oreg.: Willian Publishing, 2009.

Michelle L. Foster
Kent State University

aid and abet Aid and abet refers to the act of assisting another human being who commits, or attempts to commit, a crime. One can be found to assist another person through indirect actions, such as helping to plan the crime, or directly participating in the crime itself. One can also assist through words of encouragement, or even silence, if the person has knowledge that the crime is going to be committed.

The term *abet* literally means to encourage or assist. Traditionally, one who assisted in the commission of a crime was referred to as an *abettor.* Today, most criminal codes simply use the term *accomplice,* which carries the same meaning.

One who aids and abets another to commit a crime may be guilty of the very same crime as the person committing the crime (generally referred to as the principal). For example, if person A commits a crime, and person B aids and abets (assists) person A in committing the crime, then person B can be found guilty of the same crime as person A.

The actual extent of liability for aiding and abetting depends on the JURISDICTION. For instance, under Title 18, Section 2 of the U.S. Code, aiding and abetting liability is available where any federal crime is proven. Under state criminal laws, different degrees of liability may attach depending on the type of aid rendered to the principal of the crime, and whether or not the aider and abettor intended to aid in the commission of a particular crime. For example, a person who aids and abets a principal in the commission of a ROBBERY, in which the principal also shoots and kills another person during the robbery, may or may not be responsible for the killing of the other person depending on the state where the act occurred.

Generally speaking, three elements are required to prove aiding and abetting. First, there must be some criminal act. This is usually the act carried out by the principal (robbery or homicide in the example above). Second, the aider and abettor must have some knowledge (or MENS REA) of the underlying criminal act carried out by the principal. This knowledge can be either actual knowledge of crime itself (for example, being present during the commission of the crime), or knowledge that a crime is intended to take place (for example, aiding in the planning of the crime but not necessarily being present during its commission). Finally, the abettor must assist the principal in some manner. As stated above, this assistance can occur prior to the commission of the crime (planning), during the commission, or after the crime has been committed.

Over half a century ago, the U.S. Supreme Court, in *Nye & Nissen v. United States,* 336 U.S. 613 (1949), upheld the notion that in order to be found guilty of aiding and abetting, one must associate oneself with the criminal act, willingly participate in the act (in some capacity), and seek to succeed in the criminal endeavor. In doing so, the Court outlined the general requirements of aiding and abetting liability that is seen in various forms in today's criminal statutes.

For more information

Henning, Anna C., and Kenneth R. Thomas, coordinators. *Congressional Research Service, Reports and Issue Briefs,* "Judge Sonia Sotomayor: Analysis Selected Opinions." (June 19, 2009): 28.

Kurkland, Adam H. "To 'Aid, Abet, Counsel, Command, Induce, or Procure the Commission of an Offense': A Critique of Federal Aiding and Abetting Principles," *South Carolina Law Review* (Autumn 2005): 2005, 85.

Chad J. McGuire
University of Massachusetts, Dartmouth

airport searches Airport searches occur when airport authorities conduct preflight searches of individuals or their luggage. Airport searches raise the legal issue of whether preflight searches violate the FOURTH AMENDMENT protection to be free from unreasonable SEARCHES AND SEIZURES.

Beginning in the 1960s, the Federal Aviation Administration (FAA) established preflight screening procedures designed to prevent people from bringing weapons on board aircraft. Since the early 1970s, the federal COURTS OF APPEALS have adopted a number of different approaches that provide justification for suspicionless airport searches. While the Supreme Court has not clarified which rationale should be adopted, there is agreement among the courts that suspicionless airport searches do not violate the Fourth Amendment protection against unreasonable search and seizure. The justifications the lower courts have provided exempting preflight airport searches from the PROBABLE CAUSE and warrant requirements of the Fourth Amendment include (1) ADMINISTRATIVE SEARCH; (2) consent search; (3) lack of expectation of privacy; (4) stop-and-frisk; (5) BORDER SEARCH; and (6) general reasonableness.

1. ADMINISTRATIVE SEARCH

Searches that are conducted in order to facilitate some administrative purpose rather than a criminal investigation are exempted from the Fourth Amendment requirement of probable cause and a search warrant. The rationale for the exception to the normal requirements is that the searches are not directed at an individual person or an individual crime. In the context of airport searches, some lower courts have held that preflight screenings are administrative searches aimed at preventing weapons and explosives from being carried onboard (*U.S. v. Davis,* 482 F.2d 893 (9th Cir. 1973)). These administrative searches would differ from an individualized search of a person for evidence of a specific crime.

2. CONSENT SEARCH

As long as a person voluntarily gives consent to the authorities to conduct a search, probable cause and a warrant are not required (*SCHNECKLOTH V. BUSTAMONTE,* 412 U.S. 218 (1973). With respect to airport searches, some lower courts have reasoned that people voluntarily give consent for their bags to be searched when they know that they have to submit to a security check at the airport (*Shapiro v. State,* 390 So. 2d 344 (Fla. Sup. Ct. 1980). Unlike searches conducted without notice or choice, airport searches are avoidable by choosing not to travel by airplane (*U.S. v. Edwards,* 498 F.2d 496, 500 (2d Cir. 1974)). If, on the other hand, persons were searched without probable cause and a warrant while they were merely walking down the terminal before entering the checkpoint, that search would violate the Fourth Amendment (*Florida v. Royer,* 460 U.S. 491 (1983)).

3. LACK OF EXPECTATION OF PRIVACY

A search does not require probable cause and a search warrant if the person does not have a reasonable expectation of privacy (*KATZ V. U.S.*, 389 U.S. 347 (1967)). With respect to airport searches, the Florida Supreme Court has reasoned that individuals cannot have an expectation of privacy in their luggage when they know that airports inspect luggage (*Shapiro v. State,* 390 So. 2d 344 (Fla. Sup. Ct. 1980).

4. STOP-AND-FRISK

Some courts have analogized airport metal detectors to constitutionally permissible WARRANTLESS "stop-and-frisk" SEARCHES. The Supreme Court has held that police officers are allowed to pat down people without a warrant for the safety of the officer (*TERRY V. OHIO,* 392 U.S. 1 (1968)). Some lower courts have held this same rationale extends to the minimal intrusion of airport metal detectors in order to protect the safety of other people (*United States v. Epperson,* 454 F.2d 769 (4th Cir. 1972)).

5. BORDER SEARCH

In the interest of protecting the nation, it is constitutionally permissible to conduct a search of persons entering the country without probable cause or a warrant (*U.S. v. Ramsey,* 431 U.S. 606 (1977)). In *U.S. v. Nates,* the Ninth Circuit Court of Appeals held that the rule that authorities do not need any suspicion to search people entering the country applies to people flying out of the country as well (831 F.2d 860 (9th Cir. 1987)).

6. GENERAL REASONABLENESS

While the lower courts have applied different justifications for airport searches, there is a consensus that the risk of someone hijacking an airplane justifies the minimal intrusion of airport searches. Irrespective of the specific rationale given, courts have consistently found good-faith airport searches conducted without probable cause and a warrant reasonable when they are designed to prevent airplanes from being hijacked. The reasonableness of warrantless airport searches is bolstered when advance notice is given so that people have the opportunity to not go through the checkpoint.

For more information

Minert, Steven R. "Square Pegs, Round Hole: The Fourth Amendment and Preflight Searches of Airline Passengers in a Post-9/11 World." *Brigham Young University Law Review* 1631 (2006).

Herzog, Simcha. "Constitutional Problems Posed by Aviation Security Post September Eleventh." 6 *Florida Law Review* 361 (2005).

Eric McAdamis and Ryan C. Black
Michigan State University

Alcatraz Prison Alcatraz, also known as The Rock, is best known as the site of a federal prison. The prison, located in San Francisco Bay, gained fame for being nearly escape proof and for housing the most dangerous criminals of the mid-1930s through the early 1960s.

Isla de Los Alcatraces (Island of the Pelicans) remained an uninhabited 12-acre island of rock until 1853, when it became the first U.S. fort on the Pacific Coast. Fort Alcatraz never saw any action and by 1868 had become a prison for military offenders, drunks, and other minor criminals. In 1907, Alcatraz stopped serving as a fort and became the Pacific Branch of the U.S. Military Prison. The army built the main prison building, which houses the main cell blocks. Alcatraz remained an army prison until January 1, 1934, when it became a federal penitentiary. The first federal prisoners, 53 men, arrived on August 15, 1934, with the remainder of the 242 prisoners arriving by the end of the year.

Alcatraz acquired a reputation as the nation's toughest prison. Each cell stood eight feet long by five feet wide and contained a toilet, wash basin, and wall bunk. Wire-mesh-protected catwalks for the guards ringed the tier blocks and provided a view of every corridor and every cell door. Electronically controlled block-locks, capable of remote operation if needed, opened and closed the cell doors, corridor by corridor. Inmates were under continuous surveillance for 24 hours a day, whether they were asleep, in the recreation yard, or walking from cell block to work site. The mess hall and the kitchen were under the same roof and on the same floor as the cell blocks. The convicts ate ringed by guards and under a ceiling studded with tear gas outlets, ready for automatic use if the occasion arose. Outside of the building, guards armed with .30 caliber carbines and high-powered rifles (two guns per man) staffed five towers, the work area, the recreation yard, the rooftops, and the roadways. Psychologically, Alcatraz proved equally confining to the inmates. With no pretense given to rehabilitation, the prison was designed to be of maximum security and minimum privilege.

The prisoners were a select group who had already demonstrated that they were tough, violent, calculating, and, in many cases, apparently criminally insane. They had been rejected from other prisons because of their poor behavior. Alcatraz was essentially a dumping ground for men serving long or life terms. Many of these prisoners had shown in the past that they were willing to kill to escape prison. The imprisoned included Birdman Robert Stroud, the kidnapper Arthur "Doc" Barker, AL CAPONE, Alvin "Creepy" Karpis, the train robber Roy Gardner, and Machine Gun Kelly. Barker died at Alcatraz, shot down on the rocky shore as he attempted to swim off the island.

Attorney General Robert F. Kennedy closed the obsolete prison in 1963. By this time, Alcatraz had housed more than 1,500 prisoners. In 1969, a small group of Native-American activists occupied several empty prison buildings as a protest against the U.S. government. The prison is now a tourist attraction.

For more information

Godwin, John. *Alcatraz, 1868–1963*. Garden City, N.Y.: Doubleday, 1963.

Needham, Ted, and Howard Needham. *Alcatraz*. Millbrae, Calif.: Celestial Arts, 1976.

Caryn E. Neumann
Miami University of Ohio

alienage Alienage and immigration are central elements of U.S. national social and economic policies. Aliens are individuals from another nation who seek admission into the United States. Aliens who are U.S. residents generally have the same civil and criminal rights as given to citizens; major exceptions include voting, holding federal elective office, and serving on a JURY. CONSTITUTIONAL INTERPRETATION permits executive and legislative branches to decide about the presence of foreigners in our nation.

Immigration is an exclusive function of the national government as part of its power over foreign affairs.

In U.S. history there has been frequent societal ambivalence toward immigration. Restrictions on admission of persons from another country began in 1882 with the Chinese Exclusion Act. Since then Congress has passed a variety of acts to limit entry of certain types of individuals, such as criminals, the mentally ill, or persons from particular nations as part of a national origins quota system. The Immigration and Nationality Act of 1952 (McCarran-Walter Act) placed severe restrictions "upon the immigration and naturalization of Communists and other totalitarians." Congress may establish annual limits for immigration and may alter those limits and quotas for persons or their relatives with special skills. In 1965 Congress abolished the national quota system and established a new annual limit of 170,000 persons per year.

The U.S. Congress decides immigration policy as part of its power to regulate foreign commerce. The U.S. Supreme Court has deferred to Congress on immigration matters, and there are few constitutional limits on this legislative power. Congress establishes rules and individual qualifications for naturalization of an alien admitted to citizenship; see Article I, section 8 of the Constitution. Minors become citizens when their parents are naturalized. Naturalization matters, including admission, naturalization, and deportation of aliens, are administered by the IMMIGRATION AND NATURALIZATION SERVICE (INS) in the U.S. DEPARTMENT OF JUSTICE.

There have been frequent constitutional claims against excessive use of force and BORDER SEARCHES and seizures by the INS. On administrative issues, there have been claims of arbitrary INS practices concerning individuals seeking entry into the country. Immigration rules for deportation and those seeking admission do not always comply with the full realm of rights under the CONSTITUTION. However, the Supreme Court has ruled that DUE PROCESS guarantees apply to INS deportation hearings. An outline of general INS administrative procedures is given in *INS v. Chadha.* Executive departments play an important role in administering immigration laws. Both the Departments of State and Justice have substantial discretion to determine who may enter the United States.

For more information

Aleinkoff, Alexander T. "Federal Regulation of Aliens and the Constitution," *American Journal of International Law* 83 (1989): 862–871.

Gordon, Charles, and Harry N. Rosenfeld. *Immigration Law and Procedure.* Rev. ed. New York: Matthew Bender, 1985.

INS v. Chadha, 462 U.S. 919 (1983).

Neuman, Gerald L. *Strangers to the Constitution: Immigrants, Borders, and Fundamental Law.* Princeton, N.J.: Princeton University Press, 1996.

Steven Puro
Saint Louis University

alternative dispute resolution Alternative dispute resolution refers to a broad range of techniques used in settling conflicts between parties outside the arena of a public court. Alternative dispute resolution (ADR) methods may involve relatively few formal procedures, as in negotiation and mediation, or may, in the instance of arbitration, resemble the structure and adversarial format of a civil trial. The ultimate purpose of ADR is to produce an agreement to which the parties will be bound, avoiding litigation. However, ADR proceedings may be either binding or nonbinding and may be court-ordered or entered into voluntarily by the parties. In voluntary ADR, parties may stipulate at the outset whether the results of proceedings, such as an arbitrator's award, will be binding. In court-ordered ADR, parties enjoy the option of entering into a binding agreement at the conclusion of proceedings. Also, parties are allowed to reject the outcome of court-ordered ADR and pursue claims in a judicial forum. Moreover, ADR is favored by many disputants as a procedurally flexible, cost-effective way of resolving conflict while avoiding civil litigation.

Although in use throughout our nation's history, ADR techniques were not widely embraced by American courts until the 1970s. In the 1980s and 1990s, ADR methods became permanent fixtures in the American legal establishment as state and federal legislatures responded to the exigency of burgeoning civil dockets. In 1990 Congress encouraged the use of ADR techniques by passing the Civil Justice Reform Act, providing funds for ADR programs in the federal courts. More recently, Congress passed the Alternative Dispute Resolution Act of 1998. This legislation requires the federal courts to ensure that litigants consider non-adjudicative approaches to resolving civil disputes. As part of a broader plan to streamline government operations, in 1993 the Clinton administration called on federal administrative agencies to enhance efforts at ADR and avoid the costs of litigation. As a result, federal agencies increasingly employ forms of mediation and arbitration in resolving disputes with private citizens.

ADR is used, to varying degrees, in all state court systems. In many instances, state law or court rules require that litigants participate in one or more approaches to ADR before proceeding to trial. State law and court rules often require that parties engage in ADR in cases involving family issues or commercial relationships. Many legal scholars observe that in matters of DIVORCE and child custody, disputants are more inclined to comply with the terms of settlements reached in the non-adversarial settings of negotiation and mediation. The business community lauds ADR schemes for providing a degree of flexibility and confidentiality in settling legal disputes not ordinarily available through traditional adjudicative processes. Considering that agreements and decisions reached via ADR techniques need not be founded on legal principles, many litigants consider these options better suited to the task of securing a just outcome. ADR strategies are routinely employed in foreign trade disputes where jurisdictional ambiguities often make litigation an unwieldy exercise. Business executives often find that ADR methods are useful in preserving the highly interdependent relationships between firms so typical in today's economy.

The most common forms of ADR include pretrial settlement conferences, the relatively non-adversarial methods of negotiation and mediation, the slightly more adversarial techniques of summary jury trials and mini-trials, and arbitration, the most procedurally complex and formal of non-litigious dispute resolution strategies. Negotiation often takes place between disputing parties prior to the time that attorneys are retained, and this often precludes the need to engage in the expense and delay associated with formal pleadings and discovery. Sometimes, however, parties to a dispute employ legal counsel for the purposes of safeguarding their interests in negotiating a settlement in a civil dispute. Settlement conferences are part of standard pretrial procedures in the federal courts. In a settlement conference, a magistrate, rather than a trial judge, meets with opposing attorneys prior to the scheduled trial date and explores the possibility of a mutually acceptable resolution to the case. When successful, settlement conferences produce a formal, binding agreement between the parties, achieving the goal of avoiding a trial.

Mediation is considered a non-adversarial ADR technique. Mediation sessions are less procedurally rigid than arbitration and are designed to preserve existing legal relationships. Mediation sessions are not intended to gauge the legal strength or evidentiary weight underlying each party's position. Rather, the neutral third party, or mediator, is principally concerned with guiding the disputants toward an agreement to which both parties can accede. Thus, mediators typically seek to highlight points of agreement between parties and narrowly frame issues that produce discord. Doing so often requires that mediators meet with disputing parties in joint sessions as well as in individual meetings, typically referred to as caucuses, in a search for consensus and a sustainable agreement. Mediation sessions may be ordered by a court or arranged voluntarily by the parties. In either case, disputants are free to reject mediation agreements and proceed to litigation.

Summary jury trials are a unique and innovative form of ADR. In a summary jury trial, opposing attorneys present documentary and testimonial evidence, along with brief oral arguments, to a panel of neutral finders of fact. These panels, or "juries," then advise the parties as to the probable outcome of the case were a public trial held. Summary jury trials often occur at a time between the discovery stage of civil litigation and the beginning of an actual trial. Further, summary jury trials are comparatively more adversarial than mediation and are especially useful for litigants as indicators of the viability of their case. Despite the procedural differences between mediation and summary jury trials, both are designed to encourage out-of-court settlements and avoid the delay and expense associated with civil trials. Summary jury trials are occasionally required by court rules.

Mini-trials are similar to summary jury trials in that both settings involve the use of jurors and modifications of conventional trial settings. In addition, mini-trials often involve discovery or information-sharing procedures similar to, yet presumably less costly than, those used in civil trials. Whereas summary jury trials typically use laypersons as finders of fact, mini-trials ordinarily employ a panel of corporate executives representing the disputing parties. Acting as jurors, these executives enjoy the authority to effectuate a binding settlement in the dispute. Like mediation and summary jury trials, mini-trials serve the goal of fully informing the disputants about one another's position, a strategy designed to increase the probability of an agreement and thus obviate the need for litigation. Although frequently arranged solely by the parties, in some jurisdictions courts require mini-trials as a precondition to litigation.

The most adversarial of ADR methods, arbitration is commonly used in business and international trade disputes. Also, arbitration has proven useful in reconciling labor-management discord in a variety of employment settings. Often, parties to a CONTRACT will agree in advance not to litigate disputes over duties and obligations but to have an arbitrator produce a binding decision. If the parties to a dispute elect to participate in arbitration at the time when a disagreement occurs, a neutral third party hears opposing arguments and renders a decision, sometimes referred to as an award. Parties may agree in advance to be bound by an arbitrator's decision. Inasmuch as arbitration awards resemble jury verdicts, the hearings that precede the award often include presentation of documentary and testimonial evidence as well as questioning of witnesses.

In cases of voluntary arbitration, the principle of RES JUDICATA applies, restricting either party from future litigation in the matter. Moreover, by agreeing to participate in arbitration, disputants may waive their SEVENTH AMENDMENT right to a jury trial and agree to be bound by an arbitrator's decision. Awards rendered in binding arbitration sessions are enforceable by public courts. Unlike circumstances wherein parties agree to arbitrate a dispute, court-annexed arbitration is nonbinding and either party may reject the neutral's award. In this instance, a trial *de novo* may be held and a court resolves all legal and factual disputes in the matter. Following an arbitrator's decision, however, parties may accept an arbitrator's award and enter into a binding, enforceable agreement.

The popularity of ADR is reflected in the ascendance of several public and private sector organizations that offer standardized procedural frameworks and professional neutrals trained in dispute resolution methods. The American Arbitration Association (AAA), a private sector organization, provides a complete range of mediation and arbitration services. In addition, the AAA monitors the performance and has compiled a lengthy roster of highly qualified mediators and arbitrators with expertise in a variety of fields. The AAA reports that in 1999 the firm administered ADR services in more than 140,000 cases. In addition, the Global Arbitration Mediation Association provides directory services for parties seeking referral to ADR firms and professionals. The Federal Mediation and Conciliation Service is an independent government agency dedicated to mediating labor-management disputes in public and private sector entities. The prevalence of ADR in domestic and international arenas is likely to encourage growth in these and many related organizations.

For more information

Kheel, Theodore W. *The Keys to Conflict Negotiation: Proven Methods of Settling Disputes Voluntarily.* New York: Four Walls and Eight Windows, 1999.

Nolan-Haley, Jacqueline M. *Alternative Dispute Resolution in a Nutshell.* St. Paul, Minn.: West, 1992.

Bradley J. Best
Austin Peay State University

amendments to the U.S. Constitution Amendments to the U.S. Constitution are vital both to keeping the document up-to-date and to avoiding violence that can occur when peaceful means of constitutional change are blocked, as the colonists felt they had been at the onset of the American Revolution.

Seeking mechanisms that would respond to widely perceived necessities while resisting temporary currents of opinion, the framers of the U.S. CONSTITUTION included amending processes in Article V. This article divides the amending process into proposal and ratification stages and provides two forms of each. An amendment must be proposed by two-thirds majorities of both Houses of Congress or, in a still unused mechanism, by a special convention proposed by two-thirds of the state legislatures. Congress specifies whether amendments will be ratified by three-fourths of the state legislatures or—as in the case of the Twenty-first Amendment repealing national alcohol prohibition—by special state conventions.

Reflecting the importance of the Great Compromise between the small and large states, Article V specifies that no state shall be deprived of its equal vote in the Senate without its consent. Another so-called entrenchment clause provided that Congress would not interfere with the slave trade during the new nation's first 20 years.

Throughout the course of American history, members of Congress have introduced more than 10,000 amending proposals, many of them redundant. Congress has proposed only 33 by the necessary two-thirds majorities and, of these, only 27 have been adopted. Unratified proposals have included a provision related to congressional representation, an amendment to strip citizenship from individuals who accepted titles of nobility, an amendment (the Corwin Amendment) that would have guaranteed the continuing existence of slavery in the South, a child labor amendment, an amendment guaranteeing congressional representation for the District of Columbia, and the EQUAL RIGHTS AMENDMENT.

The initial Congress introduced the first 10 amendments, collectively known today as the BILL OF RIGHTS, and the states ratified them in 1791. These amendments emerged from the controversy between Federalist proponents of the Constitution and Anti-Federalist opponents, who had cited the omission of a bill of rights as a key fault in the new document. Although initially resisting, key Federalists, most notably James Madison, agreed to work for a Bill of Rights if the new document were adopted. In the first Congress Madison gathered together scores of state proposals, most guaranteeing individual rights, which were condensed into 12 amendments, 10 of which were ratified in 1791. Key provisions include the protections for freedom of RELIGION, speech, press, peaceable assembly, and petition in the First Amendment; the RIGHT TO BEAR ARMS in the Second Amendment; provisions against the quartering of troops in private residences in the Third Amendment; protections against unreasonable SEARCHES AND SEIZURES in the FOURTH AMENDMENT; protections for individuals accused of, or on trial for, crimes in AMENDMENTS Five through SEVEN; and the provision against CRUEL AND UNUSUAL PUNISHMENTS in the EIGHTH AMENDMENT. Reflecting Federalist fears that no set of amendments could adequately provide for all contingencies, the NINTH AMENDMENT refers to unenumerated or unlisted rights, and the Tenth Amendment cites rights retained by the states. When originally adopted, the provisions in the Bill of Rights applied only to the national government, but since the adoption of the Fourteenth Amendment with its protection against state denials of DUE PROCESS, the Supreme Court has applied, or "incorporated" almost all these provisions to the states as well. Unincorporated provisions are the Second Amendment right to bear arms, the Third Amendment provision regarding the quartering of troops, the Fifth Amendment guarantee of GRAND JURY indictment, the Seventh Amendment right to a JURY in civil cases, and the Eight Amendment provision against excessive fines and bails.

The Eleventh and Twelfth Amendments were almost contemporaneous with the Bill of Rights. The Eleventh Amendment overturned a Supreme Court decision by limiting lawsuits against the states, and the Twelfth modified the electoral college mechanism for presidential selection so as to prevent unanticipated ties in the voting that the party system had made possible.

The three amendments ratified from 1865 to 1870 responded to the events that precipitated the Civil War. The Thirteenth Amendment permanently abolished slavery. The Fourteenth Amendment overruled the *DRED SCOTT* decision of 1857 by extending CITIZENSHIP to all persons born or naturalized in the United States and prohibiting states from denying citizens their rights. The Fifteenth Amendment further specified that race was not to be used to deny individuals the RIGHT TO VOTE.

Adopted from 1913 to 1920, the next four amendments are associated with the Progressive Era in U.S. politics, which stressed reform and greater democratic participation. The Sixteenth Amendment overturned a Supreme Court decision and permitted the national income tax. The Seventeenth Amendment provided for direct election of U.S. senators, who had been previously selected by state legislatures. The Eighteenth Amendment mandated national alcohol prohibition, while the Nineteenth extended the right to vote to women, a subject that had been increasingly in the national consciousness since the Seneca Falls Convention of 1848.

The last eight amendments have dealt with a variety of subjects. The Twentieth Amendment changed the dates that new presidents and congresses take office, thus shortening the terms of so-called lame-duck members who had been voted out of office. The Twenty-first Amendment repealed national alcohol prohibition. The Twenty-second Amendment limited presidents to two full terms, or eight years, in office. The Twenty-third Amendment provided representation in the electoral college for the District of Columbia. The Twenty-fourth Amendment limited the effect of poll taxes; the Twenty-fifth Amendment provided for cases of presidential disability; and the Twenty-sixth Amendment reduced the voting age to 18.

The last amendment, the Twenty-seventh, prohibits Congress from giving itself a raise until after an intervening election. Originally proposed in 1789 as part of the Bill of Rights, the states did not ratify the amendment until 1992, after a college student named Gregory Watson became convinced that the amendment was still viable. This amendment points to the fact that Article V specified no ratification deadline. Similarly, Article V does not specify whether states can rescind ratifications of pending amendments or ratify amendments they have previously rejected.

Proposed amendments often become issues even when they are not proposed by Congress by the necessary two-thirds majorities and ratified by the states. Recent decades have witnessed vigorous debates over amendments to reverse Supreme Court decisions regarding PRAYER AND/OR BIBLE READING IN PUBLIC SCHOOLS, busing, ABORTION, and FLAG-BURNING as well as amendments to balance the federal budget, make English the official national language, and guarantee VICTIMS' RIGHTS.

Interpretations of the Constitution often change over time through judicial decisions and congressional and presidential practices. Amendments serve, however, as markers for many key changes in the Constitution and evidence of the continuing power that "We the people" can exercise through legal channels.

For more information

Palmer, Kris E. *Constitutional Amendments, 1789 to the Present*. Detroit: Gale Group, 2000.

Vile, John R. *Encyclopedia of Constitutional Amendments, Proposed Amendments, and Amending Issues, 1789–1995*. Santa Barbara, Calif.: ABC-CLIO, 1996. See also Appendix.

John R. Vile
Middle Tennessee State University

American Bar Association American Bar Association or the A.B.A. is a private, voluntary association, with headquarters in Chicago, which is the national organization for the legal profession. The A.B.A. is the largest association of professionals in the world, with more than 400,000 members, or approximately half of the lawyers in the United States.

The A.B.A. was established in 1878, in response to the industrialization of the economy, which spurred calls for the creation of stricter standards for entry into the legal profession. The standards for admission to law practice had been lax for more than a hundred years. As late as 1860, only nine of the 39 states had any educational requirements for practicing law. In those states, an aspiring lawyer served a period of apprenticeship in a law office, then sat for a rather casual oral exam, conducted by a judge, which lasted about a half hour. Often, the examinee passed because of a recommendation from a well-known lawyer, not because of professional competence. The A.B.A. urged state legislatures to require candidates for admission to the bar to pass a written "bar exam" that was more rigorous than the earlier oral exams. A.B.A. members viewed written exams as a method of improving the competence of lawyers, which remains one of the association's major goals.

Today the A.B.A. pursues that goal principally by serving as the national accrediting body for U.S. LAW SCHOOLS. Most states rely on A.B.A. accreditation to determine whether the law school attended by an applicant for admission to practice meets the educational requirements necessary for admission to the bar. Graduation from a law school that is not A.B.A.-accredited may entitle the graduate to take the bar exam in the state in which the law school is located, but it often disqualifies the graduate from taking the bar exam in other states. Therefore, the customary path to the legal profession nowadays is to earn a baccalaureate degree (B.A. or B.S.) from a four-year college and a juris doctor (J.D.) degree from an A.B.A.-accredited law school. The A.B.A.'s Section of Legal Education and Admissions to the Bar assists aspiring lawyers to find suitable law schools by publishing the *Official American Bar Association Guide to Approved Law Schools* annually.

The A.B.A. also attempts to improve the competence of lawyers by sponsoring continuing legal education programs and by publishing books, articles, pamphlets, and newsletters that address substantive areas of the law, as well as issues such as law office management and the increasing role of technology in the practice of law. Some A.B.A. publications recommend standards of conduct that lawyers should follow when they perform certain legal tasks. For example, *Standards of Conduct: Pleas of Guilty*, Third Edition (1999), establishes guidelines for PROSECUTORS and defense attorneys to use in negotiating "PLEA BARGAINS" with persons accused of crimes. In a plea bargain, the accused pleads guilty to a less serious offense than the offense that was charged originally, in exchange for receiving a less severe sentence than would have resulted from a conviction on the original charge.

The ethical standards of the legal profession are another focus of the A.B.A., and they have been for many years. In 1908 the A.B.A. adopted a code of professional ethics, and most states either accepted the A.B.A. code or something similar as their official rules for the conduct of lawyers. Today the A.B.A. periodically amends its code of ethics, known as the "Model Rules of Professional Responsibility," which states are free to accept or reject, but which most states adopt, at least in part or in modified form.

One of the most important roles that the A.B.A. plays is as an evaluator of prospective federal JUDGES. The A.B.A.'s "Committee on Federal Judiciary," which is comprised of 15 members who represent each region of the country, screens persons whom the president is considering for nomination to a federal judgeship and assigns each one a rating of "not qualified," "qualified," or "well-qualified," which the committee then makes available to the attorney general and to the Senate

Judiciary Committee for their consideration. The major function of the Committee on Federal Judiciary is to try to prevent ill-advised nominations; once the president chooses a nominee, the committee does not actively oppose that choice even if it rated the nominee "not qualified."

Despite its power and prominence, the A.B.A. faces several daunting challenges in the new millennium. Among these are: (1) making legal services more affordable; (2) making the practice of law friendlier to minorities and women, especially mothers of school-age children; and (3) addressing the public perception that our system for compensating injury victims enriches lawyers but diminishes America's economic competitiveness in the global economy. Only time will tell whether the A.B.A. is equal to these awesome challenges.

For more information

Linowitz, Sol, and Martin Mayer. *The Betrayed Profession: Lawyering at the End of the Twentieth Century.* Baltimore, Md.: Johns Hopkins University Press, 1994.

Porto, Brian L. *May It Please the Court: Judicial Processes and Politics in America.* New York: Addison Wesley Longman, 2000.

Brian L. Porto
Vermont Law School

American Civil Liberties Union The American Civil Liberties Union or the ACLU is a nonpartisan citizens' organization dedicated to the preservation and implementation of the BILL OF RIGHTS. It was founded in 1920 by political activists reacting to government attempts to stifle dissent during World War I, and it now has 300,000 members, national offices in New York City and Washington, D.C., with a staff of more than 150, affiliate offices in 50 states, and an agenda that covers all the rights protected by the CONSTITUTION.

Its underlying premise is that democracy, as embodied in the U.S. system of government and law, has two parts: rule by the majority of the people, through democratically elected representatives, and protection of the rights of the individual and of groups—even when protection means limiting the power of the majority. By this reasoning, it would be undemocratic, for example, to permit the majority to prohibit people from voting, going to certain schools or holding certain jobs because of their race, religion, political views, gender, or other irrelevant characteristics.

While the organization has persuaded state and federal courts to apply this underlying principle, that has not exempted it from the animosity of many. The reasons are twofold.

First, the ACLU has adopted numerous positions that were, and in some cases remain, controversial. Taking the entire Bill of Rights as its mandate, the organization regularly involves itself in issues such as speech (*Reno v. ACLU*, 1997), racial discrimination, separation of church and state (*Santa Fe Independent School District v. Doe*, 2000), lesbian and GAY RIGHTS (*Romer v. Evans*, 1996), arts CENSORSHIP, CAPITAL PUNISHMENT, children's rights, education reform, national security, privacy and technology, PRISONERS' RIGHTS, voting rights, women's rights (*Planned Parenthood v. Casey*, 1992), and workplace rights, electronic privacy, rights of the mentally ill, and drug policy and law enforcement issues (*Miranda v. Arizona*, 1966).

Second, the ACLU frequently defends people whose opinions are controversial or extreme (*National Socialist Party of America v. Skokie*, 1977) because it believes that once the government is empowered to violate one person's rights it can use that power against everyone.

The ACLU describes itself as the nation's first public interest LAW FIRM. The bulk of its work consists of litigation, with the combined national and affiliate offices handling more than 6,000 cases a year. The majority are the work of volunteer attorneys. They work closely with the legal staff, members of which sometimes argue cases themselves. The organization's boards of directors are similarly made up of volunteers.

In addition to bringing cases itself, the ACLU writes AMICUS CURIAE ("friend of the court") briefs in cases it considers particularly important in a specific subject area or in the development of constitutional doctrine. It argues more cases and submits more amicus briefs to the Supreme Court than any other nongovernment organization. Its high success rate accounts for its impact on both American law and the proliferation of other public interest law organizations.

For more information

Cowan, Ruth B. "Women's Rights through Litigation," *Columbia Human Rights Law Review* 8 (1976): 373–412.

Walker, Samuel. *In Defense of American Liberties: A History of the ACLU.* New York: Oxford University Press, 1990.

Philippa Strum
City University of New York

Americans with Disabilities Act The Americans with Disabilities Act or the ADA is a federal statute prohibiting discrimination based on disability in employment, state and local government, public accommodations, commercial facilities, transportation, and telecommunications. President George H. W. Bush signed the Americans with Disabilities Act (ADA) into law in 1990. Any individual who has a disability, or a relationship or association with someone with a disability, is covered by the ADA.

According to the ADA, the term *disability* refers to a physical or mental impairment that substantially limits major life activities. Anyone who has a history of such impairments, or whom others perceive to have such impairments, is protected by the provisions in the ADA. The ADA does not specify all types of disabilities that the law covers. In fact, after passage of the ADA, AIDS (acquired immunodeficiency syndrome) activists sought, and eventually won, a Court interpretation of the statute that includes AIDS as an ADA qualifying disability.

Congress divided the ADA into titles, and each specifies protections within a particular category. Title I requires employers (employing 15 or more persons) to provide equal opportunities to all employment-related benefits for qualified individuals with disabilities. The Equal Employment Opportunity Commission (EEOC) handles Title I complaints.

Title II applies to state and local governments and requires that all people with disabilities be assured access to public programs and services. The kinds of public programs and services that ADA applies to are, for example: public education, government employment, public transportation, access to the courts, and participation in elections. Title III requires businesses and nonprofit service providers to provide equal treatment to persons with disabilities. Examples of the types of public accommodations covered under Title III include: movie theaters, buses, homeless shelters, hotels, retail stores, and restaurants. Businesses running these sorts of public services are required to provide "reasonable accommodation" for people with disabilities. This is a difficult term to define, and judges have interpreted it in various ways. Generally it means that whenever possible, businesses should make adjustments to accommodate people with disabilities. If an owner can show that he or she has made an honest attempt to provide accommodations, then this will generally put them in compliance with the law. For instance, a business may be required to provide adaptations, like ramps, wider doorways, and braille menus. The U.S. Department of Justice handles complaints under both Titles II and III.

Finally, Title IV of the ADA covers telecommunication services such as television and telephone access for persons who have hearing and/or visual impairments. The purpose of this title is to ensure that people with disabilities have access to interstate and intrastate communications. Therefore, the telephone companies are required to provide devices such as telecommunications devices for the deaf (TDDs). In addition, television broadcasting companies were required to add closed captioning to federally funded public service announcements. Television manufacturers were required to make television sets capable of showing the closed captioning available to the general public. The Federal Communications Commission oversees this title.

Disability advocates heralded the passage of the ADA through Congress, and its signing into law, as a triumph. Many Americans with disabilities have benefited from the provisions of this law at work, in leisure activities, and in exercising their rights as citizens to vote in elections. Many disability interest groups are still working to educate members of the public, and persons protected by the law, on its many provisions.

For more information

(on interest group education) http://TheArc.org; and (the law itself) 42 U.S.C. section 12101 et seq.

O'Brien, Ruth. *Voices from the Edge: Narratives about the Americans with Disabilities Act.* New York: Oxford University Press, 2004.

Nancy Winemiller Basinger
University of Georgia

amicus curiae Amicus curiae is Latin for "friend of the court." The plural is amici curiae. As the name suggests, amici curiae are expected to serve the interests of the court. An amicus curiae is anyone, or any group, that has a strong interest in a case but is not one of the direct parties in a case, who seeks to provide information to the court to reinforce the arguments provided in the BRIEFS of the litigants or to provide information that those parties did not include in their briefs. This understanding of amici curiae and their role before the courts may be somewhat misleading. In practice, amici curiae have generally participated to advance their own policy objectives, rather than serving altruistic goals such as serving the needs of the court system to be fully informed.

Amicus curiae briefs can be filed in any court, state or federal, and at any level, trial or appellate. In most instances, the amicus is an attorney filing the brief on behalf of a client, but it need not be. Amicus curiae briefs can only be filed with the consent of the court in which the case is being heard, but this consent is usually granted, particularly when the consent of both litigants is provided. However, if the party submitting the brief is the federal government, state, territory, or commonwealth, consent is not required from the court. In rare circumstances, amici are allowed to participate in oral arguments.

These briefs are filed by interested third parties because decisions of the court, while directly applying only to the parties directly involved in the case, have implications beyond the case being decided. Through the doctrine of *STARE DECISIS*, or PRECEDENT, the decision in a case may be of interest to persons, businesses, or interest groups not directly involved in the case. In these instances, those who might be potentially affected may file an amicus curiae brief.

Amicus curiae briefs are more frequently filed at the appellate level than in trial courts. The reasons for this are associated with the cost of filing amicus briefs and the policy impact of becoming involved in the case. The most effective amicus curiae briefs are those with substantial legal research, containing information that the court might not otherwise obtain from the litigants. As a result, the cost to research and prepare the brief can be quite high. In addition, those filing briefs will want to participate as amicus curiae in a court where the decision will have the greatest impact, and will focus on courts of appeal rather than trial courts.

There is no limit on the number of amicus briefs that can be filed in a single case. Those cases that tend to attract the most amicus activity are those that involve issues that are highly salient to the public and involve significant issues of policy that affect large segments of the population. The first amicus brief was filed in the Supreme Court in 1821, and amicus activity was relatively rare for the next century. Even during the first half of the 20th century, amicus briefs were filed in approximately 10 percent of Supreme Court cases. As the Supreme Court heard more cases involving CIVIL LIBERTIES, and public interest groups formed to pursue policy, it is now rare for a case to reach the Supreme Court without at least one amicus brief filed. In recent years, more than 80 percent of cases heard by the Supreme Court contain at least one amicus curiae brief.

The record for the most amicus curiae briefs filed in a case heard by the Supreme Court occurred in *Webster v. Reproductive Services*, an ABORTION rights case decided in 1989. In *Webster*, there were 78 amicus curiae briefs filed by hundreds of pro-choice and antiabortion organizations, breaking the previous record of 57 briefs filed in the affirmative action case *REGENTS OF THE UNIVERSITY OF CALIFORNIA V. BAKKE* in 1978. The Court may give the arguments in the amicus curiae brief as much or as little weight as it chooses, but with the increasing number of briefs filed, the Court is certainly better informed about the potential legal, social, and political consequences of their decisions than ever before.

For more information

Merrill, Thomas, and Joseph P. Kearney. "The Influence of Amicus Curiae Briefs on the Supreme Court," *University of Pennsylvania Law Review* 148 (January 2000): 743–855.

Ennis, Bruce J. "Effective Amicus Briefs," *Catholic University Law Review* 33 (1984): 603–609.

Krislov, Samuel. "The Amicus Curiae Brief: From Friendship to Advocacy," *Yale Law Journal* 72 (March 1963): 694–721.

Scott Comparato
Southern Illinois University at Carbondale

animal rights Animal rights often refers broadly to efforts by advocates of every kind to protect nonhuman animals from exploitation by humans. But to many lawyers it refers specifically to the struggle to obtain legal rights for at least some nonhuman animals.

Twenty-first-century U.S. humans have an assortment of basic legal rights: They cannot be enslaved. Their bodies cannot be used in biomedical research without their consent. They cannot be imprisoned in steel and concrete cages if they have committed no crime. At one time Americans enslaved each other. It was only near the end of the Middle Ages that Europeans began to believe that it was wrong to enslave those who were of their own race or RELIGION. That did not stop white Christians from enslaving Muslims or Africans of any religion, but it was a start. At various times in the history of the United States, Indians, women, children, and blacks all lacked basic legal rights. Human slaves were treated as legal things, scarcely different from a chair, a dish, or a cow. Sometimes they were treated as real estate, such as houses and land. Only legal persons have legal rights and human slaves were not legal persons under the civil law. They were invisible to the civil law and so they lacked all CIVIL RIGHTS.

Legal things are often protected by the criminal law, but that does not give them any legal rights. Today a statute might make it a crime to take a baseball bat to the windshield of a car. A wrongdoer might be fined or even sent to prison, but neither the car nor the windshield would be a legal person with civil rights. Before the Civil War, many slave-holding states made it a crime to kill or grievously harm a slave. If a master violated that law, it was a criminal matter between the master and the state, not a civil one between the master and slave. The first major criminal statute that protected nonhuman animals was England's "Martin's Act," passed in 1822 to "prevent the cruel and improper treatment of Cattle." That statute has been expanded, extended, and multiplied throughout the English-speaking world. Every U.S. state has at least one. But, in almost every way, the "legal thinghood" of every nonhuman animal in the United States today is the same as it is for windshields and cars and the same as it once was for black slaves before the Civil War.

Animal rights lawyers are trying to change this. They want at least some nonhuman animals to be declared legal persons with basic legal rights. They want people to be able to protect them against enslavement, biomedical research, and imprisonment. This might be accomplished in several ways. The UNITED STATES CONSTITUTION or state constitutions might be amended, but these are unlikely places to start. More promising are the legislatures of the 50 states. Perhaps the most promising is the common law.

The common law is what judges make as they decide cases that do not interpret of statutes or constitutions. The rules that one cannot drive negligently or break a contract are just some of a large number of common law rules. How do judges decide what these rules should be? They look to three things—PRECEDENT, policy, and principle. Precedents are those cases already decided, whether yesterday or 500 years ago. Policy concerns what judges think will be the impact of their decisions on society. Principle involves what judges believe is right and wrong. By temperament and training, each judge will tend to emphasize one of these three over the others.

Precedent judges, who care most about deciding cases the way they have always been decided and in keeping the law stable, will probably not be inclined to change the legal status of nonhuman animals from legal thing to legal person. After all, nonhuman animals have been legal things for many centuries. More common in the United States are policy judges and principle judges. It can be thought that when the basic interests of a being are at stake, they should never be sacrificed to the interests of those who want to exploit them. This is exactly what occurred before the Civil War. Even Northern judges who hated slavery supported the most unfair Fugitive Slave Laws for policy reasons; they wanted to facilitate economic growth and promote national unity by not alienating the slave-holding South. Today we think they did a terrible thing as a matter of principle.

The highest principles of the common law include liberty and equality. Fundamental to liberty is the idea that certain basic interests are of immense importance. One of those interests is "autonomy." Any being able to want things and able intentionally to try to get them, and who has a sense of self complex enough to allow them to realize, however dimly, that they are living a life should have autonomy sufficient to entitle them to the legal rights to bodily integrity and bodily liberty. Their bodies cannot be used in biomedical research. They should not be imprisoned in steel and concrete cages. Species should be entirely irrelevant.

The debate over animal rights asks whether animals are property or some entity that has rights of its own. Traditionally, animals, both wild and domestic, were considered property and owners could do with them whatever they wanted. But increasingly, many communities are adopting laws enhancing penalties for animal abuse. In part, these laws have been adopted because research suggests that abuse of animals, if unchecked, often escalates into other forms of abuse. Additionally, the topic of animal rights has led to efforts to regulate factory farms, and many businesses have adopted practices to improve how they raise animals such as chickens, pigs, and cattle.

Fundamental to equality is the idea that "likes should be treated alike." We give basic legal rights even to human infants born without a brain who are not conscious or sentient. What about chimpanzees and bonobos? They feel pain and suffer. They are probably self-conscious. They act intentionally. They solve problems insightfully. They use and make tools. They flourish in rough and tumble societies so political that they are routinely dubbed "Machiavellian." They can learn symbols and numbers and understand two or three thousand English words. It is impossible both to comport with equality and give these infants rights, yet deny every legal right to chimpanzees and bonobos. And there are almost certainly others.

For more information

Sunstein, Cass R., and Martha C. Nussbaum. *Animal Rights: Current Debates and New Directions.* New York: Oxford University Press, 2005.

Wise, Steven M. *Rattling the Cage—Toward Legal Rights for Animals.* Boulder, Colo.: Perseus, 2000.

Steven Wise
Center for the Expansion of Civil Rights

anonymous tips Anonymous tips refer to calls or information law enforcement officials receive from unknown sources related to some criminal activity. While anonymous tips may be an important source of information for police, acting on them raises significant constitutional questions.

In an effort to improve communication with the population they serve and protect, many urban police departments try to involve local citizens in maintaining the peace and security of their own neighborhoods. Since residents have familiarity with the day-to-day routine in their own neighborhoods, it is easier for residents than for police to pinpoint unusual behavior, identify suspects, and bring other problems to the attention of police in a timely fashion, thereby helping prevent or at least reduce the amount of local criminal behavior. Additionally, with improved police-neighborhood communication, residents' perception of police may improve, so that the whole environment becomes less confrontational and more cooperative. Anonymous tip lines have become essential to neighborhood policing in areas as diverse as Walkill, N.Y., population, 2,000, Syracuse, N.Y., population 150,000, which has television advertising:

> [Please call the tip line with] information . . . relative to an incident that has previously occurred or one that is going to occur. [A]ll tips are confidential. . . . Because the tip line is anonymous, the sender will not receive a response. . . .

and Washington, D.C., population 600,000, where billboards display the following:

> Anyone who has information concerning a homicide, gangs, guns, or other violent offenses can call the anonymous tip line. . . . [which] is part of an ongoing effort to devise innovative ways to further reduce violence. . . .

Regardless of the above communities' response to the tip line concept, one major question about soliciting anonymous tips remains unanswered: How can law enforcement personnel assess accuracy of information obtained through anonymous tip lines, so they know how much reliance can logically be placed on tips obtained this way?

Anonymous tips have often been held to be an insufficient basis by themselves for a finding of reasonable suspicion that would justify a stop, *United States v. Robinson,* 537 F.3d 798, 802 (7th Cir., 2008). But there is no legal mandate to disallow information volunteered by anonymous tipsters. It appears that when questioning the validity of anonymous tips, the federal courts review this information on a case-by-case basis rather than applying a flat rule to every situation. The courts have held that when the identity of an anonymous tipster would be easy to determine, *United States v. Kent,* 531 F.3d 642, 648–649 (8th Cir., 2008); or the tipster provides a great deal of detail that corroborates police observations and also could not benefit from the suspect's ARREST, *Edwards v. Cabrera,* 58 F.3d 290, 294 (7th Cir., 1995), police may be justified in relying on the tipster's information. In general, courts seem to use an anonymous tip as an integral portion of a larger body of information but not as the sole source of information on which they base a decision to search or arrest a suspect, but with or without a warrant. *United States v. Torres,* 534 F.3d 207, 210–211 (3d Cir., 2008).

While the idea of protecting the identity of information sources may be relatively new to police departments, courts and state legislatures throughout the United States have dealt with this issue for many years, particularly in regard to journalists' information sources. When reporters obtain information from sources who wish to remain anonymous, courts have frequently ruled upon whether this "reporters' privilege" exists; and if the privilege exists, if it is enforceable in any context.

The landmark case on reporters' privilege is *Branzburg v. Hayes*, 408 U.S. 665 (1972). In *Branzburg*, a reporter claimed that journalism represented an expression of FREEDOM OF SPEECH and was therefore protected by the guarantee of free speech in the First Amendment to the U.S. CONSTITUTION. The reporter argued that this guarantee would be violated if a court mandated identification of a source to whom the journalist had promised confidentiality. The Supreme Court, in a 5-4 decision, found that First Amendment rights do not shield the journalist's sources from inquiry before a GRAND JURY.

However, Justice Powell's concurring opinion would have limited the applicability of the *Branzburg* decision to the facts of that case. Later decisions in the federal courts interpreted Powell's opinion to mean that journalists' privilege indeed exists, but only in the realm of civil, rather than criminal, cases. *Zerilli v. Smith*, 656 F.2d 705 (D.C. Cir., 1981).

As of 2009, 40 states and the District of Columbia have enacted laws creating at least a partial statutory shield for journalists. In the remaining 10 states, journalists can claim only a common law privilege, extracted from court decisions in those JURISDICTIONS. In some states, statutory or common law protects journalists in civil but not in criminal proceedings.

For more information

CRS Annotated Constitution, Legal Information Institute. Available online. URL: http://www.law.cornell.edu/anncon/html/amdt4frag3_user.html; and http://www.law.cornell.edu/anncon/html/amdt1bfrag1_user.html.

Paul K. McMasters, and Geoffrey R. Stone. Do Journalists Need a Better Shield? Available online. URL: http://www.firstamendmentcenter.org/commentary.aspx?id=14547.

Petro, M. J. "7th Circuit Criminal Law Alert, Anonymous Tip Arrest." Available online. URL: http://mjpetro.typepad.com/7th_circuit_alert/2009/12/criminal-forfeiture-and-restitution-bo ilerp late-rules.html.

Beth Simon Swartz
Attorney

anti-loitering laws Anti-loitering laws refer to laws making it illegal to be in a public place at certain times without a valid reason.

Laws prohibiting being in a public place without a valid reason have existed for centuries in parts of western Europe and North America. Except in times of war or civil unrest, these laws were rarely enforced. However, the 1990s saw a renewed enthusiasm for this type of legislation in the United States with many municipalities either revamping existing laws and accentuating enforcement or creating new ones. Today, most major U.S. cities as well as many smaller cities and towns have anti-loitering ordinances in place. Because so many JURISDICTIONS have enacted this type of legislation, there is no universal standard or single legal definition of "loitering." However, loitering is commonly understood today as the congregation of two or more people in public places without an apparent purpose.

The earliest incarnation of prohibitions against loitering can be traced to 14th-century English common law. These early prohibitions were designed to control the movement of peasants within towns and villages by holding them accountable for their presence outside of "dwelling places." It was believed that the criminalisation of "loitering" would guard against idleness, flight, vagrancy, or other more serious offenses. Over the course of several centuries, the prohibitions against loitering were amended many times to account for economic, demographic, and cultural shifts in Europe.

In the United States, anti-loitering legislation has also undergone significant changes in both substantive content and in enforcement strategies. Between the late 18th and mid-19th centuries, America anti-loitering legislation was designed primarily to ensure that people adhered to the tenets of hard work, temperance, and piety.

Anti-loitering laws as stand-alone pieces of legislation waned considerably beginning in the early 20th century. While such ordinances remained as part of state legislation or municipal codes, their enforcement was lax. Instead, what began to appear were proscriptions against loitering as components of other criminal or civil statues. This reflected the sentiment that being in a public place without an apparent purpose was not in and of itself a transgression, but rather that it was a symptom of, or precursor to, other forms of deviance or criminality. As such, the discourse of anti-loitering became an integral part of a variety of different criminal laws and pieces of civil legislation. Perhaps best known as a component of laws prohibiting PROSTITUTION, loitering has been included in legislation pertaining to truancy, panhandling, the sales of alcohol, curfews, narcotics, and most recently, GANGS.

As the public's fear of STREET CRIME grew exponentially in the late 1980s and early 1990s (though actual street crime was not on the rise), there was a resurgence in anti-loitering laws. Many major American cities enacted ordinances that again made being in a public place without an obvious purpose a crime, even if not accompanied by any other criminal activity (such as intoxication, soliciting, etc.). The best known of these was Chicago's Gang Congregation Ordinance (Chicago Municipal Code 8-4-015 [1992]).

Proponents of anti-loitering legislation contend that it is useful in combating street crime, particularly gang activity and drug trafficking. Opponents counter that the legislation relies too heavily on the discretion of police officers, resulting in the unfair targeting of the poor and racialized minorities. In the case of *City of Chicago v. Morales*, 527 U.S. 41 (1999), the U.S. Supreme Court ruled that the ordinance was unconstitutional.

While enthusiasm for specific anti-loitering legislation has waned somewhat among lawmakers since the Supreme Court's ruling, the use of anti-loitering provisions as part of other criminal statutes is still viewed by law enforcement officials and the general public as a valuable tool in the war on street crime.

For more information

Chambliss, William J. "A Sociological Analysis of the Law of Vagrancy," *Social Problems* 12, no. 1 (Summer 1964): 67–77.

Levi, Ron. "Making Counter-Law: On Having No Apparent Purpose in Chicago," *British Journal of Criminology* 49, no. 2 (2009): 131–149.

Schofield, Daniel L. "Gang Congregation Ordinance: Supreme Court Invalidation," *FBI Law Enforcement Bulletin* 68 no. 9 (September 1999): 28–33.

Stephen L. Muzzatti
Ryerson University

antitrust law Antitrust law refers to a cluster of federal laws that seek to inhibit private parties from improperly restraining the marketplace through large combinations or trusts of business or capital. Some argue that the goal of antitrust laws can be thought of as promoting allocative economic efficiency. That is, the goal of antitrust is to promote a market system that maximizes societal wealth by deploying resources where they are most highly valued. Others argue that antitrust is primarily designed to protect consumers from monopolists and cartel members. That is, the policy goal is to avoid artificially high prices being charged to the consumer. Whatever the normative policy goal, the laws take the form of prohibitions on a variety of actions deemed to harm or improperly restrain the market. While many states have enacted legislation that tracks the federal laws, the term generally refers to the SHERMAN ACT, the CLAYTON ACT, and the Federal Trade Commission Act.

The Sherman Act (15 U.S.C. § 1–7) makes CONTRACTS or agreements for purposes of the restraint of interstate or foreign trade illegal. The Sherman Act also prohibits monopolies and conspiracies to monopolize. By *monopoly,* the statute contemplates a consolidation of economic power which allows the suspect firm to set a price that is artificially high.

The Clayton Act (15 U.S.C. § 12–27) supplements the Sherman Act by prohibiting price discrimination when the effect is to substantially lessen competition. The Clayton Act also prohibits kickbacks and other commercial bribery or price manipulation as well as any attempt to obtain or grant kickbacks or bribes.

The Federal Trade Commission Act (15 U.S.C.A. § 41–51) creates the commission responsible for preventing the use of unfair methods of competition or deceptive trade practices.

Antitrust laws can be the basis for civil or criminal actions and can be privately or publicly enforced. In the event that a private plaintiff prevails in an antitrust action, that plaintiff is entitled to damages. Damages may take the form of injunctive relief or compensatory relief. Injunctive relief occurs when the defendant(s) is/are ordered to CEASE AND DESIST engaging in the objectionable behavior that gave rise to the litigation. Compensatory relief seeks to compensate the aggrieved party for the actions of the defendant(s).

The Clayton Act contains a treble damages provision which is designed to discourage bad behavior before it occurs. The Clayton Act awards treble damages, or triple the actual loss, to any successful plaintiff. The treble damages provision has been the principal deterrent to and punishment of anticompetitive conduct. It also serves as an incentive for private enforcement of the antitrust laws and a mechanism for retrieving ill-gotten gains. Still, the treble damages provision is not without its critics. Some economists and legal scholars argue that the statute does not encourage consumers or others to mitigate, or lessen, their damages since it awards three times the actual damages suffered. Further, since the proscribed behavior is somewhat vague, the treble damages may create a disincentive for aggressive competition. The windfall of treble damages may act as an incentive for frivolous litigation. Finally, compensating an injured party beyond their damages while penalizing a defendant in excess of the gains from misbehavior may be unfair.

For more information

Hovenkamp, H. *Federal Antitrust Policy, The Law of Competition and Its Practice.* 2nd ed. St. Paul, Minn.: West, 2000.

Ross, S. R. *Principles of Antitrust Law.* Westbury, N.Y.: Foundation Press, 1993.

Sullivan, E. T., and Harrison, J. L. *Understanding Antitrust and Its Economic Implications.* 2nd ed. New York: Matthew Bender, 1994.

Charles Anthony Smith
University of California, San Diego

Apodaca v. Oregon 406 U.S. 404 (1972) In *Apodaca v. Oregon,* the Supreme Court affirmed that conviction by a less than a unanimous JURY did not violate the SIXTH AMENDMENT's provisions for a RIGHT TO TRIAL BY JURY.

Robert Apodaca, Henry Morgan Cooper, Jr., and James Arnold Madden were convicted in Oregon of assault with a deadly weapon, BURGLARY in a dwelling, and grand LARCENY before three separate juries. Apodaca and Madden were found guilty of all charges by verdicts of 11–1, while a 10–2 jury convicted Cooper. The Oregon state constitution permitted a verdict by 10 of 12 jurors in criminal cases, except in the event of first-degree MURDER. The Oregon Court of Appeals affirmed the convictions in 1969 and the Oregon Supreme Court denied a review. All three defendants then sought a review by the U.S. Supreme Court.

The Court had earlier ruled in *Williams v. Florida,* 399 U.S. 78 (1970), that the Sixth Amendment's right to trial by jury did not require that all juries consist of 12 jurors. The Court found that the original intent of the framers of the CONSTITUTION required only an impartial panel of individuals from a cross section of the community. The Founding Fathers' aim of preventing oppression by the government could be achieved with fewer than 12 jurors. The *Apodaca* decision rested in part on the *Williams* decision.

Justice Byron White announced the *Apodaca* decision on May 22, 1972. CHIEF JUSTICE WARREN BURGER, Justice Harry Blackmun, Justice Lewis F. Powell, Jr. and Justice WILLIAM REHNQUIST joined in the opinion. Justices THURGOOD MARSHALL, WILLIAM J. BRENNAN, JR., and Potter Stewart dissented. Building on the *Williams* decision, the Court considered the function of a jury. The justices concluded that a jury provided a defendant with the protection of the judgment of his peers against the possible oppression of the state. Requiring unanimity would produce hung juries. The Court concluded that the Sixth Amendment did not require a unanimous jury because the amendment has never been held to require proof beyond a REASONABLE DOUBT in criminal cases.

The Court then considered the arguments of the defendants that a less than unanimous verdict violated the Fourteenth Amendment's requirement of a jury of peers since conviction could take place without the agreement of minority members of the community. The Court agreed that jury panels had to reflect the community. Since the views of all jurors would be considered during jury deliberations, the Court disagreed that a majority of the jury would refuse to weigh the evidence. No proof existed that a majority of jurors would vote for guilt or innocence based upon prejudice instead of the evidence.

The Court thus held that a jury had to consist of at least six people and did not demand unanimity in state trials. Five justices construed the Sixth Amendment to demand unanimity in federal criminal trials, however.

For more information

Abernathy, M. Glenn, and Barbara A. Perry. *Civil Liberties under the Constitution.* Columbia: University of South Carolina Press, 1993.

Caryn E. Neumann
Miami University of Ohio

appeal An appeal is a legal procedure by which an unsuccessful litigant in a lawsuit requests a higher court to reverse the decision made by a lower court or agency.

The term *appeal* was originally used in early English law to mean "to accuse." In the 13th century, the term was used to refer to a proceeding by which a superior court tried a case anew, without deference or reference to a lower court's decision. The term now refers to a superior court's examination of possible prejudicial error in a lower court proceeding. Potential errors that appellate courts examine may include, but are not limited to, a lower court's decision about motions, monetary awards or remedies, the admission or suppression of EVIDENCE, SENTENCING, the application of the law to the facts of the case, or the lower court's overall judgment.

The aggrieved party who is displeased with a lower court decision and initiates an appeal is called the appellant or petitioner. The party who opposes the appeal and is usually satisfied with the lower court's decision is called the appellee or respondent. To commence the appeal, the appellant must file a notice of appeal and other legal documents. An "appeal by application" is an appeal requiring permission by the appellate court before a case may be appealed, whereas an "appeal by right" requires no prior permission.

Rules of appellate procedure applicable to a reviewing court, as well as court practices, local rules, and internal operating procedures, govern an appellate court's review. Federal appellate courts follow the Federal Rules of Appellate Procedure, and state appellate courts follow their own rules of appellate procedure. Such rules and practices determine, for example, the scope of the types of cases that are appealable and to which appellate court they are appealed, the procedure by which the appeal is brought before the court, what procedures the parties must follow when appealing a case, and the standard of review that is used by the appellate court to determine what is required for a reversal of the lower court decision.

Appellate courts review cases to assure that significant and prejudicial errors made by a lower court during pretrial and trial stages are corrected, to develop the law, and to act with the ultimate goal of assuring uniformity of the law. An appellate court does not make the initial decision in a case, accept new evidence, call witnesses, or render judgments that it would have rendered if it had originally tried the case. Instead, an appellate court reviews the record of a lower tribunal proceeding (such as transcripts of testimony, documents, and the lower court's opinion) to determine whether the lower tribunal correctly applied the law to the facts of the case. Appellate review is often restricted to the appellate court's independent determination of the law, which is guided by precedent so that similar cases are similarly decided.

An appellate court rarely alters a trial JUDGE's interpretation of facts and will only alter facts when the trial court's factual findings are clearly erroneous. An appellate court almost never disturbs the trial court's conclusions about the credibility of witnesses or documents. Most appellate courts will not interfere with the discretionary decisions made by a trial court, unless the court abused its discretion. Moreover, an appellate court usually will only review legal issues that were raised in the trial court. Under exceptional circumstances, such as a clear miscarriage of justice, a legal issue that was not preserved for appeal might be reviewed for plain error. Issues that have become moot or cases that have been settled during the time period that the appeal is pending are not reviewable.

Appellate courts usually review issues from a lower court case after a final judgment in that case has been entered. However, under certain circumstances, some issues may be appealable before a trial court has issued a final judgment (known as an interlocutory appeal). The review of nonfinal judgments is limited to legal questions (such as issues of qualified immunity, subject matter jurisdiction, or constitutional questions) that must be answered before the trial court case may properly proceed.

There are different routes an appeal may take through state or federal judicial systems. Cases appealed to state appellate courts usually originate in state trial courts. Most states have more than one level of appellate courts, with the first level called an intermediate appellate court, and the highest court of the state (often called the state "Supreme Court") being on the second level. Cases appealed to federal appellate courts may originate in a U.S. district court, the highest court of a state in which a decision could be received, or a federal agency. THE U.S. COURTS OF APPEALS are intermediate appellate courts in the federal judicial system. Cases appealed to a U.S. court of appeals typically originate in a federal district court located in the geographic region of the court of appeals. The highest court of the United States is the United States Supreme Court. The United States Supreme Court, outside of narrow exceptions, accepts cases by permission only and selects only a relatively few number of appeals to review during each court term.

An appeal might be reviewed by only an intermediate appellate court; however, some cases can also be reviewed by the highest appellate court in the judicial system after the case was reviewed by an intermediate appellate court; and some cases may bypass the intermediate appellate court and be appealed directly to the highest appellate court of the judicial system. An administrative agency decision is usually reviewed by an administrative law judge before it is appealed to a trial court, and then the case may proceed through the appellate courts, such as an intermediate appellate court and then, perhaps, to the highest court in the judicial system.

APPELLATE BRIEFS are usually written by both the appellant and appellee and presented to the appellate court to assist the court in understanding the legal questions presented on appeal. The appellate court may grant the appellant and appellee an opportunity to argue their cases orally to a panel of judges, so that the parties may elaborate on the arguments presented in their

appellate briefs and answer questions asked by the judges. Oral arguments are subject to time limits that are usually established at the discretion of the appellate court.

If an appellate court affirms a lower court decision, the appellate court agrees with the decision reached by the lower court. If an appellate court modifies a lower court decision, the court agrees with the appellant that prejudicial error exists, and the appellate court changes the result reached by the lower court. If an appellate court reverses a lower court decision, the court agrees with the appellant that a legal error(s) was made, and the appellate court changes the result reached in the lower court proceeding. If an appellate court remands a case back to the lower court, the appellate court generally agrees with the appellant and directs the lower court to determine the relevant issue(s) consistent with the appellate court's decision. An appellate court might also dismiss an appeal, if, for example, the court discovers that it lacks the authority to hear the appeal.

An appellate court need not reach a unanimous decision. The majority of judges on the panel reviewing an appeal determines the result of the appeal. An appellate judge(s) who disagrees with the majority's result may write a dissenting opinion that explains areas of disagreement. A judge(s) who agrees with the result reached by the majority, but disagrees with the reasons for majority's decision, may write a concurring opinion that provides reasons for disagreement.

For more information

Hornstein, Alan D. *Appellate Advocacy in a Nutshell.* St. Paul: West Publishing, 1998.

Martineau, Robert J. *Fundamentals of Modern Appellate Advocacy.* Rochester, N.Y.: The Lawyer's Cooperative, 1985.

Neumann, Richard K. Jr. *Legal Reasoning and Legal Writing: Structure, Strategy, and Style.* Boston: Little, Brown, 1994, pp. 327–337.

Lindsley Armstrong Smith
Martin and Kieklak Law Firm
Fayetteville, Arkansas

appellate briefs Appellate briefs are written documents that present legal questions about the proceedings and final decision in a lower court case and are intended to persuade an appellate court that an error was or was not made by the lower court.

Appellate briefs assist an appellate court (a superior court of review) in understanding the facts and legal questions presented in an APPEAL of a lower court case. The briefs must conform to formal stylistic requirements that are established by the appellate court (such as: restrictions on the length of the briefs, size and font of lettering, jurisdictional statement, table of contents, table of authorities, proper legal citations, a concise statement of the relative facts of the case, and an argument section with both headings and subheadings). Appellate briefs are filed with the appellate court and provided to the opposing litigant. Appellate briefs are usually written by attorneys who represent the appellant (the litigant who is dissatisfied with a lower court decision and who brings the case to the appellate court for review) and the appellee (the litigant who is generally satisfied with a lower court decision and opposes the reversal of the decision). A brief written by a litigant, rather than a licensed attorney, is called a *pro se* brief.

An appellant provides the appellate court with a brief that consists of arguments about how the lower court decided a case inconsistently with the law, and it may include arguments that the lower court made erroneous findings of fact. Specifically, the appellant typically provides the legal question presented for review by the appellate court, the relevant facts of the case, arguments supporting reversal of the lower court decision, and legal authority supporting the arguments. The appellee, in turn, writes a brief that refutes the arguments made in the appellant's brief, discusses the deficiencies in the appellant's brief, and urges the appellate court to accept the decision of the lower court. Although the appellee's brief is usually a response to the arguments and legal authority presented in the appellant's brief, the appellee may also present other issues for the appellate court's review in the form of a cross-appeal (appeal by the appellee to modify or reverse a portion of the lower court's decision, which is usually heard at the same time as the appellant's appeal). The appellant, in turn, may then provide the appellate court with a reply brief, which refutes the arguments and/or legal authority discussed in the appellee's brief.

Individuals or associations that are not litigants in a lawsuit may also file an appellate brief, which is referred to as an amicus brief. The people or associations filing such briefs are referred to as "AMICUS CURIAE" (a friend of the court). Amici typically write an appellate brief because they wish the appellate court to consider a relevant perspective of the law and society that was not specifically addressed by a litigant, they wish to advance the argument of a litigant or to provide specific expertise on a legal issue that is to be decided by the court. The amici typically wish to influence the court's decision on a legal issue of great importance to the amici.

For more information

Hornstein, Alan D. *Appellate Advocacy in a Nutshell.* St. Paul: West, 1998, pp. 182–226.

Neumann, Richard K. Jr. *Legal Reasoning and Legal Writing: Structure, Strategy, and Style.* Boston: Little, Brown, 1994, pp. 327–337.

Lindsley Armstrong Smith
Martin and Kieklak Law Firm
Fayetteville, Arkansas

appellate jurisdiction Appellate jurisdiction is the authority of a higher court to review and revise a case that has already been decided by a lower court.

Appellate jurisdiction is distinguished from "original jurisdiction" (the jurisdiction conferred on or inherent in a court to hear a case initially). For example, if a case is not one designated within the United States Supreme Court's original jurisdiction, the Supreme Court could only hear the case through the exercise of its appellate jurisdiction. Article III, section 2 of the U.S. Constitution vests appellate jurisdiction in the Supreme Court, and 28 U.S.C.A. sections 1291–1295 vest appellate jurisdiction in the federal courts of appeals (intermediate appellate courts in the federal judicial system).

Appellate courts do not have the authority to hear every APPEAL presented to them. The federal CONSTITUTION and statutes, as well as state constitutions and statutes, create courts and designate the types of cases within the appellate jurisdiction of the courts. The structure of judicial systems, federal and in each state, provides a guide as to which court within a system has the authority to hear an appeal. For example, appellate jurisdiction does not exist in a court where an action is first brought, but it can exist in a higher court. Appellate courts may have concurrent power to hear a certain type of appeal, or a particular appellate court may be vested with the exclusive power to review a particular appeal. In effect, an appellate court must determine whether it has the authority to hear the appeal in the judicial system of which it is a part, as well as determine whether it has the jurisdiction to hear the particular appeal.

The lack of appellate jurisdiction is so important that an appellate court must dismiss an appeal of its own initiative, without the need for a litigant to first argue that appellate jurisdiction is lacking, if the court does not have the authority to hear the appeal (a *sua sponte* dismissal). Appellate courts must also determine the scope of their jurisdiction. Appellate courts have the power to decide only the law and issues presented in the particular case on appeal, rather than pronounce judgment on issues that have no practical effect on the determination of the case being appealed. Appellate courts dismiss a premature appeal—one that was presented for review before the lower court issued a final, appealable order or judgment—however, some nonfinal judgments of a lower court are reviewable under a court's appellate jurisdiction. Moreover, appellate courts lack the power to hear certain appeals, such as those that are moot or present political (rather than judicial) questions.

For more information

"Federal Courts, Original and Appellate Jurisdiction." In *American Jurisprudence.* 2nd ed. Volume 32, Section 549, Rochester, N.Y.: Lawyer's Cooperative, 1995.

Hornstein, Alan D. *Appellate Advocacy in a Nutshell.* St. Paul: West, 1998, pp. 43–47.

Lindsley Armstrong Smith
Martin and Kieklak Law Firm
Fayetteville, Arkansas

appointment and removal power (executive)

Appointment and removal power concerns presidential authority under Article II, section 2 of the CONSTITUTION—Appointments Clause—to remove subordinates in the executive branch and in administrative agencies.

The Constitution allows the president to nominate, with the advice and consent of the Senate, a wide variety of officers of the United States, including "Ambassadors, other public ministers and Consuls, Judges of the Supreme Court and all other Officers of the United States. . . ." Appointments are divided into two classes: principal and inferior officers. Presidential appointment power to carry out the executive duties of government has received a broad constitutional mandate. The president has clear authority to appoint principal officers—those requiring advice and consent of the Senate—who have major enforcement and administrative duties. Further, the president has discretion in removing administrative officials, both principal and inferior, who are directly responsible to that office. This authority is connected to the presidential requirement to "faithfully execute the laws." Congress may allow the president to appoint inferior officers on his own or through the heads of departments. The president has the authority to remove federal officers, such as local postmasters or members of independent regulatory commissions, who may have a combination of legislative, executive, and judicial powers.

The appointment and removal power can involve issues of separation of powers between the executive and the legislature. A main question is whether congressional statutes interfere with the executive's removal and appointment powers. A major conflict occurred in *Morrison v. Olson.* In this case Congress passed a law establishing the office of special prosecutor. Independent counsels from that office had authority to investigate and prosecute high ranking federal government officials or violation of federal criminal laws. The appointment and removal process was conducted by judiciary and the ATTORNEY GENERAL, and it was independent of presidential appointment or removal authority. The Court said that special prosecutors are "inferior" officers. However, the Constitution allows for some congressional interbranch appointments, where an officer of one branch is appointed by officers of another branch.

Congressional attempts to increase its own appointment and removal powers at the expense of the executive branch have been ruled unconstitutional. Congress cannot directly remove executive officials without invading the executive's removal powers. Congress can only remove principal executive officials through IMPEACHMENT and conviction. In several periods of congressional–executive conflict presidential removal power has been the central question of constitutional litigation.

For further information

Bowsher v. Synar, 478 U.S. 714 (1986).

Buckley v. Valeo, 424 U.S. 1 (1976).

Humphrey's Executor v. United States, 295 U.S. 602 (1935).

Morrison v. Olson, 484 U.S. 654 (1988).

Steven Puro
Saint Louis University

Argersinger v. Hamlin 407 U.S. 25 (1972)

The U.S. Supreme Court's holding in *Argersinger*

v. Hamlin, granted Jon Richard Argersinger's petition for a writ of habeas corpus that had been denied by the Florida Supreme Court. Argersinger, an indigent defendant, was tried before a judge on a concealed weapons charge, found guilty, and sentenced to 90 days in jail. Argersinger challenged his incarceration, claiming that his SIXTH AMENDMENT RIGHT TO COUNSEL was violated when he was denied the assistance of a state-provided attorney at trial. In the unanimous decision, the justices agreed with his position, expanding the protections afforded to criminal defendants who lacked the means to hire an attorney.

The Court's treatment of the Sixth Amendment protection of indigents began in the 1930s, when by a vote of 7–2 the justices required JUDGES in capital cases to assign counsel to those defendants incapable, either financially or intellectually, of mounting their own defense. *POWELL V. ALABAMA,* 287 U.S. 45 (1932). More than 30 years later, the justices broadened the right to counsel, requiring that states provide counsel to all poor defendants charged with a serious offense. *GIDEON V. WAINWRIGHT,* 372 U.S. 335 (1963). Left unprotected by this holding, however, was the significant pool of indigent defendants charged with minor or petty crimes who faced either jail time or fines.

In *Argersinger,* the Court rejected the argument that states were obligated only to provide indigent defendants charged with serious crimes, or FELONIES, the assistance of counsel at trial. Writing for justices, WILLIAM O. DOUGLAS emphasized that the presence of a lawyer to aid the accused is "often a requisite to the very existence of a fair trial," whether the offense is trivial or not. *Argersinger v. Hamlin,* 407 U.S. 25, 31 (1972). Citing *Baldwin v. New York,* 399 U.S. 117 (1970), Douglas observed that "the prospect of imprisonment for however short a time will seldom be viewed by the accused as a trivial or petty matter." The Court concluded that fairness dictates that "absent a knowing and intelligent waiver, no person may be imprisoned for any offense, whether classified as petty, misdemeanor or felony unless he was represented at trial." *Argersinger v. Hamlin,* 407 U.S. 25, 37 (1972).

Although the Court created a new federal constitutional requirement, the holding reserved to the states and the trial judge the management of the assignment of counsel to indigents. The clear and absolute rule announced by the justices was that no individual could be sentenced to any term of incarceration if denied the assistance of an attorney at trial. The result of the case drew the support of all nine members of the bench. However, Justices WILLIAM BRENNAN, WARREN BURGER and Lewis Powell all wrote separately to ponder the potential effect of the decision on the CRIMINAL JUSTICE SYSTEMS in the states. Brennan and Burger both expressed confidence that the states would not be overwhelmed providing this new class of defendant with appointed counsel. Powell, however, feared that the already taxed courts in the states would suffer from the new burden, leading to unfair treatment.

For more information

Galloway, John, ed. *The Supreme Court and the Rights of the Accused.* New York: Facts On File, 1973.

Garcia, Alfredo. *The Sixth Amendment in Modern American Jurisprudence: A Critical Perspective.* New York: Greenwood Press, 1992.

Charles F. Jacobs
St. Norbert College

Arizona v. Evans (514 U.S. 1 (1995) *Arizona v. Evans,* is a decision by the U.S. Supreme Court in which the Court extended the "good faith EXCEPTION" TO THE EXCLUSIONARY RULE to cases involving clerical errors of law enforcement employees that resulted in an illegal seizure of evidence. This ruling is an important ruling under the unreasonable SEARCHES AND SEIZURES clause of the FOURTH AMENDMENT to the UNITED STATES CONSTITUTION.

This case started with a rather routine traffic infraction, at which time a normal computer

search mistakenly showed an outstanding MISDEMEANOR warrant for the driver of the car. Based on this information, the automobile was searched, marijuana was found, and the individual was ARRESTED. The case went through the Arizona judiciary, with the Arizona Supreme Court eventually deciding in favor of Evans, ruling that his Fourth Amendment liberty against an unreasonable search and seizure had been violated. The U.S. Supreme Court, by a 7-2 vote, reversed the Arizona Supreme Court, finding no police misconduct.

The majority opinion for the Supreme Court was written by Chief JUSTICE WILLIAM H. REHNQUIST. The chief justice relied heavily on the previous decision in *United States v. Leon,* 468 U.S. 897 (1984), in which the Court declined to apply the exclusionary rule when the police act in "good faith" in relying on a search warrant issued by a neutral magistrate. The exclusionary rule is a standard used by the Court in Fourth Amendment cases to prevent the use of evidence gained illegally in order to convict a defendant. Chief Justice Rehnquist argued in his majority opinion in *Arizona v. Evans* that an ordinary clerical error was "harmless error" that did not rise to the level of intentional, unconstitutional behavior on the part of law enforcement officials.

Associate Justices SANDRA DAY O'CONNOR and David H. Souter wrote concurring opinions. They agreed with the Court's decision, yet cautioned their colleagues in the majority that with the advent of the computer age and an increasing reliance on technology, such clerical errors could in fact become more than just routine, in turn threatening individual liberties.

Justices JOHN PAUL STEVENS and RUTH BADER GINSBURG dissented from the Court's decision; they contended that had the clerical error not occurred Evans would not have been arrested. Therefore, the "harmless error" was in fact substantial and did rise to the level of an unconstitutional infringement on his constitutional liberty under the Fourth Amendment.

The ruling in *Evans* is a significant one, for it demonstrated the Rehnquist Court's tendency to side with law enforcement officials in its criminal justice jurisprudence. The ruling is also critical because it illustrates the Rehnquist Court's reluctance to extend the exclusionary rule as well as its determination to support the "good faith" precedent of *United States v. Leon.*

For more information

Amar, Akhil. *The Constitution and Criminal Procedure.* New Haven, Conn.: Yale University Press, 1997.

Long, Carolyn. *Mapp v. Ohio: Guarding against Unreasonable Searches and Seizures.* Lawrence: University Press of Kansas, 2005.

Stephen K. Shaw
Northwestern Nazarene University

Arizona v. Fulminante 499 U.S. 279 (1991)

In *Arizona v. Fulminante* the Supreme Court held that Oreste Fulminante's CONFESSION to the MURDER of his stepdaughter had been coerced. Although admitting the confession into EVIDENCE during Fulminante's murder trial violated the Fifth and Fourteenth AMENDMENTS TO THE UNITED STATES CONSTITUTION, the Court also held that the error was harmless and could not be used to vacate the conviction.

In the early morning of September 14, 1982, Fulminante called the Mesa, Arizona, Police Department to report that his stepdaughter, Jeneane Hunt, was missing. Two days later, she was found dead, with two gunshot wounds to the head. The police were unable to connect Fulminante to the crime, and so he moved to New Jersey, where he was later imprisoned on an unrelated gun charge. While in prison, an FBI informant, Anthony Sarivola, was instructed to befriend Fulminante to find out more about his role in the murder. Other inmates became increasingly hostile against Fulminante because of the rumors swirling around him. One evening, Sarivola offered to protect Fulminante from the other prisoners, but only if Fulminante told him what really happened. As a result, Fulminante confessed to Sarivola that he had taken the girl to the desert, where he sexually assaulted her and then shot her twice in the head. He later repeated this confession in detail to Sarivola's wife, Donna Sarivola.

After his release, Fulminante was indicted for first-degree murder. The defense moved to suppress both confessions, claiming they had been coerced. The trial court ruled the confessions were voluntary, denied the motion, and allowed them into evidence during the trial. Fulminante was ultimately convicted and sentenced to death. He appealed, and the Arizona Supreme Court ultimately held that the confessions were coerced, and that it could not apply a harmless-error test to a coerced confession. The conviction was reversed, and Fulminante was ordered to be retried without the confession.

The Supreme Court affirmed. First, the Court considered the voluntariness of the confession. Applying the "totality of the circumstances" test, the Court concluded that the confession was obtained as a result of extreme coercion because the defendant believed his life was in danger. In so ruling, the Court rejected the notion that coercion must include actual violence by a government agent; indeed, in this case, a "credible threat" of violence was sufficient. Fulminante's will to not confess was overwhelmed by the threat of physical violence, a threat facilitated by a government agent. Therefore, the confession was the product of coercion.

Five justices, however, disagreed with the Arizona Supreme Court and ruled that the harmless-error test applies to coerced confessions that are later admitted into evidence. The test asks whether a particular constitutional error—in this case, the admission of a coerced confession—did not contribute to the defendant's conviction. A majority on the Court ruled that the confession did contribute to the conviction, mostly because it was unlikely that Fulminante would have been prosecuted at all absent the inculpatory statements.

For more information

Gangi, William. "The Supreme Court and Coerced Confessions: *Arizona v. Fulminante* in Perspective." *Harvard Journal of Law and Public Policy* 16 (1993): 493.

Nasheri, Hedieh, and Victor J. DeMarco. "True Confessions?: A Critique of *Arizona v. Fulminante*," *American Journal of Criminal Law* 21, no. 2 (Winter 1994): 273–290.

David Perez
Yale Law School

Arizona v. Gant 556 U.S. 332 (2009) In *Arizona v. Gant*, the Supreme Court affirmed the Arizona Supreme Court's decision that the police search of Rodney Gant's automobile, incident to his ARREST, violated the FOURTH AMENDMENT of the CONSTITUTION. *Gant* is a significant case as it changed the rules for WARRANTLESS automobile SEARCHES incident to arrest that police had practiced for almost 30 years under *NEW YORK v. BELTON*, 453 U.S. 454 (1981).

Gant was arrested for driving with a suspended license. After handcuffing Gant and placing him in the back of a patrol car, police conducted a warrantless search of his car, relying on the *Belton* case, which held that police could search the entire passenger compartment of an automobile upon the lawful arrest of one of its occupants. *Belton* was based on the search incident to arrest rationale announced in *CHIMEL v. CALIFORNIA*, 395 U.S. 752 (1969), which justified warrantless searches following a lawful arrest on the theory that such searches were reasonable for the purposes of (1) protecting officers from any weapons the arrestee might have hidden away that might be used to harm the officer or effect an escape; and (2) preventing the arrestee from concealing and then destroying EVIDENCE of a crime. Under *Chimel*, these rationales supported the search of the person being arrested and the area within his or her reach. By the time of *Belton* in 1981, the Court observed that applying the *Chimel* reaching distance test in the context of automobiles had proven difficult. Accordingly, the Court fashioned a bright-lined rule in *Belton* that allowed officers to search the entire passenger compartment of a vehicle (including any bags, jackets, purses, etc.) upon the lawful arrest of one of the automobile's occupants. Over the years, lower courts had interpreted *Belton* to allow searches of automobiles even when the arrestee was already restrained and placed in a patrol car at the time of the search (and thus could not reach any weapons or evidence contained in the vehicle). This tension between the rationales announced in *Chimel* and the *Belton*-based search practices that went beyond those rationales provided the basis for issues in *Gant*.

The Arizona Supreme Court had held that since the *Chimel* rationales did not apply in Gant's case (since there virtually was no way he could reach weapons or destroy evidence left in the car), that *Belton* did not support the search. Yet, as the *Gant* majority acknowledged, *Belton* had for years been widely understood to allow such a search even where the arrestee could not physically reach the passenger compartment. According to the Court, this reading of *Belton* was never intended by the *Belton* case. Thus, in announcing *Gant,* the Court purported not to overturn *Belton* but merely to correct its misapplication.

In order to search an automobile as incident to the arrest of one of its recent occupants, the Court in *Gant* held that one of two scenarios must be present. First, police may search an automobile incident to the arrest of one of its occupants when the arrestee is unsecured and within reaching distance of the passenger compartment at the time of the search. In such a case, the safety and evidence concerns of *Chimel* are present, and therefore a warrantless search is justified. Second, police may search incident to arrest where it is "reasonable to believe evidence relevant to the crime of arrest might be found in the vehicle." 556 U.S. at tk. Thus, police who arrest a driver after smelling marijuana would be justified in searching the car for drugs, whereas an officer who arrests a person for driving on a suspended license may not have a reasonable belief that he or she would discover evidence of that crime by searching the automobile. Although *Belton* would have supported a search in the latter scenario, *Gant* forbids it.

For more information

Wayne R. Lafave. *Criminal Law.* St. Paul, Minn.: Thomson-West, 2003.

Rhys Hester
University of South Carolina

arms, right to bear The right to bear arms refers to the Second Amendment of the U.S. CONSTITUTION, which guarantees an individual right to own firearms. This right has also been incorporated to protect this right against limitations by state and local governments. The extent of what this individual right to bears arms means is not clear.

Historically, the right to bear arms derives from an Anglo-American legal tradition relying on citizens to fulfill many of the functions of government, from serving on JURIES to policing and protecting communities. Among the unpaid obligations of citizenship was the bearing of arms to suppress civil disorder and repel invasion. Long before the invention of firearms, Englishmen were required to be ready to assemble as bowmen in defense of the realm, and this requirement was readily transferred to colonial America. From the recruitment of Miles Standish to train and lead a Pilgrim militia to the reliance on state militias in support of the Continental army in the War for Independence, state and federal governments attempted to maintain a force capable of providing stability and security to communities and the state without recourse to standing armies.

After the Revolution this impulse continued, and it was combined with a pervasive general fear of standing armies. For these reasons the federal Constitution provided for the creation and use of militias "to execute the Laws of the Union, suppress domestic Insurrections and repel invasions," but it also specified that the states appoint militia officers and take control of training the militia "according to the discipline prescribed by Congress" (Article I, section 8). Even so, the Second Amendment attests to a lingering distrust of a consolidated government by guaranteeing the theory that "A well regulated Militia, being necessary to the security of a free State, the right of the people to keep and bear Arms, shall not be infringed." In addition to limits on Congress, many of the new states provided in their own constitutions for protecting the right to bear arms.

Although most states linked this right to a militia duty, Pennsylvania expanded the traditional language and stated, "The people have a right to bear arms for the defence of themselves and the state." As new states joined the union in the following century, many defined the right to bear arms as an individual right to SELF-DEFENSE rather than as a collective one, though not all did so. Mississippi's guarantee of 1817, that "Every citizen has a right to bear arms in defense of himself," became a model for other states before the Civil War, as fear of slave revolts and Indian resistance generated concerns for security.

Even so, individual gun ownership remained rare until after the war, when veterans returned with their mass-produced weapons and manufacturers fueled demand with heavy advertising and low prices.

Over the past century, state legislatures have protected individual gun ownership, but they retain the authority to regulate it. The Supreme Court has upheld state firearms control laws against challenges under the Second Amendment (*United States v. Cruikshank* in 1870 and *Presser v. Illinois* in 1886), as well as a model local ordinance banning handguns (*Quilici v. Village of Morton Grove* in 1983).

Until 2008, debates surrounding the meaning of the Second Amendment centered on whether it protected a collective right within the context of a militia or an individual right of ownership. The Supreme Court resolved that dispute in a controversial 5–4 decision in *DISTRICT OF COLUMBIA V. HELLER*, 554, U.S. 570 (2008), in which Justice Scalia wrote for a majority that said that the Second Amendment protected an individual right. The Court did not specify exactly what that right protected, but Scalia did indicate that it did not preclude adoption of rules that would prohibit the possession of firearms by felons and the mentally ill, or laws restricting the carrying of firearms in places such as schools and government buildings.

The *Heller* decision focused on the meaning of the Second Amendment when it came to its application against the federal government. The decision did not address whether the right to bear arms was also incorporated through the Fourteenth Amendment to restrict state and local governments. In *McDonald v. City of Chicago*, 561 U.S. (2010), the Court ruled 5-4 that this individual right was incorporated to apply to state and local governments.

As a result of *Heller* and *McDonald*, many gun ordinances are being challenged as the meaning of the Second Amendment is being clarified by state and lower federal courts.

For more information

Cornell, Saul, ed. *Whose Right to Bear Arms Did the Second Amendment Protect?* New York: St. Martin's Press, 2000.

Cottrol, Robert J., ed. *Gun Control and the Constitution: Sources and Explorations on the Second Amendment.* New York: Garland, 1994.

David Thomas Konig
Washington University in St. Louis

arraignment An arraignment is any court appearance that precedes a trial in a criminal proceeding. In a strict sense, it is defined as the hearing before a court having JURISDICTION, or judicial power to adjudicate a criminal case, in which the identity of the defendant is established and in which the charges are formally announced. The court informs the defendant of his or her rights and requests the defendant to enter a plea or reply to the charges. There are five possible pleas: Not Guilty (Innocent); Not Guilty by reason of an affirmative defense, such as self-defense, or insanity; Guilty; Nolo Contendere, or 'no contest,' which means that the defendant will be convicted; Remain standing silent, which is entered as a plea of "not guilty."

In many states, appearance is required in all events except where a simplified information is presented by the PROSECUTOR in a MISDEMEANOR. The defendant always has the right to the aid of counsel at the arraignment and at every subsequent stage of the action. Appearance by counsel instead of the charged person is permissible in any case in which the defendant is required to appear in court by summons or a traffic appearance ticket.

If the defendant appears without counsel, generally he or she must be informed of the rights listed below. The court must allow the defendant to exercise those rights and must also undertake affirmative action to ensure that those rights have been employed, where the defendant exhibits inaction.

Right to an adjournment for the purpose of obtaining counsel;

Right to communicate, free of charge, by letter or by telephone to obtain counsel or inform next of kin that a criminal charge has been entered against her;

Right to have the court appoint counsel if there is financial impairment.

At the arraignment, in the absence of an intention to dispose of the action in its entirety, the court must issue a securing order either releasing the defendant on his own recognizance or setting bail for a future appearance in the action. In the case of a felony charge, the court must allow the district attorney to object to the BAIL, or after knowledge or notice of the application and a reasonable opportunity to be heard, a failure to appear constitutes a waiver of the right to do so.

The court must also be furnished with a report from the division of criminal justice services listing the defendant's criminal record, if any, or with a police department report with respect to the defendant's prior arrest record. The report must be presented to the defendant or his legal defense counsel. In New York State, for example, if a local criminal court lacks authority to order recognizance or bail, or has denied the application for recognizance or bail, or has fixed excessive bail, then defense counsel may make an application or motion to a superior court JUDGE to vacate an existing order and enter a decree for bail or recognizance subject to notice to the DISTRICT ATTORNEY and an open court hearing in the case of a FELONY charge.

Special statutory criminal procedure provisions exist for the arraignment of corporate defendants. A "corporate summons" is a process issued by a superior court directing a corporate defendant designated in an indictment to appear before it at a designated future time in connection with an indictment. The summons must be served by a public servant, designated by the court, upon the corporation by delivering it to an officer, director, managing or general agent of such corporation authorized by law to receive service of process.

The arraignment process may also be used to ascertain whether a person or individual is a material witness. A court may issue a "material witness" order declaring that a person possesses material information in connection with a pending action and is expected not to be amenable or responsive to a SUBPOENA to appear at a later time. A prospective material witness must be informed in an arraignment about the nature and purpose of the proceeding and is entitled to a prompt hearing upon the issue of whether a decree declaring the person a material witness should be ordered. The court must also instruct the prospective material witness as to the right to legal counsel, including adjournment to obtain counsel or assignment of counsel, in case of financial hardship. If the proceeding is adjourned at the request of the prospective material witness, then the court may set bail to assure future attendance.

In *Garland v. State of Washington,* 232 U.S. 642 (1914), the defendant was retried on two information statements, one charging him for larceny of a $1,000 check, and the second for LARCENY of 1,000 U.S. dollars. No arraignment or plea was entered on the second information charge. The Court held that the object of an arraignment was to inform the accused of the charged criminal offense and to obtain an answer. Referring to English history, the Supreme Court reviewed the necessity of arraignment to validate the trial. In *U.S. v. Alvarez-Sanchez,* in spite of the absence of a state court arraignment, defendant's CONFESSION on other federal criminal acts was upheld.

For more information

Travis, Lawrance F. III. *Introduction to Criminal Justice.* 3rd ed. Cincinnati, Ohio: Anderson Publishing, 1998.

J. David Golub
Touro College
New York Institute of Technology
Kean College of New Jersey

arrest Arrest is the depriving of a person's liberty by legal authority because that person has been accused of committing a crime.

Hundreds of arrests are made on television, but what exactly is an arrest, what is required for it to be valid, and what rights does the arrested person have? Although in theory any citizen may make an arrest, due to possible legal and physical dangers law enforcement agents make nearly all arrests. When someone is deprived of freedom by being taken into custody, an arrest has occurred whether that specific word is used or not. If the suspect has no choice about whether to accompany the officer, even when the officer phrases the matter as a polite request, it is considered an arrest. Because arrests are considered seizures of the person, the FOURTH AMENDMENT's prohibition of unreasonable SEARCHES AND SEIZURES applies. Therefore, no person may be lawfully arrested without PROBABLE CAUSE, which is defined as adequate EVIDENCE to convince a reasonable person that the suspect is likely to have committed a crime. However, most arrests are made without a court-issued warrant. Such arrests are legitimate if made in a public place with probable cause. When the police go to someone's residence, however, they need an arrest warrant.

Many people incorrectly believe that an arrest is invalid unless accompanied by the Miranda warning. In fact, this warning is required only for CUSTODIAL INTERROGATION. If it is not given, any responses by the suspect cannot be used as evidence by the prosecutor but, if no questions are asked, the suspect does not have to be told of his/her rights to counsel and silence.

In *CHIMEL V. CALIFORNIA* (1969) the Supreme Court ruled that a lawful arrest allows the police to search the area within the suspect's immediate control even without a search warrant. The justification is to prevent destruction of evidence and to allow the police to safeguard themselves by seizing any weapons the suspect might grab.

The Supreme Court has expanded POLICE POWER to stop automobiles. Roadblocks to deter and apprehend drunk drivers are permitted if there is no police discretion. This means that either every vehicle or every *n*th vehicle can be stopped to determine sobriety even without probable cause. *MARYLAND V. WILSON* (1997) held that during routine traffic stops, police could order not only the driver but also passengers out of the car.

TERRY V. OHIO (1968) allowed the police to make investigatory stops of suspects on less than probable cause. Any officer with a reasonable suspicion that a crime is about to be committed can stop a suspect, frisk him/her for weapons, and ask a few questions. Only if this results in additional evidence adequate for probable cause can an arrest be made. The case of *ILLINOIS V. WARDLOW* (2000) held that unprovoked flight from the police in a high crime area justified a TERRY STOP and frisk. On the other hand, *Florida v. Royer* (1983) ruled that a person who ignores the police and goes about his/her business cannot be stopped without additional evidence.

Because evidence obtained as a result of an unlawful arrest is generally excluded from a trial, the legality of an arrest is often critical to its outcome.

For more information

Illinois v. Wardlow, 528 US 119 (2000).

Podgers, James. "Poisoned Fruit: Quest for Consistent Rule on Traffic Stop Searches," *American Bar Association Journal* 81 (February, 1995): 50–51.

Bruce E. Altschuler
State University of New York, Oswego

arrests at home Arrest at home refers to occasions when law enforcement officials arrest or take custody of individuals in their home or apartment. Individuals arrested in their homes are generally afforded more legal protections than those ARRESTED IN PUBLIC.

The police generally may not arrest individuals within private homes without a warrant. This is true regardless of the severity of the suspected offense. This principle contrasts to the rule that the police may arrest individuals in public without a warrant, and is justified by the principle that the "physical entry of the home is the chief evil against which the wording of the Fourth Amendment [see entry] is directed." *PAYTON V. NEW YORK*, 445 U.S. 573, 586 (1980).

When the police have a warrant to arrest someone within a private residence, they may enter the home to make the arrest even if they do not also have a search warrant. In some instances, this standard may allow the police to access private areas that they would not ordinarily be able to access without a search warrant. For example, if the police enter a home to arrest a suspect and see contraband, they may seize it under the PLAIN VIEW doctrine even if they did not have a warrant to search the premises.

A warrant authorizing the arrest of a suspect is limited to arrests in public and in the suspect's own home. It does not authorize an attempt to arrest the suspect in a third party's home, even if the police have reason to believe that the suspect is present at the time of the attempted arrest.

This restriction reflects a concern that the police might use an arrest warrant as a substitute for a search warrant. In other words, if the police could enter every residence a suspect is known to frequent simply because they had a warrant to arrest the suspect, they could then use the arrest warrant as an end run around the general requirement that a search warrant is necessary to enter a private residence. Such a practice would affect the privacy interests not only of the suspect, but also those of the inhabitants of the various residences where the suspect is known to spend time. Conceivably, such a practice would allow the police to enter and search every house on a street if the suspect sometimes spent time at all of them. Law enforcement interests in preventing and punishing crime and making timely arrests does not outweigh these potentially grave consequences for individual privacy.

The requirement that the police obtain a warrant for arresting an individual within a private residence arguably runs counter to historical precedent. Under common law, courts permitted warrantless arrests within private homes for felonies, and some evidence indicates that such arrests were relatively frequent. However, a majority of the Supreme Court has held that the history is inconclusive and therefore should not dictate the prevailing standards for arrest within the home.

For more information

Note. "Warrantless Entry to Arrest in Suspect's Home": *Payton v. New York, Harvard Law Review.* 178 (1980).

Payton, Christos Papapetrou. "Practical Wisdom, and the Pragmatist Judge: Is *Payton*'s Goal to Prevent Unreasonable Entries or to Effectuate Home Arrests?," *Fordham Urban Law Journal* (2007): 1,517.

Nancy Leong
William and Mary School of Law

arrests in public According to the Supreme Court in *ATWATER V. LAGO VISTA,* 532 U.S. 318 (2001), the police have broad discretion to ARREST citizens in public spaces as long as the arrest is supported by PROBABLE CAUSE that the arrestee committed a crime.

The police do not need to have a warrant before they arrest someone in public. Moreover, under the modern rule, the severity of the crime that the arrestee is suspected of committing does not affect whether the police may execute an arrest. For example, in *Atwater,* the Supreme Court held that a police officer's warrantless arrest of a woman for a MISDEMEANOR seatbelt violation punishable by a fine of less than $50 was constitutional.

The police have substantially more leeway to execute public warrantless arrests today than in the past. Common law generally prohibited the police from executing a warrantless arrest for misdemeanors without warrants, with a narrow exception for breaches of the peace committed in the presence of the arrestor immediately before the arrest. FELONY arrests were generally permitted under common law. As statutes increasingly specified that warrantless arrests were permissible for certain offenses, these rules gradually gave way to the modern rule permitting warrantless arrests regardless of the severity of the offense.

The modern rule allowing warrantless arrests is arguably in tension with the rule requiring a warrant for searches unless the search falls within one of a few limited exceptions. Justice Powell noted this "anomaly" in his concurrence in *Watson,* explaining that while "[a] search may cause only annoyance and temporary inconvenience to the law-abiding citizen," and arrest "is a serious personal intrusion regardless of whether the person seized is guilty or innocent." *United States v. Watson,* 423 U.S. 411, 428 (1976).

One possible explanation for this discrepancy is that requiring a warrant for arrests would create an impediment to effective law enforcement. If the police delayed getting a warrant even after establishing probable cause—a strategy they might pursue in order to accumulate more evidence—they would risk a court holding that a later warrantless arrest was not supported by exigency. On the other hand, if the police got a warrant immediately upon establishing probable cause and then delayed executing the warrant to continue their investigation, they would risk a court holding that the warrant had become stale.

Some public arrests culminate in a "perp walk"—a police practice of leading an arrestee through a public place with the result that the media may observe and record the arrest. Perp walks staged solely for the media violate the FOURTH AMENDMENT prohibition on unreasonable SEARCH AND SEIZURE. But perp walks undertaken for legitimate law enforcement reasons—i.e., transporting an arrestee from one location to another—do not necessarily violate arrestees' rights, and courts have held that some perp walks promote governmental interest of reducing crime by increasing public awareness of law enforcement efforts and deterring crime. *Caldarola v. County of Westchester,* 343 F.3d 570, 572–73 (2d Cir. 2003). In evaluating the constitutionality of a perp walk, courts balance these governmental interests against the arrestee's expectation of privacy.

For more information

William A. Schroeder. "Warrantless Misdemeanor Arrests and the Fourth Amendment." *Missouri Law Reviews* (1993): 77.

Nancy Leong
William and Mary School of Law

arson Arson is the act of intentionally burning or attempting to burn property or land, and may or may not include the intent to defraud. Arson targets can include houses, public buildings, vehicles, and personal property.

Arson is the fastest-growing crime in the United States due to the variety of motives. The U.S. Senate has stated that arson is the easiest crime to commit and the hardest to prevent or prove with results that directly and significantly affect average citizens by increasing insurance premiums, destroying property, increasing fatalities, and a decrease in quality of life. First-degree arson is committed when an injury or fatality results from a fire. Second-degree arson is committed when property damage or destruction results from an intentional fire (Maryland Penal Code 27, § 5(a)-(f), 1957, ch.26, s.2). Arson is a FELONY.

Suspicious fires account for nearly a third of all fires occurring in the United States, accounting for about 267,000 fires annually. It is the second-leading cause of deaths and injuries (475 and 2,000 respectively) and accounts for $1.4 billion in property loss each year. Half of all arson-related fires are set outside, one-third are set in structures, and one-fifth are started in vehicles. There are many different motivations for arson: FRAUD, revenge and prejudice, vanity, and crime concealment. Roughly half of all fire-related property damage in the United States is committed for profit. It is a low-risk, high-gain business as 9 percent of all arson cases result in ARREST and 2 percent in conviction. Insurance fraud is the most common type of arson committed for profit as there are direct financial gains for the loss of a house or property.

Revenge is another main motivator in arson cases. Feuding or disgruntled lovers, neighbors, or employees may express spite or jealousy through arson. Prejudice can also be a strong motivator for arson, and racial and religious hostility is the cause of many HATE CRIMES occurring in the United States. These are manifested in the burning of places of worship, homes, and special centers such as group homes and halfway houses.

A third motivator is the hero syndrome. An individual or employee, such as a security guard or even a fireman, may feel neglected and ignored and start a fire to then extinguish it and be a celebrated hero. Lastly, arson is often committed as a means to conceal another crime. In this spirit, vehicles used for escape are often burned to destroy FINGERPRINTS and other evidence. Tools used in the commission of another crime are often burned as well to avoid seizure.

For more information

Redsicker, D. R., and J. J. O'Connor, eds. *Practical Fire and Arson Investigation: Second Edition*. New York: Taylor & Francis, 1996.

Julie Yingling
Michigan State University

Articles of Confederation The Articles of Confederation were adopted in 1781 as the first CONSTITUTION for the United States after its independence from England.

The Articles of Confederation were drafted in stages from 1776 to 1777 but were not ratified until 1781; the Articles extended and revised the existing understanding of diffused authority and state autonomy. Richard Henry Lee, Samuel Adams, John Dickinson, and Roger Sherman, among others, assisted in the drafting of the document. Although regarded in 1781 as a reliable constitution, the accepted caricature of the Articles portrays the work as a dismal failure in all respects; the Articles could not provide for a system of popular rule or supply the young regime with the security measures that were needed to ensure its survival. Critics of the Articles usually cite the plan's inability to endow a national government with the power to levy taxes or regulate commerce, thereby discouraging all efforts at national cohesion. The Articles, in other words, embodied the political tensions within American politics during the period between the DECLARATION OF INDEPENDENCE and the Philadelphia Convention.

The Articles possessed the means for affirming popular rule, diffusing political authority, and allowing for a system of government. As in the case of the Declaration of Independence, the Articles perpetuated the original design for the territorial division of the country into independent and sovereign states, a "perpetual union." Article Two described the nature of the alliance: "Each state retains its sovereignty, freedom and independence, and every power, JURISDICTION, and right, which is not by the Confederation expressly delegated to the United States, in Congress assembled." Articles Three and Four, antecedents of the Tenth Amendment, affirmed the nature of their "league of friendship" and provided for the EXTRADITION of fugitives. Article Five presented a system of representation for the states in Congress that allowed for each state to have no less than two and no more than seven delegates. Articles Six and Seven concerned limitations upon the states regarding the conducting of foreign affairs and national security. Article Eight detailed how the costs of war would be defrayed, and Article Nine outlined the powers of Congress, the only branch of government established by the document. The last four Articles discussed various aspects of the "perpetual" union.

The Articles confirmed the centrality of the states, thus maintaining the relationship between the governed and the government at the state level instead of the national level. The Articles also provided that the respective states, not the federal government, would protect citizens' privileges and immunities. As a genuine precursor to the Tenth Amendment, the Articles limited the power of the federal government and strengthened state prerogatives.

For more information

Hoffert, Robert W. *A Politics of Tension: The Articles of Confederation and American Political Ideas.* Boulder: University Press of Colorado, 1991.

Jensen, Merrill. *The Articles of Confederation.* 1940. Reprint. Madison: University of Wisconsin Press, 1970.

Moore, Wayne D. *Constitutional Rights and Powers of the People.* Princeton, N.J.: Princeton University Press, 1996.

H. Lee Cheek, Jr.
Gainsville State College

articulable suspicion Articulable suspicion is a tool or legal standard of proof that allows law enforcement to stop and/or search citizens in a manner that differs from consensual contact and PROBABLE CAUSE. This tool is beneficial to law enforcements' ability to uncover criminal activity before it has been committed or after the fact. The officers' "hunch" that the subject was "up to no good" is not enough to detain a subject. The officer must be able to demonstrate to the court the specific reasons for the officer to believe that the subject was involved in criminal activity.

Another term for articulable suspicion is the *TERRY STOP* after *TERRY V. OHIO*, 389 U.S. 347 (1968), Supreme Court decision on these limited warrantless stop and seizures. The defendant argued that the concealed weapon seized and used as EVIDENCE to convict him was illegally obtained. He asserted his FOURTH AMENDMENT right against unreasonable SEARCH AND SEIZURE because he had not committed a crime.

The Court used the totality of the circumstances and the officer's experience to determine that the defendant's Fourth Amendment right had not been violated and upheld the conviction. The totality of circumstances can include time of day, tips from callers, location, mannerism, individuals present, dress, etc. Some of these circumstances may not be of any importance to the average person; however, to a police officer, they could spell out criminal activity or INTENT, which was the case in *Terry v. Ohio.* The defendant was convicted on intent to commit a ROBBERY.

When the police hold a suspect beyond the amount of time necessary to accomplish the reason for the stop, the seizure becomes an ARREST and must be supported by probable cause, which is more than articulable suspicion. The Supreme Court has not clearly defined when a stop becomes an arrest, and therefore the lower courts have been making these decisions on a case-by-case basis. When the courts are faced with these challenges, they consider the diligence of police in resolving their reasonable suspicion as quickly as possible, the scope and nature of the restraints placed on an individual's liberty (such as handcuffing or placing the person in the back of the patrol vehicle), and if police transported the individual to another location.

When determining the extent of detention, courts balance the degree of intrusion on the individual's liberty against the state's need to ensure the safety of both the public and law enforcement officers. The mere existence of a less intrusive means of investigation does not make a detention unreasonable. When a detainee's own actions contribute to the duration of a stop, a longer detention may be reasonable.

In using articulable suspicion, an officer is not allowed to go beyond the initial reason for a stop and frisk. For example, if an officer stops a vehicle because he or she believes it was stolen, when the vehicle is cleared as not stolen, the officer cannot subsequently search the vehicle or ask the occupants about illegal drugs present.

Articulable suspicion has been a valuable tool for law enforcement; however, limits do exist and must be considered so that a person's rights are not violated. These limited warrantless Terry stops and/or frisks may be a minor inconvenience to the average person, but to a criminal intending to or just having committed a crime, it keeps the public safe.

For more information

Calsyn, Jeremy D., et al. "Warrantless Searches and Seizures," *Georgetown Law Journal* (June 1998).

Winston D. Boswell
Boulder County, Sheriff Office, Colorado

Lyn Boswell
University of Colorado School of Public Affairs, Denver, Colorado

assault & battery Assault and battery are two distinct common law crimes that can take the form of civil TORTS or criminal offenses. They are often linked together because an assault often, but not always, precedes a battery.

An assault occurs when an individual willfully threatens another or engages in actions that place a person in fear of imminent physical injury. No actual touching or physical injury need occur. While generally a MISDEMEANOR, a simple assault can become a more serious crime when, for example, an assailant uses a weapon to instill fear of imminent physical injury.

A battery is any intentional, wrongful, and nonconsensual physical contact that results in an injury or offensive touching. Batteries can take a variety of forms, some of which are designed to address specific societal problems and carry enhanced penalties. An aggravated battery can occur when an assailant uses any sort of weapon to conduct the unlawful touching, when there is great physical harm done to a victim, or the victim falls within a certain class of persons (e.g., a police officer or teacher) regardless of the level of harm. The penalty for aggravated battery is usually a FELONY. Other particular forms of battery include sexual battery and domestic battery. Sexual battery pertains to unlawful physical contact of a sexual nature and is sometimes used when PROSECUTORS lack EVIDENCE to successfully prosecute a more serious sexual assault. Domestic battery, the unlawful touching of a domestic partner, often results in enhanced penalties as well and is designed to help combat the problem of spousal abuse.

Not all intentional touching constitutes a battery. A number of defenses can be raise do justify what might otherwise be considered unlawful physical contact. The first of these defenses is consent. This commonly occurs in sports where a certain level of contact is to be expected (e.g., boxing or football). A consent defense is not absolute, however, when public policies are violated. For example, two individuals who consent to fight each other can still each be charged with battery. Another justification would be SELF-DEFENSE. Under certain circumstances, an individual may strike another in self-defense, such as when he or she is attacked. Finally, certain individuals are empowered by law to employ a certain amount of force in the line of duty. This includes police officers, corrections officers, security officers, and merchants detaining shoplifters for authorities.

For more information

Anderson, Terry M., and Thomas J. Gardner. "Assault, Battery, and Other Crimes against the Person." In *Criminal Law,* 10th ed. New York: Wadsworth, 2009.

Brewer, James D. *The Danger from Strangers: Confronting the Threat of Assault.* New York: Insight Books, 1994.

Darren A. Wheeler
Ball State University

Jesse Beal
Ball State University

assisted reproductive technologies (ART)

Assisted reproductive technologies have challenged traditional concepts of FAMILY law by raising questions involving the legal status of a child that results from ART and the legal rights and duties of the gamete donor(s), surrogate mother, and intended custodial parents.

ART includes both low-tech artificial insemination and higher tech "test-tube baby" procedures where the egg and sperm are brought together outside of the body, such as for in vitro fertilization (IVF), gamete intrafallopian transfer (GIFT), zygote intrafallopian transfer (ZIFT), and intracytoplasmic sperm injection (ICSI).

Laws regulating ART are few and far between except for statutes and court decisions clarifying legal rights and duties in artificial insemination. New legal issues have arisen when a surrogate mother is carrying a child for another couple (who may or may not be the genetic parents) and decides that she does not want to relinquish the child, when the father is deceased and his sperm are used in ART, and when excess embryos are frozen for future implantation and one of the prospective parents no longer wishes to participate.

Surrogate mothers first came to the public's attention with the Baby M case, *In re Baby M,* 537 A.2d 1227 (N.J. 1988), in which the surrogate mother provided both the egg and the uterus. The New Jersey Supreme Court found that the surrogacy CONTRACT was invalid because it conflicted with public policy and adoption laws that prohibited the enforcement of preconception agreements. The court gave sole custody of the child to the intended custodial parents but did not terminate the parental rights of the surrogate mother. In *Johnson v. Calvert,* 851 P.2d 776 (Cal. 1993), the surrogate mother provided only the uterus and the intended custodial parents contributed the embryo; the California Supreme Court honored the preconception intention of the parties.

The ability to freeze and store sperm for later insemination after the death of the father has raised legal issues. In Louisiana, Judith Hart was conceived by GIFT three months after the death of her father. Her mother applied for Social Security survivor benefits for her based on the father's Social Security employment and earnings record. Under Louisiana and federal law, the child was not the legal heir of her father because she was not born at the time of his death, nor born within 300 days of his death. The Social Security Administration decided that survivor's benefits would be paid nevertheless, based on public policy reasons, but recognized that there were neither regulations nor law to address this issue.

As an alternative to immediate implantation, pre-embryos can be stored for future implantation by freezing them in liquid nitrogen. Thousands of these frozen pre-embryos are stored in laboratories and IVF clinics across the country. There are no clear laws on who has authority to dispose of them or what becomes of them in case of parental death, divorce, unavailability, dispute, or nonpayment of storage fees. In both *Davis v. Davis,* 842 S.W.2d 588 (Tenn. 1992) and *Kass v. Kass,* 696 N.E.2d 174 (N.Y. 1998), the couple attempted to conceive a child through IVF but divorced before they could do so. In both cases, the husband asked that the court not give the pre-embryos to the wife. In the Tennessee case, there was no prior written agreement regarding pre-embryo disposition, and the Tennessee Supreme Court weighed the procreative interests of the husband and wife and ruled that the party wishing to avoid reproduction should prevail whenever the other party has a reasonable possibility of having offspring through other means. In the New York case, the court ruled that the couple's signed written agreement prior to ART directing the IVF program to use the pre-embryos in approved research should be honored.

Laws are needed for clarifying the status of ART offspring and for assigning rights and duties of parentage in situations when gamete donors and surrogate mothers are used. The spirit and intent of the laws would have to acknowledge that the U.S. Supreme Court has recognized procreation as one of the basic CIVIL RIGHTS. An outright ban on ART would be unconstitutional because it would limit the basic right of individuals to reproduce.

For more information

Andrews, Lori B. *The Clone Age: Adventures in the New World of Reproductive Technology.* New York: Henry Holt, 1999.

Evans, Donald, ed. *Creating the Child: The Ethics, Law and Practice of Assisted Procreation.* The Hague, Netherlands: Martinus Nijhoff, 1996.

Gosden, Ralph. *Designing Babies: The Brave New World of Reproductive Technology.* New York: W. H. Freeman, 1999.

Karen Gottlieb
BioLaw
Nederland, Colorado

asylum Asylum can be sought by a person physically present in the United States who meets the definition of a refugee and fears political persecution if returned to his or her home country. A refugee is defined as "any person who is outside any country of such person's nationality or in the case of a person having no nationality, is outside any country in which such person last habitually resided, and who is unable or unwilling to avail himself or herself of the protection of that country because of persecution or a well-founded fear of persecution on account of race, religion, nationality, membership in a particular social group, or political opinion."

Asylum law was codified in the United States as part of the Refugee Act of 1980. Serious concern for the plight of refugees developed both internationally and in the United States after World War II. The definition of a refugee used by the United States comes from the 1951 United Nations Convention and 1967 Protocol Related to the Status of Refugees, which the United States signed in 1968.

Persons seeking refugee status apply from outside the United States, whereas asylum seekers apply from within the United States. Under current law, applications for asylum must be made within one year of entry unless there are extraordinary circumstances that caused delay or changed circumstances that materially effect the applicant's eligibility for asylum. Persons who meet the definition of refugee may not be granted asylum if they have been firmly resettled in a safe third country before coming to the United States. Additionally, applicants may not qualify for asylum if they themselves were persecutors, if they have been convicted of a serious crime in the United States, if there are reasons to believe they committed a serious crime outside the United States, or if they are a risk to the security of the United States. Similar restrictions apply to spouses or children of asylees who otherwise may be granted asylum if accompanying or following to join the person granted asylum status.

Persons filing for asylum in the United States may request work permission after a several month waiting period. Persons granted asylum status may file for permanent resident status after one year.

For more information

Anker, Deborah E. *The Law of Asylum in the United States.* 3rd ed. Boston: Refugee Law Center, 1999.

Bhabha, Jacqueline, and Geoffrey Coll, eds. *Asylum Law and Practice in Europe and North America.* Toronto: Federal Publications, 1992.

The Immigration and Nationality Statute, 8 U.S.C. § 1101(a)(42)(A) and 1158 (2000), and the Code of Federal Regulations, 8 C.F.R. § 208.1–208.31 (2000).

Angela McCaffrey
Hamline University
School of Law

attempt Attempt is in general the performance of an act or series of acts with the intention to achieve some end. In criminal law, the attempt to commit a crime usually means that a person acting with the level of culpability or knowledge required to commit the crime (1) purposefully engages in conduct which would constitute the crime if the attendant circumstances were as that person believes them to be (for example, buying drugs from an undercover government agent); (2) when causing a particular result is an element of the crime, does or omits to do something with the purpose of causing that result; or (3) does or omits something where the defendant believes that act or omissions is a "substantial step" in a course of conduct planned to culminate in the commission of a crime. (Model Penal Code § 5.01 [4]). As the New Jersey Supreme Court stated in *New Jersey v. Robinson,* 643 A.2d 591 (1994), "the criminalization of attempt focuses on the INTENT of the actor to cause a criminal result."

The law of attempts is of relatively recent origin in the common law, commonly dated to the 1784 decision by Lord Mansfield in *Rex v. Scofield.* It is also one of the more complex concepts in criminal law. By definition, an attempt to commit a crime means that the crime itself usually has not occurred. As set forth by the New York Court of Appeals in *New York v. Mahboubian,* 74 N.Y.2d 174 (1989), common rationales advanced for punishing attempts include that it is as appropriate to punish a person who has unsuccessfully committed a crime as one who has committed one, and that law enforcement authorities should be encouraged to stop crimes before they occur. In the case, for example, of one who attempts to commit a crime but fails to do so because of unforeseen circumstances or accident, it seems proper still to punish the perpetrator for the attempt.

In order to protect against punishing thoughts or acts that will not, without more, lead to a crime, attempt statutes as drafted by the legislatures and interpreted by the courts have sought to distinguish between actions taken in order to attempt to commit a criminal offense and actions that, while "preparatory" to a crime, are not themselves sufficient to constitute an attempt. These include the doctrines of "factual" impossibility, in which the attempted crime is unable to be completed due to some factual circumstance unknown to the actor, for example, by picking an empty pocket; and "legal" impossibility, in which the intended result of defendant's actions is not in fact a criminal offense, for example, attempting to receive stolen goods that were not in fact stolen. A person who is found to have attempted a legal impossibility generally is immune from conviction for attempt. However, one who attempted to commit a crime that was factually impossible is still subject to PUNISHMENT for an attempt to commit the contemplated crime.

While at common law attempt was considered a lesser crime than had the crime been completed, and so was accorded a lesser punishment, the current trend among state attempt statutes is to punish attempt at the same level as the crime attempted.

For more information

Kaplan, John, and Robert Weisberg. *Criminal Law: Cases and Materials.* Boston: Little, Brown, 1986, pp. 509–577.

Gerald J. Russello
Covington and Burling, New York

Attica Prison riot The Attica Prison riot, one of the most notorious and deadly uprisings behind bars, briefly focused attention on the plight of prisoners. The riot occurred in September 1971 at the Attica State Correctional Facility in New York. Forty-three men died, making it the deadliest riot in U.S. history. Four deaths were caused by prisoners, while 39 people were killed by state police officers.

At Attica, prisoners complained of harassment and brutal treatment by guards as well as poor food and a lack of adequate facilities for physical and mental health. (Subsequent investigations supported the prisoners' claims of inhumane disciplinary procedures.) As a result of changes in SENTENCING laws, many prisoners were serving longer sentences than those who had committed the same crimes in previous years. There were few meaningful activities for the prisoners, with the majority idle for most of their time. The average Attica prisoner spent 16 to 23 hours per day in his cell. Overcrowding also proved to be a concern. Attica had a capacity of 1,200, but it housed 2,225 prisoners at the time of the riot. Most of the prisoners were young, with an average age under 28. The prisoners were described by correctional personnel as more troublesome, more impatient, and more prone to violence than those incarcerated a decade earlier. Violence proved the only way to gain respect and cooperation among the prisoners, with prisoner leadership positions dependent on violent behavior. Additionally, correctional officers had no training in prison violence and seldom received more than on-the-job training.

The Attica riot arose partly out of the political consciousness. Most of the prisoners were African Americans and had begun to identify with black political movements among the free population. They believed that they were not being treated as human beings. The appointment of a new prison commissioner in January 1971 offered the hope of reform, but by September prisoners had become convinced that no change was on the horizon.

The riot broke out when prisoners refused to return to their cells as officers ordered them to do so for disciplinary reasons. Officials had not prepared for a riot. Plans and regulations at the prisons had been developed without the input of line officers. Three prisoners were killed in reprisal attacks by other prisoners as officers were taken hostage. At this point, Black Muslims within the prison established order and control, thereby preventing even more deaths. The Attica prisoners insisted on open negotiations in front of the entire prison population. They argued for demands that represented all those held there. New York governor Nelson Rockefeller became the brunt of considerable public criticism for refusing to become personally involved. Administrators decided to use violence to take back the prison. Fear and confusion among the officers as well as their emotional response led to the 39 deaths in the resulting assault.

For more information

Braswell, Michael C., Reid H. Montgomery, Jr. and Lucien X. Lombardo, eds. *Prison Violence in America.* Cincinnati: Anderson, 1994.

Featherstone, Richard Andrew. *Narratives from the 1971 Attica Prison Riot: Toward a New Theory of Correctional Disturbances.* Lewiston, N.Y.: Edwin Mellen Press, 2005.

Caryn E. Neumann
Miami University of Ohio

attorney general, U.S. The U.S. attorney general is the chief legal officer of the United States or of a state, who gives legal advice to the chief executive and to other officials. In the early years the attorney general of the United States gave legal advice to the Congress when requested. In 1819 William Wirt put a stop to this. The attorney generals serve two masters—the chief executive and the law. From time to time there can be a clash between their responsibilities to their political superior and to the public interest. The attorney general gives both legal and policy/political advice. The attorney general's interpretation of a law stands as authoritative unless overturned by judicial decision. In recent years the attorney general has been legally empowered to appoint an independent PROSECUTOR to investigate cases of high-level wrongdoing in the executive branch.

The U.S. attorney general heads the DEPARTMENT OF JUSTICE and, since the time of George Washington, is a member of the president's cabinet. In 1993 Janet Reno became the first woman attorney general in the nation's history. While some state ATTORNEYS GENERAL have gone on to the governorship (e.g., Bill Clinton in Arkansas), no federal attorney general has become president (though Robert Kennedy ran for the office in 1968, and William Wirt was the candidate of the Anti-Masonic Party in 1832). However, a number of attorneys general (Roger B. Taney, Nathan Clifford, Joseph McKenna, William Moody, James C. McReynolds, HARLAN F. STONE, Frank Murphy, Robert H. Jackson, Tom C. Clark) have become justices on the Supreme Court. Henry Stanbery (Andrew Johnson's A.G.) and Ebenezer R. Hoar (Grant's A.G.) were rejected by the Senate when nominated for the Supreme Court.

The attorney general directs the Justice Department with the assistance of the deputy attorney general, the associate attorney general, the solicitor general, and nine assistant attorneys general. On rare occasions the attorney general may represent the government before the Supreme Court, though it is usually the SOLICITOR GENERAL who appears. (It was not until December 1996 that Attorney General Reno argued a case before the Supreme Court.) The attorney general directs the work of the U.S. attorneys, the U.S. MARSHALS, and federal penal institutions. The Justice officials also make recommendations to the president concerning appointments to federal judicial positions. The attorney general, acting through the IMMIGRATION AND NATURALIZATION SERVICE, may grant ASYLUM to applicants who have well-founded fears of persecution in the country to which they would otherwise be returned.

Forty-three states have elected attorneys general; the rest are appointed. Thus it is possible in many states for the attorney general to be a member of a different political party from that of the governor. Sometimes the attorney general may refuse to represent the governor's position before the courts. Governors may need to have their own lawyers represent them where the attorneys general are at arm's length.

For more information

Baker, Nancy V. *Conflicting Loyalties: Law and Politics in the Attorney General's Office, 1789–1990*. Lawrence: University Press of Kansas, 1992.

Clayton, Cornell W. *The Politics of Justice: The Attorney General and the Making of Legal Policy*. New York: M.E. Sharpe, 1992.

Martin Gruberg
University of Wisconsin at Oshkosh

attorneys general Attorneys general government officials who serve as the chief legal officer of either the national government or a state government. Both the U.S. government and the governments of each of the 50 states have a chief legal officer that represents its legal interests in court. Commonly that official holds the title of the attorney general. Thus, the United States has an attorney general, and most states have an attorney general.

Attorneys general rarely personally appear in court on behalf of their respective governments, although for particularly important cases an attorney general may personally represent the government's interests in court. Rather, attorney generals employ and supervise the lawyers that will actually appear in court in most cases. Thus, much of an attorney general's responsibilities are administrative. While the attorney general of the United States has authority over all federal PROSECUTORS, in many states crimes are prosecuted by the local district attorneys (who are either elected officials or gubernatorial appointees), and thus state attorneys general exercise less control over criminal prosecutions than does the attorney general of the United States. Indeed, on the state level, representing the government in civil lawsuits takes up much more of the attorney general's resources than representing the government in criminal prosecutions.

Attorneys general often have other responsibilities in addition to overseeing the representation of their respective government's interests in court. They often advise the chief executive officer of the government, such as the president or the governor, regarding the legality of the chief executive officer's actions, the constitutionality and wisdom of proposed legislation, or even judicial appointments. However, attorneys general are usually viewed as representing the government rather than the chief executive, and thus there is some tension in the attorney general's various roles. Consequently, chief executives also generally hire lawyers as a part of their personal staffs who are more beholden to them as chief executive. Attorneys general, on the state level at least, often have an obligation to respond to inquiries from the legislature about the constitutionality of potential legislation. In addition, attorneys general may be responsible for governmental entities other than those that are comprised mainly of lawyers. For instance, the U.S. attorney general has responsibility for supervising law enforcement agencies, such as the FEDERAL BUREAU OF INVESTIGATION and the DRUG ENFORCEMENT AGENCY. The U.S. attorney general also supervises the IMMIGRATION AND NATURALIZATION SERVICE, which controls entry into the United States.

The attorney general of the United States is appointed with the approval of a majority of the U.S. Senate. Many state attorneys general are elected, but some are appointed by the governor with the approval of the state senate. In at least one state where the attorney general is appointed, the attorney general, once appointed, possesses some tenure protection to assure that he maintains some independence from the governor.

Sometimes citizens bring lawsuits to vindicate the rights of themselves and the public in general. In such circumstances the individual is sometimes referred to as a private attorney general.

For more information

Huston, Luther A., et al. *Roles of the Attorney General of the United States.* Washington, D.C.: American Enterprise Institute, 1968.

Ross, Lynne M., ed. *National Association of Attorneys General, State Attorneys General: Powers and Responsibilities.* Washington, D.C.: Bureau of National Affairs, 1990.

Bernard W. Bell
Professor of Law
Rutgers Law School, Newark

Atwater v. City of Lago Vista 532 U.S. 318 (2001) *Atwater v. City of Lago Vista,* is a decision by the U.S. Supreme Court in which the Court upheld the authority of the police to make a warrantless ARREST for minor criminal offenses, such as a MISDEMEANOR automobile seatbelt violation.

Gail Atwater was stopped and arrested after a police officer saw her driving her pickup truck in which neither she nor her two small children were wearing their seatbelts. She was ordered out of the truck, was verbally abused by the arresting officer in the presence of her children, and was not allowed to call a friend to whose nearby house she wished to take her children. She was taken to jail in handcuffs and was charged with driving without her seatbelt fastened, failure to fasten her children's seatbelts, driving without a license, and failure to provide proof of insurance. She pleaded no contest to the seatbelt charges and paid a $50 fine. The other charges were dismissed.

Later, she and her husband, an emergency room doctor, filed a federal CIVIL RIGHTS suit, which was dismissed by lower federal courts. The Atwaters then appealed to the Supreme Court, which by a vote of 5-4 ruled against the Atwaters. According to the Court, the Unreasonable SEARCHES AND SEIZURES Clause of the FOURTH AMENDMENT is not violated when a person is arrested for driving without the seatbelt fastened.

Associate Justice David H. Souter wrote the majority opinion for the Court. He stressed that while the officer's conduct was clearly unprofessional, it was not behavior that violated Mrs. Atwater's freedom against being unreasonably seized, as protected by the Fourth Amendment. The emphasis, according to Souter, is on the meaning of "unreasonable." What, he inquired, is the meaning of the standard of "reasonableness" in the context of the Fourth Amendment?

According to Souter and the Court's majority, there is no crystal clear, once-and-for-all meaning of "reasonable"; so much, he wrote, depends on the situation and the use of discretion by the law enforcement officer. Souter concluded it is not unreasonable in a situation not tending toward violence or a breach of the peace for a police officer to arrest someone for a misdemeanor without a warrant. "There simply is no evidence," Souter argued, "of widespread abuse of minor-offense arrest authority."

Associate Justices STEPHEN BREYER, RUTH BADER GINSBURG, SANDRA DAY O'CONNOR, and JOHN PAUL STEVENS dissented. Justice O'Connor wrote an impassioned dissent in which she emphasized the indignity of what Mrs. Atwater suffered at the hands of an overbearing police officer, and that even a minor offense can rise to the level of unconstitutional behavior. Justice O'Connor, as she often did during her Court tenure, argued for a practical, balancing approach that would take into account properly the interests of the state and the legitimate liberty interests of individuals such as Mrs. Atwater.

For more information

Yarbrough, Tinsley E. *The Rehnquist Court and The Constitution.* New York: Oxford University Press, 2001.

Yarbrough, Tinsley E. *David Hackett Souter: Traditional Republican on the Rehnquist Court.* New York: Oxford University Press, 2005.

Stephen K. Shaw
Northwestern Nazarene University,
Nampa, Idaho

automobile searches Automobile searches refer to the search of an individual's car. The Supreme Court has ruled that in general the police have far more leeway and authority to search cars and vehicles compared to someone's house or apartment.

An automobile may be searched without a warrant in three circumstances. First, when a law enforcement officer has PROBABLE CAUSE to believe an automobile contains contraband or EVIDENCE of a crime, the automobile may be searched to seize the contraband or evidence. Second, when the driver or an occupant of the vehicle is placed under ARREST, the passenger compartment of the automobile may be searched as an incident of the arrest. Third, when the automobile has been secured or seized by law enforcement, an INVENTORY SEARCH may be conducted to document its contents to protect the property of the automobile's owner and to protect law enforcement from claims of lost or stolen property. In each case, these searches are permissible pursuant to an exception to the general rule that searches may be conducted only when authorized by a warrant issued by a neutral and detached magistrate.

The FOURTH AMENDMENT to the UNITED STATES CONSTITUTION provides that "the right of the people to be secure in their persons, houses, papers and effects against unreasonable searches and seizures shall not be violated." As a general rule, searches conducted without a warrant are presumed to be unreasonable, and evidence obtained as a result of the warrantless search cannot be used against the defendant during a criminal trial. However, the U.S. Supreme Court has recognized that automobiles should be exempted from the warrant requirement.

The Supreme Court has identified two reasons that support the reasonableness of WARRANTLESS SEARCHES of automobiles when there is probable cause to believe contraband is being transported. First, automobiles are readily movable, making it impracticable for law enforcement officers to get a warrant before contraband may be transported out of the JURISDICTION. Second, automobiles offer a lowered expectation of privacy because their occupants and contents are generally in plain view of the public.

The exception for automobiles was first recognized in the Prohibition-era case of *Carroll v. United States,* 267 U.S. 132 (1925). In that case, federal agents were patrolling the roadways when they happened upon George Carroll and John Kiro, who were driving from Grand Rapids toward Detroit, Michigan, in an Oldsmobile roadster. Because Carroll and Kiro were known to bootleg liquor along that route in that particular automobile, the agents stopped them, searched their car, and found 68 bottles of illegal liquor. At their trial, Carroll and Kiro sought to have the evidence excluded on the ground that it was seized in violation of the Fourth Amendment. The trial court denied that request, and the Supreme Court affirmed.

The Supreme Court's decision rested on the distinction between the search of a house and the search of a vehicle, which the Court explained has always been recognized in its Fourth Amendment jurisprudence. The fact that a vehicle may be easily and quickly moved is a critical factor in determining whether a warrantless search is reasonable. Yet, the Court still recognized that the authority to search an automobile should not be unlimited. Therefore, the Court ruled that if the facts and circumstances would justify a reasonably cautious person to believe that a vehicle is transporting contraband, the law enforcement officer may search the automobile and seize the contraband without a warrant. In a subsequent case, *United States v. Ross,* 456 U.S. 798 (1982), the Supreme Court addressed how extensive a warrantless search could be and decided that the permissible scope of a warrantless search under the automobile exception is the same as the scope of a search conducted pursuant to a warrant. Therefore, the automobile search could include the passenger compartment, the trunk, and all containers and sub-compartments, which may contain the contraband in question.

Automobiles may also be SEARCHED INCIDENT TO A LAWFUL ARREST. This exception to the warrant requirement is an extension of the general exception for searches conducted incident to a lawful custodial arrest. In *WEEKS V. UNITED STATES,* 232 U.S. 383 (1914), the Supreme Court explained that it was always recognized in the law that a search incident to arrest could be conducted to discover the fruits or evidence of crimes. In later cases, most notably *CHIMEL V. CALIFORNIA,* 395 U.S. 752 (1969), the Court explained that the search incident to arrest was not limited to the body of the arrested person but extended also to anything within his or her control and within the immediate area within the person's reach. Ultimately, in *New York v. Belton,* 453 U.S. 454 (1981), the Supreme Court considered the application of the search incident to arrest rule to an arrest occurring in an automobile. In that case, the Court decided that when a law enforcement officer arrests the occupant of an automobile, the officer is authorized to conduct a warrantless search of the passenger compartment of the automobile and any containers inside it. This type of search is permitted so the officer may seize any weapons or contraband that may be found in the area within the occupant's reach.

Finally, impounded automobiles may be searched without a warrant to take an inventory of the automobile's contents. The Supreme Court first recognized that inventory searches are reasonable and exempted from the warrant requirement of the Fourth Amendment in *South Dakota v. Opperman,* 428 U.S. 364 (1976). In that case, the defendant's automobile was impounded due to multiple parking violations. An inventory search led to the discovery of a small amount of marijuana in the glove compartment, and the defendant was prosecuted for possession of marijuana. Ultimately, the Supreme Court concluded that the inventory search was reasonable because automobiles are afforded less protection under the Fourth Amendment and the search was conducted as part of law enforcement's caretaking role. When automobiles are seized by law enforcement, the automobiles are secured and their contents are documented. This administrative procedure is followed for four reasons: to protect the car owner's property while it is in police custody, to protect the police against claims over lost or stolen property, to protect the police from potential danger, and to determine if the automobile has been stolen. Evaluating all the circumstances at issue, the Court concluded that inventory searches are reasonable and, therefore, do not offend the Fourth Amendment's prohibition of unreasonable searches and seizures.

For more information:

Bloom, Robert M. *Searches, Seizures, and Warrants: A Reference Guide to the United States Constitution.* Westport, Conn.: Praeger, 2003.

Hubbart, Phillip A. *Making Sense of Search and Seizure Law: A Fourth Amendment Handbook.* Durham, N.C.: Carolina Academic Press, 2005.

LaFave, Wayne R. *Search and Seizure: A Treatise on the Fourth Amendment. 4th ed.* Eagan, Minn.: Thomson West, 2004.

Mark A. Fulks
Tennessee State University

B

bail and bondsman Bail is the process through which an ARRESTED person can obtain release from custody while his or her case works its way through the justice system. It is typically a monetary guarantee pledged to the court, assuring that a defendant or suspect will return to court for hearings and the trial. A bondsman is a third-party person who supplies the bail for a defendant, oftentimes for a fee.

American bail procedures originate from English common law, which relied on oath and on pledges of land or property from the defendants or their relatives to ensure that they did not flee. In the United States, each state has its own laws and constitutional provisions regarding bail. Moreover, the EIGHTH AMENDMENT to the CONSTITUTION prohibits imposing excessive bail, but it does not define what constitutes excessive bail and does not provide a right to bail.

Since 1984, the Bail Reform Act set guidelines for federal courts to consider in the decision whether to release the defendant into the community; the accused may be held without bail if the court considers him or her a threat to the community. The U.S. Supreme Court held in *UNITED STATES V. SALERNO*, 481 U.S. 739 (1987), that DUE PROCESS was not violated by the detention of individuals without bail. PRETRIAL DETENTION without bail in state courts is governed by each state's own laws.

Bail-setting processes vary by city and state, with a number of factors and actors influencing the decision. The JUDGE decides whether to RELEASE ON RECOGNIZANCE, set bail, or jail the suspect. Bail decisions depend on several factors, including the seriousness of the charges, the likelihood that the defendant will flee, any prior criminal record, and concerns about community safety.

The most common forms of bail include Release on Recognizance (ROR), surety bond, Written Promise to Appear (PTA), cash or property, or some combination. ROR means that defendants are released from jail pending a trial or APPEAL based on a written promise to appear in court. Conditional release and the unsecured bond constitute other means of release without financial requirements. The former requires the defendant to maintain contact with a pretrial release program or other form of monitoring, while the latter means that although bail is set, no money is paid to the court. The defendant will be liable for the full amount of bail in case of failure to appear.

A third party agrees to be responsible for the debt or obligation of the defendant when release is based on a surety bond. In many JURISDICTIONS, bail bondsmen provide this service, commonly for a nonrefundable fee of 10 percent of the required amount for bail. Failing to comply with the conditions set in the bail arrangement can lead to loss of the bail money and immediate return to jail. Bail bondsmen are controversial profit-seeking individuals who influence whether people in jail will gain pretrial release. Many countries, including Canada, England, and Australia, have banned commercial bail bonds as unfair and corrupt. In fact, only the Philippines and the United States allow these practices.

Individuals who fail to make bail are statistically more likely to be convicted of a crime. They also face other disadvantages in the preparation of their defense and in dealing with the CRIMINAL JUSTICE SYSTEM. In the last 50 years, numerous reform initiatives have sought to reduce the bail system's discriminatory effect upon the poor, prevent unnecessary detention prior to conviction, and prohibit excessive bail. Despite these attempts, bail remains a significant discretionary decision that can have especially significant effects on people who are too poor to pay required amounts and therefore suffer the effects of pretrial detention, including loss of jobs and inability to support their families.

For more information

Devine, F. E. *Commercial Bail Bonding: A Comparison of Common Law Alternatives.* Westport, Conn.: Praeger Publishers, 1991.

"The Truth about Commercial Bail Bonding in America." *The National Association of Pretrial Services Agencies Advocacy Brief* 1, no. 1 (August 2009).

Zoltán Levente Fejes
Michigan State University

bail revocation Bail revocation refers to the reversal of a court decision to release a suspect from jail prior to trial hearings.

The procedural rules of bail revocation can vary from state to state but generally serve as a safeguard for the public and those involved in the suspect's impending trial. Though originally designed to uphold freedoms of citizens suspected of a crime (i.e., suspects are innocent until proven guilty), bail introduces a certain amount of risk to the public's safety. Concerns over additional crimes these individuals can commit while out on bail prompted statutes outlining bail revocation procedures.

An individual who has been released on BAIL (also known as a "bond") surrenders a sum of money in exchange for temporary freedom until a trial date occurs. This exchange, often mediated by a bail bondsman, is a form of pretrial release that comes with certain rules that the suspect must abide by while awaiting trial. These rules are known as conditions of release and, depending on the nature of the crime the suspect was charged with, vary in the amount of control the court maintains over the suspect.

For example, typical conditions of release include the stipulation that no new crimes of a similar nature of the initial charge can be committed. For example, if the suspect was originally charged with ASSAULT, being involved in an assault while out on bail would violate the conditions of release. Other conditions of release can include abstinence from drugs and alcohol, confinement to a specific geographic area (e.g., cannot leave the state, city, or county), and avoiding contact with witnesses to the initial crime in which the suspect was allegedly involved. Ultimately, conditions of release are designated by the presiding JUDGE during pretrial hearings and are often arbitrated by prosecution and DEFENSE ATTORNEYS.

Bail revocation hearings are scheduled after it is found that there is reasonable suspicion that the suspect has violated one or more conditions of the original bail release agreement. For example, bail is often given with the condition that the suspect must stay within a certain geographical area in order to ensure the individual will be most likely to return to court for future trial hearings. If a suspect is found outside of the geographical area outlined in the conditions of release (e.g., they were caught speeding on a highway outside of the county in which they were required to stay), they can be taken into custody and must face a judge to discuss the violation.

During a bail revocation hearing, three outcomes are possible. First, re-release of the suspect without revision of the bail agreement can occur if the suspect was brought into custody on suspicion of violating the conditions of release, but the judge found the suspicions were unfounded. The second possible outcome concerns revision of the conditions of release and re-releasing the suspect on bail once again. Called bail modification, the conditions of release are often more strict, further constraining the freedom of the suspect but ultimately allowing him or her to return to the community while awaiting trial. The third possible outcome of a bail revocation hearing is detaining the suspect in jail and not re-releasing him or her into the community. This decision generally hinges upon whether the judge believes the suspect will uphold the conditions of release. Often, the determination that allows for PRETRIAL DETENTION coincides with the judge's belief that the individual is a flight risk (i.e., will not return to court for future trial hearings) or that the suspect will interfere with trial processes if released (e.g., influence or intimidate witnesses).

Bail revocation statutes offer additional assurance to the public that individuals released on bail are subject to many facets of judicial control. Designed to serve as an additional deterrent to engagement in criminal behavior, bail revocation provides the CRIMINAL JUSTICE SYSTEM with an additional tool for maintaining control over individuals awaiting trial. Though there are concerns over the effects of bail revocation on subsequent trial proceedings, this tool offers insurance for the risk involved with pretrial release decisions.

For more information

Saltzburg, Stephen A. *American Criminal Procedure: Cases and Commentary.* 2nd ed. St. Paul, Minn.: West, 1984.

Territo, Leonard, James B. Halsted, and Max L. Bromley. *Crime and Justice in America: A Human Perspective.* 5th ed. Boston, Mass.: Butterworth-Heinemann, 1998.

Kathryn Zafft
University of Maryland, College Park

Bailey, F. Lee (1933–) defense attorney F. Lee Bailey distinguished himself as one of America's best-known criminal DEFENSE ATTORNEYS in the 20th century. Over the course of his career, he represented defendants in many high-profile cases, successfully argued a case before the U.S. Supreme Court, and inspired generations of trial lawyers with his courtroom style.

One of his first cases garnering public attention involved Dr. SAM SHEPPARD, an Ohio physician accused of murdering his wife in 1954. The pretrial media coverage surrounding the case was so egregious and so biased against the defendant that a guilty verdict was a foregone conclusion. APPEALING Sheppard's conviction in FEDERAL COURT, Bailey argued that the prejudicial media coverage had tainted the jurors, who were not sequestered and not otherwise able to avoid the barrage of media coverage. Consequently, Bailey maintained that media coverage had undermined Sheppard's constitutional right to a fair JURY trial. The U.S. Supreme Court agreed, reversing Sheppard's conviction. Justice Tom C. Clark concluded that Sheppard had not received a fair trial. The Court held that the incessant, biased media coverage had prejudiced jurors, thereby infringing upon the defendant's DUE PROCESS protection under the Fourteenth Amendment. *Sheppard v. Maxwell,* 384 U.S. 333 (1966), forever links Bailey to media coverage and its effect on a criminal defendant's ability to receive a fair trial. The facts of the *Sheppard* case are widely believed to have inspired the 1960s television series (and the 1993 movie) *The Fugitive.*

Despite high-profile victories, Bailey's career also bears its share of high-profile defeats. In 1967, Bailey represented Albert DeSalvo in the BOSTON STRANGLER case. DeSalvo stood trial on charges of raping and MURDERING 11 women between 1962 and 1964. Bailey was unable to overcome the facts of the case, including the defendant's CONFESSION, and DeSalvo was convicted. The Boston Strangler case was Bailey's first high-profile loss.

During the 1970s, PATTY HEARST, heiress to the Hearst newspaper fortune, was an undergraduate student at the University of California, Berkeley. She was abducted by members of the SYMBIONESE LIBERATION ARMY (SLA), a terrorist group. During her captivity, Hearst participated in a number of armed bank ROBBERIES with the SLA. Following her release, Hearst stood trial for her role in the robberies. Bailey alleged that Hearst had been brainwashed by her captors into participating in the crimes that she otherwise would never have committed. Bailey's defense in this case was considered groundbreaking; though not an insanity defense, it did nonetheless seek to diminish the defendant's legal culpability due to profound emotional duress. Bailey's skill was not enough to overcome the facts, and Hearst was convicted.

In 1994, Bailey seared himself into the psyche of a new generation by serving on the defense team of O. J. SIMPSON, the former professional football star accused of murdering his ex-wife and another person. Bailey and several co-counsel comprising the "dream team" successfully defended Simpson, who was ACQUITTED of all criminal charges.

Despite disbarment in the state of Florida for improperly retaining millions of dollars in securities as compensation from a client that the U.S. government had sought to seize in 2001, Bailey's legendary career remains marked by numerous high-profile victories and defeats, and a PRECEDENT-setting Supreme Court decision. His impressive cross-examination skill also inspired generations of American trial lawyers as a real-life Perry Mason able to elicit information from witnesses they otherwise would not have divulged.

For more information

Bailey, F. Lee. *For The Defense.* New York: Signet, 1976.

———. *The Defense Never Rests.* New York: Signet, 1971.

———. *To Be a Trial Lawyer.* New York: John Wiley, 1994.

Whitten, Les. *F. Lee Bailey.* New York: Avon, 1971.

Melanie Morris
United States Government

Baker v. Carr 369 U.S. 186 (1962) *Baker v. Carr* is a "landmark" ruling of the WARREN COURT that initiated a "reapportionment revolution" in American CONSTITUTIONAL LAW and electoral politics. In his memoirs, EARL WARREN, who was CHIEF JUSTICE of the United States from 1953 to 1969, wrote that, in his opinion, the most important case during his tenure on the Supreme Court was not the school desegregation case of *BROWN V. BOARD OF EDUCATION OF TOPEKA, KANSAS;* rather, it was *Baker v. Carr.*

Prior to the case of *Baker v. Carr,* which the Supreme Court handed down on March 26, 1962, the Court and virtually all other courts of law in the country had for decades steadfastly refused to hear cases concerning legislative reapportionment. For instance, in the case of *Colegrove v. Green* in 1946, the United States Supreme Court refused to accept, under what is known as the "political question doctrine," a legislative reapportionment case from Illinois concerning that state's congressional districts in the U.S. House of Representatives. In the words of Associate Justice FELIX FRANKFURTER, who wrote the opinion for the Court in *Colegrove,* "Courts ought not to enter this political thicket." What Frankfurter meant is that the issue of legislative reapportionment was one that the political system was equipped to address, but that the judiciary was not able to address the issue in any kind of principled way. By invoking the political question doctrine, as it did in *Colegrove,* the Court declared that the issue of legislative reapportionment was a "nonjusticiable" issue.

The Court in *Baker v. Carr* changed its mind, overruled *Colegrove,* and clearly stated that, contrary to the ruling in *Colegrove,* legislative reapportionment was NOT peculiarly political and instead was a justiciable issue, one that the judiciary could address through the judicial process using well-established legal principles. Writing for the Court in *Baker v. Carr,* Associate Justice WILLIAM J. BRENNAN reasoned that when a legislature, in the light of population increases and shifts over the course of six decades, still did not reapportion legislative seats, the EQUAL PROTECTION clause of the Fourteenth Amendment offered a constitutional vehicle by which lawsuits could be brought alleging denial of political equality and voting rights. The Court in *Baker* did not decide the case from Tennessee on the merits; rather, it remanded or sent the case back to the federal trial court, thus empowering federal courts to begin accepting such reapportionment cases.

By holding in *Baker v. Carr* that reapportionment was no longer a nonjusticiable controversy, the Supreme Court soon would find itself bombarded by such cases. Over the next two years, the Court would hear close to 20 such cases, and the principle, under the Fourteenth Amendment's equal protection clause, of "one person, one vote" would soon be enshrined in American constitutional law and electoral politics. Reapportionment cases are still regularly before the Court today and often are no less controversial than they were a generation ago.

Another critical issue confronted by the Court in *Baker v. Carr* was the Court's own role in American law and politics. Dissenting in *Baker,* Justice Frankfurter argued that "there is not under our Constitution a judicial remedy for every political mischief, for every undesirable exercise of legislative power." However, by repudiating Frankfurter's thesis on legislative reapportionment announced in *Colegrove,* the Court in *Baker* not only offered a definitive statement on the meaning of the political question doctrine; the Court also committed itself to defining and ultimately policing a system of fair and responsible government in the United States.

For more information

Baker, Gordon. *The Reapportionment Revolution.* New York: Random House, 1966.

Strum, Philippa. *The Supreme Court and "Political Questions": A Study in Judicial Evasion.* Tuscaloosa: University of Alabama Press, 1974.

Stephen K. Shaw
Northwest Nazarene University

Bakke See *REGENTS OF THE UNIVERSITY OF CALIFORNIA V. BAKKE.*

bankruptcy Bankruptcy is the legal process by which the assets of insolvent debtors are identified and distributed among their creditors. The purpose of bankruptcy is to provide a fair means to satisfy the claims of creditors and permit debtors to make a fresh start without the burden of debt that brought them to insolvency in the first place. Discharge in bankruptcy is an exclusively federal power that is created and regulated by federal statues; however, because property rights are created and defined by state law, the process of bankruptcy varies from state to state. For example, some states, such as Florida, allow debtors to protect more of their property from creditors than other states. In all cases, however, bankruptcy rearranges and redefines the legal relationships between debtors and creditors.

Article one, section eight of the CONSTITUTION gives Congress the power to enact legislation regarding bankruptcy. The first bankruptcy act was adopted in 1800, with additional acts adopted in 1803, 1841,1867, 1874, then in 1898 and again in 1938. The most recent bankruptcy acts were adopted in 1978, with major revisions to it occurring with the Bankruptcy Abuse Prevention and

Consumer Protection Act of 2005. Between the 1978 and 2005 acts, Congress also composed many minor bankruptcy code revisions.

Both individuals and businesses may declare bankruptcy, and there are several different statutory schemes under which the bankruptcy process may be pursued. The most extreme approach is for the debtor to be declared insolvent and his or her assets (the bankruptcy estate) to be identified, reduced to cash, and distributed among the creditors. Bankruptcy law determines what assets may be distributed, how creditors must make their claims on those assets, and which creditors have priority in being paid from the bankruptcy estate. Once the distribution is completed, the debtor's legal obligations to the creditors are extinguished, even if the debts have not been fully paid. In other cases, bankruptcy is used to prevent individual creditors from seizing the debtor's assets and require the creditors to accept payment according to a plan approved by the bankruptcy court. Under this approach, debtors with an income that is sufficiently stable and regular to make payments can gain protection from their creditors while their debts are being paid off. Both individuals and businesses have access to these types of bankruptcies, and under both approaches creditors are often paid substantially less than the entire amount they are owed.

The bankruptcy laws have been altered several times in recent years in response to pressure, especially from the credit industry, to curb abuses of the bankruptcy remedy. Reformers have argued that the law encourages people to overspend and run up debts by offering them an easy way to discharge their liabilities while still retaining much of their property. Opponents of reform argue that the potential for abuse is already limited by the fact that debtors are entitled to file for bankruptcy only once every seven years. They also claim that the credit industry encourages individuals to spend beyond their means.

Recent bankruptcy reform effort addresses these concerns by limiting individual debtors' access to the so-called straight bankruptcy (Chapter 7) and forcing them to make use of the less liberal Chapter 13 bankruptcy, which allows debtors to discharge fewer debts and obligates them to enter into payment plans with their creditors. In addition, debtors' ability to shelter their assets is limited by setting a cap on the "homestead exemption," under which individual states determine the value of residential property that the debtor may protect from creditors. The basic goal of such reforms is to limit access to consumer bankruptcy and force debtors to be more accountable. Nevertheless, easy access to consumer credit is likely to continue to encourage debtors to spend beyond their ability to pay.

The 2005 act, as with earlier bankruptcy laws, seeks a trade-off between requiring individuals and businesses to be responsible for their debts versus discharging them and giving parties a new opportunity to make a fresh start. Some argue that the 2005 act made it more difficult for individuals to discharge debts, thereby making it more difficult to recover from the mounting personal debt many had built up on credit cards. Conversely, creditors argued that consumers should not be rewarded for overspending.

Finally, after the recession of 2008, there were efforts to change the bankruptcy laws to make it easier for homeowners to adjust their mortgage debt. These efforts did not pass Congress.

For further information

Caher, John. "Bankruptcy Reform; Congress Set to Address Perceived Debtor Abuse," *New York Law Journal* (June 1, 2000): 5.

Solomon, Robin. "A Bankruptcy Primer for Paralegals," *The Legal Intelligencer,* September 14, 2000, p. 9.

Celia A. Sgroi
State University of New York, Oswego

Barron v. Mayor of Baltimore 32 U.S. 243 (1833) *Barron v. Mayor of Baltimore* is the case in which the Supreme Court, under Chief Justice

JOHN MARSHALL, announced that the Fifth Amendment's "TAKINGS CLAUSE," which prohibits the government from taking private property unless it pays the owner "just compensation," applied only to the national government, not state governments.

In *Barron,* 32 U.S. 243, 7 Pet. 243 (1833), the plaintiff was seeking to recover damages for injuries to his "extensive and highly productive wharf" that were the result of changes in the way the city of Baltimore graded and paved streets. The wharf-owner alleged that the city's actions constituted an uncompensated taking of property, and that as a result, those actions violated the "takings clause" of the Fifth Amendment, which provides "nor shall private property be taken for public use, without just compensation." The suit was first brought in the Baltimore County Court, where after a trial, the wharf-owner was awarded $4,500 in damages. On APPEAL, the Maryland Court of Appeals reversed the trial court and dismissed the suit. The case was then appealed to the United States Supreme Court.

The Supreme Court, in an opinion written by Chief Justice John Marshall, held that "We are of [sic] opinion, that the provision in the fifth amendment to the constitution, declaring that private property shall not be taken for public use, without just compensation, is intended solely as a limitation on the exercise of power by the government of the United States, and is not applicable to the legislation of the states." Chief Justice Marshall set forth three arguments in support of this conclusion.

Marshall's first argument is that the CONSTITUTION concerns a government created by the people for themselves, not for the states. In the opinion, Marshall writes: "The people of the United States framed such a government for the United States as they supposed best adapted their situation and best calculated to promote their interests. The powers they conferred on this government were to be exercised by itself; and the limitations on power, if expressed in general terms, are naturally, and, we think, necessarily, applicable to the government created by the instrument."

Marshall's second argument is premised on the language of the takings clause. Marshall argues that when the Constitution sets forth limitations on the power of the states, as it does in Article I, section 10, it does so expressly ("no state shall pass any bill of attainder or EX POST FACTO law"). More general limitations on power, like those found in Article I, section 9, must only be applicable to the national government, otherwise the language expressly including the states in Article I, section 10 is superfluous. The takings clause of the Fifth Amendment is a general limitation and must therefore only be applicable to the national government.

Marshall's last argument is based on the concerns of the public at the time the Constitution was ratified. In the opinion, Marshall writes: "In almost every convention by which the constitution was adopted, amendments to guard against the abuse of power were recommended. These amendments demanded security against the apprehended encroachments of the general government—not against those of the local governments. In compliance with a sentiment thus generally expressed, to quiet fears thus extensively entertained, amendments were proposed by the required majority in congress, and adopted by the states. These amendments contain no expression indicating an intention to apply to the state governments."

The holding in *Barron* has since been reversed (see *Chicago, Burlington and Quincy Railroad Company v. Chicago,* 166 U.S. 226 [1897]). The Supreme Court, based on the Fourteenth Amendment's DUE PROCESS clause, has gradually incorporated most of the provisions of the first eight amendments so that they apply to state governments.

For more information

White, G. Edward. *The Marshall Court and Cultural Change 1815–1835* (abridged edition). New York: Oxford University Press, 1991.

Michael H. Walsh
Loyola University, Chicago, Illinois

Batson v. Kentucky 476 U.S. 79 (1986) *Batson v. Kentucky* was decided in 1986 by the U.S. Supreme Court. The Court decided that PROSECUTORS may not use a PEREMPTORY CHALLENGE in a racially motivated manner to exclude jurors from a criminal trial. This case represents a major shift in the Court's stance toward peremptory challenges. Prior to *Batson,* the Supreme Court largely deferred to the peremptory challenge due to its view of the importance of such a challenge. In the wake of this case, however, the Court increasingly affected the use of these types of controls over JURY composition.

James Batson was on trial in 1985 for second-degree BURGLARY and also for the receipt of stolen goods in the state of Kentucky. During the jury selection, the JUDGE conducted the VOIR DIRE portion of jury selection, when each juror's competence is questioned and the judge decides whether they stay or are dismissed. When the judge was done, there were four black men on the panel of jurors. After the judge completed his questioning of the jurors, the defense and prosecutors were allowed to use their ability of peremptory challenges, which allows them to dismiss any of the jurors without states cause. The prosecutor then proceeded to dismiss all four of the black men who were on the panel. The defense moved to discharge the jury citing Batson's SIXTH AMENDMENT right to an impartial jury of his peers and his Fourteenth Amendment rights of EQUAL PROTECTION OF THE LAW. The trial judge denied the motion, and Batson was convicted of the two counts. Batson then appealed to the Kentucky Supreme Court, which also denied the claim of unfair trial. Batson subsequently appealed to the U.S. Supreme Court, which reversed the decisions of the state courts.

The opinion of the Court was written by Justice Lewis Powell in favor of the petitioner in a 7-2 decision. The majority overruled *Swain v. Alabama,* 380 U.S. 202 (1965), which stated that explicit proof of racism on the part of the prosecutor is required. In *Swain,* the Court applied the equal protection principle to peremptory challenges. In *Batson,* Justice Powell wrote an opinion based on the Sixth and Fourteenth Amendments, and he utilized *Strauder v. West Virginia,* 100 U.S. 303 (1880), which overruled a law in West Virginia that allowed only white men to be jurors. Powell argued that "[c]ompetence to serve as a juror ultimately depends on an assessment of individual qualifications and ability impartially to consider evidence presented at trial. A person's race simply 'is unrelated to his fitness as a juror.'"

Batson cleared the way for decisions that reconsider the power of the peremptory challenge. In *Edmonson v. Leesville Concrete Co.,* 500 U.S. 614 (1991), the Court applied *Batson* to private litigants. The justices further reevaluated the peremptory challenge in *Georgia v. McCollum,* 505 U.S. 42 (1992), when they argued that neither prosecutors nor defense counsels can use a peremptory challenge to deny a person for race in criminal cases. In *J.E.B. v. Alabama Ex Rel. T. B.,* 511 U.S. 127 (1994), the Supreme Court held that potential jurors could not be excluded on a basis of gender.

Batson limited the power of the criminal prosecution to act in a racially motivated way in peremptory challenges. This case was a watershed moment in the rights of individuals. Not only did the Supreme Court protect the accused, but also the rights of the potential juror. Additional progeny also expanded the protections against gender discrimination, to prohibit both sides of a criminal dispute from using the challenge in a biased manner, and expanded these protections to civil disputes. This contraction of the powers of peremptory challenges is not without its critics, however. For example, Justice ANTONIN SCALIA argued in dissent in *McCollum* that the Supreme Court "use[s] the CONSTITUTION to destroy the ages-old right of criminal defendants to exercise peremptory challenges as they wish."

For more information

Epstein, Lee, and Thomas G. Walker. *Constitutional Law for a Changing America: Rights, Liberties, and Justice.* 6th ed. Washington, D.C.: CQ Press, 2007.

Stephanie Arrowsmith
Monmouth College

Tobias T. Gibson
Westminster College

battered women's syndrome Battered women's syndrome, sometimes referred to as "BWS," is a psychological condition often considered to be a form of post-traumatic stress in women living with consistent and/or severe relationship abuse. BWS has been offered as a defense in cases where women have been criminally charged with killing individuals who have physically abused them.

The term was first coined in the late 1970s by the feminist academic Lenore Walker in the context of the women's movement and increasing public awareness of DOMESTIC ABUSE. It describes psychological and behavioral symptoms resulting from repeated cycles of violence in an intimate relationship (see domestic abuse), creating a form of psychological paralysis that makes the victim unable to take independent action to extract herself from the abusive relationship. The term *battering and its effects* is often preferred in order to better reflect various battering patterns. Although it can occur in same-sex relationships and/or with male victims, it is overwhelmingly an affliction of women who have male partners.

BWS can be important in criminal cases in several ways. It can be used to demonstrate duress if the abuse victim is charged with a third-party crime that the abuser coerced her into committing. If an abuser is facing criminal charges for abuse and the victim later recants, BWS may also be used to explain her recantation as an effect of her circumstances, thus allowing the prosecution to proceed.

The most well known use of BWS is in a defense against a charge of ASSAULT or MURDER when the victim has attacked her abuser. It is not an independent legal defense but can be used as a component of a defense in several ways. First, BWS can be considered a mitigating circumstance. Conditions that affect one's judgment may mean that a person is found guilty of a lesser crime than murder because of diminished capacity or diminished responsibility. Experts in a trial can establish that BWS is one such condition and that the defendant was experiencing it at the time of the killing.

A second way in which BWS can be used is to bolster a claim of SELF-DEFENSE, where a defendant normally must show that she was at risk of imminent and serious bodily harm and that she reasonably believed her actions were necessary to save her own life. However, abuse victims who kill their partners often do so after the violence has abated, such as when he is sleeping, thus removing the imminent harm element. BWS can sometimes be used to demonstrate that in her current psychological state as a result of repeated severe abuse, she believed she had no other options to protect herself and that her actions were therefore reasonable and necessary for self-preservation according to her own state of mind.

The first use of BWS in court began in the late 1970s by attorneys who believed the legal process victimized battered women. The Washington Supreme Court decision *State v. Wanrow,* 559 P.2d 548 (1977), is considered a landmark case that laid the groundwork for the use of BWS in a defense. The court noted that the defendant's perception of danger and necessary force may have been different because she was a woman, and the JURY should have been instructed accordingly. JUDGES often refused to allow BWS EVIDENCE, however. In the early 1980s, the traditional legal trend began to change. In the Maine case *State v. Anaya,* 438 A.2d 892 (Me. 1981), for example, the trial judge refused to allow any BWS evidence in the defense of a woman who killed her husband, but the decision was reversed on APPEAL. Nevertheless, courts were slow to accept the concept.

BWS as a theory is criticized in several respects. Some argue that it attempts to allow abuse to excuse unjustifiable violence. Others claim that the theory actually harms abuse survivors by casting them as helpless and passive victims who belong outside the public discourse regarding their own situations. An additional criticism is that the theory belies the fact that the experiences of battered women are unique and varied.

Today, the willingness of courts to allow evidence of BWS is fairly widespread. Although it is still controversial as part of a legal defense, it has become widely accepted in courts throughout the United States. It is recognized as a legitimate part of a defense by statute in many states. Evidentiary rules on its admissibility can vary significantly with each state, however, and the scope may be limited.

For more information

Downs, Donald Alexander. *More Than Victims: Battered Women, the Syndrome Society, and the Law.* Chicago: University of Chicago Press, 1996.

Walker, Lenore. *The Battered Woman Syndrome.* 3rd ed. New York: Springer, 2009.

Deborah Anthony
University of Illinois at Springfield

Beard, Charles A. (1874–1948) political historian Charles A. Beard was among the most important American political historians of the first half of the 20th century. As a leading member of the "Progressive" school of U.S. historians, Beard was influential and active in both the scholarly and political communities and may be best known for writing *An Economic Interpretation of the Constitution of the United States* (1913).

Charles A. Beard (Library of Congress)

Beard graduated from DePauw University and studied at the University of Oxford and Cornell University before earning his Ph.D. at Columbia University in 1904. Though raised in a prosperous midwestern family, Beard quickly became involved in the working-class politics of the day, both in Britain and in the United States. Upon completing his Ph.D., Beard joined the Political Science Department at Columbia as a member of the faculty. A prolific author, Beard wrote and edited numerous books and textbooks, as well as a large number of articles and book reviews for both scholarly and popular publications.

The Progressive school of U.S. history emphasized the economic roots of politics and argued that economic conflict between popular and elite classes within society was the central feature of American political history. *An Economic Interpretation of the Constitution of the United States* is the most famous work in that vein. *An Economic*

Interpretation argued that the CONSTITUTION was part of an elite reaction to the democratizing influence of the American Revolution and was motivated by the economic interests of its supporters. Although controversial even in its own time, it was a pioneering work in examining the motivations of politicians and the political origins of the Constitution and U.S. law. Beard extended this argument in such works as *The Economic Origins of Jeffersonian Democracy* (1915), *The Economic Basis of Politics* (1922), and *The Supreme Court and the Constitution* (1912). With his wife, Mary Ritter Beard, he applied this basic approach to all of American history in the influential narrative *The Rise of American Civilization* (1927). Both Beard's specific analysis of the origins of the Constitution and his general emphasis on economic conflict in U.S. political history were challenged beginning in the 1950s by the "consensus" school, led by such historians as Louis Hartz and Daniel Boorstin, who argued for the importance and persistence of shared values in shaping U.S. politics.

The Progressive political movement, with which Beard was associated, emphasized "good government" reforms to reduce political corruption and democratize politics, while also encouraging a more activist government that would address the social and economic problems associated with industrialism and urbanization. In keeping with those concerns, Beard published such works as *American Government and Politics* (1910), *American City Government* (1912), *American Leviathan* (1930), and *The Myth of Rugged Individualism* (1932). In his early years at Columbia, Beard produced several textbooks and readers on modern European history. In 1917 Beard resigned from Columbia University in protest of the investigation and firing of a number of professors for political activities against World War I. In 1919 he helped to found the New School for Social Research. In his later years, Beard turned much of his attention to criticism of the foreign policy of Franklin Roosevelt and the U.S. entry into World War II.

For more information

Hofstadter, Richard. *The Progressive Historians: Turner, Beard, Parrington*. Chicago: University of Chicago Press, 1968.

Nore, Ellen. *Charles Beard, An Intellectual Biography*. Carbondale: Southern Illinois University Press, 1983.

Keith E. Whittington
Princeton University

Berman v. Parker 348 U.S. 26 (1954) *Berman v. Parker* was a decision by the U.S. Supreme Court that broadened federal and state governments' power of EMINENT DOMAIN. This ability to take private property for a public purpose is explicitly established by the Fifth Amendment to the U.S. CONSTITUTION:

"No person shall . . . be deprived of . . . property, without due process of law; . . . nor shall private property be taken for public use without just compensation."

Despite the Constitution's old-fashioned language, most of the document is relatively easy to understand. For instance, "just compensation" means that in situations which require a governmental body to seize privately owned land, the owner must be paid a fair price. Unfortunately, the meanings of some portions of the Fifth Amendment, such as the "public use" phrase, have been questioned for 200 years. The Constitution's failure to define this phrase compounds the fact that the wording may be interpreted in many, equally plausible, ways. Because of the confusion surrounding the meaning of "public use," this phrase has become the key issue in many courtroom controversies, including *Berman v. Parker*.

Between the end of World War II and the 1954 Supreme Court decision in *Berman v. Parker*, millions of military veterans returned to the United States, eager to use their very low interest rate, "GI" mortgages, to purchase homes. Because there was a shortage of urban residential space, veterans were forced to use their cheap mortgages on real estate outside the city limits. This non-country, but also non-city, lifestyle quickly became the American ideal, and middle-class Americans flocked to the newly invented suburbs. As a result, the suburbs flourished, while only the lowest income populace remained within city limits. The urban poor had no choice but to live in substandard, unsanitary, poorly maintained housing, owned by absentee landlords. In an effort to remedy this situation, in 1949 Congress established urban renewal as a national priority and, during the next five years, enacted additional laws and allocated federal funds for rehabilitation of blighted, poverty-stricken, urban areas.

During the 1950s, the standard urban renewal project adhered to an inflexible plan, which mandated that each project begin with the eviction of all residents and businesses, continue with demolition of all buildings in the project area, and culminate with construction of new, uniformly designed, buildings.

The plaintiff in *Berman v. Parker* was infuriated when he discovered that his profitable, long-standing neighborhood business was in an area scheduled to be razed pursuant to a neighborhood improvement plan. In an effort to halt the demolition of his livelihood, he sued the government agency which administered the plan.

The plaintiff first argued that the ongoing profitability of his business clearly demonstrated that his premises served a "public use." Hence, he stated that his property should be excepted from the plan to demolish the entire neighborhood.

The plaintiff's second argument was based on the urban renewal plan's goals, which were: beautification of the neighborhood by building safe, sanitary, building-code compliant residences; and improvement of the neighborhood's balance of commercial, residential, and municipal land uses. The plaintiff argued that these goals exceeded a reasonable interpretation of the Fifth Amendment's "public use" clause. Hence, the plaintiff stated that the urban renewal plan itself violated the constitutional limitations on eminent domain.

The Supreme Court disagreed with the plaintiff's arguments. The justices decided that even if, within the area to be revitalized, a privately owned parcel of land contains a viable business, the public's interest in completion of the project outweighs the landowner's interest in continuing his business. Furthermore, the justices found that the neighborhood improvement plan in this case would serve the public's interest by encouraging development of a neighborhood with strategically located residential buildings, churches, schools, and commercial enterprises. The Supreme Court concluded that the *Berman v. Parker* project's plan sought to use the plaintiff's land for a public purpose, within the meaning of the Fifth Amendment to the Constitution.

Since *Berman v. Parker,* the Supreme Court has continued to broaden the scope of the Fifth Amendment's "public use" clause. Whereas pre-*Berman* plans limited urban revitalization projects to recreational and residential improvements, these projects may now include, in addition to upgraded residential property, a wide variety of economic improvements, including factories, casinos, shopping malls, parking lots, and high-rise office buildings. Additionally, the trend which began with *Berman v. Parker* has shifted the focus of neighborhood improvement projects from demolition to preservation and rehabilitation of property.

For more information

"City Planning," *Microsoft Encarta Encyclopedia,* 2000 edition.

Klop, Jeremy R. *Eminent Domain.* Chapel Hill: University of North Carolina Press, 1998.

United States Code Annotated, Title 42, Section 1441, 1998 edition.

www.planning.org, Web site of the American Planning Association.

Beth Simon Swartz
Attorney

bill of attainder A bill of attainder is an act of the legislature that inflicts PUNISHMENT on specifically named persons or groups whose members can easily be determined. The CONSTITUTION, in Article I, section 9, prohibits the federal government from passing bills of attainder. The states are prohibited by Article I, section 10. These prohibitions insure that punishments are not imposed without the safeguards present in a judicial proceeding.

Historically, a bill of attainder was an act of the British parliament that imposed the death penalty on persons or a particular group, usually for treasonous activities. These legislative acts usually were accompanied by a "corruption of blood," prohibiting individuals from inheriting property from attained persons. If the punishment imposed by Parliament was less than death, the act was referred to as a "bill of pains and penalties." Although the Constitution only prohibits bills of attainder, the Supreme Court has recognized that the prohibition extends to these bills of pains and penalties. As a result, a legislative act imposing any type of punishment on individuals or specific groups falls within the prohibition.

A bill of attainder may include punishments like death, imprisonment, or the imposition of a fine, but it also extends to punishments such as the deprivation of rights or the banning of employment. For example, in *United States v. Lovett,* 328 U.S. 303 (1946), the Supreme Court found that a congressional act forbidding payment of funds to three government employees found by Congress to have engaged in subversive activity was an unconstitutional bill of attainder. It oftentimes may be difficult to determine if a legislative act directed to an individual or group is a punishment or a permissible regulation. In determining whether it is a punishment, thereby making it an unconstitutional bill of attainder, the Supreme Court has considered whether the challenged act falls within the historical understanding of punishment, whether the act furthers any nonpunitive legislative purposes, and whether there is evidence of a legislative intent to punish.

For more information

Tribe, Laurence H. *American Constitutional Law.* 2nd ed. Mineola, N.Y.: Foundation Press, 1988, pp. 641–663.

James N.G. Cauthen
The City University of New York

Bill of Rights The Bill of Rights is the first 10 AMENDMENTS TO THE U.S. CONSTITUTION and lists the basic CIVIL LIBERTIES possessed by people living in the United States. When the new U.S. CONSTITUTION was proposed in 1787, a large group of people argued against the adoption ("ratification") of the proposed federal Constitution. Because of their opposition, they became know as the "Anti-Federalists." One of their main objections was the fact that the proposed Constitution did not put specific limits on government interference with the basic political rights and freedoms of citizens. The Anti-Federalists feared that without a list of specific rights of the people, the national government would have too much power and so might end up oppressing the people by taking away their individual liberties. Supporters of the proposed Constitution, who became known as the "Federalists," publicly proposed a compromise. The Federalists asked the Anti-Federalists, as well as people undecided as to whether to support the new Constitution, to support the ratification. In exchange for their support, as soon as the Constitution was ratified, a list (a "bill") of individual rights would immediately be proposed as amendments to the document. Although only a minority of Anti-Federalists and undecided people were persuaded by this offer to support the Constitution, enough were satisfied with the compromise to tip the scales in a sufficient number of state legislatures in favor of ratification.

In keeping with the understood agreement, immediately after the Constitution was ratified, the new U.S. Congress proposed 12 amendments to the Constitution listing specific limitations on the power of the federal government. Ten of these were ratified by enough states to become amendments to the Constitution. These first 10 amendments to the U.S. Constitution are known as the Bill of Rights. The Bill of Rights lists many of the most basic political rights of persons within the United States. These rights include the FREEDOM OF SPEECH, FREEDOM OF THE PRESS, and freedom of RELIGION, as well as numerous rights of fair procedure given to criminal suspects, such as a RIGHT TO A JURY. These rights were based on the common understanding at the time of which rights were the most important and fundamental rights of individual citizens. These ideas had their origins in earlier legal documents such as the English Bill of Rights of 1689 as well as the variously worded bills of rights that already existed in the constitutions of the individual American states. In fact, the Bill of Rights found in the U.S. Constitution was drafted primarily by James Madison, who used the Virginia Bill of Rights as a rough model.

For more than a hundred years the U.S. Supreme Court, when interpreting the Bill of Rights, generally offered very little protection to the rights listed. However, beginning in the early to mid-20th century, the Supreme Court began to strongly enforce the rights contained in the Bill of Rights. Also, although the Bill of Rights was originally intended to place limits on the power of only the *federal* government, the U.S. Supreme Court has applied most of the limitations on power in the Bill of Rights to *state* governments as well. The court has done this by "incorporating" the Bill of Rights into the Fourteenth Amendment's guarantee that no *state* shall deprive any person of life, liberty, or property without "due process of law." Thus, the amount of liberty protected by the Bill of Rights has seen a slow but steady expansion in the last century.

At present, the Supreme Court has incorporated most but not all of the Bill of Rights to apply to the states. Most recently, in 2010, the Court in *McDonald v. City of Chicago,* 561 U.S. (2010), ruled that the Second Amendment RIGHT TO BEAR ARMS did apply to the states. The Third Amendment, barring the billeting of troops in homes, and the SEVENTH AMENDMENT requirement for a jury trial in civil suits, have not been incorporated.

Most other nations have analogous listings of individual rights in their national constitutions, although in many instances those rights are neither recognized nor enforced to any great degree. Regardless, generally the people of other nations look to the United States as a model of how to write and apply a bill of rights to their government and society.

For more information

Epstein, Lee, and Thomas G. Walker. *Constitutional Law for a Changing America: Rights, Liberties, and Justices.* 3rd ed. Washington, D.C.: CQ Press, 1998.

Levy, Leonard W. *Origins of the Bill of Rights.* New Haven, Conn.: Yale University Press, 1999.

Schultz, David, John R. Vile, and Michelle D. Deardorff. *Constitutional Law in Contemporary America,* vol. 2. New York: Oxford University Press, 2010.

Rick Swanson
University of Louisiana, Lafayette

Billy the Kid (ca. 1859–1881) outlaw Billy the Kid was a 19th-century outlaw whose real-life exploits have mixed with fiction to create a classic American icon.

Henry McCarty, better known as Billy the Kid, was born on November 23, 1859, and died violently on July 14, 1881, at the age of 21. McCarty rose to prominence through his actions in the Lincoln County War and the legal troubles that followed from it. Billy the Kid was hardly known during his own lifetime; he became famous when the man who killed him, Pat Garrett, and co-author M. A. Upson began to write their biography, *The Authentic Life of Billy, the Kid.* As with many of the legendary outlaws of the American West, it is difficult to discern fact from fiction in the actions ascribed to Billy the Kid. He is often credited with having killed one man for each year of his life, but the real figure is probably under a dozen, and historians are only certain about four victims. The truth about the man was further obscured by a number of popular biographies written about him and by reports that he lived on in secrecy past the time he was reported dead.

McCarty spent his early childhood in the Irish slums of New York City before moving west with his mother, Catherine McCarty, and his brother, Joseph. Henry became an outlaw in his mid-teens when he joined John Mackie in stealing horses. His criminal life escalated with the MURDER of Frank Cahill, a blacksmith that bullied the young thief. Pursued by law enforcement and Cahill's friends, McCarty adopted the name William Henry Bonney and moved to Lincoln County, New Mexico. In 1877, he went to work as a guard for the rancher John Tunstall and the following year took part in the Lincoln County War, a conflict between the Tunstall's associates and the Murphy-Dolan faction over the latter's monopoly on local commerce. When Tunstall was murdered, McCarty and other Tunstall loyalists formed a GANG known as the Regulators to track down the killers. The men were deputized but throughout the war operated on both sides of the law. When Sheriff William Brady tried to hunt down the Regulators, Billy the Kid and several others from the gang killed Brady and Deputy George Hindman.

McCarty managed to secure amnesty for his actions during the war but did not leave his life of crime. For the following two years, he was a cattle rustler, and in 1880 he killed Joe Grant, a man who came to the area to kill Billy the Kid in order to spread his own reputation. In 1881, McCarty was captured by Pat Garrett but managed a daring escape from his jail in Lincoln while awaiting execution for the murder of Sheriff Brady, killing two guards in the process. On July 14, 1881, Pat Garrett shot Billy the Kid near Fort Sumner. Details on the attack are obscure as there were no reliable witnesses, but evidence suggests that Garrett took McCarty by surprise and managed to fatally wound him without a fight.

For more information

Nolan, Frederick. *The Billy the Kid Reader.* Norman: University of Oklahoma Press, 2007.

Marcus Schulzke
State University of New York at Albany

Bivens v. Six Unknown Named Agents of Federal Bureau of Narcotics/1983 Suits 403 U.S. 388 (1971) In *Bivens v. Six Unknown Named Agents of the Federal Bureau of Narcotics,* the Supreme Court held that federal officers were not immune from federal lawsuits under 42 U.S.C. 1983 for FOURTH AMENDMENT violations. This decision is important because it gives individuals the ability to sue the federal government, especially law enforcement officials, for alleged violations of their constitutional rights.

Bivens arose when federal narcotics agents, acting without a warrant and without PROBABLE CAUSE, entered Bivens's apartment and used allegedly unreasonable force to effect his ARREST. Claiming that he suffered humiliation, embarrassment, and mental suffering, Bivens sought $15,000 in damages from each of the agents involved. The U.S. district court dismissed the suit for want of a cause of action, and its decision was upheld by the U.S. COURT OF APPEALS. Rather than claim that Bivens was without remedy, the agents argued that Bivens's right to privacy was protected by state law and therefore may only be tried in a state court under state TORT law. They also asserted that as federal officers they were immune from liability for violations under the Fourth Amendment. Justice WILLIAM BRENNAN, writing for the Court's majority, overruled the district court and court of appeals. The Court held that an alleged violation of the Fourth Amendment by a federal agent acting under the color of his authority does give rise to a federal cause of action. The ruling, in effect, provided Bivens with a federal forum to prove his allegations against the agents involved in the raid on his apartment and to seek monetary damages.

Bivens and 1983 suits (42 U.S.C 1983) involve the issue of official IMMUNITY of those who, acting under the authority of color of law, deprive a citizen of the United States a right secured under the CONSTITUTION. Section 1983 was originally part of the Civil Rights Act of 1871 which was passed by Congress to protect the newly freed slaves from Southern sheriffs and others who, acting under "color of law" deprived the former slaves of the CIVIL RIGHTS. Rather than try cases of abuse of power in state courts where an African-American plaintiff was unlikely to get a fair hearing, the law permitted a federal cause of action that could be tried in FEDERAL COURT. In *Bivens*, the issue is whether a violation of the protection against unreasonable SEARCHES AND SEIZURE is a cause of action in federal court.

The significance of *Bivens* and 1983 suits is that they hold public officials at all levels of government accountable for abuse of official power. Section 1983 states that "every person" who under color of law deprives a citizen of the United States "any rights, privileges, or immunities secured by the Constitution and laws" is liable for monetary damages to the victim. As a result, section 1983 has allowed persons incarcerated in state prisons to sue for inadequate medical treatment, overcrowded prison conditions, and countless other violations of their constitutional and civil rights. It has been used in voting rights cases and to protect the rights of students as well.

For more information

Scheb, John M., and John M. Scheb II. *Law and the Administrative Process*. Belmont, Calif.: Thomson Wadsworth, 2005.

Warren, Kenneth F. *Administrative Law in the Political System*. 3rd ed. Upper Saddle River, N.J.: Prentice Hall, 1997.

James V. Calvi
West Texas A&M University

Black, Hugo (1886–1971) Supreme Court justice Hugo Black served as associate justice for the Supreme Court from 1937 to 1971. He became known as one of the greatest "liberals" to serve on the Court during the 20th century. Black supported CIVIL LIBERTIES and political equality in numerous opinions over 34 years.

Black was born in Clay County, Alabama, on February 22, 1886. He received a law degree in 1906 and became a police court JUDGE in 1911. He was elected PROSECUTOR for Birmingham, Alabama, and later became an influential trial lawyer in Alabama. During the early 1920s he briefly joined the KU KLUX KLAN. In 1925 he was elected to the U.S. Senate where he served until 1937. During his time in the Senate, Black supported the New Deal legislation of President FRANKLIN D. ROOSEVELT and conducted congressional investigations of the utilities industry and its lobbyists.

In 1937 Roosevelt used his first opportunity to nominate Black to the Supreme Court. Black's participation in the Ku Klux Klan became an issue in his confirmation. He made a national radio broadcast saying his involvement in the Klan was minor and defending his record on racial issues. He stated that he did "number among my friends many members of the colored race. . . ."

Black immediately began to work on reversing the Court's anti–New Deal rulings and voting to support the constitutionality of administration legislation. By the early 1940s he began to develop his reputation as a civil libertarian and free speech advocate. After voting in the majority to uphold suppression of unpopular views in *Chaplinsky v. New Hampshire* (1942) and *Minersville School District v. Gobitis* (1940), Black became the Court's leading advocate of absolute protection for First Amendment freedoms.

Black's change of heart in the middle 1940s led to intellectual and personal feuds with some of his Supreme Court brethren, especially Justices FELIX FRANKFURTER and Robert Jackson. During the period of 1941 to 1953, when conservative pro-government decisions were being handed down, Black was usually in dissent, often accompanied by WILLIAM O. DOUGLAS, Frank Murphy, or Wiley Rutledge. During the years of CHIEF JUSTICE EARL WARREN, Black often authored majority opinions supporting the rights of minorities, FREEDOM OF SPEECH, and the rights of the accused. Black was particularly forceful in arguing for an "absolutist" position for First Amendment rights. Dissenting in *Roth v. United States* (1957), he stated, "But I believe this nation's security and tranquility can best be served by giving the First Amendment the same broad construction that all BILL OF RIGHTS guarantees deserve. . . ." He was equally forceful in decisions concerning FREEDOM OF THE PRESS and the RIGHT TO COUNSEL.

During the final years of his tenure on the Supreme Court, some observers argued that Black moved toward a more conservative position. While Black's absolutist position on the First Amendment never wavered, he occasionally was very limited in what he considered "speech." Black dissented from protecting Paul Cohen's jacket in the case *Cohen v. California* (1971) and in 1965 wrote the dissent *GRISWOLD V. CONNECTICUT* (1965), stating, "[The] Court talks about a constitutional 'right of privacy' as though there is some constitutional [provision] forbidding any law ever to be passed which might abridge the 'privacy' of individuals. But there is not."

Justice Hugo Black (Harris and Ewing, Collection of the Supreme Court of the United States)

Black entered his final year on the Supreme Court in declining health. He resigned on September 17, 1971, and died eight days later. Black ranks as one of the most important justices of the century, and his support for First Amendment rights has been heralded by scholars as the most devoted and articulate of any Supreme Court justice. It was ironic that Black, a typical southerner in many ways, would be a leader for racial justice and individual liberty.

For more information

Newman, Roger K. *Hugo Black: A Biography.* New York: Pantheon Books, 1994.

Simon, James F. *The Antagonists.* New York: Touchstone, 1989.

Charlie Howard
Tarleton State University

blackmail Blackmail is an illegal act that involves a demand of something of value from another person in return for not disclosing some embarrassing or shameful information about that person.

While the words *blackmail* and EXTORTION are often used as if they were synonymous, the words describe distinctly different crimes. Blackmail and extortion both require a demand for something of value. However, the threat involved in blackmail is injury to reputation, whereas the threat in extortion is of illegal harm to the object of the crime (such as injury, death, or maiming), or to loved ones or relatives, or to property (such as burning a house down).

Identifying the existence of blackmail can be problematic because as long as the threat is coincidental with the demand, the crime exists even if the threatened disclosure, in and of itself, would be legal. For example, if a male individual is secretly a cross-dresser, it would be legal, although cruel and potentially destructive to his private life and career, to broadcast this information on every imaginable media outlet. However, it would be illegal if someone told this cross-dressing male, "Give me $1 million by 5 P.M. today or I will reveal to the world that you dress in women's clothing whenever time permits." The threat would have even more potential for damage if it were expressed as, "Give me $1 million by 5 P.M. today or I will reveal to the world that you dress in women's clothing and engage in prostitution whenever time permits." The illegality exists because of the coincident demand for money and threat of disclosure of embarrassing information. Finally, this situation could descend to the depths of extortion if someone told the cross-dressing male, "Give me $1 million by 5 P.M. today or I will shoot you in the head." Now, the situation has a demand for money and a threat of illegal action and fulfills both of the requirements of extortion.

While extortion, which incorporates the threat of a criminal act, clearly falls into the criminal realm, the reasoning behind criminalization of blackmail, with its threat of legal action, is less obvious. Current legal scholars classify blackmail as criminal because:

1) In a nation with the rule of law, it is necessary to have laws to define antisocial behavior and establish penalties for engaging therein.
2) If blackmail were legal, a blackmailer could profit significantly by returning repeatedly to the same person with the threat of revealing the same secrets. Such ongoing harassment could be terribly damaging financially as well as psychologically. It is clearly necessary to have laws to deter such abhorrent behavior.

Although both blackmail and extortion are crimes in all 50 states, many of the state laws that create and define these crimes are archaic and, more important, significantly inconsistent with one another in regard to penalties.

For more information

Bartels, Daniel M., Michael T. Cahill, and Paul H. Robinson. "Competing Theories of Blackmail: An Empirical Research Critique of Criminal Law Theory." Available online. URL: http://papers.ssrn.com/sol3/papers.cfm?abstract_id=1477400; "Blackmail and Defense in Blackmail Cases." Available online. URL: http://www.theblanchlawfirm.com/NewsDetails-36/Blackmail.html?newsid=105.

Beth Simon Swartz
Attorney

Blackstone, Sir William (1723–1780) scholar Sir William Blackstone was an English JUDGE and law professor whose *Commentaries on the Laws of England* influenced the development of early American law in colonial times and after the Revolution. Blackstone published his *Commentaries* in 1765–70 while he was professor of law at Oxford University. He later served on the Court of Common Pleas in England.

The Blackstone treatise, which organized English law into basic themes, was at the time often the only law book for American lawyers as American courts slowly committed decisions to record. Almost all of the American founders had read Blackstone's *Commentaries,* and his ideas on property law, free speech, CONTRACT, and TORT law were the main bridge between English common law and the laws that the colonies enforced prior to the Revolution. Blackstone's influence after the Revolution was also significant, serving as the basis of early U.S. law in the states, defining provisions of state CONSTITUTIONS, and capturing the mind of many United States Supreme Court justices such as JOHN MARSHALL and Joseph Story.

Sir William Blackstone (Library of Congress)

For more information

Freedman, Lawrence M. *A History of American Law.* New York: Simon & Schuster, 1973.

Wm. Osler McCarthy
Supreme Court of Texas
University of Texas, Austin

Blakely v. Washington 542 U.S. 296 (2004)

The U.S. Supreme Court revolutionized SENTENCING practices in states with criminal SENTENCING GUIDELINES in *Blakely v. Washington.* In that case, it ruled that JUDGES are restricted in their ability to impose sentences more severe than prescribed in sentencing guidelines.

In *Blakely v. Washington,* Ralph Blakely, Jr. pleaded guilty to kidnapping of his estranged wife, which held a maximum sentence, by statute, of 53 months. In the state of Washington, sentences are decided by judges under the guidance of a sentencing guideline. Sentencing guidelines are determined by a grid of legal factors—namely, prior criminal history and severity of current conviction. It significantly restricts judges as compared to INDETERMINATE SENTENCING systems in which judges can decide a sentence within a larger range of statutory minimum and maximum sentences. However, judges still retain a fair amount of discretional authority by departing from the guideline cell to which the prior record and current conviction mandates. A downward departure allows for the judge to decrease the sentence below the sentencing guideline range minimum. An upward departure allows for the judge to increase the sentence above the sentencing guideline range maximum. This type of sentence was referred to as an "exceptional" sentence. In *Blakely,* the trial judge heard facts and imposed an "exceptional" sentence of 90 months because the defendant acted with "deliberate cruelty."

On APPEAL, the defendant claimed that this exceptional sentence without a JURY determination of the facts on which the judge based his decision is a violation of the SIXTH AMENDMENT RIGHT TO A JURY TRIAL. The Supreme Court in *Blakely* used *Apprendi v. New Jersey,* 530 U.S. 466 (2000), as a precedent to address the defendant's claim. The Court found that upward departures from the prescribed guideline range maximum by a preponderance of the evidence violated the defendant's right to a jury trial and the right to have facts against him proven beyond a REASONABLE DOUBT. Although the facts in *Apprendi* addressed a statutory maximum beyond which the judge could not sentence the defendant without a jury determination of the facts with a burden of beyond a reasonable doubt, the Court in *Blakely* focused on the *prescribed* nature of the sentencing guidelines in the state of Washington—much like statutory prescriptions.

The Court in *Blakely* addressed the purpose of the protection of the defendant's right to jury trial in sentencing decisions. They concluded that the jury acts as a check against the judicial sentencing power. Although determinate sentencing—such as Washington's sentencing guidelines—did limit judicial DISCRETION, the Court claimed that "determinate judicial-fact-finding schemes entail less judicial power than indeterminate schemes, but more judicial power than determinate *jury*-factfinding schemes."

Therefore, if a judge wants to increase the sentence above the sentencing guideline range maximum, he or she must have a jury determine the facts upon which this decision can be based. Additionally, the jury must use the burden of beyond a reasonable doubt to determine if these facts exist and are credible.

Blakely is important precedent for future sentencing guideline cases such as *United States v. Booker,* 543 U.S. 220 (2005), *United States v. Fanfan* (consolidated with *Booker*), and in *Tapia v. United States* 564 U.S. _ (2011). In *Blakely,* the Court stated that the federal sentencing guidelines were still presumed valid. In *Booker* and *Fanfan,* it decided that the federal sentencing guidelines were now merely voluntary—not presumptive. Finally, in *Tapia* the Court ruled that judges may not depart from sentencing guidelines in order to encourage rehabilitation of an offender.

For more information

Pettit, Carol A. "Writing the Book[er] on Blakely: the Challenge to the Federal Sentencing Guidelines," *Tulsa Law Review* 41 (Winter 2005): 365–404.

Jeremy Ball
Boise State University

Bolling v. Sharpe 347 U.S. 497 (1954) *Bolling v. Sharpe* was a unanimous, 9-0, United States Supreme Court decision declaring racial SEGREGATION in the public schools of Washington, D.C., to be unconstitutional.

Bolling basically provided a unique solution and legal rationale to desegregate public schools in the District of Columbia. Interestingly, this case was decided shortly after the landmark Supreme Court decision of *BROWN V. BOARD OF EDUCATION OF TOPEKA, KANSAS,* in which the Court ruled that separate public schools for blacks and whites were inherently unequal and therefore violated the EQUAL PROTECTION clause of the Fourteenth Amendment to the CONSTITUTION. The *Brown* decision is famous for providing a legal PRECEDENT to desegregate public schools around the country and particularly in the South.

On the heels of the *Brown* decision, the *Bolling* case seemed to be simple on its face. If schools were to be desegregated by the *Brown* decision, then why was Washington, D.C., any different? The case is unique and important because the Supreme Court found a problem in the District's special status in America. Washington, D.C., was not a state, so the equal protection clause of the Fourteenth Amendment did not apply, given its language of "nor shall any state deprive . . . the equal protection of the laws." Since Washington, D.C., was not a state, this presented a problem of finding the correct legal authority to rule against segregation (as in *Brown*).

In the unanimous opinion by CHIEF JUSTICE EARL WARREN, the Court ruled that the D.C. public schools should be desegregated like other schools throughout America. The problem of finding a controlling legal authority for the District was solved by making use of the DUE PROCESS clause of the Fifth Amendment of the Constitution where it states that "no person shall . . . be deprived of life, liberty, or property without due process of the law." The Fifth Amendment provided a solution that remedied the problems of Washington, D.C., because much of the District is controlled by actions of the U.S. Congress. Since the Fifth Amendment applied to the federal government, it was deemed to be applicable to the District.

Therefore, writing for the Court, Chief Justice Warren argued that while the Fourteenth and the Fifth Amendments are not the same, "both . . . [stem] . . . from our American ideal of fairness, [and] are not mutually exclusive." Furthermore, "discrimination may be so unjustifiable as to be violative of due process" and it would be unthinkable to "impose a lesser duty" in the District of Columbia than in the rest of the United States. Thus, in a pragmatic fashion the Court used the available law to desegregate the schools throughout America.

For more information

Kluger, Richard. *Simple Justice: The History of Brown v. Board of Education and Black America's Struggle for Equality.* New York: Knopf, 1976.

Roger Hartley
University of Arizona

bond A bond is a widely used and versatile financial instrument, and it appears in an enormous number of varieties. The use of bonds is a common occurrence in commercial transactions, in order to raise money for a corporation or government without diluting EQUITY ownership.

In general, a bond is a written document that certifies or evidences a debt for which the debtor, who is almost always the issuer of the bond, promises to pay interest on the debt at a set rate for a set period. Upon the expiration of the period of the bond, which in general can range anywhere from one to 30 years, the issuer will pay the full, or "face," amount of the debt to the bondholder. However, bonds have been developed into many different types: Some pay no interest at all, some adjust the interest rate during the period, and others pay interest dependent on other factors such as the issuer's financial condition. This flexibility has made issuing bonds a common financial strategy for raising funds.

A bond is therefore a type of security. Unlike stock, however, possession of a bond does not confer on the bondholder equity or ownership in the issuer. Once the bond is paid at the end of the period, the relationship between the issuer and the bondholder is ended. Like stocks, bonds are traded widely in the public markets, and the markets have developed unique trading procedures for bonds. For example, bonds can be divided into two parts. One part represents the face value paid at the end of the term, and the other represents the stream of interest payments due until the term of the bond expires. These are traded separately and the pieces are "bundled" together with similar pieces from other bonds. There are several companies that rate bonds according to their investment value, with Triple A (AAA) bonds having the highest rating.

When issued by a private company, bonds are generally secured by collateral. The most common form of collateral is mortgages on real property, although any other item of value can serve as collateral, or "security," for a bond. If the issuer defaults on the debt by failing to pay either interest payments or the face amount, the collateral can then be used to repay the bondholders. Bonds are very often issued by the federal government or state governments as well. These types of bonds are generally backed by the "full faith and credit" of that government rather than specific collateral. The most common type of government bonds are called "General Obligation Bonds" and are issued to raise funds for overall governmental operations. Many state and local governments will issue bonds, however, for specific projects, such as highway maintenance, school funding, or building construction.

Aside from this common commercial use, bonds are also used for several purposes in the law. The most common example is the posting of a bond in exchange for the temporary release of a defendant under indictment but not yet tried. The bond is issued, in an amount set by the JUDGE or according to statute, as a security for the defendant to remain available for trial and to prevent flight to escape trial. Bonds are also used in civil disputes. A judge can require a party seeking extraordinary or injunctive relief before a trial to post a bond in order to protect the other party to the dispute should the party seeking the relief fail to prevail on the merits of the case.

For more information

Black's Law Dictionary. 6th ed. St. Paul, Minn.: West, 1990, pp. 178–181, 847.

Reddy, Michael T. *Securities Operations.* 2d ed. Upper Saddle River, N.J.: Prentice Hall, 1995.

Gerald J. Russello
Covington and Burling, New York

Bonnie and Clyde Bonnie Parker and Clyde Barrow were well-known criminals who traveled with their GANG through the central United States during the Great Depression years. Their famous crime spree began with a series of ROBBERIES early in 1932 and ended with their deaths in a police ambush in Louisiana on May 23, 1934. Many of their crimes involved banks and small businesses. A number of MURDERS were committed during the spree, including as many as nine law enforcement officers.

Bonnie Parker was born on October 1, 1910, in Rowena, Texas. Clyde Barrow was born on March 24, 1909, in Ellis County, Texas. Both were raised in poverty with seriously dysfunctional families. Parker's father died while she was a child; she married in 1926 just short of her 16th birthday. She was first jailed in 1932 in Kaufman County, Texas, charged with an unsuccessful robbery. She was released after a county GRAND JURY failed to indict her. Barrow was first arrested in 1926 for the theft of an automobile. He was subsequently arrested and jailed many times over the next several years.

The famous crime spree began on April 30, 1932, with the robbery of a small business in Hillsboro, Texas. The business owner was murdered during this robbery. Other crimes followed in Oklahoma and Missouri, including the murder of law enforcement officers in both states.

A popular romantic mythology surrounding Bonnie and Clyde began and grew as their exploits were publicized. In part, the myth was based on unexpected instances of kindness. The use of a Browning automatic rifle by Clyde Barrow as his preferred firearm added another element to the Bonnie and Clyde mythology.

Members of the Barrow gang were frequently captured. Clyde Barrow's brother, Buck, was seriously wounded near Kansas City, Missouri. Buck's wife, Blanche, was hurt during the same shootout. Both were later captured in Iowa, while the rest of the Barrow gang escaped. Buck Barrow died soon after.

The murderous spree returned to Texas in 1934 with the Barrow gang dramatically freeing prison inmates from a Texas corrections facility. Murders of several Texas law enforcement officers soon followed. The very viciousness of these attacks somewhat soured the public opinion of Bonnie and Clyde.

Bonnie and Clyde were killed on May 23, 1934, in Bienville Parish, Louisiana. The pair were ambushed by a group of Texas and Louisiana law enforcement officers. The officers issued no warning prior to opening fire. Clyde Barrow apparently died instantly; Bonnie Parker was shot several times and died in some agony.

Bonnie and Clyde were buried in separate cemeteries in Dallas, Texas. Their deaths and burial seemed to revitalize the legends that had originally grown up around their exploits and the crime spree. That legend was reinforced by Arthur Penn's 1967 film starring Warren Beatty and Faye Dunaway. A Bonnie and Clyde Festival is held annually in Gibsland, Louisiana, on a weekend near to the date of the pair's death. The festival includes a reenactment of the law enforcement ambush.

For more information

Guinn, Jeff. *Go Down Together: The True, Untold Story of Bonnie and Clyde.* New York: Simon & Schuster, 2009.

Phillips, John Neal. *Running with Bonnie & Clyde: The Ten Fast Years of Ralph Fults.* Norman: University of Oklahoma Press, 2002.

Steele, Philip, and Marie Barrow Scoma. *The Family Story of Bonnie and Clyde.* Gretna, La.: Pelican, 2000.

Jerry E. Stephens
U.S. Court of Appeals, for the 10th Circuit

boot camp Boot camps are one form of PUNISHMENT used to deter criminal activity.

Sometimes called shock incarceration, a boot camp takes its name from military basic training where recruits are trained for military life. The physical work, order, and discipline are thought to provide selected inmates with more structure and motivation to stop criminal behavior. Many boot camps offer inmates who graduate from the program a reduction in sentence and a release to PROBATION or PAROLE.

Boot camps are managed by local, state, and federal juvenile and adult corrections programs. Ranges of time in boot camp run from as short as a month to six months duration. Many boot camps provide not only the work and discipline environment but a battery of motivational programming, education, and training classes with enhanced counseling, job placement training, and prerelease programs.

Boot camps are very tightly organized with a full day of activity for the inmates, often starting early in the morning, with physical training, breakfast, work, lunch, work and programming, dinner, more programming, and counseling and group meetings, followed by time for cleaning clothes and the living spaces, and finally sleep. A 5:00 A.M. to 10:30 P.M. day six or seven days a week is not unheard of.

While boot camps are touted for a reduction in RECIDIVISM, the figures need to be looked at carefully. Many boot camps are tailored for less serious offenders, many of whom would not fail on probation or parole in the first place. This factor, combined with the duration and intensity of the boot camp experience, seems to lead to good outcomes. Also important is the fact that boot camps provide a reduction in the length of time served for many offenders, and this releases funds from the JURISDICTION to be used elsewhere.

Boot camps also appeal to those who would like to be tough on crime. These inmates are not sitting around in jail or prison, watching television or doing other nonproductive activity. The boot camp inmates are working hard, often in public works projects that support the communities from which they came. Overall, boot camps have been quite popular with correctional administrators who see these programs as "win/win" situations; the jurisdiction benefits from the work and the success of the offenders on release, and the inmates benefit by being give new skills and motivation to do better.

For more information

Ravenell, Teresa E. "Left, Left, Left, Right Left: The Search for Rights and Remedies in Juvenile Boot Camps," *Columbia Journal of Law and Social Problems* 35 (Summer 2002): 347–370.

Bruce Bikle
California State University at Sacramento

border searches Border searches are searches of persons and items conducted at international borders of their functional equivalents. Border searches generally are exempt from the FOURTH AMENDMENT warrant requirements.

The Fourth Amendment of the UNITED STATES CONSTITUTION provides protection against unreasonable SEARCHES AND SEIZURES. In most circumstances, a reasonable search requires PROBABLE CAUSE and a warrant. Due to the interest a sovereign nation has in protecting itself, border searches are exempted from the requirement of probable cause and a search warrant (*U.S. v. Ramsey,* 431 U.S. 606 (1977)). Warrantless and suspicionless border searches are justified by the long-standing and widely accepted rationale that a nation should have the power to control who and what comes through its borders. The national security interest in keeping stolen and illicit material out of the country outweighs the intrusion a border search presents to one's privacy. *United States v. Montoya de Hernandez,* 473 U.S. 531 (1985).

At the borders of the United States, the Customs and Border Protection (CBP) agency enjoys broad authority to search people and objects crossing the border without any specific suspicion. The objects the CBP can legally search at the border without probable cause or a warrant include, but are not limited to, vehicles, computers, PDA's, memory cards, and other portable electronic devices. *United States v. Flores-Montano,* 541 U.S. 149, 152–55 (2004); *United States v. Ickes,* 393 F.3d 501, 504 (4th Cir. 2005). The CBP also has the authority to make photocopies of any documents or letters that it examines during a border search. *United States v. Fortna,* 796 F.2d 724, 738–39 (5th Cir. 1986).

There are limits to the exemptions of the probable cause and warrant requirements granted to border searches. Routine border searches such as bag or vehicle searches, drug sniffs, and pat downs may be conducted without any suspicion or warrant. On the other hand, more physically intrusive, nonroutine searches such as cavity searches, STRIP SEARCHES, and detentions require reasonable suspicion on behalf of the CBP. *United States v. Montoya de Hernandez,* 473 U.S. 531 (1985). While the greater privacy invasion involved in nonroutine border searches implicates the Fourth Amendment protection from unreasonable search and seizures, the standard of probable cause and a warrant is still not required. Rather, the CBP need only have a "reasonable suspicion" to conduct the invasive nonroutine category of border searches. Reasonable suspicion amounts to some level of legitimate suspicion less than probable cause. The justification for this lowered standard for even the more invasive, nonroutine variety of border searches is that illegal border activity such as drug smuggling is rarely apparent at first blush and any higher standard would jeopardize border integrity.

For more information

Gilmore, Kelly A. "Preserving the Border Search Doctrine in a Digital World: Reproducing Electronic Evidence at the Border," *Brooklyn Law Review* 72 (2007): 759.

Eric McAdamis and Ryan C. Black
Michigan State University

Bork, Robert H. (1927–) Supreme Court nominee Robert H. Bork is best known for being among the most controversial appointments to the Supreme Court in the 20th century. Robert Bork has served as professor of law at Yale University (1962–73, 1977–81), SOLICITOR GENERAL of the United States (1973–77), and as a JUDGE for the U.S. Circuit Court of Appeals for the District of Columbia (1982–88). He was nominated for the U.S. Supreme Court by President Ronald Reagan on July 1, 1987, to replace the retiring justice, Lewis Powell. The Senate rejected Bork's nomination on October 23, 1987, by a 58-42 vote. Justice Powell had become known as a relatively moderate justice who held the swing position on the Court on a number of controversial issues. The nomination of Bork to replace Powell seemed to symbolize the Reagan administration's strategy of appointing conservatives to the federal judiciary. Given the importance of Powell's seat to the balance of the Court and the outcome of the 1986 elections, in which the Democrats regained the majority of the Senate, the Senate confirmation process was unusually long, public, and contentious. After being rejected by the Senate for the seat on the Supreme Court, Bork resigned from his seat on the Circuit Court in 1988. ANTHONY KENNEDY was later appointed and confirmed to fill Justice Powell's seat on the Court. Presidents have subsequently been careful to avoid a similar confirmation battle over their judicial nominations by choosing less well known or less controversial candidates.

Bork is a judicial conservative and a leading advocate of the view that the CONSTITUTION should be interpreted in accord with the "original intentions" of the founders who drafted and ratified it. This was also a prominent position of the Reagan administration, but it is generally controversial. This originalist approach to constitutional interpretation urges the Court to enforce the Constitution only as it would have been understood at the time it was adopted and to exercise judicial restraint by refusing to strike down laws that do not clearly violate the Constitution. Critics of originalism argue that such deference to historical understandings is impractical and would have the effect of reducing protections to CIVIL LIBERTIES. After leaving the judiciary, Bork further explained and defended his approach to the Constitution in a book, *The Tempting of America*.

Bork received his law degree from the University of Chicago in 1953, and before becoming involved in constitutional issues he worked in ANTITRUST LAW, concerned with regulating monopolies. At Chicago, Bork was influenced by the early "law and economics" movement, which sought to apply economic theories to the law and often opposed government intervention in the marketplace. His first book, *The Antitrust Paradox*, was a critique of activist antitrust policy and argued that the primary goal of antitrust law should be to benefit consumers. As solicitor general, Bork is best known for carrying out President Richard Nixon's order to fire special PROSECUTOR Archibald Cox, who was investigating the Watergate scandal and had sued to obtain tapes of White House conversations. The public outcry over the dismissal of Cox led to the appointment of a new special prosecutor, the start of an IMPEACHMENT investigation, and eventual legislation providing for independent counsels to investigate executive misconduct.

For more information

Bork, Robert H. *The Tempting of America: The Political Seduction of the Law.* New York: Free Press, 1990.

Bork, Robert H. *Slouching toward Gomorrah: Modern Liberalism and American Decline.* New York: HarperCollins, 1990.

Keith E. Whittington
Princeton University

Boston Strangler Albert DeSalvo (1931–1973), better known as the Boston Strangler, confessed to 11 of the 13 rape-murders that terrified Boston between June 14, 1962, and January 4, 1964. He is one of the most notorious serial rapists and killers in U.S. history.

Anna Slesers, a 55-year-old woman, became the first victim of the Strangler. Attacked in her home, she was raped with an unknown object, strangled with her bathrobe belt, and positioned to expose her vagina to anyone entering her apartment. The next five victims fit the same pattern as the Slesers killing: European-American women between the ages of 65 and 87 who had allowed the assailant into their homes, raped with no semen present, strangled with one of their own items, and often positioned to shock. The seventh killing linked to the Strangler, that of 21-year-old African-American student Sophie Clark, ended suspicions that the murderer was a "mother killer." Mary Sullivan, the 19-year-old final victim, was raped with a broom handle and positioned with a greeting card at her feet. Foreign-object rape, fairly common, further humiliates the victim while amplifying the power of the attacker. The use of an object may also indicate that the attacker is impotent.

By this point and in response to the general hysteria, the Massachusetts ATTORNEY GENERAL Edward Brooke had taken over the investigation. Police soon focused on DeSalvo, a married father of two charged with attempted rape. DeSalvo admitted to being the Green Man, who raped women in four states while wearing green work pants. He soon confessed to most of the Boston attacks, possibly in an effort to claim the reward money.

No physical evidence linked DeSalvo to the crimes, and no witnesses could identify him. Forensic experts expressed doubts that one man committed all of the killings. However, DeSalvo provided details of the CRIME SCENES and convinced his attorney, F. LEE BAILEY, of his guilt. DeSalvo also fits the profile of a serial rapist in that he was a white male of European ancestry who targeted white females, attacked them in their homes, lived with a partner, and had been married at least once.

DeSalvo stood trial only for the Green Man crimes and received a life sentence. Sent to

Walpole State Prison in 1967, he was murdered in the infirmary a few years later.

For more information

Frank, Gerold. *The Boston Strangler.* New York: New American Library, 1988.

Caryn E. Neumann
Miami University of Ohio

Bowers v. Hardwick 478 U.S. 186 (1986) *Bowers v. Hardwick* was a case in which the U.S. Supreme Court declared states could criminalize homosexual sodomy and was the first case ever to reach the Supreme Court involving the rights of gays and lesbians. In that case, a police officer had gone to the residence of Michael Hardwick to serve him with a warrant for failure to keep a court date. One of Hardwick's housemates allowed the officer to search the house for him. The officer passed a bedroom door and saw Hardwick engaged in homosexual sodomy (anal sex with another man). The officer arrested Hardwick for violating a Georgia law that prohibited the practice of oral or anal sex. Hardwick challenged the law as violating his constitutional right to privacy.

The Supreme Court, by a 5-4 vote, held there is no constitutional right to engage in "consensual homosexual sodomy." The majority opinion, written by Justice White, declared the right of privacy includes only those rights "deeply rooted in the Nation's history and tradition." Sodomy did not meet that definition because it was a crime under the common law and had been outlawed by all 13 original colonies, all 50 states as recently as 1961, and 24 states as of 1986. Nor did it matter to the Court that Hardwick's conduct occurred in the privacy of the home. The Court stated that it could not grant a right to engage in "VICTIMLESS" CRIMES between consenting adults in the home because such a right would allow the use of drugs, as well as other sex crimes such as adultery, incest, and PROSTITUTION.

The dissenting opinion, written by Justice Brennan, attacked the majority for mischaracterizing the basic issue involved in the case. The real issue according to the dissent was whether adults have a right to control the nature of their intimate relationships with others. The dissent believed "the right of an individual to conduct relationships in the intimacy of his or her own home" is at "the heart of the CONSTITUTION's protection of privacy."

Although the *Bowers* case allowed states to continue to criminalize homosexual sodomy, since 1986 many state legislatures have repealed their laws against homosexual sodomy. Several other state supreme courts have ruled that their states' anti-sodomy laws are unconstitutional, based on other constitutional rights such as EQUAL PROTECTION under the U.S. Constitution, or based on a right of privacy or equal protection found in their own state constitutions rather than in the U.S. Constitution.

ROMER V. EVANS (1996), called into question the continued vitality of the holding in *Bowers*. In *Romer*, the Court declared unconstitutional an amendment to the Colorado Constitution that prohibited local governments within Colorado from offering gays and lesbians protection against discrimination. The Court said this violated the equal protection clause of the U.S. Constitution. The Colorado amendment was so far-reaching in its consequences, it was "inexplicable by anything but animus" toward gays and lesbians, and hostility toward a group, the Court declared, is not a valid reason for denying that group equal protection of the law. However, the majority in *Romer* neither discussed nor even cited *Bowers*. This left unanswered the question of whether the Court would find that anti-sodomy laws, or any other laws that discriminate on the basis of sexual orientation, are based merely on hostility toward gays and thus would be unconstitutional under the equal protection clause. Given the increasing pressure across the nation for equal rights under the law for gays and lesbians, it is undoubtedly just a matter of time before the Court will confront this issue again.

Bowers was a controversial decision. Many state courts, including Kentucky, Georgia, and Minnesota, had reached rulings contrary to the *Bowers* decision based on their own state constitutions. *Bowers* was overturned in *Lawrence v. Texas,* 539 U.S. 558 (2003). In that case, the Court explicitly overturned *Bowers,* ruling that adults choosing to engage in homosexual relations are protected under the DUE PROCESS clause of the Fourteenth Amendment. Many supporters of gay and lesbian rights heralded *Lawrence* and the overturning of *Bowers* as an important victory for equality.

For more information

Pinello, Daniel R. *Gay Rights and American Law.* New York: Cambridge University Press, 2003.

Rick Swanson
University of Louisiana, Lafayette

Bradwell v. Illinois 83 U.S. 130 (1873)

Bradwell v. Illinois is the case in which the United States Supreme Court held that the Illinois Supreme Court's decision to deny Mrs. Bradwell a license to practice law solely because she was a woman did not violate the PRIVILEGES AND IMMUNITIES CLAUSES of the Fourteenth Amendment. However, the case is more often remembered for the concurring opinion written by Justice Bradley wherein he opined "the paramount destiny and mission of woman are to fulfil the noble and benign offices of wife and mother. This is the law of the Creator."

At issue in *Bradwell v. Illinois,* 16 Wall. (83 U.S.) 130 (1873), was whether the Illinois Supreme Court's decision to deny Mrs. Bradwell a license to practice law solely because she was a woman violated the Privileges and Immunities Clause (not the EQUAL PROTECTION clause) of the Fourteenth Amendment. The majority opinion, written by Justice Miller, held that "the right to practice law in the courts of a State is one of those powers which are not transferred for its protection to the Federal government, and its exercise is in no manner governed or controlled by citizenship of the United States in the party seeking such license." The holding was based on the extremely narrow construction of the privileges and immunities clauses announced by the Supreme Court one day earlier in the SLAUGHTERHOUSE CASES (1873).

Justice Bradley began his opinion with an attempt to undermine the basis of Mrs. Bradwell's claim that women can engage in any and every profession of civil life. He did so by writing "the civil law, and nature herself, has always recognized a wide difference in the respective spheres and destinies of man and woman. *Man is, or should be, woman's protector and defender. The natural and proper timidity and delicacy which belongs to the female sex evidently unfits it for many of the occupations of civil life.*"

He then added that the "constitution of the family organization, which is founded in the divine ordinance, as well as in the nature of things, indicates the domestic sphere as that which properly belongs to the domain and functions of womanhood."

Having laid out these patriarchal notions about the nature of life, Justice Bradley's opinion then focused on the issue of whether denying a woman a license to practice law solely because she is a woman was contrary to the privileges and immunities clauses. He reasoned that it did not because the "*paramount destiny and mission of woman are to fulfil* (sic) *the noble and benign offices of wife and mother. This is the law of the Creator. And the rules of civil society must be adapted to the general constitution of things, and cannot be based upon exceptional cases.*" Therefore, he concluded the opinion by proclaiming "[i]n the nature of things it is not every citizen of every age, sex and condition that is qualified for every calling and position. It is the prerogative of the legislator to prescribe regulations founded on nature, reason, and experience for the due admission of qualified persons to the professions and callings demanding special skill and confidence. This fairly belongs to the police power of the State; in my opinion, in view of the peculiar characteristics, destiny, and mission of woman, it is within the province of the legislature to ordain what offices, positions, and callings shall be filled and discharged by men, and shall receive the benefit of those energies and responsibilities, and that decision and firmness which are presumed to predominate in the sterner sex."

While the Supreme Court has never altered its restrictive view of the privileges and immunities clauses, the decision in *Bradwell* has been overturned as a result of the Supreme Court's holding that the equal protection clause of the Fourteenth Amendment prohibits discrimination against women. It should also be noted that Mrs. Bradwell was later admitted to the bar of the state of Illinois (1890) and, somewhat ironically, to the bar of the Supreme Court of the United States (1892).

For more information

Craig v. Boren, 429 U.S. 190 (1976).

Mississippi University for Women v. Hogan, 458 U.S. 718 (1982).

Reed v. Reed, 404 U.S. 71 (1971).

Michael H. Walsh
Senior Lecturer, Political Science Dept.
Loyola University, Chicago

Brady rule In 1963, the Supreme Court in *Brady v. Maryland,* 373 U.S. 83 (1963), held that the prosecution's withholding of EVIDENCE violates DUE PROCESS when "the evidence is material to guilt or punishment" irrespective of the good faith or bad faith of the prosecution. The result of this decision is that in criminal trials the prosecution has an obligation to disclose its evidence to the defense, especially that which would indicate the innocence of the person charged with a crime.

In *Brady,* Brady and his companion, Boblit, were prosecuted for MURDER. Brady admitted being involved in the murder but claimed Boblit had done the actual killing. Brady was convicted for murder and APPEALED, asserting that the prosecution had withheld a statement by Boblit confessing that he had done the killing by himself. Because Brady had already admitted his involvement in the killing, the only issue on appeal was whether the information should have been turned over as relevant to the question of punishment. The Court held that, although the statement was not exculpatory, it was material to the level of PUNISHMENT Brady should be given.

In 1995, the Supreme Court in *Kyles v. Whitley,* 514 U.S. 419 (1995), extended the duty of disclosure to evidence in the possession of the entire prosecution team, including investigative and other government agencies. Additionally, the Court held that failure on the part of the government to disclose *Brady* material requires a new trial, or a new SENTENCING hearing, if disclosure of the evidence creates a reasonable probability of a different result. Subsequent Supreme Court decisions also elaborated the *Brady* obligations to include the duty to disclose IMPEACHMENT evidence and the duty to disclose favorable evidence in the absence of a request by the accused.

Brady marked an important shift from a strictly ADVERSARIAL PROCESS to a more innocence-focused inquisitorial system. The prosecution "team" is no longer allowed to withhold exculpatory evidence in an attempt to "win" the case. Instead, the focus of the prosecution is to uncover the truth, even if the truth proves the defendant is innocent. Although this is the law in theory, in practice it is often much more problematic. Prosecutors are still adversarial-minded, making it difficult for them to be in the position to turn over evidence that is harmful to their case. Moreover, determining what is deemed "material" such that it must be turned over to the defense has been the subject of a glut of litigation. Additionally, it is difficult for defendants to gain access to documents that might contain exculpatory information because documents pertaining to their case are usually spread across many different agencies and the defendant often does not know what evidence exists.

While *Brady* did mark a valuable step toward innocence-focused investigation, as long as the system as a whole remains primarily adversarial, there will continue to be hurdles surrounding the *Brady* rule.

For more information

Bibas, Stephanos. "The Story of Brady v. Maryland: From Adversarial Gameship Toward the Search for Innocence?," *University of Pennsylvania Law Review* 81 (2005).

Rebecca E. Paddock
William S. Boyd School of Law, University of Nevada–Las Vegas

Brandeis, Louis D. (1856–1941) Supreme Court justice Louis D. Brandeis was a lawyer and Supreme Court justice who helped change the course of law in the United States. Born in Louisville, Kentucky, Brandeis enrolled at Harvard Law School when he was 18. Shortly after he left Harvard in 1878 he opened a law partnership in Boston. There he developed a novel approach to the role of the lawyer.

Brandeis assumed that to assess his small business clients' needs he had to understand not only their immediate problems but the economic context in which they arose. That belief illuminated his legal philosophy, which held that law had to be consistent with societal needs and that societal needs could be assessed only through an accumulation of facts. The fact-filled briefs he presented to courts, a novelty in his day, later became the basis for the modern American approach to law.

He also believed that law had to be moral in order to be valid, and that attorneys had an obligation to work on behalf of the people rather than as employees for wealthy corporations. That led in 1893 to his beginning a simultaneous career in public service, beginning with a 10-year fight against the attempt of the Boston Elevated Railway to acquire a monopoly over Boston's transportation system. His decision not to take fees for public service helped create the American *pro bono* ("for the public good") tradition and led to the media's dubbing him the "People's Attorney." He redesigned Massachusetts' utilities laws, invented Savings Bank Life Insurance so that workers could provide for their families, designed much of President Woodrow Wilson's antitrust policy, advised President FRANKLIN ROOSEVELT to enact unemployment insurance, and advocated legalization of unions, minimum wage and maximum hours laws, public ownership of Alaska's natural resources, and public works projects during the depression of the 1930s.

Wilson nominated Brandeis to the Supreme Court in 1916—the first time a Jew had been nominated—and he took his seat later that year. A colleague called Brandeis an "implacable democrat"; another commented that to Brandeis, "democracy is not a political program. It is a religion." His unceasing accumulation of facts had convinced him that freedom was endangered by concentration of power, whether in the hands of government or of corporations. As a justice, therefore, he usually favored action by the states over that by the federal government, balancing corporate power with union power, encouraging competition among businesses, and permitting experimentation with laws designed to aid workers (*New State Ice v. Liebmann,* 1932; *Liggett v. Lee,* 1933). He insisted that the Court exercise self-restraint (*Ashwander v. TVA,* 1936) and not substitute its opinion for reasonable attempts by legislatures to solve societal problems (*Jay Burns v. Bryan,* 1924). At the same time, he joined the Court whenever it struck down what he felt was a level of governmental assumption of power not contemplated by the CONSTITUTION or inconsistent with democracy (*Schecter v. U.S.,* 1935).

Brandeis's democratic ideal included an emphasis on the rights of the individual, particularly as they affected human dignity and the ability of people to participate in the democratic process. He and his law partner coined the phrase "the right to be let alone" in an 1890

Justice Louis D. Brandeis (Harris and Ewing, Collection of the Supreme Court of the United States)

article about privacy. He drew on it as a justice when the Court upheld what it saw as the government's constitutional power to wiretap at will. A furious Brandeis insisted in dissent that the Founding Fathers had included the "right to be let alone" in the Constitution (*Olmstead v. United States*, 1928). In later years the Supreme Court came to agree and has repeatedly cited Brandeis in affirming a constitutional right to privacy.

He considered free speech an absolute necessity if citizens were to have access to ideas and be able to make intelligent choices among them. His dissenting opinions in a number of 1920s cases, arguing that unpopular and even potentially dangerous views had to be permitted to preserve democracy, were adopted by the Supreme Court in the 1960s and are largely responsible for the United States's permissive speech jurisprudence (*Whitney v. California*, 1927; *Brandenburg v. Ohio*, 1969).

When Brandeis resigned from the Court in 1939, he left behind a tradition of lawyers contributing their efforts to public service, a jurisprudence based on interpreting the Constitution in light of societal facts, an insistence on privacy and free speech that gradually became the law of the land, an emphasis on individual dignity, and his certainty that, given the efforts of active democrats, liberty would indeed prevail.

For more information

Mason, Alpheus Thomas. *Brandeis: A Free Man's Life*. New York: Viking, 1946.

Strum, Philippa. *Louis D. Brandeis: Justice for the People*. Cambridge, Mass.: Harvard University Press, 1984.

———, ed. *Brandeis on Democracy*. Lawrence: University Press of Kansas, 1994.

Philippa Strum
City University of New York

Brandeis brief Brandeis brief refers to a legal BRIEF that emphasizes sociological and economic information rather than legal principles. It takes its name from LOUIS D. BRANDEIS, the lawyer and later Supreme Court justice who created it.

During the late 19th century and the first years of the 20th century American courts developed the doctrine of LIBERTY OF CONTRACT. They interpreted the word *liberty* in the Constitution's Fourteenth Amendment ("No state shall . . . deprive any person of life, liberty, or property without DUE PROCESS of law") to mean that employers and employees were free to enter into whatever contractual relationship they liked. Liberty of contract therefore precluded state regulation of hours, wages, and other working conditions.

When the courts of Oregon used the doctrine to strike down a state statute establishing a 10-hour workday for women in laundries and factories, the National Consumers' League hired Brandeis to APPEAL the decision. In 1905 the Supreme Court had endorsed the doctrine

(LOCHNER V. NEW YORK), saying that a law limiting men's working hours had no relationship to health and safety. Brandeis decided his only hope was to argue that women needed a greater level of protection than did men for the sake of their own health and safety and that of society. He and his colleagues, including his sister-in-law Josephine Goldmark, therefore devised a brief that devoted only two pages to legal PRECEDENTS and went on to present more than 100 pages containing sociological, economic, and physiological data about the effect of long working hours on the health of women. The tactic worked. Justice David Brewer acknowledged the brief in his opinion for the Court (*MULLER V. OREGON*, 1908), and Brandeis won his case.

The Brandeis brief was subsequently utilized by lawyers to sustain other regulations of working conditions. In 1954 attorneys in *BROWN V. BOARD OF EDUCATION* drew on the social and behavioral sciences to demonstrate the negative effects of segregated schooling on the ability of African-American children to learn, and CHIEF JUSTICE EARL WARREN cited their EVIDENCE in his landmark decision overturning the "SEPARATE BUT EQUAL" doctrine.

Brandeis's assumption that the law must reflect societal realities and that one of the lawyer's functions is to present those realities to the court has since gained general acceptance, and the Brandeis brief has become the norm for lawyers arguing constitutional cases.

For more information

Strum, Philippa. *Louis D. Brandeis: Justice for the People.* Cambridge, Mass.: Harvard University Press, 1984, chap. 8.

Woloch, Nancy. *Muller v. Oregon.* New York: Bedford Books, 1996.

Philippa Strum
City University of New York

Brandenburg v. Ohio 395 U.S. 444 (1969)

Brandenburg v. Ohio is an important Supreme Court case that established significant guidelines for free speech under the First Amendment.

In this case the Supreme Court ruled that a statute which purports to punish mere advocacy speech, or which forbids assembly to advocate with others, violates both the First and Fourteenth Amendments. A state may forbid speech or assembly only where advocacy is directed to incite or produce imminent lawless action.

Clarence Brandenburg, the leader of an Ohio KU KLUX KLAN group, was convicted, fined $1,000, and sentenced to one to 10 years in prison under Ohio's 1919 criminal syndicalism statute. The Klan leader had invited a Cincinnati television reporter and cameraman to attend and record a rally at which the participants burned a large wooden cross and carried firearms. The Klan leader was taped making derogatory remarks about Negroes and Jews and speaking of the possibility of "revengeance" (sic). In 1919, when the Ohio statute was written, the CONSTITUTION did not guarantee a right to speech that advocated illegal acts or violence. Any speech that "tended" to cause a violation of the law could be punished.

With *Brandenburg,* the Court found that the Ohio Criminal Syndicalism Act went beyond the "clear and present danger" standard that Justice Holmes had advocated in *SCHENK V. UNITED STATES,* 249 U.S. 47 (1919). Under that test, speech, even mere advocacy, could be limited if it posed a clear and present danger. The Court found that while Mr. Brandenburg was advocating action, he was not inciting imminent lawless action. With this new test, speech may not be suppressed or punished unless it is intended to produce "imminent lawless action" and it is "likely to produce such action." Otherwise, the First and Fourteenth Amendments protect even speech and assembly which advocate violence.

The *Brandenburg* imminent lawless test that was developed by this case effectively meant an end to most laws that seek to punish the advocacy of ideas, thereby protecting all types of speech and speakers from censorship.

For more information

Greenawalt, Kent. *Fighting Words: Individuals, Communities, and Liberties of Speech.* Princeton, N.J.: Princeton University Press, 1995.

Harrison, Maureen, and Gilbert, Steve, eds. *Freedom of Speech Decisions of the United States Supreme Court.* First Amendment Decisions Series, Carlsbad, Calif.: Excellent Books, 1996.

Wolfson, Nicholas. *Hate Speech, Sex Speech, Free Speech.* Westport, Conn.: Praeger, 1997.

Paul Kuritz
Bates College

Brennan, William J., Jr. (1906–1997) Supreme Court justice William Brennan was one of the most significant justices ever to serve on the U.S. Supreme Court and a dominant force for expanding constitutional rights during his tenure from 1956 to 1990. His decisions advocated a reading of the BILL OF RIGHTS that would recognize and expand the "human dignity" of individuals, and his approach to the CONSTITUTION called for interpreting it according to society's changing values.

Born in Newark, New Jersey, in 1906, Brennan was the son of a labor organizer who became a successful political leader in Newark. Brennan, who eschewed politics, attended the Wharton School at the University of Pennsylvania and Harvard Law School. He joined a major Newark law firm in the 1930s and developed an expertise in the emerging field of LABOR LAW but on the side of management. During World War II, he enlisted in the army and served as a labor and manpower specialist in Washington, D.C. After the war he returned to practice in Newark and became involved in efforts to reform the state judicial system. In 1949 he became a trial JUDGE in the newly revamped state court system, and he advanced quickly to the appeals court and in 1952 to the state supreme court.

In 1956 Brennan, a Democrat, was picked by President Dwight Eisenhower, a Republican, for a seat on the United States Supreme Court to replace the retiring Justice Sherman Minton. Eisenhower wanted to appoint a Catholic and a Democrat to help cement his support among independent and Democratic voters in the Northeast in the 1956 presidential election. Eisenhower's sentiment expressed a few years later, that he was disappointed at how liberal Brennan proved to be, was misplaced since Brennan was chosen for his impact on the election rather than on the Court.

Brennan quickly won the trust of CHIEF JUSTICE EARL WARREN and earned the respect of other justices. He demonstrated a remarkable ability to bring justices together to form important majorities in case after case. His warm, friendly manner and ready accessibility to colleagues made him extraordinarily effective in the Court's internal deliberations and opinion-drafting.

Among his major decisions, Brennan wrote *BAKER V. CARR* (1962), which paved the way for the

Justice William J. Brennan, Jr. (Robert Oakes, National Geographical Society, Collection of the Supreme Court of the United States)

Supreme Court to reapportion state legislatures to achieve "one person, one vote." He authored *NEW YORK TIMES V. SULLIVAN* (1964), which said that criticism of public officials was protected by the First Amendment guarantee of FREEDOM OF SPEECH. He led the Court's application of provisions of the Bill of Rights to the states through the DUE PROCESS clause of the Fourteenth Amendment, known as "INCORPORATION." He wrote the decision in *Craig v. Boren* (1976), which subjected gender discrimination to greater scrutiny under the Fourteenth Amendment EQUAL PROTECTION clause. He wrote major decisions upholding AFFIRMATIVE ACTION, striking down loyalty oaths for public employees, and requiring due process for individuals receiving welfare, food stamps, and other government assistance. As a dissenter, he argued for the unconstitutionality of the death penalty and for the First Amendment protection of obscene materials.

After Earl Warren retired, and first WARREN E. BURGER became chief justice in 1969 and then WILLIAM H. REHNQUIST in 1986, the Court grew more conservative; Brennan found himself more often in dissent, but he continued to muster surprising victories. Brennan retired after he suffered a stroke in 1990, still forging majorities down to his last day on the bench. He died in 1997.

For more information

Cushman, Clare, ed. *The Supreme Court Justices: Illustrated Biographies, 1789–1995.* 2nd ed. Washington, D.C.: Congressional Quarterly Books, 1995.

Marion, David E. *The Jurisprudence of William J Brennan, Jr.* Lanham, Md.: Rowman and Littlefield, 1997.

Rosenkranz, E. Joshua, ed. *Reason and Passion: Justice Brennan's Enduring Influence.* New York: W. W. Norton, 1997.

Stern, Seth, and Stephen Wermiel. *Justice Brennan: Liberal Champion.* New York: Houghton Mifflin Harcourt, 2010.

Stephen Wermiel
American University, Washington College of Law

Breyer, Stephen Gerald (1938–) Supreme Court justice Stephen Gerald Breyer was nominated to the Supreme Court by President Bill Clinton in April 1994 and was confirmed by Congress in July 1994.

A native of San Francisco, Breyer earned an A.B. from Stanford University in 1959. He continued his education in England, where he earned a B.A. in philosophy and economics at Oxford University in 1961. On his return to the United States, Breyer enrolled in Harvard Law School, from which he graduated magna cum laude in 1964. He has been married since 1967 and has three children. He is an avid bicyclist and also enjoys cooking and recreational reading.

Stephen Breyer started his professional career by accepting a prestigious Supreme Court clerkship, a position coveted by every newly graduated attorney. During his clerkship, Breyer assisted Supreme Court justice Arthur Goldberg with writing the Court's decision in *GRISWOLD V. CONNECTICUT*, a landmark, right-to-privacy case.

In early 1967 Breyer became an assistant professor at Harvard Law School. He was promoted to a full professorship in 1970. However, in 1967, soon after he started teaching at Harvard, Breyer was offered a Washington, D.C.-based position as assistant U.S. attorney general. Breyer also accepted that employment and continued to commute between Boston and Washington, D.C., until 1980.

Stephen Breyer gained visibility in 1974 by serving as an assistant special PROSECUTOR on the Watergate Special Prosecution Force, a task group formed to investigate the possibility of impeaching President Richard M. Nixon. After the Watergate prosecution team completed its mission, Breyer accepted employment as a senior aide to Senator Edward M. Kennedy, chairman of the Senate Judiciary Committee. Breyer demonstrated that his talent and work ethic enabled him to excel not only with employment in the judicial and executive branches of government but also with work at the legislative branch. Less than one year after starting work with Senator

Kennedy, Breyer was promoted to special counsel to the Judiciary Committee. He was promoted to chief counsel to that committee in 1979.

During this time period, Stephen Breyer's unorthodox, creative methods of solving both legal questions and practical problems impressed both Republican and Democratic committee members. Because senators from both sides of the aisle respected Breyer's talent for innovative reasoning and willingness to assert independent, nonpartisan ideas, the senators trusted him to convert legislative stalemates into mutually acceptable solutions. Breyer soon earned a reputation for being Congress's most skillful consensus builder.

During his tenure with the Judiciary Committee, Breyer became well known for his groundbreaking work in deregulating the airline and trucking industries. He also initiated long-term projects in the dissimilar fields of prison reform and fair housing law, with the ambitious goal of updating, reorganizing, and rewriting these statutes

In October 1980, during the presidential campaign in which Democratic president Jimmy Carter sought reelection, Stephen Breyer was one of several individuals nominated by the president to fill vacant judicial positions in federal courts. Unfortunately, President Ronald Reagan, a Republican, won the election before Congress had time to finalize these appointments. Following the usual practice of a new president whose political affiliation differs from his predecessor's, in January 1981 President Reagan "cleaned house." With one exception, he nullified the appointments made by Carter but not confirmed by Congress. The exception was the only nominee who had support from both political parties: Stephen Breyer. His new title, "justice of the U.S. COURT OF APPEALS," was confirmed in early 1981.

Throughout his 13-year tenure at the U.S. Court of Appeals, Stephen Breyer's judicial opinions reflected his pragmatism and distrust of broad legal theory. His work also clearly demonstrated that he was a political moderate and an advocate of judicial restraint. Breyer's name became well recognized by the general public as well as by attorneys and politicians because of his unusual talent for expressing complex legal concepts in language that bright high school students could comprehend.

While serving in the Court of Appeals, Breyer participated in the work of the U.S. Sentencing Commission, a group of U.S. Court of Appeals judges who were responsible for the revision of the federal guidelines consulted by JUDGES when imposing criminal sentences. The revised guidelines, which took effect in 1987, reflect Breyer's idea that the sentence recommended for a particular crime should be based on national averages of sentences in similar cases. Unlike his other work, these guidelines have been widely criticized as being too rigid, since they do not permit any input of judicial DISCRETION.

Breyer's performance on the Supreme Court evinces a moderate ideology amid an overall tendency to align with the Court's liberal bloc. He typically assumes a probusiness position in antitrust cases, expressing a suspicion of government regulation of private business activity. His dislike of government regulatory schemes is muted, however, in cases involving environmental protection legislation. Justice Breyer has generally supported AFFIRMATIVE ACTION plans, joining Justice Ginsberg's dissent in the *Adarand Contractors v. Pena* (1995) decision. Several of Breyer's recent decisions angered conservatives who supported his nomination. Justice Breyer wrote the majority opinion in *Stenberg v. Carhart* (2000), the controversial partial-birth abortion case in which the Court reaffirmed the essential features of *ROE V. WADE* (1973). Furthermore, Breyer recorded liberal votes in *Chicago v. Morales* (1999), *ILLINOIS V. WARDLOW* (2000), and *DICKERSON V. UNITED STATES* (2000), three highly publicized cases involving the rights of criminal defendants.

Breyer continues to be identified with the more liberal wing of the Supreme Court, generally voting to support ABORTION and GAY RIGHTS and opposing the death penalty. He has also emerged as the intellectual foil of ANTONIN SCALIA, often criticizing the latter for his approaches to constitutional and statutory interpretation. Breyer has authored several books describing his views on these subjects, including *Making Democracy Work: A Judge's View,* and *Active Liberty: Interpreting Our Democratic Constitution.*

For more information

Breyer, Stephen G. *Making Democracy Work: A Judge's View.* New York: Knopf, 2010.

Breyer, Stephen G. *Active Liberty: Interpreting Our Democratic Constitution.* New York: Vintage Books, 2006.

Beth S. Swartz, J. D.
Bradley J. Best
Austin Peay State University

brief Brief describes two different types of legal documents. Generally the term refers to written documents submitted to a court to advocate a particular disposition of a motion or a case. Such briefs may be directed to either an appellate court or a trial JUDGE. The term *brief* also refers to a summary of a legal decision setting forth the disposition of the case and its underlying facts; the court's holding, i.e., the rule of law established by the case; and the rationale underlying the court's decision. Briefs are an essential part of the appellate process—the process by which judges' rulings undergo review for errors. Litigants may APPEAL a judicial decision to an appellate court, which will determine whether the judicial ruling should be upheld, reversed, or resolved in some other manner.

APPELLATE BRIEFS, briefs submitted to appellate courts, enable the lawyers for the various parties to the lawsuit to give a written explanation of their argument that the appellate court should either uphold or overturn the decision rendered by the lower court. The precise form of appellate briefs varies somewhat depending on the appellate court to which the brief will be submitted. Generally, however, appellate briefs consist of a statement of the legal issues that must be resolved, a description of the relevant factual background, and a legal argument that details the legal bases for ruling in the party's favor. The factual section of an appellate brief includes citations to the portions of the record supporting the factual assertions made in the brief. The record consists of the legal documents filed in the trial court, trial testimony, trial exhibits, and the decisions rendered by the trial court. The argument section of appellate briefs includes citations to cases, statutes, regulations, and other legal authorities that support the statements of law made as a part of the argument. Though lawyers for the parties to a case often have the opportunity to present oral arguments before appellate courts once they have filed their appellate briefs, appellate judges rely much more heavily on briefs than on oral argument.

Briefs submitted at the trial level are ordinarily less formal than appellate briefs, and they are often referred to as memoranda of law. Whenever a party to a lawsuit seeks an order from the court, the party must file a motion and ordinarily must submit a brief justifying the order sought. Such briefs, or memoranda of law, generally consist of a section setting forth the facts relevant to the motion and a legal argument establishing the party's legal entitlement to prevail on its motion, supported by citations to legal authorities. The other parties in the case can then submit responsive briefs or memoranda of law setting forth facts and legal arguments justifying denial of the motion. Sometimes parties also submit trial briefs—briefs to familiarize a judge with the facts parties expect to present and the legal basis for their claims in a trial over which a judge will preside.

Lawyers occasionally use the term *brief* to refer to a formal summary of a legal decision. Such a brief, also known as a case brief, sets forth the issue presented by a case, the disposition of the case, the relevant facts, the legal principle established by the case, and the rationale for the court's decision. Case briefs are not submitted to judges but rather are a form of note taking. Law students often prepare case briefs to prepare for class.

For more information

Porter, Karen K., et al. *Introduction to Legal Writing and Oral Advocacy.* New York: Matthew Bender, 1989.

Shapo, Helene S., Marilyn R. Walter, and Elizabeth Fajans. *Writing and Analysis in the Law.* 4th ed. Westbury, N.Y.: Foundation Press, 1999.

Bernard W. Bell
Rutgers Law School (Newark)

broken windows theory of crime The broken windows theory states that major crimes often escalate from minor ones and that the best way to address the former is to prosecute and take seriously more minor crimes. The theory eventually became very important to police practice in the 1980s and 1990s.

Broken windows theory was derived from an experiment conducted by Philip Zimbardo (1969), in which an abandoned automobile was placed in a high-crime neighborhood where it remained untouched for a week until part of it was smashed by a researcher. Within a few hours of the initial damage, the car was destroyed. The theory posits that in certain neighborhoods if a broken window remains unrepaired, then it alerts others that this is the norm, and breaking more windows becomes more acceptable; in other words, a failure to enforce minor public offenses contributes to a downward spiral in which residents become less involved and withdrawn from the community, thereby allowing for crime and vandalism to proliferate; and moreover, that disorder is indirectly linked to serious crime.

The theory was derived by Wilson and Kelling (1982) from the findings of a foot-patrol experiment conducted in Newark, New Jersey, by police administrators and social scientists. While swapping police officers from patrol cars to walking beats did not reduce the amount of crime in those neighborhoods as expected, residents did experience positive outcomes. Residents in neighborhoods that had foot patrols felt more secure, believed that crime had decreased, and appeared to take fewer precautions to protect themselves from criminal activities. While the use of patrol cars increases police mobility, expediting the response time to citizen service calls and strengthening the control of central command, they also act as a barrier between the officer and the community. An officer on foot patrol is unable to separate himself or herself from the street, allowing for greater integration into the neighborhood, along with greater accessibility by residents, thus fostering a sense of collective identity in which both formal and informal actors are collaborating at improving their community.

Wilson and Kelling (1982) found that the level of disorder in a neighborhood provides a signal to motivated offenders that there is a lack of concern about the neighborhood. This indicates that there is a lack of social control, either formal (i.e. police officers) or informal (i.e. neighbors, family), which reduces the chances for apprehension. Therefore, offenders will target disorderly neighborhoods to commit offenses because the costs of their illegal actions are greatly reduced or eliminated.

The theory predicts that a sequence of events (i.e. windows breaking) will then ensue: first, the ongoing accumulation of disorder in the neighborhood; second, individuals will perceive that violent crime is increasing and become more fearful of their community; third, the increased levels of fear will inhibit individuals from intervening in the neighborhood, limiting their use of public space; fourth, residential turnover will ensue, with individuals who are able to move away replaced by individuals who are not attached to the neighborhood; finally, serious crime (this includes drug dealing, PROSTITUTION, ROBBERIES, CAR THEFT, assorted violent crimes) will inevitably increase.

Broken windows theory is primarily concerned with two forms of disorder: physical and social. Physical disorder represents the level of maintenance for a neighborhood's physical environment. This includes the condition of buildings, property surrounding the buildings, and vacant lots. Social disorder is the pattern of social activities, or interactions, which is visible to the public and considered to be "deviant" or "inappropriate" to most individuals. This can include the presence of "non-violent people, nor, necessarily, criminal, but disreputable or obstreperous or unpredictable people: panhandlers, drunks, addicts, rowdy teenagers, prostitutes, loiterers, the mentally disturbed."

Just as the physical disorder of a neighborhood is predicted to be a cue to potential offenders (both minor and serious) of the ability to act without restraint, social disorder is predicted to have a similar effect. The ignoring of and lack of intervention on certain types of unacceptable social interaction will encourage problematic behavior and crime. As individuals become more fearful of crime occurring, they become detached from the neighborhood, thus eroding the amount of informal social control, which will allow criminal activities to flourish.

Emerging simultaneously with broken windows theory was the philosophy of COMMUNITY POLICING. While the media has conflated these two philosophies, they are quite distinct. Community policing strives for both citizens and law enforcement to be equal partners in the construction and implementation of policies aimed at ameliorating the neighborhood. Wilson and Kelling argue, however, that while citizens can aid reducing crime, the principal component required to fight crime is the use of formal social controls, specifically the police. Historically, the mission of the police was as "watchmen" concerned with maintaining order, primarily from fire, wild animals, and inappropriate behavior. Within the last 40 years, this role has changed to focus on fighting crime. Wilson and Kelling articulate that the role of the police is to reinforce the informal social control of the neighborhood. The encouragement of law enforcement agencies to engage in the order maintenance aspect of policing needs to be retained and promoted in order to deter crime.

While there have been many critiques of broken windows theory, such as Sampson and Cohen (1988), Harcourt (2001), and Taylor (2001), which have found that aggressive policing of street offenses, thus removing disorder, is not significant in reducing the amount of crime. William Bratton (former chief of the Los Angeles Police Department from 2002 to 2009) and George Kelling (professor of criminal justice at Rutgers University) both strongly argue that the criticisms of broken windows theory are due to the misrepresentation of the theory, in which the effects on disorder on serious crime has been measured as a direct connection instead of the stated indirect link (Bratton and Kelling, 2006). Bratton attests that emphasizing order restoration has been the foundation to his crime reduction strategies, in both New York and Los Angeles, which have reduced the number of homicides and overall crime within both cities during his tenure.

For more information

Bratton, William J., and George L. Kelling. "There Are No Cracks in the Broken Windows: Ideological Academics Are Trying to Undermine a Perfectly Good Idea." *National Review Online* (28 February 2006). Available online. URL: www.nationalreview.com.

Cordner, Gary. "Community Policing: Elements and Effects." In *Community Policing: Contemporary Readings*, edited by Geoffrey Alpert and Alex Piquero, 45–62. Prospect Heights, Ill.: Waveland Press, 1998.

Harcourt, Bernard E. *Illusions of Order: The False Promise of Broken Windows Policing*. Cambridge, Mass.: Harvard University Press, 2001.

Police Foundation. *The Newark Foot Patrol Experiment*. Washington, D.C.: Police Foundation, 1981.

Sampson, Robert J., and Jacqueline Cohen. "Deterrence Effect of the Police in Crime: A Replication and Theoretical Extension." *Law and Society Review* (1988): 166.

Skogan, Wesley. *Disorder and Decline: Crime and the Spiral of Decay in American Neighborhoods*. Berkeley & Los Angeles: University of California Press, 1990.

St. Jean, Peter K. B. *Pockets of Crime: Broken Windows, Collective Efficacy, and the Criminal Point of View*. Chicago: University of Chicago Press, 2007.

Taylor, Ralph. *Breaking Away from Broken Windows: Baltimore Neighborhoods and the Nationwide Fight against Crime, Grime, Fear, and Decline*. Boulder, Colo.: Westview Press, 2001.

Wilson, James Q., and George L. Kelling. "Broken Windows." *Atlantic* (March) 29–38.

Zimbardo, Philip. "The Human Choice: Individualism, Reason, and Order versus Deindividuation, Impulse, and Chaos." *Nebraska Symposium on Motivation* 17, edited by W. J. Arnold and D. Levine, 237–307. Lincoln: University of Nebraska Press, 1969.

Matthew Valasi
University of California, Irvine

Brown v. Board of Education of Topeka, Kansas 347 U.S. 484 (1954) *Brown v. Board of Education of Topeka, Kansas* was the case in which the Supreme Court declared that racial SEGREGATION in the public schools violated the CONSTITUTION of the United States.

The Fourteenth Amendment to the U.S. Constitution states, "No state shall . . . deny to any person within its jurisdiction the EQUAL PROTECTION of the laws." The amendment became part of the Constitution in the immediate aftermath of the Civil War. Soon after its adoption a number of southern and border states passed laws mandating racial segregation in public facilities. In 1896 the Supreme Court found that so long as the facilities provided for members of different races were equal, segregation itself did not violate the equal protection clause (*PLESSY V. FERGUSON*). This "SEPARATE BUT EQUAL" doctrine was used as the legal justification for segregation laws for more than half a century.

In 1952, 17 states and the District of Columbia segregated their public schools. Linda Brown was an eight-year-old African-American girl who lived near an all-white elementary school in Topeka. Though her parents wanted her to attend that school, she was not allowed to do so because of her race. Linda sued, through her parents, to have Topeka's school segregation laws declared unconstitutional. The Supreme Court combined Linda's case with four others and issued its decision on May 17, 1954.

On behalf of a unanimous Court, CHIEF JUSTICE EARL WARREN wrote that even if the physical facilities provided to members of different races were equal, modern psychological research demonstrated that legal segregation, itself, conveyed a governmental message to those who were kept out of schools attended by the white majority. "[T]he policy of separating the races is usually interpreted as denoting the inferiority of the negro group. A sense of inferiority affects the motivation of a child to learn. . . . Separate educational facilities are inherently unequal."

Legal segregation did not end with the *Brown* decision. The Court recognized that the states would need time to develop plans for eliminating their dual school systems. In *Brown v. Board of Education II* (1955) the Court told local school boards to move toward that goal "with all deliberate speed."

Some school boards ended segregation quickly. Most did not. Critics of *Brown II* scolded the Court for its failure to foresee the fact that segregationist diehards would treat the decision as an invitation to proceed with "all deliberation and no speed." As late as 1992 the state of Mississippi was before the Court because it was continuing to maintain a dual university system (*United States v. Fordice*).

Though *Brown I* and *II* did not end legal segregation immediately, they removed its constitutional underpinning and put the full backing of the Constitution behind the CIVIL RIGHTS MOVEMENT in the United States.

For more information

Karst, Kenneth L. *Belonging to America: Equal Citizenship and the Constitution*. New Haven, Conn.: Yale University Press, 1989.

Peltason, Jack. *Fifty-Eight Lonely Men*. Urbana: University of Illinois Press, 1971.

Woodward, C. Vann. *The Strange Career of Jim Crow*. 3d ed. New York: Oxford University Press, 1974.

William H. Coogan
University of Southern Maine

BTK killer Dennis Rader, the BTK killer, was born in 1945 and ARRESTED in 2004. From 1974 to 1991, he committed 10 murders in Wichita, Kansas, and ATTEMPTED several others. He is currently serving nine life sentences in prison.

The name BTK killer, which stands for Bind, Torture, Kill, was chosen by Rader himself and used in his first letter to police. It was one of a number of nicknames that Rader chose for himself, and it became popular through the media's use of it. During his years as a SERIAL KILLER, Rader maintained the appearance of being a model citizen. He performed a number of roles in his local community of Park City, Kansas, including president of the Lutheran Church congregation, working as the town compliance officer, and serving as a Boy Scout leader. This normal life and the long periods that Rader spent between murders helped him to hide from law enforcement. Two restraining orders filed against him by women that he was STALKING and the severity of disciplinary actions while serving for the Park City Compliance Department were the only indications of his violent character.

Rader's first victims were four members of the Otero family. He later admitted in court that the murders were poorly planned. Rader's original intent was to sexually assault Mrs. Otero or her daughter, Josephine, but he was surprised to find the father and son at home with them. After cutting the house's phone lines, Rader entered through the back door, held the family at gunpoint, then strangled each of the family members with plastic bags and cord. Rader sent his first message to the police to claim responsibility for the Otero murders. Sending such letters became one of his defining characteristics, and during his three decades of activity he frequently communicated with law enforcement and the media to stay in public view.

His letters taunted police and dared them to predict his next move. They also gave detailed reports of the murder of each victim and admitted to attempted murders that went unnoticed. One letter expressed his desire to kill Anna Williams, who only avoided death by returning home late, by which time Rader had already left her home.

Rader was arrested in 2004, when, after 13 years of silence, he resumed sending letters to the police and prompted a resumption of the investigation with the new tool of DNA analysis. Initially, police compared the samples to DNA taken from more than 1,000 local men but did not find a match. Rader only made himself a suspect when he sent a disk to police that included documents made under the name Dennis and showed a connection to the church where Rader worked. Police collected DNA taken from Rader's daughter during a visit to the doctor, which gave them enough evidence to make the arrest. In 2005, he pled guilty to 10 murders and was sentenced to serve 10 life sentences in prison. Rader was spared the death penalty as all his victims were killed before it was reinstated.

For more information

Wenzl, Roy. *Bind, Torture, Kill: The Inside Story of BTK, the Serial Killer Next Door*. New York: Harper, 2008.

Marcus Schulzke
State University of New York at Albany

Buckley v. Valeo 424 U.S. 1 (1976) *Buckley v. Valeo* is the Supreme Court case that established the basic guidelines for the current system of financing campaigns for federal office in the United States.

At issue were the 1974 amendments to the Federal Election Campaign Act (FECA) of 1971. The Court upheld limits on the amounts that individuals and political action committees could contribute to candidates, requirements for reporting receipts and spending by candidates, and the system for publicly financing the presidential election campaigns. The ruling struck down spending limits for candidates and independent persons and groups, as well as restrictions on the use of personal wealth to fund campaign activity.

There are two key results of this ruling pertaining to financing campaigns for federal office. First, it confirmed the right of Congress to legislatively set limits on contributions to candidates. The Court further reinforced the idea that contribution limits were constitutional in *Nixon, Attorney General of Missouri, et al. v. Shrink Missouri Government PAC, et al.*, 528 U.S. 1033 (2000) where the Court expressly stated that *Buckley* was the authority on this matter and extended the right of regulating the amount of contributions to state legislatures as well.

The most significant feature of the case is the linkage of money and spending to political speech and the First Amendment. To quote the decision:

> A restriction on the amount of money a person or group can spend on political communication during a campaign necessarily reduces the quantity of expression by restricting the number of issues discussed, the depth of their exploration, and the size of the audience reached. This is because virtually every means of communicating ideas in today's mass society requires the expenditure of money.

This linkage of political speech to money makes any attempt to fully regulate campaign finance extremely difficult, as it would require getting around the First Amendment. As such, Congress has no way of legislating a cap on spending by candidates, nor can it limit the amounts spent by independent groups. A 1996 case, *Colorado Republican Federal Campaign Committee, et al. v. Federal Election Commission,* 518 U.S. 604 (1996), further clarified the issue by ruling that political parties could collect and spend unlimited funds for "party building" exercises. The combined effects of *Buckley* and *Colorado Republican* have created the significant influx of soft money (i.e., unregulated campaign contributions and spending) into campaigns since the 1996 electoral cycle.

In sum: it is constitutionally allowable to limit how much can be given to a candidate, but the amount that candidate spends cannot be capped. Further, groups and individuals acting independently from a candidate cannot be limited in the amount they spend.

The Court did allow an exception to its strictures against limiting campaign spending. Spending ceilings were upheld in the case of the partial public financing of presidential primaries and the complete public financing of the general election campaign for president on the basis that the system was voluntary in nature. Candidates could choose to receive the funds and therefore be required to conform to limits, or candidates could avoid the limits by not accepting public monies.

Of secondary importance to the basic rules of the game for campaign finance, it is also worth noting that the case struck down the method of selecting the Federal Election Commission (FEC), which gave the president pro tempore and the Speaker of the House the authority to appoint two members each to the commission. The Court held that this violated the appointment clause of the CONSTITUTION (art. 2, sec. 2, cl. 2). As a result, the Court ordered the Congress to reformulate the appointment provisions to the FEC, although the Court did uphold any existing rulings made by that body.

The ruling was *per curiam* (unsigned), in which all members of the Court joined at least in part, excepting Justice Stevens, who took no part in the consideration or decision of the case.

Since it was decided in 1976, *Buckley* has remained the major precedent regarding campaign financing and spending. It has consistently guided Supreme and lower federal and state court decisions. An effort to overturn *Buckley* was rejected by the Court in *Randall v. Sorrell*, 548 U.S. 230 (2006). In that case, Vermont sought to impose mandatory expenditure caps on political campaigns. In rejecting these caps as unconstitutional, the Supreme Court reaffirmed the central rulings of *Buckley*.

For more information

Schultz, David, John R. Vile, and Michelle D. Deardorff. *Constitutional Law in Contemporary America*, vol. 1. New York: Oxford University Press, 2010.

Steven L. Taylor
Assistant Professor of Political Science
Troy State University

bullying and anti-bullying laws Bullying refers to the act of a student or students physically or verbally abusing another student. Many states, cities, and school districts have adopted laws or rules aimed at preventing such behavior.

Bullying is an act of intimidation or aggression directed at a weaker individual. The caricature of the schoolyard bully no longer tells the whole story. The type of intimidation or aggressive behavior included in bullying has expanded beyond the schoolyard. Bullying may include mockery; being the subject of rumors; being threatened with harm; being pushed, shoved, tripped, or spit on; being pressured into doing things a person does not want to do; being excluded; being sexually harassed, or having property destroyed purposefully. Suicides and MURDERS have been attributed to bullying. Bullying no longer has to take place in person; it can also include using the Web, Twitter, or social networks such as Facebook.

There were several school shootings in the 1990s that were committed by students who complained of being bullied. Since the 1999 shootings at COLUMBINE High School, bullying is no longer dismissed as a childish phase. Investigations into the background of the two Columbine students, who killed both teachers and classmates, revealed that they had been bullied. Educators, employers, administrators, legislators, law enforcement officials, and parents have become involved in attempting to curtail and treat aggressive and intimidating behavior. More than 40 states explicitly prohibit bullying either through legislation or education policy. The Bully Police Web site tracks anti-bullying legislation and rates each state's attempts to prohibit bullying. The full text of the laws are available on this Web site.

Data on bullying are compiled annually by the National Center for Education Statistics (NCES) in its publication, *Indicators of School Crime and Safety*. Before 2000, statistics on acts of intimidation and bullying were not tallied separately in the publication. Since the school shootings, the report contains numerous tables on bullying.

Reports of bullying have increased over the past decade. About one-third of the students surveyed in the *Indicators of School Crime and Safety* reported that they had been bullied. These incidences occurred primarily on school grounds. The idea of place has taken on new meaning, however, with the advent of online communication.

Since the age of the INTERNET, bullying is no longer confined to personal attacks in the schoolyard or workplace. Cyberbullying has become an Internet reality: instant messaging, e-mails, MySpace, Facebook, and other social networking technologies have provided a medium for bullying, sometimes allowing the bully to act with anonymity. Some states have amended their laws or education policies to include cyberbullying. In an ironic turn of events, the bully may no longer be the stronger intimidating character. The anonymity of the Internet shields the cyberbully, although, according to the lawsuits that have been filed thus far, most online bullying seems to stem from face-to-face occurrences.

Another aspect of bullying is sexual harassment. In *Aurelia Davis v. Monroe County Board of Education,* 526 U.S. 629 (1999), the Supreme Court held that a school district could be held liable for damages under Title IX of the Education Amendments of 1972 for sexual harassment. The Court granted monetary damages to Ms. Davis because it found that school officials had failed to stop the sexual harassment of her fifth grade daughter by a fellow student.

An important consideration is whether the curtailment of off-campus Internet speech hinders free speech and blocks First Amendment rights. The courts have determined that Web sites or other cyber communications that did not pose a realistic threat to another could be deemed to be free speech.

Workplace bullying, often called harassment, may take more subtle forms than that of student bullying. Usually passive and nonphysical in nature, the harassment may be manifested by gossip, unfair workloads, unfair performance appraisals, sexual harassment, denial of promotions or raises, and other practices leading to a hostile work environment. As with student bullying, the workplace has been affected by cyberbullying.

While legislators and administrators are attempting to heed the desperate calls of the bullied, especially post-Columbine, merely passing laws and policies are ineffective methods if there is no enforcement behind them.

For more information

Bully Police USA. Available online. URL: http://www.bullypolice.org. Accessed November 30, 2009.

Feinberg, Ted, and Nicole Robey. "Cyberbullying," *Principal Leadership* 9, no. 1 (2008): 10–14.

U.S. Department of Education. National Center for Education Statistics. *Indicators of School Crime and Safety.* Washington, D.C.: U.S. Government Printing Office, 2008. Available online. URL: http://www/nces.ed.gov. Accessed November 30, 2009.

Rosemary L. Meszaros
Western Kentucky University

burden of proof Burden of proof refers to the legal concept that requires an accuser to establish some level of proof in order to substantiate a legal claim. The amount of proof required depends on whether one is being charged civilly or criminally.

In the United States, there is a general presumption that a person accused of violating a law (or right) is presumed innocent until proven guilty (or in the civil context, proven to have committed some kind of civil wrong—generally referred to as a *TORT*).

In the criminal context, the burden of proof required is high. The standard required to prove one guilty of a criminal act requires sufficient EVIDENCE to prove the accused committed the act beyond a REASONABLE DOUBT. In terms of a percentage, this generally means the evidence must show the accused is 99 percent or more guilty of the alleged criminal act. The reason the burden of proof is so high in criminal proceedings is because of the consequences of being found guilty, which can include a prison sentence, which includes the removal of the individual's personal liberties guaranteed by the UNITED STATES CONSTITUTION.

In the civil context, the burden of proof required is lower than in the criminal context. The general standard applied to many civil actions is the plaintiff (the person bringing the claim) must show it is more probable than not that the defendant (the person being accused) violated some legal standard. This standard is sometimes referred to as a PREPONDERANCE OF THE EVIDENCE standard. Again, from a percentage standpoint, this means the plaintiff must prove the defendant violated a standard by approximately 51 percent or more. The reason the burden is lower in civil cases is because, unlike the potential for jail time in criminal cases, a defendant who is found responsible for a civil wrong must pay money damages, and there is generally no possibility of being sent to prison.

There is another burden of proof standard sometimes used in both criminal and civil cases.

This standard, clear and convincing evidence, requires the accuser to present sufficient evidence to show it is substantially more likely than not that the accused has committed the alleged act. This standard requires a greater showing than the preponderance of evidence standard, but less than the beyond a reasonable doubt standard. Some have suggested, percentage-wise, this means the evidence must show it is at least 75 percent likely the accused committed the act.

The standards of proof identified above generally relate to the legal burden of proof placed on the accuser to prove a charge or claim against an accused. There is also what is referred to as an evidentiary burden of proof in American law, which refers to the specific pieces of evidence presented at a trial. Like the overall burden of proof required to prove the guilt of the accused, sufficient proof must be presented on each piece of evidence presented during the trial that is being relied on, in total, to support a judgment. These two concepts, a legal and evidentiary burden, together form the burden of proof in our American legal system.

For more information

Ruotolo, Lyndsay V. "Due Process of Law in Sentencing," *New York Law School Law Review* (Summer 2009): 655.

Sotomayor, Sonia. "Criminal Law," *Congressional Research Service, Reports and Issue Briefs* (June 2009).

Chad J. McGuire
University of Massachusetts, Dartmouth.

Bureau of Alcohol, Tobacco, and Firearms

The Bureau of Alcohol, Tobacco, Firearms, and Explosives (ATF) is a U.S. government agency, housed in the DEPARTMENT OF JUSTICE since 2003. Its self-described mission is to protect communities "from violent criminals, criminal organizations, the illegal use and trafficking of firearms, the illegal use and storage of explosives, acts of arson (see entry) and bombings, acts of terrorism (see entry), and the illegal diversion of alcohol and tobacco products."

From 1972 until 2003, it was called the Bureau of Alcohol, Tobacco, and Firearms and located in the Treasury Department. It was moved to Justice and given its new name, reflecting its increased emphasis on bombings and explosives, by the Homeland Security Act of 2002. (It is still commonly referred to as ATF.)

The decision not to place it in the new DEPARTMENT OF HOMELAND SECURITY reflected its mission overlap with that of the FBI, already part of Justice, and a desire to improve ATF-FBI coordination and erase longstanding tensions that even flared as both agencies rushed to respond to the 2001 terrorist attacks. At the same time, suggestions in Congress for totally merging the two agencies have always met with opposition from both, presumably because of desires to protect turf, identity, and culture.

The ATF's roots extend back to the beginning of the Republic when alcohol began to be taxed to pay war debts. Its antecedents acquired a mix of tasks ranging from tax collection to pursuit of lawbreakers. Its history is one of reorganizations, reforms, mergers, and name changes. In 1862, an Office of Internal Revenue containing an Alcohol Tax Unit was created within the Treasury Department to tax alcohol and tobacco products and to hire law enforcement officials to apprehend tax evaders. The passage of the Eighteenth Amendment in 1919 raised its profile and expanded its responsibilities. This led to creation of a Prohibition Unit, which soon became a bureau, but shortly thereafter was dissolved and its duties divided between new entities in Justice and Treasury. The repeal of PROHIBITION in 1933 transformed it into the Federal Alcohol Administration, once again in Treasury; it merged with Treasury's Alcohol Tax Unit in 1940. Even after the end of Prohibition, the unit's investigators continued to work "moonshine" cases, especially in states with dry counties. In 1941, it acquired authority under the National Firearms Act to pursue firearms violations. This role expanded in the 1960s, and its image became increasingly that of an agency with expertise in explosives and firearms. The ATF was separated from what had become the Internal Revenue Service and became an independent bureau within the Treasury Department in 1972, and Congress expanded its powers several times since.

ATF became controversial because of the highly publicized events at Ruby Ridge, Idaho, (1992) and the Branch Davidian Compound near Waco, Texas (1993). These raised questions, particularly among the gun lobby, civil libertarians, and antigovernment activists about ATF's methods and leadership and the very matter of ATF intervention in these situations. More generally, ATF has been accused by the gun lobby of persecuting "ordinary citizens." However, ATF has its defenders and won support for its role in investigating the 1993 World Trade Center and 1995 OKLAHOMA CITY BOMBINGS.

Since its 2003 relocation, ATF continues its dual role of law enforcement and regulation. It aids local law enforcement officials in pursuing violent criminals, investigates many arson and explosives incidents, traces crime guns, maintains large arson and explosives databases, provides training for other law enforcement agencies, and maintains sophisticated forensics laboratories. It also continues its tense competitive-cooperative relation with the FBI—a rivalry some dismiss as a bureaucratic food-fight and others find dangerously detrimental to the fight against terrorism.

For more information

Bumgarner, Jeffrey B. *Federal Agents: The Growth of Federal Law Enforcement in America.* Westport, Conn.: Praeger, 2006.

Bureau of Alcohol, Tobacco, Firearms, and Explosives. Available online. URL: http://www.atf.gov/

Vizzard, William J. *In the Cross Fire: A Political History of the Bureau of Alcohol, Tobacco, and Firearms.* Boulder, Colo.: Lynne Rienner, 1997.

Jane G. Rainey
Eastern Kentucky University

Burger, Warren E. (1907–1995) chief justice of the Supreme Court Warren E. Burger served as the 15th CHIEF JUSTICE of the United States from June 10, 1969, to July 10, 1986. He was born on Constitution Day, September 17, 1907; he died June 29, 1995.

Burger's life was a Horatio Alger story. The fourth of seven children, he picked tomatoes on the family farm near St. Paul, Minnesota, and he had a number of odd jobs, including a daily newspaper route. He turned down a scholarship to Princeton because he could not have worked to contribute to the family finances. Instead, he attended the University of Minnesota at night and then St. Paul College of Law (now William Mitchell) where he graduated in 1931 magna cum laude. He did so well in LAW SCHOOL that the faculty appointed him an adjunct professor, and he taught there for 17 years while practicing law in St. Paul.

His practice was primarily corporate, real estate, and probate. He became active in local civic affairs and Republican Party politics. He was the floor manager for Minnesota governor Harold Stassen's 1948 and 1952 campaigns for the presidential nomination, which brought him to the attention of national party leaders. President Eisenhower's ATTORNEY GENERAL, Herbert Brownell, named Burger assistant attorney general of the Civil Division at the DEPARTMENT OF JUSTICE, where he earned a reputation for industry and loyalty.

In 1955 Burger was appointed to the U.S. COURT OF APPEALS for the District of Columbia. He began speaking and writing about the perennial problems facing the judicial system: crime and corrections, overloaded dockets, and delays. These activities brought him to the attention of President Nixon, who had campaigned against the activism of the WARREN COURT and for "law and order."

Chief Justice Burger was widely viewed as a conservative jurist who presided over a conservative court. But the Burger Court did not overrule Warren Court decisions on CONSTITUTIONAL LAW, managing only to refrain from extending them.

Chief Justice Warren E. Burger (Harris and Ewing, Collection of the Supreme Court of the United States)

Furthermore, in many new and controversial areas, the Burger Court rushed in where the Warren Court had feared to tread: the issues of ABORTION, AFFIRMATIVE ACTION, and the death penalty.

The chief justice seemed to tack back and forth, unwilling or unable to chart a clear course either for his own constitutional jurisprudence or for the Court's. His judicial performance was certainly better than his contemporary critics would allow and not appreciably different from many of his colleagues. Still, he was not a great justice. The Burger Court likely will go down in history as a transitional period between the liberal Warren Court and the conservative Rehnquist Court, both of which enjoyed considerably greater acclaim—and significant controversy—for their visions of the CONSTITUTION.

At his Senate confirmation hearing, Burger pledged to take seriously the title of being "chief justice of the United States." He kept this promise by using the prestige and influence of his office to initiate countless reforms of the federal and state courts. Indeed, his indefatigable work to improve the administration of the courts—more than his judicial decisions or opinions—was his most important contribution to JUSTICE. History will credit him with leading the modernization of the nation's court system.

Burger's last great public service was as chairman of the Commission on the Bicentennial of the U.S. Constitution. In the foreword to the pocket Constitution the commission published, he wrote, "For 200 years this Constitution's ordered liberty has unleashed the energies and talents of people to create a good life." That describes his own life and career as a jurist, administrator, and public servant to improve the cause of justice.

For more information

Blasi, Vincent, ed. *The Burger Court—The Counter-Revolution That Wasn't.* New Haven, Conn.: Yale University Press, 1983.

Lamb, Charles M., and Stephen C. Halpern, eds. *The Burger Court—Political and Judicial Profiles.* Champaign: University of Illinois Press, 1991.

Schwartz, Bernard, ed. *The Burger Court—Counter-Revolution or Confirmation?* New York: Oxford University Press, 1998.

Woodward, Bob, and Scott Armstrong. *The Brethren—Inside the Supreme Court.* New York: Simon & Schuster, 1979.

Thomas E. Baker
University of Scranton

Burger court The Burger court refers to the U.S. Supreme Court under the CHIEF JUSTICE WARREN BURGER from 1969 to 1986. The Court was more conservative or less defendant-orientated on criminal DUE PROCESS issues compared to that under CHIEF JUSTICE EARL WARREN.

When Richard Nixon campaigned for the presidency in 1968, he emphasized the theme of "law and order." Specifically, Nixon capitalized on the public's anxiety about rising crime, racial tensions, campus disturbances, and antiwar protests to advocate for changes in the courts as a response to those concerns. In particular, Nixon promised to appoint JUDGES who were "strict constructionists," who would not expand the definitions of the constitutional rights of the accused. Like many conservatives, Nixon argued that decisions by the WARREN COURT, such as *MAPP V. OHIO*, 367 U.S. 643 (1961), and *MIRANDA V. ARIZONA*, 384 U.S. 436 (1966), had "tied the hands of the police" and "let criminals walk free." He was faced with an immediate opportunity to reconfigure the Supreme Court as the office of chief justice of the United States awaited a nominee.

Earl Warren, who had served as chief justice since 1963 and who was closely identified with the Court's due process revolution, announced his intention to retire in 1968. President LYNDON JOHNSON's choice to succeed Warren, Abe Fortas, withdrew from consideration because of financial improprieties. As it was too late in Johnson's term to see another nominee confirmed, the choice of chief justice fell to Nixon, who selected Warren Burger in May 1969.

A native of Minnesota with a conservative judicial record, Burger served on the U.S. COURT OF APPEALS for the District of Columbia, where he had frequently written opinions that were critical of rulings by the Warren Court. Burger was easily confirmed by the Senate and took the oath of office on June 23, 1969. Burger served as chief justice for 17 years. During that time, the Court moved to the right as Burger was joined by three other Nixon appointees: Harry Blackmun, Lewis Powell, and WILLIAM REHNQUIST; one justice, JOHN PAUL STEVENS, appointed by Gerald Ford; and Ronald Reagan's first appointee, SANDRA DAY O'CONNOR. Although they revisited many of the criminal justice issues considered by the Warren Court, the Burger court did not overturn *Mapp* or *Miranda*. Instead, they narrowed the application of those decisions. In the area of CAPITAL PUNISHMENT, however, it may be argued that the Burger court widened the Court's constitutional oversight.

SEARCH AND SEIZURE

In *Mapp v. Ohio*, 367 U.S. 643 (1961), the Court had ruled that improperly seized EVIDENCE must be excluded at trial. Critics claimed that this exclusionary rule allowed criminals to be set free simply because police officers made mistakes. The Burger court ruled on the admissibility of evidence a number of times, and although they did not abolish the exclusionary rule, they seriously modified it. For example *SCHNECKLOTH V. BUSTAMONTE*, 412 U.S. 218 (1973), held that although consent may be necessary for some WARRANTLESS SEARCHES, a suspect's consent may be valid even though he or she is unaware of the right to withhold consent. *Schneckloth* reflects the majority's willingness to distinguish FOURTH AMENDMENT rights from rights invoked during trial and to downgrade the importance of the former. Likewise, the Court greatly increased the opportunities for police to SEARCH SUSPECTS INCIDENT TO ARREST even for a traffic violation in *United States v. Robinson*, 414 U.S. 218 (1973), and to conduct warrantless searches on automobiles and their contents.

A most significant Fourth Amendment decision was *United States v. Leon*, 468 U.S. 897 (1984). Many opponents of the exclusionary rule have argued for a "good faith exception," where an honest mistake by police would allow otherwise illegally seized evidence to be offered in court. In *Leon*, the justices went partway toward such a total exception by allowing evidence obtained with an invalid search warrant to be used without restriction. Here the majority seemed to argue that if the purpose of the exclusionary rule is to deter illegal searches by the police, an honest mistake requires no deterrence, and therefore its results should not be banned from trial.

CONFESSIONS AND ATTORNEYS

The Burger court also addressed the scope of *Miranda*. Restricting its application, they ruled in *Harris v. New York*, 401 U.S. 222 (1971), that a statement made without the required warning might be used to impeach the testimony of a defendant who took the stand in his own defense. On the other hand, in *Brewer v. Williams*, 430 U.S. 387 (1977), the majority in a 5–4 decision excluded the statements of a defendant who, while being transported by police, led them to his victim's body. The officers had promised the suspect's attorney not to interrogate him, but one of them, knowing of the suspect's religious convictions, commented that it was tragic to see the little girl victim denied a Christian burial. Additionally, in *RHODE ISLAND V. INNIS*, 466 U.S. 291 (1980), the Court found that the *Miranda* protections are activated whenever a person in custody is "subjected to either express questioning or its equivalent." The Burger court strengthened *Miranda* safeguards when they held in *Edwards v. Arizona*, 451 U.S. 477 (1981), that once a suspect invokes his or her RIGHT TO COUNSEL, the police cannot continue questioning.

In another decision that expanded rather than limited the rights of the accused, the Court determined in *ARGERSINGER V. HAMLIN*, 407 U.S. 25 (1972), that the SIXTH AMENDMENT required that indigent defendants be provided counsel in MISDEMEANOR as well as FELONY trials if imprisonment could result.

CAPITAL PUNISHMENT

Perhaps the area where the Burger court most confounded predictions was in bringing the states' use of the death penalty under constitutional scrutiny. In 1972, the Court heard three capital cases grouped together as *FURMAN V. GEORGIA*, 408 U.S. 238 (1972). For the first time in its history, the Supreme Court considered whether the death penalty violated the EIGHTH AMENDMENT ban on CRUEL AND UNUSUAL PUNISHMENT. In a 5-4 decision, with each justice writing a separate opinion, they found the death penalty *as administered* unconstitutional. The reasoning of the justices varied from those who believed the punishment was inherently unconstitutional to the position that it was flawed when it was administered in a random and discriminatory way. The ruling practically invited the states to rewrite their capital statutes to meet the Court's concern about unbridled DISCRETION. Among the two major approaches chosen by the states, the Court preferred the version that allowed for more guidance to judges and JURIES involved in a bifurcated trial separating the guilt phase from the SENTENCING phase. They upheld such a law in *GREGG V. GEORGIA*, 428 U.S. 153 (1976). On the same day, the Court rejected mandatory death sentences in *Woodson v. North Carolina*, 428 U.S. 280 (1976), as such laws treated defendants as a "faceless, undifferentiated mass." Ultimately the Burger court's death penalty jurisprudence brought the use of capital punishment under the supervision of the Supreme Court, which would determine its conformity with the CONSTITUTION.

BURGER AS CHIEF JUSTICE

Those who thought the Supreme Court under the leadership of Chief Justice Burger would reverse the "rights revolution" of the Warren court were probably disappointed. At most, during those years, the Court modified and limited certain rights of the accused. It was a period of retrenchment rather than repeal. A more conservative Court would emerge after Burger's retirement when William Rehnquist became chief justice and Presidents Reagan and Bush appointed Justices Scalia, Kennedy, and Thomas.

For more information

Abraham, Henry J. *Justices, Presidents, and Senators: A History of U.S. Supreme Court Appointments from Washington to Bush II*. 5th ed. Lanham, Md.: Rowman and Littlefield, 2008.

Lamb, Charles M., and Stephen C. Halpern, eds. *The Burger Court: Political and Judicial Profiles*. Urbana: University of Illinois Press, 1991.

Maltz, Earl M. *The Chief Justiceship of Warren Burger, 1969–1986*. Columbia: University of South Carolina Press, 2000.

Wasby, Stephen L. *Continuity and Change: From the Warren Court to the Burger Court*. Pacific Palisades, Calif.: Goodyear, 1976.

Mary Welek Atwell
Radford University

burglary Burglary is a criminal offense consisting of the breaking and entering in the nighttime of another's dwelling place, with the INTENT to commit a FELONY inside. As the old adage states, "a man's home is his castle." It is the enjoyment of this castle, free from the midnight terror of an intruder, that the outlawing of burglary was designed to protect. Thus, the essence of the crime of burglary at common law is the violation of the security of the dwelling house, rather than a crime against property.

To prove common-law burglary, the state must meet all of the elements of the offense, which requires proof that the perpetrator's actions consisted of: (1) breaking, (2) entering, (3) a dwelling house, (4) in the nighttime, and (5) with the intent to commit a felony. To constitute a "breaking," one need not pry a lock or destroy property to gain entry. Pushing open an unlatched or partially opened door or window is sufficient. The breaking may even occur once the perpetrator has entered the house, or it may occur in an outbuilding near the premises. Of course, the entry must be without the consent of the owner of the premises. However, the dwelling need not be occupied at the time of the entry, so long as it is suitable for residential purposes and the occupant has the intent to return. The breaking must occur "at night," which is generally understood to mean that the sky contains insufficient sunlight to discern a person's face.

To be guilty of burglary, the perpetrator need not actually commit the intended felony. He need not carry away any goods. It is enough simply to enter the premises with the requisite intent. The intended felony may be one of a number of offenses, including LARCENY, rape, ASSAULT, or arson. The state generally may prove intent by circumstantial EVIDENCE, and if no explanation for the breaking and entering is apparent, a JURY may infer the perpetrator's intent was to commit larceny.

Under modern criminal statutes, many of the strict definitional rules of common-law burglary have been relaxed or abandoned. For example, in many states, mere entry into an occupied building or structure is sufficient; the "breaking" requirement has either been abandoned or it is stated as an alternative to entering (e.g., *breaking or entering*). Moreover, the common-law requirement for breaking into a "dwelling house" has been relaxed in many states. Many statutes define burglary to include the entry with intent to commit a crime into any "building," including stores and other business establishments. Indeed, in a number of states, the entry into a motor vehicle, railroad car, or vessel may constitute burglary. Also, the requirement that the offense occur "at night" generally has been eliminated; the unlawful entry may now occur at any time, day or night. Finally, the perpetrator need not intend to commit a felony to be guilty of burglary; it is now sufficient if the perpetrator intents to commit any crime, including petty larceny.

Interestingly, even in those states that have substantially modified the definition of burglary, the impact of the common law is still felt. Many states impose greater penalties on the perpetrator if the burglary occurs at night, or in a dwelling house, or if the perpetrator intended to commit a felony.

For more information

Torcia, Charles E. *Wharton's Criminal Law.* 15th ed., vol. 3. New York: Clark Boardman Callaghan, 1995.

Nathanael Causey
Assistant Professor of Law
United States Military Academy
West Point, New York

Burton, Harold Hitz (1888–1964) Supreme Court justice Harold Hitz Burton served as an associate justice of the United States Supreme Court in 1945–54, where he represented a moderate judicial approach, neither predictably liberal nor predictably conservative.

Burton was born in 1888 near Boston, where his father served as dean of the faculty at the Massachusetts Institute of Technology. After attending Bowdoin College, where he excelled as a student and as an athlete, Burton graduated from Harvard Law School. He then married Selma Florence Smith and joined her uncle's law firm in Cleveland, Ohio. He served with the Allied forces in Europe during World War I and afterward returned to private practice and civil affairs in Cleveland. He was elected to the Ohio legislature as a Republican in 1929 and became mayor of Cleveland in 1934. There he earned a reputation for integrity and economy. In 1940 Burton won a seat in the U.S. Senate where he served until his appointment to the Court. While in the Senate, Burton was a member of Harry S Truman's special committee to investigate the national defense. In addition to disclosing FRAUD and abuse in war CONTRACTS, the committee fostered a camaraderie between Truman and Burton that doubtless contributed to Truman's decision to make Burton his first appointment to the Supreme Court.

Burton's record in the Senate reflected the same values that would characterize his behavior on the bench. He was a moderate who supported CIVIL RIGHTS for African Americans and an internationalist who opposed communism. His character as a tireless worker who paid painstaking attention to detail followed him from the legislature to the judiciary. Truman's nomination of the Republican Burton to the Court was intended as a conciliatory gesture. His name was brought to the Senate in the midst of debate on an unemployment bill. He was confirmed unanimously without hearings, debate, or objection.

Burton served under CHIEF JUSTICES HARLAN FISKE STONE, FRED VINSON, and EARL WARREN, and during his tenure he observed the Court becoming more concerned with civil rights and CIVIL LIBERTIES. He wrote the Court's opinion in *Henderson v. United States* (1954), holding that SEGREGATION in railway dining cars violated the INTERSTATE COMMERCE ACT. He was an early supporter of overturning the "SEPARATE BUT EQUAL" principles of *PLESSY V. FERGUSON* and outlawing school segregation in *BROWN V. BOARD OF EDUCATION* (1954). Burton kept a diary during the Court's conferences on segregation, which has been a valuable source for understanding how Warren built consensus for the unanimous ruling. Burton's votes were mixed in cases where the civil liberties of suspected communists were at issue. In *Emspak v. United States* (1955) he voted with the majority to support the Fifth Amendment rights of witnesses before congressional committees. Burton also joined the majority in *Ullman v. United States* (1956), which upheld the Immunity Act limiting the use of Fifth Amendment protections in testimony before GRAND JURIES investigating threats to national security. In *Yates v. United States* (1957) Burton voted to limit the application of the Smith Act, which had outlawed the organizing activities of the Communist Party, but Burton's vote was cast on narrow procedural grounds. He did not agree with

Justice Harold Hitz Burton (Harris and Ewing, Collection of the Supreme Court of the United States)

Justices Black and Douglas that the Smith Act itself violated the First Amendment.

Burton disagreed with one of the Warren Court's early decisions applying the BILL OF RIGHTS to the states through the Fourteenth Amendment DUE PROCESS clause. In *Griffin v. Illinois* (1956) Burton dissented when the Court held that denying trial transcripts to indigent defendants violated due process. He would leave criminal procedure to be determined by the states.

Burton's votes on cases related to the economy are also evidence of his independence and non-ideological position. He opposed his good friend Truman's seizure of steel mills during a strike in *Youngstown Steel and Tube v. Sawyer* (1952). With the majority of the Court, Burton believed that the president could not seize private property in peacetime. During his first term on the Court, he wrote the opinion in *American Tobacco Company v. United States* (1946), holding that the tobacco industry formed a CONSPIRACY in violation of the SHERMAN ANTITRUST ACT. In two later dissents he took positions on both sides of the application of the Sherman Act. In *United States v. E. I. DuPont* (1957) Burton held that duPont should not be charged with monopolistic practices for a stock acquisition 40 years earlier. In *Toolson v. New York Yankees* (1953) he was in the minority who argued that major league baseball was a business subject to ANTITRUST LAWS.

Burton retired from the Court in 1958. He died in Washington, D.C., in 1964.

For more information

Berry, Mary Frances. *Stability, Security, and Continuity: Mr. Justice Burton and Decision Making in the Supreme Court 1945–1958*. Westport, Conn.: Greenwood Press, 1978.

Schwartz, Bernard, with Stephan Lesher. *Inside the Warren Court*. Garden City, N.Y.: Doubleday, 1983.

Mary Welek Atwell
Radford University

C

California v. Hodari D. 499 U.S. 621 (1991) In *California v. Hodari D.*, the Supreme Court held that a mere show of authority, without the application of physical force, is not a seizure within the meaning of the FOURTH AMENDMENT.

In *Hodari D.*, two police officers came upon several youths who surrounded a small red car. When the youths saw the officers approaching, all, including Hodari, took flight. As he was about to be overtaken by one of the officers, Hodari tossed away a small rock that later turned out to be cocaine. At his juvenile hearing, Hodari requested that the EVIDENCE be suppressed as a result of an illegal seizure. Hodari argued that once the officer displayed a "show of authority," a seizure had taken place under the Fourth Amendment and that the officer lacked PROBABLE CAUSE to seize him. The request was denied, but the trial JUDGE's ruling was later reversed by the California Court of Appeals. The California Supreme Court denied review, and the state appealed to the U.S. Supreme Court.

Justice ANTONIN SCALIA, writing for the majority, asserted that the only issue before the Court was whether at the time he dropped the cocaine Hodari had been "seized" within the meaning of the Fourth Amendment. Scalia wrote that the California Court of Appeals erred when it ruled that the officer's "show of authority" constituted a seizure under the Fourth Amendment. Justice Scalia noted that when an officer orders a person to stop, that person is seized only if he or she either complies with the order or is physically restrained by the officer. In this case, Hodari failed to comply with the officer's show of authority and was brought under physical control after the cocaine had been abandoned. Because the cocaine had been abandoned before the seizure occurred, it cannot be the fruit of an unreasonable SEARCH AND SEIZURE.

Interestingly, the Court sidesteps the issue whether the officer had probable cause to chase Hodari. The question whether Hodari's flight alone was sufficient to establish probable cause to make an investigative stop [*TERRY V. OHIO*, 382 U.S. 1 (1968)] is disposed of in a footnote. The issue was finally resolved in *ILLINOIS V. WARDLOW*, 528 U.S. 119 (2000), when the Court ruled that mere flight does provide sufficient probable cause for an investigative stop.

In dissent, Justice JOHN PAUL STEVENS argued that the majority mistakes an ARREST for an attempted arrest, a distinction made at common law. Just as an ASSAULT at common law does not require physical contact, neither does an attempted arrest. Assault is the threat of harm and does not require actual touching. If an attempted arrest is illegal at its inception, as Stevens maintained this was, the cocaine should be excluded under the exclusionary rule.

For more information

Aker, James R., and David C. Brody. *Criminal Procedure: A Contemporary Perspective.* Gaithersburg, Md.: Aspen, 1999.

Klein, Irving J. *Constitutional Law for Criminal Justice Professionals.* 3rd ed. South Miami, Fla.: Coral Gables, 1993.

James V. Calvi
West Texas A&M University

cameras in public places Cameras in public places refer to the use of surveillance cameras by the government in order to monitor streets, parks, and buildings for criminal activity. Local governments are increasingly using cameras to monitor public places, raising, for some, issues of privacy.

The average New Yorker is caught on camera 200 times per day. At first glance, the surveillance provided by these cameras does not appear to affect a person's reasonable expectation of privacy. After all, a camera in a public place merely captures still images or video of things taking place in public, where people already have only a limited expectation of privacy.

But cameras provide options that the eyes of an observer do not: Images may be magnified, digitally enhanced, viewed or replayed repeatedly, preserved forever, and perhaps even posted on the INTERNET for anyone to view. Cameras therefore create a greater intrusion on privacy, one that courts have acknowledged. As one court, *Sanders v. Am. Broad. Cos.*, 978 P.2d 67, 72 (Cal. 1999), explained, "The mere fact that a person can be seen by someone does not automatically mean that he or she can legally be forced to be subject to being seen by everyone." Although no court has invalidated the use of a camera in a public place, many have raised concerns about the effect on privacy of having cameras everywhere.

Cameras serve law enforcement ends. In some instances, unattended still or video cameras are installed permanently in high-crime areas. The footage from these cameras later serves as a valuable tool for the police in identifying and prosecuting criminals. After cameras were mounted in high-crime areas in Tacoma, Washington, and Baltimore, Maryland, police reported a significant drop in crime. Even if the actual crime is not captured on camera, the suspect may be identified entering or leaving a building around the time that a crime was known to have been committed. In one high-profile incident, a bank ATM camera captured footage of a truck outside Oklahoma City's federal office building just before the explosion that killed 167 people. Ultimately, that information helped police track down bomber Timothy McVeigh.

Most recently, Google Earth and Google Streetview have attracted attention for the comprehensive and detailed visual information they make available on the Internet. Personal images—such as images of pets or furniture captured through windows—is sometimes visible through the street-level views of homes, while even fenced backyards are visible through aerial satellite images. A couple recently sued Google, raising privacy and trespass claims, for making images of their home available online; however, their suit was dismissed.

Despite the privacy concerns about Google Earth and Google Streetview, these tools nonetheless help law enforcement solve crimes. As one of many examples, a Florida man was charged with illegally dumping a boat near his home after a deputy used images from Google Earth to locate the boat in the man's backyard.

The prevalence of cameras ultimately raises questions about the definition of a reasonable expectation of privacy in an age where surveillance is routine. Does a reasonable person continue to expect that he or she has any real privacy in public? Or has technology now limited our expectations of privacy to the confines of our home?

For more information

Clark, M. Wesley. "Pole Cameras and Surreptitious Surveillance," *FBI Law Enforcement Bulletin* 23 (2009).

Kallen, Stuart A., ed. *Are Privacy Rights Being Violated?* Detroit: Greenhaven, 2005.

Nancy Leong
William and Mary School of Law

capital punishment Capital punishment refers to the use of death or the taking of the life of a person found guilty of committing a crime, such as MURDER. The use of capital punishment is controversial, raising significant constitutional, ethical, and political issues.

The United States is one of the few modern democracies that retains the use of capital punishment. As of August 2009, 35 states as well as the U.S. military and the federal government authorize the death penalty. Fifteen states and the District of Columbia prohibit its use. The vast majority of executions (967 of 1,171) during the last three decades have taken place in the South, with 542 in Texas and Virginia alone. Thus, it may be argued that although the death penalty survives in the United States, it is largely a regional and even a local phenomenon.

During the modern period dating from 1977, the annual number of executions reached a high of 98 in 1999. Since that date, the number of people put to death each year has declined with 37 executions in 2008. Likewise, the number of death sentences handed down by JURIES has dropped from 328 in 1994 to 111 in 2008. There

Executions in the United States, 1930–2009

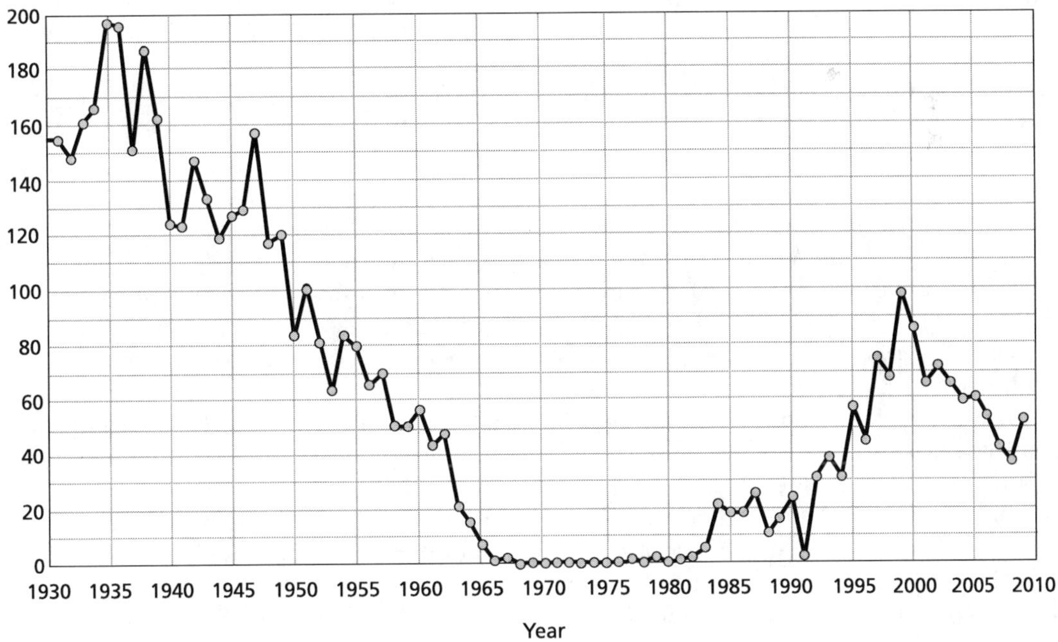

is no simple explanation for the reduction in the numbers of executions and death sentences, although the cost of capital punishment may be a factor in some cases. Additionally, all death penalty states now offer the alternative of life without PAROLE. Juries may be more inclined to sentence someone to prison than to sentence him or her to death, especially as more information about wrongful convictions has become available. At least 153 people have been exonerated and freed from death row since 1977. Such cases probably contribute to questions about the accuracy and fairness of the system.

Many questions have been raised regarding the influence of race on the application of the death penalty. There is clearly a racial disparity among those sentenced to death. While African Americans make up approximately 12 percent of the U.S. population, they constitute 42 percent of those on death row. A number of studies have shown that the race of the victim is also a significant factor in death penalty cases. Among cases resulting in execution, nearly 80 percent of the victims were white, although nationally only 50 percent of murder victims are white.

ESSENTIAL CASES: *FURMAN* AND *GREGG*

Although each state has the choice of whether or not to provide for the death penalty in its laws, all must operate within the framework of the U.S. CONSTITUTION as it has been interpreted by the Supreme Court. When one examines the law of capital punishment in the contemporary era, the 1972 case *FURMAN V. GEORGIA*, 408 U.S. 238 (1972), marks the beginning of the Court's involvement with the issue.

Prior to hearing arguments in *Furman*, the Court had handed down a series of rulings that effectively applied the BILL OF RIGHTS to the states, including the EIGHTH AMENDMENT prohibition of CRUEL AND UNUSUAL PUNISHMENT. However, the Court had not considered the question of whether the death penalty itself could be considered cruel and unusual, and therefore unconstitutional. In 1972, the justices ruled on three cases grouped under the heading *Furman v. Georgia*. Each member of the Court wrote a separate opinion. Some focused on racial discrimination, others on the unguided discretion of JURIES in death cases. However, a majority of five agreed that capital punishment *as administered by the states* violated the Eighth Amendment because its application was arbitrary and capricious. There were two possible outcomes after the ruling in *Furman*. Either the death penalty could be permanently abolished, or the states could rewrite their capital statutes to address the issue of arbitrariness.

Within a short time, more than two-thirds of the states created new laws to govern the application of the death penalty. Several chose to make the sentence mandatory for all first degree murders. The Court rejected this approach in *Woodson v. North Carolina*, 428 U.S. 280 (1976), holding that mandatory death sentences violated evolving standards of decency that mandated that each defendant merited individual consideration. Instead, the Court endorsed the approach in new Georgia and Texas laws in *GREGG V. GEORGIA*, 438 U.S. 153 (1976), and *Jurek v. Texas*, 428 U.S. 262 (1976). *Gregg* was a 7-2 decision, which found that the Georgia law addressed the problems with arbitrariness by listing the specific categories of capital offenses; by providing that trials would be divided into separate phases to determine guilt and sentencing; by listing aggravating circumstances; and by providing for direct review of capital cases by state supreme courts. With such provisions, it was assumed that jury deliberations and verdicts would be guided rather than capricious.

Since 1976, the Court has not revisited the issue of whether capital punishment overall is unconstitutional. Rather, subsequent Courts have woven an elaborate system of laws to guide its application. In the process, it has also stated that its imposition on certain individuals for specific crimes is not permitted.

PROPORTIONALITY

Prior to *Furman*, death had often been the punishment for rape, particularly when the victim was white and the accused rapist was African American. One of the earliest post-*Gregg* cases, *Coker v. Georgia,* 433 U.S. 584 (1977), concerned the constitutionality of capital punishment for the rape of an adult women. At the time, Georgia was the only state to treat such rapes as capital crimes. In *Coker,* the Court ruled that such sentences were disproportionate and violated evolving standards of decency. However, *Coker* did not resolve the issue of whether the rape of a child could merit a capital sentence. The Supreme Court addressed that issue in *Kennedy v. Louisiana,* 07-343 (2008). In that case, the Court ruled that if murder was not involved, capital punishment violated the Eighth Amendment's ban on cruel and unusual punishment, even if the victim was a child. They held that as only six states provided a death sentence for child rape, the national consensus opposed such punishments. They also pointed out that as no one had been executed for rape since 1964, such a sanction violated contemporary standards of decency.

The Court has also addressed the issue of whether an accomplice to murder who did not actually kill anyone may be sentenced to death. In *Edmund v. Florida,* 458 U.S. 782 (1982), the Court held that capital punishment for an accomplice who played a minor role in the murder but did not kill or intend to kill was disproportionate and therefore unconstitutional. The Court revisited the issue in *Tison v. Arizona,* 481 U.S. 137 (1987), in which a majority found that a defendant who was a major participant in a murder but did not actually kill could be sentenced to death.

WHO IS ELIGIBLE FOR DEATH?

The Supreme Court has determined that the execution of certain categories of defendants violated the Eighth Amendment ban on cruel and unusual punishment. In *Atkins v. Virginia,* 536 U.S. 304 (2002), the Court ruled against capital punishment for persons with mental retardation. However, the justices left it up to the individual states to determine whether an individual was mentally retarded. Thus, definitions and procedures vary widely among the states. On the other hand, the Court's ruling in *ROPER V. SIMMONS,* 543 U.S. 551 (2005), is quite clear. The justices held that the execution of anyone who was less than 18 years of age at the time of the crime was unconstitutional.

The Court has not resolved the issue of whether it is permissible to put someone to death if he or she was severely mentally ill at the time of the crime. In *Ford v. Wainwright,* 477 U.S. 399 (1986), the justices decided it was unconstitutional to execute a person who was insane at the time of death. However, they have not determined whether the state may medicate someone so he or she will be sufficiently sane to be executed.

May the state execute a person who is actually innocent? Most people would reject that idea. Some argue that the decline in public support for capital punishment from 80 percent in 1994 to 65 percent in 2006 is partly due to concern about wrongful convictions. However, the Supreme Court has never directly addressed the issue of executing an innocent person. In *HERRERA V. COLLINS,* 506 U.S. 390 (1993), the justices held that a defendant making a claim of innocence must show an independent violation of constitutional rights. He would not be granted an APPEAL simply because he could provide EVIDENCE that he was factually innocent. Although several justices wrote that executing an innocent person would be "perilously close to simple murder," the majority did not take that position.

With respect to the issue of race, in 1987 the Court considered whether statistical evidence of racial bias was sufficient to challenge the constitutionality of the death penalty. In *MCCLESKEY V. KEMP,* 481 U.S. 279 (1987), the defendant argued that the Baldus Study, a comprehensive statistical analysis, showed that the race of the victim had a significant bearing on the application of the death penalty and that therefore the capital system was permeated with racism. If McCleskey's claim had been upheld, it might have undermined the constitutionality of capital punishment. However, the Court decided that statistical evidence was insufficient and that each individual defendant must prove racial bias in his or her case.

THE METHOD OF EXECUTION

Since the death penalty was reinstated in 1976, more than 1,000 of the executions have been by lethal injection. In *Baze v. Rees,* 07-5439 (2008), the Court determined that death by the three-drug cocktail used in 30 states did not violate the ban on cruel and unusual punishment. Despite claims that the procedure, especially when administered by untrained correctional personnel, carried a risk of significant pain, the Court decided that lethal injection did not involve an "objectively intolerable" risk of serious harm. The majority noted that the Court has never ruled that a particular method of execution is unconstitutional; instead, it has left such decisions to the states.

DETERRENCE

A survey of CRIMINOLOGISTS in 2009 indicated that more than 88 percent of those surveyed believed that the death penalty was not a deterrent to murder. More than 80 percent of the executions since 1976 have taken place in the South, yet the southern states have the highest murder rates in the country.

For more information

Bohm, Robert M. *Death Quest II: An Introduction to the Theory and Practice of Capital Punishment in the United States.* New York: Lexis-Nexis, 2005.

Del Carmen, Rolando V., Scott Vollum, Kelly Cheeseman, Durant Frantzen, and Claudia San Miguel. *The Death Penalty: Constitutional Issues, Commentaries, and Case Briefs.* New York: Lexis-Nexis, 2005.

Paternoster, Raymond, Robert Brame, and Sarah Bacon. *The Death Penalty: America's Experience with Capital Punishment.* New York: Oxford University Press, 2008.

Mary Welek Atwell
Radford University

Capone, Alphonse (1899–1947) organized crime leader Alphonse Capone was born on January 17, 1899, in Brooklyn, New York. He eventually became the icon of notorious American gangsters.

While intelligent and capable as Capone's leadership of the Capone organization would demonstrate, he had little use for school. He left at age 14 to join the James Street GANG, where he became close friends with Johnny Torrio and Lucky Luciano.

While working in a Brooklyn saloon as a bouncer, Capone was slashed in the cheek several times with a straight razor, giving him an ugly scar and eventually the public nickname of Scarface. In order to avoid a MURDER charge, he moved in 1918 to Chicago, Illinois, at the invitation of Torrio, who had been working there for his uncle Big Jim Colosimo since 1909.

Capone worked for Torrio's uncle as bag man and enforcer. Seeing the opportunities PROHIBITION was creating for bootlegging, Torrio and Capone killed Colosimo in order to gain control of his organization. Numerous gangland slayings gave the Torrio-Capone organization complete control of the Chicago South Side.

Madison Street in downtown Chicago was the dividing line between the Torrio-Capone organization and their rival, the Charles Dion O'Banion gang on the North Side. The two organizations fought for control. Capone had O'Banion murdered on November 8, 1924. In retaliation, the O'Banion mobsters critically wounded Torrio on January 24, 1925. Recovered, he left Chicago for an extended vacation in Europe, leaving Capone as leader of the Capone organization.

Capone continued to expand his bootlegging operations with the connivance of elected officials, corrupt police, and others greedy for money. He supported local politicians favorable to him, sought to control local elections with thugs who intimated voters that were not supporters, sometimes intimidating, beating, or killing them.

On September 20, 1926, the O'Banion gang tried to kill Capone. In reply, Capone recruited members of the Purple Gang of Detroit to kill North Side gang leader, Brian "Bugs" Moran, in a garage Moran used for bootlegging activities. The killers dressed as police officers gunned down the seven men there in the Saint Valentine's Day (1929) massacre.

Capone was in Florida at the time of the Saint Valentine's Day massacre, but the federal government was seeking to put him behind bars. In 1928, Elliot Ness and his "Untouchables" had begun constant raids on Capone's bootlegging operations. In 1931, the Internal Revenue Service had Capone indicted for income tax evasion. During the October trial, the entire original JURY had to be replaced because it had been bribed. Convicted and sentenced to 11 years imprisonment at hard labor, he spent two years in the Atlanta penitentiary before being sent to ALCATRAZ. He was PAROLED November 19, 1939, suffering from paresis caused by syphilis. He went to his Palm Island, Florida, home, where he died on January 25, 1947.

For more information

Bergreen, Laurence. *Capone: The Man and the Era.* New York: Simon & Schuster, 1994.

Kobler, John. *Capone: The Life and World of Al Capone.* New York: Putnam, 1971.

Andrew J. Waskey
Dalton State College

Cardozo, Benjamin (1870–1938) Supreme Court justice Benjamin Cardozo was an associate justice of the United States Supreme Court from 1932 to 1938 who gained an international reputation for his efforts to reconcile CONSTITUTIONAL INTERPRETATION with the social and economic challenges of the New Deal. Cardozo was born to a prominent Sephardic Jewish family in New York City on May 24, 1870. Educated at Columbia College and Law School, he was admitted to the New York Bar in 1891 at the age of 21 and went into private practice in New York City.

Cardozo was elected to the New York Supreme Court in 1913, where he served briefly before receiving a temporary appointment to the New York Court of Appeals, the state's highest court. He was elected to the Court of Appeals in his own right in 1918 and became chief JUDGE in 1927. Under his leadership, the New York Court of Appeals developed a reputation as one of the leading courts in the nation, and Cardozo was widely regarded as one of the nation's premier common-law judges, especially in the areas of TORT and CONTRACT law. In *MacPherson v. Buick* (1916), for example, Cardozo established the foundations of modern PRODUCT LIABILITY law, while *Palsgraf v. Long Island Railroad* (1928) established the principle that negligence must be founded upon the foreseeability of harm to the injured party, and *Ultrameres Corporation v. Touche* (1931) extended protections against FRAUD to third parties.

Justice Benjamin Cardozo (Harris and Ewing, Collection of the Supreme Court of the United States)

On February 15, 1932, President Herbert Hoover appointed Cardozo to replace retiring justice OLIVER WENDELL HOLMES on the United States Supreme Court. Cardozo joined a court that soon found itself sharply divided over how to treat the New Deal legislation emerging from the FRANKLIN ROOSEVELT administration. As a leading member of the Court's liberal wing, Cardozo often maintained that Congress and the states should be accorded considerable deference in dealing with the nation's economic crises. In attempting to reconcile the traditional principles of U.S. CONSTITUTIONAL LAW to the changed conditions of the 1930s and to uphold key elements of the New Deal, Cardozo often found himself joining justices LOUIS D. BRANDEIS and Harlan Fiske Stone in dissent.

Cardozo was instrumental in leading the Court toward a more pragmatic, less abstract interpretation of the nature of FEDERALISM, away from the system of mutually exclusive rights and powers that had defined the relationships between the states and the federal government toward a relationship in which the rights and powers of the two layers of government would be understood as overlapping and concurrent. In *Steward Machine Co. v. Davis* (1937) and *Helvering v. Davis* (1937), Cardozo wrote for the Court in upholding the Social Security Act of 1935 based on Congress's authority under the taxing and spending clauses of the CONSTITUTION, while his majority opinion in 1937's *PALKO V. CONNECTICUT* laid out the Court's rationale for the INCORPORATION of elements of the BILL OF RIGHTS into the Fourteenth Amendment and the application of those constitutional protections to state actions.

In addition to the 150 opinions that he wrote during his six years on the U.S. Supreme Court, Cardozo was also the author of *The Nature of the Judicial Process* (1921), *The Growth of the Law* (1924), *Paradoxes of Legal Science* (1928), and *Law and Literature* (1931). He died in Port Chester, New York, on July 9, 1938, following a heart attack and a stroke.

For more information

Kaufman, Andrew L. *Cardozo.* Cambridge, Mass.: Harvard University Press, 1998.

Pollard, Joseph P. *Mr. Justice Cardozo.* 1935. Reprint. Westport, Conn.: Greenwood Press, 1970.

William D. Baker
Arkansas School for Mathematics and Science

career criminal Career criminal is a concept that refers to the series of criminal and delinquent acts committed by an individual from childhood through adolescence and adulthood.

A 1972 Philadelphia study found that only 6 percent of juveniles accounted for more than 50 percent of all juvenile contacts with police and 70 percent of all juvenile contacts involving FELONY offenses (Wolfgang, Figlio, and Sellin, 1972). This study led to the theory that a small number of career criminals account for a disproportionate amount of crime. Four main elements apply to the study of career criminals: participation, frequency, seriousness, and career length. Participation refers to the proportion of the population at large that is involved in offending behavior. Frequency is the rate of offending of active offenders. Seriousness refers to the magnitude of the offenses committed by a particular individual. Career length refers to the length of active offending time on the part of the offender.

The concept of career criminals stems from life-course theory. Life-course theory was founded by the Gluecks and examined desistence and criminality in 500 boys in Massachusetts in the 1920s and 1930s, following them through their 30s. Whether or not the young men engaged in criminal behavior was attributed to their bonds to society. While social bonds vary for individuals and by age, crime and delinquency were more likely to be expressed in those with weak bonds. Further, life-course theory builds on the fact that age and crime are highly correlated, causing criminal involvement to peak in midadolescence and decline in early adulthood. Turning points, such as marriage, graduation, starting a new job, having children, etc.) stop individuals from continuing to engage in criminal activities. Some individuals, however, do not stop engaging in criminal activities and offend through adulthood, becoming a career criminal (Sampson and Laub, 1993).

Research indicates that there is a small population who engages in deviant behavior at every stage in life. These individuals have an early onset of misbehavior that may be expressed differently due to varying opportunities. This population not only faces problems at every stage in life, but their access to conventional opportunities is further compounded by past criminal behavior (Moffitt, 1993: 679).

The study of career criminals has powerful implications. Because a small number of offenders account for a disproportionately large and severe amount of crime, effectively controlling this small number of offenders could significantly reduce crime rates. However, efforts to identify and predict career criminals have been largely unsuccessful.

Effectively studying career criminals requires the use of longitudinal data. Narrow perspectives using cross-sectional data on adolescents have dominated criminology, making the study of life course perspectives rather difficult (Sampson and Laub, 1993: 23).

For more information

Sampson, R. J., and J. H. Laub. *Crime in the Making: Pathways and Turning Points through Life.* Cambridge, Mass.: Harvard University Press, 1993.

Julie Yingling
Michigan State University

car theft and jacking Carjacking characterizes a compound crime that includes both ROBBERY and vehicle THEFT. The term became popular after some violent carjacking attacks and increased media attention in the 1980s. Perpetrators of this variety of motor vehicle theft apply the use of force and fear in the constructive presence of the owner. VICTIMIZATION may involve a secondary crime scene, and further crimes such as rape, aggravated ASSAULT, kidnapping, and MURDER.

The Susan Smith case received considerable media attention after she claimed a black man hijacked the car she was driving with her children still restrained in their car seats. This false reporting was an attempt to cover up the murder of her two sons, ages three, and 14 months, their lifeless bodies eventually found at the bottom of a lake. Police investigators replicated the alleged carjacking scenario and determined Susan had approximately 30 minutes to change the deadly course of events.

Police investigators are alert to the possibility of false carjacking and vehicle theft reports that attempt to conceal additional crimes. The police dealt with someone who suffered from bipolar mood disorder in the Susan Smith case. Eventually, her tearless plea and grammar syntax, specifically verb tense usage, "my children *needed* me," confirmed investigator suspicions of Susan's attempts to cover up the murders.

CARJACKING: LEGAL ELEMENTS

The police must verify that the crime of carjacking actually took place and prove the elements of the crime. For example, under Illinois law (720 ILCS 5/18–3), a person commits the FELONY of carjacking, "when he or she takes a motor vehicle from the person or immediate presence of another by the use of force or by threatening the imminent use of force." Car theft involves the taking of the vehicle without the owner's presence and the absence of robbery elements.

Aggravated vehicle carjacking provisions of Illinois law (720 ILCS 5/18 4) focuses on youthful or elderly victims and being armed with a weapon or firearm. The emphasis is on the level of force during the commission of the carjacking offense. Moreover, the offender causes great bodily harm, permanent disability, permanent disfigurement, or death of another person.

CARJACKING: CRIME ANALYSIS

According to the U.S. DEPARTMENT JUSTICE, Bureau of Justice Statistics, carjacking rates are highest in urban areas. Approximately 93 percent occur in cities or suburbs. Approximately 15 murders a year involve car theft, but not all are carjacking. Approximately 63 percent occur within five miles of the victim's home. Males commit 93 percent of carjacking offenses.

Weapons are the most obvious means of attack in 74 percent of carjacking cases. Offenders use firearms in 45 percent of the cases, knives in 11 percent, and other weapons in 18 percent of the cases. The victim resisted the offender in two-thirds of the carjacking crimes.

In conclusion, in approximately 24 percent of the cases, victims attempted confrontational resistance, such as threatening, attacking the offender, or trying to capture the offender. Law enforcement agencies need to discourage this kind of tombstone courage through active crime prevention campaigns.

For more information

Klaus, Nancy. *Carjacking, 1993–2002.* Washington, D.C.: U.S. Department Justice, Bureau of Justice Statistics, National Crime Victimization Survey, 2004. Available online. URL: http: bjs.odjp.usdoj.gov.

Thomas E. Baker
University of Scranton

cease and desist order A cease and desist order is an official court decree directing a party to refrain from engaging in some conduct or activity that is found to be detrimental to another party, a designated group, or the community as a whole. This order is generally sought by governmental administrative agencies as an enforcement tool to enjoin illegal and harmful conduct committed against people, legal entities, property, and the environment.

Federal agencies that have imposed such orders include but are not limited to the Federal Trade Commission, the National Labor Relations Board, the SECURITIES AND EXCHANGE COMMISSION, and the International Trade Commission. For example, the FTC will impose such an order where an entity such as a partnership, corporation, or other person or individual has been found guilty of unfair methods of competition and unfair or deceptive acts or practices, such as "price discrimination," in interstate commerce. Civil penalties for the violations of cease and desist orders may be recovered in subsequent civil proceedings.

After receiving DUE PROCESS in an administrative agency hearing, a defendant ordered by an administrative law JUDGE to refrain from continuing specifically defined illegal practices in violation of a federal statute may contest the findings and the decision by seeking JUDICIAL REVIEW of any cease and desist order but must continue to comply with the order, which may include the filing of annual or special reports or providing specific disclosure of internal proprietary information. The UNITED STATES COURT OF APPEALS for the relevant circuit has exclusive JURISDICTION to affirm, enforce, modify, or set aside such judicial order. The United States Supreme Court may grant a valid petition to review the validity of such an order.

For more information

The Administrative Procedure Act (APA) 5 U.S.C. § 551 et Seq. Administrative Law and Regulatory Policy: Problems, Text, and Cases, by Breyer, Stewart, and Sunstein.

J. David Golub
Touro College,
New York Institute of Technology, Kean College of New Jersey

censorship Censorship is legal banning of the publication or distribution of printed or recorded materials by the government.

Once a relatively straightforward constitutional concept, censorship has become an increasingly contested issue. Anglo-American constitutional discourse traditionally saw governmental censorship as a regrettable (though occasionally necessary) departure from the overriding normative goal of providing constitutional protection for the widest possible "free exchange of ideas." Censorship, in this frame, signified external governmental restraint on the internal preferences of individuals to speak or write "their own mind."

More recently, critical theorists who embrace continental literary and political theory have treated censorship as a linguistic practice. By that any one person's expression inevitably depends on shared understandings with others and on culturally constructed conventions of what kinds of utterances count as meaningful discourse. From this perspective, the question is not whether there is censorship but, rather, what kinds of censorship are in force and what is their effect on the existing distribution of power and knowledge.

Debate over censorship emerged in relationship to prior restraints imposed by governmental officials. The English licensing system, in which an official censor decided what publications were allowed to go to press, provided the classic example. Although licensing disappeared during the 17th century, the issue of prior restraints remained a central concern of U.S. constitutional doctrine. Litigation over forms of prior restraint that could seem analogous to licensing appeared in a variety of circumstances: INJUNCTIONS against libelous publications (*Near v. Minnesota* [1931]); local ordinances that required speakers or persons distributing printed matter to obtain special licenses (*Marsh v. Alabama* [1946]); licensing arrangements aimed at entertainment with sexually explicit content (*Joseph Burstyn, Inc. v. Wilson* [1951]); laws against "hate speech" (*R.A.V. v. St. Paul* [1992]); congressional limitations on political expenditures (*Buckley v. Valeo* [1976]); and, in the famous "Pentagon Papers case," an injunction against publication of a secret history of U.S. involvement in Vietnam (*New York Times Co. v. United States* [1971]).

Although the U.S. Supreme Court ruled in favor of "freedom of expression" and against "censorship" in all these cases, even celebrants of the anticensorship position acknowledged a countertradition. The Court, for example, allowed public school officials to censor student publications (*Hazelwood School District v. Kuhlmeier* [1980]) and upheld a contractual arrangement that barred current or retired CIA officers from publishing anything that had not been cleared by the agency (*Snepp v. U.S.* [1980]). According to the traditional anticensorship position, decisions such as this simply meant that the Court would, in a few, very narrowly defined, special circumstances, allow governmental censorship.

Critics of this perspective, however, insist that discussions of censorship cannot be limited by the classical concept of governmental action or focused on allegedly neutral constitutional doctrines and on "core principles" such as the requirement that government regulation not "create an external chill" on free discussion. Constitutional debate over censorship has never been simply about expression per se, the critical view argues, but has always involved political decisions about the proper distribution of social power. Expression does not achieve protection because, in some abstract constitutional calculus, it involves the "free" exchange of ideas but because the political agenda to which the expression is connected seems legitimate to those powerful people who possess the potential to censor it. Disputes about expression over the INTERNET, for instance, have highlighted the ways in which traditional copyright law both restricts and enables expression. Critics also argue that it is no accident that, during the last 30 years, the Supreme Court has struck down governmental measures aimed at reining in large political expenditures and laws designed to combat racist and pornographic speech and has upheld regulations aimed at protecting the national security bureaucracy.

More broadly, critics note that the traditional idea of censorship, with its focus on governmental action, ignores the day-to-day regulation of expression by powerful private groups. Media conglomerates routinely decide what counts as "news" and what kinds of cultural products seem worthy of distribution, while corporations of all kinds possess broad power to regulate—and even effectively silence—the expression of their employees. A marketplace of ideas, even if entirely freed from governmental restraints, would hardly qualify as a "free" one, in this critical view.

The critical perspective on censorship suggests no clear set of constitutional principles or legal doctrines. Indeed, because it emphasizes the complex social-linguistic networks through which expression is articulated and received, it tends to place in the foreground the inability of universal principles, such as "no prior restraints" or the freest possible "exchange of ideas," to untangle the complex, censorship-related issues such as "hate speech." As a consequence, this critical perspective, though well represented in legal-constitutional scholarship, has yet to find its way into legal-constitutional doctrine, which is still closely tied to the traditional concept of eliminating "governmental censorship" of "the exchange of ideas." This long-established view of censorship, its supporters maintain, still constitutes one of the bulwarks of American constitutionalism.

But it is the rise of the Web and Internet as a new communications tool that has raised new questions about censorship. Specifically, the concern is access or exposure of minors to sexually suggestive materials. The 1996 Communications Decency Act (CDA) sought to regulate the distribution of pornographic materials, but it was declared unconstitutional in *Reno v. ACLU,* (521 U.S. 844, 1997). Congress then passed the Child Online Protection Act, but again in *Ashcroft v. American Civil Liberties Union,* 542 U.S. 656 (2004), the Court again ruled that efforts to regulate nonobscene but sexually explicit material on the Web violated the First Amendment.

Finally, the perceived increase in violence associated with video games has led to demands to regulate them. In 2005 the state of California sought to restrict the sale of violent video games to individuals under the age of 18. But in *Brown v. Entertainment Merchants Association* 564 U.S. _ (2011), the Supreme Court ruled that violent video games are a form of protected speech under the First Amendment and, therefore, the California law was unconstitutional.

For more information

Burt, Richard, ed. *The Administration of Aesthetics: Censorship, Political Criticism, and the Public Sphere.* Minneapolis: University of Minnesota Press, 1994.

Jansen, Sue Curry. *Censorship: The Knot That Binds Power and Knowledge.* New York: Oxford University Press, 1991.

Post, Robert C. *Censorship and Silencing: Practices of Cultural Regulation.* Los Angeles: J. Paul Getty Museum, 1998.

Norman L. Rosenberg
Macalester College

certiorari, writ of A writ of certiorari is a discretionary writ—an order with the force of law—that has long been in use in English and American judicial practice. Pronounced *sir*-sho-*rare*-ee, certiorari is a Latin term literally meaning "to be informed of; to be made certain." As the word suggests, a writ of certiorari requires a lower court to provide a higher court with the record of a specific judicial proceeding so that the higher court can review, "be informed" about that record, and "made certain" that the lower court's judgment is free from legal errors.

In England writs of certiorari originally were issued at the monarch's prerogative to remedy an official's abuse of authority or neglect of duty. English use of such writs evolved gradually to where private individuals could apply to chancery courts beginning in the 14th century and then, in the 16th century, to the Court of Queen's Bench and, after 1857, to the High Court to persuade jurists to issue a writ of certiorari commanding jurists in lower courts to certify—return—their proceedings so that their actions could be reviewed.

In the United States, writs of certiorari (or their equivalent) are an important discretionary avenue of review in state and federal courts. Two states, Oklahoma and Rhode Island, specify writs of certiorari as a possible way to obtain review of provisional (interlocutory) judgments of lower courts. While some states have statutorily abolished the term *certiorari* in lieu of an appellate "petition of review" (Alaska, Idaho), a "writ of supervisory control" (Montana), or commonly a petition for "leave to APPEAL," these actions are similar in nature and purpose to certiorari. At the federal level, about 90 percent of the cases that come to the U.S. Supreme Court arrive via petitions for a writ of certiorari (or "cert." for short). The procedure governing consideration of writs of certiorari, found in Part III, rule 10 of the Rules of the Supreme Court, specifies: "Review on a writ of certiorari is not a matter of right, but of judicial DISCRETION." The Supreme Court usually decides to "deny cert.," rejecting 90 percent of petitions for writs of certiorari filed. It has not always had complete discretion to choose the cases it would hear. Prior to the Judiciary Act of 1891, which created intermediate federal courts of appeal, the Supreme Court had no control over its docket. The 1925 Judiciary Act ("Judges' Bill") expanded the Court's certiorari JURISDICTION while mandatory appeals were severely restricted.

Because the Supreme Court has complete discretion to grant or to deny "cert.," it consequently has broad authority to set its own agenda. The seven formal rules pertaining to its jurisdiction on writs of certiorari (Part III, rules 10–16) provide meager insight into the practical factors shaping how justices determine which cases to decide. Students of judicial decision making have devoted considerable attention to exploring this aspect of the black box that envelops the choices justices make. The prevailing view is that all judicial choices, including decisions on "cert." petitions, result from "strategic" interactions among the justices which entail each jurist pursuing policy goals interdependently with colleagues within the context of internal and external social rules (institutions) which structure judicial practices. Over the past two decades, the Supreme Court has exercised its discretion to deny "cert.," thereby restricting appellate access while, at the same time, the number of cases filed has soared. By the mid-1990s more than 6,500 new cases were filed annually while the Court granted "cert." to fewer than 5 percent.

For more information

Epstein, Lee, and Jack Knight. *The Choices Justices Make.* Washington, D.C.: Congressional Quarterly Press, 1998.

Provine, Doris Marie. "Certiorari." In Janosik, Robert J., ed., *Encyclopedia of the American Judicial System,* 3 vols. New York: Charles Scribner's Sons, 1987, II: 783–794.

James C. Foster
Department of Political Science
Oregon State University

Chase, Samuel (1741–1811) Supreme Court justice Samuel Chase was an associate justice of the United States Supreme Court and the only member of the Supreme Court ever to be impeached by the House of Representatives.

A native of Maryland, Chase had long been active in state politics and was a leading supporter of the American Revolution in Maryland. He was a member of the state legislative assembly (1764–84), a member of the Continental Congress (1774–78, 1784–85), and a signer of the DECLARATION OF INDEPENDENCE. As a member of the Maryland ratification convention, he opposed the ratification of the U.S. CONSTITUTION but later became an ardent Federalist and a supporter of the new Constitution. He was the chief JUDGE of the Maryland General Court (1791–96), during which time he became involved in a brief scandal and was the subject of an IMPEACHMENT investigation by the Maryland legislature.

Justice Samuel Chase (Painting by Jarvis, and engraving by H. B. Hall, Collection of the Supreme Court of the United States)

In 1796 Chase was appointed to the Supreme Court by President George Washington to fill the seat vacated by John Blair. He was the ninth justice appointed to the Court, and he held the seat until his death in 1811. Chase wrote the lead opinion in the important case of *Ware v. Hylton* (1796), which declared federal treaties to be superior to conflicting state laws. Chase wrote a provocative opinion in the case of *Calder v. Bull* (1798) that foreshadowed the Court's declaration of a power of JUDICIAL REVIEW in the later case of *MARBURY V. MADISON* (1803), as well as later debates over "substantive DUE PROCESS." In *Calder,* Chase argued that legislative power was limited by "certain vital principles in our free republican government," even if those principles had not been explicitly included in the constitutional text. In the case of *United States v. Worrall* (1798), Chase wrote an early opinion denying the existence of a federal common law of crimes, which would have allowed federal prosecutions based on judge-made law rather than a specific statute.

In 1804 Chase was impeached by the House of Representatives, but he was acquitted by a four-vote margin in a trial by the Senate in 1805. In the two years prior to the elections of 1800, Chase had been particularly aggressive, and some thought biased, in conducting criminal trials of various opponents of the Federalist administration. Chase had also actively participated in the reelection campaign of President John Adams in 1800. In 1803 he delivered an inflammatory political speech to a GRAND JURY in Maryland. Based on these events, the Jeffersonians, who had won the congressional and presidential elections of 1800, impeached Chase for abusing his judicial office and using it in a partisan manner. His eventual ACQUITTAL both eased fears that the impeachment power would be used to undermine judicial independence and discouraged federal judges from further involvement in partisan politics.

For more information

Presser, Stephen. *The Original Misunderstanding: The English, the Americans, and the Dialectic of Federalist Jurisprudence.* Durham, N.C.: Carolina Academic Press, 1991.

Rehnquist, William H. *Grand Inquests: The Historic Impeachments of Justice Samuel Chase and President Andrew Johnson.* New York: William Morrow, 1992.

Keith E. Whittington
Princeton University

chemical castration Chemical castration refers to a criminal PUNISHMENT imposed on individuals convicted of some SEX CRIMES such as rape. The use of this punishment is controversial on several counts, including the criticism that its imposition assumes that sex crimes are about sex and not power or aggression.

Chemical castration aims to reduce RECIDIVISM among male sexual criminals by reducing their levels of testosterone. The difficulties of stopping recidivism in sex criminals prompted some legal authorities to advise that SEX OFFENDERS be given medications that reduce the intensity of sexual drives. The term *chemical castration* is actually a misnomer, since no castration in fact occurs when a drug is used. The drug most often employed, an Upjohn product called Depo-Provera, lowers the testosterone level in men and thus reduces sex drive. When use of the drug stops, the sex drive returns to a normal level.

The procedure has a fairly long history, though it only became widespread in the 1990s. R. M. Foote first administrated progesterone hormonal compounds to men in 1944 to reduce testosterone levels. The procedure stayed largely forgotten until John Money decided to try it with sex offenders in the late 1960s. The drug, medroxyprogesterone acetate (MPA), that Money used is not medically approved for rendering men impotent. It is supposed to be used to reduce abnormal levels of sex drive, to return sexual fantasies to normal levels, to permit patients to control their socially prohibited urges, and to allow them relief from the intrusive ideas and urges that they have great difficulty controlling.

The brand name Depo-Provera applies to depot medroxyprogesterone acetate (DMPA). It is a birth control drug that is normally prescribed to women. Depo-Provera gained national attention in 1983, when a Texas JURY sentenced convicted rapist Joseph Frank Smith to 10 years of PROBATION instead of prison after he volunteered to undergo Depo-Provera therapy. Smith, known as the "ski mask rapist," had been convicted for raping the same woman twice. Smith moved to the Richmond, Virginia, area after his conviction. He appeared on the television news magazine show *60 Minutes* as an example of the success of chemical castration. However, while on Depo-Provera and while promoting himself as the poster child for sex offender rehabilitation, Smith continued his career as a rapist. In 1998, he pled guilty to committing two sex crimes. Virginia authorities suspected that he really committed 75. Smith received a 40-year sentence for breaking and entering, aggravated sexual battery, and two counts of ATTEMPTed oral and anal sodomy in a June 1993 attack on a five-year-old girl.

Despite the heavily publicized Smith debacle, a number of states proceeded to pursue chemical castration. In 1996, California became the first state to mandate the procedure. The California legislature required any pedophile who had been convicted twice to be periodically injected, after release from prison, with a drug that inhibited sex drive. Sex offenders who voluntarily submitted to surgical castration were exempt. THE AMERICAN CIVIL LIBERTIES UNION (ACLU) objected to the California law as well as subsequent state ones that mandated castration for several reasons. The EIGHTH AMENDMENT prohibits CRUEL AND UNUSUAL PUNISHMENT, which may cover the side effects of chemical castration drugs. The drugs have also been linked to high blood pressure, shrinkage of the testicles, diabetes, heart problems, and irregular gallbladder functioning. Other critics of chemical castration argue that the treatment misses the underlying problem because rape is a crime of power and not the result of uncontrollable sexual urges.

For more information

Taylor, Gary. *Castration: An Abbreviated History of Western Manhood*. New York: Routledge, 2002.

Caryn E. Neumann
Miami University of Ohio

chief justice Chief justice is the title of the Supreme Court justice nominated by the president to lead the rest of the Court. The chief justice has both formal and informal powers that shape how the Court functions.

The position of chief justice was mentioned in the CONSTITUTION under the IMPEACHMENT clause and was formally created by the Judiciary Act of 1789. Neither, however, mentions the scope of duties or powers of the chief justice. The role of the chief justice has been developed over the course of 200 years by the individuals who have filled the post. The position of chief justice is often referred to as *primus inter pares,* Latin for first among equals. This is not entirely accurate, though. The chief justice does have unique responsibilities and powers that set the position apart from the associate justices. In addition to hearing and deciding cases with the rest of the justices, the chief justice's role can be divided into three parts: formal, informal, and extrajudicial.

The chief justice's formal powers include being able to assign who will write the opinion in a case (if they are in the majority), controlling and managing discussion of the cases in the weekly private conference, and determining whether either side presenting oral arguments in a case can go over their allotted time. Additionally, the chief justice handles a myriad of administrative duties ranging from oversight of the premises of the Supreme Court to reviewing work conditions for Court employees.

These formal powers are just the beginning, though. The chief justice's informal powers are based on his or her ability to lead the rest of the Court. Chief Justices JOHN MARSHALL, Charles Evans Hughes, and EARL WARREN were renowned for their ability to get majorities together for major cases through persuasion, example, and conviction, while Chief Justices Edward White and FRED VINSON are regarded as largely ineffective leaders. Conversely, both WARREN BURGER and WILLIAM REHNQUIST are credited with excellent management skills in overseeing not just the Supreme Court but the entire federal court system.

The chief justice is the most highly visible of the justices, and his actions and beliefs carry an added weight not only on the Court but also in the public. It is this visibility that is key to the chief justice's extrajudicial functions. The chief justice is involved in lobbying Congress for funding for the judicial branch, developing standards for judicial ethics at all federal court levels, leading the conference of all the federal court JUDGES, and presiding over impeachment trials in the Senate. These extrajudicial functions are critical to establishing and maintaining the stature of the Supreme Court and play an important role in the operation of the Court.

There have been 17 chief justices since the adoption of the Constitution. In chronological order, they are:

John Jay (1789–1795)
John Rutledge (1795)
Oliver Ellsworth (1796–1800)
John Marshall (1801–1835)
Roger Brooke Taney (1836–1864)
Salmon Portland Chase (1864–1873)
Morrison Remick Waite (1874–1888)
Melville Weston Fuller (1888–1910)
Edward Douglass White (1910–1921)
William Howard Taft (1921–1930)
Charles Evans Hughes (1930–1941)
Harlan Fiske Stone (1941–1946)
Fred M. Vinson (1946–1953)
Earl Warren (1953–1969)
Warren Earl Burger (1969–1986)
William H. Rehnquist (1986–2005)
John G. Roberts, Jr. (2005–)

For more information

Fish, Peter Graham. *The Office of Chief Justice.* Charlottesville: White Burkett Miller Center, University of Virginia, 1984.

Steamer, Robert J. *Chief Justice: Leadership and the Supreme Court.* Columbia: University of South Carolina Press, 1986.

Christopher Shortell
University of California, San Diego

child abuse Child abuse is mistreatment of a child. Child abuse is a criminal offense that can take many forms.

There are three levels of child abuse: collective, institutional, and individual. Collective abuse is a large-scale, cultural issue and involves ignoring the natural and legal rights of children.

Institutional abuse occurs at the level of social institutions such as schools and social welfare programs. Individual abuse is harm done to a child by someone with authority over the child and usually involves a parent or caregiver.

Abuse is generally viewed as a pattern of behavior, though it can be a one-time event. There are four categories of abusive behaviors: physical, emotional, sexual, and neglect.

Physical abuse describes any act that results in a nonaccidental injury by a person who is providing care for a child. INTENT to injure a child is not central to the definition, though the act must be willful. Physically abusive actions include throwing things, hitting, kicking, biting, shaking, burning, etc. It is behavior that can cause physical injury or death.

Emotional abuse, sometimes referred to as psychological abuse, is that which does harm to the child's sense of self, self-esteem, or emotional well-being. Emotional abuse includes rejecting, terrorizing, denying stimulation, isolating, degrading, and devaluing a child. It is present when a caregiver inadequately nurtures, is inattentive to the child's development, and/or shows a lack of concern about maladaptive behavior.

Sexual abuse refers to a wide range of behaviors that involve sexual contact or interaction between a child and an adult. It can be intrafamilial, within the FAMILY; or extrafamilial, someone external to the family who is known or unknown to the child. Sexually abusive behaviors include rape, voyeurism, pornography, fondling, and exhibitionism.

Neglect differs from other forms of abuse in that it is passive. Neglect is an act of omission rather than commission. It involves not meeting a child's physical, emotional, medical, or educational needs. Neglect is the most common form of abuse.

Each year about 800,000 or nearly 10 percent of all children, are officially determined to have been abused or neglected. It is important to note that many more children are abused, though their VICTIMIZATION goes unreported. Of reported cases, more than half are age seven or younger. Girls account for 52 percent of reports and boys 48 percent. A majority of cases involve neglect. It is responsible for 59 percent of cases, physical abuse 11 percent, sexual abuse 8 percent, emotional abuse 5 percent, and 13 percent involve multiple forms. Other types of abuse such as abandonment account for 4 percent. Minority children, including African-American, Native-American, and Hispanic children are slightly more likely to be reported abused. Asian children have the lowest rates.

Approximately 1,600 children die annually as a result of abuse or neglect. Children under age four account for 76 percent of all abuse fatalities. Parents are responsible for 70 percent of these fatalities. Head injuries are the most common fatal injury suffered by children in these cases.

Parents are the primary perpetrators of child abuse. They are responsible for 74 percent of reported cases of abuse. Mothers are the most likely perpetrators of child abuse, though in many case children are abused by both parents. Younger parents are more likely than older parents to mistreat children. Parents who suffered abuse in childhood have a tendency to engage in violent behavior. The presence of substance abuse also increases the likelihood that abuse will occur in a home. Additionally, caregivers who are isolated from their extended families and lack a support in stressful situations are more likely to abuse their children. Additional characteristics of parents who abuse their children include depression, spousal tension, unrealistic expectations of children, and high anxiety.

The effects of child abuse are cumulative. The longer the abuse lasts, the more enduring the effect on the child. The effects of child abuse are short and long term and include behavioral, emotional, and physical problems. Short-term effects include regression, running away, lower intellectual functioning, and difficulty with interpersonal relationships, among others. Possible long-term effects include post-traumatic stress disorder (PTSD), delinquent or criminal behavior, substance abuse, mood and personality disorders, and low self-esteem.

There is no single, identifiable cause of child abuse. It is a complex problem. Attempts to explain abuse can be placed into three categories. First, the psychopathological model places emphasis on the characteristics of the abuser as the primary cause of abuse. It focuses on characteristics of the abusive parent, such as mental illness or personality traits. Second, the interactional model focuses on family structure and the role of the child. It argues that when a child fails to meet parental expectations abuse may occur. Third, the sociocultural model stresses society as the primary cause of abuse. It emphasizes cultural factors such as social learning, poverty, lack of education, and other social problems.

Child abuse prevention strategies involve all levels of society. Some programs, such as community awareness campaigns, are designed to educate the public about child abuse. School-based education programs are efforts to assist children in preventing, recognizing, and reporting their own abuse. The most common approaches focus on improving parental competence. These initiatives attempt to improve parenting skills of at-risk caregivers with the hope of reducing abuse rates.

Child abuse occurs in private and can easily be hidden. When it is discovered, various public welfare and law enforcement agencies respond. All states have mandatory reporting laws that require teachers, doctors, and others to report suspected abuse. These statutes allow a child to be removed from the home if in imminent danger. When abuse is deemed present, the case can be handled by social services or processed by criminal, family, or juvenile court. Statutes in many states classify child abuse as a FELONY offense.

The Child Abuse Prevention and Treatment Act (CAPTA) provides federal funds to states for services to mistreated children and their parents. The act has improved the legal frameworks under which social service agencies function. Official responses to substantiated claims of child abuse usually involve Child Protective Services (CPS) and/or the CRIMINAL JUSTICE SYSTEM. CPS focuses on protecting the child by investigating reports, providing treatment for offenders, coordinating with other agencies, and offering prevention programs.

The criminal justice system is a more punitive approach that can involve incarceration, PROBATION, and diversion programs. Most people who mistreat children are not prosecuted for their crimes. Cases are most likely to be prosecuted when they involve severe abuse and the defendant has a prior criminal record. Only 10 percent of child abuse cases proceed to trial. PLEA BARGAINING for a lesser sentence is common. This is due in part to the difficulties PROSECUTORS face with these types of cases. Physical EVIDENCE is rarely available, and often the victim is the only witness. The credibility of child witnesses is often questioned. The National Center for Prosecution of Child Abuse was established in 1985 to provide training and resources for investigators and prosecutors in an effort to increase the number of successful child abuse prosecutions.

For more information

Barnett, Ola, Cindy L. Miller-Perrin, and Robin D. Perrin. *Family Violence Across the Lifespan: An Introduction.* 2nd ed. Thousand Oaks, Calif.: SAGE, 2005.

Wallace, Harvey. *Family Violence: Legal, Medical, and Social Perspectives.* Boston: Pearson, 2008.

Karen S. Miller
West Virginia Wesleyan College

child pornography Child pornography, generally defined as sexually explicit materials made by exploiting children, is not protected by the First Amendment.

Child pornography is a fairly new legal concept. It was not until *New York v. Ferber* (1982) that sexually explicit material involving underage individuals became a separate category outside the confines of mainstream OBSCENITY law. In that case, the Supreme Court found that the involvement of children in the production of child pornography was psychologically and physically harmful to them. Consequently, the constitutional protections required in obscenity prosecutions did not apply in child pornography cases. *Ferber* and subsequent cases held that child pornography had no redeeming social significance and that mere possession or viewing of child pornography could be a crime.

Federal and state laws have tried to keep pace with new concerns and technologies. The original federal law enacted in 1977 criminalized interstate commercial child pornography. However, child pornography was not a major commercial enterprise: Only one person was convicted under the law in nine years. In 1984 Congress broadened the law to include noncommercial sexual exploitation of children. Subsequently the law was modified to outlaw the electronic transmission of child pornography.

Prior to 1996 the actual participation of children in the production of pornography was the *sine qua non* of the regulation scheme. However, in 1996 Congress shifted its focus from defining child pornography in terms of the harm inflicted upon real children to a determination that child pornography was evil in and of itself, whether it involved real children or not. Congress argued that even simulated child pornography increases the activities of child molesters and pedophiles. The law was declared unconstitutional in December 1999 by the Ninth UNITED STATES COURT OF APPEALS.

Despite the near universal abhorrence of child pornography, its regulation poses several problems. Neither the word *child* nor the word *pornography* has a universal meaning. Different cultures define childhood differently. In some countries a person ceases to be a child at age 13. In other countries marriage at any age makes one an adult. Prior to 1984, U.S. child pornography laws did not apply if the participants were over the age of 16—now it is 18. Even today age requirements are not uniform in the states. The variety of definitions is a major problem if governments attempt to apply their laws to producers or distributors of materials available on the INTERNET.

Determining what constitutes child pornography is also difficult. For some, any picture of a naked child is child pornography, can have no redeeming social value, and must be outlawed. This perception has led to the prosecution of such works as *Radiant Identities* and *The Last Day of Summer* by photographer Jock Sturges, *The Age of Innocence* by French photographer David Hamilton, and the Academy Award–winning film, *The Tin Drum*.

Most Americans, and the courts, would not go to that extreme. To do so would make all parents with pictures of their naked children criminals. Because drawing the line between the need to prevent the sexual exploitation of children and the right to take nonexploitative pictures of children is critical but difficult, the battle to define child pornography will continue.

For more information

Akdeniz, Yaman. *Regulation of Child Pornography on the Internet: Cases and Materials*. Available online. URL: http://www. cyber-rights.org/reports/child.htm. Last updated December 1999. Copyright Yaman Akdeniz, 1996–1999.

William E. Brigman, Ph.D.
University of Houston—Downtown

Chimel v. California 395 U.S. 752 (1969) In *Chimel v. California*, the Court reversed the WARRANTLESS SEARCH of a defendant's home, ruling that it exceeded what was permitted by the FOURTH AMENDMENT. The *Chimel* case marked a new era of jurisprudence by limiting the scope of SEARCHES INCIDENT TO ARREST to the area within the arrestee's reaching distance. As a result, law enforcement can no longer search entire rooms and dwellings solely on the basis of the ARREST as the Supreme Court had sometimes allowed prior to *Chimel*.

Police suspected Chimel in a coin shop BURGLARY and obtained a warrant for his arrest but did not procure a warrant to search his home. Upon arresting Chimel, police thoroughly searched his house (including all three bedrooms, the attic, garage, and a workshop) under the search incident to arrest doctrine. Since *United States v. Rabinowitz,* 339 U.S. 56 (1950), police generally had been allowed to search the area under the arrestee's control whenever they made a lawful arrest of the individual. This "area of control" often had been construed to include the entire dwelling occupied by the individual.

Justice Stewart, the author of the *Chimel* majority opinion, traced the history of the search incident to arrest doctrine and admitted that the Court's decisions under the doctrine had been "far from inconsistent." *Chimel,* 395 U.S. at 755. Since first mentioning the doctrine in 1914 up until *Chimel* in 1969, the Court had developed two inconsistent views of searches incident to arrest. As the *Chimel* majority discussed, at times the doctrine was construed as an expansive right by the police to search multiple rooms under the control of the arrestee, while in other cases the Court struck down similar searches as violating the Fourth Amendment prohibition on unreasonable SEARCHES AND SEIZURES. Although the expansive version of the doctrine had prevailed since *Rabinowitz,* the *Chimel* Court found a more restricted refinement of search incident to arrest better in keeping with the ideals embodied in the Fourth Amendment. Accordingly, the *Chimel* decision marked a significant shift in search incident to arrest law.

The *Chimel* Court ruled that it was reasonable for an officer to conduct a limited search of an arrestee in order to remove weapons that might harm the officer or aid in an arrestee's escape. Further, a search of the person of the arrestee was reasonable so that the officer might discover any EVIDENCE that the arrestee could conceal or destroy. As an extension of these principles, it followed that officers could search the area in the arrestee's immediate control—defined as "the area from which he might gain possession of a weapon or destructible evidence"—in order to preserve officer safety and prevent escape and the destruction of evidence. 395 U.S. at 766. However, broad searches of areas beyond the immediate control of the arrestee were declared unreasonable. Accordingly, since *Chimel,* police can no longer search beyond the arrestee's area of reach unless they possess a search warrant or unless the search falls within one of the other recognized exceptions to the warrant requirement (for example: consent searches, PLAIN VIEW searches, the automobile exception, TERRY STOPS, and exigent circumstances, among others).

For more information

Tomkovicz, J. J. "Divining and Designing the Future of Search Incident to Arrest Doctrine: Avoiding Instability, Irrationality, and Infidelity," *University of Illinois Law Review* (2007): 1417–1475.

Rhys Hester
University of South Carolina

choice theories of crime Choice theories of crime are those that view offenders as being calculative in their actions, essentially weighing the costs and benefits of a crime prior to committing the offense. If the benefits (i.e., stolen goods) of the crime outweigh the costs (i.e., prison sentence), then a person may be more inclined to offend. Conversely, if the costs of the crime outweigh the benefits, then the person will be less likely to commit the criminal act. This argument relies on the assumption that human beings constantly seek out pleasure while attempting to avoid any form of pain.

Choice theories are descendent from the 18th-century "classical school" of CRIMINOLOGY, which emphasized free will and rationality on the part of the criminal actor (Hagan, 2008). This idea would regain popularity in the 1970s and 1980s due, in part, to the perceived failure of rehabilitation programs of the 1960s, which viewed the offender as a victim of society rather than a calculative criminal, as argued in choice theories. Today, an entire group of theories are referred to as choice theories, including routine activities theory (Cohen and Felson, 1979), rational choice theory (Cornish and Clarke, 1986), and lifestyle theory (Hindelang, Gottfredson, and Garofalo, 1978).

What separates choice theories from many other perspectives is that while numerous theories of crime make the assumption that offenders dramatically differ from everyone else in society based on some enduring characteristic (i.e., antisocial personality), choice theories reject this idea and instead argue that *any* person is capable of committing crime as long as the benefits outweigh the costs in practically *any* situation (Nagin and Paternoster, 1993). Overall, there are two main ideas within the framework of choice theories: They place emphasis on the idea that individuals rationally choose whatever behavior they perform based on information collected prior to the crime, and they argue that an individual's choice to be deviant can be controlled by society through the fear of PUNISHMENT. This latter component is generally referred to as DETERRENCE and is generated when the costs of an act outweigh the potential benefit gained from completion of the act. Therefore, when the punishment generated from a crime is too great and not worth the potential reward, the person is said to be deterred from committing the crime.

Choice theories view all human beings as rational actors who calculate the cost and benefit of every action prior to committing criminal acts. These calculations are rational in nature and are based on the assumption that individuals will inherently strive to gain the maximum amount of pleasure while simultaneously attempting to avoid any form of pain. For instance, burglars must weigh the benefit of stealing others' property, which may take little time and effort to accomplish, against the potential to be ARRESTED and sent to prison. However, an individual's rationality is never perfect but may be limited, or bounded, when knowledge of the costs and benefits is incomplete or inaccurate (Cornish and Clarke, 1986). For instance, criminals may be unaware of the consequences for stealing because they are not aware of the formal punishment generally handed out by the government.

While an individual's choice is always driven by a hunger for pleasure, these choices are constrained by a fear that the act will be followed by some form of pain or punishment; when the pain or punishment prevents the person from committing crime, they are said to be deterred. Choice theories rely on two forms of deterrence in order to prevent crime. General deterrence is aimed at society as a whole in order to deter crime through the use of formal punishments (i.e., laws) or informal punishments (i.e., shaming). Specific deterrence, on the other hand, is aimed at preventing an already apprehended person from committing crime in the future.

While the above forms of deterrence would restrict a person's decision to commit crime, deterrence may also come in the form of taking the benefits (i.e., the goods to be stolen) out of an individual's calculations. For instance, parking garages might take the benefits of the crime away as potential thieves cannot view the goods (automobiles) prior to taking them, not allowing a calculation of the costs and benefits prior to the crime. Choice theories can also rely on any number of other deterrents as long as they either restrict a person's decision to commit crime or take the benefits of the crime out of the equation.

For more information

Cohen, Lawrence E., and Marcus Felson. "Social Change and Crime Rate Trends: A Routine Activities Approach," *American Sociological Review* 44 (1979): 588–607.

Cornish, Derek B., and Ronald V. Clarke. *The Reasoning Criminal.* New York: Springer-Verlag, 1986.

Hagan, Frank E. *Introduction to Criminology: Theories, Methods, and Criminal Behavior.* 6th ed. Los Angeles: SAGE, 2008.

Hindelang, Michael J., Michael Gottfredson, and James Garofalo. *Victims of Personal Crime: An Empirical*

Foundation for a Theory of Personal Victimization. Cambridge, Mass.: Ballinger, 1978.

Nagin, Daniel S., and Raymond Paternoster. "Enduring Individual Differences and Rational Choice Theories of Crime," *Law and Society Review* 27 (1993): 467–496.

Williams, Frank P. III, and Marilyn D. McShane. *Criminological Theory.* 4th ed. Upper Saddle River, N.J.: Pearson, 2004.

Matthew DeGarmo
Washington State University

citizenship Citizenship is defined in the Fourteenth Amendment to the CONSTITUTION, which states, "All persons born or naturalized in the United States, and subject to the JURISDICTION thereof, are citizens of the United States and of the State wherein they reside." Prior to the ratification of the Fourteenth Amendment in 1868, the Constitution had been silent on the definition of national citizenship, leaving that issue to the states to determine.

The Supreme Court addressed the definition of citizenship in *DRED SCOTT V. SANDFORD,* 60 U.S. 393 (1857). In this infamous decision authored by Chief Justice Taney, the Court ruled that persons of African descent could never be citizens of the United States. The Fourteenth Amendment was enacted in part to overturn this decision and thus provide a national definition of citizenship.

After passage of the Fourteenth Amendment, however, some issues regarding the definition of citizenship still remained. In *Elk v. Wilkins,* 112 U.S. 94 (1884), the Supreme Court ruled that Native Americans were not automatically citizens, because as members of tribes they were not wholly "subject to the jurisdiction" of the federal government. Congress later reversed this decision. In *United States v. Wong Kim Ark,* 169 U.S. 649 (1898), the Court ruled that persons of Asian ancestry born in the United States were citizens despite the fact that federal laws in force until 1952 prohibited Asians from becoming naturalized citizens.

The Court has also had to face questions regarding the rights of noncitizens. In *Yick Wo v. Hopkins,* 118 U.S. 356 (1886), a unanimous Court ruled that the EQUAL PROTECTION clause of the Fourteenth Amendment applies to noncitizens as well as to citizens. In *Graham v. Richardson,* 403 U.S. 365 (1971), the Court held that ALIENAGE, like race, was a suspect classification under the equal protection clause, requiring STRICT SCRUTINY and analysis. Under strict scrutiny, the state must prove that laws drawing distinctions based on citizenship must serve compelling governmental interests. Thus the Court ruled that it was unconstitutional for states to deny welfare benefits to noncitizens. In *In re Griffiths,* 413 U.S. 717 (1973), the Court also applied the strict scrutiny standard, holding that states may not prohibit noncitizen resident aliens from practicing law.

However, in *Sugarman v. Dougall,* 413 U.S. 634 (1973), the Court stated that noncitizens could be barred from some elective and nonelective positions in state governments, although states could not prohibit noncitizens from holding certain civil service jobs. Justice Blackmun, writing for the Court, stated that noncitizens could be barred from governmental positions that involve the formulation, execution, or review of broad public policy, since these political functions go to the heart of representative government. Later cases upheld state prohibitions on noncitizens becoming state troopers, public school teachers, and deputy probation officers, but rejected such citizenship requirements for notaries public.

In 2010 and 2011, as concerns about ILLEGAL ALIENS immigration heated up, some have called for the adoption of legislation or amending the Constitution to deny birthright citizenship to children of illegal aliens born in the United States. The argument for those advocating these measures is that granting birthright citizenship to these children creates incentives for individuals to enter the United States illegally. Opponents argue that such legislation would effectively create a two-tier level of citizenship, effectively denying some individuals equal protection under the law.

For more information

Carens, Joseph H. "Who Belongs? Theoretical and Legal Questions about Birthright Citizenship in the United States," *University of Toronto Law Journal* 37 (1987): 413.

Shklar, Judith N. *American Citizenship: The Quest for Inclusion.* Cambridge, Mass.: Harvard University Press, 1995.

Mark C. Miller
Clark University

civil action A civil action is a noncriminal lawsuit filed in a court.

Rule 2 of the Federal Rules of Civil Procedure provides that there shall only be one form of noncriminal action (i.e., lawsuit) known as a "civil action." Most states have a similar provision. To appreciate the significance of having only a single form of action, one must understand how it departs from traditional practice.

Historically, there were two separate judicial systems in Anglo-American law. Courts of law were empowered only to award monetary damages. Courts of EQUITY, on the other hand, could order a party to perform certain actions (like convey a piece of real estate) or not perform certain actions (such as not building a fence which blocks access to someone else's property). Thus, the choice of court and whether one files an "action" at law or a "suit" in equity largely depended upon the type of relief being sought.

In courts of law, there were a wide variety of forms of action with names like *assumpsit* (to recover damages for the breach of a promise) and *trover* (to receive compensation for goods wrongfully used by another person). Each form had technical requirements that could trap the unwary draftsman and cause an action to be dismissed.

Federal courts, as well as the courts in most states, now have JURISDICTION over both legal and equitable claims. Moreover, the numerous and complex forms of action have been replaced by a single form—the civil action. To initiate a civil action, one simply files a complaint with the court which contains a "short and plain statement" as to why one is entitled to relief. The technical forms of pleading have been abolished.

For more information

Federal Civil Judicial Procedure and Rules (2000).

Reppy, Alison. *Introduction to Civil Procedure: Actions and Pleading at Common Law.* Buffalo, N.Y.: Dennis, 1954.

Danton Asher Berube
Yale University

civil commitment for sex offenders Civil commitment for sex offenders is a method of incarcerating SEX OFFENDERS after their criminal sentence has been served because it is believed that they are mentally ill and cannot be released from detention. This civil commitment is very controversial and raises numerous legal issues.

Under American law, a person who is considered dangerous due to a mental illness may be involuntarily committed to a mental institution. Involuntary commitment is a matter of civil, not criminal, law because a person so committed is not being punished but rather incapacitated and treated. Constitutional DUE PROCESS doctrine governs the process to an extent, ensuring that a person is not unreasonably or unnecessarily committed. Furthermore, a person who ceases to be a danger because of his or her mental illness must be released.

Mentally ill persons who are sexually dangerous may be involuntarily committed under a state's general commitment legislation. States also may enact legislation focused specifically on sexually dangerous persons. In recent years, several states have, with some controversy, empowered PROSECUTORS to initiate commitment proceedings against a convicted sex offender shortly before the end of his or her prison sentence. See, e.g.,

Sexually Violent Predator Act of 1994 (Kan. Stat. Ann. §59-29a01 *et seq.*). The primary argument against these new-style statutes is that they, in effect, impose a life sentence for sex offenses, violating constitutional due process and DOUBLE JEOPARDY rights—in other words, a person is punished twice for the same crime by being involuntarily committed to a mental institution.

In a series of decisions (*Kansas v. Hendricks,* 521 U.S. 346, [1997]; *Seling v. Young,* 531 U.S. 250, [2001]; *Kansas v. Crane,* 534 U.S. 407, [2002]), the Supreme Court issued guidelines for assessing the constitutionality of sex offender commitment statutes.

First, a state commitment statute is presumed to be nonpunitive in nature unless there is strong EVIDENCE that it is motivated by retribution or DETERRENCE. Involuntary commitment of mentally ill and sexually dangerous persons in order to protect the public is a legitimate government end and is not per se punitive.

Second, a statute is more likely to be seen as nonpunitive if it offers the possibility of eventual release into the community through treatment and offers the same procedural safeguards provided by general civil commitment statutes. This does not mean, however, that sexually dangerous persons can be committed only if they are likely to respond to treatment. States have never been required to offer some guarantee of eventual release to the mentally ill. Therefore, the possibility that a convicted sex offender is likely to never be cured and released is not itself constitutionally problematic, so long as the length of his or her confinement is directly related to the mental disorder that served as the basis for commitment.

Third, a state may define sexual deviance, for purposes of commitment, more broadly than professionally accepted diagnostic categories. For example, Kansas's statute allows for the commitment of those who are sexually dangerous due to a "mental abnormality" or a "personality disorder." Legislatures have traditionally had broad discretion to determine what qualifies as a mental illness or malady that would justify potential civil commitment. At the same time, involuntary commitment statutes for sexually dangerous persons may be used only on people who are shown to have "a special and serious lack of ability to control behavior" based on a mental disorder. This requirement prevents broadly worded commitment statutes from being used as an alternative or supplemental form of PUNISHMENT for typical criminals who are expected to RECIDIVATE upon release.

For more information

Cantone, Jason A. "Rational Enough to Punish, But Too Irrational to Release: The Integrity of Sex Offender Civil Commitment," *Drake Law Review* 57 (2009): 693–727.

James Daniel Fisher
Edinboro University of Pennsylvania

civil disobedience Civil disobedience is an unlawful act, committed in public, based on nonviolence and performed in a conscientious manner with a willingness to accept PUNISHMENT. American author Henry David Thoreau first introduced the idea of civil disobedience in his 1849 essay, "Civil Disobedience." Thoreau's refusal to pay taxes in protest against slavery and the U.S. war against Mexico resulted in his ARREST and his acquiescence to punishment typical of a civilly disobedient act.

Civil disobedience involves breaking a law. No one crime category defines a civilly disobedient act. Civil disobedience may involve violation of noise ordinances, trespass laws, tax payment laws, traffic laws, and so on. Any deliberate violations of the law performed in public could represent civil disobedience. Expression of radical viewpoints and vehement oral disagreement with a law are not sufficient. An act of civil disobedience requires the performance of a legally forbidden act. The civil disobedient knowingly breaks the law based on a moral evaluation of the law.

Not every act that violates the law is based on civil disobedience. The act of civil disobedience, unlike the act of armed ROBBERY, is not undertaken for private gain. Instead, those who engage in civil disobedient protests will voluntarily suffer legal punishments, financial losses, and in some instances personal humiliation. Acts of civil disobedience are based on a cause or larger principles for which the civil disobedient is willing to make personal sacrifices. Usually, those who employ civil disobedience have exhausted all legal avenues to change.

A willingness to accept punishment is essential. This distinguishes civil disobedient acts from the acts of common criminals, such as thieves. Civil disobedience, then, is a conscientious act. Conscientious means that the protestor honestly believes that what he or she is doing is correct. Weighing the consequences of violating the law, civil disobedients knowingly break the law based on what they believe is right.

Civil disobedience is an act usually performed in public. To make a statement for the cause or principle for which they stand, those who are civilly disobedient must break the law in public. A protestor who burns his military draft card at home may have broken the law but has not made a public statement of protesting a war. By breaking the law in public, the protestor makes a public statement and expresses a willingness to take responsibility for that act in an attempt to remedy injustice. Some acts of civil disobedience may be clandestine by necessity such as the disobedient protest during the Civil War when Northern citizens systematically violated slave system laws by building the Underground Railroad. Generally, however, civil disobedience must be public, to educate fellow citizens about the injustices of the law being broken.

Civil disobedience is usually nonviolent. Most protestors who engage in civil disobedience abhor violence. Violent acts often invoke fear and may alienate significant parts of the population to whom civil disobedients wish to make a conscientious appeal. Although violence may attract greater media coverage and public attention, it also scares people and may place those who commit such acts in a negative light. Most adherents to civil disobedience eschew violence and view deliberate use of nonviolent methods, such as passive resistance, as more effective ways to register an honest disagreement with a law. Violence is often associated with revolution and the rejection of authority or repudiation of a regime. Civil disobedience does not seek death, destruction, and the overthrow of government. Its aim is to point out injustices associated with the law or a set of laws, not to create instability.

Civil disobedience has been employed on the left and the right of the ideological spectrum. Antiabortion protestors, large numbers of whom are associated with the Religious Right, employed civil disobedience in the 1980s and into the 1990s by blocking access to abortion clinics. Protestors in the 1960s and 1970s used civil disobedience to register their concerns about the Vietnam War. Environmental protection activists in the 1980s and 1990s have used civil disobedience by laying down their bodies in front of logging trucks. MARTIN LUTHER KING'S CIVIL RIGHTS MOVEMENT in the 1960s used the tactics of civil disobedience to overturn JIM CROW SEGREGATION LAWS.

For more information

Cohen, Carl. *Civil Disobedience: Conscience, Tactics and the Law.* New York: Columbia University Press, 1971.

Herngren, Per (trans. Margaret Rainey). *Path of Resistance: The Practice of Civil Disobedience.* Philadelphia: New Society Publishers, 1993.

Ruth Ann Strickland
Professor, Political Science and
Criminal Justice Department
Appalachian State University

civil forfeiture Civil forfeiture refers to the authority of state and federal legislators to seize property related to criminal activities. An action in which the government seeks to seize assets connected to criminal activity is called civil forfeiture.

Civil forfeiture means property purchased, or maintained, with proceeds from a criminal activity, or property used to commit the crime, is seized by the government and converted either to government use or sold and the proceeds retained by the government. Forfeiture statutes were enacted as a means of divesting large-scale criminal enterprises, such as drug cartels and the MAFIA, of the proceeds and property related to their criminal activity. Generally, large-scale criminal enterprises net significant proceeds and, therefore, acquire assets, such as property. The legal theory is that "but for" the criminal enterprise, the criminal would not have the means to acquire or maintain the property and therefore the property is directly related to the criminal activity. This connection is legally referred to as the "nexus" between the criminal activity and the asset. The government must prove, by a PREPONDERANCE OF EVIDENCE, the existence of this nexus. The government seizure of property has raised concerns by opponents, including the constitutional prohibition against DOUBLE JEOPARDY (being twice tried for the same crime), government abuse, and fear that innocent owners will be deprived of their lawful property.

Direct nexus between the property and the criminal activity is generally demonstrated by seizing property that was used to commit the crime. Initially, law enforcement officials seized airplanes, boats, and other vehicles used to transport illegal narcotics. Following successful defense of these seizures, law enforcement officials expanded seizures to include homes, cash, investments, and other items that law enforcement officials asserted were the profits from the crimes. Courts required law enforcement officials to demonstrate the direct nexus between the criminal acts and the profits. These were generally demonstrated by a lack of employment or legal income of the criminal and the assets. However, criminal enterprises have adapted.

Criminal enterprises have modified their approach to property ownership as a result of forfeiture statutes. Where homes, cars, boats, and airplanes were once owned entirely by the criminal enterprise, such ownership has been modified to insert "innocent owners," such as banks or landlords. Law enforcement officials have struggled to prove the required direct nexus between the profit from the crimes and property when the owner is a bank, landlord, or company. As a result, courts have required officials to prove the "innocent owner" was, or should have been, aware of the criminal enterprise before the seizure is upheld. Generally, this is proven by demonstrating the owner was "willfully blind"—intentionally unaware of the activities—or otherwise should have known of the criminal activity (leasing property to someone who has no source of income).

Opponents of these statutes think seizure of property from someone who is otherwise subject to sanctions for his or her criminal activity is unconstitutional as a result of double jeopardy. Courts have generally upheld the seizure on the theory that the defendants are not subject to further incarceration as a result of the asset forfeiture, but the critical element that has aided in the defense of these actions is that they have not been tied, pleaded, or otherwise connected to the criminal sanctions. However, this remains an evolving area of the law.

For more information

Leonard, W. Levy. *A License to Steal: The Forfeiture of Property.* Chapel Hill: University of North Carolina Press, 1995.

Young, Simon M.N. *Civil Forfeiture of Criminal Property: Legal Measures for Targeting the Proceeds of Crime.* Northhampton, Mass.: Edward Elgar, 2009.

Mark McClain
Central Washington University

civil liberties Civil liberties refer to a person's freedom from arbitrary government interference.

In the United States, civil liberties are based on the BILL OF RIGHTS, the first 10 AMENDMENTS TO THE U.S. CONSTITUTION. "Government," sometimes called "the State," in this sense includes government in all its forms—public schools, police, public health systems, and all government agencies on any level, and may include private persons who act on behalf of the government. The Bill of Rights specifically *denies* government the power to do certain acts and applies to all persons in the United States, not just citizens.

U.S. government is based on two conflicting ideas: (1) that the majority rules, and (2) that the power of the majority must be limited so as to preserve civil liberties. For example, according to (1), the majority of voters can approve a law that bans a certain RELIGION, but under (2) that law would be invalid and unenforceable because of the First Amendment guarantee of freedom of religion. Similarly, even widely accepted civil liberties are not absolute and are limited by the rights of other individuals and by the concept of public safety. It is sometimes very difficult to determine where one person's freedom should end and another person's freedom should begin; courts repeatedly struggle with these limitations and conflicts.

The civil liberties guaranteed by the Bill of Rights and further developed by statute and by court decisions include:

First Amendment rights: freedom of expression, of speech, and of the press; FREEDOM OF ASSOCIATION AND ASSEMBLY; freedom of religion and freedom *from* religion; freedom to complain to the government and ask for assistance or correction of a problem.

FOURTH AMENDMENT: freedom from unreasonable government SEARCHES AND SEIZURES of one's home, office, personal possessions, documents, and records.

Fifth Amendment: freedom from SELF-INCRIMINATION; freedom from DOUBLE JEOPARDY; right to not be deprived of life, liberty, or property without DUE PROCESS of law; right to fair payment for private property that the government takes for public use.

SIXTH, Seventh and EIGHTH Amendments: rights to fair treatment if one is accused of a crime; rights to fair court procedures.

In addition, through laws enacted by legislatures and through court rulings based on the Bill of Rights, civil liberties now include:

Right to equal treatment under law (nondiscrimination): applies in schools, the workplace, the courts, and the voting booth, as well as most public accommodations such as hotels, restaurants, public transportation, and most businesses.

Right to due process: right to be treated fairly when facing criminal charges or other serious accusations that could result in loss of liberty, property, schooling, housing, benefits, or other major interests.

Right to privacy: right to pursue and make decisions about one's personal life without government interference.

For more information

Carey, Eve, Alan H. Levine, Janet R. Price, and Norman Dorsen. *The Rights of Students: ACLU Handbook for Young Americans.* New York: Puffin Books, 1997.

Gara, Joel M., David Goldberger, Gary M. Stern, and Norton H. Halperin. *The Right to Protest: The Basic ACLU Guide to Free Expression.* Carbondale: Southern Illinois University Press, 1991.

Lynn, Barry, Marc D. Stern, and Oliver S. Thomas. *The Right to Religious Liberty: The Basic ACLU Guide to Religious Rights.* 2nd ed. Carbondale: Southern Illinois University Press, 1995.

McDonald, Laughlin, and John A. Powell. *The Rights of Racial Minorities: The Basic ACLU Guide to Racial Minority Rights.* 2nd ed. Carbondale: Southern Illinois University Press, 1993.

Ross, Susan Deller, Isabelle Katz Pinzler, Deborah A. Ellis, and Kary L. Moss. *The Rights of Women: The Basic ACLU Guide to Women's Rights.* 3rd ed. Carbondale: Southern Illinois University Press, 1993.

Schultz, David, John R. Vile, and Michelle D. Deardorff. *Constitutional Law in Contemporary America,* vol. 2. New York: Oxford University Press, 2010.

Elsa M. Shartsis
Attorney

civil procedure Civil procedure is the body of laws and rules that govern how courts handle noncriminal lawsuits. Each court system has its own set of rules, and there are often significant variations between the federal rules and those of various states. Their fundamental purpose, however, is the same. As stated in Rule 1 of the Federal Rules of Civil Procedure, they seek "to secure the just, speedy, and inexpensive determination of every action."

Civil procedure provides the answers to a number of fundamental questions that arise in almost every civil action, including: Which court has the power to hear the case (JURISDICTION)? How are the issues to be litigated or framed (pleadings)? What information must the parties provide to each other (discovery)? What relief may the parties seek from the court short of a trial (motions)? How is the lawsuit itself conducted (trial procedure)?

There is no more fundamental issue in civil procedure than which court has jurisdiction over a given dispute. Jurisdiction is literally "the power to speak," and without it, any action or judgment by a court is wholly invalid. There are two distinct types of jurisdiction—subject matter and personal. Subject matter jurisdiction defines the types of issues and cases a court can hear. Civil courts, for example, generally do not have subject matter jurisdiction over criminal cases. Another common subject matter limitation has to do with the dollar amount at issue—thus in some states a "SMALL CLAIMS" COURT may be prohibited from hearing disputes involving more than $5,000 or $10,000.

Personal jurisdiction, on the other hand, refers to the power of a court to issue an order or render a judgment which is binding upon a particular party. As a general rule, for example, a New York court would lack personal jurisdiction over a person who resided in California. But a state court can acquire personal jurisdiction over nonresidents if they have sufficient contacts with the state, such as doing business there or causing an accident within the state's borders. Moreover, unlike subject matter jurisdiction, a lack of personal jurisdiction may be waived by a party. Without subject matter jurisdiction over the type of dispute and personal jurisdiction over the parties, a court lacks the authority to hear and resolve a case.

Parties to a lawsuit use pleadings to advise each other and the court of the factual and legal questions at issue in the case. The plaintiff—i.e., the person bringing suit—files a complaint, which sets forth the factual allegations that the plaintiff contends give rise to liability on the part of the defendant. The defendant then files an answer, which admits or denies each of the plaintiff's allegations. The answer is also used to raise affirmative defenses to the lawsuit. For example, the defendants might admit that they breached a CONTRACT but claim that the plaintiff waited too long to file suit, thereby raising the STATUTE OF LIMITATIONS as an affirmative defense.

Pleadings, however, are merely a rough outline of the facts in dispute between the parties. In order to speed up trials, the rules of civil procedure require that parties exchange detailed information with one another through a process known as discovery. Perhaps the most common of these information-exchanging techniques is the DEPOSITION. During a deposition, the witness is asked questions under oath and the answers are transcribed by a court reporter. Other discovery methods include interrogatories—written questions which must be answered by the other party—and requests for production of documents—which identify papers and related items that one party must disclose to the other. Discovery can be the most time-consuming and expensive step in the litigation process. It has the advantages, however, of streamlining the trial itself, avoiding unfair surprises, and even facilitating settlement once the parties understand the proof in each other's favor.

Most civil cases never reach the trial stage. Instead, they are either settled by the parties or disposed of by motion. A motion is simply a request by a party for a court order. If, for example, a defendant needs more time to prepare an answer, he could file a motion with the court asking for an extension. The two most important motions under the rules of civil procedure are the motion to dismiss and the motion for summary judgment. They are called dispositive motions because they allow the court to dispose of a case—i.e., rule on the merits—without having to conduct a trial. In a motion to dismiss, the defendant is asking the court to dismiss the plaintiff's lawsuit because, even assuming the facts are as the plaintiff alleges, she is legally not entitled to any relief. A motion for summary judgment, on the other hand, is generally filed at the conclusion of discovery. It asks the court to render a judgment in favor of the moving party on the ground that the moving party is entitled to win even if all of the disputed facts are construed in the light most favorable to the nonmoving party.

If a case does proceed to trial, the rules of civil procedure describe whether there will be a JURY, how the jury is selected, the type of verdict to be rendered, etc. It is important to note, however, that some of the most important issues at trial do not involve civil procedure at all. Instead, questions related to the kinds of information that can be considered by the JUDGE or jury are governed by the law and rules of EVIDENCE, which is considered to be a quite distinct field from civil procedure.

Civil procedure, in short, may be thought of as the rules by which the game of litigation is played. Many of the requirements are technical and may even appear arbitrary. For the careless lawyer they can be a trap, while master strategists are able to use them to their clients' advantage. But in the end they are an absolute necessity because without rules, the game could not be played.

For more information

Federal Civil Judicial Procedure and Rules, 2000.

Friedenthal, Jack H., et al. *Civil Procedure.* 3rd ed. St. Paul, Minn.: West, 1999.

Danton Asher Berube
Yale University

civil rights Civil rights mandate equal treatment of citizens by other members of society. In contemporary American political life, a person has a civil right to be treated similarly to all other citizens, without being discriminated against for reasons of (in the language of Title VII of the 1964 Civil Rights Act) race, color, religion, sex, or national origin. This was not always the case. The history of civil rights in the United States is the checkered story of outsiders struggling to be included as equal participants in society.

Civil rights struggles are conventionally traced to the end of the Civil War and ratification of the EQUAL PROTECTION clause of the Fourteenth Amendment in 1868. In fact, civil rights are implicit in the language of the 1776 DECLARATION OF INDEPENDENCE: "We hold these truths to be self-evident, that all men are created equal. . . ." In the 1830s William Lloyd Garrison, editor of *The Liberator,* insisted on civil rights for blacks as well as the immediate abolition of slavery. The 1848 Seneca Falls Declaration of Rights and Sentiments was adopted by a group of women gathered to consider the "social, civil, and religious condition and rights of women." It proclaimed "that all men and women are created equal." In the depths of the Civil War, in November 1863, ABRAHAM LINCOLN reaffirmed at Gettysburg that the American nation was "dedicated to the proposition that all men are created equal." Thus, the language of the equal protection clause is the heritage of nearly a century of civil rights struggles. That clause holds that "No State shall . . . deny to any person within its JURISDICTION the equal protection of the laws."

For more than three-quarters of a century after its ratification—between 1868 and the mid-1940s—the principle of equal CITIZENSHIP at the core of the equal protection clause was in eclipse. In the late 19th and early 20th centuries, civil rights struggles against JIM CROW LAWS and for women's suffrage took place in the shadow of the Supreme Court's indifferent neglect and legal defeat of civil rights, and in the teeth of fierce social resistance. Ironically, changing judicial and social attitudes toward civil rights was signaled in a 1944 Supreme Court decision upholding the constitutionality, under the equal protection clause, of the exclusion and confinement of over 70,000 American citizens of Japanese descent. In the course of validating these wartime restrictions in KOREMATSU V. UNITED STATES, 323 U.S. 214, the Court observed: "all legal restrictions which curtail the civil rights of a single racial group are immediately suspect" and should be given "the most rigid scrutiny."

Constitutional civil rights, under the equal protection clause, emerged in the second half of the 20th century in conjunction with the CIVIL RIGHTS MOVEMENT and the Women's movement. Both these civil rights struggles and the Supreme Court's interpretation of the equal protection clause evolved from initially challenging laws requiring discrimination on the basis of race and sex, to advocating and, in the Court's case scrutinizing, positive government responses to remedy the consequences of past discrimination. As the focus of activism and law shifted in the 1970s, civil rights debates again sharpened. The consensus against SEGREGATION and universal suffrage unraveled. Policies such as busing and AFFIRMATIVE ACTION generated controversy and incurred resistance. Further fueling civil rights disputes was the rise of the GAY RIGHTS movement following the 1969 Stonewall riots in New York City. Although disparate treatment of people based on their race or their gender—both characteristics generally and legally assumed to be innate—is widely understood to violate civil rights, many view differential treatment of gays and lesbians as a rejection of their lifestyle choices.

Finally, other groups, such as those with physical handicaps, have also fought for civil rights and equal treatment. The passage of the Americans with Disability Act (ADA) in 1990 is viewed by many as equivalent to a civil rights act for those with physical handicaps.

For more information

Evans, Sara M. *Born for Liberty: A History of Women in America.* New York: Free Press, 1997.

Kluger, Richard. *Simple Justice: The History of Brown v. Board of Education and Black America's Struggle for Equality.* New York: Knopf, 1975.

McGlen, Nancy E., and O'Connor, Karen. *Women, Politics, and American Society.* 2nd ed. Upper Saddle River, N.J.: Prentice Hall, 1998.

Schultz, David, John R. Vile, and Michelle D. Deardorff. *Constitutional Law in Contemporary America,* vol. 1. New York: Oxford University Press, 2010.

Wilkinson, J. Harvie III. *From Brown to Bakke: The Supreme Court and School Integration, 1945–1978.* New York: Oxford University Press, 1979.

James C. Foster
Department of Political Science
Oregon State University

Civil Rights movement The Civil Rights movement was a legal, political, social, and economic struggle for equality for African Americans during the 20th century peaking in the period from the mid-1950s to the mid-1960s. Its effects have permanently changed the legal, political, and social structure of America.

The modern Civil Rights movement began in December 1955, with the Montgomery, Alabama, bus boycott. A year later the Supreme Court declared the policy of racial SEGREGATION in public bus seating to be unconstitutional in *Gayle v. Browder,* 352 U.S. 903 (1956). The Reverend MARTIN LUTHER KING emerged as the leader of the movement and as head of the Southern Christian Leadership Conference (SCLC).

The Civil Rights Act of 1957 (42 U.S.C.A., sect. 1975) established the Civil Rights Commission as an independent agency. Its reports and recommendations have often been the basis of new civil rights legislation.

In the 1950s the movement centered on legal maneuvering. Frustrated with the slow pace of change, some groups took direct action. In 1960 black and white college students in Greensboro, North Carolina, engaged in "sit-in" demonstrations at the "whites only" lunch counter at the local Woolworth store. Quickly the sit-in movement was copied in many other places. ARRESTS for violating segregation laws were eventually dismissed by the courts on the grounds that these laws were unconstitutional, e.g., *Peterson v. City of Greenville,* 373 U.S. 244 (1963), et al.

The Civil Rights Act of 1960 (42 U.S.C.A., sect. 1971) provided for the appointment of referees to help African Americans register to vote. It also granted the right to sue those obstructing the right.

In 1961 the Congress of Racial Equality (CORE) launched "Freedom Rides" with racially mixed groups on buses traveling through the South in order to demonstrate that segregation at bus stations violated the rights of African Americans engaged in interstate travel. In September 1961 the Interstate COMMERCE COMMISSION outlawed racial segregation in interstate transportation.

In 1963 Martin Luther King led a march on Washington, D.C., pressing for equal rights. The next summer Congress passed the Civil Rights Act of 1964 (42 U.S.C.A., sect. 2000a et seq.), which outlawed discrimination in public accommodations on the basis of the COMMERCE CLAUSE OF THE CONSTITUTION (Article I, section 8, clause 3).

In 1965 Congress passed the VOTING RIGHTS ACT OF 1965 (42 U.S.C.A., sect. 1973) prohibiting discrimination in voting and outlawing literacy tests. It also provided federal supervision of voting in the South.

After 1965 the Civil Rights movement began to decline as it changed from a movement to end racial segregation in the South to a movement for social and economic equality throughout the whole country. Demands for AFFIRMATIVE ACTION in employment and other areas of life created a "white backlash" with charges that non-African Americans were now victims of "reverse discrimination." The movement further fragmented with ideological disputes among its leaders.

The movement endured throughout the remainder of the century, steadily achieving its original goal of racial equality.

For more information

Davis, Abraham L., and Barbara L. Graham. *The Supreme Court, Race and Civil Rights.* Thousand Oaks, Calif.: SAGE, 1995.

Weisbrot, Robert. *Freedom Bound: A History of America's Civil Rights Movement.* New York; Plume, 1991.

Andrew J. Waskey
Dalton State College

class action A class action is a lawsuit brought by or against a limited number of individuals or entities as representatives of a much larger group of similarly situated individuals or entities too numerous to include each separately.

Class action lawsuits frequently generate significant attention in the media, and because they often involve claims by hundreds, thousands, or even millions of people, the costs to the defendants (usually large corporations) can be tremendous. The objects of recent notable class actions include discriminatory employment practices, leaking silicon breast implants, disease-causing asbestos insulation, and defective automobile tires. A suit has even been filed on behalf of pay-per-view customers who were allegedly shortchanged when Mike Tyson was disqualified for biting Evander Holyfield in their 1997 boxing match.

In federal courts, there are four prerequisites which must be met in order to file a class action lawsuit. (Many states have similar rules.) First, there must be so many members of the proposed class that joining them individually in the lawsuit is impractical. Second, there must be questions of fact or law which are common to all members of the proposed class. Third, the claims or defenses of the selected representatives must be typical of those of the proposed class. Fourth, the selected representatives must be able to fairly and adequately protect the interests of the proposed class.

Even after these four prerequisites are met, a class action will not be permitted unless it also satisfies at least one of the following four additional conditions. One, there is a risk that separate lawsuits by individual members of the class would subject the opposing party to inconsistent standards of conduct. Two, there is a chance that separate lawsuits would resolve for all practical purposes the rights or obligations of other class members or would impair their ability to protect their legal interests (when, for example, there is a limited fund which is insufficient to satisfy all of the potential claims). Three, injunctive or declaratory relief is appropriate because the opposing party has treated or refused to treat the members of the class consistently. Four, the suit is characterized more by common questions of fact or law than by different questions for each member of the class and using a class action is fairer and more efficient than the available alternatives.

In class actions arising under the last condition—i.e., those involving common questions of law or fact—members of the class must be given notice of the lawsuit by the best means practicable. For members who can be specifically identified through reasonable investigation, the notice must be sent to them individually. For others, notice is usually in the form of mass media advertisements. Among other things, the notice must advise the class members that they have the right to withdraw from the class and that, if they fail to do so, they will be bound by the court's judgment.

JUDGES are given broad DISCRETION to manage class action lawsuits to make them both as fair and efficient as possible. The judge must also agree before a class action can be dismissed or settled, and all members of the class must be given notice of the proposed dismissal or settlement.

Class action lawsuits are often controversial. Defendants sometimes claim that they are filed by greedy lawyers more interested in their own legal fees than they are in protecting the rights of class members. While such abuses undoubtedly occur on occasion, in the modern age where goods and services are delivered to millions of consumers nationally, the class action is often the only feasible mechanism of providing JUSTICE for all.

For more information

Dickerson, Hon. Thomas A. *Class Actions: The Law of 50 States.* New York: Law Journal Seminars Press, 2000.

Yeazell, Stephen C. *From Medieval Group Litigation to the Modern Class Action.* New Haven, Conn.: Yale University Press, 1987.

Danton Asher Berube
Yale University

class and crime Class and crime refers to the various connections between social economic status and crime and how class affects who commits crime, why, and who the victims are.

There is an implied link between class and crime. However, this link is complex and is contingent in how class and crime are defined and measured. An array of factors have been used to demonstrate a class-crime link as well as show the role that class has on the types of crimes committed. These factors can be divided into two sets, individual-level and geographic factors. Individual-level factors include wealth, income, occupation, employment status, household and FAMILY structure, existence of having received public assistance or residing in public housing. Geographic factors consists of rate of home ownership, median value of homes, rate of absolute and/or relative poverty, ethnic heterogeneity, relative deprivation, and existence of strong or weak social networks or social supports.

The relationship between class and crime has been examined in three ways: first, by looking at the effect that economic conditions have on crimes rates, particularly if it increases during economic downturns; second, by understanding the social class background of prisoners or past offenders. Official ARREST data demonstrates a relationship between socioeconomic status and crime, finding that the lower the socioeconomic status, the greater the crime rate. However, these findings do not mean that socioeconomic status alone predicts criminal behavior. Thus, a third approach compares crime rates with the socioeconomic characteristics within geographic areas, particularly, the rates of poverty and disadvantage. A main theme of liberal CRIMINOLOGY finds that criminal behavior increases with decreasing economic opportunities for individuals within a geographic area.

Studies have found that low socioeconomic status combined with community-level dynamics such as residential mobility, ethnic heterogeneity, economic deprivation, and the existence of weak social ties or support, leads to increased feelings of relative or concentrated deprivation and mental stress. In return, these contributing factors can influence criminal behavior. For the youth, a combination of these factors has been found to increase rates of delinquency. By looking at aggregate measures of household income within specific areas, studies have also found that crime rates tend to be higher in communities with residents of low socioeconomic status. Therefore, in order to understand the link between crime and socioeconomic status, one cannot rely solely on individual-level factors such as socioeconomic status but must also take into account the community contextual factors and the feelings of deprivation that result from living in a socially and economically marginalized area. Other factors that have been found to contribute to increased rates of criminal behavior are the existence of higher rates of police concentration in low-income and minority areas.

Criminal behaviors are most commonly defined as blue or WHITE-COLLAR CRIMES. These classifications are a function of the opportunities available to potential offenders. For example, those employed in unskilled occupations and/or residing in low-income geographic areas have fewer opportunities to exploit than individuals of higher status, with skilled employment, and/or residing in higher income areas. The term *white-collar crime* was introduced in the 1940s to bring attention to the types of crimes committed by individuals from higher social groups and which are often overlooked by officials. White-collar crimes are also synonymous with corporate crimes such as FRAUD, bribery, INSIDER TRADING, EMBEZZLEMENT, and FORGERY in that the opportunities to engage in these criminal behaviors are more available to white-collar than blue-collar employees.

Unlike blue-collar crimes, white-collar criminals can more easily disguise their offenses by using their affluence and legitimacy. This key distinction is in contrast to blue-collar crimes, which tend to be more obvious and therefore attract more police attention. Because crime measurements are often obtained from official data by police, court, or correctional facilities, many argue this has contributed to biased measurements in that blue-collar crimes are more represented in official crime measurements than are white-collar crimes. Additionally, at the same time that blue-collar crimes such as MURDER, ARSON, BURGLARY, THEFT, ASSAULT, rape, and VANDALISM are overrepresented in official crime measurements, they are also often attributed to antisocial behaviors and psychological, associational, and structural factors like those mentioned earlier.

Many argue that there is an inherent problem in the way that the relationship between class and crime is understood, the most important reason being the double standard between white-collar and blue-collar crimes. Besides the concern that white-collar crimes are more easily disguised and not always reported, there are additional factors that explain why white-collar criminals are often overlooked. Many argue that due to their higher social status they are able to afford the best legal representation. Additionally, those accused of white-collar criminal offenses are more likely to have access to or friendships with powerful elites in the government or business sector who can help obtain a favorable outcome for those accused. Furthermore, those in power may also create or implement laws and behaviors that can ensure that particular white-collar criminal behaviors are not clearly defined or strictly enforced. Reports have shown that in relation to police effort to address blue-collar crimes, very little police effort goes into fighting white-collar crimes and that enforcement often falls into the hands of government agencies that often act only as watchdogs.

Another reason that explains the difference in the treatment of white-and blue-collar crimes is that criminal penalties are most commonly associated with the degree of physical force or violence involved rather than to the scale of monetary loss. Therefore, because white-collar criminals often do not have to resort to violence, they can escape receiving severe criminal penalties. This means that someone who mugs a victim and steals the person's wallet is more likely to be harshly punished than a white-collar employee who embezzles millions of dollars from shareholders or an employer.

By looking at the relationship between class and crime, officials have also been able to predict which groups are more likely to be victims of violent crime. Although, crime rates and individual risks of VICTIMIZATION greatly vary according to social context, individuals of low socioeconomic status residing in marginalized geographic areas with low economic opportunities are generally associated with higher rates of criminal victimization. Studies have identified areas of economic marginality and deprivation so pervasive that all residents, despite personal lifestyles and routine activities, may be equally at risk of victimization. Therefore, it is important to examined the micro social context when determining the link between class and crime because it can determine how other factors influence individuals' risk of victimization.

Official census data have found that black males are overrepresented in both victimization and offender figures, bringing the factor of race into the discussion of the link between class and crime. However, studies show that rather than confirming that crime is more a function of biological or cultural characteristics, it is economic deprivation that affects the intraracial homicide rates for whites and blacks, particularly the separation and isolation of large segments of social groups based on income.

Understanding the complex relationship between class and crime continues to generate much research and debate. Recent studies have begun to examine the relationship between socioeconomic status and specific offenses and specific types of offenses. This new path in research may lead to greater coherence in the understanding of the relationship between class and crime. Among the factors lacking in this debate is the development of a standard measure for social class as well as greater attention paid to the kinds of questions being asked when analyzing official data. Nevertheless, many think that this issue will remain controversial because of the implications it suggests for social policies addressing crime as well as preventing criminal behaviors.

For more information

Cloward, R. and Ohlin, L. *Delinquency and Opportunity.* New York: Free Press, 1960.

Merton, Robert K. *Social Theory and Social Structure.* 2nd rev. ed. New York: Free Press, 1968.

Nye, Ivan, and James F. Short, Jr. "Scaling Delinquent Behavior," *American Sociological Review* 22 (1957).

Wilneida Negrón
CUNY Graduate Center

classical theory of crime Attributed to the Italian philosopher Cesare, marquis de Beccaria (March 12, 1738–November 28, 1794), the classical theory or classical school of crime is an outgrowth of the Enlightenment and its emphasis on individual liberty and rationalism within an ordered society. Those following this school argue that crime is a conscious, rational decision by a person who is seeking to maximize his or her pleasure, or "utility" in meeting physical or social needs. Weighing the costs and benefits of committing a given crime, a person will commit a crime if the penalty is (1) uncertain to occur, or (2) disproportionately moderate in the face of the crime, or (3) unlikely to occur immediately after the crime was committed. The essence of the classical theory is the assumption that people are rational actors, and that they exercise free will in choosing criminal behavior.

ORIGINS OF THE CLASSICAL THEORY

The Enlightenment (about 1650 to 1804) was a period of physical and social scientific development. Advances in biology led to the discovery of vaccines for smallpox and cowpox; developments in mathematics produced new theories in calculus and economics. The social sciences advanced with developments in legal theory, political theory, and social theory. Among the most important were developments in criminal justice theory, including ideas of crime and PUNISHMENT, training in law and legal theory; and efforts to end practices such as debtors' prisons and cruel punishments within the navies and militaries of the world.

During the medieval period and the early Renaissance, most people believed that criminal behavior was the consequence of man's inherent sin nature. Punishments for crimes were often inconsistent and dependent upon whichever JUDGE had heard a given case. It was common for judges to order such practices as whippings and mutilations to compel a suspect to confess to a crime or series of crimes. The administration of JUSTICE was capricious and often corrupted by bribery. The rise of Enlightenment ideas and of a growing middle class pushed many philosophers to consider a system of justice that was fair, proportionate, and rational. In the midst of this revolution in thinking, Cesare Beccaria published *On Crimes and Punishments*, the book most scholars consider the founding statement of modern CRIMINOLOGY.

CESARE BECCARIA AND *ON CRIMES AND PUNISHMENTS*

Beccaria was born into a middle-class family and was classically educated. He entered the Jesuit college in Parma to study mathematics but soon changed his emphasis to economics. Influenced by Montesquieu and Bentham, Beccaria believed that government was a social CONTRACT between government and the governed and believed that policy should promote utility, a philosophy promoting the greatest happiness (not good) for the greatest number. He published a number of works outlining his philosophy, but his treatise on crime stands as his greatest work. Toward the end of his life, he served as chair of law at Palentine College and served in the Italian government as an economic adviser.

On Crimes and Punishment is the first statement of Enlightenment principles applied to crime. The work calls for a complete reform of the Italian penal system, from eliminating the death penalty to reform of the judicial system, calling for a new theory that grounded justice on Enlightenment principles of rational humanism. Beccaria called for such reforms as making punishments proportionate to the crime committed; an end to the death penalty; the decriminalization of suicide; and for a penal code designed to deter crime, rather than to punish it. The work was remarkably influential and became the basis for the classical theory of crime.

TENETS OF THE CLASSICAL THEORY OF CRIME

Beccaria's work outlined a theory of criminal justice that attempted to balance the need for social order with the Enlightenment's concern for protecting individuals from the power of government. Thus, the theory begins with the assumption that individuals exercise free will, that they choose their lives and actions. Under this assumption, individuals will choose to commit a crime as long as the benefits of that action outweigh the costs of trial and incarceration. Because crime is a conscious choice, those who commit crimes should be held responsible for their actions. The CRIMINAL JUSTICE SYSTEM should deter criminal acts and should seek to punish those who commit crimes. Followers of the classical theory of crime reject the notion that social forces can compel a person to choose crime. Classical theorists generally do not believe in RESTORATIVE JUSTICE or in REHABILITATION. Since crime is a rational calculation, the penal system should provide certain, proportional punishment for crimes. It reflects the modern notion of allowing the punishment to fit the crime.

The classical theory of crime also introduced modern ideas of the judiciary. First, the judiciary should be independent of influences from either the executive or the legislative branches of government. Judges are to be independent in order to administer justice fairly. Second, the criminal procedure from ARREST, to trial, to decision and APPEAL should be open for public inspection, and all judicial proceedings should be recorded for review. Third, courts must follow the rule of law, meaning that all defendants enter a trial presumed to be innocent and tried only for those offenses defined by statute. During the medieval period, it was possible for one to be tried for an offense that did not exist in the law. Finally, classical theorists argue that because of the loss of liberty that results in a criminal conviction, courts must interpret criminal statutes using a strict rule of construction: The judiciary must not interpret a law to include an offense not specifically addressed in a given statute or law.

The classical theory of crime also outlined new ideas about how judges decide cases. Judges are to have a great degree of DISCRETION, or freedom, in deciding how laws apply to specific cases; judges must have some discretion to exercise mercy. This discretion is limited, however, by codes of judicial ethics, statutory intent, and legislative rules, i.e., limited by the concept of the rule of law. Judges must give sentences of determinate length as specified by the law. Once again, this is a repudiation of the medieval practice of permitting a magistrate or judge to extend or shorten a person's sentence based on personal biases or bribes.

The classical theory of crime dominated legal thinking until the 20th century. With the development of scientific methods, newer theories of crime arose; however, most of them owe their existence to Beccaria and his followers. One line of theory, the rational choice school, is considered a descendant of the classical model. Other schools of thought such as legal positivism, social learning theory anomie, and gender theory reject the individual responsibility assumption in classical theory, arguing that crime is a sociological phenomenon rather than a decision-making one.

Classical criminal theory remains influential today, especially in public discourse over issues of crime and punishment, mandatory sentencing, and the causes of crime. While it is no longer a dominant theory in criminal justice, its tenets form much of the institutional basis of Western criminal justice, defendant rights, and criminal procedure.

For more information

Haining, Robert. *Spatial Data Analysis: Theory and Practice.* Cambridge: Cambridge University Press, 2003.

Radzinowicz, Leon. *Adventures In Criminology.* New York: Routledge, 2002.

Michael P. Bobic
West Virginia Wesleyan College

Clayton Act Clayton Act refers to a group of federal laws (15 U.S.C. 12–27) which supplement the SHERMAN ACT in proscribing unlawful restraints of trade and monopolies. It is part of the cluster of laws referred to as "ANTITRUST LAWS." The Clayton Act was enacted on October 15, 1914, and has been amended since only to make technical changes. These changes include allowing plaintiffs to recover interest on damages (1980) and allowing foreign governments to recover treble damages in certain circumstances (1982).

The Clayton Act prohibits price discrimination that may substantially lessen competition or may tend to create a monopoly. By "price discrimination," the statute contemplates different consumers being charged different prices for the same good for reasons not connected to the cost of the good. The rationale behind the policy objective of preventing price discrimination is that it is economically inefficient. The inefficiency leads to higher prices for consumers and a lessening of competition.

Price discrimination can take many different forms and is prohibited regardless of whether the buyer or seller initiates the unlawful pricing. Some examples of price discrimination are tie-ins, bribes, rebates, and discount prices. A tie-in occurs when the purchase of one product is tied to the purchase of another. For example, a seller of printer toner might require customers to also purchase paper as a condition of toner sales. Such a requirement might lessen competition in the paper market. Bribes occur when some customers are given an incentive to purchase not available to all customers in proportionally equal terms. Rebates are similar to bribes but are more directly associated with the product. Sometimes these types of prohibited behavior overlap. For example, a movie distributor might require a chain of theaters to run an unpopular movie in order to run a blockbuster (a tie-in) but give a rebate on advertising associated with the popular movie.

Discount pricing generally arises in the context of either vertical or horizontal integration. Vertical integration occurs when a seller moves up or down in a line of commerce. For example, if a distributor entered the retail sales market it would move down the line of commerce. If that distributor entered the manufacturing market, it would move up the line of commerce. Discount pricing arises when one level in the vertical line offers to another level a discount not available to competitors. Horizontal integration occurs when a seller expands at one level in the line of commerce. For example, if a distributor merged with several other distributors, it would expand at one level in the line of commerce. Discount pricing arises when the newly expanded distributor provides discounts not available to competitors. Only vertical and horizontal integration that substantially lessens competition is prohibited.

The Clayton Act also provides for a private cause of action so that individuals who are injured by the proscribed behavior may sue for damages. The act provides for compensatory damages, injunctive relief, and treble damages. Compensatory damages seek to place the aggrieved party in the position they would have been in had the violations not occurred. Injunctive relief takes the form of a court order prohibiting continued violations of the law. Treble damages serve as a PUNISHMENT for any violation of the act. The treble damages provision triples the award of actual damages.

For more information

Hovencamp, H. *Federal Antitrust Policy: The Law of Competition and Its Practice.* 2nd ed. St. Paul, Minn.: West, 2000.

Ross, S. R. *Principles of Antitrust Law.* Westbury, N.Y.: Foundation Press, 1993.

Sullivan, E. T., and Harrison, J. L. *Understanding Antitrust and Its Economic Implications.* 2nd ed. New York: Matthew Bender, 1994.

Anthony Smith,
University of California, San Diego

clear and convincing evidence Clear and convincing evidence is a standard of proof that is more rigorous than the one that is generally employed in civil litigation.

In the ADVERSARIAL PROCESS of court proceedings, the litigants on both sides present their versions of incidents or transactions that occurred somewhere else at some time in the past. How is a fact finder (JUDGE or JURY) supposed to determine the truth among these conflicting versions of events? What is required is some formula by which fact finders can consider how convinced they are by the proof that has been submitted in the trial or hearing. In court, judges and juries are guided by standards of proof or degrees of belief that govern various types of cases. These range from the least rigorous "PREPONDERANCE OF THE EVIDENCE" used in most civil cases to the most rigorous "beyond a REASONABLE DOUBT" standard used in criminal cases. Somewhere in between is "clear and convincing evidence," a standard of proof that is employed when proof by a preponderance of the evidence is not considered to be demanding enough. Standards of proof are generally established by statutes and case law. According to the U.S. Supreme Court, a standard of proof "serves to allocate the risk of error between the litigants and to indicate the relative importance attached to the ultimate decision" (*Addington v. Texas,* 441 U.S. 418 [1979]). Preponderance of the evidence is the appropriate standard of proof for ordinary civil lawsuits because it allocates the risk of loss equally between the parties. Sometimes, however, rights or interests of such importance are involved in a civil suit that one side deserves greater protection than the other. In such instances, stated the Supreme Court, the clear and convincing evidence standard provides "a middle level of BURDEN OF PROOF that strikes a fair balance between the rights of the individual and the legitimate concerns of the state" (*Addington,* 441 U.S. 418).

Clear and convincing evidence is used in cases in which the rights to be determined or issues to be decided are more serious than whether one party or another is entitled to money, such as a significant deprivation of liberty or the loss of important personal rights. For example, determination of paternity must be by clear and convincing evidence, as must termination of parental rights. Civil commitment of a mentally ill person requires proof by clear and convincing evidence, as does the determination as to whether an incompetent person who is terminally ill may have life-sustaining treatment withheld or withdrawn. The clear and convincing evidence standard is also used in civil cases involving adverse possession of property, libel and slander, and FRAUD and deceit. In all these instances, it is considered necessary for the fact finder to be more certain of which litigant is right than in ordinary civil cases. But how does a fact finder decide what constitutes proof by clear and convincing evidence? How does a judge instruct a jury about the standard, and how does the judge apply the standard in a bench trial? A survey of judges found that most regarded proof by clear and convincing evidence to be about a 75 percent certainty. According to one recent federal court decision, "'clear and convincing evidence' is that quantum of proof which produces in the mind of the trier of fact a firm belief or conviction as to the truth of the allegations sought to be established, evidence so clear, direct and weighty, and convincing as to enable the fact finder to come to a clear conviction, without hesitancy, of the truth of the precise facts in issue" (*Elliott Associates, L.P. v. Republic of Peru,* 12 F.Supp.2d 328 [1998]). All courts agree that proof by clear and convincing evidence is something less than "beyond a reasonable doubt" and more than "preponderance of the evidence," but the precise meaning of the standard and how it should be applied are issues that must be reevaluated frequently.

For more information

Addington v. Texas, 441 U.S. 418 (1979).

McCauliff, C. M. A. "Burdens of Proof: Degrees of Belief, Quanta of Evidence, or Constitutional Guarantees?" *Vanderbilt Law Review* 35 (November 1982): 1293–1334.

Santosky v. Kramer, 455 U.S. 745 (1982).

Celia A. Sgroi
State University of New York, Oswego

Clinton cops The term *Clinton cops* has come to mean those officers hired under the Community Oriented Policing Services (COPS) program established as part of the Violent Crime Control and Law Enforcement Act of 1994. The term comes from President Bill Clinton's promise that the program would place 100,000 police officers in communities by 2004. While the program has been remarkably successful in placing officers on the streets, especially in poor, urban communities, it has never achieved the goal of 100,000 officers. Most estimates place the total number hired at between 37,000 to 92,000 new officers serving in communities that would not be able to afford them otherwise.

President Clinton's claim that the program would place 100,000 officers on the streets was unfortunate, as the program does more than hire police officers. In essence, the Community Oriented Policing Services program is a grants program assisting communities in funding numerous COMMUNITY-POLICING programs, from hiring officers to updating computer systems, to purchasing new police cars, to improving officer training. Taken as a whole, the COPS program appears to have been successful in three areas: hiring new officers, providing improved technology, and providing civilian aids so that desk officers could do more patrolling.

Critics of the COPS program charge it with several types of failures. Most analysts agree that the COPS program has been subject to waste and FRAUD. An audit in 2002 of just 3 percent of COPS grants found fraud in close to 30 percent of programs funded. States and communities complain that they are required to keep officers on the beat for one year after COPS funding ceases. Despite these problems, the Obama administration has asked Congress to continue the program, requesting funding for three more years.

The evidence remains controversial, but the COPS program seems to have been one factor of many in reducing crime during the 1990s and into the 21st century. There are numerous theories about why this would be the case. Until the middle 1990s, most social scientists disputed the claim that police officers reduced crime, noting that officers seldom catch criminals in the midst of a crime, and that many types of crime, including petit THEFT, go unsolved. However, other studies indicate that targeted use of police officers, for example in high-crime "hot spots," can indeed reduce crime. Scholars also point to many other factors occurring at the same time, including changes in gun laws, stricter penalties for crime, and increased incarceration.

For more information

Eisler, Peter, and Kevin Johnson. "10 Years and $10B Later, COPS Drawing Scrutiny." *USA Today* (10 April 2005) A1.

Ludwig, Jane, and John J. Donohue, III. "More COPS," *Brookings Institute Policy Brief* 158 (2009).

The COPS Grants and Information Web Page. Available online. URL: http://www.cops.usdoj.gov/.

Michael P. Bobic
West Virginia Wesleyan College

Clinton v. Jones 520 U.S. 681 (1997) *Clinton v. Jones,* decided by a unanimous Supreme Court, held that a sitting president has no constitutional right to put off, until he leaves office, a civil lawsuit alleging he engaged in harmful conduct in his private life.

Paula Jones sued President Bill Clinton in 1994 for making "abhorrent," unsuccessful sexual advances toward her in 1991, when Clinton was governor of Arkansas and Jones was a state employee. On two grounds, the president asked the courts to delay all pretrial proceedings and the trial itself until after he left office. First, the president argued that the separation of powers doctrine prevented the courts from imposing on a sitting president by requiring him to defend himself in court. Second, the president claimed that if the case were allowed to proceed, the need to defend himself in court would divert critical time and attention from his presidential duties, a problem that could only grow worse as the Court's decision would encourage others to sue the president.

The Supreme Court rejected these claims, stating that the drain on the president's time and attention would be minimal (at least in this case) and that a decision to allow the lawsuit to proceed would be "unlikely" to encourage many others to sue the president. The Court emphasized that a president may not be sued for his official acts as president in order to protect him from fear that his actions on behalf of the public might result in his being sued—as the Court had ruled in *Nixon v. Fitzgerald*, 457 U.S. 73 (1982). But the justices saw no such public interest in protecting a president from lawsuits based on his private behaviors.

The ruling did not result in further lawsuits against President Clinton in his remaining three and a half years in office. Such lawsuits can, however, severely embarrass a president. The pretrial proceedings in the Jones suit unearthed President Clinton's extramarital affair with Monica Lewinsky while in office. His apparent desire to conceal that relationship and his prevarications while under oath in response to questioning on that subject led to his IMPEACHMENT by the House of Representatives (but later ACQUITTAL by the Senate).

Clinton and Jones eventually settled out of court when Clinton paid Jones $850,000.

For more information

Kasten, Martin. "Summons at 1600: *Clinton v. Jones*' Impact on the American Presidency," *Arkansas Law Review* 51 (1998): 551–74.

Rozell, Mark J., and Wilcox Clyde, eds. *The Clinton Scandal and the Future of American Government*. Washington, D.C.: Georgetown University Press, 2000.

Weeden, L. Darnell. "The President and Mrs. Jones Were in Federal Court: The Litigation Established No Constitutional Immunity for President Clinton," *George Mason Law Review* 7 (Winter 1999): 361–387.

Michael Cominskey
Pennsylvania State University

Collin v. Smith 578 F.2d 1197 (1978) *Collin v. Smith* is a famous case taking place in Skokie, Illinois, a Chicago suburb, and it was the scene of a two-year struggle in the 1970s over a planned march by an American Nazi group that was strongly opposed by a large group of Holocaust survivors. The bitter dispute put the First Amendment to one of its toughest tests and has come to symbolize the tension between FREEDOM OF SPEECH and freedom from unwanted speech.

The village of Skokie had a population of 70,000 in 1977, and by most estimates 30,000 of those residents were Jewish, including 6,000 Holocaust survivors and their families. It was in this community that Frank Collin, leader of the Chicago-based Nazi group, National Socialist Party of America, planned to march on May 1, 1977. Word of the planned march triggered alarms throughout the Holocaust survivors' community.

A prolonged legal battle ensued; before it was finished, the case went to the Supreme Court three times and up and down in the state and federal courts. The end result was, first, a ruling that an INJUNCTION issued to stop the march was unconstitutional, and second, a decision by Collin to call off the march.

Faced with the planned march, Skokie invoked a local ordinance that prohibited distributing materials that promote hate, that barred parade permits to groups portraying or inciting hatred based on RELIGION and other factors, and that disallowed demonstrations by political groups wearing military uniforms.

An Illinois trial JUDGE issued an injunction to stop the march, an appeals court agreed, and the state supreme court refused to hear an expedited APPEAL, meaning the injunction against the march remained in effect. The U.S. Supreme Court, in *National Socialist Party of America v. Village of Skokie*, 432 U.S. 43 (1977), ruled 5-4 that the failure of the Illinois Supreme Court to give expedited review to the injunction had an effect similar to an unconstitutional prior restraint of freedom of speech.

With the march still on hold, the high court sent the case back to the state courts. The Illinois Supreme Court, in *Village of Skokie v. National Socialist Party of America,* 373 N.E.2d 21 (1978), said the First Amendment protected the march, even if there was potential for violence from hostile onlookers, and also protected display of the Nazi swastika. Meanwhile, Collin challenged the constitutionality of the Skokie ordinances and won in a decision of the U.S. COURT OF APPEALS for the Seventh Circuit, *Collin v. Smith,* 578 F.2d 1197 (1978). The Supreme Court refused to hear the case, *Smith v. Collin,* 436 U.S. 953 (1978). Collin's march had been rescheduled, but after winning the principle in various courts that his demonstration was protected by the First Amendment, he called off the plans to march in Skokie.

Throughout the legal proceedings, courts accepted the view that the First Amendment requires content-neutral regulation and does not permit suppression of speech because of opposition to content. To press this point, Collin enlisted the help of the AMERICAN CIVIL LIBERTIES UNION, which was criticized by some of its members for representing a Nazi, and which saw a loss of membership and contributions.

For more information

Smolla, Rodney A. *Smolla and Nimmer on Freedom of Speech.* Deer Field, Ill.: Clark Boardman Callaghan, 1996.

Strum, Philippa. *When the Nazis Came to Skokie: Freedom for Speech We Hate.* Lawrence: University Press of Kansas, 1999.

Stephen Wermiel
American University, Washington College of Law

Columbine shootings The Columbine shootings refer to the killing and injuring of several individuals at Columbine High School in 1999. This incident represents the single most lethal shooting at a school in American history.

On Tuesday, April 20, 1999, 12 students and a teacher were killed at Columbine High School, near Denver, Colorado. Twenty-four others were injured, three of them while seeking to escape. The official report was released on May 15, 2000, explaining that two students, by the name of Eric Harris and Dylan Klebold, acting alone, engaged in a killing spree before committing suicide. However, a closer analysis of local news coverage and official reports reveals that the issue is far more complex than what was first thought, and we are left with more questions than answers.

To begin, numerous EYEWITNESSES reported to the *Denver Post,* to the *Denver Rocky Mountain News* and to the FBI that the shooting went on for two to four hours, whereas the official report states that "it ended after 45 minutes." Second, it is not clear how two teenagers alone could have placed throughout the high school "95 homemade explosive devices," including two 20-pound propane tank-bombs, all at the same time and unnoticed, while carrying four shotguns and 9mm handguns and plenty of ammunition. Unfortunately, a custodian was replacing the security camera videotape at precisely the time when Harris and Klebold entered the cafeteria. Still, more than 50 eye and ear witnesses provided EVIDENCE that five to eight shooters were involved, and some of them have identified by name two other participants, members of the infamous, so-called Trenchcoat Mafia—ostensibly "a group of disgruntled Goths." Even the reasons given for the killing spree, namely the intense and bitter rivalry between jock culture and goth culture, leave much to be desired if one considers that Harris and Klebold shot randomly and planned to blow up the entire school, hoping to kill more than 500 people in an act of domestic TERRORISM that would "outdo" what Timothy McVeigh and Terry Nichols did in Oklahoma City, almost exactly four years earlier, on April 19, 1995. The two murderous students also wanted to hijack an airplane at Denver

Evidence connected to the Columbine massacre on display for the first time (Getty Images)

International Airport and, of all things, slam it into a New York skyscraper.

Based on the available data, the Denver journalist Dave Cullen has concluded that Harris fits the profile of the psychopath, that is, a person devoid of empathy, authoritarian, egomaniac, manipulative, predatorial, and lacking feelings of remorse or guilt. Instead, Klebold resembles more closely the angry, depressive, and introvert suicidal type. It is, nevertheless, always important to warn readers against the logical fallacy of psychological reductionism in the study of extreme behavior.

Psychologists have pointed out that Harris did not display several of the traits typically associated with a psychopath, and it is equally possible that as victims of BULLYING they were mainly motivated by an unquenchable desire to take revenge and to "kickstart a revolution" of oppressed students as themselves, as they declared in the videos they made before conducting the assault. This would be more in line with political terrorism. Incidentally, the date of the rampage coincided with Adolf Hitler's birthday, and Harris was reportedly obsessed with Nazi Germany memorabilia, something that might corroborate the suggestion that with their avenger attitude they sought JUSTICE by destroying the people and institutions they held responsible for their oppression. What one can infer from reading his diary is that Harris was indeed enraged with jocks and humanity in general: "Everyone is always making fun of me because of how I look, how fucking weak I am, and shit, well I will get you all back: ultimate fucking revenge here."

Yet bullying is common, and school shootings are relatively infrequent. This means that there are no neat, exhaustive explanations for what happened that day, and any tentative observations are subject to revision. Constantly subjected to gay-baiting and to a total desecration of their masculine ideals in a hypermasculinity-focused environment, Harris and Klebold might have been overly concerned about the danger of being exposed as fallible males. It is possible that they eventually resorted to violence to prove their manhood and thereby heal the narcissistic wound they had suffered. This kind of violence could stem, at least in part, from a worldview in which vigorous antagonism and the desire to seize, exploit, and put oneself above morality are praised as virtues instead of being lambasted as malignant vices. If so, the shooters could be understood as thoughtless, ideological creatures, pushed by aesthetically and psychologically pleasant but seriously misguided and intoxicating fictions of masculine purity, authenticity, and integrity to overcome their perhaps congenitally weak inhibitions, making them immune to moral considerations.

For more information

Cullen, Dave. *Columbine*. New York: Twelve-Grand Central/Hachette, 2009.

Kass, Jeff. *Columbine: A True Crime Story, a Victim, the Killers and the Nation's Search for Answers*. Denver: Ghost Road Press, 2009.

Larkin, Ralph W. *Comprehending Columbine*. Philadelphia: Temple University Press, 2007.

Stefano Fait
Fondazione Museo Storico del Trentino, Trento, Italy

the commerce clause The commerce clause of the U.S. CONSTITUTION gives Congress the power to regulate many activities between the United States and other countries and within the United States. It was the outgrowth of the concern over commercial strife that precipitated the call for the Constitutional Convention. Despite this, the Constitution deals with commerce with deceptive brevity. Article I, section 8, clause 3 states: "Congress shall have the power to regulate commerce with foreign nations, and among the several states, and with the Indian tribes." This positive, but imprecise, grant of power to Congress is limited somewhat by a prohibition against export taxes and a requirement that the ports of no state shall have preferred status.

It should be noted that the terms are not defined. What is "commerce"? What is "commerce among the states"? What is the meaning of "regulate"? Today we have an elaborate framework to answer these and similar questions, but that framework has been developed through experience and adjudication.

Congress began the regulation of foreign commerce immediately but waited almost a century before it began serious regulation of domestic commerce with the INTERSTATE COMMERCE ACT of 1887. As a result, the bulk of constitutional adjudication regarding commerce involved state regulation. That topic is covered elsewhere. In this section, the focus is on federal power over commerce.

In *GIBBONS V. OGDEN*, 22 U.S. (9 Wheat.)1 (1824), which was the first major commerce case to be decided by the Supreme Court, CHIEF JUSTICE JOHN MARSHALL broadly defined commerce as "commerce which concerns more States than one." Only those activities that had no effect outside of a single state were beyond congressional JURISDICTION. Under this conceptualization, Congress could regulate business that operated within a single state if it had an effect outside the state.

Marshall's "effects" test to determine the limits of congressional power over commerce was subsequently subverted into a dichotomy between "intrastate" and "interstate" commerce. The process began when Chief Justice Taney, a states-righter, in the *License Cases*, 46 U.S. (5 How.) 504 (1847), wrote of "internal or domestic commerce, which belongs to the States, and over which Congress can exercise no control." This apparently innocuous restatement creates a geographic basis for the division of the commerce power between the states and the federal government.

However, since Congress did not actively pursue its powers over "commerce among the States" for almost a century, the interstate/intrastate distinction presented few problems. And when Congress entered the field with the Interstate Commerce Act of 1887, it entered the area of interstate transportation where its domain was largely uncontested. But when Congress attempted to use the commerce power to regulate activities other than transportation, the dichotomy between interstate and intrastate became important.

Under the restrictive concept of interstate commerce, Congress could regulate an activity within a state only if Congress could establish that the local activity had a "direct" effect on interstate commerce. An "indirect" effect would not suffice to authorize congressional action even though that "indirect" effect was nationwide. As a result, mining, manufacturing, and agriculture were beyond congressional control. For example, in 1895 the Supreme Court ruled that a trust which controlled virtually all sugar production in the United States was not subject to federal ANTITRUST LAWS because manufacture was not commerce (*United States v. E. C. Knight Co.*, 156 U.S. 1 [1895]).

In the early 1900s the Supreme Court ruled that the Chicago stockyards, although located within one city, had a direct impact on interstate commerce and upheld federal regulation. It also upheld prohibitively high federal taxation on oleomargarine colored to look like butter and approved the exclusion of lottery tickets from interstate commerce.

However, few federal laws were upheld, and in 1918 the Court returned to the more restrictive position. *HAMMER V. DAGENHART*, 247 U.S. 251 (1918), held that Congress could not exclude child-made products from interstate commerce because it was attempting to regulate manufacture. Congressional attempts to place heavy taxes on companies that used child labor also failed.

Thus, when President Roosevelt and Congress launched the New Deal in 1933, the constitutional status of congressional power over commerce, or the Supreme Court's interpretation thereof, was somewhat ambiguous but generally hostile to federal attempts to use the commerce clause as a way to regulate any aspect of manufacturing, mining, or agriculture. In *Schechter Poultry Corp. v. United States*, 295 U.S.495 (1935), and a series of other cases, the Court used the narrow construction to strike down the major legislation undergirding the New Deal: Although Congress could regulate railroad transportation, it could not create a pension plan for railroad workers; federal regulation of agricultural production was unconstitutional because production did not have a direct impact on interstate commerce; and production codes regulating working conditions and wages were outside the scope of congressional power because production was not directly related to interstate commerce. In short, the Court refused to acknowledge that local activity had any meaningful or "direct" impact on commerce among the states and ruled Congress had no power to act under the commerce clause.

However, apparently responding to President Roosevelt's threat to pack the Supreme Court, it reversed its position in 1937 and upheld legislation very similar to that which it had voided only a few months before. Abandoning the "direct" and "indirect" distinction, the Court endorsed an "effects" theory that appeared to give Congress virtually unlimited power over all aspects of commercial activity. From 1937 to 1995 the Supreme Court, with one exception that was subsequently overturned, upheld the far-reaching application of the commerce clause to all aspects of life, most notably its use to end racial discrimination at all levels.

In 1995 the Supreme Court suddenly reversed course. In *U.S. v. Lopez*, 514 U.S. 549 (1995), it struck down the Gun Free School Zones Act of 1990, holding that the possession of a gun on school grounds was not an economic activity that would have a substantial effect on interstate commerce. To uphold the law, the Court said, would be to convert congressional commerce clause authority into a general POLICE POWER of the sort held only by the states. The Court followed up five years later by striking down the federal VIOLENCE AGAINST WOMEN ACT in *U.S. v. Morrison*, 529 U.S. 598 (2000).

The majority opinions in the two cases not only reject the broad power of Congress to regulate commerce, which was uncontested from 1937 to 1995 and appears to resurrect the "direct" and "indirect" effect distinction, but the language is also reminiscent of the rhetoric of dual FEDERALISM which dominated prior to the New Deal. *Lopez* and *Morrison* may be the opening rounds in a new constitutional revolution that will dramatically reduce the power of the federal government under the commerce clause. As the 21st century begins, it is impossible to foretell the outcome of the new struggle over the meaning of the commerce clause. An area of CONSTITUTIONAL INTERPRETATION that had been settled for two-thirds of a century is in flux.

One sign of the potential revolution that these decisions may portend surrounded legal challenges beginning in 2010 to the Patient Protection and Affordable Care Act. The act, labeled by its critics as "Obamacare," was a major piece of legislation adopted by Congress to provide more individuals with health-care coverage in the United States. Among the act's major provisions is a mandate requiring individuals to purchase insurance if they are not otherwise covered by their employer or some other program. Critics of the mandate argue that Congress lacks the authority under the commerce clause to require individuals to purchase insurance. In support of their arguments, they cite *Lopez* and *Morrison*. Conversely, supporters argue that decisions not to purchase health care do affect instate commerce, and they cite a host of New Deal cases as PRECEDENT.

In 2010, three federal district courts split on the constitutionality of that individual purchase mandate, with two upholding it as a valid exercise of commerce clause authority and one rejecting it. In 2011, one federal court of appeals upheld the act as a valid regulation of commerce. The issue as it is addressed by the courts, eventually including the Supreme Court, will clarify the scope of the commerce clause for years to come.

For more information

Gunther, Gerald, and Kathleen M. Sullivan. "The Commerce Power." In *Constitutional Law.* 13th ed. Westbury, N.Y.: Foundation Press, 1997.

Schultz, David, John R. Vile, and Michelle D. Deardorff. *Constitutional Law in Contemporary America,* vol. 1. New York: Oxford University Press, 2010.

William E. Brigman
University of Houston—Downtown

commercial speech Commercial speech is defined by the U.S. Supreme Court as speech characterized by: (1) an advertisement (2) that refers to a specific product and (3) the speaker is economically motivated.

In *Valentine v. Chrestensen* (1942), the first commercial speech case to come before it, the U.S. Supreme Court held that "purely commercial advertising" was not entitled to any protection by the First Amendment. However, in two cases in the mid-1970s, the Court rejected the rationale of *Valentine* and began to hold that commercial speech had some First Amendment protection, albeit not to the same degree as "core" political speech.

In *Bigelow v. Virginia* (1975) and *Virginia State Board of Pharmacy v. Virginia Citizens Consumer Council, Inc.* (1976), the Supreme Court concluded that society has a strong interest in the free flow of commercial information, such as the availability of ABORTIONS (in *Bigelow*) and the prices of prescription drugs (in *Virginia State Board of Pharmacy*). Therefore, such commercial speech enjoyed the protection of the First Amendment. At the same time, however, the Court held that certain restrictions on commercial speech would be permissible, such as a prohibition on false or misleading ads or advertisements of illegal products or services.

Since these two landmark decisions, the Supreme Court has held the First Amendment's commercial speech protection to apply to advertising by lawyers (*Bates v. State Bar of Arizona,*

1977), advertisements for contraceptives (*Bolger v. Youngs Drug Products Corporation,* 1983), labels listing alcoholic content (*Rubin v. Coors Brewing Company,* 1995), and the advertisement of liquor prices (*44 Liquormart Inc. v. Rhode Island,* 1996). Conversely, the Court has sometimes accepted restrictions on commercial speech, such as upholding a federal law prohibiting broadcasters from advertising other states' lotteries in states that do not allow lotteries (*United States v. Edge Broadcasting Company,* 1993).

If, under the First Amendment, the government may regulate or even prohibit some forms of commercial speech but not others, it was incumbent upon the Court to develop a test or standard to make that determination; this it did in *Central Hudson Gas & Electric Corporation v. Public Service Commission of New York* (1980). In that case, the justices developed a four-part test to determine when commercial speech could be regulated by the government. The first element of this test is to determine whether the commercial speech is protected by the First Amendment. This is achieved by asking whether the speech concerns lawful activity and is not misleading. If the answer is "yes," then the commercial speech at issue has First Amendment protection. A court would then examine the government's regulation to determine (1) if the government's interest in regulating the speech is substantial, (2) whether the regulation actually works in a way that advances that interest, and (3) whether the regulation is not more extensive than necessary to serve that interest. All three of these elements must be proved by the government in order for it to regulate commercial speech. A single "no" on any of these three questions will result in the commercial speech regulations being declared an unconstitutional violation of the First Amendment's FREEDOM OF SPEECH protections.

Although the Supreme Court backtracked on the four-part *Central Hudson Gas* test in *Posadas de Puerto Rico Associates v. Tourism Company of Puerto Rico* in 1986, 10 years later in *44 Liquormart* it disavowed *Posadas* and returned to the *Central Hudson Gas* test, which remains the standard in commercial speech cases.

For more information

DeVore, P. Cameron. *Advertising and Commercial Speech: A First Amendment Guide.* New York: PLI Press, 1999.

Shiffrin, Steven H., and Jesse H. Choper. *The First Amendment: Cases, Comments, Questions.* St. Paul, Minn.: West, 1991.

Michael W. Bowers
University of Nevada, Las Vegas

community corrections Community corrections refers to correctional programs and activities that are alternatives to incarceration for offenders at various stages of the criminal justice process. They were developed because traditional incarceration was not effective in reducing crime or RECIDIVISM. Community corrections involve the supervision of individuals who are facing conviction or offenders who have already been convicted of a crime. Interest in community corrections has grown in the past several decades as PRISON POPULATIONS have rapidly increased. All programs are intended to address the issues that led to the offender's criminal behavior and to hold the offender accountable for the offense while protecting the public.

Community corrections include a variety of programs and approaches, among them RESTITUTION programs, fine options programs, PROBATION, intensive supervision, substance abuse treatment, community service, conditional sentence programs, BOOT CAMPS, attendance center programs, ELECTRONIC MONITORING, community-based centers, halfway houses, and PAROLE. These programs can be delivered individually, coupled, or used in sequence. The probation or parole officer can make decisions about the effectiveness and appropriateness of a current alternative.

Community corrections programs have been developed as (1) a means of cost savings by reducing prison populations, (2) to improve

SENTENCING outcomes, including reduced recidivism, (3) for humanitarian reasons, and (4) to respond to public opinion. Their ability to obtain these outcomes varies greatly.

The argument for cost savings is that it is less expensive to supervise an offender in the community than to incarcerate him or her. Since up to 90 percent of prison costs are fixed (buildings and staff), identifiable short-term savings can be realized only if alternatives to incarceration result in a JURISDICTION not having to construct more prisons or jails, does not have to pay fees to other jurisdictions for incarcerating convicted offenders, or is able to close a facility or a portion of a facility when the prison population is reduced. Long-term savings, which are more difficult to measure, can result from the reduction in recidivism, and thus the long-term reduction in crime and criminal convictions and incarceration.

Two of the strongest arguments for community corrections are that they are more effective in reducing recidivism and are more humanitarian. They allow the offender to remain in and have a more successful reintegration into the community, through educational and vocational programs and counseling. They are seen as being more responsive to the needs of the offenders, the victims, and the community. Community corrections avoid the undesirable effects of incarceration, including stigmatization and exposure to other criminals.

Community corrections are used primarily for less serious offenders or for offenders for whom the likelihood of REHABILITATION is greatest. Their purpose is to punish and at the same time to change behavior. The demands of a community corrections program may be more difficult for an offender to meet than simply spending time behind bars, but they may also allow the offender to develop the necessary skills and abilities to live a lawful and useful life. Some of the more common community corrections programs are:

- Alternative measures programs, also known as diversion or conditional sentence programs, where the offender agrees to a kind of contractual agreement to answer for his or her crime. If the terms of the agreement are met, the offender never formally enters THE CRIMINAL JUSTICE SYSTEM.
- Restitution programs require the offender to pay the victim for damages or loss. These programs may be a part of larger RESTORATIVE JUSTICE programs, where the offender and the victim meet regularly and come to terms with their roles as offender and victim. Often this involves some kind of forgiveness by the victim.
- Fine options programs require the offender to pay fines that reflect actual costs incurred by the victim, as well as intangible costs (sometimes referred to as "pain and suffering").
- Community service programs require the offender to perform work in the community.
- Probation provides for the supervision of the offender in the community, with attached behavioral conditions. (See entry on probation.)
- Boot camps are intensive training programs that involve strict discipline as well as counseling and education or skill training. They are intended to provide offenders with structure and self-control that they may have lacked in their family or home environment. Boot camps are used primarily with younger offenders.
- Attendance centers or day reporting centers are nonresidential community facilities to which the offender is required to report for supervision or programs. Educational and vocational programs may be offered at an attendance center, as well as substance abuse counseling, anger management counseling, community service, victim restitution programs, and a wide variety of other personal and vocational development programs.
- Community-based centers or halfway houses are residential facilities in the community. Offenders are required to be in the center or house in the evening, but they can leave during the day for work, education, or training.

- Electronic monitoring involves fitting an offender with an ankle bracelet that transmits signals of his or her whereabouts to a correctional officer or monitoring facility. Depending on the terms of the sentence, the offender may be able to hold a job or attend school while being monitored but cannot leave a prescribed area.
- Comprehensive sanction centers were developed by the Federal Bureau of Prisons to provide for more structured community-based programs that more closely control inmates' access to the community. The strictest level of supervision is 24-hour confinement; this differs from traditional incarceration, however, because the facilities are smaller, located in communities, and include programming in which the offenders are required to participate.
- Parole is also considered a community corrections program because it is the extension of corrections in the community after a period of incarceration.

There are two major obstacles to the use of community corrections. First, JUDGES may be unwilling to sentence offenders to such programs, either because they believe that the programs are not effective, or because they believe there are insufficient public resources to support additional offenders in existing programs. This is a kind of "catch-22" since the development and support of programs depends on judges' willingness to include them in sentencing options.

The second obstacle is greater: public opinion. In general the public supports PUNISHMENTS that hold offenders accountable, supervise and monitor them, and increase the likelihood that they will not reoffend. The public needs to be assured that community corrections are "real" sentences and that the alternatives do not significant increase the risks to public safety. General support for community corrections may be eroded by a NIMBY (not in my backyard) attitude—that such programs are acceptable but *not* in one's own neighborhood or community. Because citizen support in community corrections is essential to the programs' survival, it is important that citizens have information about the circumstances of cases and the probability of success of a program in rehabilitating an offender. Involvement of citizens in providing programs also increases community support.

Community corrections offer treatment programs that may be available in prison as well, but, in general, treatment programs are more effective when delivered in a community setting, not in a prison. In addition, community corrections include employment and community service options not available to incarcerated offenders. They also maintain FAMILY ties, which usually are essential for the long-term rehabilitation of offenders. Community corrections allow for some offenders to avoid incarceration altogether and for others to be reintegrated into the community more successfully.

For more information

Alarid, Leanne Fiftal, Paul F. Cromwell, and Rolando V. Del Carmen. *Community-Based Corrections.* 4th ed. Belmont, Calif.: Wadsworth, 2010.

Hauser, Robert D. *Community Corrections.* Thousand Oaks, Calif.: SAGE, 2009.

Susan C. Paddock
University of Wisconsin–Madison

community notification laws Community notification laws contributed to the development and enforcement of SEX OFFENDER registries. These laws were adapted from the Jacob Wetterling Crimes against Children and Sexually Violent Offender Registration Act passed as part of the Federal Violent Crime Control and Law Enforcement Act of 1994. The Wetterling Act allowed law enforcement authorities to track and locate convicted sex offenders. Community notification laws go one step further by allowing for information about sex offenders to be made available to the public.

Community notification laws were implemented in response to the 1994 rape and MURDER of seven-year-old Megan Kanka. On July 29, 1994, in Hamilton Township, New Jersey, Megan was deceived into going to the house of her neighbor, who promised her she could see his new puppy. Her neighbor was the convicted sex offender Jesse Timmendequas, who had recently served time in prison for aggravated ASSAULT and ATTEMPTED sexual assault against a child.

Due to public outcry and three months after her death, the New Jersey Legislature passed the community notification law known as Megan's Law, NJSA 2C:7-1 through 7-ll. On May 17, 1996, President Bill Clinton signed a federal version of the law, Megan's Law (H.R. 2137). The amendment provided states with minimum national standards to follow in developing community notification systems for sex offenders living in the state. The law also applies to all sex offenders regardless whether their victims are children or adults.

Courts or registering agencies are generally responsible for notifying offenders of their obligation to register with their local law enforcement or corrections agency upon their release. The information required for the registries include the offender's name, address, birth date, Social Security information, physical description, FINGERPRINTS, and photographs. Other information that may be required is a list of previous convictions and samples of DNA. Once offenders register with their local agency, the information is sent to a centralized registry administered by state police or a state bureau. An offender's profile can last 10 years in this registry. However, if an offender has been classified as a "sexual predator" or been convicted of additional sexual offenses, lifetime registration may be required.

Although all sex offender registries have to meet federal guidelines, variation exists among states. Additional information provided to the public may vary between the registries as well as how this information is released to the public. For example, some states do not provide information online and instead require that citizens contact their local law enforcement agencies to learn about sex offenders in their area. Other states maintain extensive and searchable online registries with detailed information about offenders. The information available online for the public may include the name, address, a photo of the offender, physical description of the offender, as well as information about past convictions and/or gender of past victims. In some cases, law enforcement officials directly notify prior victims, neighbors, schools, and community groups about registered sex offenders entering their communities. Law enforcement agencies have also used newspapers, television, radio, and community events to notify the general public.

Critics of community notification laws question their effectiveness. Many find the enactment of these laws as a political response that does little to prevent or reduce sexual assaults and offenses. Some studies have found that most victims of sexual offenses are assaulted by someone they already know, such as a FAMILY member, friend, or acquaintance. There are also concerns regarding the high costs associated with the implementation and maintenance of a law that has had no demonstrated effect.

The data also show that the laws have a negative effect on offender's ability to reintegrate into society and have an unintended negative effect on the offenders' families, past victims, and the community. There is also concern that these laws provide a false sense of security and ignore other preventative measures that could be taken to prevent sexual assaults and rehabilitate sexual offenders. Instead, critics recommend eliminating community notification laws and implementing a confidential notification system. Other recommendations call for proper SENTENCING and treatment for sex offenders, improvements in monitoring systems within PROBATION and PAROLE agencies, and laws targeting proper supervision of children.

The U.S. Supreme Court has addressed the constitutionality of community notification laws. However, in both *Connecticut Dept. of Public Safety v. Doe*, 538 U.S. 1 (2003), and in *Smith v.*

Doe, 538 U.S. 84 (2003), the Court found that sex offenders' constitutional rights were not violated by community notification laws. In general, there is still strong public support for community notification laws regardless of the consequences to the offender or other individuals.

For more information

FBI Web site, which links to all state sex offender registry Web sites. Available online. URL: http://www.fbi.gov/hq/cid/cac/states.htm.

Zgoba, Kristen, Melissa Dalessandro, Bonita Veysey, and Philip Witt. *Megan's Law: Assessing the Practical and Monetary Efficacy.* Washington, D.C.: National Institute of Justice, 2008.

Levenson, Jill S., and Leo P. Cotter. "The Effect of Megan's Law on Sex Offender Reintegration," *Journal of Contemporary Criminal Justice* 21, no. 1: 49–66.

Wilneida Negrón
CUNY Graduate Center

community policing The term *community policing* is used to describe a set of police values, strategies, and organizational reforms aimed at increasing police-community relations. It is also known as PROBLEM-ORIENTED POLICING and/or neighborhood-oriented policing. This style of policing was instituted in many American cities in the 1990s, and some advocates credit it with reducing the crime rate in the United States. Critics contend that community policing is more about public relations and that its effect on crime is debatable.

During the social unrest of the 1960s, police departments looked for ways to improve police-community relations as well as address the growing isolation between police departments and the communities they served. Team policing strategies were the first attempt at addressing this dilemma and laid the groundwork for community policing. Team policing sought to assign a geographic area to a team of police officers who would work together to learn about the neighborhood and its residents. After some initial pilot projects, team policing initiatives were discontinued. Responsible for their failure was the contradiction between an emphasis on long-term problem solving versus the need for fast response to incidents and problems within a community. Like team policing, community policing recognizes the importance of greater cooperation between the public and the police.

Community policing became an official federal policy with the passage of the Violent Crime Control and Law Enforcement Act of 1994. The crime bill authorized the U.S. ATTORNEY GENERAL to make grants to states, local governments, and other public and private entities to increase police presence through "community policing." In return, police departments were expected to invest time and energy in developing new internal management and information technology structures aimed at developing stronger bonds to the communities they serve.

Community policing strategies may be implemented in different ways. However, they all share a core value in promoting cooperation and mutual responsibility between the police and the public to work together to address safety, social disorder, and quality of life. The emphasis on values of cooperation and mutual responsibility has spurred an organizational model for police reform aimed at building stronger bonds between the police and neighborhood residents.

Police departments are faced with an array of complex crime and violence issues affecting communities. More recently, public safety problems such as illegal drugs, GANG violence, MURDERS, muggings, and BURGLARIES have challenged dominant forms of policing based on central management structures that are detached from the communities they serve. As a result, decentralizing policing management structures was seen as a key way to embed the police within the communities they serve and to promote collaboration between residents and other government and community leaders. Often at the frontline of community relations are the patrol and street officers; therefore, policing management structures often have to be adjusted in order to give patrol officers greater discretion in addressing community concerns. This strategy is in contrast to centralized top-down policing management structures in that patrol officers could assume managerial responsibility for the delivery of police services to their assigned area.

Another key component in departmental restructuring is the utilization of information-technology tools not only to increase information sharing within police departments but also between the police and neighborhood residents. The computer software COMPSTAT is an example of an information-technology system created to promote the decentralization of decision making from the top echelons to precincts at the neighborhood level.

Besides the internal reorganization of police departments, community policing strategies require that the police devote a considerable amount of energy developing new programs and activities that encourage problem solving and information sharing between the police and neighborhood residents. Necessary for the development of this relationship is trust between both parties. This goal has proved to be difficult, especially in neighborhoods with internal conflicts or where relations with the police have been strained. For example, a community policing strategy of increasing police presence in a community may be initially met with suspicion by residents.

However, many have found that over time an increase in the accessibility of the police to the public contributes to the development of trusting relationships. Regular community meetings and forums between the police and the public have been found to promote consensus building by allowing residents to provide input into police activities, as well as to identify urgent concerns and ways to resolve them. Many find that providing opportunities for the public and police to set priorities and develop common solutions increases police accountability to the public. Other activities that bring the police closer to the community include having street officers patrol by foot, bicycle, scooter, horseback, etc. within their assigned geographic regions. In addition, special community-based units are sometimes created to provide a range of crisis intervention services, which further bring the police closer to the community.

Developing and implementing community policing activities and strategies requires energy, creativity, understanding, and patience of all involved. Residents may also seek to develop their own activities to work with the police in addressing community issues. The most well known community-based crime prevention group is Neighborhood Watch. The activities of Neighborhood Watch are centered on working closely with the police to organize and train residents on crime reporting and detection of criminal activity. These efforts contribute to increase surveillance of neighborhoods. Signs are also placed in selected areas to designate them as areas covered by Neighborhood Watch.

Advocates of community policing highlight many benefits of these strategies. They find that increased cooperation between police and residents does lead to improvements in crime prevention. Also, increased participation of the public augments police accountability to the community, which further supports the development of cooperative relationships. Others highlight that community policing strategies encourage the recruitment of women and minorities into police work as police departments seek to improve community relations. The internal reorganization of police departments seeking to implement community policing strategies have also been found to increase police morale and retention as a result of an increase in positive contacts between officers and the people in the community who value their presence and service to the community. Street officers may also experience an increase in their professional standing since community policing requires them to have a broader range of analytic, management, and communication skills needed to carry out their duties successfully.

Critics are less optimistic of community policing strategies. They find the term *community policing* to be vague and lacking real programmatic clarity. As a result, they argue that any range of activities, whether complex or simple, can be classified as community policing. This lack of conceptual clarity leads to the concern that community policing strategies rarely unify the many programmatic elements that it requires. Critics are also not optimistic of more formal community policing programs, finding that the police and the public face an uphill battle in developing effective and long-lasting collaborations, and that in most cases, it is rarely achieved. At the same time, many feel that as popularity of community policing continues to grow, many will only pay lip service to it and do little follow-up to implement the necessary structure and partnerships required to follow it through. Because of these reasons, many feel it is impossible to trace the effect of community policing strategies and crime prevention and reduction.

Despite the obstacles faced when implementing community policing strategies and lack of evidence on its effect on crime prevention, many observers expect the movement to continue to grow. The perceived benefits of this strategy present an important opportunity for the police and the public to develop a cooperative and mutually beneficial relationship, one in which the public benefits by increased crime prevention and police accountability, and in return the police benefit from increased legitimacy, morale, and professional standing.

For more information

Kelling, G. L., M. H. Moore, S. D. Greene, Jr. *Community Policing: Rhetoric or Reality.* New York: Praeger, 1988.

Trojanowicz, R., V. E. Kappeler, L. K. Gaines, B. Bucqueroux, and R. Sluden. *Community Policing: A Contemporary Perspective.* 2nd ed. Cincinnati, Ohio: Anderson, 1990.

Wilneida Negrón
CUNY Graduate Center

comparable worth Comparable worth is a method an employer can use to determine the proper wage for a worker or group of workers. Using a point rating system, all jobs in a plant or agency are evaluated and given points according to the level of knowledge, skill, and responsibility required to do the job. Workers in jobs with similar point ratings receive the same base or hourly pay. An example taken from a Minnesota state job survey:

COMPARABLE WORTH

Job	Job Rating
Delivery Van Driver (mostly men)	117 points
Clerk Typist (mostly women)	117 points

At the end of the 20th century, women working full-time in the United States earned about 75 cents for every dollar earned by men. Some women's groups, labor unions, and legislators want to use a "comparable worth point system" to remedy this pay inequity in the public sector. Critics charge that implementing comparable worth would drive up the cost of government and pay rates are only one factor motivating a worker to prefer one job over another. They claim women freely choose certain types of lower paying jobs.

Other methods employers use to fix pay levels include:

(a) Equal pay for equal work in which all van drivers are on one pay rate and all secretaries are on another (lower) rate.
(b) Union-Management Contract wage rates which specify the base wage rate for each category of worker.
(c) Market-based "prevailing rate" in which the employer pays van drivers what they can earn elsewhere in the area and uses the same calculation to fix (lower) pay rates for secretaries. Advocates of pay comparability want federal workers to get

the same base pay, the prevailing rate, as those doing the same work for nongovernment employers in that area.

(d) Federally mandated wage rates, such as the federal minimum wage, determine the wage rate for many workers.

Since 1963 U.S. courts have embraced equal pay for equal work but have refused to support the concept of "comparable worth." The DEPARTMENT OF JUSTICE holds as of 2000 that the comparable worth argument does not establish a cause for action under federal law. The Equal Employment Opportunities Commission (EEOC) consistently has turned aside complaints based on comparable worth arguments. In the *Wards Cove* case (1989), the Supreme Court refused to recognize pay differences by gender as deliberate attempts to discriminate.

For more information

Nigro, Lloyd, and Felix Nigro. *The New Public Personnel Administration.* 5th ed. Itasca, Ill.: Peacock, 2000.

Gayle Avant
Baylor University

compelling governmental interests Compelling governmental interests are the very important public or governmental objectives that may sometimes allow the state to override constitutional rights even where STRICT SCRUTINY is called for. Those values must be so important that they may be termed compelling.

The basic idea is that some public needs are so important that they sometimes justify suspending, limiting, or curtailing constitutional rights. The notion that constitutional rights may have to be limited by public necessity is at least as old as the republic. It was a way of expressing the conviction that the needs of the community override individual needs. In its modern form it entered into constitutional doctrine over a period of years from the era of World War II culminating in a fairly well developed and explicit statement in a Supreme Court opinion in *Shelton v. Tucker* in 1960.

The Court, however, has not elaborated standards for the designation of compelling government interests or overriding public purposes. They are not described in the text of the CONSTITUTION. And they are not understood in the Rehnquist Court in the same way they were understood in prior courts. Thus, for example, the BURGER COURT treated racial integration as a compelling government interest but the Rehnquist court does not. Thus it is not possible to describe compelling governmental interests with any certainty.

Nevertheless, there are several things that can be said. First, by governmental interests we mean public interests. Compelling governmental interests are only about those things that the government does on behalf of the public.

Second, many, though not all, of the interests that the Court has actually found to be compelling seem to be related to constitutional values like life, liberty, and property. Thus, for example, national security protects all constitutional values, and it has repeatedly been held to be a compelling government interest.

Third, the Court interprets these values as justifying the need to restrict constitutionally specified rights but not to justify the announcement of fundamental rights. Thus the Court has overridden protections of the First Amendment because of what it has treated as the compelling public interest in indoctrinated schoolchildren, but it has refused to find that there is any fundamental right to education.

Fourth, compelling interests are part of *strict scrutiny*, a form of *balancing* designed to protect constitutional rights from limitation except in the case of the most important considerations.

There are, however, several justices who have expressed the view that constitutional issues should be decided by categories rather than by balancing. Those justices have been very critical of the notion of compelling interests. Others argue that categorical tests merely hide the balancing taking place.

For the present, strict scrutiny and compelling government interests remain a part, if a somewhat muddy part, of CONSTITUTIONAL LAW.

For more information

Gottlieb, Stephen E. "Compelling Governmental Interests: An Essential but Unanalyzed Term in Constitutional Adjudication," *Boston University Law Review* 68 (1988): 917.

———, ed. *Public Values in Constitutional Law.* Ann Arbor: University of Michigan Press, 1993.

Stephen E. Gottlieb
Albany Law School

CompStat Computerized statistics, known as CompStat, is a computer-based technology system that gathers and plots information on criminal activity according to the day, time, location, victim, and perpetrator. CompStat is also an organizational tool for policing that is used to address crime and other quality-of-life issues as well as to help police departments better manage their staff and resources. Since the 1990s, police departments in the United States have been incorporating CompStat into their work. Advocates of CompStat argue it has contributed to sharp drops in crime in the cities in which it was used; and many have hailed it as a new model of modern policing, which stresses accountability at all levels of a police department.

CompStat is based on principles of community policing and the BROKEN WINDOWS THEORY by George Kelling, which promotes the decentralization of police management in order to give precincts greater discretion over the communities they serve. Although CompStat shares many tenets of COMMUNITY POLICING, police departments that use it have also found it to be compatible with traditional crime-fighting policing models.

CompStat was first used by the New York City Police Department in 1994. Its development and implementation was overseen by Police Commissioner William Bratton, who later went on to become the police commissioner of the Los Angeles Police Force in 2002 and implemented CompStat there. CompStat is also used in other major metropolitan cities, including Philadelphia, Minneapolis, and Baltimore, Maryland.

CompStat relies upon geographic information systems (GIS) and database management systems to collect and analyze daily crime reports. This information is then mapped out, making it easy for the police to identify key problem areas, crime patterns, and trends according to location, victims involved, perpetrators, and time of day. This information allows the police to respond more rapidly and effectively to crime and quality-of-life problems. A second component of CompStat is weekly or biweekly meetings between central management and police chiefs from local precincts. These meetings allow for vital information sharing and problem solving to discuss and develop crime-reduction strategies. These meetings also ensure that precincts are attuned to the needs of the communities they serve and that central management is also more informed of the needs of local precincts. CompStat also promotes accountability at all levels of a police department by holding management accountable for outcomes.

Critics of CompStat are less keen to fully credit it for crime reduction in the cities where implemented. They find that the computer-based technology aspect of CompStat is often implemented without the necessary restructuring of management and accountability systems between central management and local precincts. Others have found that CompStat has a small effect on crime reduction. Reports have identified that during the implementation of CompStat other policing and societal changes were taking place that could have had an effect on the reduction of crime for a given area. Additional contributing factors identified have been better training of police officers, the deployment of additional police force, decentralization of management, more efficient and effective handling of backlogged warrants, and overall national or state-wide changing trends in crime patterns from either economic growth or other factors. In New York City, Mayor Rudolph Giuliani's zero-tolerance policy against petty crime is also listed among the many key contributing factors in the reduction of crime in the city.

For more information

Bratton, William, and Peter Knobler. *The Turnaround: How America's Top Cop Reversed the Crime Epidemic.* New York: Random House, 1998.

Levitt, Steven. "Understanding Why Crime Fell in the 1990's: Four Factors That Explain the Decline and Six That Do Not," *Journal of Economic Perspectives,* 18, no. 1 (Winter 2004): 163–190.

Wilneida Negrón
CUNY Graduate Center

concurrent sentences Concurrent sentences refer to a SENTENCING procedure in which persons convicted on multiple crimes serve the sentence or prison time for them simultaneously.

The purpose of sentencing is to provide a punitive consequence for each convicted offense. When offenders are convicted of multiple offenses and/or multiple counts of offenses at the same time, the JUDGE may impose concurrent or consecutive sentences. Concurrent sentences begin at the same time and are served simultaneously; the length of the longer sentence imposed determines the length of the full sentence. Alternatively, consecutive sentences, also referred to as cumulative sentences, are served one after the other. In the United States, there is variation across states and the federal system regarding when to use concurrent or consecutive sentences. Most often, the trial court judge has DISCRETION in determining which kind of sentences to impose. Several factors may be taken into account: the nature of the crimes committed, the time of the events, characteristics of the offender such as prior criminal history, characteristics of the victim including age, and other mitigating or aggravating factors. Yet, state legislation also dictates and provides guidelines for the selection of these sentences. For example, some states have developed legislation with a presumption of one kind of sentence over the other unless mitigating or aggravating factors provide reason to depart. In addition, state legislation in the form of criminal statutes sometimes mandates consecutive sentences for particular crimes.

This issue is complicated when an offender obtains convictions from multiple JURISDICTIONS and, in particular, from both a state and a federal jurisdiction. The UNITED STATES CODE 18 §3584 presents the federal legislation pertaining to consecutive or concurrent sentences and allows for judicial discretion in district courts to the extent that related federal SENTENCING GUIDELINES are considered in 18 U.S.C. §3553(a), 3584(b), and section 5G1.3, which include prohibitions against imposition of concurrent incarceration sentences for select crimes (e.g., involving a firearm).

For more information

Demleitner, N. V., D. A. Berman, M. L. Miller, and R. F. Wright. *Sentencing Law and Policy: Cases, Statutes, and Guidelines.* New York: Aspen, 2004.

Goffette, E. E. "Sovereignty in Sentencing: Concurrent and Consecutive Sentencing of a Defendant Subject to Simultaneous State and Federal Jurisdiction," *Valparaiso University Law Review* 37 (2005): 1035.

Jennifer Sumner
Pennsylvania State University, Harrisburg

condominium A condominium is a form of ownership of real property with the following characteristics: (1) exclusive ownership of a designated unit within a development, (2) an undivided interest in common areas, and (3) a common system of governance and assessment for the development. The word is sometimes used to refer to the entire development or to a specific unit within the development.

Condominium developments are often associated with high-rise apartments; however, this form of ownership has also been used for the development of detached single FAMILY residential neighborhoods and commercial and industrial projects. A development is the entire parcel subjected to the condominium form of ownership, including all structures on that parcel. The condominium regime is a creature of statute, and all 50 states have specific legislation authorizing condominium ownership.

The two basic documents involved in the creation of a condominium development are the declaration and the bylaws. A declaration is a written document filed with the county records keeper that includes such items as a legal description of the development, a general description of each unit, a description of the common elements, voting rights of each unit owner, the creation of an association comprised of all unit owners, and the method of assessments for common expenses. The bylaws establish the methods by which the condominium development will be administered, usually including the method of calling the unit owners to assemble, the process for the election of a board of directors of the association, and the rules for the regulation, maintenance, and repair of the common areas. Some JURISDICTIONS also require that a plat survey of the condominium development be recorded.

Individual unit ownership is central to the condominium concept. Each unit can be separately owned, mortgaged, and taxed. Utilizing this concept, an apartment in a high-rise building can be transformed into a separate real estate parcel. The rest of the condominium development, other than the individual units, is considered the common area or common element. The common elements are subject to mutual rights of support, access, use, and enjoyment by all unit owners. However, limited common elements may be designated which primarily benefit one or more but not all of the unit owners. Examples of common elements are parking lots and pools. Examples of limited common elements are specific stalls in the parking lot or attached balconies.

The extent of a unit owner's undivided interest in the common elements is usually expressed in a percentage. A typical method of determining this percentage is to divide the value of each unit by the value of the property as a whole. Quite often this percentage also establishes the amount of the assessment for which the unit owner is responsible.

The management of a condominium development is usually under the control of an association of unit owners. These unit owners typically have an annual meeting at which time they elect a board of directors. The board of directors are responsible for maintaining, repairing, and insuring the common areas and determining and collecting the assessments to pay for the same.

For more information

American Jurisprudence. 2nd ed., vol. 15A, *Condominiums and Cooperative Apartments.* Rochester, N.Y.: Lawyer's Cooperative, 1976.

Rohan, Patrick J., and Melvin A. Reskin. *Real Estate Transactions: Condominium Law and Practice.* New York: Matthew Bender, 1999.

David M. Reddy
shareholder in the law firm of
Sweet and Reddy, S.C., of Elkhorn, Wis.

confessions Confessions refer to situations in which individuals accused of crimes admit to their guilt. Confessions are an important means of solving crimes in the United States, but what counts as a valid confession is often in legal dispute.

One critical function of any justice system is to determine the guilt or innocence of criminal suspects. Confessions play a key role in this determination. In early English common law, the court allowed confessions as EVIDENCE of guilt, even when the police used torture tactics to obtain the confession. Over time, however, the United States has recognized the unreliability of coerced or FALSE CONFESSIONS. In response, the United States developed laws in an attempt to prevent the prosecution from using unreliable confessions against the defendant in violation of their CIVIL RIGHTS. Additionally, U.S. courts created the exclusionary rule as a remedy. The exclusionary rule is a JUDGE-made doctrine that prohibits the introduction at a criminal trial of evidence obtained in violation of the defendant's civil rights. Over the years, the U.S. Supreme Court has found protections for confessions in the Fifth Amendment right against SELF-INCRIMINATION and the SIXTH AMENDMENT RIGHT TO COUNSEL.

The Supreme Court first invoked the UNITED STATES CONSTITUTION to support the requirement that confessions be voluntary in *Bram v. United States*, 168 U.S. 532 (1897). In *Bram*, the Court applied the Fifth Amendment privilege against self-incrimination and held that any amount of influence exerted to obtain a confession rendered the confession involuntary and thus inadmissible. Additionally, the Court held any threats or direct or implied promises by law enforcement amounted to impermissible influence and resulting confessions were inadmissible. In *Malloy v. Hogan*, 378 U.S. 1 (1964), the Court held the Fifth Amendment privilege against self-incrimination, which had previously applied only to federal courts, also applied to state courts. Subsequent courts either chose a bright line test finding certain techniques were per se coercive or they adopted a totality of the circumstances test that considered various factors, including the vulnerability of the suspect, to determine whether the confession was voluntary.

The Supreme Court also found protections for confessions in the Sixth Amendment to the Constitution. In *MASSIAH V. UNITED STATES*, 377 U.S. 201 (1964), the Supreme Court held the Sixth Amendment right to counsel applied to the criminal suspect after the suspect had been formally charged. In the same year, the Court in *ESCOBEDO V. ILLINOIS*, 378 U.S. 478 (1964), expanded this right to include interrogations prior to formal charges. Consequently, if a suspect invokes his or her right to counsel, police and prosecutors cannot question the suspect without counsel present. The theory is that to ensure a fair trial, the individual must be afforded a representative knowledgeable of the law and the procedure to provide guidance and protection through the criminal process.

Two years later, the Supreme Court handed down its landmark decision *MIRANDA V. ARIZONA*, 384 U.S. 436 (1966), finding police custody was inherently coercive and, as such, suspects should be informed of their constitutional rights prior to any interrogation. Those rights included the right to remain silent and the right to retain counsel. The Court held the suspect may choose to waive his or her rights, but the waiver must be done voluntarily, knowingly, and intelligently. Consequently, if law enforcement did not inform the suspect of his or her rights prior to interrogation or the suspect did not voluntarily waive those rights, any confession obtained would be inadmissible. The theory behind *Miranda* is that often individuals are unaware of the protections the Constitution affords them. The decision in *Miranda* prompted huge criticism by individuals who felt the decision undermined the efficiency of the police and would result in an increase in crime. However, over the years, *Miranda* warnings have become common knowledge and are widely accepted.

Today, there is still an ongoing debate over the boundaries of constitutional protections. Even with the constitutional protections afforded individuals, false confessions occur on a regular basis, prompting the argument that the current laws do not protect individuals enough. Alternatively, some argue the constitutional rights afford individuals too much protection, which interferes in police investigations and results in the acquittal of guilty criminals. Regardless of one's side of the debate, confessions play a key function in the criminal justice process, and the Court's role is to carefully balance the individual's constitutional rights with society's interest in punishing those who commit crimes.

For more information

Grano, Joseph D. *Confessions, Truth and the Law.* Ann Arbor: University of Michigan Press, 2003.

Mirfield, Peter. *Silence, Confessions and Improperly Obtained Evidence.* Oxford: Oxford University Press, 1997.

Rebecca E. Paddock
William S. Boyd School of Law, University of Nevada–Las Vegas

conflict theories of crime Conflicts theories of crime assume that the causes of crime and lawless behavior are rooted in social conflicts such as class or race.

Like many other criminological and sociological theories, conflict theory has evolved through contributions from dynamic theorists, academics, and social pioneers. Unlike other theories, however, conflict theory retreats from the notion that social order is established and maintained through the investment in a social contract. Instead, it proposes that conflict, rather than consensus, is the cornerstone of society, with conflicting groups battling for resources, power, and authority. Setting forth one of the most comprehensive arguments for conflict theory, George Vold (1958, 204) argued that "As social interaction processes grind their way through varying kinds of uneasy adjustment to a more or less stable equilibrium of balanced forces in opposition, the resulting condition of relative stability is what is usually called social or social organization."

Consensus theories such as positivism lay their foundations in the belief that society is held together by the common acceptance of right and wrong. As a consequence, law reflects the necessary constraints and permission to retain that order. Conversely, conflict theory argues that law is a reflection of economic, social, and political inequality, with the powerful using law to impose their desired will on society at large. Academically, conflict theory has evolved through three main forms, with each subsequent offering building from the previous manifestation.

Culture conflict, based most notably in the work of Thorsten Sellin (1938), introduced the concept that within modern societies conflict between varying groups causes crime. He found in his studies that the expansion of population and increasing urbanization created social anonymity, isolation, and a wide variety of competing groups. As a consequence, regardless of behavioral fashions, groups inevitably violate the norms or culture of other groups. Law, Sellin found, was a direct reflection of the most powerful norms used by one group to subjugate the domain of others. Building on the work of Sellin, the previously mentioned George Vold (1958) extended the notion of culture conflict to political organization, or group conflict. Viewing the law as the ultimate expression of group power, Vold examined political lobbying and influence through the lens of conflict. He theorized that groups strive to strengthen their political position by lobbying policy makers to enact laws reflecting their norms. In turn, their interests are satisfied while the behavior and attitudes of other groups are curbed. As a result, the law and its ongoing enforcement needs to be recognized as a reflection of the ongoing conflicts between groups, with criminalization representing the extent of political power held by certain groups at any given time.

Examples of cultural and group conflict over the past 50 years can be seen in historical issues involving SEGREGATION, ABORTION, and war, with more contemporary manifestations being seen in protests over global economics and the World Trade Organization (WTO), the International Monetary Fund (IMF), and the World Bank. The law in each case of conflict has been used as an intermediary, with the outcome ultimately favoring one set of norms.

Beginning in the 1960s and continuing through the early 1970s, several criminological theorists expanded the breadth and depth of conflict theory to include the concept of social class within the discussion. Using pluralistic notions such as lower, middle, and upper class, individuals such as Austin Turk (1969), William Chambliss (1975), and Richard Quinney (1970) intimately described the definition and enforcement of criminal law as a purposeful act favoring the ruling classes. Heavily inspired by Marxist theory, class conflict theory described criminal law as purposeful oppression and repression of the lower classes. Moreover, it examined capitalism as the catalyst for law, asserting that law was an instrument of the state to maintain social order and divert the attention of the working class away from their ongoing repression. Crime as an act itself is seen as inert, regardless of the behavior, and was categorized as such only when it interfered with the interests of the ruling class. As Richard Quinney (1970, 16) surmised "criminal definitions describe behaviours that conflict with the interests of segments of society that have the power to shape public policy." The assertions of class conflict theory have added an understanding of why in a capitalist state certain behaviors are deemed criminal, while others are not. Moreover, it has expanded on how capitalism is more likely to produce certain patterns of criminal activity such as theft and other economic crime.

To examine crime and the law within the scope of conflict theory is to understand both as the ongoing struggle between different sets of interests. With norms, morals, and culture constantly changing, the law can be seen as a reflection of those who hold the power to dictate "appropriate" behavior and beliefs. It stresses that to ultimately understand the law, one must understand the interests served in criminalization and the power, legitimacy, and authority involved in the administration of criminal law.

The heyday of conflict criminology was the tumultuous 1960s in the United States, when political and social uproar over war, civil rights, and human rights threatened the national political structure. By the 1970s, it was largely rendered moot by new developments in critical CRIMINOLOGY and the New Criminology. However, the principles of conflict theory remain in many contemporary applications. The struggle of interest groups in the discussion regarding the targeting and isolation of segmented groups of society, using law as a repressive tool and the privatization of prisons in the United States, has expounded some core principles of conflict theory. Theorists such as Michael Hallett (2006), Randall Shelden (2001), and Jonathan Simon (2006) continue to expose the law as the manifestation of conflict and criminalization as a tool of the powerful.

For more information

Chambliss, William. "Toward a Political Economy of Crime," *Theory and Society* 2 (1975): 149–170.

Hallett, Michael. *Private Prisons in America.* Champaign: University of Illinois Press, 2006.

Quinney, Richard. *The Social Reality of Crime.* Boston: Little, Brown, 1970.

Sellin, Thorsten. *Culture, Conflict and Crime.* New York: Social Science Research Council, 1938.

Shelden, Rundall. *Controlling the Dangerous Classes: A Critical Introduction to the History of Criminal Justice.* Ann Arbor: University of Michigan Press, 2001.

Simon, Jonathan. *Governing through Crime.* New York: Oxford University Press, 2007.

Turk, Austin. *Criminality and the Legal Order.* Chicago: Rand McNally, 1969.

Vold, George. *Theoretical Criminology.* New York: Oxford University Press, 1958.

Mitch Walker
Queens University Belfast

the confrontation clause The confrontation clause is the guarantee, contained in the SIXTH AMENDMENT of the U.S. CONSTITUTION, that "the accused shall enjoy the right . . . to be confronted with the witnesses against him." In practice, the confrontation clause guarantees the right to cross-examine witnesses and protection against the admission of HEARSAY. Both are key elements of the adversarial CRIMINAL JUSTICE SYSTEM used in the United States.

The exact origin of the confrontation right remains a subject of debate, but sufficient evidence exists to demonstrate its long history.

The Romans routinely allowed the accused to meet their accusers face-to-face in judicial proceedings. Several references to these rights also appear in English common law. The right to confront, suggests one writer, is rooted in laws governing the admission of ex parte (from one party) testimony, cross-examination, and criminal law procedures from the reign of Mary I called the Marian Statutes (Kry, 2009). The framers of the U.S. Constitution were certainly aware of the existence of such a practice in common law and saw fit to include it as part of the BILL OF RIGHTS.

Whatever the provenance of the right in Western legal tradition, an important issue that is closely tied to the right to confront is that of hearsay EVIDENCE, second-hand information a witness did not see or hear directly. The introduction of hearsay evidence potentially defeats the purpose of the confrontation clause since the accused cannot directly confront the original source of the hearsay information. English common law treated hearsay evidence as inadmissible as it was generally considered untrustworthy. The United States has continued this tradition. Article VIII of the Federal Rules of Evidence provides definitions and rules for hearsay. According to the rules, hearsay is not admissible in courts except in carefully circumscribed instances such as cases involving "excited utterances" or public and family records.

Supreme Court doctrine regarding the admission of hearsay evidence has been in a state of flux in recent decades. *Bruton v. United States,* 391 U.S. 123 (1968), was a major decision by the WARREN COURT concerning the admission of a nontestifying codefendant's CONFESSION at a joint trial. The Court held that such admissions violated the defendant's constitutional right to confront, establishing a strict definition of hearsay. For the next 40 years, under the Warren and BURGER COURTS, treatment of hearsay in confrontation doctrine vacillated, but with what some authors saw as a tendency to restrict the *Bruton* doctrine, which had the effect of making it easier to introduce hearsay evidence in a trial setting. One example of this is the case of *Ohio v. Roberts,* 448 U.S. 56 (1980). In the majority decision for the Court, Justice Harry Blackmun established a test that would allow the admission of hearsay as long as it met two requirements: The witness providing the hearsay statement must be demonstrably unavailable, and the statement must be "generally reliable." This represents a trend following *Bruton* that one author describes as regarding the confrontation clause as "nothing more than a 'constitutional hearsay rule' subject to many hearsay exceptions" (Garcia, 94).

In 2004, the Rehnquist court reversed course from cases such as *Roberts* and chose to expand the definition of hearsay once more. In an opinion authored by Justice ANTONIN SCALIA, the Court rendered a unanimous decision in *Crawford v. Washington,* 541 U.S. 36 (2004), which held that the use of a prerecorded statement by a witness to a crime as evidence was unconstitutional. The Court reasoned that the framers of the Constitution had intended the Sixth Amendment to prevent the use of out-of-court testimony against defendants by giving the accused the right to confront, or cross-examine, witnesses. This decision narrowed or overturned previous rulings that expanded the admission of hearsay such as *Roberts,* applying a strict interpretation of the Sixth Amendment. This decision has caused much speculation among the legal community as to how the hearsay rule should now be applied (Kirst, 2009).

Recent cases have raised a number of important confrontation clause issues that the Supreme Court continues to address. One especially difficult issue revolves around how the courts choose to handle the delicate situation of a child's testimony in cases where the child is allegedly a victim of sexual abuse. Courts have attempted to deal with this issue using a variety of techniques. Prerecorded or video-recorded statements, closed-circuit television, and interviewing have all been tried with varying degrees of success. The Supreme Court's responses to these techniques have varied from case to case. In *Coy v. Iowa,* 487 U.S. 1012 (1988), the Court held that the use of a screen to shield minor victims of sexual assault during the trial of their accused attacker violated the defendant's confrontation right. However, two years later the Court in *Maryland v. Craig,* 497 U.S. 836 (1990), upheld the use of closed-circuit testimony to protect the well-being of children testifying in cases. Writing for the Court, Justice SANDRA DAY O'CONNOR reasoned that the right of the accused to directly confront the accuser was not absolute and that certain "competing interests," such as the well-being of the child, may vitiate a defendant's confrontation clause rights.

Another issue involves the use of scientific evidence in courts. The case of *Melendez-Diaz v. Massachusetts,* 557 U.S. (2009), concerned the admission of a laboratory report into evidence. A split Court ruled that as the defendant was not able to directly confront the technicians who had created the report such evidence constituted a violation of his Sixth Amendment rights. The dissenting justices in the case criticized the majority for summarily ignoring longstanding rules that allow the admission of scientific evidence without the need for testimony. Both of these areas, child testimony and scientific evidence, illustrate the complex balancing that the courts must do to protect the confrontation rights of the accused while remaining sensitive to other competing interests in the criminal justice system.

For more information

Garcia, Alfredo. *The Sixth Amendment in Modern American Jurisprudence.* New York: Greenwood Press, 1992.

Kirst, Roger. "Crawford and Beyond: Exploring the Future of the Confrontation Clause in Light of Its Past: Does Crawford Provide a Stable Foundation for Confrontation Doctrine?" *Brooklyn Law Review* 71 (Fall 2005): 35–103.

Kry, Robert. "Confrontation under the Marian Statutes." *Brooklyn Law Review* 72 (Winter 2007): 493–555.

Roberson, Cliff. *Constitutional Law and Criminal Justice.* Boca Raton, Fla.: CRC Press, 2009.

Darren A. Wheeler and Eric Vandervort
Ball State University

consent and waiver Consent and waiver are two examples of the general FOURTH AMENDMENT requirement that a warrant is required for a search.

During a law enforcement contact for any reason, a police officer must have a warrant, reasonable suspicion or PROBABLE CAUSE to search a person, place, or thing for EVIDENCE of a crime or criminal activity. The Fourth Amendment to the UNITED STATES CONSTITUTION protects every citizen from unlawful SEARCHES AND SEIZURES without a warrant. Consent and waiver is the simplest type of WARRANTLESS SEARCH that law enforcement uses to circumvent the necessity for reasonable suspicion or probable cause.

Consent and waiver is particular effective in light of the fact that law enforcement agents are not required to warn people of their right against SELF-INCRIMINATION, i.e. *Miranda* rights, *MIRANDA V. ARIZONA,* 384 U.S. 436 (1966). Because *Miranda* rights are not given, a person may not realize that he or she has the right to withdraw their consent at almost any time during the search. The only exception is when a person enters an area where there is an expectation that a search will occur, such as in an airport or prison. The withdrawal of consent does not have to be in writing and may be a simple statement such as, "That's enough, I want you to stop," as in the case of *United States v. Baily,* 227 F.3d 792 (2000). However, once a police officer finds probable cause or can develop a reasonable suspicion, the individual has lost the right to stop the search because the police have now developed reasons to search without consent.

Consent to search will be held valid even though police officers did not properly identify themselves, for example, in cases involving undercover officers or informers. A person may give consent for an officer to search his or her person or property when the officer lacks lawful authority. The person must have the authority to give consent to search property. In other words, if a person owns a residence but rents a room out to another person, the owner can only give consent to search common areas and areas under his or her control. The owner has no authority to give consent to search a renter's room. The person giving consent does not need to be the person who is ultimately charged or even suspected. However, consent can also be taken away by the same individual at any time.

Waiver is simply the written confirmation that the individual waives his or her constitutional rights to be protected from unlawful searches. Law enforcement has found that the use of written consent to search waivers is valuable in court and can be used to rebut testimony from the defendant that consent was not given. However, because the waiver gives up strong constitutional rights, the consent must be freely and voluntarily given without coercion or duress by the police. This means that if the person giving the consent was a suspect before the search, not reading *Miranda* rights to this person may make the consent invalid because it is then considered not to be freely and voluntarily given. In addition, waving a piece of paper purporting to be a search warrant when it is not will invalidate any consent a person gives under those pretenses.

Many people are afraid to refuse to consent to a search, thinking it will make them more suspicious. Although this action may make the person more suspicious, a police officer does not gain any additional authority for conducting a warrantless search. Simply refusing to consent to a search does not give rise to a reasonable suspicion of probable cause, as in the case of *United States vs. Fuentes,* 379 F. Supp. 1145 (S.D. Tex. 1974). Furthermore, it does not give police the right to detain someone while awaiting a drug sniffing dog or for other police officers to arrive so they can figure out a legitimate reason to conduct a search. However, deception by the police will not automatically invalidate a search.

The courts recognize that deception is a valuable tool of police investigations. If a law enforcement officer uses fictitious circumstances or fictitious charges, this will not automatically negate the consent because the person is still clearly aware of the fact that the officers are investigating a crime. However, there are cases in which the courts have ruled that the deception was so manipulative that the defendant's consent did not validate the search. For example, in the case of *State of Florida vs. McCord,* 833 So.2d 828 (4th DCA 2002), the detective assigned to investigate armed ROBBERIES met with the defendant and told him he was a suspect in a rape case and that he could exclude himself from rape investigation by providing a saliva sample. The detective acknowledged that the rape never occurred and that he fabricated the charge to obtain defendant's consent to search. This deception, coupled with the fact that the defendant was in jail, was so manipulative that defendant's "consent" did not "validate the search."

For more information

Lafave, Wayne R. *Criminal Law.* St. Paul, Minn.: Thomson-West, 2003.

Mark Allan
RTI International, LGP3—Iraq

consent order A consent order is a signed document, approved by a court, which limits or terminates continued prosecution of alleged illegal conduct in exchange for an agreement to refrain from committing future similar acts or violations of some statutory law. It is basically a CONTRACT between the plaintiff, usually the PROSECUTOR or attorney representing the government, and the defendant, the alleged wrongdoer, subject to the watchful eye of a JUDGE, in which the parties exchange promises to end civil or criminal proceedings for a pledge not to commit any similar future conduct, alleged to violate federal or state statutory law, such as securities patents, antitrust acts, and EMPLOYMENT LAWS. More often, a consent order is reached at or during the investigation stage of a proceeding brought by a government agency. The agency agrees to terminate the investigation without a determination as to whether a particular statute has been violated, under authority derived from the ADMINISTRATIVE PROCEDURES ACT. A settlement agreement is reached, with no further prosecutorial action.

Generally, the defendants refuse to admit wrongdoing, by pleading *nolo contendere,* but acquiesce to sign and adhere to the order to avoid a lengthy court battle. As a matter of public policy, the government has incentives to conserve judicial resources, including court time and taxpayer dollars, in situations that are civil in character, and where the opponents have significant financial resources and legal talent to wage extensive protracted litigation, because the alleged misconduct is open to legal interpretation and differing opinions, or there is a lack of clear and specific judicial PRECEDENT found in the case law, or because of the vagueness and ambiguity of the written statutes signed into law by either the United States Congress or the state legislatures. The parties to the consent order may also agree that the defendants, as a condition for the termination of continued prosecution, may be required to undertake some additional corrective measures designed to promote and enhance what is presumed to be in the best interests of the community as a whole.

For example, the New York Times Company and the Equal Employment Opportunity Commission specifically declared in a recent consent order that it was the ". . . aim of the parties to correct the statistical imbalance . . ." of minorities and women employed as junior pressmen at the *Times,* by making a good faith effort to increase employment opportunities for females and members of minority groups and to achieve a goal of 25% minority and female representation. A consent decree may be opposed by intervenors, such as labor unions, which are affected, directly or indirectly, by the actual terms and conditions of the consent order, if they can demonstrate legally tangible, material injury. In most cases courts retain JURISDICTION during the stated time period in which the consent decree shall remain in force. The court is also available to enforce the contractual provisions and also permit parties to apply for further relief in the form of orders and directions that may be necessary to effectuate the terms and conditions of the consent decree.

Under the 1988 Omnibus Trade and Competitiveness Act, the International Trade Commission, the agency created and authorized to assist the executive branch of the government in carrying out, executing, and enforcing the federal laws in connection with international commerce, is empowered by its own longstanding practice and specific express statutory authority under 19 U.S.C. §1337 to issue and enforce consent orders. A consent order may be enforced, modified, or revoked by civil penalty proceedings.

A consent agreement between a federal agency and an entity or person, corporate or otherwise, including an individual, constitutes a restraint of federal or state power, and is thus subject to federal or state remedy by penalty or enforcement, in the event of the breach and violation of its contractual terms and provisions.

For more information

Breyer, Stephen. *Breaking the Vicious Circle: Towards Effective Risk Regulation.* Cambridge, Mass.: Harvard University Press, 1995.

J. David Golub
Touro College
New York Institute of Technology
Kean College of New Jersey

conspiracy Conspiracy is an agreement or mutual understanding between two or more persons to either engage in an unlawful or criminal act, to perform an act that may be innocent in itself but becomes unlawful when done by a group of people, or to use illegal means to achieve something that in itself is lawful. The agreement must be made voluntarily and with an intent to participate in furthering a common purpose. Mere knowledge or approval in the absence of an actual agreement to cooperate does not constitute a conspiracy. The charge of conspiracy is a powerful legal tool that can be used to construct a broad umbrella of criminal liability while providing PROSECUTORS flexibility to handle complex, amorphous, and sophisticated criminal conspiracies such as terrorist cells, drug distribution networks, elections, and quiz shows.

Federal statutes require an overt act that moves the conspirators toward completion of their plan. The charge of conspiracy stands alone or can be an additional charge. For example, persons can be charged for homicide and for planning a homicide simultaneously. The law seeks to punish conspiracies substantively and separately because not only does it require two or more persons agreeing to commit a crime, but also the potential for crime increases the danger that may be faced by the public. To prove a conspiracy, those involved must have agreed to the plan before all the actions have been taken, or what occurs may be simply a series of independent illegal acts. A conspiracy can be criminal if the planning and carrying out of illegal activities occurs, or it may give rise to a civil lawsuit for damages if someone suffers injury because of the conspiracy. If a group of people, for example, sell a used product as new, they could be prosecuted not only for FRAUD, but also for conspiracy.

In addition, a purchaser of the product can sue for damages for the fraud and conspiracy. If a coconspirator dies prior to the indictment or trial, the surviving coconspirator may still be charged with conspiracy. A husband and wife can be guilty of conspiracy. A corporation is considered a person for conspiracy purposes, so a corporation can be guilty of conspiracy, but it cannot conspire with itself. For example, if two or more employees within a corporation conspire to break the law and subsequently commit an act in furtherance of the conspiracy, the corporation itself is not criminally liable for conspiracy. Many legal experts criticize the concept of conspiracy as too wide-ranging and, in practice, see the concept expanded beyond reasonable interpretations.

For more information

Alexander, David. *Conspiracies and Cover-Ups*. Berkeley, Calif.: Berkeley Penguin Books, 2002.

Fichtelberg, Aaron. "Conspiracy and International Criminal Justice," *Criminal Law Forum* 7, no. 2 (2006).

McConnachie, James, and Robin Tudge. *The Rough Guide to Conspiracy Theories*. Berkeley, Calif.: Rough Guides, 2005.

Newton, Michael. *The Encyclopedia of Conspiracies and Conspiracy Theories*. New York: Checkmark Books, 2005.

Elizabeth Sharpe Overman
Jackson State University, Jackson, Mississippi

constitution *Constitution* is a word that Americans redefined at the end of the 18th century to mean the written fundamental law that establishes, organizes, empowers, and limits the government. Every republic ever since—the world over—has borrowed from its principles of government of the people, by the people, and for the people.

By force of arms, the American Revolution repudiated the British constitution. In England the word *constitution* simply referred to the country's history of government and how its institutions developed. The term was merely descriptive of how the Crown and Parliament ruled against a background of great events and great laws, like the Magna Carta and the Bill of Rights of 1689. The English system depended on unwritten understandings and traditions, like the common law, but it was based on the fundamental idea of parliamentary supremacy. This worked to the satisfaction of most Englishmen but certainly not the colonists. Great Britain to this day does not have a written constitutional document. There the word *constitution* still means no more nor no less than how in fact the government is organized and functions.

By force of ideas, American constitutionalism reimagined the relationship between government and the individual and codified the new social compact in a written document that is higher law. "It may be a reflection on human nature that such devices should be necessary to control the abuses of government. But what is government itself but the greatest of all reflections of human nature?" James Madison asked rhetorically in *Federalist Papers number 51*. He continued, "If men were angels, no government would be necessary. If angels were to govern men, neither external nor internal controls on government would be necessary. In framing a government which is to be administered by men over men, the great difficulty lies in this: you must first enable government to control the governed; and in the next place oblige it to control itself." Resolving this difficulty has been the lasting achievement of the CONSTITUTION.

Americans had been practiced at writing state constitutions after the Revolution, but their first effort at a national constitution, the ARTICLES OF CONFEDERATION, left much to be desired. Indeed, the founders became possessed with a sense of crisis about whether their bold experiment in self-government would fail, done in by foreign conquest or undone by domestic corruption.

The novel political theory of the Constitution was to draw legitimacy from popular sovereignty and the consent of the governed. The source of ultimate power was the people rather than the legislature. Consequently, the framers patented the convention as the proper mechanism for constitution-making. They met in the Philadelphia Convention of 1787 to draft the Constitution. They held conventions in each of the states to ratify it. "We the People" ordained and established the Constitution.

"A written constitution" was for its time "the greatest improvement on political institutions," according to CHIEF JUSTICE JOHN MARSHALL. The greatest innovation of the American regime was to create a document that was itself normative. The written document constitutes the institutions of government, establishes their powers, and limits their function. The will of the people, expressed in the written Constitution, is superior and paramount to the will of the people's representatives expressed in mere statutes. The institutions of government—the state governments and all three branches of the federal government—must adhere to the rule of law that is the Constitution. This political innovation completed what the Revolution had begun.

Mistrustful of the excesses of both human nature and government power, the framers relied on a wonderful clockwork design of checks and balances to protect individual liberty while at the same time energizing the national government. They put in place a republican democracy, characterized by regular elections and limited terms for representatives. The national government was a government of limited and enumerated powers; what Congress could do and could not do was spelled out in Article I, for example.

FEDERALISM—the idea that two sovereign governments could govern the same territory at the same time—was their invention. The great powers of nationhood—such as waging war and making peace, taxing and spending for the general welfare—were assigned to the national government. Other important powers, however, were left to state governments.

Separation of powers divided the national branches into three branches—legislative, executive, and judicial—with elaborate checks and balances on each other. For example, the president nominates Supreme Court justices with the advice and consent of the Senate. The most powerful branch, Congress, was subdivided into two houses as a further restraint.

It was a government the framers hoped would be strong enough to allow the United States to take its rightful place among the nations of the world and, at the same time, would be restrained enough to preserve individual liberty. In Article V the framers proscribed the process for constitutional change through the amending process, evidencing their expectation that the Constitution would be permanent and paramount. As part of the politics of ratification, the founding generation added a BILL OF RIGHTS in 1791 for good measure.

The framers of the Constitution were children of the Enlightenment. They believed in the inevitability of progress through the application of right reason, as exemplified in the Constitution. Their Constitution was the first written constitution in history and today our Constitution remains the oldest written constitution in the world. British prime minister William Gladstone delivered the fitting *dictum* that the Constitution of 1787 was "the most wonderful work ever struck off at a given time by the brain and purpose of man."

For more information

Baker, Thomas E. *"The Most Wonderful Work . . ."—Our Constitution Interpreted.* St. Paul, Minn.: West, 1996.

McDonald, Forrest. *Novus Ordo Seclorum—The Intellectual Origins of the Constitution.* Lawrence: University Press of Kansas, 1985.

Wood, Gordon S. *The Creation of the American Republic, 1776–1787.* New York: W. W. Norton, 1969.

Thomas E. Baker
University of Scranton

Constitution, U.S. The U.S. Constitution was drafted as the nation's charter in 1787. This document functions as the supreme law, which trumps any conflicting federal, state, or local laws.

Prior to the creation of the Constitution, the United States was ineffectively governed by the ARTICLES OF CONFEDERATION, which allowed states to remain sovereign governments and choose to work together only when it suited their needs. In contrast, the Constitution provides for a sovereign national government with subordinate yet somewhat independent state governments.

The Constitution consists of a preamble, seven articles, and 27 amendments. The preamble establishes that this document's purpose is to preserve the union by the rule of laws which emanate from the will of the people. The seven articles define the branches and powers of the federal government, specify that powers which are not assigned to the federal government are reserved for the states, and emphasize that no law may conflict with the federal Constitution. The first 10 amendments are known as the BILL OF RIGHTS because they focus on the rights of individuals, such as FREEDOM OF SPEECH and the right to DUE PROCESS. Although specific individual rights are enumerated in the Bill of Rights, the NINTH AMENDMENT explicitly guarantees that individuals retain other basic rights as well. Seventeen more amendments have been added since the creation of the Bill of Rights, dealing with issues ranging from the repeal of PROHIBITION to voting.

Two methods for amending the Constitution are established in Article V. However, all of the amendments to date have resulted from the following method: two-thirds of both houses of Congress have voted to propose an amendment and then the amendment has been ratified by three-fourths of the states. The alternate method for amending the Constitution is that two-thirds of the states can request that Congress call a convention where amendments can be proposed. The ratification process for amendments proposed at a convention is the same as that for those proposed by Congress. That the Constitution has only been amended 27 times since it was written demonstrates the document's inherent adaptability to changing circumstances.

Because the Constitution is a concise document dealing with broad general issues, its meaning for current events must often be inferred from the text. The responsibility for this task lies with the Supreme Court, which first articulated and exercised this power in *MARBURY V. MADISON* (1803) by ruling that a law passed by Congress was invalid due to its inconsistency with the Court's interpretation of the Constitution. For example, one of the Court's most controversial modern decisions, *ROE V. WADE* (1973), which established a woman's right to choose to have an ABORTION, stems from the Court's inference that privacy is one of the fundamental personal rights guaranteed by the Constitution.

For more information

U.S. founding documents. Available online. URL: www.law.emory.edu/federal/

The U.S. Constitution. Available online. URL: USConstitution.net

Martha M. Lafferty
Tennessee Fair Housing Council

constitutional interpretation Constitutional interpretation includes both the practical application of the CONSTITUTION, the academic study of this process, and the normative study of how the Constitution ought or should be understood. As a matter of practical application, officials in all three branches of government—legislative, executive, and judicial—engage in constitutional interpretation. Congressmen and senators often debate not only whether certain pieces of legislation can survive the courts but also whether that legislation is truly in keeping with the principles of the Constitution. Many issues of recent fierce debate, including ABORTION rights, school prayer, AFFIRMATIVE ACTION, FLAG-BURNING, and hate speech have spurred discussion in Congress and the states about the proper understanding of the Constitution. The executive, the branch of government least identified with constitutional interpretation, also exercises this important function. Issues ranging from war powers to presidential IMMUNITY to state power, to constitutional limits on Supreme Court power, all depend largely on the meaning of the Constitution.

Of the three branches of government, under the U.S. Constitution the judiciary, that is, the Supreme Court and lesser federal courts, bears the primary responsibility for interpreting what the Constitution means. In *MARBURY V. MADISON* (1803) the Supreme Court said it was in the province of the Supreme Court to determine whether an act of Congress violates the Constitution. The next time the Supreme Court declared an act of Congress unconstitutional was in *DRED SCOTT V. SANDFORD* (1857), a case that helped to precipitate the Civil War. Although constitutional interpretation is not a power expressly granted to the courts, since *Marbury v. Madison* it has been recognized as a fact of the U.S. political system and has become a major role for the Supreme Court, especially in the 20th century.

State supreme courts also engage in constitutional interpretation when they interpret state constitutions to see if state laws conflict with their state's constitution or with the U.S. Constitution, which they are bound to uphold. However, the Supreme Court does not review cases that are purely questions of state law; rather, it has JURISDICTION over cases involving federal law and claims relating to the Constitution. Since so many cases can be seen as having a constitutional dimension, the Supreme Court has a wide berth of cases it may hear and wide discretion to decide whether to hear them.

Two major categories of theory can be identified in constitutional interpretation. The first, originalism, holds that the Constitution has a fixed meaning and that the proper business of the courts is to interpret what that meaning says about a particular constitutional claim. Originalism can be broadly divided into intent originalism and textualism, although there is considerable variety even in these categories. Intent originalism emphasizes historical tradition, particularly the views held at the time of the founding. Intent originalists include CHIEF JUSTICE WILLIAM REHNQUIST and JUDGE ROBERT BORK, who has written extensively on intent originalism. A core criticism of intent originalism is based on the question of which originalists' intent to follow: the framers of the Constitution at the Constitutional Convention or the members of the ratifying conventions in the states. Moreover, can we know what the intent of the framers (and ratifiers) of the Constitution and its amendments mean (such as what they meant by *liberty*) when the words way have meant quite different things to these individuals, and the problems of the nation and the role of government change over time.

Textualism focuses exclusively on the words of the Constitution as a guide to interpretation; it is also called literalism. Both liberals and conservatives have been textualists: Justice HUGO BLACK on the left, and Justices ANTONIN SCALIA and CLARENCE THOMAS, Supreme Court justices in 2000, on the right. Black's textualism led to the application of the guarantees of the BILL OF RIGHTS through the Fourteenth Amendment. Where the meaning of a clause simply could not be determined by its reading, Black opted for the plain meaning by the consensus of the day. Justices Scalia and Thomas, by contrast, use a more historical form of textualism, arguing for the understanding of the phrase in the Constitution at the time of the founding when a simple reading of its words and phrases fails. Black, Scalia, and Thomas all share the view that free speech is an absolute and that the courts have no business defining what life, liberty, and property means in the Fourteenth Amendment DUE PROCESS clause, interpretations that have resulted in the Supreme Court defining a right to privacy and right to ABORTION choices.

Non-originalism counts an even greater variety of approaches to constitutional interpretation than does originalism. Broadly speaking, these approaches have in common a view of a "living Constitution," enunciated in the words of non-originalist Justice WILLIAM BRENNAN, and first described by Chief Justice JOHN MARSHALL in the following oft-quoted words in *McCulloch v. Maryland* (1819): "We must never forget that it is a constitution we are expounding." The above phrase came after Marshall had argued that the Constitution contained a general outline of the federal government's structure and powers, from which the rest of its powers could be deduced; it was not a complex legal code with detailed rules and powers to meet every exigency.

Pragmatism, postmodernism, critical theory, deconstruction, civic republicanism, liberalism, and economic approaches to law all are schools of non-originalist theories of interpretation. Two of the most important non-originalist theories are representation-reinforcement and the moral reading of the Constitution. Representation-reinforcement, put forth by John Hart Ely in *Democracy and Distrust,* holds that the courts ought to keep the political process open, particularly for minorities. Vigorous enforcement of the equal protection clause and the protection of free speech are hallmarks of representation-reinforcement, which opposes the Court placing into law its definition of what such terms as *life, liberty,* and *property* mean.

Ronald Dworkin, a prominent constitutional theorist and legal philosopher, developed the moral reading of the constitution. In numerous books and articles, Dworkin argues that there are two kinds of constitutional provisions: the specific and the open-ended. The Third Amendment, barring quartering of troops in civilian homes during peacetime, is a specific directive. The EIGHTH AMENDMENT, in contrast, is open-ended because the phrase "CRUEL AND UNUSUAL" has no clear meaning. The meaning, Dworkin argues, can only be determined by strenuous moral argument. Dworkin's theory supports substantive due process.

Non-originalism has many more adherents than does originalism. Justices WILLIAM O. DOUGLAS and William Brennan are examples of non-originalist justices, as are EARL WARREN, Arthur Goldberg, Abe Fortas, THURGOOD MARSHALL, and Harry Blackmun.

In the last few years, the most vocal originalists have included Justices Antonin Scalia, Clarence Thomas, and former chief Justice William

Rehnquist. Non-originalists have included Justice SANDRA DAY O'CONNOR, JOHN PAUL STEVENS, and STEPHEN BREYER. Breyer and Scalia have often clashed on the role of original intent when reading the Constitution. Chief Justice John Roberts and Justice Samuel Alito often seem to invoke originalist claims, while Justices Sonia Sotomayor and Elena Kagan have been less willing to appeal to original intent and more to other values when interpreting the Constitution.

Finally, it is important to note that the U.S. Constitution forbids any action by government officials, at any level, that is not compatible with the Constitution, as interpreted. Therefore, every legal question may raise a constitutional question, and any action by public officials may or may not be enforceable, depending on whether or not it has been found to be in violation of the Constitution.

For more information

Bork, Robert. *The Tempting of America: The Political Seduction of Law.* New York: Free Press, 1990.

Dworkin, Ronald. *Law's Empire.* Cambridge, Mass.: Harvard University Press, 1986.

Ely, John Hart. *Democracy and Distrust.* Cambridge, Mass.: Harvard University Press, 1980.

Kahn, Ronald. *The Supreme Court and Constitutional Theory, 1953–1993.* Lawrence: University Press of Kansas, 1994.

Ronald Kahn
Oberlin College

constitutional law Constitutional law is a body of public law that includes the CONSTITUTION itself and the amendments to the original document as well as judicial decisions and legislative enactments that apply to and interpret that document and its amendments. All of the different types of constitutional law must be in harmony with the Constitution itself. Any legislative enactment or judicial decision that is in violation of a constitutional provision is deemed to be null and void. Thus, constitutional law is the supreme law of our society. The defining feature of both constitutions and constitutional law is that they provide limitations on the power of government. This branch of law also defines and organizes the powers of government and distributes the authorities and functions of government among various political and legal actors.

In the United States constitutional law is a very large component of the law in existence. While short by some standards, the Constitution of the United States provides for numerous procedural and substantive requirements to which governmental actors must adhere. These requirements are found most clearly explained in the first three articles of the Constitution. Each of these articles lays out the constitutional law respecting one of the three constitutional branches of government.

The AMENDMENTS TO THE CONSTITUTION are also highly regulative of governmental relationships both in terms of the federal state relationship and with respect to the relationship between the government and individual citizens. These additions to the basic corpus of the Constitution have been added over time, but they represent the same type of fundamental legal authority as the original text of the Constitution.

While the Constitution and the subsequent amendments provide a framework for governmental interaction, they are frequently void and are certainly not self-interpreting rules. As a result of the vagueness of some of the constitutional provisions, courts become involved in determining the meaning of the Constitution. The Supreme Court of the United States has been an important actor in promulgating constitutional law by interpreting and applying that document to specific cases brought to them. Many of the most famous decisions that have been made by the Supreme Court have been interpretations of the Constitution and are therefore part of the body of constitutional law.

Whatever its source, constitutional law is the fundamental law of a nation or state. This area of law defines the general plan for government.

Constitutional law defines the spheres of governmental power and places limitations on that power. It defines and regulates the relationship between government and individuals. It is the standard that must be met by all other laws.

For more information

O'Brien, David M. *Constitutional Law and Politics: Struggles for Power and Governmental Responsibility.* New York: W. W. Norton, 1991.

Pritchett, C. Herman. *Constitutional Law of the Federal System.* Upper Saddle River N.J.: Prentice Hall, 1984.

David A. May
Eastern Washington University

contempt Contempt is the offense of disobeying an order issued by a court of law.

U.S. JUDGES have inherent authority to punish contempt, an authority that distinguishes a judicial from an administrative body. DUE PROCESS requires only that contemners be given fair notice and are afforded a public hearing, which, however, may take place on the spot and immediately prior to SENTENCING. Contempt may be charged against anyone present during judicial proceedings, or against persons who, away from the courtroom, act in a manner that interferes with the orderly processes of JUSTICE. Both types, respectively "direct" and "indirect," may be punished by any reasonable means, normally fine or imprisonment or both. A contempt order seldom will be overruled by a higher court, and then only if it was committed outside the issuing judge's JURISDICTION, not for reasons of error.

Although the division is not precise, judges often categorize contempts as civil and criminal. While all contempt orders vindicate the court's dignity, civil contempts are considered those committed "in the face of the court," punished on a motion by an opposing party and imposed in the latter's interest. Civil punishments are intended to be coercive, and they continue until the court's order is obeyed. Criminal contempts are more frequently committed away from the courtroom and punished in the interests of the public. They are generally fixed in amount and duration. Punishment for criminal contempt may be limited and provided special procedures by statute; Congress first established such limits on federal courts in 1831.

Contempt convictions figure in many of the highlights of American legal history. Famous contemners include Passmore Williamson, abolitionist; Eugene Debs, leader of the Pullman strike; Ross Barnett, anti–civil rights governor of Mississippi; William Jefferson Clinton, president of the United States. (The English tradition is equally notable: Charles I was executed for, among other things, contempt of court.) The first volume of *U.S. Reports* includes a Pennsylvania Supreme Court decision fining and imprisoning a Philadelphia editor for contempt after he publically accused local judges of political bias (*Respublica v. Oswald,* 1 U.S. 319 [1788]). The leading contempt case, *Anderson v. Dunn* (19 U.S. 204 [1821]), upheld the order of Henry Clay, Speaker of the U.S. House of Representatives, imprisoning a private citizen during his interrogation by the House for attempted bribery.

One of the longest punishments for contempt in American history, seven and one-half years in Maryland state prison (1988–95), was imposed on Jacqueline Bouknight, a welfare recipient who refused to accede to the court's order that she reveal the whereabouts of her son. Previously accused of CHILD ABUSE, she claimed her Fifth Amendment right against SELF-INCRIMINATION. However, the U.S. Supreme Court held that the local court's order was for compelling reasons unrelated to criminal law enforcement (*Baltimore City Department of Social Services v. Bouknight,* 493 U.S. 549 [1990]), and denied the APPEAL.

In 1994 in *International Union, United Mine Workers v. Bagwell,* 512 U.S. 821, the U.S. Supreme Court muted the civil-criminal court distinction in the interests of greater procedural protection. The Court unanimously decided that a punishment of monetary fines, graduated upward over successive incidents of the union's disobedience of an order prohibiting certain disruptive practices associated with a coal strike and payable to the state of Virginia as recompense for policing costs, was criminal, despite having been expressly designated by the issuing court as civil. Because the fines, once incurred, could not be purged in the usual method of compliance with the order, they were punitive, under the Constitution requiring TRIAL BY JURY.

For more information

Dobbs, Dan B. "Contempt of Court: A Survey," *Cornell Law Review* 56 (1971): 183.

Dudley, Earl C. "Getting beyond the Civil/Criminal Distinction: A New Approach to the Regulation of Indirect Contempts," *Virginia Law Review* 79 (1993): 1025.

Wells, John. "Authority of the Trial Judge," *Georgetown Law Journal* 88 (2000): 1389.

Karen Orren
University of California at Los Angeles

contingency fee Contingency fee refers to an arrangement between lawyer and client in a civil lawsuit in which the payment of attorney's fees is conditioned upon the successful outcome of the case. In essence, a contingent-fee agreement is a contract whereby the attorney agrees to be paid out of the proceeds of the successful lawsuit or not at all. The lawyer may also agree to advance payment of all fees and expenses connected with the civil action. Contingency fees are considered to be valid except where prohibited by law, considered to be against public policy, or obtained by FRAUD, mistake, or duress. For example, contingent-free agreements are not permitted in criminal cases, and in most JURISDICTIONS they are not permitted in DIVORCE or alimony proceedings. The fee agreed upon is generally a percentage of the award recovered by the plaintiff in the lawsuit. Contingent fees may range from 25% to 40% of the plaintiff's recovery. The fee must be considered reasonable and not excessive, and courts may and do examine contingent-fee arrangements to determine whether they are reasonable. Contingency fees raise ethical problems for lawyers, who are generally not supposed to have a property interest in litigation they bring on behalf of their clients. Contingent-fee arrangements are an exception to this rule. Moreover, contingency fees are limited by the rule of professional ethics that prohibits the charging of excessive fees. However, the risk the lawyer assumes in a contingent-fee case may be reflected in the amount he can charge. The U.S. Supreme Court has observed: "Fees for legal services in litigation may be either 'certain' or 'contingent' (or some hybrid of the two). A fee is certain if it is payable without regard to the outcome of the suit; it is contingent if the obligation to pay depends on a particular result's being obtained. Under the most common contingent-fee CONTRACT for litigation, the attorney receives no payment for his services if his client loses" (*City of Burlington v. Dague*, 505 U.S. 563 [1992]).

Whether a contingency fee will be considered reasonable and not excessive depends on the particular difficulty of the case and the amount of work the lawyer must do, as well as the degree of likelihood that the client will succeed at trial. Civil litigation, especially when it involves large companies, is extremely expensive, and successful attorneys charge high fees for their services. Without contingent-fee agreements, many potential plaintiffs would be unable to sue the persons or companies that injured them. However, contingency fees are controversial and continue to be a hotly debated issue in the legal system. Many people claim that contingent-fee agreements cause excessive litigation and larger demands for damages. According to the many critics of the practice, contingency fees encourage lawyers to pursue weak or frivolous cases and mislead clients about their chances of success. Contingency fee lawyers are seen as "hired guns" who reap enormous fees. Indeed, there have been cases in which contingency-fee lawyers have brought CLASS ACTIONS in which the attorney's fees reached $100 million. The question is whether the benefit of opening up litigation to lower-income plaintiffs is outweighed by the potential for abuse. Legislatures and courts regulate contingency fee practices, but the controversy is likely to continue as long as large damages awards and high attorneys' fees are handed out by the courts.

For more information

Kritzer, Herbert M. "Contingency Fee Lawyers as Gatekeepers in the Civil Justice System," *Judicature* 81, no. 1 (July/August 1997): 22–29.

Celia A. Sgroi
State University of New York, Oswego

contract Contract is the term for an agreement between two or more parties to exchange goods or services for money or other goods or services.

For a contract to be formed there must be a promise for a promise. For example, Jones saying, "I will sell you my gold fountain pen for $200" has made an offer to hand over the pen in exchange for currency in that denomination in ordinary business terms. If Smith then says, either verbally or in writing, "I will take it at that price," an immediate contract is entered into. But, if Smith says, "I will take it for $195 (or some other sum)," he has made a counter/offer and there is not a contract.

If Smith says, "I will take the pen on next Friday if White pays me $200 by then," Smith has made a conditional acceptance, which is nevertheless binding when White pays. If White does not pay the money by the time specified, the condition has not been met and the acceptance is void. Even if Smith receives $200 from some other source, the contract is still void because it specified a payment by White.

In order for a contract to be binding, there must be some consideration, that is, something must be given in exchange for the goods or services received. Thus the $200 is consideration for the pen. Consideration may be something other than money, such as other goods or labor performed for the offer or the object accepted. Labor to be performed may be paid for by money or goods. Among family members or other social relations, the consideration may be "natural love and affection."

Contracts may be mutual or unilateral. Most business contracts that are bargained for, such as commodities or real estate, are said to be "arm's-length" and are mutual. An example of a unilateral contract is an employee manual in which the employer sets the terms.

A contract is usually made between two parties but may be made for the benefit of someone else, called a third party beneficiary. For example, a parent may enter into an agreement with a college to pay an offspring's tuition.

A meretricious contract is one that accomplishes an illegal purpose. Thus, a contract to sell street drugs is illegal and therefore is unenforceable in court. Examples of other meretricious contracts would be for engaging in PROSTITUTION or for the sale of fertilized human embryos.

A contract may not be enforceable for a number of reasons. A failure of consideration is the term used when performance on one side is not completed. Jones fails to deliver the gold pen upon tender of $200 in U.S. currency. Smith tenders not cash but a check which is returned for insufficient funds. The pen may have been stolen and Jones cannot deliver, and therefore the contract fails for impossibility of performance. There may be a mutual mistake of fact, such as the pen turning out to be other than gold.

A unilateral mistake of fact may not render a contract unenforceable, particularly if Jones, for instance, did nothing to foster the impression that the pen was gold. On the other hand, a court may declare a contract unenforceable if there was such a disconnection between the perceived bargain and what was exchanged that no reasonable person would make such an agreement.

If the price offered for the pen was $20,000 and the pen turned out to be a salesman's promotional giveaway, the contract would be considered voidable if not actually void because the price offered is substantially in excess of the value of the pen. In this instance the court might consider the contract to be an "adhesion contract," that is, one which so heavily favors one side that a reasonable person might think the contract was coerced or involuntary.

Most contracts are explicit in their terms and are called express contracts, as in Jones being willing sell Smith the pen for an agreed price. Some contract terms, however, are implied. A contract to form a partnership for profit implies a covenant of fair dealing and honesty, such as not disclosing business strategy to a competitor to the disadvantage of the partnership.

Most contracts are in writing, although some are not, particularly those dealing with land or for value in an amount greater than that determined by statute. Agreements for an amount smaller than the statutory amount need not be written. If people do not write the contract but behave as if there is one, the courts may find that a contract existed anyway.

For more information

American Jurisprudence. 2nd ed., vol. 17A. *Contracts.* St. Paul, Minn.: West, 1988–.

Miller, Roger LeRoy, and Gaylord A. Jentz. *Business Law Today.* 5th ed. St. Paul, Minn.: West, 2000.

Stanley M. Morris
Attorney
Cortez, Colorado

cooperative A cooperative is a corporation formed to hold title to real property. The shareholders of the corporation are in turn entitled to long-term proprietary leases for units within the property.

A cooperative is usually set up by a sponsor or promoter. The sponsor must follow the state law regarding incorporation of a cooperative. The cooperative corporation is customarily a nonprofit corporation; it issues stock and is governed by a board of directors.

Generally, there are three documents needed to establish a cooperative: (1) the plan of cooperative organization, (2) the proprietary lease, and (3) the bylaws.

The plan of cooperative organization describes the property and identifies the sponsor. It can specify the method of allocation of the corporation's stock. For example, a certain number of shares of the cooperative can be allocated to each unit of the property. Purchasers of those certain stock certificates are then entitled to long-term proprietary leases for the corresponding unit. The plan also usually contains conditions for the purchase of stock, arrangements that have been made for management of the property, and the corporate details.

Owners of a cooperative do not own real estate. Instead, they own stock, which entitles them to use the property according to the terms of their proprietary lease. An essential provision of the proprietary lease is the payment of rent. The amount of the rent is determined by the board of directors and is used to pay the common expenses of the cooperative. The proprietary lease usually contains a provision that prevents the assignment of the lease to another without approval of the board of directors.

The bylaws establish the operating procedures for the board of directors, including the methods of calling shareholders meetings, the process for the election of the board of directors of the association, and the formula for the determination of the amount of rent. A typical method for determining the amount of rent is for the board of directors to estimate the total amount necessary to pay such expenses as real estate taxes, insurance, wages, and utility costs for the ensuing calendar year. That total divided by the number of shareholders represents the annual rent for the tenant-shareholder.

An important question relating to cooperative corporations is whether the corporation is subject to security regulations. Generally it is unlawful for a promoter to offer stock for sale without first registering such stock with the appropriate securities regulator. Some states specifically exempt cooperatives from such registration. Other states have waived the registration requirement, using the analysis that a security is an investment with an expected return, whereas there is no such expectation with the purchase of stock in a cooperative. This is true because purchasers generally make their decision whether to purchase cooperative stock on the basis of a desire to reside in the cooperative unit, not the prospects of profit.

For more information

American Jurisprudence. 2nd ed. vol. 15A. *Condominiums and Co-Operative Apartments.* St. Paul, Minn.: West, 1976.

Rabkin, Jacob, and Mark H. Johnson. *Current Legal Forms with Tax Analysis.* New York: Matthew Bender, 1994.

David M. Reddy
Sweet and Reddy, S.C.
Elkhorn, Wisconsin

coroner (medical examiner) A coroner, serving as a medical examiner, is a public officer whose purpose is to investigate instances of violent, unusual, or otherwise unexpected deaths.

While in general most people think of coroners investigating criminal homicides, they may also have a duty to investigate unexplained deaths of infants or children and the deaths of individuals held in law enforcement custody. The coroner may be responsible for transporting the deceased and issuing death certificates. An autopsy is generally performed to establish the identity, cause, and time of the individual's death. If the coroner determines that the individual may have been a victim of a homicide, the coroner presents EVIDENCE to law enforcement officials, who then carry out the criminal investigation. The coroner is required to remain objective in his or her investigation, without undue influence from law enforcement. The coroner must also document a chain of custody for any and all evidentiary items that may be used in court.

Depending upon the coroner's JURISDICTION, he or she may also have additional powers and duties. In many jurisdictions, coroners work within the area's law enforcement agencies. This allows them additional privileges, such as bearing arms in public and quicker access to records. Also, coroners may have the responsibility to issue arrest warrants for possible MURDERS. In a few of the smaller districts that follow this model, the sheriff may serve as the coroner.

Coroners' duties in the courtroom play a vital role in the judiciary process. While in court, they testify as EXPERT WITNESS to many aspects of the case. They provide key insight into the physical elements of the homicide, such as the details to the type of death. The coroners also provide interpretations of the forensic data that could indicate important factors of the case. For example, a coroner may state an opinion clarifying whether the defendant's physical strength and size was adequate to carry out the alleged murder. Outside of the courtroom, the coroner's detailed information helps the government track the numerous types of murders from year to year and, in some instances, diseases representing public health threats. Coroners may also identify population members that typically become victims, as well as the time of day and year that specific murders are more prevalent.

The education of coroners varies greatly according to the criteria set by their jurisdiction. In districts where the coroner acts as a medical examiner, he or she is normally required to hold a medical degree. Most coroners also hold additional education focused on forensic sciences and legal training. These well-qualified medical coroners are usually appointed in hopes to make the career more professional and prestigious. Sparsely populated districts often hold less strict educational requirements for a coroner, where it may only be necessary for him or her to hold a high school diploma in conjunction with some job training. These coroners usually serve a broader variety of roles, which may include law enforcement or court official duties. An election is usually used to select this type of coroner.

For more information

The National Institutes of Health. "Life Works: Coroner and Medical Examiner." Available online. URL: http://science.education.nih.gov/LifeWorks.nsf.

National Association of Medical Examiners. Available online. URL: http://thename.org.

Emily Greenelsh and Todd Collins
Western Carolina University

corporal punishment Corporal punishment generally refers to the use of force to inflict physical pain on an individual with the intent to discipline and change undesired behavior. Corporal punishment is generally differentiated based on who is committing the act of punishment. In general, private agents (such as parents or private school teachers) can engage in corporal punishment. In addition, public agents (such as public school officials or public prison officials) can also engage in acts of corporal punishment. We separate between public and private actions because each triggers different legal considerations.

The major form of private corporal punishment is generally referred to as corporal punishment in the home. This includes situations in which the parents use force (for instance, spanking) as a means of disciplining their children. Currently, there are no laws in the United States outlawing the use of corporal punishment in the home between a parent and child. However, this should be contrasted with CHILD ABUSE, which differs from corporal punishment by the degree, or intensity, of harm inflicted upon the child. Generally speaking, corporal punishment is not allowed privately between adults, and such actions (adult to adult) are usually categorized as a battery, or other cognizable legal harm (both civilly and criminally).

There are two major categories of public corporal punishment: school corporal punishment and judicial corporal punishment. School corporal punishment refers to instances in which school officials use force to inflict pain as a means of punishment and/or behavior modification. This can occur in the classroom or in other settings, such as forcing students to engage in excessive physical exercise. Judicial corporal punishment refers to government-sanctioned corporal punishment derived from an official government action. The basic example includes a court judgment that provides for corporal punishment as part of a sentence, as is done in death penalty cases (where death is the form of punishment), or in other cases in which the court orders convicted defendants to engage in laborious activities as a condition of their sentence.

A major limitation on the use of corporal punishment by public officials is the EIGHTH AMENDMENT to the UNITED STATES CONSTITUTION, which prohibits the government from engaging in acts that result in CRUEL AND UNUSUAL PUNISHMENT to an individual. Many legal cases have been brought, for instance, claiming the use of the death penalty by states and the federal government violates the Eight Amendment because it is cruel and unusual punishment. Cases have also been brought against public schools, claiming that certain acts of corporal punishment by school officials go too far, resulting in cruel and unusual punishment in violation of the Eighth Amendment.

In one famous case, *Ingraham v. Wright*, 430 U.S. 651 (1977), the U.S. Supreme Court reviewed a claim by a 14-year-old student, James Ingraham, claiming Florida's public school system's policy allowing corporal punishment violated the Eighth Amendment prohibition against cruel and unusual punishment. James was sent to the principal's office for rowdy behavior and ultimately received paddling as a punishment. The paddling resulted in bruising on his buttocks. The U.S. Supreme Court ruled that corporal punishment, in general, was constitutional, indicating the Eighth Amendment was primarily intended as a protection for convicted criminals. The Court also indicated an aggrieved child could look to state law and bring civil and criminal complaints against school officials when their actions go too far, resulting in a violation of law toward the student. Since the *Ingraham* decision, a number of states have passed specific laws prohibiting the use of corporal punishment in public schools. Currently, 20 states still allow the use of corporal punishment in public schools.

As stated in the *Ingraham* opinion, the Eighth Amendment is most applicable to protections afforded to convicted criminals. Thus, the use of judicial corporal punishment is constantly challenged, especially in the prison context, including the types of punishments that can be levied against a convicted criminal. Prohibited categories of corporal punishment from criminal convictions based on U.S. Supreme Court opinions include: executing minors and incompetents; burning and disembowelment; drawing and quartering; as well as public dissecting. See *Wilkerson v. Utah*, 99 U.S. 130 (1978); *Atkins v. Virginia*, 536 U.S. 304 (2002); *ROPER V. SIMMONS*, 543 U.S. 551 (2005). Other categories where excessive corporal punishment might be found in imprisonment cases include: a "gross disproportionality" between the crime and the sentence (*HARMELIN V. MICHIGAN*, 501 U.S. 957 [1991]); excessively hard and painful labor during incarceration (*Weems v. United States*, 217 U.S. 349 [1910]); and jail sentences for addictions to narcotics (*ROBINSON V. CALIFORNIA*, 370 U.S. 660 [1962]).

For more information

Bitensky, Susan H. "The Poverty of Precedent for School Corporal Punishment's Constitutionality under the Eighth Amendment," *University of Cincinnati Law Review* (Summer 2009): 1327.

Henning, Anna Cir, and Kenneth R. Thomas, Coordinators. "Judge Sonia Sotomayor: Analysis of Selected Opinions." *Congressional Research Service, Reports and Issue Briefs* (June 19, 2009): 28.

Sachs, Deana P. "State Actors Beating Children: A Call for Judicial Relief," *University of California David Law Review* (April 2009): 1165.

Chad J. McGuire
University of Massachusetts, Dartmouth.

counterfeiting Counterfeiting is the making of false currency and offering it as legitimate. SIR WILLIAM BLACKSTONE, an English common law legal scholar defined high TREASON as, "When disloyalty rears its crest as to attack majesty itself." At common law, counterfeiting was high treason. Counterfeiting of the Great Seal characterized an attack against the king. Initially, the term *FORGERY* defined the making of false documents or the falsification of existing documents.

Almost every type of tangible personal property that cannot be subject to forgery can be subject to counterfeiting. There are areas in counterfeiting that overlap forgery, even though forgery does not overlap counterfeiting. The similarities between these offenses can create uncertainty or suggest a gap in legal coverage. Federal statutes prohibit counterfeiting; forgery, or false making of securities and obligations, and the creation of fictitious obligations (18 U.S.C. §514).

Modern statutes advocate that counterfeiting is a FELONY because it affects government functions. Counterfeiting occurs when the object "bears such a likeness or resemblance to any of the genuine obligations or securities issued under the authority of the United States as is calculated to deceive an honest, sensible and unsuspecting person of ordinary observation and care when dealing with a person supposed to be upright and honest." *United States v Wethington*, 141F.3rd 284,287 (6th Cir. 1998).

Counterfeiting generally refers to "a crime based upon a preexisting genuine instrument." Forgery does not always "carry such presumption but indicates that there is a genuine or real obligor in existence whose obligation has been simulated." *Stinson v. United States*, 316 F.2d

554 (5th Cir. 1963); see also 18 U.S.C. §513(c). Counterfeiting and forgery have similar attributes in the same chapter of the UNITED STATES CODE. Occasionally, the courts use the legal concepts interchangeably. Refer to the legal terminology below as an example of the statutory wording:

The federal government aggressively investigates and prosecutes offenders who engage in counterfeit activities. "Counterfeiting bills, coins, or alteration of genuine currency, the possession of forged monies with intent to distribute, and the possession of printed reproductions (even photographs) of federal currency, postage stamps, or U.S. securities are punishable by fine and/or up to 15 years in prison. The forgery, trafficking, or alteration of U.S. bonds or checks is punishable by fines and or up to 10 years in prison."

State statutory law punishes those who counterfeit items other than money. Examples of such counterfeit items include municipal bonds, corporate securities, and counterfeit labels of consumer goods. Counterfeit consumer goods are imitations, and usually there is intent to defraud and offer the goods as genuine. Individuals trafficking counterfeit products take advantage of the established worth of the imitated product, such as clothing, software, pharmaceuticals, and electronics. The counterfeited item results in a trademark, logo, or brand name patent infringement. The federal government has similar legislation regarding counterfeit goods, trademarks, logos, labels, and brand names, etc.

In conclusion, the U.S. Secret Service is responsible for the investigation of counterfeiting. The agents refer to working these investigations as "funny money" cases.

For more information

Kersten, Jason. *The Art of Making Money: The Story of a Master Counterfeiter.* New York: Gotham Press, 2009.

Thomas E. Baker
University of Scranton

County of Riverside v. McLaughlin 500 U.S. 44 (1991) In the *County of Riverside v. McLaughlin,* the Court reversed a decision by the district court and the U.S. COURT OF APPEALS that had determined a PROBABLE CAUSE hearing must take place in 36 hours. In their 5-4 decision, the Court determined a probable cause hearing, when a person is ARRESTED without a warrant, must take place within 48 hours of arrest.

In this case, Donald Lee McLaughlin had been incarcerated in the Riverside County Jail in California. He later filed a complaint in the U.S. District Court for the Central District of California claiming his FOURTH AMENDMENT guarantee to a prompt determination of whether probable cause existed for his arrest was violated. The complaint was filed to represent McLaughlin and other individuals being detained in the Riverside County Jail without an arrest warrant. The argument made by McLaughlin's lawyers was the period between arrest and the determination of probable cause for that arrest (through a probable cause hearing, which is combined with ARRAIGNMENT in Riverside County) violated the "prompt" rule established by the Fourth Amendment and further reaffirmed in *Gerstein v. Pugh,* 420 U.S. 103 (1975).

It was Riverside County policy to hold the arraignment/probable cause hearing within two days of the arrest. Yet, there was the potential that due to weekends and holidays (which were not included in the computation) more than two days could pass. For example, as noted by Justice SANDRA DAY O'CONNOR, who delivered the opinion of the Court, "over a Thanksgiving holiday, a 7-day delay is possible." *County of Riverside v. McLaughlin,* 500 U.S. 44 (1991).

In its finding, the Court rejected the premise by the lower courts that a prompt probable cause hearing was to be held within 36 hours of an individual's arrest without a warrant. This 36-hour principle was established by the district court and reaffirmed by the U.S. Court of Appeals for the Ninth Circuit. In the Court's decision, a balance between the administrative nature of bringing individuals before a magistrate to determine probable cause and attempting to protect an individual's right to determination of probable cause for arrest was struck. Reiterating the principle of promptness outlined in *Gerstein v. Pugh*, 420 U.S. 103 (1975), the Court noted the lower courts had selectively taken from *Gerstein* to create their 36-hour rule. Instead, the majority of the Court argued there were no procedural guidelines that were imposed on the states. Due to variation across various JURISDICTIONS, there needed to be flexibility in the application of the right to a prompt probable cause hearing. Yet, the Court also argued the current policy by the County of Riverside did not comply completely with the balance struck in *Gerstein*. In not taking into account delays due to weekends and holidays, the Court argued Riverside could potentially be sued for violations of the 48-hour principle established in the Court's decision.

The significance was the establishment of a time limit for bringing individuals before a probable cause hearing. Since this case, a violation of the 48-hour principle is referred to as a Riverside violation. Later cases, such as *POWELL V. NEVADA*, 511 U.S. 79 (1994), determined this principle must be applied retroactively to any case that occurred prior to the ruling. It also noted delays in gaining probable cause hearings had not yet been solved. Within the war on TERRORISM, both scholars and lawyers have reviewed the 48-hour principle. This has been in reference to whether individuals being detained on terrorism-related charges are required to be brought before a JUDGE to determine probable cause.

For more information

Chavey, Victoria W. "The Forty-Eight Hour Rule and *County of Riverside v. McLaughlin*," *Boston University Law Review* 72 (1992): 403.

Lalmalani, S. G. "Extraordinary Rendition Meets the U.S. Citizen: United States Responsibility under the Fourth Amendment," *Connecticut Public Interest Law Journal* 5, no. 5 (2005).

Kevin E. Grisham
California State University, San Bernardino

courts of appeals, U.S. The U.S. courts of appeals are the middle-level court of the FEDERAL COURT SYSTEM.

Established by the Evarts Act in 1891, they were intended as appellate courts only; that is, rather than hold trials they only review the cases from lower courts and establish whether there were any errors at trial. Originally created to alleviate the workload of the higher U.S. Supreme Court and to review the decisions of the lower U.S. district courts, these courts have become increasing important in the federal judicial hierarchy. Because most legal decisions never make it to the Supreme Court (less than 100 or so cases per year), the U.S. court of appeals have been largely charged with *interpreting* doctrines of national policy and ensuring that national policies fit local or regional concerns.

In the century since they were established, they have been constantly restructured to accommodate an ever increasing caseload. This increase in caseload largely reflects the expansion of federal law and litigation, as well as the increasing JURISDICTION of federal courts, rate of appeals, quantity of federal litigation, and complexity of federal law. The number of circuits has increased from nine to 13 and the authorized judgeships from 22 to 167 to accommodate the current 54,000 cases filed per year. LAW CLERKS and permanent staff attorneys are another addition; virtually unknown in these courts in the 1930s, there are now more than 800 law clerks and 150 staff attorneys assigned to these courts.

Each of the 13 circuits has its own court. The states and territories are divided into numbered circuits, each of which contains three or more states, with the District of Columbia having a circuit in itself. The number of JUDGES in each circuit ranges from six in the First Circuit (e.g., New England and Puerto Rico) to 28 in the Ninth Circuit (e.g., from Alaska to Arizona), with a total of 167.

For the most part, these courts do not have the option of choosing which cases they will review (unlike the U.S. Supreme Court). Instead, questions of error occurring from the lower courts are mandatorily decided by rotating panels of three judges. However, in cases of great importance or ones that divided the panel of judges (about 100 cases per year), a majority vote can choose to hear (or rehear) a case *en banc,* which is participation by all the judges in that particular circuit. As with all federal judges, these judges are nominated by the president and confirmed by the Senate.

Since the 1960s, the volume of cases coming to these courts has increased dramatically, creating great strains on their ability to handle the caseload; their caseload has increased from approximately 33,000 cases in 1985, 54,000 in 1998, 60,000 in 2009, and then 57,000 in 2010. This increase is largely due to the fact that these courts are the intermediate court of the federal judiciary; they handle the disparity between the less than 200 cases that the higher Supreme Court decides each year and the enormous increase in cases at the lower district court level. Much of the strain between these two levels must be absorbed by the appellate courts if a uniformity of national law is to be maintained. Congress has responded with several measures: increasing the number of appellate judgeships, authorizing *en banc* procedures, splitting circuits, and creating the federal circuit are some examples. Nonetheless, the strains in the workload of these courts continue.

For more information

Kuersten, Ashlyn, and Songer, Donald. *Guide to the U.S. Courts of Appeals.* New York: Garland Press, 2000.

Ashlyn K. Kuersten
Western Michigan University

crack-cocaine disparity The crack-cocaine disparity refers to different PUNISHMENTS received for the possession of the same amounts of each of these substances, with crack possession receiving significantly more severe punishment. Some contend that the differences in punishment are racially motivated, whereas others contend that they are reflective of the severity of the crimes surrounding possession of one versus another.

Throughout the early 1970s, the United States embarked on a federal war on drugs under the leadership of President Nixon. The effects of this policy resulted in the creation of the DRUG ENFORCEMENT ADMINISTRATION in 1973 equipped with the mission to stop drug trafficking. Under strict drug penalties, drug use became a crime with thousands being locked up in jails and prisons. The origins of crack cocaine into America's poorest communities have been blamed by many on the Reagan administration's involvement in overthrowing a Marxist Nicaraguan government in the late 1970s by introducing crack in U.S. cities in order to support the Freedom Fighters. As a result of this, some argue, crack exploded on the drug market, especially in poor communities. Later in the 1980s, the Anti-Drug Abuse Acts called for harsh mandatory SENTENCING for low-level offenders of crack cocaine that was drastically different from penalties for powder cocaine users.

Crack and powder cocaine are two forms of the same drug base. The difference between them lies in how crack cocaine is man-made versus powder cocaine, which is in its traditional form. Crack cocaine is derived by cooking the powder until it crystallizes into rocks. The rocks are then sold on the market at a much cheaper cost than powder cocaine, making it more readily available to urban and poor communities across the United States. In the 1980s, this created a crack explosion in some of the poorest U.S. communities. As a result, the Anti-Drug Abuse Acts were passed to criminalize those who used, abused, and sold crack cocaine, leading to high rates of ARREST and incarceration, predominantly among poor blacks and Hispanics. On the other hand, powder cocaine is the choice of white-collar drug users. Since its inception, only those who could afford it can buy it. Many argue that the effects of crack cocaine versus powder cocaine are the same, and therefore penalty structures ought to be identical.

The Anti-Drug Abuse Act of 1986 penalizes crack cocaine at significantly greater weight than powder cocaine. A mandatory minimum five-year sentence is the penalty for being convicted with five grams of crack cocaine; the same five-year penalty applies to powder cocaine only when an offense involves 500 grams of cocaine, or 100 times the crack minimum for sentencing. The average crack-cocaine sentence is several years longer than powder-cocaine offenses.

This disparity in penalization has racial and social justice implications. For example, crack cocaine users are sentenced to mandatory terms in prisons, unlike powder cocaine users. Furthermore, in crack cocaine cases, the JUDGE has no right to intervene to reduce sentencing for low-level drug offenders, regardless of the level of severity. For example, African Americans have been the primary target of crack cocaine mandatory sentences despite the fact that crack users are largely white or other minorities, and despite the fact that powder cocaine users are predominantly white. To further affect the sentencing issue, of those incarcerated for crack cocaine, a majority of offenders have low-level involvement in the drug market, such as street peddlers and lookouts. Concern about this racial disparity led the Minnesota Supreme Court in *State v. Russell*, 477 N.W.2d 886 (Minn.1991), to declare sentencing differences between convictions for crack and cocaine possession to violate the Minnesota constitution's version of the EQUAL PROTECTION clause.

In part because of cases like *Russell*, a new outlook on the disparities in sentencing for crack cocaine and powder cocaine has emerged. This new movement regarding the inequalities and unfair penalization structures has resulted in advocates and policy makers interested in ending the sentencing disparity. In 2010, this disparity was largely eliminated at the federal level, although in many states it still persists.

For more information

American Civil Liberties Union. Available online. URL: http://www.aclu.org/drugpolicy/sentencing/index.html.

Grogger, J., and M. Willis. "The Emergence of Crack Cocaine and the Rise in Urban Crime Rates," *Review of Economics and Statistics*, 82, no. 4 (2000): 519–529.

The Sentencing Project. Available online. URL: http://www.sentencingproject.org/doc/dp_crack_sentencing.pdf.

Leila Sadeghi
Center for Executive Leadership in Government, Rutgers University, New Brunswick

crime and international law Crime and international law refers to the prosecution of crimes that cross national borders. These types of crimes raise difficult issues surrounding the application of appropriate laws as well as the apprehension and trial of those accused of these crimes.

Crimes can be committed at both the domestic level and international level. In addressing the criminal behavior at these two levels, one will notice an overlap between the international legal system and domestic legal systems. In the case of domestic criminal behavior, countries can generally tackle the issue with local laws and the local legal system. When criminal behavior occurs at the international level and/or has international implications, how to address the matter becomes more complicated. In the case of crimes that have international implications, the issues that arise in the overlap between domestic and international legal systems are significant. The issue of the universal JURISDICTION principle, application of international law within the United States and the participation of the United States in the prevention of international criminal acts (i.e., participation in the International Criminal Court) are three of these issues.

One of the core issues facing the American legal system is the application of the universal jurisdiction principle. Often, the United States has incorporated legal principles from international conventions and treaties into U.S. federal code. Thereby, the extension of international law into the American legal system has persisted for many years. Yet, as noted by recent debates over whether the United States should sign and ratify the Rome Statute (1998) and therefore became a party to the International Criminal Court, the issue of universal jurisdiction is not agreed upon in the United States.

Early in the history of the U.S. legal system, court decisions began to establish a principle whereby "[. . .] the character of an act as lawful or unlawful must be determined wholly by the law of the country where the act is done." *American Banana Company v. United Fruit Company,* 213 U.S. 347 (1909). These early decisions by the U.S. Supreme Court tended to not favor the position of adopting the universal jurisdiction principle by the United States. Yet, in *U.S. v. Bowman,* 260 U.S. 94 (1922), the permissibility of the application of U.S. law outside of the territorial borders was established. In this case, the Court noted to determine whether U.S. law can be applied outside of its border should be based on part of the intent of the congressional act.

However, these positions have shifted in the U.S. legal system over the years. In recent years, the criminal statutes found in the U.S. legal system could have worldwide implications. Using the principles outlined in *Bowman,* this principle has been applied when pursuing individuals committing transnational acts that violate both international law and/or the U.S. federal code. An example of this can be seen in the pursuit, apprehension, and detention of the former Panamanian president Manuel Noriega. *United States v. Noriega,* 746 F. Supp. 1506 (S.D. Fla. 1990). An additional example can be seen in the case of *U.S. v. Vasquez-Velasco,* 15 F. 3d. 833 (1994). These cases and many other examples suggest there is no clear adoption of the principle of universal jurisdiction in the U.S. legal system. Application of U.S. code occurs outside of the U.S. territorial boundaries, but the United States continues to explore the role of the U.S. legal system when addressing international law within its borders.

As a party to a significant amount of multilateral treaties and conventions, the United States is obligated to adhere to the principles of those documents. Yet, the question remains: How are violations of the principles of these documents to be addressed within U.S. courts? In some countries, violations of international criminal law can be addressed in their legal systems. According to Amnesty International USA, as of 2009, 125 countries follow this international legal standard. Since the end of World War II, many countries began to fight against violations of international criminal law. This has been accomplished through the ARREST, detention, or EXTRADITION of individuals committing particular ordinary crimes (e.g., MURDER, THEFT, hijacking, and hostage taking) or crimes that affect the international system (e.g., genocide, crimes against humanity, torture, and WAR CRIMES). Some of the countries that have been involved in this approach have included the United States, Canada, the United Kingdom, France, Mexico, and Belgium. In some cases, countries have allowed individuals affected by crimes that violate international law to sue those responsible in their court system. An example where this has been applied in the United States is the civil lawsuit involving Nicolas Carranza, the former vice-minister of defense of El Salvador. He was sued successfully in a U.S. federal court in 2005. This suit was for acts of torture and murder that were committed by soldiers under his command in El Salvador's civil war in the 1980s. With the new war on TERRORISM, the future application of international law at the domestic level is an issue to be determined. Particular activities used by countries in the war on terrorism could amount to violations of international criminal law. Whether these violations are addressed in other countries' domestic courts remains to be seen.

With the International Criminal Court (ICC) coming into effect in 2002, the future of international criminal law and the use of the ICC to address criminal behavior have been discussed further. This has been particular true in the U.S.

legal system given the U.S. government's apprehension to sign and ratify the Rome Statute. Like the United States, countries can still choose to prosecute individuals in domestic courts when there have been violation of international criminal law. Yet, when countries cannot or choose not to arrest, detain, and/or prosecute individuals for violations of international criminal law, the ICC can normally intervene. Yet, in the case where a country has not ratified the Rome Statute, if a United Nations (UN) Security Council referral has not occurred, the ICC cannot intervene if nationals of the nonratifying country committed the crime. This is additionally true when the crime occurred within the territorial boundaries of the country. This is particularly important as the United States as of 2009 has not ratified the Rome Statute, and under the Bush administration, the United States unsigned the Rome Statute.

As of 2009, the ICC has indicted 14 people. The international criminal cases involving these individuals come from Uganda, the Democratic Republic of the Congo, and the Central African Republic. Each of these countries referred the cases in their countries to the ICC. Additionally, the UN Security Council has referred a case involving Sudan, which is not a party to the Rome Statute. In the case of Sudan, one of the individuals whom the ICC has issued an arrest warrant for is the current Sudanese president Omar al-Bashir. This is for crimes against humanity and war crimes committed in the Darfur region of Sudan. Bashir is the first-ever head of state to be prosecuted by the ICC. This has created some questions concerning the issue of sovereignty and the role of international criminal law within countries and related to a country's behavior. This latter question has been at the core of the discussion within the American legal and policy community.

Even as the United States helped in the post–World War II environment to shape international criminal law and the ICC, policy makers have been concerned that becoming a party to the Rome Statute could undermine U.S. sovereignty. Furthermore, there was a concern the ICC could become politicized, and it could be used against the United States. In addition, there was a concern that the ICC may prosecute action by U.S. military personnel as war crimes or crimes of aggression. This issue was addressed in a limited fashion by unilateral international agreements between the United States and other countries where U.S. military personnel are located. These agreements allow the United States to retain jurisdiction over their personnel when they commit crimes outside of the United States. An example is the Republic of the Philippines–U.S. Visiting Forces Agreement (1999). With the current war on terrorism, these concerns over U.S. military activities abroad and whether they could be brought before either the ICC or another country's court continue.

For more information

American Banana Company v. United Fruit Company, 213 U.S. 347 (1909).

Ferdinandusse, Ward N. *Direct Application of International Criminal Law in National Courts.* Cambridge: Cambridge University Press, 2006.

Reydams, L. *Universal Jurisdiction: International and Municipal Legal Perspectives.* Oxford: Oxford University Press, 2003.

Sewall, Sarah, and Carl Kaysen, eds. *The United States and the International Criminal Court: National Security and International Law.* Lanham, Md.: Rowman and Littlefield, 2000.

United States v. Bowman, 260 U.S. 94 (1922).

United States v. Noriega, 746 F. Supp. 1506 (S.D. Fla. 1990).

United States v. Vasquez-Velasco, 15 F. 3d. 833 (1994).

Kevin E. Grisham
California State University, San Bernardino

crime and school Crime and school refers to the committing of illegal acts in schools. Although many assume that criminal behavior is a serious and growing phenomenon, the crime rate in schools has actually dropped over the last few decades in the United States.

Schools in the United States are safe havens for students to engage in teaching and learning, and to learn social norms and behaviors within the context of the school environment. Throughout the late 1980s through today, school crime has been a factor in disrupting the learning process but also a threat to the safety of other students, faculty, and staff. Crime in schools is not limited to VIOLENT CRIMES. It includes a host of other crimes such as GANG presence and/or activity, possession and/or use of drugs or alcohol, sexual harassment, and more. Ensuring safe schools has become the mantra for many school districts and state policies. School safety programs and workshops have been developed in response to crime in the school environment. In many schools, faculty and staff are required to undergo school safety professional development for prevention purposes.

A majority of schools across the country have experienced some form of crime on school property. Despite a majority of crimes in schools classified as nonfatal, a few have resulted in fatal outcomes. Carrying weapons or firearms to schools was a major phenomenon from the mid 1990s through today. Guns in particular have become more readily available in communities and hence in the hands of children and adolescents in schools. Crime in schools can be linked to a variety of indicators. For example, some argue that urban areas, given higher crime rates than suburban areas, will experience more crime in schools. In this case, the physical environment is a factor. In another example, school crime can be linked to the presence of gangs and/or gang activity in the community. Other factors can include parents and FAMILY structure, attention-seeking behavior, or feelings of depression or isolation.

Over the past 15 years, school crime has witnessed an up-and-down trend. School crime was most prevalent in the early 1990s, peaked in 1995, and steadily declined since then. More recently, state and national school crime trends have scaled back.

Looking back to the 1989 NATIONAL CRIME VICTIMIZATION SURVEY (NCVS), only 9 percent of students reported being victims of crime. At the same time, roughly 15 percent of students reported that gangs were present in their schools, and 12 percent of those reported routine fights involving gangs. Then in 1998, the National Center on Education Statistics (NCES), coupled with the Bureau of Justice Statistics (BJS), analyzed 1989 and 1995 NCVS data and found that while the rate of students reporting being victims of crime remained stable between the two years, the number of students who reported experiencing violent crime increased. Also of interest was a sharp rise in the number of students reporting a problem involving VICTIMIZATION coupled with drugs, gangs, or guns in the school environment. The number of students who reported that gangs were present in their schools also increased significantly to 28 percent. In a second joint study between the BJS and NCES, from 1993 to 1998, the overall victimization rate decreased. Students who reported being victimized also declined. Gangs and carrying guns have also declined in schools since the early 1990s. In 2000, a report by the U.S. Departments of Education and Justice paints a more compelling picture of the trends. According to this report, overall the levels of school crime have declined since 1995.

The word *crime* connotes a variety of instances that may occur in schools. This list is not exhaustive, yet the majority of crimes typically include victimization, physical attacks or fights, verbal name-calling (e.g., hate words), BULLYING; drug and alcohol possession, use, or distribution; possession or use of weapons; sexual harassment; verbal abuse of teachers; and vandalization.

The role of crime in schools varies according to many indicators, for example, the higher the rate of students qualifying for free and reduced lunch, discipline problems, truancy, and the presence of weapons. The population size of schools is also a factor in the rate of crime.

In general, the presence of any of these issues can create a school environment that is disruptive and out of control, and often corruptive toward other students. In time, many of these situations become permanent and can affect student achievement and overall safety for students and teachers.

Schools can respond to different incidents of varying degree in several ways. The most often used method involves disciplinary action against a student. This can include school suspension for greater than five days, in-school suspension (where students leave their regular classroom but is suspended within school), expulsion (where a student is removed with no service from their school) or zero tolerance (automatic expulsion), or an out-of-school transfer (where the student is transferred to a specialized school). Some parents use home schooling as a prevention method to ensure their children are safe.

Schools also use a variety of safety measures that include specific procedures and programs that ensure the safety of staff and students. Some of these programs continue to deter school crime as the trends have demonstrated. Other schools use a variety of prevention methods that assist in securing safety, such as requiring students to enter through monitoring devices, installing sophisticated camera monitoring systems, and hiring guards and police to monitor school grounds and observe entrances and exits. In the future, schools most likely will continue to experience stronger safety measures, including a sharp rise in police or security presence on school grounds.

Overall, bringing a variety of stakeholders to the table to combat school crime is an ideal approach. Administrators, parents, teachers, children, community activists, citizens, local business owners, academics, and researchers, as well as state and local officials ought to participate in the process. Many of these individuals are responsible for the day-to-day operations of schools and students and have a unique understanding of school processes. Through collaboration, effective policies, programs, and prevention methods can be designed that have a sustaining effect on reducing school crime rates and school violence.

For more information

National Center for Education Statistics. U.S. Department of Education, Institute of Education Sciences. "Indicators of Crime and Safety 2008," Available online. URL: http://nces.ed.gov/programs/crimeindicators/crimeindicators2008/.

National and State School Crime Trends. "SystemStats. Spring, 2001." Available online. URL: http://www.ncgccd.org/systemstats/spring01p65.pdf.

Leila Sadeghi
Center for Executive Leadership in Government,
Rutgers University, New Brunswick.

crime control model The crime control model is one of two theories of the criminal process. This model stems from the classical, conservative view that imprisonment is necessary to control crime and antisocial behavior. The alternative view is the DUE PROCESS model, which focuses on the rights of individuals in society.

Émile Durkheim (1858–1917), a French philosopher, advocated for the crime control model. He believed that to be productive members of society, everyone was required to live within society's rules. If a crime was committed, the offender had to receive a PUNISHMENT equivalent to the offense for the rest of society to become whole. The crime control model advances the notion that when a person commits a crime, that person knowingly and willingly commits the act and, therefore, owes a debt to society that needs to be repaid. The focus is on the victims as opposed to the offender. The victims of a crime include not only the person who was subjected to the crime but also the rest of members of the community as well (Vold, Bernard, and Snipes, 2002).

Thus, crime control strategies approach punishment as being necessary and a way to restore and solidify social order. Punishing criminals reinforces law-abiding citizens' commitment to the system. Sentences that are not deemed harsh enough or proportionate to the criminal act could have a negative effect on the community. Leniency toward offenders could lead to dissention within the ranks of the majority (Vold, et al., 2002). As such, an assurance that offenders will be caught, convicted, and sentenced could be a deterrent against committing criminal acts. This process restores order, and other members of the community could be satisfied that the system is working. Offenders deserve to be punished; this view toward crime can also be understood by the use of the phrase *just deserts*. Simply stated, if a person commits a crime that person should expect to be punished and deserves to be punished.

This dominant view of punishment became popular in the 1970s and 1980s. Prior to the switch in strategy, REHABILITATION was the practice in the CRIMINAL JUSTICE SYSTEM. The goal of correctional institutions was to enable offenders to return to society as law-abiding citizens and not reoffend. However, SENTENCING goals changed in the 1980s from rehabilitation to incapacitation. The switch in ideology occurred for many reasons, all of which can be traced to a dissatisfaction with the effectiveness of the rehabilitation model. Correctional institutions were failing at rehabilitation; PAROLE was clearly not working because reoffending rates were high. Crime was still rampant and a problem.

Even more damaging to the rehabilitation model was the prominent study released by Robert Martinson in 1974. His report claimed that crime reduction strategies were ineffective, and the view that "nothing works" to reduce crime began to take hold. Martinson's study was the information needed to fuel a movement for a change. Thus, the problems of rising and more violent crime, as well as claims that the current rehabilitative efforts were ineffective, made it easy for a policy change to move to the forefront.

These factors, in combination with Ronald Reagan's pronouncement of a "war on crime," pushed the crime control model back into practice. Thus, a return to the utilitarian philosophy of punishment again reclaimed the focus of institutions trying to control crime. Changes in criminal sanctions included tougher, longer sentences for offenses, mandatory minimum sentences for certain crimes, and three-strikes laws for FELONIES. Mandatory minimum sentences refer to the length of a sentence an offender receives for a particular crime. Three-strikes laws consist of laws targeted toward repeat offenders to remove them from the community to keep citizens safe and to deter criminal activity (Riedel and Welsh, *Criminal Violence: Patterns, Causes and Prevention* 2nd ed., 2008). The expected result from more stringent laws was that people would be deterred from committing crimes for fear of punishment. The laws were also to have the added effect of reducing future reoffending by criminals released from prison. Reoffending would be deterred because offenders were expected to be afraid to be rearrested and sent back to prison.

A side effect to these changes in criminal justice policies, referred to as "get-tough policies," created a surge in the amount of offenders incarcerated in the prison system. The possible unintended consequence of increased incarceration rates and mandatory minimum sentences led to overcrowding in correctional institutions. To alleviate the overcrowding problem, more prisons had to be built to house those offenders sanctioned under the new laws.

The effectiveness of these crime control strategies has been debated in recent decades. Advocates of the get-tough policies claim that the reduction in crime rates demonstrated that the sentencing practices worked. However, critiques of the policies claim that mandatory minimum sentences did not deter crime. Further, a reduction in crime rates did not occur immediately when the laws were established. For example, sentences for VIOLENT CRIMES tripled; however, the rate of violent crime did not decrease during this time period (Beckett and Sasson, 2004). Thus, even though a person committing a violent crime could be expected to receive a prison sentence three times longer than would have been received prior to the policy changes, that person was not deterred from committing the act. Again, due to the perceived ineffectiveness of preventing crime, criminal justice agencies returned to the rehabilitative ideal in the 1990s. The "nothing works" view was replaced with a focus on what works to prevent crime. Currently, deterring crime is still a goal, however now in a modified form. A blended approach, one focusing on the offender and the community is practiced as the mechanism for crime control today.

For more information

Beckett, Katherine, and Theodore Sasson. *The Politics of Injustice: Crime and Punishment in America.* 2nd ed. SAGE, 2004.

Martinson, Robert. "What Works? Questions and Answers about Prison Reform." *National Affairs* 35 (Spring 1974). Available online. URL: www.nationalaffairs.com/public_interest/detail/what-worksquestions-and-answers-about-pr ison-ref. Accessed August 17, 2011.

Vold, George B., Thomas J. Bernard, and Jeffrey B. Snipes. *Theoretical Criminology.* 5th ed. New York: Oxford University Press, 2002.

Michelle L. Foster
Kent State University

crime in the workplace Crime in the workplace refers to the commission of illegal activity in the factory, office, etc. The types and incidence of crime has enormous variation across workplaces and is often difficult to estimate.

Crime in the workplace can take many forms, spans the range of seriousness, and is committed by a wide variety of individuals and groups. It victimizes employers, employees, customers, related businesses, governmental agencies, and others, including the larger economy and the environment. What links these diverse activities and actors is where the criminal activity takes place, in the workplace of the perpetrator(s).

An employee who arrives at his or her workplace armed and opens fire on those present is the most dramatic form of workplace crime. There are other ways in which persons are killed in their workplace because of the criminal activities of others that are not nearly as dramatic and rarely make it onto the evening news or a police scanner. Violations of worker safety and health laws lead to the injury and death of thousands of workers in the United States every year, far more than the number injured or killed in workplace shootings. These violations are criminal and usually perpetrated by company officers, management employees, and/or their proxies.

Other crimes committed in the workplace can lead to the death or injury of persons and/or other beings outside the workplace. Using banned substances in the production of goods, the violation of safety rules that lead to explosions or other dangerous events (such as running an oil tanker aground), violations of ENVIRONMENTAL LAWS, and similar crimes not only endanger those within the workplace but also those near, in the path of, or within the customer stream of the workplace in which the crime was committed.

Substantial economic harm can come to those near and far from a workplace in which fraudulent activities are taking place. Enron is perhaps the most notorious example for which the books have all but been closed. In this corporation, the use of creative to criminal accounting practices supported by its outside auditors resulted in the demise of this corporation, its auditing firm, the savings of many employees, and the savings of others directly or indirectly invested in the company. The banking crisis that hit the United States in 2008 is ongoing as of this writing, but allegations and suspicions of violations of law in service to the profits of banking interests abound. The complex structure of financial schemes and apparent lack of regulation of these may or may not result in criminal charges.

Individuals caught up in some of the more exotic investment strategies, such as Bernie

Madoff, have faced criminal charges. This particular individual and his alleged crimes in his workplace affected the financial security of many persons and entities. These crimes not only affect individual investors who may or may not know of the risks at hand but also pensioners whose employers have invested their pensions in markets affected by FRAUD and other financial crimes that greatly reduce or entirely wipe out the value of those investments.

More mundane financial crimes occur when companies collude on pricing, smaller frauds are committed within small business, employers do not pay workers established wages, or employees EMBEZZLE or otherwise steal money from their employees. Failure to properly fund retirement accounts or to maintain other benefits as promised to employees may also be criminal acts and are typically perpetrated by management personnel in their workplace.

The nonviolent workplace crimes that receive the most attention from police and the public include petty THEFT by employees, low-level embezzlement, and similar activities. Low-level employees who steal money or property from their workplaces do not typically get rich from their efforts as their high-level counterparts often do, but they are at greater risk of detection. Surveillance efforts originally aimed at shoplifters and other nonemployees are often used to catch small-time workplace thieves. Response to these crimes is often loss of employment but can include criminal prosecution. Low-level employees engaged in workplace crimes are more likely than their upper-level counterparts to be caught, fired, prosecuted, imprisoned, and to serve long sentences. This reflects general criminal justice responses.

Theories regarding the reasons for workplace crime are almost as numerous and diverse as the crimes themselves. It is impossible to use one theory to cover all of these crimes. But, if one takes a methodical approach and categorizes the crimes, it is easier to locate appropriate theoretical approaches.

A worker who kills her boss after being fired is clearly more driven by passion than reason. While a financial executive who finds a way to pilfer large sums of money from his companies' retirement fund while using a complex computer program to prevent detection is clearly more reasoned in his approach. A waiter who is not given meals while on the job as he knows is customary in his profession and begins taking home expensive bottles of wine to balance this slight is a different character than either of the other two. Therefore, it is vital that workplace crimes be properly categorized and examined for common threads prior to attempting a theoretical analysis. This has proved difficult within CRIMINOLOGY as definitions and categories often depend on perspective.

A CRIMINOLOGIST with a strict law-and-order stance would not necessarily draw a distinction between the pilfering financial executive and the waiter, while a more critical criminologist might see some similarities between the waiter and the killer while placing the financial executive in an entirely different category. Controlling workplace crime will depend on the ability to understand it through theoretical analysis and empirical study. Both present a challenge.

Empirical study requires reliable and valid data; these are difficult to attain. Many workplace crimes go undetected, and many detected are not reported. Those reported are often generically coded (workplace theft with general theft) making them indistinguishable within databases. Workplace violence (like other violent crimes) is most likely to be reported, and these are identified and compiled by the Bureau of Justice Statistics and readily available on its Web site.

For more information

Geis, Gilbert, Robert F. Meier, and Lawrence M. Salinger. *White Collar Crime: Classic and Contemporary.* New York: Free Press, 1995.

Loretta Capeheart
Northeastern Illinois University

crime scene A crime scene is the physical space where a crime occurs. Crime scenes can be classified based on many characteristics, including the type of crime, time sequence, location, and size.

The location where a crime began is known as the primary crime scene with all subsequent locations involved in the crime referred to as secondary crime scenes. In terms of size, crime scenes range from microscopic, which are individual, and at times minute, pieces of EVIDENCE, to macroscopic crime scenes, which include all of the overlapping and intersecting locations that exist within a larger crime scene. For example, the location where a MURDER took place is the primary crime scene, while the car that was used to transport the body and the location where the body was eventually buried are secondary crime scenes. Microscopic crime scenes include the body itself, the specific gunshot wounds, the trace evidence found on the body, such as small bloodstains embedded in a suspect's clothing, and the bullet casing found on the ground. The macroscopic crime scene includes all of the microscopic crime scenes that exist together within one location—in this case, the room where the shooting took place. No two crime scenes are identical, and they can include such varied spaces as a house that has been robbed, a series of cities involved in a SERIAL KILLER investigation, or an individual check in the case of FRAUD.

Though crime scenes vary greatly, all crime scene investigation follows a similar systematic procedure guided by law enforcement experience and legal guidelines. This process includes the securing of the crime scene by initial responders; the recognition, documentation, collection, and preservation of physical evidence; and crime scene reconstruction. Following organized protocol during crime scene investigation is necessary for the successful use of physical evidence by forensic scientists and criminal investigators.

Protocol must be followed from the moment the first officer arrives and begins the preliminary investigation of the crime scene. This officer has many responsibilities, including assisting any victims on the scene; arresting any suspects still on-site; locating, documenting, separating, and interviewing witnesses; and securing and maintaining the crime scene.

The Locard Exchange Principle states that whenever two objects come into contact, each will transfer matter to the other, linking them physically. For example, if a person walks into a carpeted room, he or she will pick up carpet fibers on the shoes, and hair from the head will drop to the floor. Because of this principle, the physical evidence at a crime scene can potentially link the suspect, victim, and crime scene to one another. Therefore, the careful maintenance of a secure crime scene prevents anyone from entering a crime scene and moving, altering, destroying, or contaminating physical evidence present at the scene. Careful preservation of evidence at the scene allows it to be documented, collected, and analyzed by crime scene investigators and forensic scientists just as it was found when the initial responder arrived at the crime scene.

Once the crime scene is secure, all potentially relevant physical evidence must be identified and documented. Evidence at a crime scene generally falls into one of two classifications: corpus delicti, which refers to evidence that establishes that a crime has been committed, and associative evidence, which links a suspect with a crime. The process of identifying evidence begins with an initial walk-through once the crime scene investigator arrives at the scene. Often, this is done with the first responder in order to take note of initial details and any elements at the crime scene that may have been altered or contaminated since the first responder arrived. Next, a careful and systematic survey of the crime scene is made to locate all potential physical evidence at the scene. This may be done using directional search patterns such as spirals or grids, or zone-based crime scene surveys, depending on which strategy best fits the characteristics of the individual crime scene.

Once evidence is identified, crime scene documentation occurs through a combination of note taking, photographic and video collection, and sketching of the scene. Crime scene note taking is a continual process throughout the criminal investigation and involves detailing information regarding who was involved or witnessed the crime, when and where the crime took place, what evidence has been located, and all information regarding how the event occurred. These notes are important because they can detail both what was observable by crime scene investigators as well as what was missing. Crime scene photographs are extremely important in order to provide an accurate visual record of the crime scene. Pictures must carefully document the macroscopic crime scene, particular midrange sections of the scene, and close-up details, including individual pieces of evidence. Video of the crime scene, though generally less detailed, provides a single visual representation of the relationships between various parts of a crime scene. Finally, investigators sketch the crime scene in order to incorporate scale and measurements into the documentation of the evidence and overall visualization of the crime scene. Each form of documentation is conducted during the systematic crime scene investigation, and each provides different information that may be used by investigators and forensic scientists. Once all documentation is complete, one officer is placed in charge of carefully collecting and recording all physical evidence at the crime scene following specific protocol in order to maintain the integrity of the evidence and allow its use in the ongoing investigation and its admissibility in court.

Crime scene reconstruction is the final stage in crime scene investigation procedure. Through the data collected at the crime scene and the scientific evaluation of the physical evidence conducted in the forensic laboratory, investigators are able to formulate and test hypotheses regarding the details of a crime and the identity of suspects. A reconstruction can only be as good as the information available, and the quality of that information is based on the successful execution of the crime scene investigation procedure. The crime scene is the one area that brings together the work of criminal justice professionals, including law enforcement officers, forensic scientists, and legal authorities to identify and analyze evidence and efficiently and effectively solve crime.

For more information

Fisher, Barry A. J. *Techniques of Crime Scene Investigation.* 7th ed. New York: Taylor and Francis, 2003.

James, Stuart H., and Jon J. Nordby, eds. *Forensic Science: An Introduction to Scientific and Investigative Techniques.* New York: Taylor and Francis, 2003.

Lyman, Michael D. *Criminal Investigation: The Art and the Science.* 4th ed. Upper Saddle River, N.J.: Pearson, 2005.

Ben Epstein
CUNY Graduate Center

crime theories CRIMINOLOGISTS use theories to explain why crimes occur, to suggest ways for preventing crimes from happening, or to reduce their incidence when they are unavoidable. Many criminological theories have been developed over the last four centuries. They were inspired by the accepted school of thought of the day.

The classical CRIMINOLOGY of the 18th century inspired the development of the rational choice and DETERRENCE THEORY. Nineteenth-century positivism inspired biological, psychological, and biosocial trait theories. Twentieth-century constructivism informed the sociological theories of crime. Lastly, critical theory motivated the emergence of labeling, conflict, and FEMINIST THEORIES. Some of these theories have been rejected by the scientific community. Others have been adjusted to accommodate recent research findings. In addition, integrated forms of crime theories have been debated since the 1970s.

The classical school of criminology was influenced by the social contract thinkers of the 17th and 18th centuries. Thomas Hobbes (1588–1679), John Locke (1632–1704), and Jean-Jacques Rousseau (1712–78) proposed a theory of social order they referred to as the social contract. The social contract is an unwritten agreement between the state and its citizens. It expresses the rights and obligations of each and endows the state with the legitimate authority of intervening when a violation of the contract occurs. Laws are the embodiment of the social contract; they help maintain social order. When citizens elect to defy these laws, the JUSTICE system punishes them to maintain order.

Cesare Beccaria (1738–94) and Jeremy Bentham (1748–1832) applied the principles of the social contract to early criminology. They argued that individuals are rational and calculating beings. They have the option of obeying the law or defying it. To determine their course of action, they will weigh the costs against the benefits of committing a crime. If they find that the expected benefits of crime outweigh the size of the PUNISHMENT, they will carry out the offense. If the consequences outweigh the benefits, individuals will refrain from committing the act. Becarria cautioned that punishments should be proportional to the crime committed to prevent criminals from engaging in serious criminal behavior. If the punishment imposed for THEFT is equal to the punishment imposed for MURDER, thieves will be tempted to slay the witness to decrease the likelihood of being identified as the malefactor. Deterrence theory was criticized for overlooking other properties of punishment that may be relevant for deterring crime. Furthermore, deterrence was faulted for assuming that all individuals process the information in a similar fashion and, therefore, perceive rewards and punishments in the same way. In recent years, deterrence has been expanded to include informal sanctions such as the potential of losing one's employment status, friends, and family.

The ability to choose one's fate, a key assumption of deterrence theory, dissolves in 19th-century positivist explanations of crime. Positivism assumes that deterministic forces beyond the individual's capacity influence behavior. Positivists believe they can observe and directly measure social phenomena much the same way they observe and measure the natural sciences. They use scientific method to observe and identify causal relationships between individual observable features and the incidence of crime.

For instance, trait theorists (see TRAIT THEORIES OF CRIME) assert that basic biological and psychological differences distinguish criminals from noncriminals. The biologist Franz Joseph Gall (1758–1828) examined the shape of a person's skull to predict criminality, and the biologist Cesare Lombroso (1835–1909) argued that criminals were physically inferior to noncriminals. Biological theories persist today in the form of modern biosocial theories. Modern biosocial theoreticians focus on the role of diet, vitamin deficiencies, and birth complications to make inferences about the relationship between biochemical conditions and crime. Other research suggests that brain chemistry and hormones may influence criminal behavior.

Like biological trait theorists, who believe that individual bodily dysfunctions encourage criminal behavior, psychological trait theorists suggest that deficiencies in the cognitive development of individuals lead to antisocial behavior. The cognitive perspective, for instance, stipulates that individuals construct and interpret the world around them. In turn, these interpretations inform individual behavior and choices. Cognitively deficient individuals process information about the world less efficiently and will behave in a nonconformist and illegitimate way. Nowadays, neo-behavioral psychologists claim that criminal behavior is not inherent but rather learned through processes of reward or punishment.

Over the decades, criminology has progressively distanced itself from biological and psychological trait theories. Trait theories like eugenics provided policy makers with the veil of science to pass sterilization policies that targeted "socially inadequate people." Today's biosocial and psychological theories argue that compliance with the law is the result of an individual's environment rather than his or her genetic makeup and heritability.

The urbanization, industrialization, and immigration of the early 20th century brought about rapid social changes that have contributed to the disintegration of the social norms and cohesion of cities. Unlike positivistic trait theories that looked at individual biological and psychological properties to understand criminal behavior, sociological theories of crime studied the social environment and the socialization of individuals to explain offending behavior. Social disorganization theory, for instance, asked why crime is more prevalent in certain neighborhoods rather than in others. Sociologists of the University of Chicago, Robert Park (1864–1944) and Ernest Watson Burgess (1886–1966), proposed a theory that viewed the city as a natural ecological community. They hypothesized that crime was the common outcome where informal social control was absent.

Strain theories are another product of the 20th-century social dynamics. Strain theorists assert that people exhibit criminal behavior when they are pressured or strained. Robert King Merton (1910–2003) argued that the United States has a high crime rate because people are expected to be economically successful. Structural limitations such as economic and racial disparities may lead individuals to seek success through alternative illegitimate means.

The differential association theory developed by Edwin H. Sutherland (1883–1950) posits that individuals learn criminal behaviors and criminal INTENT through interaction and communication with intimate personal groups and peers. The media is another documented agent of socialization. If individuals are exposed to criminal behavior for prolonged periods of time and criminal socialization takes precedence over other types of socialization processes, individuals are more likely to become criminals themselves.

Control theories, like social learning theories, place the onus of the explanation of criminal behavior on social processes. They surmise that people commit deviant behavior because nothing stops them from engaging in inappropriate behavior. Travis Hirschi (born April 15, 1935) claims that delinquent acts occur when an individual's bond to society is weakened. For Hirschi, the social bond is composed of four elements: attachment to others, commitment to conventional activities or goals, involvement in conventional activities, and beliefs in the rules of society.

While control theories stress the power of social bonds in maintaining order, the critical perspectives question the value of social structures altogether. Critical theorists or Marxist criminologists were inspired by the 1960s CIVIL RIGHTS MOVEMENT, the Vietnam antiwar movement, and the women's movement. Instead of studying the psychological and ideological features of deviants and the social structure within which they are nested, they point to the capacity of powerful social institutions to "construct" crime and criminality. These institutions place the weight of the blame on the individual rather than on the criminal act committed or the structures that produced it.

LABELING THEORY is a strand of critical theory. It suggests that the way society views and judges an individual's behavior determines what constitutes a deviant and unacceptable act and what does not. Society ascribes stigmatizing labels to individuals who commit these acts (e.g. "criminal"). When this societal appraisal is internalized by the offender, a lifestyle of criminality becomes a self-fulfilling prophecy.

CONFLICT THEORY, another strand of critical theory, questions the fairness of the system itself. Its proponents conjecture that market economies produce social and economic inequalities. The resulting pressures create the conditions favorable for criminality. The poor, the unemployed, racial minorities, youths, and males are predisposed to noncompliance because of the inequality of the system itself. Conflict theorists explain that laws do not exist for the collective good. Rather, they represent the interests of the powerful.

Feminist criminal theories purport that sexism is a more important form of oppression than other social inequalities denounced by the labeling or conflict theories. Sexism cuts across ethnic, racial, and class lines. The feminist perspective studies how gender inequalities structure criminal and noncriminal options. Of the many feminist theories, the emancipation theory alleges that the women's liberation movement has opened more opportunities to women to participate in the legitimate and illegitimate activities of society alike. Radical feminist criminology, on the other hand, maintains that the legal system upholds male authority over women. Women victims are revictimized by the male-dominant justice system when they seek solace against the offenses that have been committed against them. The product of radical feminist criminology was increased federal funding for battered women's shelters and harsher penalties for batterers.

In the 1970s, a number of criminologists called for the theoretical integration or combination of two or more preexistent theories of crimes. Integrated theories are based on conceptual similarities or how two or more theories make the same predictions. One example of integrated theories is Elliott, Ageton, and Cantor's (1979) fusion of strain, social control, and social learning perspectives. These authors speculate that strain or the social pressure to outperform in FAMILY and schools weakens social bonds with positive peer groups, which in turn promotes differential association with delinquent peers and encourages the likelihood of delinquent behavior.

For more information

Curran, Daniel J., and Claire M. Renzetti. *Theories of Crime*. 2nd ed. Boston: Allyn and Bacon, 2001.

Elliott, Delbert, Susan Ageton, and Rachelle Canton. "An Integrated Theoretical Perspective on Delinquent Behavior," *Journal of Research on Crime and Delinquency* (1979): 3–27.

Hirschi, Travis. *Causes of Delinquency*. New Brunswick, N.J.: Transaction Publishers, 2002.

Kubrin, Charis, Thomas D. Stucky, and Marvin D. Krohn. *Researching Theories of Crime and Deviance*. New York: Oxford University Press, 2009.

Merton, Robert King. *Social Theory and Social Structure*. New York: Free Press, 1968.

Park, Robert, R. D. McKenzie, and Ernest Burgess. *The City: Suggestions for the Study of Human Nature in the Urban Environment*. Chicago: University of Chicago Press, 1925.

Sutherland, Edwin H. *Principles of Criminology*. Chicago: University of Chicago Press, 1924.

Marie-Jose Louis Tayah
Kent State University

criminal justice system The criminal justice system consists of those governmental and private agencies and personnel whose main functions are to deter and prevent crime; investigate reported crimes; apprehend, prosecute, and defend criminal suspects; adjudicate criminal charges and sentence convicted offenders; and maintain correctional custody over adjudicated offenders.

The primary components of the criminal justice system are police departments, PROSECUTORS' offices, DEFENSE ATTORNEYS, courts, correctional departments (including PROBATION and PAROLE divisions and penal institutions), and appellate courts. Criminal justice agencies are distributed among local, state, and federal governments.

There is no one integrated criminal justice system. Each state and the federal government has its separate court systems and its corrections departments. State prosecutors are mostly county elected officials who hire assistant prosecutors as needed, although the attorney general's office in each state may prosecute some crimes. The police are highly fragmented. Most law enforcement agencies are units of local government, although each county has a sheriff's office; each state has a state police organization, and there are approximately 50 federal law enforcement agencies. This complexity causes some friction

American Criminal Justice System

What is the sequence of events in the criminal justice system?

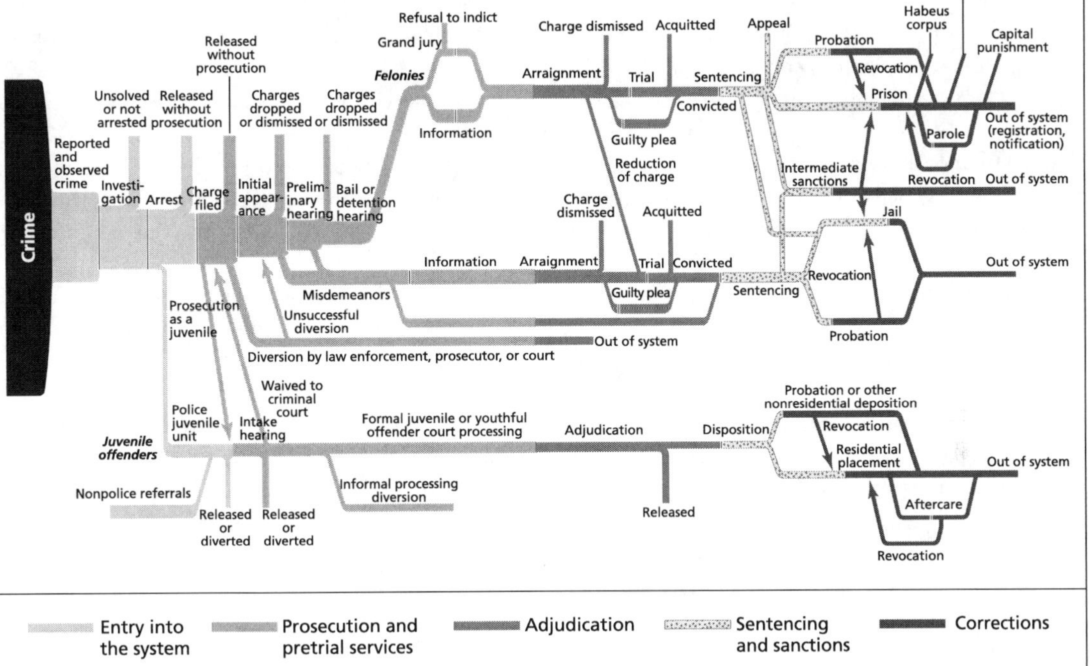

in criminal justice operations, but a good deal of cooperation and coordination among agencies allows the system to function.

The largest component of the criminal justice system is the police, which in 1996 employed more than 900,000 employees, including more than 700,000 sworn full-time officers, spread among 18,800 federal, state, and local law enforcement agencies. The next largest component is corrections, with about 650,000 employees in 1996. State court prosecutors' offices employed about 71,000 attorneys, investigators, and support staff. The total employment in the judicial branch exceeds 400,000 persons, but the number of judicial officers is smaller. The United States Supreme Court and state courts of last resort are staffed by 360 justices and JUDGES. Below these courts, 39 states have intermediate appellate courts (850 judges) and the 12 circuits of the U.S. COURT OF APPEALS (180 judges). Trial courts are divided between courts of general JURISDICTION that try FELONY cases (9,000 state judges; 650 federal district court judges) and courts of limited jurisdiction (18,000 state judicial officers; 500 federal magistrates).

The governmental expenditure for all criminal justice agencies in 1996 was $120 billion. The largest single component was local law enforcement ($38 billion), followed by state correctional expenditures ($29 billion). Expenditure by function in 1996 was police protection—$53 billion; judicial and legal—$26 billion; and corrections—$41 billion. Local government expends 52.3 percent of the total criminal justice budget, state government 33.2 percent, and the federal government 14.5 percent.

Different models of the criminal justice system help to explain its functioning. A model developed by the President's Commission on Law Enforcement and Administration of Justice in 1967 first popularized the idea of a system by portraying criminal justice as a sort of conveyor belt in a flowchart. It depicted a large number of known crimes that lead to a smaller number of apprehensions that are then processed through the adult and juvenile criminal justice systems. At each point in the process a certain number of individuals drop out because of dismissals or ACQUITTALS, and some who are conditionally released on probation or parole are recycled back into the system.

Another model—the wedding cake model—indicates that the popular concept of crime is not accurate; the criminal justice system deals with a much larger number of crimes of minor disorder than serious threats to life and safety. At the top of the wedding cake are those very few notorious and extremely serious crimes that linger in the popular imagination, such as the double MURDER prosecution and acquittal of O. J. SIMPSON. The second layer includes the violent FELONIES of murder, MANSLAUGHTER, rape, ROBBERY, and aggravated ASSAULT. These crimes constituted 4.7 percent of all ARRESTS in 1997. Next in seriousness are BURGLARY and felony PROPERTY CRIMES—13.2 percent of arrests. The remaining 82.1 percent of arrests were for MISDEMEANOR assault and property crimes, vice crimes, drug offenses, driving offenses, juvenile runaway and curfew violations, and a large number of miscellaneous offenses.

Clearly, the work of criminal justice system personnel includes hundreds, if not thousands, of different tasks. Nevertheless, criminal justice system operations include several unique or distinctive characteristics. First, the system is based on the government's monopoly of the legitimate use of *force.* Contrary to popular entertainment, most criminal justice processes, including arrest, do not involve the overt use of force—most persons who are arrested go along without physical resistance. Nevertheless, the system is pervaded by the show of force, including the police officer's gun, handcuffs, and badge, the judge's somber robes, and prison walls. A suspect, defendant, or convicted person who resists can expect to be subdued with physical force. Next, much of the criminal justice system is *routinized* into administrative subsystems, such as PLEA BARGAINING, that make the system more efficient than a full use of the model. Another characteristic is the high degree of *DISCRETION* that is available to criminal justice officers, which goes counter to the popular idea that each important aspect of the criminal justice system is controlled by unambiguous laws. Also, the *effectiveness* of the criminal justice system is determined not only by its ability to suppress crime and identify offenders but by its fairness and *justice.* In this regard it is important that agents of the system follow legal and constitutional mandates, that methods deemed unfair not be used, and that persistent problems, such as racial disparities in arrest and SENTENCING, be minimized.

For more information

Bureau of Justice Statistics. Available online. URL: http://www.ojp.usdoj.gov/bjs/.

National Criminal Justice Reference Service (NCJRS) Web site. Available online. URL: http://www.ncjrs.org/ncjhome.htm.

Senna, Joseph, and Larry J. Siegel. *Introduction to Criminal Justice.* Rev. ed. Toronto: International Thompson Publishers, 1999.

Walker, Samuel. *Taming the System: The Control of Discretion in Criminal Justice, 1950–1990.* New York: Oxford University Press, 1993.

Marvin Zalman
Wayne State University

criminologist A criminologist is someone who researches or works professionally in fields concerning the causes and methods of preventing crime, the treatment of criminals, or the judicial, criminal justice, and law enforcement systems.

While CRIMINOLOGY is a broad field of scientific study, a criminologist could be any academic or professional who conducts research in criminology or applies it to a real-world crime-related discipline. Regardless of their specific professional title, all criminologists seek to understand crime as a social phenomenon. Criminologists explore complex questions such as: what theories of crime causation led to the criminal action; why is certain deviant behavior deemed illegal while others are not; what treatments of criminals are most effective in rehabilitation; how does crime affect the FAMILY and neighborhood in which it takes place; what strategies are most effective for peaceful conflict resolution; and whether the potential benefits of new law enforcement techniques or corrections facilities are worth the costs involved in their implementation. Criminologists use scientific research methods to study and resolve specific questions concerning the causes of criminal behavior as well as the apprehension, prosecution, and treatment of criminals.

Many social scientists, including psychologists, sociologists, economists, legal scholars, and political scientists are criminologists who apply scientific methodology to the study of crime. For instance, sociologists explore the relationship between crime and society, often called cultural criminology. Cultural criminology involves the ways in which criminal activities are interrelated with political systems, law enforcement techniques, and media on a daily basis. Economists and political scientists investigate the countless policy and budgetary implications of crime prevention and the CRIMINAL JUSTICE SYSTEM. Meanwhile, psychologists who work with law enforcement personnel, prisoners, and those affected by crime are central to research on criminal rehabilitation, behavior modification, and the social impact of crime. Regardless of their specific discipline, scholars from across the social sciences are also involved in the ongoing theoretical debate regarding criminal causation.

Beyond academic research, professionals throughout the criminal justice system apply criminology to the process of lawmaking, law enforcement, and the treatment of prisoners. Lawmakers write crime statutes based, in part, on research regarding the societal effect of particular deviant behavior. Criminal defense and prosecuting attorneys apply the social, economic, and cultural factors surrounding accused criminal activity to persuade JUDGES of the guilt or innocence of the defendant. Judges, therefore, determine verdicts and the appropriate treatment for those found guilty by interpreting the laws and the actions of the accused within their social context. Each of these individuals can be considered criminologists because of the way they utilize criminological research. Those who work within law enforcement are also criminologists. Every day they are on the job, police officers and detectives apply research on trends of various types of crime, motivations of criminals, and effective methods of criminal apprehension. Forensic scientists and MEDICAL EXAMINERS use physical and biological sciences to examine CRIME SCENE EVIDENCE, known as criminalistics. Their work is useful throughout the criminal justice system. Finally, corrections officers and others working in prisons use research on penology, the study of crime and the PUNISHMENT of prisoners, to improve the effectiveness of prison systems in protecting the public and effectively rehabilitating criminals. Each of these criminologists work to deter crime and limit its effect on society as well as to effectively apprehend, prosecute, and treat criminals.

For more information

Adler, Reda, Gerhard O.W. Mueller, and William Laufer. *Criminology and the Criminal Justice System.* 4th ed. New York: McGraw Hill, 2001.

Siegel, Larry J. *Criminology: Theories, Patterns, and Typologies.* 10th ed. Florence, Ky.: Cengage Learning, 2008.

Vold, George B., Thomas J. Bernard, and Jeffrey B. Snipes. *Theoretical Criminology.* 5th ed. New York: Oxford University Press, 2002.

Wright, Richard A., and J. Mitchell Miller, eds. *Encyclopedia of Criminology.* New York: Routledge, 2005.

Ben Epstein
CUNY Graduate Center

criminology Criminology is the study of crime and its causes, societal implications, and methods of prevention. The goals of those who study criminology may include understanding the relationship between a society and the norms and laws that govern it, the causes and methods of criminal behavior, and how to treat criminals and prevent future crime.

One common misconception of criminology is that it deals only with STREET CRIMES, such as MURDERS and ROBBERIES. In reality, criminologists study all types of crime, including TERRORISM, racial or ethnically motivated HATE CRIMES, crimes against the environment, and WHITE COLLAR CRIMES such as corporate FRAUD and INSIDER TRADING. Regardless of the type of crime, criminologists investigate the social, legal, political, and behavioral contexts surrounding the criminal act. The sociologist Edwin Sutherland, a pioneer in American criminology, offered the most widely accepted summary of this broad body of knowledge in 1924, when he defined criminology as "including within its scope the process of making laws, of breaking laws, and of reacting toward the breaking of laws."

The process of making laws involves the decision to elevate a particular deviant behavior, which violates social norms, to the level of a criminal behavior, punishable by law. CRIMINOLOGISTS study who is responsible for those decisions and what factors come into play in making the decisions. When looking at the development of criminal law, criminologists make a distinction between two conflicting views: the consensus model, which believes that lawmaking occurs because the majority of society agrees that a particular deviant act should be made illegal, and the conflict model, which concludes that a small group of powerful elites dictate what is illegal for the rest of society. The study of the process of breaking laws includes the multiple variables that contribute to criminal behavior. Scholars who research how society reacts to the breaking of laws apply their work to increasing the effectiveness of CRIMINAL JUSTICE SYSTEMS around the world as well as the improved treatment of the criminals within those systems.

Criminology is the application of science to the phenomenon of crime. As such, it is primarily a part of the social, or behavioral, sciences, including sociology, psychology, political science, economics, and law. These social sciences help criminologists evaluate the process of lawmaking, the causes and social implications of criminal activity, and which methods of crime prevention and rehabilitation are most effective. Though criminology falls primarily under the heading of social sciences, it also includes important work in the physical sciences, known as criminalistics, which is applied specifically to criminal investigation. This includes the work of MEDICAL EXAMINERS and forensic scientists who examine CRIME SCENE EVIDENCE. The work of these physical and biological scientists is vital to the criminal justice system as well as to the analysis of criminal behavior, the legal process of determining guilt or innocence, and determining the appropriate forms of treatment or rehabilitation.

Criminology seeks to find facts about crime, and those facts are explained through theories that describe the relationship between observable phenomena. There are many competing theories as to why crime occurs and what society should do about it, which leads to substantial debate and controversy within the broad field of criminology. There are three broad categories that help to organize the diverse theoretical arguments regarding the causation of crime. First is classical criminology, which argues that humans are intelligent and that rational choice dictates behavior. As a result, crime is seen as a product of the choice of the individual who weighs the potential benefits of the criminal activity against the potential costs. Under this theory, more severe PUNISHMENTS would increase costs for the potential criminal and therefore reduce the likelihood that they choose criminal behavior.

Next is positivist criminology, which argues that behavior is due to biological, psychological, or social factors outside of the individual's control, which have come together to determine the criminal behavior.

Finally, there is the broad theoretical position that criminal behavior is created by criminal law. Advocates for this perspective argue that no behavior can be defined as morally right or morally wrong. As such, any behavior is criminal only insofar as the laws of a society deem it so. According to this theory, what differentiates criminal behavior from all other behavior are simply laws of each society and the criminal justice system that enforces them. For instance, two different actions that are equally harmful to society may be viewed completely differently in the eyes of the laws of two separate societies. Additionally, two people with different socioeconomic, racial, ethnic, or gender characteristics who are charged with the same crime may be treated differently as they move through the criminal justice system.

For centuries, philosophers, legal scholars, and political theorists have developed theories regarding the causes of crime and the treatment of criminals. However, criminology as a practice can be traced back only to the mid-19th century, when Henry Mayhew and Thomas Plint first explored the relationship between social class and criminal behavior in England. These social reformers created the concept of the criminal class and aimed to persuade the government and philanthropists that there was a difference between those who deserved public or private assistance and those who required only punishment and surveillance. Modern scientific criminology began in earnest in 1876, when the Italian Cesare Lombroso applied the work of Charles Darwin to the biology of criminals, arguing that criminal impulses were hereditary. The term *criminology* was first introduced in 1885 by the Italian law professor Raffaele Garofalo. Criminology then became an academic subject, or series of subjects, taught in universities around the world. The specific focus on social or behavioral scientific methods related to crime, law, and society was strengthened when Edwin Sutherland introduced the theory of differential association in 1939. The theory of differential association argues that one's behavior, and specifically criminal behavior, is a result of social interactions and the culture in which one is raised (Adler, Mueller, and Laufer, 8–10). This powerful and controversial theory of crime causation has been debated and tested ever since it was introduced. With this shift toward social scientific approaches, criminologists have largely rejected some early theories, including the hereditary and biological causation of criminal activity. Since the 1960s, the technological resources of criminologists have greatly improved, scientific approaches have become far more specialized, and the study of criminal justice has become increasingly intertwined with criminology. However, the overall goals and scientific nature of criminology have remained relatively stable.

The increasingly close relationship between criminology and the criminal justice system has become confusing. Both areas involve scholars and scientists who are interested in crime and society and who use similar scientific methods. Furthermore, the overarching goals of each are the same: to understand what causes criminal behavior and to reduce crime and the impact of criminal acts on society at large. Although these two fields are closely related, they are distinct in a few important ways. Criminal justice, which emerged in the United States in the 1960s, is a very young field of study compared to criminology. It focuses on recognition of crime and how to hold criminals accountable. Criminal justice scholars are primarily interested in the role of institutions and policy in this process. This is a more narrow focus than criminology, which is also interested in the various causes and societal impact of crime. Therefore, the two perspectives may view the same action, for example the arrest of a 30-year-old man for drug trafficking, through different lenses. The arresting officer, who is a central player in the criminal justice system, is interested in removing the dangers caused by that illegal activity. Criminal justice scholars would study this event to see if the ARREST helped to control drug trafficking today and deter future drug-related crimes. Meanwhile, the criminologist might study this same arrest to see what factors likely led this man to break the law and how his arrest may affect his children or neighbors.

For more information

Adler, Reda, Gerhard O.W. Mueller, and William Laufer. *Criminology and the Criminal Justice System*. 4th ed. New York: McGraw Hill, 2001.

Siegel, Larry J. *Criminology: Theories, Patterns, and Typologies*. 10th ed. Florence, Ky.: Cengage Learning, 2008.

Suthenland, Edwin H. *Principles of Criminology*. Chicago: University of Chicago Press, 1924.

Vold, George B., Thomas J. Bernard, and Jeffrey B. Snipes. *Theoretical Criminology*. 5th ed. New York: Oxford University Press, 2002.

Wright, Richard A., and J. Mitchell Miller, eds. *Encyclopedia of Criminology*. New York: Routledge, 2005.

Ben Epstein
CUNY Graduate Center

critical criminology *Critical theory* is a term that encompasses a wide variety of contemporary left critiques of criminal justice practice, CRIMINOLOGY, and society itself. Such critical perspectives (most are not properly termed *theories*) include CONFLICT, left-realism, feminism, peacemaking, and postmodern/cultural criminology. These theories are criticized as untestable, sometimes unreadable, and romantic, yet survive on the edge of the criminological mainstream and have made contributions to understanding crime and humanizing the CRIMINAL JUSTICE SYSTEM.

All social sciences were profoundly influenced by the social and academic conflicts of the 1960s. Radical critique and points of view proliferated and flourished in this era. Somewhat late to the fray, a few RADICAL CRIMINOLOGISTS and scholars were convinced that a Marxian conflict model of social relations or other conflict-based representations of social realities and criminal justice were apposite to the criminal justice endeavor. These individuals were concerned with how law creation, enforcement, and judicial practice benefit the ruling class and bureaucracies and acts as oppressive realities to all others in society. Specifically, law and the criminal justice system are weapons in the establishment and maintenance of dominant class hegemony. From this point of view, crime is the product, or by-product, of economic and social inequality. Even noneconomic crimes flow out of frustration, alienation, and anger fostered by this dynamic. The power structure, of course, defines crimes as behaviors that threaten their class interest. In this setting, the interests of the underclass are underrepresented, if represented at all.

Other scholars embraced a more general critique of social order without embracing a Marxian framework. Feminists of different persuasions were also part of this general trend. These views were variously known as "conflict," "radical" or more generally, "critical" criminology. The latter was the preferred term because not all radical criminologists embraced a Marxist, feminist, or conflict view but preferred to embrace a generally critical stance toward the criminal justice enterprise and the field of criminology itself. Representing what has always been a minority viewpoint in the field, scholars such as Richard Quinney, William Chambliss, Austin Turk, Ian Taylor, Jock Young, and Paul Walton brought this point of view into short-lived currency in the late 1970s. But, the field of criminology itself, however liberal, did not sustain this as a mainstream current, and critical criminology fell on lean times in later decades. The supposed radical views of some of these scholars made employment in criminal justice agencies and academic departments problematic. Indeed, the criminology program at the University of California at Berkeley was closed in the mid-1970s by Governor Ronald Reagan in reaction to its reputation as a nucleus of radicalism and critique.

Many manifestations grew out of the critical criminology of the 1970s. The most prominent themes, or currents, that are influential today are conflict, left-realism, feminism, peacemaking, and postmodern/cultural criminology.

Modern conflict theorists have embraced and extended the general points outlined above. Their concerns include advocating various reforms such as GUN CONTROL, the abolition of CAPITAL PUNISHMENT, ending MANDATORY SENTENCING and prison building, more COMMUNITY POLICING, and decriminalization of drug offenses. The hope is, if these reforms become reality, that government will become less oppressive and that society will become less violent and punitive.

Left-realism suggests that other critical criminologists have ignored the real effect of crime on the poor. That is, in criticizing the established order and pointing to the lower-class victim as a "rebel" of a sort, the predatory criminal has been romanticized. The very real harm he or she does is minimized. From this point of view, realism is needed in the way criminals and criminal justice policy is viewed. Left-realists are concerned that conservative prescriptions for crime were sweeping left critiques aside and that a more practical set of solutions needed to be formulated from their own point of view. STREET CRIME is real and can be countered with community policing, victim-centered programs, RESTITUTION, community service sentencing, crime prevention, and minimal use of penal sanctions. This current of thought is less critical of capitalism and more focused on building a more humane criminal justice response to crime.

Feminist criminologists have raised a number of serious issues in the historically male-dominated criminological enterprise and continue to do so. Some maintain that the law itself is male-oriented and point to the dominance of males in all areas of criminal justice practice. Even more apposite is the point that criminological theory, the backbone of the discipline, is "his story," as well, that is, representative of male interests and concerns, by and about males, and written for a male audience. The field has certainly been male dominated, and in theory texts, female voices are conspicuous by their virtual absence. Courses about GENDER AND CRIME are bringing new balance and clarity to classes formerly taught in ways perhaps unconsciously biased and sexist. Feminist scholars and female criminal justice professionals are making major contributions to theory and practice and make up a large share of the contemporary professional audience.

Peacemaking criminology such as left-realism advocates less punitive alternatives to the penal sanction and the criminal justice system. Such practices as mediation, reconciliation, and conflict resolution all work toward the goal of reintegrating the offender into society. Peacemakers take a Buddhist stance of addressing "suffering" and thereby reducing the underlying cause of crime. Thus, reform emerges out of both critical and religious traditions. The criminal justice system is based on coercion and violence. These foundations must be replaced with nonviolence and love as way to achieve lasting freedom from crime and attendant suffering. Peacemaking is a perspective—a way of looking at crime and the criminal justice enterprise—and as such offers no real theory of crime beyond that stated above.

Postmodernism is a movement encompassing all literary and social science discourse. In criminology, it has several signal manifestations. Postmodernist criminology, borrowing from anthropology, is focused on the relativity of values, rules, and laws. That is, rules are a product of a total society, including its media. It follows then that media is a prime focus of postmodernist study. Postmodernism also acknowledges that what is understood as reality is characterized by change, and flux, and much interpretation. Postmodernists are skeptical toward science and scientific methods. In criminology, they are particularly acerbic about the dominance of statistics and the ongoing derogation of qualitative methods in the field. Such criminologists are generally in favor of "deconstructing" and demystifying criminology and criminological practice through study of the media and reconstructing existing criminal justice theoretical and practice structures in ways more consistent with what they see as the essence of human nature.

Cultural criminology, a major manifestation of postmodernist criminology, focuses on deviant subcultures—so-called edgework, that is, studying groups on the edge of society, from an "edgy" perspective. Such research brings issues like excitement and the quasi-sexual thrill that deviant behavior can engender. In short, society provides limited access to thrills. Seeking excitement outside of socially approved values and activities is a form of active rebellion against the oppressively bland nature of approved reality.

For more information

Chambliss, William, and Milton Mankoff. *Whose Law? Whose Order?* New York: John Wiley. 1996.

Einstader, Werner, and Stuart Henry. *Criminological Theory: An Analysis of Its Underlying Assumptions.* Fort Worth, Tex.: Hartcourt Brace, 1995.

Quinney, Richard. *Critique of Legal Order.* New York: Little, Brown, 1994.

Schwartz, Martin D., and Suzanne E. Hatty. *Controversies in Critical Criminology,* Cincinnati, Ohio: Anderson, 2003.

Taylor, Ian, Paul Walton, and Jack Young. *The New Criminology: For a Social Theory of Deviance.* London: Routledge, 1971.

Turk, Austin. *Criminality and Legal Order.* Chicago: Rand McNally, 1969.

Frederick Hawley
Western Carolina University

cross burning Cross burning is the erection and burning of a crosslike figure, often with the INTENT to intimidate others. Cross burning in the United States has a long history associated with racism and HATE CRIMES.

Cross burning is conduct that has a number of purposes and meanings. The act itself is the process by which a Christian cross is built from flammable material and set ablaze. Most commonly associated with the KU KLUX KLAN, a notorious American hate group, cross burning serves as an element of a highly ritualistic initiation ceremony for new members. Today, however, the display of a burning cross is recognized more directly as a threat or warning directed at disfavored groups or individuals by hate groups and organizations supportive of white supremacy. Policy makers in more than a dozen states, concerned about intimidation and violence associated with cross burning, have enacted statutes that allow the criminal prosecution of individuals who engage in the practice. Although more than a quarter of the states have established these prohibitions, there is little uniformity among their laws. Some limit only the burning of crosses, while other states ban the burning of additional religious symbols. Other differences include varying criminal culpability depending upon whether or not the cross burning occurs on private or public property, and whether or not property owners sanction the activity.

Bans on cross burning are a type of hate crime law that criminalizes conduct that threatens the rights and safety of individuals or enhances penalties for existing crimes that are committed against members of a particular religious, racial, or ethnic group. Hate crimes, however, are not without their critics. Many claim that such laws go beyond the mere prohibition of conduct but also affect First Amendment speech rights. As a result, the U.S. Supreme Court has been asked to weigh in on the constitutionality of cross burning prohibitions on two notable occasions. In the case of *R.A.V. v. ST. PAUL, MINNESOTA,* 505 U.S. 377 (1992), a unanimous Court held that a St. Paul ordinance was an impermissible restriction on speech. The controversy erupted when Robert Viktora burned a crudely fashioned cross on the lawn of an African-American FAMILY. He was arrested and charged with violating the St. Paul Bias-Motivated Crime ordinance that prohibited certain speech or conduct, including the act of burning a cross, which might produce fear or anger among particular minority groups. In a holding written for a unanimous Court, Justice ANTONIN SCALIA argued that the law discriminated based upon the content of the speech and hence was violative of the First Amendment.

In 2003, the Court was again asked to determine the constitutionality of hate speech regulation in *Virginia v. Black,* 538 U.S. 343. At issue was a 1952 Virginia statute that outlawed the burning of a cross with the intent to intimidate. The law was enforced against three men who participated in the burning of crosses in two separate incidents. Unlike the decision in *R.A.V.,* the Court held that the Virginia ban on cross burning passed constitutional muster. Noting that speech rights are not absolute, Justice SANDRA DAY O'CONNOR argued that intimidation, like fighting words and true threats, is a proscribable form of speech. This deviation from the holding in *R.A.V.,* however, created both a fractious majority and produced dissenting votes from three justices who argued that the state law discriminated based on content in the same manner as in the St. Paul ordinance. The exception created to the *R.A.V.* case by the majority was based in large measure on the historical record concerning the powerful and dangerous nature of the message created by a burning cross. As a result of this pair of Court decisions, there remains some lingering uncertainty about the constitutionality of existing state court cross burning prohibitions.

For more information

Levin, Jack, and Jack McDevitt. *Hate Crimes Revisited: America's War on Those Who Are Different.* Boulder, Colo.: Westview Press, 2002.

Sunstein, Cass R. *Democracy and the Problem of Free Speech.* New York: Free Press, 1993.

Charles F. Jacob
St. Norbert College

cruel and unusual punishment Cruel and unusual punishment is prohibited by the UNITED STATES CONSTITUTION'S EIGHTH and Fourteenth Amendments and most every state constitution.

The prohibition against the infliction of cruel and unusual punishment was originally drawn from the English Declaration [Bill] of Rights of 1689 in order to curtail inhumane tortures and other barbarous methods of punishment. The Eighth Amendment, however, is not tied just to methods of punishment thought to be cruel and unusual at the time the Constitution was drafted; as concepts of dignity and civility evolve in our culture, and as public opinion in society changes and evolves regarding human JUSTICE, so do the notions of what is considered cruel and unusual under the Eighth Amendment.

The prohibition against the infliction of cruel and unusual punishment extends beyond just physically appalling punishments and embodies broad and idealistic ideas of dignity, civilized principles, humanity, and decency, against which a court must evaluate criminal SENTENCING measures. Punishments considered incompatible with EVOLVING STANDARDS OF DECENCY or that involve unnecessary and wanton infliction of pain are found to violate the Eighth Amendment.

Also related to Eighth Amendment guarantees is the notion that every punishment should be properly proportionate to the crime. For example, it would be thought inhumane to impose capital punishment for a simple parking violation or evasion of taxes. Thus, an extreme punishment relative to the criminal act may also contravene the Eighth Amendment. A penalty that is more extreme than any previously inflicted will be deemed excessive, cruel, and unusual. Likewise, punishments that never before existed in this country or which modern public sentiments regard as cruel will also be found violative of the Eighth Amendment.

The idea of prohibiting torturous or heinous punishments is largely supported throughout U.S. history. How exactly to define what will constitute such heinous punishment, on the other hand, has been the subject of much debate. For example, in some instances of sex offenses, sterilization of criminals by vasectomy has been found to be cruel and unusual punishment while, in other cases, it has been upheld as a valid punishment. In addition, the death penalty has been said by many to violate the constitutional guarantee against the imposition of cruel and unusual punishment; as such, it is unlawful in several states. Still, the United States Supreme Court has not found that the death penalty necessarily violates the Eighth Amendment, unless it is inflicted in a painful or inhumane manner. However, the Supreme Court has ruled that the death penalty is a violation of this amendment in cases of punishment for rape, for minors, and those who are mentally retarded.

While it has been said that efforts to exactly define the term "cruel and unusual punishment" will prove difficult at best, the courts continue to formulate certain recognizable tests or standards for determining whether a given punishment attains cruel and unusual proportions. For instance, the earliest test, and the one that is still most frequently used for determining whether a punishment offends the Eighth Amendment, is consideration of the "inherent cruelty" of a given punishment. Nevertheless, as society's notion of humanity and decency in penal treatment develops over time, changes will be reflected in limits regarding methods of punishment, resulting in continuous reassessment of cruel and unusual punishment.

For more information

Banner, Stuart. *The Death Penalty: An American History.* Cambridge, Mass.: Harvard University Press, 2003.

"'Nor Cruel and Unusual Punishments Inflicted': The Original Meaning," *California Law Review* 57 (1969): 839.

"The Cruel and Unusual Clause and the Substantive Criminal Law," *Harvard Law Review* 79 (1966): 635.

Kristin L. Stewart
Attorney

CSI effect The *CSI effect* is a phrase used by criminal justice officials, the popular press, and academic CRIMINOLOGISTS to describe the influence of the television show *Crime Scene Investigation* and its variants and imitators. The influence is most often thought to be felt on *juries* in criminal cases regarding the expectation about EVIDENCE and how the criminal justice process should operate.

The original program, begun in 2000, presented a mediagenic cast that included an intense leading man (initially played by William Petersen), several attractive young technicians, and a sexy ex-stripper. Offshoots, set in New York and Miami, have continued to use the same formula with notable success. Typically, the CSI technicians go into the field to gather evidence, then solve the crime through the use of extremely arcane, sophisticated, and expensive methods. Often they collar the offender themselves, leaving the more traditional police officers in the dust. Though this has been criticized by criminologists and those knowledgeable about evidence collection and analysis techniques and the realities of police work, the program has had a significant influence.

JUDGES and PROSECUTORS have noted that media-saturated juries are not satisfied with traditional testimony and evidence. They want to see more sophisticated evidence and that validated by the EXPERT TESTIMONY of CRIME SCENE investigators, who are unequivocal about their testimony. This is what is popularly known as the CSI effect. The practical significance is that the people who make up juries have very unrealistic expectations of police departments and the quality of real crime scene evidence and those who collect it. Simply put, municipal governments cannot support the level of analysis that the television programs suggest is available and even commonplace. Even state crime labs often cannot approximate the image that Hollywood suggests as the norm and almost always have a tremendous backlog. These television programs are, in effect, science fiction, in that they portray plausible worlds and technology that is not really operational. Ironically, they are generating demand for CSI technicians in local law enforcement and have raised the status of that formerly lowly specialty within criminal justice agencies.

Another effect is that criminals have gotten much more thorough in covering their tracks following a crime event. Using various chemical agents to disguise blood and other bodily fluids is increasingly common among criminals who plan ahead. Some also burn crime scenes to destroy FINGERPRINTS and other evidence. Often, good police work and evidence gathering leads to the capture and conviction of these media-savvy malefactors.

Criminologists have noted that CRIMINOLOGY and criminal justice programs have been flooded with eager young people who seek careers in the very limited subfield of evidence collection and analysis. These students are frequently frustrated by the academic and theoretical foci of university programs. They are better advised to major in a mainstream science discipline such as chemistry, biology, or better still, premed, then go on to get a master's degree in a hard science. As a response to student demand, many universities now feature undergraduate forensics courses taught by sociology and criminologists who are frankly teaching outside their areas of competence. Some universities offer more science-oriented FORENSIC SCIENCE programs, which are more demanding of science competence than are traditional criminal justice curricula. Ironically, the growth of these programs was fueled by the success of the television programs, and they, in turn, are helping to fuel demand for CSI technicians by departments that heretofore had sent their lab work to the state lab. It is a case where life imitates art; that is, the pseudo-reality created by media is becoming the actual, practical reality, and crime scene investigation has emerged from obscurity into the mainstream.

For more information

Durnal, Evan W. "Crime Scene Investigation (as seen on TV)," *Forensic Science International* 199, (2010): 1–5.

Thomas, Andrew P. "The CSI Effect: Fact or Fiction," *Yale Law Journal* 115 (2006): 70. Available online. URL: http://www.thepocketpart.org/2006/02/thomas.html.

Toobin, Jeffrey. "The CSI Effect: The Truth about Forensic Science," *New Yorker* (7 May 2007). Available online. URL: http://www.newyorker.com/reporting/2007/05/07/070507fa_fact_toobin.

Frederick Hawley
Western Carolina University

custodial interrogation The phrase *custodial interrogation* is a legal term of art that became pivotal in the criminal law when it was used in the U.S. Supreme Court case MIRANDA V. ARIZONA, 384 U.S. 436, 16 L. Ed. 2d 694, 86 S. Ct. 1602 (1966). In *Miranda,* the Court announced the bright line rule that law enforcement officers must inform citizens of certain rights whenever the officers intend to engage in a custodial interrogation. Any statements given by a suspect during a custodial interrogation and without the benefit of *Miranda* warnings cannot be used against the suspect at trial.

In order for *Miranda* to apply, the citizen must be both interrogated and be in law enforcement custody. This is because the *Miranda* Court was primarily concerned with the inherent coercion brought to bear when a citizen was held incommunicado and subject to interrogation in a situation where the police were in control.

A person is in custody when there is a "formal arrest or a restraint on freedom of movement associated with a formal arrest" *(Miranda)*. The determination of whether a person is in custody for purposes of *Miranda* is done by looking at the totality of circumstances and determining, based on those circumstances, whether a reasonable person would have felt free to leave the encounter with law enforcement. *Thompson v. Keohane,* 516 U.S. 99, 116 S. Ct. 457, 133 L. Ed. 2d 383 (1995). It is not necessary that persons be held in a government detention facility for them to be in custody. The inquiry is concerned with the citizen's ability to freely quit the encounter with law enforcement. In addition, when interrogating minors, the Supreme Court ruled in *J. D. B. v. North Carolina,* 564 U.S. _ (2011), that age is a factor that must be considered in determining if custody exists for the purpose of giving a *Miranda* warning.

An interrogation occurs whenever a law enforcement officer expressly questions a person or uses any actions or words that are reasonably likely to elicit an incriminating response from the suspect. *RHODE ISLAND V. INNIS,* 446 U.S. 291, 64 L. Ed. 2d 297, 100 S. Ct. 1682 (1980). An interrogation can come in a form other than traditional questions and answers. For example, in *Brewer v Williams,* 430 U.S. 387, 51 L. Ed. 2d 424, 97 S. Ct. 1232, the suspect was believed to have kidnapped and killed a child. After the defendant was taken into police custody, two detectives, who knew of the suspect's strong religious beliefs, told the defendant, among other things, that it was important to give the child a "good Christian burial." In response to the detective's speech expounding on this theme, the defendant led the detectives to the body. The Supreme Court found that the speech amounted to interrogation, noting that the detective "deliberately and designedly set out to elicit information . . . just as surely as if . . . he had formally interrogated him."

For more information

Clymer, Steven D. "Are Police Free to Disregard Miranda?," *Yale Law Journal* 112 (2002): 447–552.

Smith, J. V. "The Threshold Question in Applying Miranda: What Constitutes Custodial Interrogation?," *South Carolina Law Review* 25 (1974): 699, 711–714.

Cassandra L. McKeown
University of South Dakota

cyber crime Cyber crime refers to crimes such as FORGERY or identity theft committed over the INTERNET or the Web. These types of crimes are new in the last decade or so, and they constitute one of the fastest-growing types of crimes in the United States and across the world.

The advances made in computer technology over the past 30 years have been nothing short of phenomenal. The advent of cheaper, more user-friendly computers and software packages have made it a veritable necessity in the everyday functions of many individuals throughout the world. Computers in modern society have been developed with the goals of speed, portability, and affordability in mind. This proliferation of computers and computing technology throughout the world has not been without consequence. As more and more individuals, corporations, and governments move further along in the digitizing of most, if not all, information, the need to find effective methods of protection for that data has been an ever-increasing concern. These new technologies that have simplified life in many ways have also created a new realm for criminal action. Cyber crime is a concern that nations throughout the world have not been able to escape. Cyber crime is defined as "various criminal behaviors that are intended to damage or destroy computer networks, fraudulently obtain money and other commodities, and disrupt normal business operations" (Regoli and Hewitt, 489).

While the definition provided broadly explains what cyber crime is, it fails to grasp the actions that typically qualify. The DEPARTMENT OF JUSTICE has created three broad classifications of cyber crime and a list of actions that meet the criteria of each category (Rantala, 2). The first category provided by Rantala focuses on cyber attacks. The actions that qualify as cyber attacks include the use of viruses, denial of service attacks, and sabotage and VANDALISM. The second category deals primarily with cyber THEFT, which involves the use of a computer in the act of illegal obtainment of money or other valuable materials, including intellectual and copyrighted property. The third category is generically titled "other security computer incidents." The actions contained within this category include hacking, spamming, spoofing, phishing, and the spreading of spyware.

A general review of cyber crime statistics illustrates the reason for concern that many individuals, corporations, and governments have. Chris Hale asserts that globally more than $500 billion is lost to cyber crime, and that only a fraction (about 10 percent) of the victims actually file a report with the police (Regoli and Hewitt, 489). In 2005, 67 percent of businesses in the United States uncovered at least one type of cyber attack, 11 percent were victims of cyber theft, and 24 percent detected other computer incidents, all of which added up to a loss of approximately $867 million (Rantala, 1). In 2008, the Internet Crime Complaint Center, an office of the FEDERAL BUREAU OF INVESTIGATION, reported that 275,284 complaints were received from individuals concerning cyber crime (Internet Crime Complaint Center, 1). Of those complaints 72,940 were referred for criminal investigation, costing individuals in the United States a total of $264.6 million. While these statistics by no means present a conclusive understanding of the effect cyber crime has on individuals, corporations, and governments, they do provide an illustration of the urgency that surrounds this issue for many in society.

In order to effectively combat against the consequences that result from cyber crime, the U.S. Department of Justice has created the Computer Crime and Intellectual Property Section, which currently has two initiatives in place. The first focuses on the implementation of federal law concerning computer crimes, and the second deals primarily with intellectual property. It is within these two areas that most federal criminal statutes concerning cyber crime are found. The first stand-alone computer crime statute enacted by Congress was the Computer Fraud and Abuse Act of 1986 (18 U.S.C. 130). This act, still in effect today, currently criminalizes many of the activities discussed above, including the use of a computer to gain access to information for the purpose of financial or material gain, and the infliction of intentional damage, just to name a few. In 1998, Congress passed legislation concerning the problem of identity theft. The Identity Theft and Assumption Deterrence Act of 1998 [18 U.S.C. 1028 (a)(7)] provides the ability to prosecute those participating in this act through the use of a computer in the federal court system. In 2003, Congress passed the CAN-SPAM Act [Pub. L. No. 108–187, 117 Stat. 2699 (2003)], which provides for both criminal and civil redress against individuals sending large quantities of unsolicited email. Many other statutes fall under the cyber crime initiative within the Computer Crime and Intellectual Property Section. This is merely a sample of that legislation.

The intellectual property initiative of the Computer Crime and Intellectual Property Section is also grounded in federal law. Again, it is virtually impossible to discuss all of the federal statutes that play a role in this initiative, however a brief sample can be compiled. One statute that can be found in the mainstream media over the past 10 years is the copyright violations that occur due to the bootlegging of both protected music (18 U.S.C. 2319A) and movies (18 U.S. C. 2319B). The proliferation of computers and software has opened up a new domain that allows protected music and movies to be traded openly, which violates the copyright protection of the work. Other federal statutes have made it a crime to use a computer to reproduce protected labels, designs, and layouts (18 U.S.C. 2318).

Computers have become a fundamental part of the modern world. Computer manufacturers continue to build machines that are smaller, faster, lighter, and more cost effective than those produced in the previous generations. While progress in this industry makes information gathering, storage, and distribution easier, it also comes with significant threats. Cyber crime has become a part of the global reality and likely will continue to be so in the foreseeable future. This brief overview of cyber crime is designed only to provide an introduction to the topic. The issues surrounding cyber crime are complex and are not bound by the borders of any one nation.

For more information

CAN-SPAM, Act Pub. L. No. 108–187, 117 Stat. 2699 (2003).

Computer Crime and Intellectual Property Section. *Prosecuting Computer Crimes.* Washington, D.C.: Office of Legal Education, Executive Office for United States Attorneys, 2007.

Computer Fraud and Abuse Act of 1986, 18 U.S.C. 130 (1986).

Identity Theft and Assumption Deterrence Act of 1998, 18 U.S.C. 1028 (a)(7).

Internet Crime Complaint Center. *2008 Internet Crime Report.* Washington, D.C.: Bureau of Justice Assistance, 2008.

Rantala, R. R. *Bureau of Justice Statistics Report: Cybercrime against Businesses, 2005.* U.S. Department of Justice. Washington, D.C.: Office of Justice Programs, 2008.

Regoli, R. M., and J. D. Hewitt. *Exploring Criminal Justice.* Boston: Jones and Bartlett, 2008.

Robert Kenneth Sammons
Northern Arizona University

D

D.A.R.E. (Drug Resistance Education Program) The Drug Resistance Education Program was created in 1983 as a joint project of the Los Angeles Police Department and the Los Angeles Unified School District. Initially, it was designed as a substance abuse prevention program for grades K-12, utilizing a core of 17 hour-long weekly lectures and exercises taught by police officers to 5th and 6th graders. Today, D.A.R.E. also contains components of GANG resistance, parent education, and after-school recreation. At one time, it was universally popular, with almost all students attending colleges and universities completing the program while in middle school.

Educators initially were enthusiastic about D.A.R.E., though results on its effectiveness were sketchy. An examination of studies on effectiveness of the program revealed that only eight previous studies of 18 examined were sufficiently rigorous to merit inclusion in the overall study. The studies that were examined showed that students learned quite a bit about drug use, but that what they learned apparently had little effect on whether they would use drugs or not. Interactive programs were found to be superior in that respect. It was suggested that long-term follow-up studies would show a greater effect on drug behavior, but this hope proved to be illusory as well. Moreover, as time passed, the already modest program effects decreased rather than increased. More studies conducted along the same lines suggest similarly dismal outcomes. CRIMINOLOGISTS and academic experts are almost unanimous in their skepticism about the program. The general assessment is that the extremely low effectiveness of the program cannot justify its high costs in terms of person hours, expense, and time lost to students. Most experts advocate other approaches. Still, D.A.R.E. survives.

Objections center on a number of issues. Police officers generally teach the course. Criminologists and drug education experts question their qualifications and skill in pedagogy and knowledge of the subject matter. Officers selected for this task may simply not be trained or personally disposed to be effective educators. Juvenile work has traditionally been a low-status specialty in police work, and in certain departments teaching in the program may be perceived as an extreme form of being a "kiddy cop." It sometimes happens then that officers selected may be low status, underachievers, and those with personal or organizational issues. Most experts in the field believe that teachers might produce more uniformly positive outcomes. Nevertheless, educators support having police in their schools in order to deter gang problems and handle disciplinary issues. Furthermore, police departments typically use the class as a forum for gathering intelligence about student drug use, drug sales, and gang activities in the school and surrounding communities. Therefore, an apparently secondary function of D.A.R.E. as an adjunct to community policing in schools is a critical, latent, and unexplored dimension. This naturally upsets some parents and civil libertarians who see police presence in schools as unwarranted and intrusive. Other parents feel that drug abuse education is the province of the parents and not appropriately taught in schools.

For more information

Ennett, Susan T., Nancy S. Tobler, Christopher L. Ringwalt, and Robert L. Flewelling. "How Effective Is Drug Abuse Resistance Education? A Meta-Analysis of Project DARE Outcome Evaluation," *American Journal of Public Health* 84, no. 9 (September 1994) 1,394–1,401.

National Institute of Justice. *The D.A.R.E. Program: A Review of Prevalence, User Satisfaction, and Effectiveness.* Washington, D.C.: Department of Justice, 1994.

West, Steven L., and Keri K. O'Neal. "Project D.A.R.E. Outcome Effectiveness Revisited," *American Journal of Public Health.* 94, no. 6 (June 2004): 1,027–1,029.

Frederick Hawley
Western Carolina University

Darrow, Clarence (1857–1938) defense attorney Clarence Darrow was the most famous lawyer in the United States during his lifetime and is still considered one of the greatest lawyers of the 20th century. "Darrow for the defense" became a rallying cry as he turned civil and criminal trials into captivating social drama.

Born in rural Ohio, Darrow was heavily influenced by his father, whom he called "the village infidel" for his nonconformist attitudes and behavior. Darrow attended, ironically, a Methodist college for one year, taught public school for three years, attended the University of Michigan LAW SCHOOL for one year, served a clerkship, then entered legal practice at the age of 21.

Darrow really began to make his mark as a lawyer when he moved to what his hometown newspaper called the nation's "most wicked city"—Chicago. When he took up the cause of Eugene V. Debs, a leading American socialist and president of the American Railway Union, during the 1894 Pullman strike, Darrow began to establish his reputation as a skillful orator and defender of the downtrodden and the despised.

For the next two decades, Darrow especially championed cases involving labor and the working class: the Amalgamated Woodworkers Union, the United Mine Workers, the American Federation of Miners, ironworkers, and Chicago's switchboard operators. In the 1920s, however, Darrow became even more famous through his criminal defense litigation, defending the privileged and the defiled alike—rich teenage murderers, anarchists, socialists, African Americans, and communists, and, in the "trial of the century," a Tennessee teacher by the name of John Scopes, in the 1925 Scopes Monkey Trial.

Darrow, who also wrote two novels and longed for the literary life more than a life as a lawyer, was motivated mainly by empathy and ambition. His professional life demonstrated a perplexing mix of altruism and cynicism. The "Great Defender," the "People's Attorney," the "Attorney for the Damned" believed that criminal defendants were primarily products of their environment and that they were ill rather than evil. He saw crime as a symptom of illness, even a sick society, instead of a question of guilt.

Clearly, it is his courtroom behavior, especially his closing arguments, for which Darrow is most remembered and regarded, even to the point of his achieving iconic status in the annals of American law. In 1908, for instance, Darrow became heavily involved in the criminal trial of William "Big Bill" Haywood of the American Federation of Miners. Haywood stood trial for murdering a former governor of Idaho during labor disputes in the Rocky Mountain West. Darrow delivered a 12-hour-long closing argument to the JURY in Boise, Idaho, which returned a verdict of not guilty

Arguably, Darrow's most famous courtroom oration, although in a losing cause legally, was in the Scopes trial, in which he defended John Scopes, who was found guilty of violating the Tennessee law forbidding the teaching of evolution, and championed modernity over William Jennings Bryan's antirevolutionary views in the "trial of the century."

For more information

Darrow, Clarence. *The Essential Words and Writings of Clarence Darrow.* Edited by Edward J. Larson. New York: Random House, 2007.

Stone, Irving. *Clarence Darrow for the Defense.* Garden City, N.Y.: Doubleday, 1941.

Stephen K. Shaw
Northwest Nazarene University, Nampa, Idaho

Dartmouth College v. Woodward 17 U.S. 4 (1819) *Dartmouth College v. Woodward* was an important early decision that helped to establish both the supremacy of the CONSTITUTION over the state legislatures and the role of the Supreme Court as the Constitution's ultimate interpreter.

Decided in 1819, this famous case paired the legendary advocacy of DANIEL WEBSTER and the judicial genius of CHIEF JUSTICE JOHN MARSHALL. Their nation-building collaboration set in motion the law of the modern corporation, capitalism, and higher education.

It began as a New Hampshire *cause célèbre.* Dartmouth College had been chartered in 1769, in the name of the Crown, to bring Christianity and education to the Indians; later, it became a Congregationalist Church college for whites. The college had the misfortune, however, to became embroiled in state partisan politics. In 1815 the trustees, who were Federalists, removed the president of the college, John Wheelock, son of the founder and first president. The next year, the governor and legislature—Jeffersonian Republicans and political opponents of the Federalists—determined to oust the Federalist trustees once and for all. They passed new state laws revising the royal charter to transform the private college into a public university with new trustees who would be politically appointed. For a time, the two sets of trustees wrangled for control and the campus became a chaos of altercations and confrontations, including physical occupations and changing of the locks of the buildings. The faculty and students were divided between the old college and the new university. Eventually they took their fight to court.

Before the Supreme Court, Daniel Webster, a loyal graduate of the college, invoked the protection of the CONTRACT clause in Article I, section 10 of the Constitution. He contended that the original charter to the college had been a contract, and the 1815 state statute purporting to amend the charter was a "Law impairing the Obligation of Contracts" of the kind prohibited by that clause. In closing, Webster appeared to choke up with emotion to implore the rapt bench, "It is, sir, I have said, a small college, and yet there are those that love it."

Marshall owned the whole of the argument, for himself and for the Court, which ruled that a grant of corporate powers was a contract within the meaning of the Constitution and a state legislature had no power to avoid it. The college was a private corporation with vested property rights. Indeed, for the next 100 years the contract clause was the principal provision the Court would use to invalidate state laws that infringed on private property.

A leading magazine of the day remarked, "Perhaps no judicial proceedings in this country ever involved more important consequences."

The decision extended national judicial power at the expense of state legislative power. It afforded constitutional protection to private economic and social actors, business corporations, and nonprofit corporations alike, against regulation by state legislatures. It validated private colleges and consequently encouraged legislatures to charter state institutions of higher education. In its aftermath, the prestige and influence of the Supreme Court and Chief Justice Marshall were enhanced considerably.

For more information

Dartmouth College v. Woodward, 17 U.S. (4 Wheat.) 518 (1818).

Garraty, John A. *Quarrels That Have Shaped the Constitution.* New York: Harper and Row, 1987.

McCloskey, Robert G. *The American Supreme Court.* Rev. 2nd ed. Chicago: University of Chicago, 1994.

Smith, Jean Edward. *John Marshall, Definer of a Nation.* New York: Henry Holt, 1996.

White, G. Edward. *History of the Supreme Court of the United States,* vols. 3–4, *The Marshall Court and Cultural Change.* New York: Macmillan, 1988.

Thomas E. Baker
University of Scranton

date rape Date rape is a form of acquaintance rape in which a romantic relationship leads to a sexual attack. The vast majority of rapes are acquaintance rapes, thereby making date rape into a fairly common type of sexual assault. Date rape can overlap with STATUTORY RAPE, or sexual intercourse with an unmarried individual who is under the age of consent. Date rape frequently occurs in situations involving alcohol or DATE RAPE DRUGS, such as ketamine, or Special K, and gammahydroxybutyrate, or GHB.

Date rape only entered the public consciousness in the 1980s. In 1982, Mary P. Koss of Kent State University in Ohio completed a scientific survey of sexual aggression and VICTIMIZATION. The subsequent report in a national magazine, *Ms.*, brought widespread notice of the prevalence of rapes since Koss concluded that one in four women were the victims of rape. Most of these attacks were acquaintance rapes. In 1987, the law professor Susan Estrich introduced the terms *date rape* and *acquaintance rape* in her book *Real Rape.* As Estrich noted, date rapes are not always taken seriously because they do not fit the classic rape scenario of a stranger leaping out from the bushes. Both the public and the CRIMINAL JUSTICE SYSTEM tend to minimize rapes that are not aggravated assaults and that "only" involve a man forcing a woman to have sex without her consent. If only stranger rapes were counted, rape would be a fairly rare occurrence.

Date rapes are a particular problem on college campuses, where there are large dating pools. Estrich's book prompted colleges and universities all over the country to hold discussions on date rape to teach young women to be clear about their intentions and young men to seek explicit consent for sexual activities. The phrase, "No means no," became common as a result. Many colleges combine alcohol education with date rape prevention because alcohol is a greater factor in many of these attacks than date rape drugs.

Date rapes are rarely reported to the authorities. If victims do report these assaults, rape is most likely to be charged and tried only when the following conditions are met: a prompt report to the police, the existence of witnesses who can testify to similar crimes committed by the suspect, physical injury to the survivor, and corroboration of the individual's story. This differential treatment of survivors of acquaintance rape has been documented by a number of researchers studying different aspects of the criminal justice system. The thoroughness of a police investigation, the choice of whether or not to prosecute a charge, the likelihood that the defendant will be convicted, and the likelihood of incarceration have all been shown to vary significantly along acquaintance rape/stranger rape lines.

For more information

Estrich, Susan. *Real Rape: How the Legal System Victimizes Women Who Say No.* Cambridge, Mass.: Harvard University Press, 1987.

Neumann, Caryn E. *Sexual Crime.* Santa Barbara, Calif.: ABC-CLIO, 2010.

Warshaw, Robin. *I Never Called It Rape: The* Ms. *Report on Recognizing, Fighting, and Surviving Date and Acquaintance Rape.* New York: HarperCollins, 1994.

Caryn E. Neumann
Miami University of Ohio

date rape drugs Date rape drugs are substances that make it easier for an attacker to subdue a victim. Date rape drugs include Ecstasy, ketamine, gammahydroxybutyrate, and rohypnol as well as alcohol.

Ecstasy is the popular name for 3,4-methylenedioxymethamphetamine (MDMA). It is generally ingested in the form of tablet or capsule with the pills occasionally crushed into a powder than can be snorted, smoked, or injected. MDMA came on the market as an appetite suppressant but also proved popular as a medicinal means of helping people to establish intimate relationships. This latter use makes it a popular date rape drug. People who are under the effect of Ecstasy exhibit increased self-confidence, euphoria, and have a strong desire to be touched by others, including strangers. The drug impairs judgment, thereby facilitating sexual contact that might otherwise seem high risk. The effects are heightened when MDMA is combined with alcohol.

Ketamine, also known as Special K, Vitamin K, and Cat Valium, is an injectable anesthetic designed to alleviate chronic pain, such as that experienced by terminal cancer patients. Most of the ketamine sold legally at the millennium is for veterinary anesthetic use. Ketamine is usually ingested in liquid form or smoked with marijuana or tobacco. If ketamine is placed in someone's drink, the usual form of delivery by sexual predators, the initial reaction may occur between 10 and 20 minutes after ingestion. The maximum effect peaks between one and six hours, but the effects can last for up to 48 hours. The long time frame gives a rapist enough time to attack and to flee the scene. The drug causes a dreamlike state, hallucinations, poor attention, numbness, and paralysis.

Gammahydroxybutyrate, or GHB, is a central nervous system depressant. Initially sold in the 1960s as an anesthetic, it caused too many deaths to remain on the legal market. GHB produces euphoria and an increased sexual drive as well as amnesia and muscle relaxation. The effects begin within 10 to 20 minutes after ingestion and can last for four hours. GHB is often put into a victim's drink. It has a salty taste that can be masked in a mixed drink.

Rohypnol is the most dangerous of the date rape drugs because it is tasteless, odorless, and dissolves easily in carbonated beverages. It is marketed legally as treatment for insomnia and a presurgical anesthetic. A dose of rohypnol as small as a milligram can impair an individual for eight to 12 hours. Rohypnol removes the ability of a victim to defend against or to identify an attacker since it causes muscle relaxation, difficulty in moving and speaking, and blackouts.

The fact that alcohol is a legal drug may mask its dangers. It remains as one of the most significant factors in date rape. A 1994 study by the Columbia University Center on Addiction and Substance Abuse concluded that 90 percent of all reported campus rapes occurred when alcohol had been used by the assailant, the victim, or both.

For more information

Liska, Ken. *Drugs and the Human Body: With Implications for Society.* Upper Saddle River, N.J.: Pearson Prentice Hall, 2009.

McKim, William A. *Drugs and Behavior: An Introduction to Behavioral Pharmacology.* Upper Saddle River, N.J.: Pearson Education, 2007.

Caryn E. Neumann
Miami University of Ohio

Daubert v. Merrell Dow Pharmaceuticals

509 U.S. 579 (1993) In *Daubert v. Merrell Dow Pharmaceuticals,* the leading U.S. Supreme Court decision on the admissibility of EXPERT TESTIMONY at trial, the Court transferred the determination of scientific validity from the science community to the purview of judicial DISCRETION.

In *Daubert,* the Court concluded that the 1923 *Frye* rule, which allowed expert testimony to be admitted if it was "generally accepted" by the scientific community, was superseded by Rule 702 of the FEDERAL RULES OF EVIDENCE, which provided that "[i]f scientific, technical, or other specialized knowledge will assist the trier of fact to understand the evidence or to determine a fact in issue, a witness qualified as an expert by knowledge, skill, experience, training, or education, may testify thereto in the form of an opinion or otherwise." The result of *Daubert* is that federal district JUDGES now play a larger "gatekeeping" role in the admission of scientific evidence.

The legal dispute arose when Jason Daubert and Eric Schuller, children with birth defects, and their parents sued Merrell Dow Pharmaceuticals, alleging that the mothers' ingestion of the company's antinausea drug, Bendectin, caused the birth defects. Merrell sought to have the lawsuit dismissed, citing the absence of evidence demonstrating a connection between Bendectin and birth defects. To support its contention, Merrell submitted an affidavit from Steven H. Lamm, a leading researcher on exposure to chemicals, that concluded that a thorough review of the literature found no study establishing a connection between Bendectin and birth defects.

In response to the Lamm affidavit, Daubert submitted testimony from eight experts who concluded, after recalculating existing statistical studies and examining test tube and animal experiments, that Bendectin can cause birth defects. The district court judge ruled in favor of Merrell and dismissed Daubert's expert testimony.

On review, the U.S. Court of Appeals for the Ninth Circuit affirmed the district court, ruling that *Frye v. United States,* 54 App. D.C. 46 (1923), a U.S. Court of Appeals for the District of Columbia Circuit decision, created the proper standard for determining when scientific evidence could be admitted at trial. According to the *Frye* rule, expert opinion is inadmissible unless the technique is "generally accepted" as reliable in the relevant scientific community. Because Daubert's eight expert witnesses reached conclusions using methods not "generally accepted" in the epidemiological community, the Ninth Circuit agreed with the trial court.

On APPEAL to the U.S. Supreme Court, the justices concluded that Section 702 of the Federal Rules of Evidence superseded the *Frye* rule. While federal judges no longer are required to determine whether expert testimony is "generally accepted" in the scientific community, judges still serve as the vital "gatekeeper" for expert testimony. Writing for the seven-member majority, Justice Blackmun noted this "gatekeeping" function, maintaining that "under the Rules the trial judge must ensure that any and all scientific testimony or evidence admitted is not only relevant, but reliable." For Justice Blackmun, Rule 702 "clearly contemplates some degree of regulation of the subjects and theories about which an expert may testify," because judges must assist in determining what is "scientific" and whether the "knowledge will assist the trier of fact to understand the evidence or to determine a fact in issue." *Daubert v. Merrell Dow Pharmaceuticals,* 509 U.S. 579, 587. Therefore, this rule places responsibility on the judge to determine whether the evidence is reliable and relevant to the facts at issue at trial and whether the expert has the appropriate qualifications to render scientific knowledge.

Writing in a separate opinion, CHIEF JUSTICE WILLIAM H. REHNQUIST, who was joined by Justice Stevens, agreed with the majority that the Federal Rules of Evidence replaced the *Frye* rule but took issue with the majority's decision to go further by providing "general observations" about judges' responsibilities under the Federal Rules of Evidence. Chief Justice Rehnquist cautioned that the majority opinion seemed to impose on federal judges "either the obligation or authority to become amateur scientists," since judges are now apparently expected to evaluate the "scientific status of a theory," i.e., whether it is "falsifiable," a scientific term that the chief justice suspected judges were as unfamiliar with as he was.

Daubert v. Merrell Dow Pharmaceuticals is significant because it created a uniform rule for federal judges to apply when determining whether expert testimony should be admitted at trial. However, lawyers and experts were unsure how the judicial "gatekeeping" function might affect the admissibility of evidence. According to a 2001 RAND Institute for Civil Justice study, after *Daubert*, federal judges "scrutinized reliability more carefully and applied stricter standards in deciding whether to admit expert evidence" (xv) and "the proportion of expert evidence excluded" increased (54). In sum, *Daubert* caused a fundamental shift in the admissibility of expert testimony and created additional questions with which courts are now wrestling.

For more information

Dixon, Lloyd, and Brian Gill. *Changes in the Standards for Admitting Expert Evidence in Federal Civil Cases since the* Daubert *Decision*. RAND Institute for Civil Justice, 2001.

Golan, Tal. "Symposium: A Cross-Disciplinary Look at Scientific Truth: What's the Law to Do? Revisiting the History of Scientific Expert Testimony," *Brooklyn Law Review* 73 (Spring 2008): 874.

Kyle L. Kreider
Wilkes University

Declaration of Independence The Declaration of Independence was adopted by the Second Continental Congress on July 4, 1776, and it declared and enumerated the reasons for the independence of the American colonies from Great Britain, advocated government by consent of the people, and then defended human rights, the right of self-government, and the right of people to rebel against any tyrannical government.

Drawing from the natural rights doctrine of the English philosopher John Locke, the original draft was written largely by Thomas Jefferson but also included the writings of John Adams, Benjamin Franklin, Roger Sherman, and Robert Livingston. Writing in characteristically eloquent prose, Jefferson sought to capture the authentic revolutionary spirit of the times. Several years after the Revolution, Jefferson stated that the Declaration "was intended to be an expression of the American mind." Jefferson and his coauthors believed that the Declaration embodied political ideals that the great majority of Americans cherished.

The Declaration of Independence is based on a novel theory of the political rights of American colonists within the British Empire. As British subjects, the colonists believed fervently that they possessed the same rights as their "British brethren," but, as subjects, they were also legally obligated to obey King George III and Parliament. This state of affairs posed a problem for those who wished to separate from England. If Americans were British subjects, by what right could they claim to be "one people" who were "separate and equal" from other nations? In an attempt to resolve this dilemma, Benjamin Franklin put forth the theory in 1768 that the American colonies were originally established as separate and sovereign states within the British Empire. Franklin argued that the colonial governments owed allegiance only to the king (as did other states or nations within the British Commonwealth), not to the British Parliament. American colonists, therefore, could justify separation *from the King* by invoking the same rights enjoyed by British citizens. This theory, which is embodied in the Declaration, accounts for the fact that it contains a list of charges against the king, not Parliament, and for the fact that the Declaration justifies separation on the ground that Americans, as a free people, had been denied their rights by the king.

The first four sentences of the Declaration put forth a concise justification of the right of revolution which would appear to be derived from the political philosophy of the 17th-century Englishman John Locke (see Locke's *Second Treatise on Civil Government,* 1690). The first sentence of the Declaration asserts the intention of the American colonies "to dissolve the political bands which have connected them with another, and to assume among the powers of the earth, the separate and equal station to which the Laws of Nature and of Nature's God entitle them." Americans in Jefferson's time would have understood that "the Laws of Nature and of Nature's God" referred to natural laws, that is, universal moral principles based on reason.

The Declaration's second sentence enumerates the specific principles that justify a "separate and equal station": "We hold these truths to be self-evident, that all men are created equal, that they are endowed by their Creator with certain unalienable Rights, that among these are Life, Liberty, and the pursuit of Happiness." Jefferson's phrase, "all men are created equal" (today we would say "all people"), was meant to convey the idea that every person, by virtue of being a human being, possessed the same natural rights. John Locke argued that God created people with equal rights in the "state of nature," which existed before people decided to form governments. Upon leaving the state of nature, people retained certain natural (God-given or unalienable) rights—such as the rights to life, liberty, and property—that cannot be given up or alienated in political society. The concept of natural or unalienable rights therefore assumes that the powers of government must be limited.

In the third sentence, we encounter Locke's theory of legitimate government, which resonated strongly with the beliefs and experience of the American colonists: "That to secure these rights, Governments are instituted among Men, deriving their just powers from the consent of the governed." People left the state of nature, according to Locke, to better secure their natural rights by instituting laws and courts, which would impartially apply the law. In forming a "social contract" among themselves, they agreed to create a government to protect those unalienable rights. American colonists believed, as did Locke, that government should be based upon the consent of the governed and should be held accountable by the people.

The fourth sentence of the Declaration articulates a justification for revolution based on Lockean social contract theory: "That whenever any Form of Government becomes destructive of these ends, it is the Right of the People to alter or abolish it, and to institute new Government, laying its foundation on such principles, and organizing its powers in such form, as to them shall seem most likely to effect their Safety and Happiness." According to Locke's theory, when the terms of the social contract have been violated by the government, the people have the right to "alter or abolish it." Revolution could be justified, according to the Declaration, because the king had violated the terms of the social contract by denying or usurping the natural rights of the colonists. The list of charges against the king in the Declaration enumerate these transgressions, which, among others, included taxation without representation, suspending or dissolving colonial governments, denying the RIGHT OF TRIAL BY JURY, and subverting the rule of law by appointing JUDGES that were not impartial.

Jefferson's reference to "men" throughout the Declaration of Independence was understood by his contemporaries to exclude women and males who were not recognized as members of political society, such as slaves and American Indians. This fact cannot be overlooked without seriously distorting the historical context within which the Declaration was written. However, throughout the 19th and 20th centuries, leaders of CIVIL RIGHTS MOVEMENTS for women, African Americans, and other disenfranchised groups regularly invoked the universalistic principles of the Declaration in support of their causes. Today, the natural rights language employed by Jefferson is interpreted to include all people regardless of their gender, race, or ethnic heritage. This is perhaps the main reason that the Declaration of Independence continues to be one of the most important statements of basic human rights ever written.

For more information

Becker, Carl L. *The Declaration of Independence: A Study in the History of Political Ideas.* New York: Vintage, 1958.

Maier, Pauline. *American Scripture: Making the Declaration of Independence.* New York: Knopf; Distributed by Random House, 1997.

Wood, Gordon S. *The Creation of the American Republic, 1776–1787.* New York: W. W. Norton, 1972.

Scott R. Bowman
California State University, Los Angeles

declaratory judgment A declaratory judgment refers to a court decision that clarifies the rights and responsibilities of the parties to a lawsuit. It is an articulation of the legal relationships among the litigants.

A declaratory judgment does not, however, require the parties to do anything based on the court's enunciation of those rights and responsibilities. This is in contrast to most court cases in which the litigants are requesting the court to order some sort of active relief for alleged injuries; for example, monetary damages. A litigant may seek a declaratory judgment if she is uncertain about her legal obligations and does not wish to inadvertently run afoul of the law. For example, a party wishing to terminate a complicated sales CONTRACT may seek clarification from the courts on the requirements for doing so.

As a general rule, courts are hesitant to issue declaratory judgments. In fact, the United States Supreme Court, in the 1928 case of *Willing v. Chicago Auditorium Association,* 277 U.S. 274, suggested that federal courts were severely limited in issuing declaratory judgments under Article III of the CONSTITUTION. The language of Article III can be interpreted to imply that only actual (as opposed to hypothetical) cases with real controversy between the parties are within the purview of the federal courts. The United States Supreme Court has subsequently taken a less restrictive view of the permissibility of declaratory judgments. However, for a federal court to issue a declaratory judgment, there still must be an actual controversy and not merely a hypothetical dispute at issue.

Congress specifically authorized federal courts to issue declaratory judgments with passage of the Federal Declaratory Judgment Act of 1934. Declaratory judgments are permissible for all civil issues except for federal tax cases. In the 1937 case of *Aetna Life Ins. Co. of Hartford, Conn. v. Haworth,* 300 U.S. 227, the Supreme Court explicitly considered the constitutionality of the act. The Court upheld the constitutionality of the act, basing its decision on the fact that it limited the use of declaratory judgments to actual controversies. Deciding what constitutes an actual controversy has proven not to be a straightforward matter to determine, but there is evidence that the Court is less likely to resolve major constitutional questions with their use. For example, the Court declined to issue a declaratory judgment in the 1961 case of *Poe v. Ullman,* 367 U.S. 497, to determine the constitutionality of Connecticut's law against contraceptive devices. However, a scant four year later the Court reversed a doctor's conviction for dispensing contraceptives to a married couple in violation of Connecticut law in the landmark case of *GRISWOLD V. CONNECTICUT,* 381 U.S. 479 (1965).

A declaratory judgment is distinct from an advisory judgment, in which a court addresses a question of law in the absence of an actual controversy, a practice the Court has consistently declined to engage in. While each state regulates the issuance of declaratory judgments by its own courts in accordance with its own laws, state practice generally parallels federal practice.

For more information

Hazard, Geoffrey C. Jr., and Michele Taruffo. *American Civil Procedure: An Introduction.* New Haven, Conn.: Yale University Press, 1993.

Silberman, Linda J., and Allan R. Stein. *Civil Procedure: Theory and Practice.* Gaithersburg, Md.: Aspen Law and Business, 2001.

Wendy L. Martinek
SUNY, Binghamton

defamation Defamation is the law that protects a person's reputation or his or her good name from ridicule.

A statement that defames someone is one that causes others to avoid the defamed person. This area of the law is centuries old. Perhaps its earliest enforcement was in the notorious Court of the Star Chamber in England in the 1400s, when the defamer was ordered to pay money to someone whose reputation he sullied and often would be maimed or imprisoned. Truth was no defense—the fact that another's reputation was attacked was all that mattered. In the Middle Ages dueling often settled disputes caused by such attacks on reputation. By the mid-1600s two separate types of defamation had emerged in the English law: LIBEL, which was defamation by writing, and slander, which was defamation by spoken word. As they developed, these related TORTS, or civil wrongs, were largely the same. A person who claimed he was slandered, however, had to prove the slanderous statement led to financial harm—cost him money. That was because spoken insults could be quickly forgotten and were limited by how many people might hear them and, not least, such insults could crowd the courts with people demanding redress. With libel, on the other hand, the written disparagement was more permanent and could be transmitted to large numbers of people.

As with all early American law, the law of defamation was established in the various states by English "common law." Despite free speech guarantees of the U.S. CONSTITUTION in the First Amendment, defamation law developed exclusively in state courts. It even encompassed seditious libel, a criminal offense that punished disparaging remarks about government officials. For the most part, however, the free speech heritage of the American Revolution established truth as a defense that took root in U.S. law. A true statement could harm a person's reputation, to be sure, but the defamer would not be liable because it was true. Once the person who claimed to be defamed proved that a false statement was written about him and that by its nature it would call his reputation into question, then the harm was presumed—his defamer had to pay, even if no one believed the statement and even if the defamer made the false statement without knowing it was false.

In most states libel protects the reputation of a person defamed by a television or radio broadcast, even though the defamatory statement is spoken, not written. The reason for this is that the statement reaches a wider audience than the law of slander originally intended and, in theory at least, would cause more damage.

The scope of defamation (at least libel) was radically changed beginning in 1964 with the U.S. Supreme Court's decision in *NEW YORK TIMES CO. V. SULLIVAN*, 376 U.S. 254, 84 S.Ct. 710, 11 L.Ed.2d 686 (1964). In this decision the Supreme Court for the first time held that state libel laws must meet certain free speech protections under the First Amendment. The *Sullivan* case required what English common law and state law did not, that the person defamed must prove his defamer was at fault. In *Sullivan,* concerned only with libel lawsuits filed by public officials when the defamatory statement related to their public duties, the Court determined that the public official claiming to have been defamed must prove that the person who defamed him knew the statement was false or recklessly disregarded whether it was true or not. Later decisions amplifying the rule in *Sullivan* established that fault must be proven in all libel cases, at least against the mass media.

For more information

Rosini, Neil J. *The Practical Guide to Libel Law.* New York: Praeger, 1991.

Wm. Osler McCarthy
Supreme Court of Texas
University of Texas, Austin

defense attorney Defense attorney refers to the legal counsel who represents a defendant in either a civil or criminal case. A defense attorney is also referred to as defense counsel or defense lawyer. In either a civil or criminal case, it is the defense attorney's job to protect the interests of the defendant in the case.

The United States has an adversarial system of justice, which places the JUDGE in the position of neutral decision maker and attorneys for plaintiffs against those of the defendant. It is the job of the attorneys to bring forth EVIDENCE in support of their position and to argue the law. The plaintiff has the BURDEN OF PROOF in both civil and criminal trials.

In civil trials, the plaintiff must prove by a PREPONDERANCE OF THE EVIDENCE that the defendant is liable, while in criminal trials the plaintiff (the PROSECUTOR) must prove beyond a REASONABLE DOUBT that the defendant is guilty. In either case, it is the job of the defense attorney to counter the claims of the plaintiff and defend the defendant. Defense attorneys do not only work during the trial; rather, it is their job to defend their clients from the beginning through the end of the case. They not only appear in court but work with PLEA BARGAINING, settlements, answering pleadings, researching evidence, and interviewing witnesses.

In civil trials, defense attorneys appear in any number of types of cases. They may appear as defense counsel for large corporations, for individuals, small businesses, and government agencies. Most lawsuits filed, whether it be against an individual, business, or the government, will require a defense attorney. Defense attorneys are therefore a mixed group of lawyers. Although some civil attorneys specialize in defense work, many may simply be lawyers who represent a client on a regular basis (i.e., doing legal CONTRACTS) and find themselves in the position of defending their client as a part of that relationship.

The SIXTH AMENDMENT to the UNITED STATES CONSTITUTION protects a defendant's right to counsel in criminal cases. In criminal matters, defense attorneys must counter the prosecution's claim of guilt. Most defense attorneys in criminal matters specialize in criminal law. Many defense attorneys in criminal law are former prosecutors. Some defense attorneys work privately or in law firms, while some work for the state as part of a program to provide legal services for indigent defendants. The most widely used of these programs is called a PUBLIC DEFENDER program.

Defense attorneys in criminal law face a hard decision. In many cases, they know their clients will not benefit from a trial. For some of these defendants, working out a plea bargain may be in their best interests. In this way, a defendant who admits guilt or a defendant who faces a strong prosecutorial case may be able to reduce the time spent in prison through a reduction of charges or sentence. On the other hand, defense attorneys will typically recommend trial for those defendants where either there is a strong chance of ACQUITTAL or where there is a very high prison sentence. In either of these cases, a defense attorney may find that his or her client's interests would best be served by a trial by JURY (*see* Neubauer, 1997).

Defense attorneys, and especially criminal defense attorneys, often face a particularly harsh public image, which is based on the competing morals in public life. On one hand, the public wants to see those who are guilty punished. Defense attorneys often represent clients who they believe to be guilty. For example, a civil lawyer may represent a car manufacturer who caused the death of a child through negligence or a criminal lawyer may represent a murderer found standing over a dead body. In either case, the public may be outraged at the person who defends the actions of the defendant, i.e., the defense attorney, especially when an attorney earns an acquittal for their client.

On the other hand, the public does not want to see innocent people go to jail or pay large fines. In this view, defense attorneys who rigorously defend their clients are only doing their job. After all, most people would want a good defense attorney if they stood accused. In addition, in many cases the lawyer simply does not know whether the client is innocent or guilty but simply must work the case based upon what the client professes to be the truth (*see* Tarr, 1999).

For more information

Neubauer, David W. *Judicial Process: Law Courts, and Politics in the United States.* New York: Harcourt Brace College, 1997.

Tarr, G. Alan. *Judicial Process and Judicial Policymaking.* Boston: West/Wadsworth, 1999.

Joy A. Willis
Michigan State University
Graduate Researcher

Defense of Marriage Act (DOMA) The Defense of Marriage Act defines marriage for federal purposes as "the union between one man and one woman." Passage of this act by Congress in 1996 also added a provision to the *U.S. Code* that permits one state to refuse to recognize a same-sex marriage which is valid under the laws of another state.

Congress passed DOMA primarily in response to *Baehr v. Lewin,* a case in which the Hawaii Supreme Court held that under that state's constitution, a marriage statute which restricts the status and benefits of marriage to male-female couples discriminates on the basis of sex. With the *Baehr* decision in 1993, Congress and advocates on both sides of the same-sex marriage debate assumed that it would only be a matter of time before same-sex marriage was a matter of course in Hawaii. Addressing this potential occurrence became a major issue in the 1996 elections, ultimately leading to the passage of DOMA at the federal level and similar laws in many states.

DOMA is unique in several ways. First, marriage regulations have historically been a matter of state law, not federal. Second, DOMA was passed in response to a perceived problem that does not yet exist. That is, while the law purports to regulate marriage, it was really enacted as a response to the possibility of same-sex marriage, which, as of this writing, has been legalized in only a few states. Third, on its face this act appears to directly conflict with the full faith and credit clause of Article IV of the U.S. Constitution. That clause requires that "Full Faith and Credit shall be given in each state to the public Acts, Records, and judicial Proceedings of every other state" and only gives Congress the power to regulate the "Manner in which such Acts, Records and Proceedings shall be proved and the Effect thereof."

Marriage has been a status that has historically led to some departures from the full faith and credit so that while marriages that are valid in the state where performed are generally valid in any other state, such marriages do not have to be recognized in another state if they violate that state's "strong public policy." However, never before has Congress simply declared that any state may categorically refuse to recognize a marriage that is valid in the state where performed.

On January 31, 2000, the Supreme Court of Vermont ruled in *Baker v. State* that it is discrimination under the common benefits clause of the Vermont Constitution to deny same-sex couples the same benefits as male-female couples. Accordingly the Vermont legislature enacted a law which gives gay and lesbian couples the same benefits that are available to heterosexual couples under state law, such as tax benefits, inheritance rights, and the legal right to make medical decisions on behalf of a partner. Vermont stopped short, however, of conferring the status of "marriage" on same-sex couples and instead allows same-sex couples to register their "civil unions." Unlike marriages, these civil unions are not recognized by other states and confer no benefits under federal law. In light of Vermont's civil union law, it was only a matter of time before one or more states granted same-sex couples the right to marry. Such an occurrence will undoubtedly lead to legal challenges of DOMA on several grounds, including but not limited to claims that DOMA violates the full faith and credit clause and regulates an area more appropriately left to regulation by the states.

Subsequent to the Vermont *Baker* decision, the Massachusetts Supreme Court in *Goodridge v. Department of Public Health*, 440 Mass. 309 (2003), ruled that precluding same-sex couples from marrying violated its state constitution. As a result same-sex couples have been able to marry in that state. Other states, including Iowa, Connecticut, and New York, either by court decision or legislation, have also changed their laws to allow same-sex couples to marry.

As a result of the *Goodridge* decision, many states adopted their own defense of marriage acts in 2004. As of 2010, 37 states have their own DOMAs.

Critics of the federal and state DOMAs contend that these laws violate either the EQUAL PROTECTION or PRIVILEGES OR IMMUNITIES provision of the Fourteenth Amendment. In July 2010, a federal district court judge declared the federal DOMA unconstitutional, contending it violated the rights of states under the Tenth Amendment. As more states recognize the rights of same-sex couples to marry, the legal and political future of DOMA remains uncertain.

For more information

Kersch, Ken I. "Full Faith and Credit for Same-Sex Marriage?" *Political Science Quarterly* 112 (Spring 1997).

Strasser, Mark P. *Legally Wed: Same-Sex Marriage & the Constitution*. Ithaca, N.Y.: Cornell University Press, April 1996.

Martha M. Lafferty
Staff Attorney
Tennessee Fair Housing Council

Department of Homeland Security The Department of Homeland Security (DHS) is a cabinet-level organization within the United States government that is responsible for protecting the nation's infrastructure from man-made and natural disasters. The formal mission of the department is to "prevent terrorist attacks within the United States, reduce the vulnerability of the United States to terrorism, and minimize the damage, and assist in the recovery, from terrorist attacks that do occur within the United States."

The Department of Homeland Security is an outgrowth of the Office of Homeland Security, which was established by President George W. Bush in the aftermath of the September 11, 2001, terrorist attacks. Senator Joseph Lieberman introduced a bill to establish the Department of National Homeland Security on October 11, 2001. The department was formally established when the Homeland Security Act of 2002 (Public Law 107–296) was passed as a law on November 25, 2002.

The former Pennsylvania governor Tom Ridge, who had been heading the Office of Homeland Security, was by appointed to the position of secretary of DHS by President Bush. The department officially opened its doors on January 24, 2003, after 24 federal government entities and their more than 180,000 employees were merged. This was the largest government restructuring since 1947, when President Truman joined the branches of the armed forces to create the Department of Defense.

The 24 agencies that created DHS were;

Animal and Plant Health Inspection Service; Border Patrol; CBRN Countermeasures Programs; Citizenship and Immigration Services; Coast Guard; Customs Service; Domestic Emergency Support Teams; Energy Security and Assurance Program; Environmental Measurements Laboratory; Federal Computer Incident Response Center; Federal Emergency Management Agency; Federal Law Enforcement Training Center; Federal Protective Service; Immigration

U.S. Department of Homeland Security

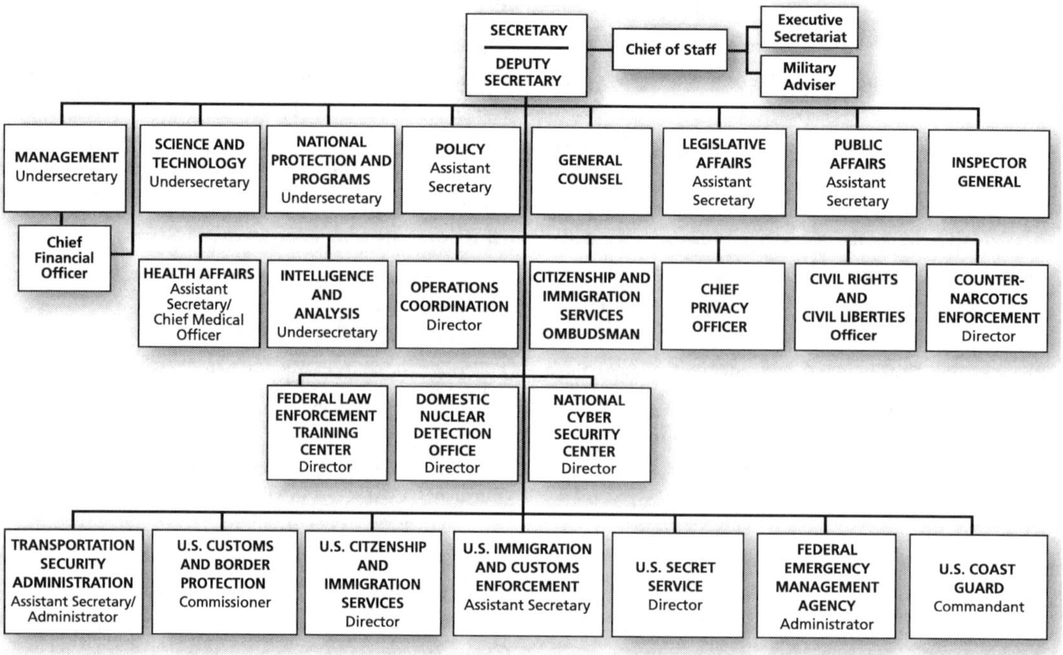

Source: Department of Homeland Security. "Homeland Security Organizational Chart." Available online. URL: http//www.dhs.gov/xlibrary/assets/DHS_OrgChart.pdf. Posted April 1, 2007.

and Customs Enforcement; National BW Defense Analysis Center; National Communications System; National Domestic Preparedness Office; National Protection and Programs Directorate; Nuclear Incident Response Team; Office for Domestic Preparedness; Plum Island Animal Disease Center; Secret Service; Strategic National Stockpile and the National Disaster Medical System; Transportation Security Administration; Notably absent from the list of absorbed agencies are the Federal Bureau of Investigation, National Security Agency, and Central Intelligence Agency, which continue to perform counterintelligence tasks separately from DHS.

Structurally, the department is divided into five directorates and three mission agencies. The directorates include: information and infrastructure, border and transportation security, science and technology, emergency response, and management; DHS mission agencies are Coast Guard, U.S. Citizenship and Immigration Services, and U.S. Secret Service.

The Department of Homeland Security employs more than 200,000 individuals, making it the third-largest cabinet-level organization behind the Departments of Defense and Veterans Affairs. Michael Chertoff succeeded Ridge as secretary of DHS in 2005 and was followed by Janet Napolitano, who was appointed by President Barack Obama in 2009. The 2010 budget for DHS is $55,115,227.

For more information

Bullock, Jane A., George D. Haddow, Damon Coppola, Erdem Ergin, Lissa Westerman, and Sarp Yeletaysi. *Introduction to Homeland Security.* 2nd ed. China: Elsevier, 2006.

Sauter, Mark A., and James Jay Carafano. *Homeland Security: A Complete Guide to Understanding, Preventing, and Surviving Terrorism.* New York: McGraw Hill, 2005.

U.S. Department of Homeland Security. "Brief Documentary History of the Department of Homeland Security," Available online. URL: <http://www.dhs.gov/xlibrary/assets/brief_documentary_history_of_dhs_2001_2008.pdf.

Megan Collins
University of Maryland

deposition Deposition is the term for sworn testimony taken before a court reporter who takes down and eventually transcribes oral testimony.

A deposition is part of the phase of the lawsuit called "discovery," which is the process by which a party to a lawsuit finds out the breadth and scope of the other party's case. A deposition is scheduled shortly after the start of a lawsuit for the purpose of preserving testimony and exploring the strengths and weaknesses of the opponent's witnesses and, by extension, the outline of the case. A party or a witness, the "deponent," is summoned into a private conference room or law library. Lawyers for each party are present, as is a court reporter. The court reporter is a notary public or some other official authorized to administer oaths or affirmations. The reporter is also a skilled stenographic note taker who takes down what is said word-for-word. Except for the swearing in of the deponent, the reporter takes no other active part in the process beyond recording the proceedings.

Once the witness is sworn, the lead attorney for the opposing side will begin asking questions of the witness. There is no presiding officer present to determine whether a question is proper or not. If a question is thought to be improper, the attorney for the deponent may object, stating his grounds based upon the rules of EVIDENCE. The deponent will then answer the question. Later, a JUDGE may decide whether the question was proper. Because a deposition can also be used as an instrument of settlement, by exposing both strengths and weaknesses of a deponent's testimony, judges are often very reluctant to strike questions or answers.

Some JURISDICTIONS impose little or no restriction on the type or number of questions that can be asked or the length of the depositions. If the side being deposed feels that the interrogation is oppressive or is being used only for purposes of pressure, the party can apply to the court for orders restricting the manner, length, or even the nature of the questioning. These are called "protective orders."

During a trial a deposition may be used to "impeach" a witness, which is the process of pointing out differences in the witness's courtroom testimony and his deposition testimony. Depositions may also be used to refresh the memory of a friendly witness. If the person whose deposition has been taken is unavailable because of illness, death, or being otherwise excused, the deposition may be read into the record as if it were the testimony of the person given on that day. As many depositions are now videotaped, this has become popular because the judge or JURY not only can hear the witness but observe the witness's demeanor and appearance as well.

Depositions are only one of the tools that attorneys use during the discovery phase. They are used most often because they produce the most immediate response. Other tools are written interrogatories, motions to require production of documents for inspection or copying, production of tangible objects for testing, or inspection of real property. Interrogatories often produce the opponent's "best" answer and therefore lack the spontaneity of an oral deposition.

For more information

American Jurisprudence. 2nd ed., vol. 23. *Depositions and Discovery.* St. Paul, Minn.: West, 1998.

Consult the statutes and rules of civil procedure in your state.

Stanley M. Morris
Attorney at Law
Cortez, Colorado

determinate sentencing Determinate sentencing is a system of PUNISHMENT that establishes fixed periods of incarceration for criminal offenders. The sentences are typically fashioned by legislatures or legislatively created sentencing commissions with the goals of deterring criminal behavior through the imposition of more certain penalties and reducing bias that leads to disparity in sentencing, often based on race, ethnicity, and gender.

Frequently referred to as "just deserts," determinate sentencing is intended to impose a term of incarceration that correlates with the seriousness of the crime. Unlike INDETERMINATE SENTENCING methods, JUDGES guided by determinate approaches are vested with little or no DISCRETION when imposing a prison term on offenders who are expected to fulfill most, if not all, of the original sentence established by law.

The term *determinate sentencing* may be applied to a number of sentencing approaches adopted by the states and the federal government since the use of variable, or indeterminate, sentences fell into disfavor in the early 1970s. Among the more commonly used alternatives adopted at the federal level and by at least 21 states is the SENTENCING GUIDELINE system. Also called structured sentencing, the system requires judges to evaluate the severity of the offense and the criminal history of the offender when determining a criminal sentence. A sentencing grid or matrix guides judges to the correct sentence for the combination of the two variables and provides a predetermined sentence or sentencing range. Judges may deviate from the recommended sentence, but only if circumstances warrant a variance and the departure is justified by the sentencing judge, usually through a written opinion. In most JURISDICTIONS employing guidelines, offenders are not eligible for PAROLE or other significant reductions to the original sentence. Credits for good behavior may reduce the overall length of incarceration, but typically 85 percent of the sentence is completed. Although adopted by more than 40 percent of the states, the constitutional validity of the approach has been called into question in several cases presented to the U.S. Supreme Court. In decisions announced in 2004 and 2005, the justices held that structured sentencing systems create SIXTH AMENDMENT difficulties if judges impose sentences longer than prescribed by the guidelines and based upon facts not proven to a JURY beyond a REASONABLE DOUBT.

Other determinate sentences schemes include mandatory and MANDATORY MINIMUM SENTENCES as well as two- and three-strike provisions. These approaches, unlike a systemic guideline structure, apply a rigid sentencing requirement only to a select group of offenses or offenders. Mandatory sentences require judges to impose a statutorily prescribed period of incarceration for a particular crime and severely restrict or eliminate the discretion of the judge. Two- and three-strike provisions require judges to mete out a lengthy sentence, often 25 years or more, to predicate offenders who violate a particular category of the criminal code on two or three occasions.

Despite the general popularity of determinate sentencing structures, critics have voiced concerns about the utility of the approach. Although determinate systems curb judicial bias and limit discretion, that discretion often shifts to other actors in the system, usually PROSECUTORS, who exercise similar partiality over other decision processes in the system. Evidence also suggests that sentences have become much harsher, leading to PRISON OVERCROWDING and other burdens on departments of corrections.

For more information

Griset, Pamela. *Determinate Sentencing: The Promise and the Reality of Retributive Justice.* Albany: State University of New York Press, 1991.

Morris, Norval, and Michael Tonry. *Between Prison and Probation: Intermediate Punishments in a Rational Sentencing System.* New York: Oxford University Press, 1990.

Charles F. Jacobs
St. Norbert College

deterrence theory Deterrence theory is a theory of crime that posits that individuals will be restrained from crime by swift, certain, and severe PUNISHMENTS. It is a CLASSICAL THEORY OF CRIME, and presumes that humans are rational, self-interested, and exercise free will in making decisions to break the law.

Deterrence can take two forms: specific and general. Specific deterrence is the result of punishment on an individual; as the result of negative consequences (incarceration, PROBATION, fines, etc.) the offender will abstain from the behaviors that resulted in the punishment in order to avoid the punishment a second time. Specific deterrence operates to prevent RECIDIVISM, or reoffending. Specific deterrence can be thought of as an "I'm not doing that again!" phenomenon.

General deterrence is the result of an individual's punishment on others; each person who receives punishment for criminal or delinquent behavior stands as an example to everyone else. General deterrence is meant as a preventative measure. Members of the public observe how others are treated for breaking the law and think, "I'm not doing that because I don't want to face those consequences!"

Deterrence theory can be traced back to the work of two influential Enlightenment thinkers: Cesare Beccaria and Jeremy Bentham. Beccaria, an Italian penal reformer, suggested in his 1764 essay *On Crimes and Punishments* that men are naturally predisposed to crime and deviance due to "the passions of the individual" (Beccaria, 1775 [1992], 19). In order to "counterbalance" and restrain these passions, Beccaria argued that the state must create swift, certain, and severe punishments. He also argued strongly that punishments should be proportional to the crime and of the least severity possible to achieve deterrence: "The degree of the punishment, and the consequences of a crime, ought to be so contrived, as to have the greatest possible effect on others, with the least possible pain to the delinquent" (Beccaria, 51). This "effect on others," of course, is what would now be called general deterrence.

Jeremy Bentham, an English philosopher and reformer, wrote about the "utility principle" in 1781. According to Bentham, "Nature has placed mankind under the governance of two sovereign masters, pain and pleasure" (1781, [2000], 14). As rational beings, men will seek to maximize pleasure and minimize pain. While the benefits of crime may sometimes be high, crime can be deterred by making the costs of crime (e.g., punishments) greater than the potential benefits.

Adherents to deterrence theory mostly philosophized about the concept until criminologists such as Jack Gibbs (1968) and Charles Tittle (1969) began to conduct empirical research on the phenomenon. Early on, the effect and presence of deterrence was determined by comparing crime rates in various states via the FBI'S UNIFORM CRIME REPORTS. The certainty of punishment in each state was measured using a ratio of the number of ARRESTS to the number of crimes known to the police, or the number of convictions to the number of crimes known. Severity was measured by the average sentence length for various crimes. Measuring across states with different levels of certainty, severity, and crime rates, these early efforts generally found that JURISDICTIONS with a high certainty of punishment had lower crime rates. Results on severity were mixed, with most studies finding a lesser effect of severity (compared with the effects of certainty), and some finding no significant effect of severity on crime rates at all. Many theorists have criticized these early studies, however, for relying too heavily on official statistics from police and corrections agencies. Measures of certainty of punishment, such as arrest or conviction rates, are particularly vulnerable to distortion since each local police department and PROSECUTOR's office makes decisions about whom to arrest and prosecute, and local police are responsible for counting their own crimes and reporting them to the FBI.

Deterrence theory was later expanded to consider an individual's perceptions of punishments in making crime decisions, rather than simply the objective levels of punishment or arrest rates in a jurisdiction (see Waldo and Chiricos, 1972). Offenders—and the public in general—are very unlikely to know such facts and figures, and most modern deterrence theorists acknowledge that efforts to measure a deterrent effect are much better aimed at what people think are the likelihood and severity of sanctions (Kleck et al., 2005). These perceptual deterrence studies also generally found support for a deterrent effect of perceived certainty and weaker support for a deterrent effect of perceived severity.

Lawrence Sherman (1990) examined the deterrent effects of police policies that concentrate enforcement efforts on one "hot spot" of crime. Sherman (1990) and others have found that such efforts can have a significant deterrent effect. There is often, however, a rapid decay of the deterrent effect, perhaps as offenders learn that their risk is lower than they originally perceived. Sherman notes that there is some residual deterrence observed, however, even after such crackdowns are ended.

Perceptions are not created in a vacuum. Researchers, including Mark Stafford and Mark Warr (1993), expanded the reach of deterrence theory by determining whether individuals had personal or vicarious experience with punishment, which may have had a role in the formation of their perceptions about the certainty or severity of punishment. Specifically, Stafford and Warr (1993) determined whether survey respondents had been caught, had committed crime but had not been caught, knew of someone who had been caught, or knew of someone who had committed a crime but had not been caught. Studies on experience and risk perception have generally found that those who had "gotten away with" delinquent and criminal acts had lower perceptions of certainty and were more likely to offend. This kind of study raises important questions, however, including whether perceptions of low certainty of punishment come before offending, or if avoiding apprehension and punishment are what create perceptions of low certainty of punishment. Panel studies, in which perceptions of certainty and severity are measured months or years before respondents are asked to report on their criminal and deviant behavior, have found very little support for the deterrent effects of either certainty or severity.

Other scholars assert that the panel study design is a flawed way to measure risk perceptions since those perceptions are often situationally induced. Researchers such as Greg Pogarsky (2002) used vignettes to assess both a respondents' present perception of risk and their response to questions about what they would do in a detailed scenario involving the potential for crime. These studies have repeatedly found support for a deterrent effect of perceptions of risk on the likelihood of offending.

Some scholars have reconceptualized deterrence theory to include informal sanctions such as social stigma, job loss, or moral condemnation. Some CRIMINOLOGISTS have suggested that these informal sanctions have a greater effect than formal legal sanctions in deterring some crime, such as drunk driving (Pogarsky, 2002). These reconceptualizations can blur the line between deterrence theory and rational choice theory. They are distinct, however, in that traditional deterrence theory is concerned primarily with costs, while rational choice theory is concerned with both costs and benefits.

The current consensus among criminologists is that there is a significant deterrent effect of the certainty of sanctions and a weaker effect of severity (Nagin, 1998). Swiftness, which has not been as widely studied, is generally found to have little or no deterrent effect. Regardless of the criminological research, there is widespread acceptance among criminal justice policy makers, politicians, and the general public of deterrence theory. This is in part because the policy implications are simple and comport with notions of "just deserts"—in order to reduce crime, the state needs to increase the likelihood of apprehension (more police) and the length of sentences (mandatory minimums, three strikes, etc.). It remains to be demonstrated, however, that such criminal justice policies are directly related to what criminologists have identified as perhaps the most important aspect of deterrence: perceptions of certainty or severity.

Furthermore, some crimes may be more easily deterred than others. Instrumental or goal-oriented crime (such as THEFT) are probably better deterred by legal sanctions than is VIOLENT CRIME. There is a significant body of research demonstrating that the ultimate sanction—the death penalty—has no significant effect on MURDER rates (Paternoster, Brame, and Bacon, 2007).

For more information

Beccaria, Cesare. *An Essay on Crimes and Punishments.* 1775. Boston: Branden, 1992.

Bentham, Jeremy. *An Introduction to the Principles of Morals and Legislation.* 1781. Kitchener, Ont.: Batoche Books, 2000.

Gibbs, J. P. "Crime, Punishment, and Deterrence," *Social Science Quarterly* 48 (1968): 515–530.

Kleck, Gary, Brion Sever, Spencer Li, and Marc Gertz. "The Missing Link in General Deterrence Research." *Criminology* 43 (2005): 623–660.

Nagin, Daniel. "Criminal Deterrence Research at the Outset of the Twenty-first Century." In *Crime and Justice: A Review of Research,* edited by Michael Tonry, 51–92. Chicago: University of Chicago Press, 1998.

Paternoster, Raymond, Robert Brame, and Sarah Bacon. *The Death Penalty: America's Experience with Capital Punishment.* New York: Oxford University Press, 2007.

Paternoster, Raymond. "The Deterrent Effect of the Perceived Certainty and Severity of Punishment: A Review of the Evidence and Issues," *Justice Quarterly* 4 (1987): 173–217.

Pogarsky, Greg. "Identifying 'Deterrable' Offenders: Implications for Research on Deterrence. *Justice Quarterly* 19 (2002): 431–452.

Sherman, Lawrence W. "Police Crackdowns: Initial and Residual Deterrence." In *Crime and Justice: A Review of Research,* edited by Michael Tonry, 10–39. Chicago: University of Chicago Press, 1999.

Stafford, Mark, and Mark Warr. "A Reconceptualization of General and Specific Deterrence," *Journal of Research in Crime and Delinquency* 30 (1993): 123–135.

Tittle, Charles. "Crime Rates and Legal Sanctions," *Social Problems* 16 (1969): 409–423.

Waldo, Gordon, and Theodore Chiricos. "Perceived Penal Sanction and Self-Reported Criminality: A Neglected Approach to Deterrence Research." *Social Problems* 19 (1972): 522–540.

David I. Hull
St. Anselm College

Diallo, Amadou (1975–1999) police brutality victim Amadou Diallo was a New York City immigrant shot and killed by police officers in that city in 1999. His killing was controversial, raising serious questions about POLICE BRUTALITY, racism, and excessive use of force.

In the early morning hours of February 4, 1999, Amadou Diallo, an unarmed 23-year-old legal immigrant street peddler from Guinea, was killed in a hail of 41 bullets in front of his home in the Bronx, New York, by four white plainclothes New York City police officers of the Street Crimes Unit. Allegedly believing a wallet Diallou was displaying to be a weapon, the officers' bullets hit the man 19 times.

In the subsequent public outrage at the event, the Street Crimes Unit was eventually disbanded, the four officers were indicted, and the events of that evening were sensationally represented in the press throughout the world as indicative of police brutality and RACIAL PROFILING.

At the time of his death, Diallo was in the United States on a student visa and had applied to the immigration authorities for a change in status to that of asylee. He was standing in front of the building where he lived when a police unit was cruising the area in an unmarked vehicle, purportedly seeking a serial rapist in the area. Believing Diallo to match the description of the person they sought, the officers exited their vehicle and approached him.

He fled to the outside steps of his apartment building.

The police claimed that they identified themselves and asked him to stop and show his hands. One of the officers shouted "gun" as Diallo moved his hand from his jacket pocket, and all the officers opened fire. One of the officers tripped on the steps, and the others claimed to believe he had been shot.

The officers' trial on MURDER and reckless endangerment charges was moved to Albany, New York, because of excessive pretrial publicity in New York City. A year after the events of February 1999, after two days of JURY deliberations, the four officers were ACQUITTED of all charges on February 25, 2000. In the aftermath of the event, as well as after the change of venue and the verdict, demonstrations were held at Police Plaza in New York City, and many well-known respected citizens were among those ARRESTED during the protests. The charges against all of them were ultimately dropped.

A large civil settlement was reached with Diallo's family. In 2003, Amadou Diallo's mother, Kadiatou, published a memoir.

For more information

Diallo, Kadiatou. *My Heart Will Cross This Ocean: My Story, My Son, Amadou.* New York: Ballatine, 2004.

Rokki Knee Carr
Attorney, Stone Ridge, New York

Dickerson v. United States 530 U.S. 428 (2000) In *Dickerson v. United States,* the U.S. Supreme Court addressed a fundamental issue raised by the landmark decision *MIRANDA V. ARIZONA,* 384 U.S. 436 (1966): Can legislatures, including Congress, waive the requirement that police provide a *Miranda* warning to suspects before interrogating them in custody? The Court answered no.

The Fifth Amendment's right against SELF-INCRIMINATION, among other things, prohibits the police from interrogating a person against his or her will. Involuntarily obtained statements are generally inadmissible at trial. Prior to *Miranda v. Arizona,* the Supreme Court used a general "voluntariness test" to determine the constitutionality of a CUSTODIAL INTERROGATION: Given the totality of the circumstances, was the defendant's statement obtained voluntarily?

In 1966, the Court in *Miranda* held that the voluntariness test alone did not sufficiently protect a suspect's right against self-incrimination. The Court reasoned that being in police custody is inherently coercive; custodial interrogations, therefore, are presumptively unconstitutional. This inherent coerciveness, however, is counterbalanced if the suspect is informed of his or her constitutional rights before being questioned. If the suspect understands and voluntarily waives those rights, the interrogation can go forward.

In instituting a preinterrogation warning requirement, the Court suggested a standard statement the police could use, now commonly known as the *Miranda* warning. The Court noted, however, that this specific statement did not have to be used. In fact, Congress and state governments have the authority to create alternative procedural requirements governing custodial interrogation so long as they are equally protective of a suspect's right against self-incrimination. This is the part of the *Miranda* decision that gave rise to the *Dickerson* case.

In 1968, the federal government enacted 18 U.S.C. §3501. Under §3501, federal trial JUDGES may admit a statement obtained from interrogation if given voluntarily, even in the absence of a preinterrogation warning. Section 3501 was largely ignored and fell into relative obscurity. Approximately 30 years later, Charles Thomas Dickerson, accused of several federal crimes, was interrogated by federal agents without being given the standard *Miranda* warning. He filed a motion to have his incriminating statements suppressed. A federal trial court judge granted Dickerson's motion, but the Fourth Circuit Court of Appeals reversed, holding under §3501 that

Dickerson's statements were admissible if "voluntary," despite the absence of a *Miranda* warning.

The issue at the heart of *Dickerson* is the nature of *Miranda*'s requirement of a preinterrogation warning. Does the Fifth Amendment specifically require that a preinterrogation warning of some type be given to suspects? Or is the preinterrogation warning one method, but not the only method, for enforcing the dictates of the Fifth Amendment? Could it be replaced with an alternative set of procedures by federal or state legislation? In a 7–2 decision, the Court held that *Miranda* intended, and the Fifth Amendment requires, that the police must issue a preinterrogation warning to suspects. Section 3501 is not, therefore, a constitutional substitution for procedures prescribed in *Miranda*.

The Court acknowledged that several post-*Miranda* decisions characterized the preinterrogation warning as being of a nonconstitutional nature, allowing for Congress to institute alternative methods to ensure the voluntary nature of custodial interrogations. Nevertheless, the Court reasoned, in practice the Supreme Court and other courts have treated the *Miranda* requirement of a preinterrogation warning as constitutional doctrine rather than an amendable policy of the FEDERAL COURT SYSTEM.

The Court held that, at a minimum, the CONSTITUTION requires that the police inform a suspect in custody that he or she has a right to remain silent; the police must also inform the suspect that the police will respect the suspect's constitutional rights. The police are not constitutionally required to use the specific wording of the warning famously suggested in the *Miranda* decision. Given that §3501 does not require any kind of warning or assurance before interrogation, the Court saw the legislation as an attempt to return to an inadequate, general, pre-*Miranda* voluntariness test.

The opinion of the Court asserted that, even if members of the Court might disagree with the *Miranda* decision the principle of STARE DECISIS required the Court to uphold *Miranda* presumptively. As one reason for upholding stare decisis in this case, the Court noted the embedded nature of the *Miranda* warnings in police procedure and popular culture.

For more information

Lafave, Wayne R. *Criminal Law.* St. Paul, Minn.: Thomson-West, 2003.

James Daniel Fisher
Edinboro University of Pennsylvania

Dillinger, John (1903–1934) bank robber John Dillinger, a bank robber of the 1930s, became Public Enemy Number One to the FEDERAL BUREAU OF INVESTIGATION (FBI). He was killed by FBI agents in 1934 in a famous shootout outside a movie theater. Dillinger became almost a folk hero during the Great Depression of the 1930s.

Born in Indiana on June 22, 1903, Dillinger struggled to find his place. After bouncing from job to job and going absent without leave from the navy, he spent nine years in prison for beating and robbing a grocer. Upon being PAROLED in May 1933, Dillinger went on a crime spree with the knowledge and friends that he had acquired while behind bars.

After botching a ROBBERY in Monticello, Indiana, Dillinger and his GANG successfully robbed at least five banks in Indiana and Ohio. The gang netted more than $50,000, much of which went for fine clothes, fast cars, and women. Dillinger also became a suspect in three other bank robberies before being arrested in September in Dayton, Ohio. Jailed in Lima, Ohio, Dillinger escaped when several of his friends killed the sheriff. To reequip themselves for more bank robberies, the Dillinger gang raided two police stations in Indiana to obtain machine guns and bulletproof vests. They stole $75,000 from a Greencastle, Indiana, bank before heading for Chicago.

By this time, Dillinger had become both a notorious outlaw and a folk hero. Bankers, who were widely blamed for the misery of the Great

Depression, had few friends among the general public. Dillinger, a handsome and charismatic man with a strong sense of humor, stole from the bad guys. While he never gave money to the poor, Dillinger had the image of an antihero just like Robin Hood. He also had some talents as a trickster. ARRESTED in Tucson, Arizona, in January 1934 for robbery and the killing of an East Chicago policeman, Dillinger was EXTRADITED to Indiana. He escaped from the Crown Point jail by whittling a toy gun out of wood, blackening it with shoe polish, then driving off in the sheriff's personal car.

Dillinger, who discussed his funeral arrangements with his father on a visit home, realized that his crime spree could have only one ending. After several more robberies and shootouts, Dillinger returned to Chicago. Betrayed by an acquaintance, the famous "lady in red," Dillinger was shot to death by FBI agents while leaving the Biograph Theater on July 22, 1934.

For more information

Gorn, Elliott J. *Dillinger's Wild Ride: The Year That Made America's Public Enemy Number One*. New York: Oxford University Press, 2009.

Caryn E. Neumann
Miami University of Ohio

diplomatic immunity Diplomatic immunity refers to a general privilege of foreign officials such as ambassadors to be free from prosecution for criminal and civil law violations while in the United States.

Diplomats, such as ambassadors, counsels, ministers, or envoys are the official representatives of foreign governments. They are granted privileged protections from ASSAULTS, harassments, threats, or indignities, including insults. They are also, with few exceptions, exempt from prosecution for violations of criminal law or from civil suits.

The basic aim of diplomatic immunity is to facilitate international relations. It also serves as a mutual protection for the diplomatic personnel because harsh treatment by a host country may be reciprocated in response.

Diplomatic immunity almost always extends to the spouses and children of diplomatic personnel as well as to those who work at the embassy. However, there are levels of immunity. Those who work at lower-level embassy job may have immunity limited to actions connected with their jobs. The amount of immunity granted is usually associated with the amount that is needed for performing their duties.

If a person protected by diplomatic immunity is ARRESTED, SUBPOENAED, or charged with a crime, his or her country can file a diplomatic protest. This is usually sufficient to block legal action. Diplomatic immunity is not a license to abuse the laws of the host country. Compliance with local laws is expected of diplomatic personnel; however, diplomats assigned to the United Nations or posted in Washington, D.C., have been notorious for violating parking ordinances and other traffic regulations. Some diplomatic missions have failed to pay rents on offices or residences. They cannot be evicted because the Foreign Sovereign Immunities Act (1976) forbids attachments or execution of civil judgments. CIVIL ACTIONS such as DIVORCE can usually proceed only with the permission of the diplomat's government.

American law enforcement officials are encouraged to thoroughly investigate serious crimes committed by those protected by diplomatic immunity. It is not unusual for the State Department to declare them persona non grata, to enter their names in the National Crime Information Center (NCIC), and to issue a warrant for their arrest if they should return.

The current international agreement on diplomatic immunity is the Vienna Convention of Diplomatic Relations, adopted on April 8, 1961, at the United Nations Conference on Diplomatic Intercourse and Immunities (March 2 to April 14). The convention was modified by an extension, the Vienna Convention on the Law of

Treaties between States and International Organizations or between International Organizations (VCLTIO) on March 21, 1986.

Diplomatic immunity in the United States is codified in the Diplomatic Relations Act of 1978 (22 U. S. C. A. § 254). The act replaced the diplomatic immunity law adopted in 1790. American practice is to be generous with diplomatic immunity in order to protect American diplomats abroad where rights are less respected.

For more information

Alebeek, Rosanne Van. *The Immunities of States and Their Officials in International Criminal Law.* New York: Oxford University Press, 2008.

Baker, J. Craig. *Immunities from Jurisdiction in International Law.* New York: Oxford University Press, 2009.

Frey, Linda S., and Marsha L. Frey. *The History of Diplomatic Immunity.* Columbus: Ohio State University Press, 1999.

Andrew J. Waskey
Dalton State College

discretion Discretion is the professional judgment used by criminal justice authorities to choose a course of action, or not to act at all, based on the particular circumstances of the situation. It is one of the most necessary, yet controversial, concepts in the lexicon of law.

JUDGES have broad discretion to dismiss a case, grant or deny motions, sign warrants, and sentence criminals. SENTENCING GUIDELINES, which set a minimum and maximum sentence for each crime, grant judges the power to use their judgment to decide the appropriate penalty for each case. However, many conservatives believe that judges issue lighter sentences than warranted by the crime committed. Consequently, many states have passed mandatory sentencing laws which require a uniform sentence for all who are convicted of a particular crime.

PROSECUTORS are granted wide discretionary latitude to decide what charges to file against the accused. They may decide not to prosecute, known as *nolle prosequi,* even where there is sufficient EVIDENCE against the accused to proceed. Or, the prosecutor might use his discretionary power to drop the case after the accused has been formally charged. They can also decide whether or not to PLEA BARGAIN with a suspect, or which members of a crime ring ARRESTED for the same crime will be offered a plea bargain. Prosecutors may not file charges for any number of reasons, including insufficient evidence, reluctant witnesses, and violations of the accused's DUE PROCESS rights. Some have criticized the failure of DISTRICT ATTORNEYS to prosecute more cases, but legislative efforts to reign in prosecutorial discretion have been largely unsuccessful.

Though the law formally grants discretionary power to judges and prosecutors, it expects the police to fully enforce all criminal laws. However, the reality of police work in a free society makes this impractical; officers learn to use their judgment to selectively enforce the laws based on the circumstances of each case. An officer on the beat might find it wiser to disperse a group of unruly teenagers with a warning than to book them on disorderly conduct charges.

Properly utilized, discretion is the power of judges, prosecutors, and the police to make decisions that depart from the letter of the law in situations where the uniform application of the law would not produce a just result. However, discretion can be used in improper ways, including corruption and discrimination. While police routinely develop profiles of certain types of criminals based on the concept of reasonable suspicion, the use of RACIAL PROFILING is an abuse of this power. Recent revelations that the New Jersey State Police routinely stopped black motorists on the New Jersey Turnpike based on the color of their skin is a prime example of how the abuse of police discretion can demoralize its victims and foment distrust of the police and the law.

For more information

Hawkins, Keith, ed. *The Uses of Discretion.* New York: Oxford University Press, 1992.

Ohlin, Lloyd E., and Frank J. Remington. *Discretion in Criminal Justice: The Tension between Individualization and Uniformity.* Albany: State University of New York Press, 1993.

Vernon Mogensen
Kingsborough Community College, CUNY

district attorney The district attorney is the elected or appointed official responsible for conducting criminal proceedings against an accused person. Whether called "district attorney," "state's attorney," "chief PROSECUTOR," "commonwealth attorney," "county attorney," or "solicitor," this person prosecutes criminal cases and defends the state or local bodies in suits brought against them.

The prosecutor has a wide range of choices in the handling of criminal defendants, the scheduling of cases for trials, the acceptance of PLEA BARGAINS, etc. In states with the GRAND JURY system, the prosecutors are responsible for bringing EVIDENCE before that body. (In states where grand juries are not used, the district attorney brings charges in the form of an "information" or "presentment.") Courts have obligated the prosecutors to share evidence with the defense. (The goal is JUSTICE, not victory by whatever means. A special power of the prosecutor is to ask the court to dismiss a case if there is insufficient evidence to secure a conviction. Yet a successful record as a prosecutor could lead to high political office or to a judgeship. Thus there is a desire to make a record.)

In all but five states, the district attorneys are elected (generally for four-year terms with the possibility of reelection). Usually, like sheriffs, they are selected in partisan elections (though a case can be made for their being nonpartisan). In three states (Alaska, Delaware, and Rhode Island) there are no local prosecutors; responsibility is centralized at the state level.

Each of the 94 judicial districts of the United States is headed by a U.S. attorney, appointed by the president for a four-year term. It is customary for the U.S. attorneys to resign if the opposition party wins the White House. Ramsey Clark proposed selecting U.S. attorneys from the ranks of career civil servants; this would have insulated them from political pressures and would develop nationally uniform standards of prosecution. (Though nominated by the president, the prerogative of selecting them has largely shifted to the senators in the state where they are to serve, from the same political party as the president.) They prosecute federal crimes in FEDERAL COURTS.

For more information

Eisenstein, James. *Counsel for the United States: U.S. Attorneys in the Political and Legal Systems.* Baltimore: Johns Hopkins University Press, 1978.

Jacoby, Joan E. *The American Prosecutor: A Search for Identity.* Lexington, Mass.: Lexington Books, 1980.

Stewart, James B. *The Prosecutors: Inside the Offices of the Government's Most Powerful Lawyers.* New York: Simon and Schuster, 1987.

Martin Gruberg
University of Wisconsin at Oshkosh

District of Columbia v. Heller 554 U.S. 570–(2008) In *District of Columbia v. Heller,* the Supreme Court ruled in a 5–4 decision that the District of Columbia's law forbidding possession of a usable handgun in one's home was a violation of the Second Amendment, as was the law's provision that any legal firearm in the home must be either disassembled or be put in an inoperable condition by use of a trigger lock. The case was significant because, unlike other parts of the BILL OF RIGHTS, the Second Amendment has received scant attention historically from the Court despite several opportunities to define its meaning and scope.

The majority opinion was written by Justice ANTONIN SCALIA, who painstakingly analyzed the wording of the Second Amendment ("A well-regulated militia, being necessary to the security of a free state, the right of the people to keep and bear arms, shall not be infringed."), focusing on the relation between the prefatory clause about the militia and the operative clause about the right to keep and bear arms. He concluded that the reference to a militia in the prefatory clause did not restrict the right in the operative clause to a military-related right only; nor did the phrase "keep and bear," which he defined as possessing and using but not necessarily in a military context. Rather, it was a guarantee of an "individual right to possess and carry weapons in case of confrontation." If the phrase meant serving as a soldier it would have included "against . . ." with the name of the enemy. Moreover, this was a preexisting right that was merely being codified by the Second Amendment. Scalia based this conclusion on English history and contrasted the wording to Article I of the CONSTITUTION as evidence that the militia was preexisting, unlike the army that Congress was empowered to create. While the prefatory clause suggested that the reason for including the Second Amendment was to protect against elimination of the militia by a tyrannical government, this did not mean, according to Scalia, that it was the only reason for the right to bear arms. The other major reason was the right of SELF-DEFENSE—the "first law of nature." Therefore, the D.C. law was rendered unconstitutional by the fact that handguns were the weapon of choice for self-defense and on the basis that the home is where the need for self-defense is greatest

Justice JOHN PAUL STEVENS and Justice STEPHEN BREYER both wrote dissenting opinion, in which all of the other dissenters joined. Justice Stevens chose to dwell on the militia-related nature of the amendment, and he found no evidence that the authors of the Bill of Rights had intended to include the common law right of self-defense in it. Examining the amendment's drafting history, he found that several efforts to expand the Second Amendment rights had been rejected. In his exegesis of the amendment's language, he concluded that to "bear arms" meant to serve as a soldier and that "to keep and bear" was one concept, not two. Moreover, this was consistent with the framers' concern with military power and reflected two potentially contradictory themes emerging from debates on the Constitution—fears about a national standing army and worry about an ill-trained militia. Finally he pointed to PRECEDENT, particularly the sawed-off shotgun case, *U.S. v. Miller,* 307 U.S. 174 ((1939), in which a unanimous Court found the Second Amendment's purpose clearly to be protecting militias.

Justice Breyer argued that even if the Second Amendment protected more than militias, its protections were no more absolute than those of the First Amendment, and he thought the District's carefully tailored gun restrictions were therefore legitimate and that "a self-defense assumption is the *beginning,* rather than the *end,* of any constitutional inquiry." To him, such an inquiry pointed to an "interest-balancing" approach between competing public interests.

In vigorously attacking the dissenting arguments of Justice Stevens, Scalia took his ammunition from English history, early commentaries on the Second Amendment, and the few prior gun-related cases. Likewise, he rejected Breyer's "balancing of interests" guideline as not even being an available option for government because the Second Amendment had foreclosed it. However, he agreed that the Second Amendment's operative phrase was not absolute and that the problems of gun-related violence could be addressed in other ways that would pass muster under the Second Amendment.

The case attracted many AMICUS CURIAE BRIEFS on both sides. Briefs for Heller ranged from predictable conservative groups, including the National Rifle Association and the Eagle Forum to the less well known such as the Pink Pistols and Gays and Lesbians for Individual Liberty, and Jews for the Preservation of Firearms. Among predictable supporters of the District were the Brady Center to Prevent Gun Violence, and the NAACP Legal Defense and Educational

Fund. Among the less familiar were the American Association of Suicidology and the Society of Adolescent Medicine. Law enforcement organizations were found on both sides as were members of Congress.

As Scalia himself acknowledged, this case did not resolve all Second Amendment issues, and several other cases were already in the pipeline, testing, among other matters, what weapons could claim Second Amendment protection and whether the Second Amendment now applied to the states—a matter not addressed since the District of Columbia is not a state. However, in a subsequent case, *McDonald v. City of Chicago*, 561 U.S. _ (2010), the Supreme Court did rule that the Second Amendment was INCORPORATED through the Fourteenth Amendment's DUE PROCESS clause to apply to the states, and therefore the city's law banning the possession of handguns was unconstitutional.

For more information

Spitzer, Robert J. *The Politics of Gun Control*. 4th ed. Washington, D.C.: CQ Press, 2008.

Tushnet, Mark V. *Out of Range: Why the Constitution Can't End the Battle over Guns*. New York: Oxford University Press, 2007.

Jane G. Rainey
Eastern Kentucky University

divorce Divorce is the legal dissolving of a marriage by a court of law.

Divorce was unavailable under the JURISDICTION of English courts prior to the reign of King Henry VII, and while parliamentary divorces during the latter 17th century did exist, they were very rare. By the early 20th century, however, all U.S. states (except South Carolina, which did not permit permanent divorce until 1948) had enacted laws authorizing courts to dissolve marriages for justifiable legal grounds; these grounds usually included adultery, cruelty, desertion, incurable insanity, or voluntary separation for a period of time.

But it was relatively easy to subvert these state requirements, at least for those with sufficient means. Couples who wished to divorce could establish temporary domicile in a more permissive jurisdiction or stage a courtroom charade to fit one of the justifiable legal grounds for divorce. For those without sufficient resources to stage productions in courts, informal separation was the only alternative. Divorce policy in almost all Western countries was either completely revised or substantially reformed after 1960. In the United States, California adopted the first divorce code in 1969 that dispensed entirely with fault-based divorce; it recognized circumstances for divorce where no fault, responsibility, or offense was attributed by law to either spouse.

There had been examples of no-fault provisions in former divorce codes (e.g., divorce by mutual agreement or reasons of incompatibility, insanity, impotence, and unavoidable absence), yet these grounds for divorce did place responsibility on one of the spouses, even if fault was not actually attributed. No-fault divorce codes are different; fault is not attributed to either spouse, and it does not require one of the spouses to be considered innocent and the other guilty. Simply, it recognizes the permanent breakdown of the marriage. Every state has now instituted no-fault procedures based on an irreparable breakdown of the marriage or on some other no-fault criterion, such as separation for a relatively short interval.

No-fault divorce does not rest on the precise circumstances that produced the breakdown of the marriage but simply on the fact of the breakdown. Most laws specify a period during which a couple must have lived separately and the marriage has ceased to have practical meaning; thus, most of the onus of defining the breakdown is given to the spouses themselves and not the courts. This is a profound change in divorce law because it overcomes the centuries-long principle that divorce must be closely regulated by the church or state. Additionally, other changes have followed; alimony has now been severely limited. Spousal maintenance generally is avoided entirely or limited to only brief rehabilitative periods. In theory, equality between the parties can be more easily accomplished through distribution of existing assets rather than future income. Today, only about a sixth of all divorcing women have received maintenance, and two-thirds of the awards have been for limited duration, averaging about two years.

Today, about half of all contemporary marriages will end in divorce, and 60 percent of all children will spend time in single-parent homes.

For more information

Phillips, Roderick. *Putting Asunder: A History of Divorce in Western Society.* New York: Cambridge University Press, 1988.

Rhode, Deborah L. *Justice and Gender: Sex Discrimination and the Law.* New York: Cambridge University Press, 1989.

Ashlyn K. Kuersten
Western Michigan University

DNA evidence DNA is the unique genetic code that makes up each individual. DNA is increasingly being used in law enforcement as evidence to identify and solve crimes and to identify criminals. Over the last two decades deoxyribonucleic acid (DNA) has played an ever-increasing role in the CRIMINAL JUSTICE SYSTEM and in the media, either through TV shows such as *CSI,* or in criminal proceedings themselves, often leading to the wrongfully convicted being exonerated (i.e. an exclusion). At the time of writing, there have been more than 200 people exonerated via DNA evidence.

DNA is present in all human cells, and if bodily secretions are present at a CRIME SCENE (e.g. semen, blood, hair [with skin tags], and saliva), this DNA can be treated in crime labs in order to obtain a DNA profile of a possible perpetrator. This evidence, as stated above, has been used to exculpate an innocent person but can also be used to show that the particular defendant charged was indeed the guilty party (i.e., an inclusion). Common sources of DNA from crime scenes can include blunt force weapons (blood), masks in which an individual has sweated in or left hair, cigarette butt leaving saliva, semen in the victim's vagina in a rape case or, also in the case of rape, semen left in a condom; bed sheets may also yield hair, blood, or semen depending upon the type and nature of the crime.

DNA is found in human chromosomes and is, except in the case of identical twins, a very good indicator of the mathematical chances of the supplier of the DNA at any given crime scene. It is found in, and is the primary component of, human chromosomes of which there are usually 23 pairs in the human cell. It is found in either the cell nuclei or in mitochondria, the cells "engines."

To extract DNA from a sample to produce a profile, there are three main techniques that can be used: Polymerase chain reaction (PCR), restriction fragment length polymorphisms (RFLPs), and short tandem repeats (STRs). In addition, the DNA found in the cells mitochondria (mtDNA) can also be obtained; however, this has the limitation of only being inherited from the mother, and so all offspring from a given female will have the same mtDNA profile. The advantage of mtDNA is that less of a sample of fluid or tissue is needed to create a profile as there tends to be more of such DNA in any given evidentiary sample. PCR copies a section of DNA when it is outside the cell itself and leads to several million of such copies. In RFLPs are "cut out" sections of DNA using what is known as a restriction enzyme; commonly about 30 of these sections are needed to make a profile as these sections are then multiplied several thousand times. However, perhaps the most modern and reliable method of obtaining DNA is by using the STR method. In this method, small areas on the chromosomes, known as loci, are seen to repeat themselves along the chromosome. According to Saferstein (2010), these STRs are about five "base-pairs" long and, therefore, each STR need only be around 400 bases in length. As these replicated strands are much shorter than those produced in RFLP, it is much easier to store them as evidence without their being adulterated over time. When the profile is needed, these STRs can be replicated using the PCR method. Not only is the STR method easier from both a practical and evidentiary standpoint, but less DNA material is needed to be recovered from a crime scene, where the amount of such material may well be scarce.

Some estimates posit that less than 100th of the biological material is needed for an STR processing method as opposed to RFLP. Finally, mtDNA, as stated above, is only heritable from the mother of the DNA donor. This has been found especially helpful in older cases when this method, which requires very little DNA evidence at all, was not available. Another advantage of DNA in "cold cases" is that once DNA evidence is gathered, the DNA profile is entered into a system known as the Combined DNA Index System (CODIS). This can be used to match a particular suspect to a particular crime; or, it may lead law enforcement to suspect an individual who, prior to the discovery of the evidence, was not even a suspect in the crime. Further, DNA can be used for the identification of human remains.

One of the most high-profile examples of the use of DNA evidence in a criminal proceeding was found in the 1994 MURDER trial of O.J. SIMPSON, who was charged with the murder of his wife, from whom he was separated, and her friend Ronald Goldman. Both of the victims had been viciously attacked with a knife and, the police theorized, that Simpson had cut his hand on the knife during the attack, leaving a trail of his own blood leading away from the murder scene to his house. Further, blood that matched both victims was found in Simpson's car, and the famous glove found at the Simpson residence also had blood on it, which matched the DNA profile of Nicole Brown-Simpson and Goldman. On its face, it would appear that this would be enough to convict O.J. Simpson for the double homicide; however, due to prosecution's poor record keeping and the defense's accusations of evidence tampering by the police department led to enough REASONABLE DOUBT to cause the JURY to return a not-guilty verdict in the case.

When crime scene units are processing a scene and suspect that biological evidence may be present, it is vital that such items of evidence are placed in a paper bag and not a plastic bag. This is due to the moisture, or sweating, of the evidence in a plastic bag, leading to the possible degradation of the evidence. Further, DNA can be affected by warmth or sunlight, and so while the scene is being processed, care must be taken to avoid leaving the evidence in the sun or in a hot squad car, for example. The environment of the evidence, as well as the chain of custody, must be meticulously documented in order to avoid the DEFENSE ATTORNEY bringing into question the integrity of the evidence itself. In many chain of custody cases the JUDGE has excluded such evidence for poor record keeping, and so the state's DISTRICT ATTORNEY must have robust systems in place to avoid such problems.

Finally, it should be noted that DNA is not a panacea for the criminal justice system. There have been cases of poor evidence-keeping facilities with leaking roofs and incorrect temperatures (e.g., the Houston Crime Lab) and individual examiners who have been found unprofessional at best, fraudulently at worst, such as Fred Zain of West Virginia and Joyce Gilchrist of Oklahoma.

For more information

Saferstein, R. *Criminalistics: An Introduction to Forensic Science*. Upper Saddle River, N.J.: Person Prentice Hall, 2007. Available online. URL: http://www.howstuffworks.com/genetic-science/dna-evidence.htm.

Gavin Lee
University of California at Irvine

DNA testing DNA testing has revolutionized the fields of law enforcement and criminal justice due to its ability to link a suspect's DNA with DNA CRIME SCENE EVIDENCE by matching "genetic markers." A genetic marker is a segment of DNA that can vary between people. The human DNA (*d*eoxyribo*n*ucleic *a*cid) molecule is a person's "genetic blueprint" and is composed of more than three billion base pairs. Approximately 99.9 percent of the base pair sequences is identical in all humans. The remaining 0.1 percent of DNA consists of many different repetitive base pair sequences varying in length from individual to individual that can be used as genetic markers. If enough genetic markers are tested, the probability of two people (excluding identical twins) having the same combination is infinitesimally small because of the great amount of variation in the genetic markers.

There are two major DNA testing technologies: restriction fragment length polymorphism (RFLP) and polymerase chain reaction (PCR). Both RFLP and PCR technologies are based on recognition of repetitive base pair sequences, but there are differences between the two technologies. RFLP typing, the older technology, identifies extremely long stretches of DNA segments called variable number tandem repeats (VNTR). The disadvantages of RFLP technology are that relatively large amounts of DNA are needed and the DNA cannot be degraded. PCR technology, which makes many copies of the DNA in a crime scene sample, can handle small (as small as the head of a pin) or degraded biological samples. PCR typing recognizes small stretches of repetitive DNA sequences known as short tandem repeats (STRs) that are too short for RFLP analysis. Geneticists estimate there are more than 30,000 STR regions, which makes PCR STR technology a powerful forensic tool. Statistical estimates suggest that typing information from 12 different STR markers allows unique identification of an individual. PCR technology also is used to type mitochondrial (as opposed to the more common nuclear) DNA. DNA testing is usually done on body fluids (for example, blood, semen, or saliva), but mitochondrial DNA (mtDNA) typing also can be performed on bone fragments, tooth, hair, and other biological trace evidence.

In 1986 Dr. Alec Jeffries of England pioneered the use of genetic markers in law enforcement when he first excluded a suspect in a case of rape and MURDER and later identified the perpetrator through DNA testing. Identification through matching of DNA sequences has been admitted as evidence in U.S. courts since 1989. The United States is currently building a nationwide DNA marker database called CODIS, *CO*mbined *D*NA *I*ndex *S*ystem. CODIS can link serial VIOLENT CRIMES that may have occurred in different JURISDICTIONS and can identify suspects by matching DNA EVIDENCE left at crime scenes to convicted offenders whose DNA markers are already in the database. An unforeseen consequence of DNA testing is that closed criminal cases are being reopened because post-conviction DNA testing has exonerated defendants wrongfully convicted and already serving a sentence. For example, the Innocence Project has been used to acquit approximately 200 individuals convicted for murder and sentenced to be executed based on DNA evidence.

Concerns about privacy rights and fear that DNA testing may be used to screen insurance applicants and discriminate against employees who have certain DNA traits has led to the passage of state and federal legislation regarding its use. In 2008, President George W. Bush signed the Genetic Information Nondiscrimination Act, which would preclude discrimination by employers and insurance companies based on specific DNA information of individuals.

For more information

Inman, Keith, and Norah Rudin. *An Introduction to Forensic DNA Analysis*. Boca Raton, Fla.: CRC Press, 1997.

Coleman, Howard, and Eric Swenson. *DNA in the Courtroom: A Trial Watcher's Guide*. Seattle, Wash.: Genelex Corporation, 1994.

Convicted by Juries, Exonerated by Science: Case Studies in the Use of DNA Evidence to Establish Innocence after Trial. Washington, D.C.: National Institute of Justice, U.S. Department of Justice, 1996.

Genetics Privacy and Legislation. Available online. URL: http://www.ornl.gov/sci/techresources/Human_Genome/elsi/legislat.shtml.

Karen Gottlieb
BioLaw
Nederland, Colorado

domestic abuse Domestic abuse, commonly known as DOMESTIC VIOLENCE or FAMILY violence, is the abuse of a current or former spouse, intimate partner, child, or elder. Typically, it refers to abuse of a spouse or intimate partner, as the other types are more commonly known as CHILD ABUSE and elder abuse. The abuse can be physical, sexual, verbal, emotional, mental, or financial, and often involves a combination of these. A common pattern develops whereby a person is deprived of basic rights, isolated from friends, family, and work, intimidated, coerced, with daily life controlled. This type of abuse is usually systematic and repeated, and various methods are used to control the victim. Typical domestic abuse situations involve what is called a cycle of violence, where tension in the relationship builds up and the victim attempts to appease the abuser, then a violent explosion occurs when the abuser lashes out at the victim, followed by a honeymoon period, during which the abuser apologizes and claims he will reform. The cycle then repeats itself.

There is no general consensus on the causes of domestic violence. Some attribute the phenomenon to individual relationship characteristics and dysfunction, including issues such as alcohol and drug use, inability to handle stress, and personality traits. Others point to society at large as instituting and perpetuating a patriarchal system whereby masculinity is linked with aggressiveness, violence, and lingering notions of domination of women.

Domestic abuse is commonly thought of as having a male perpetrator and female victim. While female-to-male violence and same-sex relationship violence does occur, studies show that the common perception is largely accurate. According to Coltrane and Adams, women are seven to 14 times more likely to be abused by their partners than are men, and three-quarters of all reported family violence involves female victims. Victims with injuries are even more likely to be women. The prevalence of domestic abuse in the United States is difficult to determine since it ranks among the most unreported crimes; statistics are therefore not always accurate. However, recent studies show that women experience 5.3 million violent episodes every year, resulting in 2 million injuries. An estimated one in four women are abused by a partner at some point in their lives.

The consequences of domestic abuse are significant for the victims, their children, families, and society, including an estimated $5.8 billion per year in medical expenses and lost productivity, according to Coltrane. The effects of abuse are both short- and long-term and include physical injury, damage to mental health, financial harm, child behavioral problems, and death. Children witnessing abuse are also more likely to become victims and abusers themselves. Victims faced with abuse sometimes turn to coping mechanisms such as alcohol, drugs, and eating disorders.

Laws regarding domestic abuse experienced significant change in the 20th century. Historically, domestic abuse was not a crime. Under the common law doctrine of coverture, women belonged to their husbands, who were permitted to treat their wives however they wished. There also existed a belief that the family was private in nature and the state should not interfere in its dealings. In 1824, for example, the Mississippi Supreme Court held that a husband had the legal right to physically "chastise" his wife, though the beatings were supposed to be "reasonable." *Bradley v. State,* 1 Miss 156 (1824). A common standard known as the "rule of thumb" held that a man was permitted to beat his wife as long as he used a rod no thicker than his thumb. A wife's only recourse to spousal abuse was to file for

DIVORCE, but the abuse had to be severe, repeated, and clearly proven before she could qualify. Usually life-threatening abuse was required.

Domestic abuse did not become a matter of social awareness until the 1970s, when it began to be recognized as a public concern. The first battered women's shelters began to open at that time. Even when laws were modernized and victims were awarded protection (RESTRAINING ORDERS), however, enforcement remained a problem, as police and PROSECUTORS often simply ignored the issue. The official law enforcement approach was typically one of crisis intervention rather than ARREST and prosecution.

Currently, every state considers domestic abuse a crime and allows the victim to file for a civil protection order. Ensuring compliance with these laws and effective prosecution of violations is a continuing concern. New developments in state laws include mandatory arrest and prosecution (taking away police and prosecutorial discretion), criminal no-contact orders, and requiring health-care providers to report domestic violence. Most states now also allow a spouse to bring a TORT action against the other for harm suffered as a result of abuse. Other resources include counseling and batterer treatment programs, although they have questionable results in terms of preventing future violence. Many experts suggest that more needs to be done to eliminate patriarchal values that increase the incidence of domestic abuse.

For more information

Coltrane, Scott, and Michelle Adams. *Gender and Families*. Lanham, Md.: Rowman and Littlefield, 2008.

Morao, Karen. "Domestic Violence and the State," *Georgetown Journal of Gender and the Law* 7 (2006): 787.

Stark, Evan. *Coercive Control: The Entrapment of Women in Personal Life*. New York: Oxford University Press, 2007.

Deborah Anthony
University of Illinois at Springfield

domestic partnership law Domestic partnership law regulates the rights and responsibilities of an unmarried couple who live together in a committed, exclusive relationship and who are financially interdependent. Much, but not all, domestic partnership law applies to same-sex couples only.

Many public and private employers offer fringe benefits to the domestic partners of their employees. Federal law treats the most popular of those benefits—such as medical and dental insurance, moving expense reimbursement, and leave time for bereavement and illness of a partner—differently from spousal benefits. Under the COBRA program, which allows employees to continue medical insurance at their own expense after leaving a company, spousal coverage can be continued; domestic partnership coverage cannot. The FAMILY AND MEDICAL LEAVE ACT of 1993 allows employees to take up to 12 weeks of unpaid leave to care for ill relatives. Domestic partners are not considered relatives, so they are not covered by the act. The Internal Revenue Service counts the value of the medical, dental, and hospital insurance for an employee's domestic partner as part of the employee's income. It does not do so for an employee's spouse.

Many state statutes and local ordinances establish domestic partnership benefit programs for public employees. Some local governments—the city of San Francisco is one—require contractors doing business with the city to make domestic partner benefits available to their employees. The state of Vermont requires insurance companies doing business in the state to offer the same benefits to domestic partners that they do to spouses.

To be eligible for domestic partner benefits, the couple ordinarily files an affidavit stating that neither is already married, that both are of legal age, are not close blood relatives, share a close personal relationship, are jointly responsible for each other's emotional and financial welfare, live together, and plan to remain in the relationship indefinitely.

The most comprehensive form of domestic partnership is the civil union—a marriage in all but name. Parties to a civil union are subject to the entire body of domestic relations law, including DIVORCE, child custody and support, and property division on the dissolution of the union. The parties can adopt children. If either one has a natural child during the period in which the union is in effect, both parties are considered parents. Each can administer the other's estate. Each has the right to visit the other in a hospital and to make decisions about the other's care. A survivor can collect damages for the wrongful death of a partner. The parties are entitled to file joint state, but not federal, tax returns.

For more information

DeLeon, Richard. "San Francisco and Domestic Partners: New Fields of Battle in the Culture Wars." In *Culture Wars and Politics,* edited by Elaine B. Sharp. Lawrence: University Press of Kansas, 1999.

Rutherford, Elizabeth A. "Domestic Partner Benefits: Are You Doing It Right?" *Employee Relations Law Journal* 23 (Summer 1997): 125–32.

Wriggins, Jennifer. "Marriage Law and Family Law: Autonomy, Interdependence, and Couples of the Same Gender." *Boston College Law Review* 61 (March 2000): 265–325.

William H. Coogan
University of Southern Maine

domestic violence Domestic violence is violence that occurs within a FAMILY, quasi family, or intimate relationship. The victim or defendant may be family members by blood or marriage, married couples, former spouses with children, or cohabitants.

In the late 1970s sociologists and psychologists began to recognize and study this societal ailment. Traditionally, victims and perpetrators of domestic violence kept their problems behind closed doors and outsiders did not concern themselves with "the problems of other families." In the 1980s the societal outlook rapidly began to change and domestic violence was recognized as the public and private wrong that it is. This resulted in increased state and federal activism in the area of domestic violence by enacting new legislation or stringently enforcing existing statutes.

Domestic violence takes several forms. It includes physical abuse such as punching, choking, smacking, pushing, forced sexual acts, and using weapons. The violence can also be verbal or psychological. In such case, the perpetrator threatens to harm the victim or someone close to the victim, repeatedly insults, degrades, and attacks the self-esteem of the victim, tells confidential information, limits the victim's contact with others, controls and monitors the whereabouts of the victim, and/or injures pets and causes damage to other property of the victim. It is not uncommon for victims to simultaneously suffer several forms of abuse at the hands of the perpetrator.

Power and control are the objective of the abuser. When the abuser senses that the power and control are waning, the abuser resorts to the above forms of domestic violence to try to reinforce and reestablish control. Abusive relationships run a continuous and familiar cycle. It begins with a tension-building stage. At this time the batterer is frustrated and becomes increasingly jealous or irritable. The victim tries very hard to pacify the batterer, trying to anticipate the batterer's desires and needs and to avoid any agitation.

Stage two is an abusive incident. Violence is most severe at this point. The victim may make police or other outside contacts at this point. The third stage, often referred to as the "honeymoon stage," involves obsessive attempts by the batterer to reestablish the loving, intimate relationship. It often includes promises to discontinue the abusive behavior, promises to change, great remorse, and sometimes a willingness to attend counseling. The batterer will be extremely apologetic and might admit to having overreacted but usually blames some external stressor. Once the relationship is reestablished, the batterer may continue to exhibit intensely loving and nurturing behavior. At some point in time, the batterer will regress and the couple will return to stage one of the cycle.

Studies on the incidence of violence in homes estimate that at least 30 percent of all women will suffer from some form of violence in an adult relationship. For 10 percent of these women, the violence will be so severe that they worry for their personal safety and life. Police forces across North America report that 95 percent of the victims of domestic violence are women and children.

Victims may file a civil or criminal complaint or both to aid in obtaining relief from a batterer. The primary difference lies in the relief that is available to the victim. Either the victim or the police may file criminal warrants. The police will always prepare either an incident report or a police report. Depending on the nature and circumstances of the incident, the police will obtain a warrant for the ARREST of the batterer or will direct the victim to take a copy of the report and make application to the appropriate court for a warrant. The police will take the accused into custody upon execution of the warrant and perform the normal criminal processing (arrest, fingerprinting, presentation for initial BAIL hearing, ARRAIGNMENT, and finally trial). The end result of a criminal proceeding can be PROBATION, incarceration, or dismissal. The court may also, as part of the bail proceeding or probation, prohibit contact between the victim and the accused. Once a criminal complaint is signed, the state takes control of the prosecution. The victim becomes the state's witness and can no longer solely make decisions regarding the prosecution of the case.

In comparison, when a civil petition/complaint is filed, the batterer is not subject to police involvement. The complaint is always filed by the victim or a representative of the victim (counsel or guardian in some cases). The batterer will not be subject to incarceration or probation, but the court can order that there be no contact with the victim. It should be noted that violation of a civil order will result in criminal charges, which could then subject the accused to penalties and sanctions including incarceration or probation. The victim is afforded a much broader spectrum of remedies under a civil order. For example, victims may request any of the following: no contact with the victim, victim's children, or relatives. In addition to face-to-face contact, the "no contact" may include phone, mail, or third party. Civil relief may also include a prohibition against harassing the victim or those closely connected with the victim; a turn-in of firearms by a specific date and time; staying away from victim's residence, property, or workplace; temporary custody of children; possession of marital property; temporary child support or support for the victim. It may also set forth visitation schedules and circumstances under which visitation will occur, or whether it will occur at all.

For more information

Bancroft, Lundy. *Why Does He Do That?: Inside the Minds of Angry and Controlling Men.* New York: Berkley Trade, 2003.

Davidson, Terry, ed. *Conjugal Crime: Understanding and Changing the Wifebeating Pattern.* New York: Hawthorne Books, 1978.

Pfouts, J. H., J. H. Scopler, and H. C. Henley, Jr. "Forgotten Victims of Family Violence," *Social Work* (July 1982).

Loretta M. Young
Family Court of State of Delaware

double jeopardy Double jeopardy is a legal concept that protects an individual from repeated government prosecution for the same set of acts. It is usually raised by the accused as a procedural defense to an attempted government prosecution.

An example for illustrative purposes might include the following: Person A is accused and tried for the MURDER of person B. After a trial, person A is found innocent of the crime by a JURY of peers. After being found innocent, the government chooses to prosecute person A again for the very same crime, the murder of person B. Because of the first trial and ACQUITTAL, person A could defend this second attempted prosecution on the grounds of double jeopardy.

The main legal principle supporting double jeopardy derives from the common law tradition that persons accused of a crime by the government could defend against the accusation by indicating they had already been tried for the same crime based on the same set of facts. In the United States, this common law tradition has been codified through the passage of the Fifth Amendment to the UNITED STATES CONSTITUTION, which states in relevant part, "[no person shall] be subject for the same offense to be twice put in jeopardy of life or limb." This section is sometimes referred to as the double jeopardy clause.

The U.S. Supreme Court has indicated the double jeopardy clause protects against three distinct abuses: "[1] a second prosecution for the same offense after acquittal; [2] a second prosecution for the same offense after conviction; and [3] multiple punishments for the same offense." *U.S. v. Halper,* 490 U.S. 435, 440 (1989). Double jeopardy serves as an important protection against excessive government conduct.

There are exceptions to the double jeopardy defense. For example, double jeopardy only applies to final judgments reached in a criminal proceeding. In addition, double jeopardy does not apply if fraudulent conduct occurred during the first criminal proceeding. Also, double jeopardy does not prevent a different legal suit based on the same facts. Finally, double jeopardy does not apply to proceedings brought in different JURISDICTIONS.

Only final judgments are subject to double jeopardy protections. Final judgments occur only when a trial has been fully completed and a judgment has been rendered. For example, a final judgment occurs when a jury renders an actual verdict. When a trial has not been fully completed, as when a jury cannot come to a unanimous verdict (also known as a hung jury), there is no final judgment, and double jeopardy does not apply. In such cases, the government may retry the accused.

A trial may also fail to be completed because of FRAUD during the proceeding. An example might be when a JUDGE or jury member is found to have accepted a bribe to alter the final outcome of the trial. In such cases, even though a final judgment was rendered, the trial is considered void due to fraud. As such, the accused can be retried for the crime without implicating double jeopardy protections.

Double jeopardy also does not prevent a different legal suit based on the same facts. An accused is protected from multiple prosecutions in the same jurisdiction for the same acts under double jeopardy, but this protection does not extend to different venues. For example, an accused may be tried and acquitted of criminal charges in state A criminal court for murder, but then subsequently tried for wrongful death based on the same acts in state A civil court. The main difference here is the first trial was in a criminal court venue of state A, while the second trial was in a civil court venue of state A. There is no double jeopardy implications in this example because civil and criminal courts are different venues with different legal standards.

Finally, double jeopardy is also limited by the jurisdiction in which the claim is brought. For example, the federal government is considered to be a separate jurisdiction from each state. In addition, each state is considered to have different jurisdiction from other states. This is known as FEDERALISM. Federalism affects double jeopardy because it allows a person to be charged with the same crime so long as the subsequent charge is based on a different jurisdiction. For example, person A could be charged and tried for the murder of person B in both federal and state courts (or in two or more separate state courts depending on the facts of the case).

For more information

Rudstein, David S. *Double Jeopardy: A Reference Guide to the United States Constitution.* (2004).

Chad J. McGuire
University of Massachusetts, Dartmouth

Douglas, William O. (1898–1980) Supreme Court justice William O. Douglas sat on the United States Supreme Court in five different decades from 1939 to 1975 championing individual rights and liberties. Never one to shy away from controversy, his writings both on and off the Court demonstrate a commitment to unpopular causes and underdogs. While admirers point to his fierce independence and many opinions supporting liberal ideals, his critics branded him a judicial activist, more interested in self-promotion than coalition-building.

He was born in Maine, Minnesota, October 16, 1898, and spent most of his youth in Yakima, Washington. His father, a Presbyterian minister, died when he was six, and Douglas experienced a childhood of poverty and illness, eventually overcoming infantile paralysis. After serving in World War I, he worked to put himself through school, earning a B.A. from Whitman College in 1920 and a law degree from Columbia in 1925. After practicing law for two years, Douglas taught at Columbia Law School and then at Yale. An academic at the time of the burgeoning LEGAL REALIST movement, Douglas was influenced by its main precept that the law is malleable and can be used as an instrument for social change. He began his government service pressing for reform on the SECURITIES EXCHANGE COMMISSION in 1936 and served as its head until President FRANKLIN ROOSEVELT selected him for the U.S. Supreme Court in 1939.

In his early years as a member of the Court, Douglas joined the other Roosevelt appointees in upholding New Deal policies, largely in the area of LABOR LAW and business regulation. During World War II, Douglas struggled with his commitment to individual rights and the war effort. In *WEST VIRGINIA V. BARNETTE*, 319 U.S. 624 (1943), he reversed his earlier position on the issue and voted to overturn compulsory flag salute and pledge of allegiance laws for public schools. Though he supported individual rights in *Barnette,* he upheld the constitutionality of Japanese-American internment in *KOREMATSU V. UNITED STATES*, 323 U.S. 214 (1944) —a decision he vacillated on and ultimately regretted.

Perhaps Douglas's most important and controversial opinion was written for the Court in *GRISWOLD V. CONNECTICUT*, 381 U.S. 479 (1965). In striking down a state prohibition on aiding, abetting, or counseling the use of contraception, Douglas articulated a broad constitutional right to privacy. He held that the "specific guarantees in the BILL OF RIGHTS have penumbras, formed by emanations from those guarantees that help give them life and substance." He argued that the various guarantees spelled out in the CONSTITUTION,

Justice William O. Douglas (Harris and Ewing, Collection of the Supreme Court of the United States)

such as the FOURTH AMENDMENT's protection against illegal SEARCH AND SEIZURE, "create zones of privacy." He asked, "would we allow the police to search the sacred precincts of marital bedrooms for telltale signs of the use of contraceptives? The very idea is repulsive to the notions of privacy surrounding the marriage relationship." Critics argued that Douglas had overstepped his constitutional duty in creating a right that is not found in the document. Despite its controversy, *Griswold* remains good law and has been cited as precedent in other controversial opinions. For example, with Douglas in the majority, the Court declared in *ROE V. WADE*, 410 U.S. 113 (1973), that a woman's right to privacy includes the right to have an ABORTION.

In his later years on the bench, Douglas became more isolated and seemed to lose interest in the work of the Court. He married four times, traveled the world, championed environmental causes, wrote for popular audiences, and survived an IMPEACHMENT attempt. At the age of 76 Douglas suffered a debilitating stroke. Though he tried to remain on the bench, he quickly showed that he was not up to the task. Douglas's colleagues formally voted to take away his power, and he retired from the Court eight months after his stroke on November 12, 1975. He died on January 19, 1980, and was buried in Arlington National Cemetery, near the graves of Justices OLIVER WENDELL HOLMES, JR., Potter Stewart, WILLIAM J. BRENNAN, and THURGOOD MARSHALL. His headstone reads, "Private U.S. Army." In his record 36 plus years on the high Court, Douglas proved independent, uncompromising, and controversial.

For more information

Douglas, William O. *The Court Years 1939–1975: The Autobiography of William O. Douglas*. New York: Random House, 1980.

Simon, James F. *Independent Journey: The Life of William O. Douglas*. New York: Harper and Row, 1980.

Urofsky, Melvin I., ed. *The Douglas Letters: Selections from the Private Papers of Justice William O. Douglas*. Bethesda, Md.: Adler and Adler, 1987.

Wasby, Stephen L., ed. *"He Shall Not Pass This Way Again": The Legacy of Justice William O. Douglas*. Pittsburgh, Pa.: University of Pittsburgh Press, 1990.

Artemus Ward
California State University, Chico

Dred Scott v. Sandford 60 U.S. 393 (1857) *Dred Scott v. Sandford* is a notorious Supreme Court decision that held that an African-American slave could not sue for his freedom in FEDERAL COURT because he was property and not a citizen. However, in attempting to settle definitively the controversy over slavery in the territories, CHIEF JUSTICE Roger B. Taney shattered the legislative consensus crafted as a result of the KANSAS-NEBRASKA ACT, triggered scathing condemnations and outrage among antislavery forces, and propelled the nation further toward civil war.

In 1846 Dred Scott, a slave, filed suit for his freedom against his owner in a Missouri state court, alleging that, having lived with his former master, an army surgeon, in the free state of Illinois and in Wisconsin Territory, he was legally free under Missouri law. The lower court ruled in Scott's favor, based on several PRECEDENTS in the state's case law recognizing that slaves in Missouri were entitled to freedom by virtue of prior residence in a free state or territory. However, despite the fact that the established legal principle in Missouri was "once free, always free," the Missouri Supreme Court overturned the lower court decision. Scott, with the backing of white abolitionist supporters, APPEALED the decision to the United States Supreme Court.

The Court might easily have sidestepped the controversial political issue; an 1851 Supreme Court decision had affirmed that state courts had the power to determine the status of African Americans within their JURISDICTIONS, and the federal merits of the case were questionable. However, Chief Justice Taney, a proslavery jurist from Maryland, was determined that the Court would succeed where the nation's political institutions had failed in resolving unequivocally the national controversy over slavery in the territories.

The Court's decision was handed down on March 6, 1857. Writing for a 7-2 majority, Taney declared that, because Scott was a slave, he was not a citizen of the United States and had no standing to sue in federal court; Scott's suit was therefore dismissed for lack of jurisdiction. Taney asserted that the nation's founders had never envisioned CITIZENSHIP for African Americans, who he described as "beings of an inferior order" with "no rights which the white man was bound to respect."

Furthermore, the Court's majority affirmed that Scott's status as a slave had not changed as a result of his residency in Illinois and Wisconsin. Because the Fifth Amendment prohibits Congress from depriving citizens of their property without DUE PROCESS of law, Taney wrote, slaves could be taken into any territory, free or otherwise, without affecting their legal status as private property. Therefore, Taney determined that Congress had exceeded its constitutional authority in the Missouri Compromise of 1820 when it had prohibited slavery in part of the territories, and that act was accordingly declared invalid.

Despite the fact that the Missouri Compromise had been repealed by the Kansas-Nebraska Act in 1854, the sectional compromise had enjoyed widespread support in the North for decades, and the Supreme Court's decision was widely denounced and condemned in the media, Congress, and the abolitionist movement as a proslavery conspiracy to extend the "peculiar institution" nationwide. Although popular among proslavery forces in the South, Taney's decision undermined the authority and prestige of the Supreme Court, shattered any possibility of peaceful compromise between pro- and antislavery interests, and spurred the growth of the new Republican Party. It would ultimately take the Civil War and the passage of the Thirteenth and Fourteenth Amendments to overturn the effects of the *Dred Scott* decision.

For more information

Ehrlich, Walter. *They Have No Rights: Dred Scott's Struggle for Freedom.* Westport, Conn.: Greenwood, 1979.

Fehrenbacher, Don Edward. *Slavery, Law, and Politics: The Dred Scott Case in Historical Perspective.* New York: Oxford University Press, 1981.

Potter, David M. *The Impending Crisis, 1848–1861.* New York: HarperCollins, 1976.

William D. Baker
Arkansas School for Mathematics and Science

driving under the influence/driving while intoxicated (DUI/DWI) Driving under the influence, called driving while intoxicated in some states, is a state's prohibition against driving a motor vehicle while impaired by alcohol or other substances. Most states have established multiple statutory provisions that establish the crime of driving under the influence: a presumed blood alcohol level (.08 in most cases), impaired by substances, or a demonstrated level of impairment that causes a driver to be unable to safely operate a motor vehicle. While driving under the influence is generally a MISDEMEANOR or gross misdemeanor, many states have also enacted compounding legislation, meaning increased sanctions for subsequent convictions, including FELONY-level punishment. Further, because driving is a state-granted privilege, many states have imposed civil sanctions as well.

A presumptive level of impairment has been established in most states and is generally expressed by a blood alcohol concentration (BAC). The presumptive level for most states is a BAC of greater than .08; however, some states have established .10 or higher as their presumptive impairment level. In order to ensure scientific certainty in the BAC level of a driver, states have established strict protocol for managing equipment, administering and testing drivers, and review of the results. However, because alcohol affects people differently, and some people refuse to participate in the testing procedure altogether, a driver can be convicted of driving while intoxicated by demonstrating they are too impaired to safely operate a motor vehicle.

In most states, a driver can be convicted of driving while intoxicated if an officer can demonstrate that the driver's ability to operate a motor vehicle was affected by alcohol or drugs. Generally, this is established through an officer's testimony of a driver's performance during Standard Field Sobriety Tests (SFSTs), which have been established by the National Transportation Safety Board. These tests are administered at the time of the traffic stop and form the justification for an officer's ARREST.

Drivers may also be convicted of driving under the influence as a result of drug use, including impairment from prescription and over-the-counter medications. When drug use is suspected, officers with specialized training, called drug recognition experts, evaluate the driver's symptoms and responses to SFSTs before making an arrest determination. Because it is impossible to determine drug use from a BAC test, officers request a health-care provider to draw blood, which is sent for analysis by a state's crime lab. The fact that a test is not immediately available for the officer to make a determination of the drug that caused the impairment, a driver may nevertheless be arrested for DUI. The state, then, is required to produce the results before trial.

While criminal sanctions result from convictions, most states impose additional civil sanctions, which may include suspension of a driver's operational privilege, the requirement of an ignition interlock device (a device that requires a breath sample to start a vehicle and random breath samples while operating the vehicle), high-risk automobile insurance, and completion of a substance abuse program. The civil sanctions are imposed in an administrative setting through a state's licensing program and operate separately from the criminal sanctions. While hearings may be requested, they are less formal and require a lesser BURDEN OF PROOF—PREPONDERANCE OF EVIDENCE rather that beyond a REASONABLE DOUBT for criminal matters.

Whether it is the increased criminal justice response or the social stigma, states have seen dramatic reductions in alcohol-related vehicle fatalities; however, the number of criminal convictions for driving under the influence remains relatively stagnant.

For more information

Jacobs, James B. *Drunk Driving: An American Dilemma.* Chicago: University of Chicago Press, 1992.

Jolly, David N. *DUI / DWI: The History of Driving under the Influence.* Parker, Colo.: Outskirts Press, 2009.

Mark McClain
Central Washington University

drug courts Drug courts are a type of problem-solving court that has sought to reform traditional PUNISHMENT-oriented approaches to drug-related crime by taking a holistic approach to SENTENCING and treating addicted offenders.

The crack cocaine epidemic of the 1980s overwhelmed courts and prisons in many states with drug-related offenses and a high percentage of offenders who were chemically addicted. Drug offenders accounted for 72 percent of the increase in the federal prison population, with similar loads in state systems. Without adequate treatment in overcrowded prisons, released offenders frequently return to criminal activity and drug use.

To break the cycle, in 1989, Miami-Dade County in Florida began experimenting with an alternative to prison for nonviolent, substance-abusing offenders. The objective was to provide intensive social services and monitoring in order to provide recovery and return offenders to the community as productive citizens. For the courts, the program offered the prospect of significantly lower RECIDIVISM rates, with fewer reARRESTS and convictions. The drug courts were also thought to be cost-effective, despite the initial costs of the intervention, as rehabilitated offenders made less demand on law enforcement, courts, and social services.

The program proved popular, and its use has spread rapidly since 1989. A decade later, there were 472 drug courts, and by 2009 there were well over 2,000, across all 50 states, serving more than 100,000 offenders at any given time. Accumulating research has confirmed the success of the approach, with lower rearrest rates for drug court participants, lower crime rates, and net savings to taxpayers over the long term. Though states may vary some features of drug courts, such as eligibility criteria for participants, the Ten Key Components were established by the National Association of Drug Court Professionals in 1997 and disseminated by the U.S. DEPARTMENT OF JUSTICE.

The basic model now widely accepted stipulates that drug courts form a nonadversarial team, including prosecution, defense counsel, JUDGES, chemical health professionals, and any other professionals deemed necessary to help the participant through rehabilitation. Eligible participants are identified early and must agree to treatment, frequent meetings with the team, and frequent DRUG TESTS. Judicial supervision remains intensive. The carrot of services and emotional support is matched by the stick of escalating sanctions for recidivism or a return to drug use. Failed drug tests can mean removal from the drug court program. Meetings and drug tests typically are less frequent as participants approach "graduation" to a drug-free life.

Adult offenders remain the largest single target population for drug courts, though the model has been extended in many JURISDICTIONS to JUVENILE OFFENDERS. Further variants on drug courts have propagated, including a FAMILY model, where cases involve the parental rights of substance abusers, a tribal model for drug use on Indian tribes, and most recently, Veterans Treatment Court, involving services through Veteran Affairs offices and using veterans as mentors. Hybrid drug courts have extended intervention to DWI offenses, seeking to change the behavior of repeat alcohol-dependent offenders.

For more information

"Painting the Current Picture: A National Report Card on Drug Courts and Other Problem-Solving Court Programs in the United States," *National Drug Court Institute,* 2, no. 1 (May 2008). Available online. URL: http://www.ndci.org/ndci-home/.

Office of National Drug Control Policy. "Drug Courts." Available online. URL: http://www.whitehouse-drugpolicy.gov/enforce/DrugCourt.html.

Caroline Ettinger and

Patrick Schmidt
Macalester College

drug decriminalization Decriminalizing drugs involves making narcotic drug use legal. The decriminalization of drugs is hotly debated, and there are a number of advantages and disadvantages that go along with legalizing drugs. Whether one is in favor or against the policy, it is important to think in terms of social costs and the potential harm or benefit that can be gained by the proposed change.

Not to be confused with decriminalization, the use of MEDICAL MARIJUANA for certain medical conditions is currently legal in 14 states in the United States. A problem with this state legislation is that even though medical marijuana is considered legal in these states, the use of the drug had been a violation of federal law. This paradox between state and federal institutions has raised concern by those using marijuana for medical reasons because these persons can be ARRESTED under federal law. In October 2009, a decision was released by the DEPARTMENT OF JUSTICE that people would not be prosecuted for medical marijuana use in states where it is legal. Some argue that this decision may be the one that begins a movement toward decriminalization.

If all illicit drugs are legalized, there are a number of factors that need to be considered. Would the U.S. FOOD AND DRUG ADMINISTRATION be the agency in charge of monitoring narcotics? Would a new agency have to be established to govern such processes? Who will be responsible for these costs? How will the drugs be manufactured? How will they be distributed and made available? Could the drugs be purchased at convenience stores or only at dispensaries? How would taxes be charged on the goods? Should an age limit be placed on the purchase and use of drugs, as there is with alcohol and tobacco? If there is an age limit, what age is safer to consume narcotics? These are just a few questions that need to be considered and addressed if drug use is legalized.

For those in favor of legalizing illicit drugs, one of their main reasons for wanting the law changed is that the drugs are illegal. By making the drugs legal, addicts will no longer have to suffer the stigma associated with being an addict. Addicts could be more open about their addiction and more likely to seek help. Resources could also be made available for persons who may fear addiction, and they could receive assistance to continue to be productive citizens and good workers. Persons who use illicit drugs for the sole purpose of pain relief would no longer be viewed as criminal. They could obtain their pain medication via legitimate means and not take the chance of being arrested and ruining their lives and families lives. Drugs could be purchased in safer mixtures and in safer locations. Drug dealers would not be trying to sell drugs to children. Drug users would no longer have to chance getting a bad mixture of heroin and risking a stroke or brain death. Users would know exactly what they are taking, how much, and it would be clean and not mixed with a potentially deadly poison.

Further, it is believed that crime would be reduced in several ways. An immediate reduction in crime will occur because drug arrests for possession will cease. The only drug arrests that may occur would be of persons considered under age, if an age limit was established for persons under the influence or if a law were established limiting persons from driving while under the influence, as is currently the case with established DUI/DWI laws. Attacks, shootings, and stabbings may decrease because persons will no longer be involved in drug deals in drug houses or in alleys. Distributions from drug cartels could cease entirely, and more legitimate means could be established to obtain drugs from South American countries. Additionally, consumers would no longer be at a disadvantage in terms of cost. It is likely that prices will be more fixed instead of being established by the drug dealer who is seeking only to make a profit.

Disadvantages for decriminalizing drugs are also complex. One of the main disadvantages stated by those against legalization is that drugs will be easier to get not only for children but for everyone. People may be more prone to try harder drugs than they normally would if the drugs had not been made legal. Thus, more persons, some who may be unsuspecting or unwise to the effects, may become addicts. Drug use would become more acceptable, and citizens may become more tolerant of drug-addicted lifestyles.

Another key issue with decriminalizing drugs cited by those against the policy is how much is too much. What should be a legal limit? Can a legal limit even be established? Alcohol, for example, has a legal limit set by states. Anyone over that limit and caught operating a motor vehicle is charged with a crime. This limit also helps drivers know, in general theory, how much alcohol can be consumed to be considered safe. A legal limit would need to be set for drug users as well. The problems are, however, how can the legal limit be established, and how could the users be tested? It is easy to test the amount of alcohol consumed because the test is conducted via a breathalyzer. However, drug tests are currently conducted with urine screenings, blood screenings, and hair follicle examinations. These tests indicate only positive drug use or no drug use. The date of use and amount of use cannot be established. For example, a person under the influence of alcohol can take a breathalyzer test and the out-

A member of the U.S. Coast Guard protects more than 11.5 tons of cocaine before a press conference. (Coast Guard)

put will be the blood alcohol content. Current drug tests do not provide that detail. It is not possible to tell if a drug user is currently under the influence of a drug. Of course, there are the standard visual cues that can be examined such as bloodshot eyes, slowed speech, difficulty concentrating, etc., but it is possible for a person not under the influence of any illegal substance to have all of those problems just from being exhausted.

The drug decriminalization debate is complex, and there are considerable arguments from both camps that justify enacting the policy or doing away with the idea altogether. However, whichever direction is taken, persons have to come to a consensus on various issues dealing with production, distribution, taxing, availability, age limitations, legal limits, etc.

For more information

Abadinsky, Howard. *Drug Use and Abuse: A Comprehensive Introduction*. 6th ed. Belmont, Calif.: Thomson Wadsworth, 2008.

Inciardi, James A., and Karen McElrath. *The American Drug Scene: An Anthology*. New York: Oxford University Press, 2007.

Michelle L. Foster
Kent State University

Drug Enforcement Administration (DEA)

The Drug Enforcement Administration (DEA), a federal agency, was created in 1973 and is housed in the DEPARTMENT OF JUSTICE. It was a direct offshoot of the Department of Justice's Bureau of Narcotics and Dangerous Drugs (1968–73). However, its ancestors include a variety of agencies created in the first half of the 20th century. Among these were the Bureau of PROHIBITION, Bureau of Narcotics, and Bureau of Internal Revenue in the Treasury Department, and the Bureau of Drug Abuse Control in the FOOD AND DRUG ADMINISTRATION. The U.S. Customs Service also played a role with regard to international drug trafficking. A growing awareness of the interrelation between the domestic and international drug abuse scenes as well as allegations of interagency rivalry in addressing drug problems led to the creation of the DEA with the goal of consolidating and coordinating federal drug control activities and enforcing the Controlled Substances Act, part of the Comprehensive Drug Prevention and Control Act passed into law in 1970.

The "war on drugs" begun during the presidency of Ronald Reagan with increased penalties for even first-time drug offenders began to expand the presence and powers of the DEA, so that by the 1990s more than half of the prisoners in federal prisons were violators of federal drug laws. In addition to enforcing federal drug laws, the DEA also plays a key role in intelligence gathering about drug trafficking, particularly as related to immigration and border traffic. By the early 21st century, the DEA's special agents numbered more than 5,000.

The DEA has conducted major operations involving drug-producing countries of South America because of their proximity and access to U.S. illegal drug markets. However, its international activities extend beyond the Western Hemisphere and include offices in more than 60 countries. The DEA has also been drawn into the protracted United States-led war against al-Qaeda and the Taliban in Afghanistan because of the massive Afghan opium production and trade, and DEA special agents are numbered among the Afghan war casualties.

The DEA has been cloaked in controversy throughout its life for several reasons. First, a vocal and substantial minority of the American public who use or have used illegal drugs support decriminalization of some or all illicit drugs and resent DEA's long reach in targeting small grassroots-level drug users. Second, in recent years, federal and state laws have clashed over the use of MEDICAL MARIJUANA—legal under some state laws but a violation of federal law. A third source of controversy, particularly for civil libertarians, arises from the power of the ATTORNEY GENERAL to assign other unspecified law enforcement duties to the DEA (along with a number of other agencies). This creates the paradox that the DEA, although an agency with narrow, well-defined powers, also has the potential to be drawn into a larger web of law enforcement activities. Finally, there has been criticism from insiders about instances of mismanagement and incompetence that allegedly caused bungled operations and unnecessarily increased the already considerable risk to DEA undercover agents battling powerful drug cartels. Similar criticisms have been leveled about rivalry between the DEA and other agencies such as the CIA and FBI with similar and potentially overlapping missions. Meanwhile, DEA supporters argue that despite these problems, the DEA has been successful at what it does and that its overall activities have the net effect of increasing the cost for customers of street drugs, thus helping to curtail illicit drug use.

For more information

Bumgarner, Jeffrey B. *Federal Agents: The Growth of Federal Law Enforcement in America.* Westport, Conn.: Praeger, 2006.

Levine, Michael. *Deep Cover: The Inside Story of How DEA Infighting, Incompetence and Subterfuge Lost Us the Biggest Battle of the Drug War.* New York: Delacorte Press, 1990.

U.S. Drug Enforcement Administration. Available online. URL: http://www.usdoj.gov/dea/index.htm.

Jane G. Rainey
Eastern Kentucky University

drug sniff and searches Drug sniff and searches are a category of searches that employ the use of narcotic-detection dogs. The FOURTH AMENDMENT of the UNITED STATES CONSTITUTION provides protection against unreasonable SEARCHES AND SEIZURES. In most circumstances, in order for a search to be deemed reasonable it must be conducted based on PROBABLE CAUSE and with the authority of a warrant. Canine drug sniff and searches, depending on the circumstances, often provide an exception to the probable cause and warrant requirements.

The Supreme Court has held in *U.S. v. Place*, 462 U.S. 696 (1983), that narcotic-detection sniff tests conducted by trained drug dogs, at least in public, are not considered searches within the meaning of the Fourth Amendment because they do not involve a legitimate intrusion of the privacy interest a person has in the property being sniffed. Moreover, drug sniffs are not considered searches because they do not reveal anything more than the presence or absence of narcotics. Therefore, as the Court stated in *Place*, "[T]he owner of the property is not subjected to the embarrassment and inconvenience entailed in less discriminate and more intrusive investigative methods."

As drug sniffs are not considered searches within the ambit of the Fourth Amendment, they may be conducted without suspicion or a warrant. If a drug sniff results in a drug dog being alerted to the presence of narcotics, the police authorities would then have established the reasonable suspicion necessary to justify a full search of the property or items under investigation.

Drug sniff and searches have perhaps been used most commonly in the context of traffic stops. In *Illinois v. Caballes*, 543 U.S. 405 (2005), the Court stated that once a vehicle has been pulled over in a routine traffic stop, the police may employ the aid of a drug sniff dog to walk around the outside of the vehicle without any need to justify a particular suspicion of criminal activity. Other areas where police commonly employ suspicionless drug sniffs include BORDER patrol checkpoints, schools, and airports.

In *City of Indianapolis v. Edmond*, 531 U.S. 32 (2000), the Supreme Court ruled that while police are justified in using drug dogs pursuant to a legitimate traffic stop, the police may not set up roadblocks and checkpoints designed solely for the purpose of uncovering EVIDENCE of general criminal activity. The difference between the two situations is that routine traffic stops are considered legitimate seizures within the meaning of the Fourth Amendment, while checkpoints aimed at general crime control are not. Checkpoints are constitutional only when their primary purpose is to ensure the safety of the roads; they may, for example, include checks for licenses, vehicle fitness, DRIVING UNDER THE INFLUENCE, etc. The added use of a drug dog at such a checkpoint does not create a search, but rather the design and motive of the checkpoint itself would constitute an unreasonable seizure under the Fourth Amendment.

The Supreme Court has never considered the issue of whether drug sniffs of people would be considered a search within the meaning of the Fourth Amendment. Using narcotic-detection dogs to sniff people may very well compromise the very kind of privacy interest that is not present in property drug sniffs. If drug sniffs of people were considered searches, then they would require probable cause and a warrant. What is clear, however, is that it is constitutionally permissible for drug dogs to sniff personal items and vehicles without any kind of suspicion or warrant. If based on that drug sniff, according to *United States v. Turpin*, 920 F.2d 1377 (8th Cir. 1990), the dog becomes alerted to the presence of narcotics, the police would then have the justifiable reasonable suspicion necessary to search the person to whom those items belonged.

The use of suspicionless drug sniffs has received criticism by some commentators because the use of the dogs could be analogized to sensory enhancement technology that would violate the Fourth Amendment. In *KYLLO V. U.S.*, 533 U.S. 27 (2001), the police used a thermal-imaging device to gain information about marijuana-growing devices within a person's home. This police activity was held to violate the resident's reasonable expectation of privacy under the Fourth Amendment because the homeowner would not expect members of the general public to have access to the kind of sensory-enhancing technology employed by the police. Similar arguments have been made with respect to the use of drug dogs. On the other hand, *Kyllo* may be distinguished from drug sniff situations in that the technology employed in *Kyllo* was aimed at the privacy of the home.

For more information

Bell, Michael. "Caballes, Place, and Economic Rin-tin-tincentives: The Effect of Canine Sniff Jurisprudence on the Demand for and Development of Search Technology." *Brooklyn Law Review* 279 (2006).

Hunt II., Cecil J. "Calling in the Dogs: Suspicionless Sniff Searches and Reasonable Expectations of Privacy." *Western Reserve Law Review* 56 (2005): 285.

Eric McAdamis and Ryan C. Black
Michigan State University

drug testing Drug testing refers to the analysis of a biological specimen to detect the presence of illegal or nonprescribed substances within an individual. In the American CRIMINAL JUSTICE SYSTEM, drug testing is generally used to determine adherence to conditions of PROBATION or PAROLE, terms of release on BAIL, and within prison settings. The justice system uses three primary methods of drug testing: urinalysis, oral fluid (i.e. saliva), and hair testing.

There are a variety of illegal and prescribed drugs that drug testing can detect, and specific analyses can be tailored to the individual being tested. Most often, the criminal justice system is concerned with testing for the presence of popular illegal substances and prescription drugs. Cocaine, opiates (e.g., heroin, morphine, codeine), delta-9-tetrahydrocannabinol (THC) (i.e., marijuana), phencyclidine (PCP), and benzodiazipines (e.g., Xanax©, Valium©, Ativan©) are the most common drugs tested for in the criminal justice system. Each specific drug has a different half-life (i.e., time it takes to leave the individual's system), and different testing methods are more or less sensitive to the presence of the drug.

Urinalysis (UA) is the most popular drug testing method used by criminal justice practitioners. Those authorized to administer drug testing follow strict protocols to ensure specimens are not tampered with or altered. These protocols often require personnel to search individuals prior to giving a specimen to detect the presence of tampering devices or prepared urine. Instant UA tests provide information about temperature and dilution, two common indicators of tampering. UA tests are sent to a laboratory for more detailed testing of the concentrations of drugs and can detect the presence of substances up to 72 hours from use. Chronic use of marijuana can often be detected for up to 30 days.

The oral fluid testing method consists of a swab of the inside of the individual's mouth. Saliva is then tested to detect the presence of drugs. This method can detect the presence of most drugs if administered within 24 hours of substance use. Recent research has found that though there is a perception among criminal justice practitioners that oral fluid testing is not as effective as urinalysis, this testing method is as effective as urinalysis with the exception of remote use of marijuana (Yacoubian and Cone, 2006). The only drawback of oral fluid testing is that only use within 24 hours of the test will be detected. If criminal justice practitioners (e.g., probation or parole officers) are concerned with use that may have occurred more than 24 hours from the time of testing, urinalysis or hair testing would be necessary.

Drug testing using a sample of hair is primarily used when historical detection of substance use is of concern. This method detects the presence of drugs from seven to 90 days of use. Hair testing is not commonly used in probation or parole settings, especially when drug testing is an ongoing and frequent requirement. The effectiveness of this drug testing method is similar to both oral fluid testing and urinalysis.

The criminal justice system uses drug testing in a variety of settings, most often by parole and probation practitioners. Individuals placed on parole or probation usually have conditions to abide by in order to remain in good standing throughout their sentence length. Random drug testing administered by probation and parole officers checks for compliance. If drug tests detect the presence of illegal, or nonprescribed drugs, offenders are subject to revocation of parole or probation as a technical violation of the conditions of their SENTENCING agreement.

For more information

Fowler, Louise. *Drugs, Crime and the Drug Treatment and Testing Order: Issues in Community and Criminal Justice.* New York: NAPO, 2002.

Inciardi, James A. "Screening and Assessment for Alcohol and Other Drug Abuse among Adults in the Criminal Justice System," *Treatment Improvement Protocol (TIP)*. Washington, D.C.: U.S. Dept. of Heath and Human Services, 1994.

Kathryn Zafft
University of Maryland College Park

due process and crime The due process clauses of the Fifth and Fourteenth Amendments respectively protect defendants in both the federal and state CRIMINAL JUSTICE SYSTEMS by constraining the powers of prosecutorial authorities in accordance with the BILL OF RIGHTS. Specifically, these due process guarantees forbid federal or state officials from depriving an individual of "life, liberty, or property" without adhering to certain procedural safeguards and principles enumerated in the FOURTH, Fifth, SIXTH, and EIGHTH AMENDMENTS to the UNITED STATES CONSTITUTION.

Ratified on December 15, 1791, the Fifth Amendment served as a check on the powers of the federal government. In relevant part, the Fifth Amendment states, "nor shall any person . . . be deprived of life, liberty, or property without the due process of law[.]" This due process clause of the Fifth Amendment shields criminal defendants in the federal court system with the protections outlined in the Bill of Rights. Notably, the due process clause of the Fifth Amendment curtails only the powers of the federal government and protects only criminal defendants facing federal prosecution. Thus, the ratification of the Fifth Amendment had no effect on state or local criminal justice systems according to *BARRON V. THE MAYOR AND CITY COUNCIL OF BALTIMORE*, 32 U.S. (7 Pet.) 243 (1833).

Following the Civil War, the United States again amended its Constitution. Commonly known as the RECONSTRUCTION Amendments or the Civil War Amendments, the Thirteenth, Fourteenth, and Fifteenth Amendments were legislative attempts to halt widespread racial discrimination against African Americans. Of these measures, the Fourteenth Amendment proved the most drastic constraint on state powers. In relevant part, the Fourteenth Amendment states, "nor shall any State deprive any person of life, liberty, or property without due process of law" (sec. 1). Through this due process clause of the Fourteenth Amendment, the Supreme Court has applied the Bill of Rights to the states in a series of landmark decisions.

The Fourth, Fifth, Sixth, and Eighth Amendments to the United States Constitution establish limits on federal and state authorities who pursue criminal prosecutions and impose sanctions for criminal convictions. Though such limits once served only to protect criminal defendants in the federal court system, some have since been INCORPORATED or applied to the states by the Supreme Court through the Fourteenth Amendment, limiting the powers of state authorities and protecting criminal defendants in state court systems.

INCORPORATING THE FOURTH AMENDMENT

In the field of constitutional criminal procedure, MAPP V. OHIO, 367 U.S. 643 (1963), is perhaps the most influential Supreme Court decision contemplating the Fourth Amendment. In *Mapp,* the Supreme Court held that the Fourth Amendment applies to the states through the due process clause of the Fourteenth Amendment. Thus, as a result of the Court's decree in *Mapp,* state actions that constitute "unreasonable searches and seizures" are constitutionally impermissible, and EVIDENCE acquired as a result of such actions is excludable in subsequent criminal proceedings. See also *Ker v. California,* 374 U.S. 23 (1963). Further, in *Aguilar v. Texas,* 378 U.S. 108 (1964), the Supreme Court held that the warrant requirements of the Fourth Amendment commanded state compliance in accordance with the due process clause of the Fourteenth Amendment.

INCORPORATING THE FIFTH AMENDMENT

In a series of other notable decisions, the Supreme Court has applied the provisions of the Fifth Amendment to the states through the due process clause of the Fourteenth Amendment. The Fifth Amendment states, in part, that "no person . . . shall . . . be subject for the same offence to be twice put in jeopardy of life or limb; nor shall be compelled in any criminal case to be a witness against himself." In *Benton v. Maryland,* 395 U.S. 784 (1969), the Court held that the Fifth Amendment's prohibition against DOUBLE JEOPARDY governed both federal and state criminal procedure. Additionally, in *Malloy v. Hogan,* 378 U.S. 1 (1968), the Court concluded that the Fifth Amendment banned compelled SELF-INCRIMINATION in both federal and state criminal prosecutions. Hence, the due process clause of the Fourteenth Amendment provides Fifth Amendment protections to state criminal defendants.

INCORPORATING THE SIXTH AMENDMENT

The Sixth Amendment guarantees a criminal defendant the right to 1) a speedy and public trial; 2) an impartial JURY; 3) notice of charges; 4) confront adverse witnesses; 5) compulsory process for obtaining witnesses; and 6) assistance of counsel. While federal criminal defendants have benefited from the guarantees of the Sixth Amendment since its enactment, the Supreme Court, again through the due process clause of the Fourteenth Amendment, has since extended Sixth Amendment rights to state criminal defendants.

The most prominent Supreme Court holdings regarding the Sixth Amendment are DUNCAN V. LOUISIANA, 391 U.S. 145 (1968), and GIDEON V. WAINWRIGHT, 372 U.S. 335 (1963). In *Duncan,* the Court took up the issue of whether a defendant has the right to a jury in state criminal proceedings. Ultimately, the Court held that the Sixth Amendment guarantees that all criminal defendants, federal or state, have the right to an impartial tribunal. In *Gideon,* the Court established another fundamental principle of criminal procedure. There, the Court held that all criminal defendants charged with a FELONY have the RIGHT TO COUNSEL. Moreover, in *Gideon,* the Court also noted that the right to counsel necessarily requires that counsel possess a measurable level of competence.

Other less notable cases further solidified state criminal defendants' rights to Sixth Amendment protections. For example, in *Klopfer v. North Carolina,* 386 U.S. 213 (1967), the Court held that, like federal criminal defendants, individuals charged with a crime in state court have the right to a speedy trial. The Court has also concluded, in *In re Oliver,* 333 U.S. 257 (1948), that state criminal defendants have the right to a public trial and have the right to notice of the charges against which they must defend. And finally, in *Pointer v. Texas,* 380 U.S. 400 (1965), and *Washington v. Texas,* 388 U.S. 14 (1967), respectively, the Supreme Court extended the Sixth Amendment such that state criminal defendants also enjoy the right to confront adverse witnesses and to compulsory process for obtaining both adversarial and favorable witnesses.

INCORPORATING THE EIGHTH AMENDMENT

In part, the Eighth Amendment prohibits the infliction of "CRUEL AND UNUSUAL PUNISHMENTS." In *ROBINSON V. CALIFORNIA*, 370 U.S. 660 (1962), through the due process clause of the Fourteenth Amendment, the Supreme Court extended to the states the "cruel and unusual punishments" provision of the Eighth Amendment, holding that certain penalties or sanctions would violate a state prisoner's constitutional protections.

UNINCORPORATED PROVISIONS

Currently, two noteworthy constitutional provisions found in the Bill of Rights serve to protect federal criminal defendants but do not protect those individuals facing state criminal prosecution. In *HURTADO V. CALIFORNIA*, 110 U.S. 516 (1884), the Supreme Court concluded that the Fifth Amendment right to "presentment or indictment by a GRAND JURY" does not apply to the states. In *Hurtado*, the Court held that an indictment filed by a DISTRICT ATTORNEY is constitutionally permissible, thereby granting significant DISCRETION to state authorities while exposing state criminal defendants to potentially unsubstantiated prosecution. Additionally, in *Schilb v. Kuebel*, 404 U.S. 357 (1971), the Supreme Court, while noting the likelihood that the Eighth Amendment's prohibition on "excessive bail" would apply to the states via the Fourteenth Amendment, stopped short of officially extending this protection to those charged with a crime in state criminal court. Therefore, while the Bill of Rights insulates federal criminal defendants from excessive bail, the Court has not afforded state criminal defendants that same security.

For more information

Cohen, W., J. D. Varat, and V. Amar. *Constitutional Law: Cases and Materials*. 12th ed. New York: Foundation Press, 2005.

Tribe, L. H. *American Constitutional Law.* Mineola, N.Y.: Foundation Press, 1978.

James M. Binnall
University of California at Irvine

Duncan v. Louisiana 391 U.S. 145 (1968) In *Duncan v. Louisiana*, the Supreme Court held that the SIXTH AMENDMENT RIGHT TO A JURY TRIAL is applicable to the states through the DUE PROCESS clause of the Fourteenth Amendment.

Gary Duncan was convicted of simple BATTERY, which at the time was a MISDEMEANOR under Louisiana law punishable by a maximum sentence of two years and a $300 fine. Duncan requested and was denied a JURY trial. Louisiana law permitted jury trials only in cases of CAPITAL PUNISHMENT or where imprisonment at hard labor was imposed. He was convicted after a bench trial and sentenced to serve 60 days and pay a $150 fine. The Louisiana Supreme Court rejected his APPEAL, and he sought review in the U.S. Supreme Court.

The question whether a specific provision of the BILL OF RIGHTS is made applicable to the states through the due process clause of the Fourteenth Amendment focuses on the fundamental nature of the right. Justice Byron White, writing for the majority, noted that every state that ratified the original CONSTITUTION had a provision guaranteeing a jury trial in serious criminal cases. In addition, every state admitted into the Union has included such a provision, and there has been no serious movement in the states to remove the right to a jury trial in a criminal case from state constitutions. Justice White acknowledges that in *Maxwell v. Dow*, 176 U.S. 581 (1900), the Court held that no provision of the Bill of Rights applies to the states a position Justice

White asserted has long since been repudiated. Although in *PALKO V. CONNECTICUT*, 302 U.S. 319 (1937), the Court indicated that the right to jury trial was not obligatory to the states, Justice White dismissed the comments there as mere dicta and not binding upon the Court.

The Court rejected Louisiana's claim that because Duncan's sentence was much less than the two-year imprisonment and the $300 fine the law permitted due process was not violated. Louisiana is free to determine the PUNISHMENT for violations of her laws. Nevertheless, due process requires a jury trial for serious offenses. Although the Court refused to fix a hard-and-fast rule about what constituted a serious offense, it strongly hinted that the federal standard of six months imprisonment for misdemeanor offenses should be considered the standard.

In dissent, Justice JOHN M. HARLAN asserted that the question was not whether the jury trial was an ancient or noble institution. The question is whether Louisiana may afford only a bench trial for offenses it deems petty. Justice Harlan notes that one aspect of American FEDERALISM is the freedom of states to adopt criminal procedures and punishments to the particular needs of individual states.

For more information

Murphy, Walter F. C., Herman Pritichett, and Lee Epstein. *Courts, Judges, & Politics: An Introduction to the Judicial Process*. 5th ed. New York: McGraw-Hill, 2002.

Abraham, Henry J. *The Judicial Process*. 7th ed. New York: Oxford University Press, 1998.

James V. Calvi
West Texas A&M University

E

Eighth Amendment The Eighth Amendment to the UNITED STATES' CONSTITUTION states "Excessive bail shall not be required nor excessive fines imposed, nor cruel and unusual punishments inflicted." Historically, this amendment was intended to protect criminals and those accused of crimes, individuals who cannot easily protect themselves, from two practices the founding fathers deemed unfair. The prohibition against excessive bail and fines was in reaction to a common judicial practice of holding prisoners for indefinite periods of time before trial by setting extremely high bail. A prohibition against cruel and unusual punishment was added to prevent punishments such as drawing and quartering, branding, and ear cropping.

In legal terms, the ideas in the Eighth Amendment can be traced back to the principle of *lex talionis* (retaliation), whereby a person's PUNISHMENT should equal the hurt he has caused his neighbor. This principle can be found in Magna Carta as well as in 13th- and 14th-century documents. The wording of the Eighth Amendment can be found almost verbatim in the English Bill of Rights of 1689. Legislative and judicial discussions around the time of the Constitution indicate that the intent of this amendment was to prevent the establishment of punishments that were disproportionate to the crime.

Of the prohibitions in the Eighth Amendment, the prohibition against "cruel and unusual punishment" has received the most philosophical and legal debate. Philosophically, one must consider the moral, cultural, and temporal subjectivity of the "cruel and unusual" clause. Even when the Constitution was drafted, many of the punishments considered cruel and unusual but allowed by law, such as branding and ear cropping, had already fallen out of use because they were considered too barbaric. In other words, punishments that are widely acceptable at one point in time are considered cruel at another. The Supreme Court acknowledged the changing nature of the "cruel and unusual" punishment clause of the Eighth Amendment in *Trop v. Dulles*, 356 U.S. 86 (1958), through the phrase "EVOLVING STANDARDS OF DECENCY." Because the concept of cruelty evolves with society, the courts must interpret and apply "cruel and unusual" according to the current standards of society. This requires the courts to walk a fine line between reflecting and upholding society's standards and adjudicating morals. To meet this challenge in an impartial way, the Supreme Court has measured the evolving public attitude toward CAPITAL PUNISHMENT by assessing the enactment or repeal of laws across the states as well as the frequency with which courts applied particular punishments.

A philosophical debate also centers on the use of *and* in the "cruel and unusual" phrase. Can a punishment be cruel but applied so frequently that it is usual and, therefore, not prohibited? Although the Supreme Court raised this question in *Trop v. Dulles,* an answer was not provided until later cases that were also assessing changes in the standards of cruelty. The Supreme Court in *Stanford v. Kentucky,* 492 U.S. 361 (1989), clarified that a punishment must meet the standards of both cruelty and unusual application to be prohibited by the Eighth Amendment. Because a majority of states allowed juvenile execution, the punishment was not unusual and, therefore, upheld by the Court. *HARMELIN V. MICHIGAN,* 501 U.S. 957 (1991), further clarified that the intent of the Eighth Amendment was to prevent the use of punishments that were both cruel and not commonly used. In *Harmelin,* the Supreme Court acknowledged that a punishment may be cruel but usually applied and, therefore, not against the Eighth Amendment.

Legally, the U.S. Supreme Court has taken on the task of both interpreting and applying the Eighth Amendment's prohibition against cruel and unusual punishment. In three cases, the justices attempted to interpret the "cruel and unusual" clause in order to provide guidelines to determine whether or not a punishment was indeed cruel and unusual. Justice WILLIAM BRENNAN's concurring opinion in *FURMAN V. GEORGIA,* 408 U.S. 238 (1972), which upheld capital punishment, established a set of guidelines for determining whether a punishment was "cruel and unusual," namely that it cannot violate human dignity, that it cannot be imposed arbitrarily, it must be acceptable in contemporary society, and that it must be proportional to the crime. The Supreme Court further defined proportionality of punishment in *SOLEM V. HELM,* 463 U.S. 267 (1983), by stating that the gravity of the punishment must meet the gravity of the crime, that the punishment must be similar to punishments for similar crimes in the same JURISDICTION, and the punishment must be similar to the punishment for the same crime in other jurisdictions. The Supreme Court reversed this position in *Harmelin v. Michigan,* 501 U.S. 957 (1991), ruling that a mandatory life sentence may be cruel but not unusual and, therefore, not prohibited by the Eighth Amendment.

The Supreme Court has applied the "cruel and unusual" clause of the Eighth Amendment to both particular punishments and the SENTENCING process. In *Weems v. United States,* 408 U.S. 238 (1910), the Supreme Court overturned a Philippine punishment as being disproportionate to the crime. Revocation of CITIZENSHIP was deemed "cruel and unusual" in *Trop v. Dulles,* 356 U.S. 86 (1958), because it removed the person from society and, therefore, forced him to forfeit rights and the protection of those rights associated with governments. Although a majority opinion could not be reached, the Supreme Court justices rejected the claim that California's "three strikes" law resulted in a cruel and unusual punishment in *Ewing v. California,* 538 U.S. 11 (2003).

Because of the irrevocable nature of a capital punishment sentence, the Supreme Court has provided numerous guidelines on the sentencing process. A mandatory death sentence was found unconstitutional in *Woodson v. North Carolina,* 428 U.S. 280 (1976), because it did not consider the character of the defendant or the circumstances of the crime. This requirement to consider character, circumstances, and other mitigating factors was further clarified in *Roberts v. Louisiana,* 431 U.S. 633 (1977), *Lockett v. Ohio,* 438 U.S. 586 (1978), and *Abdul-Kabir v. Quarterman,* 550 U.S. 233 (2007). In *Eddings v. Oklahoma,* 455 U.S. 104 (1982), the Supreme Court expanded mitigating considerations to include the defendant's emotional problems and violent FAMILY background. This was further expanded in *Smith v. Texas,* 543 U.S. 37 (2004), to include EVIDENCE of learning disabilities and a low IQ. In *Johnson v. Mississippi,* 486 U.S. 578 (1988), the Supreme Court ruled that consideration of prior imprisonment was prejudicial because it did not necessarily mean that the person was guilty of prior acts. The ability of the defendant to present residual doubts about guilt and emphasis of good behavior was affirmed in *Franklin v. Lynaugh,* 487 U.S. 164 (1988). The Supreme Court also emphasized that instructions to the JURY and state statutes cannot be vague in *Maynard v. Cartwright,* 486 U.S. 356 (1988), and *Stringer v. Black,* 503 U.S. 222 (1992). Prior notice of a capital punishment sentence must be made to the defendant, according to *Lankford v. Idaho,* 500 U.S. 110 (1991), because it would affect the preparation and arguments during sentencing. In *Harmelin v. Michigan,* the Supreme Court ruled that sentencing in capital punishment cases must be individualized.

The Supreme Court also limited these same guidelines. In *Booth v. Maryland,* the Supreme Court found that consideration of a victim impact statement would increase the risk that a capital punishment sentence would be arbitrarily imposed. According to *Buchanan v. Angelone,* 522 U.S. 269 (1988), and *Harris v. Alabama,* 513 U.S. 504 (1995), instructions to the jury did not have to specifically indicate how to weigh aggravating and mitigating circumstances as long as they provided enough information to prevent arbitrary sentencing. Evidence presented during sentencing can be limited by the state to evidence presented during the trial, thus precluding entry of new evidence that could raise REASONABLE DOUBT of guilt according to *Oregon v. Guzek,* 546 U.S. 517 (2006).

Claims that capital punishment is cruel and unusual have been rejected by the Supreme Court, although the justices have limited both the application of capital punishment and the procedures used in capital punishment cases. In each of these cases, the Supreme Court clearly relies on evidence of the changing morals of the American public. Looking specifically at the constitutionality of capital punishment, the Supreme Court upheld the practice in *Furman v. Georgia,* 408 U.S. 238 (1972). This case was before the Court at a time when support for capital punishment was low, although the practice was still supported by a majority of the public. Reviewing the lethal injection method of execution, the Supreme Court ruled in *Blaze v. Rees,* 553 U.S. 35 (2008), that the defendants did not meet the BURDEN OF PROOF required to rule it cruel and unusual punishment. However, the Court further stipulated that continuing to use any method of execution when documentation proved a readily available and feasibly adopted method was available would constitute cruel and unusual punishment. In *Coker v. Georgia,* 433 U.S. 584 (1977), the Supreme Court found that since Georgia was the only state to authorize the death penalty for rape, and that Georgia imposed the death penalty for only 10 percent of the rape cases, death was an excessive punishment for rape. Since only eight jurisdictions allowed capital punishment for a vicious FELONY, the Supreme Court ruled that it was not appropriate when the defendant participated in the crime but not MURDER in *Edmund v. Florida,* 458 U.S. 782 (1982). Similarly, in *Kennedy v. Louisiana,* 128 S. Ct. 2641 (2008), the Supreme Court found that the death penalty for child rape did not fulfill the goals of retribution and deterrence and that there was a national consensus against capital punishment for child rape.

Prohibition of capital punishment for juveniles and the mentally impaired occurred over an extended period of time. In *Thompson v. Oklahoma,* 487 U.S. 815 (1988), the Supreme Court prohibited the death penalty for those under the age of 16 because their lack of experience and education rendered them less able to evaluate the consequences of their conduct. As a result, capital punishment of those under age 16 failed to meet the goal of deterrence. However, the following year, the Court ruled in *Stanford v. Kentucky,* 492 U.S. 361 (1989), that the states were not prohibited from executing juveniles since the majority of states allowed the practice and there was no modern or historical evidence against the execution of juveniles. More recently, in ROPER V. SIMMONS, 543 U.S. 551 (2005), the Supreme Court ruled that the death penalty for those under age 18 is prohibited by the Eighth Amendment. The Court justified this decision on two grounds. First, the Court noted the number of states that either prohibited capital punishment or prevented its use on juveniles. It was noted that of the remaining states juveniles were sentenced to execution infrequently. Second, the Court ruled that citizens did not feel juveniles to have the same culpability as adults because their sense of responsibility and character were underdeveloped and they were more susceptible to pressure from their peers and other groups.

The Supreme Court first acknowledged the complexity of mental impairment in its relation to capital punishment in *Penry v. Lynaugh*, 492 U.S. 302 (1989). The Court ruled that it could not set a new prohibition on mental retardation. Although the defendant was competent to stand trial, consult with his attorney, and understand the proceedings, the intelligence level of the defendant should have been considered as a mitigating factor during sentencing. Thirteen years later, in *Atkins v. Virginia*, 536 U.S. 304 (2002), the Supreme Court found execution of the mentally retarded cruel and unusual punishment for two reasons. First, the Court found evidence of a growing consensus against executions of the mentally retarded as evidenced by the increased number of prohibitions against such executions, the infrequency of such executions, and opposition by RELIGIONS, professional, and world communities. Second, the deterrent effect of capital punishment is compromised by the diminished abilities of the mentally retarded. The mentally retarded are also less capable of effectively arguing mitigating circumstances, thus increasing the likelihood that they will be wrongfully executed. However, as in *Penry v. Lynaugh*, the Court acknowledged that not all mentally retarded are similarly impaired and left it to the states to legislate appropriately. The Supreme Court began reviewing the states' rules in *Tennard v. Dretke*, 542 U.S. 274 (2004), which overturned a capital punishment sentence because, although the defendant's low IQ was presented as a mitigating factor, the jury was instructed only to consider the deliberate nature of the crime and the probability of future crimes. In *Panetti v. Quarterman*, 551 U.S. 930 (2007), the Supreme Court overturned the standard used by the Fifth Circuit, which required an understanding between the crime and punishment. The defendant illustrated that this standard was too restrictive since the defendant's delusions prevented him from understanding that he was being executed for murder, thus preventing capital punishment from serving its retributive purpose.

Finally, in cases such as in *Brown v. Plata*, 563 U.S. __ (2011), the Supreme Court ruled that the overcrowding of jail and prison facilities can constitute a variation of the Eighth Amendment. In that case, the California prison system had twice the number of inmates the facilities were designed to hold to allow for safe and sanitary detention.

As illustrated, the interpretation of "cruel and unusual punishment" is evolving in both the legislative and the judicial sense, with the Supreme Court evolving its decisions to ensure that the interpretation of the Eighth Amendment meets the standards of society.

For more information

Brodenhamer, David J., and James W. Ely. *The Bill of Rights in Modern America* Bloomington: Indiana University Press, 2008.

Levy, Leonard William. *Origins of the Bill of Rights.* New Haven, Conn.: Yale University Press, 1999.

Smith, Rich. *The Eighth Amendment.* Edina, Minn.: ABDO, 2008.

Kathleen Barrett
Georgia State University

Eisenstadt v. Baird 405 U.S. 438 (1972) *Eisenstadt v. Baird* is an important Supreme Court decision that reversed William Baird's conviction for distributing a contraceptive.

Eisenstadt v. Baird bridges the Court's privacy decision in GRISWOLD V. CONNECTICUT, 381 U.S. 479 (1965), with its controversial landmark ABORTION rights decision, *ROE V. WADE*, 410 U.S. 113 (1973). Although concerned with contraception—like *Griswold*—*dictum* (a nonbinding statement made in the course of rendering a decision) in Justice WILLIAM J. BRENNAN's plurality opinion in *Eisenstadt v. Baird* broadened the right of privacy in ways that paved the way for *Roe*.

Prominent birth control advocate William Baird was ARRESTED, first for exhibiting contraceptive articles in the course of delivering a lecture on contraception to a group of students at Boston University and, second, for giving a young woman a package of Emko vaginal foam at the close of his talk. He was convicted of violating a Massachusetts statute that provides a maximum five-year term of imprisonment for "whoever . . . gives away . . . any drug, medicine, instrument or article whatever for the prevention of conception. . . ." except "[a] registered physician may administer to or prescribe for any married person drugs or articles intended for the prevention of pregnancy or conception." The Massachusetts Supreme Judicial Court unanimously set aside the conviction for exhibiting contraceptives on the ground that it violated Baird's First Amendment rights, but by a 4–3 vote sustained the conviction for giving away the foam. Baird filed a petition for a federal writ of habeas corpus, which the District Court dismissed. On appeal, however, the COURT OF APPEALS for the First Circuit vacated the dismissal and remanded the action with directions to grant the writ discharging Baird. Eisenstadt, the sheriff of Suffolk County, Massachusetts, APPEALED to the U.S. Supreme Court.

Eisenstadt v. Baird was decided by a 6–1 vote. Justices Powell and Rehnquist did not participate. CHIEF JUSTICE Burger dissented. Of the six justices voting to affirm the First Circuit Court of Appeals, two (White and Blackmun) argued that Baird's conviction could not stand because, under *Griswold*, Baird had a constitutionally protected right to distribute contraceptives to married persons and, "nothing has been placed in the [trial] record to indicate [the recipient's] marital Status," thereby depriving "us of knowing whether Baird was in fact convicted for making a constitutionally protected distribution of Emko to a married person."

Three justices (Douglas, Marshall, and Stewart) joined Justice Brennan's opinion. Justice Brennan held that Baird's conviction violated the Fourteenth Amendment EQUAL PROTECTION clause because there exists no "ground of difference that rationally explains the different treatment accorded married and unmarried persons under Massachusetts General Laws . . . [and] whatever the rights of the individual to access to contraceptives may be, the rights must be the same for the unmarried and the married alike." Having resolved the constitutional status of the Massachusetts law, Justice Brennan added:

> If under *Griswold* the distribution of contraceptives to married persons cannot be prohibited, a ban on distribution to unmarried persons would be equally impermissible. It is true that in *Griswold* the right of privacy in question inhered in the marital relationship. Yet the marital couple is not an independent entity with a mind and heart of its own, but an association of two individuals each with a separate intellectual and emotional makeup. If the right of privacy means anything, it is the right of the individual, married or single, to be free from unwarranted governmental intrusion into matters so fundamentally affecting a person as the decision whether to bear or beget a child.

Brennan's expansive reading of *Griswold* as bearing on the decision "whether to bear . . . a child" opened the door for the argument in *Roe v. Wade* that women—married or unmarried—had a constitutional right to choose an abortion.

For more information

Goldstein, Leslie Friedman. *Contemporary Cases in Women's Rights*. Madison: University of Wisconsin Press, 1994, chap. 1.

James C. Foster
Department of Political Science
Oregon State University

electronic monitoring Electronic monitoring is a type of COMMUNITY CORRECTIONS program that is used as an alternative to incarceration. Offenders who are on PROBATION or PAROLE can be placed on supervised release using electronic monitoring. Offenders receiving this type of sanction are typically nonviolent offenders, often with a drug conviction. Sometimes referred to as "house arrest," electronic monitoring was one measure of supervision developed to address the concerns of overcrowding in correctional institutions that occurred in the 1970s and 1980s.

Electronic monitoring consists of a device that is usually worn around the ankle of an offender for the purposes of keeping track of the person's location. The device sends a signal to the agency in charge of monitoring. The signal can be either active, which is a continuous signal, or passive, which is a signal set to dial at repeated intervals. In either case, if the signal is broken, the offender is considered to not be in an approved location. If this occurs, that person is considered to be in violation. It is possible to remove the electronic device by cutting it. If the monitoring device is removed without permission prior to the end of the sentence, the offender is considered to be in violation as well.

Other perceived benefits to electronic monitoring were cost-effectiveness, reduction in reoffending and harm to the offender. The electronic technology was considered to be cost-effective because it reduced the amount of individual monitoring necessary with home visits by a probation or parole officer. Further, the charges for this type of supervision are borne by the offender or his or her FAMILY and are not very costly. In addition, community supervision was one tool believed to prevent or reduce the harshness of the prison environment and could enable a higher likelihood of success by not returning to criminal activity.

Practitioners and academics agree that effectiveness in reducing reoffending behavior is questionable. However, supervised release, when used in combination with other services specific to the offenders' needs, may be more beneficial with reducing the likelihood of returning to criminal activity. For example, if drug-addicted offenders receive drug counseling and attend therapy sessions and other services to meet their needs, it may be a smoother transition for them. Lastly, recent advances with electronic monitoring technology have expanded the scope of monitoring offenders' locations to protect victims. Devices having this capability can alert victims if the offender is near the victim's area. This is especially helpful in cases where the victim suffered some form of abuse by the offender.

For more information

MacKenzie, Doris Layton. *What Works in Corrections: Reducing the Criminal Activities of Offenders and Delinquents*. New York: Cambridge University Press, 2006.

Siegel, Larry J. *Introduction to Criminal Justice*. 12th ed. Belmont, Calif.: Wadsworth, 2009.

Michelle L. Foster
Kent State University

Ellsworth, Oliver (1745–1807) chief justice of the United States Oliver Ellsworth served as a state JUDGE, representative to the Second Continental Congress, the Constitutional Convention, senator, ambassador, and third CHIEF JUSTICE of the United States Supreme Court. He was born in Windsor, Connecticut, on April 29, 1745. Graduating from the College of New Jersey (later Princeton University) in 1766, he soon began "reading the law." In 1771 he commenced legal practice in Windsor.

His career developed with a number of legal and political appointments. While serving as state attorney of Hartford County he was chosen in 1777 to represent Connecticut in the Second Continental Congress.

Beginning in May of 1787 Ellsworth served at the Constitutional Convention in Philadelphia. His service is best remembered for coauthoring (with Roger Sherman) the Connecticut Compromise, which resolved conflicts between the small and large states over representation in the two houses of Congress. Ellsworth also contributed the term "United States" to the new CONSTITUTION.

In 1789 Ellsworth became one of Connecticut's first two U.S. senators. As chair of the Rules Committee he helped to formulate the new Senate's rules. He also chaired the conference committee, which drafted the BILL OF RIGHTS, and he was the principal author of the Judiciary Act of 1789 (1 *Statutes* 73), creating the organizational structure of the FEDERAL COURT SYSTEM.

On March 4, 1796, President George Washington appointed Ellsworth to the U.S. Supreme Court. His very limited service was solid. With only partial success, he persuaded members of the Court to issue a single *per curiam* decision for a case rather than *seriatim* decisions (i.e., individual members of the Court each issuing an opinion). In 1796 Ellsworth issued a decision in the case of *United States v. La Vengeance* (3 Dallas 297) that outlined and increased the boundaries of federal admiralty JURISDICTION.

The Ellsworth court also ruled that its appellate jurisdiction must be prescribed through statutory elaboration by Congress. This view of the Court's appellate jurisdiction arose in a case involving the issue of whether an EQUITY degree should come to the Court by a writ of error or a writ of appeal. Ellsworth reasoned that a writ of APPEAL is a process of civil law origin and removes a cause entirely, subjecting the facts as well as the law to review and retrial. A writ of error on the other hand is a process of common-law origin, and it removes nothing for reexamination but the law, *Wiscart v. Dauchy*, 3 Dallas 321 (1796).

Chief Justice Oliver Ellsworth (Engraved after a portrait by Chappell, Collection of the Supreme Court of the United States)

In 1799 Ellsworth was sent on an ambassadorial mission to stop French privateering of U.S. shipping. While in France his health failed. He resigned his chief justiceship on October 16, 1800, and returned home. He died at Windsor, November 26, 1807.

For more information

Brown, William Garrott. *Life of Oliver Ellsworth.* New York: Da Capo Press, 1970.

Casto, William R. *The Supreme Court in the Early Republic: The Chief Justiceships of John Jay and Oliver Ellsworth.* Columbia: University of South Carolina Press, 1995.

Andrew J. Waskey
Dalton State College

Emancipation Proclamation The Emancipation Proclamation declared "forever free" slaves residing in the rebellious Confederate states. In the short term, because the Confederacy was at war with the Union in 1862, the Emancipation Proclamation liberated no one. Its immediate significance was that it served as ABRAHAM LINCOLN's adroit tactical response to threatening political pressures being exerted on him from domestic and foreign sources. There actually are two Emancipation Proclamations, Lincoln's more well-known announcement made on September 22, 1862, and his proclamation implementing that preliminary declaration on New Year's Day, 1863.

In 1862 circumstances were dire for both the Union cause and Lincoln's presidency. The Federal army could find neither military leadership nor battlefield victory. Abroad, European governments were growing impatient with the Union blockade of Southern ports and increasingly inclined to bestow diplomatic recognition on the Confederacy. At home, George B. McClellan, one of Lincoln's own generals, was positioning himself eventually to run against the president in the 1864 election. Constitutionally, Lincoln was hemmed in by the fugitive slave clause (Article IV, section 2), which required federal officials to return runaways, and *DRED SCOTT V. SANFORD*, 19 Howard 393 (1857), where seven Supreme Court justices had declared, among other inflammatory things, that Congress had no constitutional authority to ban slavery in the territories, which it had done in the 1820 Missouri Compromise. Never one to be deterred from his transcendent goal of preserving the Union—either by the letter of constitutional provisions, or a Supreme Court with which he disagreed—Lincoln chafed to seize the initiative back from his various opponents.

The vehicle he drafted to serve this purpose reflected practical, policy, and philosophical considerations. As a practical matter, Lincoln needed to make a bold move to placate abolitionists complaining that he was soft on the issue of slavery, and to outflank potential electoral opponents like McClellan who were agitating for concessions to the Confederacy. Tenuous foreign relations with England and France required Lincoln to fashion a policy that would provide these wavering nations with a reason for not allying with the Confederacy. Philosophically, Lincoln was torn. On the one hand, he was a long-time opponent of extension of slavery into the territories—a position rooted in his embrace of the "freedom national" doctrine that liberty is the universal human condition, slavery an aberration. On the other hand, Lincoln was deeply skeptical about blacks' capacities and about the ability of freed slaves and whites to live together in a single nation.

His proclamation, drafted in secret in July 1862, began by citing his constitutional authority as "commander-in-chief of the army and navy" and by reaffirming his conviction that the "object" of the Civil War was "practically restoring the constitutional relation between the United States and each of the States." Lincoln then threw down a symbolic gauntlet. By January 1, 1863, "all persons held as slaves within any State . . . the people whereof shall then be in rebellion against the United States, shall be then, thenceforward, and forever free. . . ." Between July and September, Lincoln waited impatiently for an occasion to make his proclamation public. When Union and Confederate forces fought each other to a bloody draw at Antietam Creek, Lincoln declared victory and issued his proclamation. In one grand gesture, Lincoln converted the Civil War from a brutal fratricidal feud into a high moral crusade.

In the short run, the Emancipation Proclamation's effect was largely symbolic because it freed no slaves immediately. It did serve Lincoln's purposes of placating critics at home and undercutting potential enemies abroad. In the longer term, the Emancipation Proclamation galvanized Northerners to persevere until victory was won and, after Appomattox, it laid the groundwork for the 1865 Thirteenth Amendment to

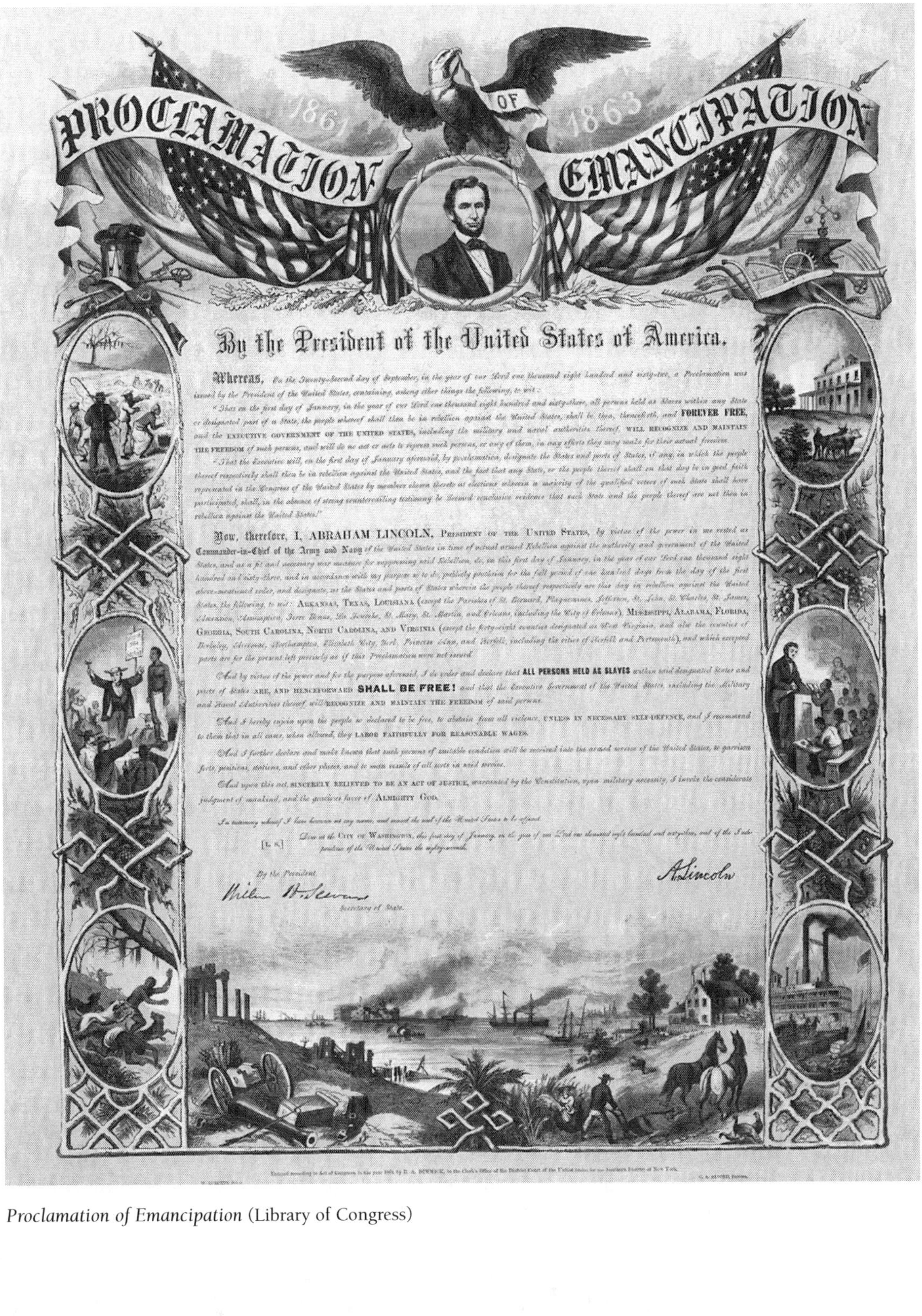

Proclamation of Emancipation (Library of Congress)

the Constitution, which declares that "[n]either slavery nor involuntary servitude . . . shall exist within the United States."

For more information

Belz, Herman. *Emancipation and Equal Rights: Politics and Constitutionalism in the Civil War Era.* New York: W. W. Norton, 1978.

Wiecek, William M. *The Sources of Anti-slavery Constitutionalism in America, 1760–1848.* Ithaca, N.Y.: Cornell University Press, 1977.

James C. Foster
Department of Political Science
Oregon State University

embezzlement Embezzlement is "the crime of misappropriating money or property entrusted to one's care, custody, or control" (Reiman, 128). A simpler description would be that it is a form of THEFT. It is separated from other thefts mainly because of the way that it is done and the persons who do it.

If someone were to stop you on a dark street and demand all the cash in your wallet, that would clearly be theft. However, if you give an insurance agent the contents of your wallet in exchange for an insurance policy and the agent then decides to use your money to buy a new pair of shoes instead, that is embezzlement. The "funds" are said to have been "misappropriated" or an instance of "conversion" has taken place.

Similarly, a bank employee who has access to multiple accounts may decide to take a little money from several accounts and place that money belonging to other people into an account where he can access it for personal use. This money has been stolen, but the crime committed is embezzlement.

A chief financial officer (CFO) entrusted with investing employee retirement monies may decide to take a part of the profits from those investments. If she removes money from an account that she does not own but has been entrusted to oversee, and places that money into her individual account for her individual benefit, this is a form of theft. However, it is usually referred to as "misappropriation of funds," and the crime committed is embezzlement.

Embezzlement can occur in any industry in which there is a motivated offender and access to money or other transferable assets. Data on embezzlement losses are difficult to ascertain because of a lack of reporting, a lack of central data collection, and the diversity of ways in which these crimes are handled. However, in 2003, the U.S. Chamber of Commerce estimated losses due to embezzlement at $15.2 billion (Reiman, 127).

Persons ARRESTED for embezzlement are less likely to face prison time for their crimes than are run-of-the-mill thieves. When imprisoned, their sentences are far shorter. However, they tend to steal far more money than other thieves, and as a group they have a much greater effect upon the economy than do other thieves.

Laws prohibiting those entrusted with the property of others from taking it for their own use originated in England in the 1400s. A series of laws evolved over the ensuing 300 years until laws prohibiting embezzlement by banking employees were established and are the basis of the more current legal prohibitions.

For more information

Friedrichs, David O. *Trusted Criminals: White Collar Crime in Contemporary Society.* Belmont, Calif.: Thomson Higher Education, 2007.

Reiman, Jeffrey. *The Rich Get Richer and the Poor Get Prison.* Boston: Allyn and Bacon, 2007.

Loretta Capeheart
Northeastern Illinois University

eminent domain Eminent domain is the power of the government to take a person's property for public use, even over the objection of the owner.

All variety of governments claim this authority. The power of eminent domain allows for a variety of government projects designed to improve the quality of life for the public generally. For example, the government may need to take someone's property in order to make way for a road to ease traffic congestion, or a farm may have to be flooded in order to build a dam to generate electricity or to create a lake for public recreation. In these situations, the government uses its power of eminent domain to take possession of the property.

Eminent domain gives the government considerable authority to interfere with individuals' property rights. In the United States, this power is constrained by the TAKINGS CLAUSE, that section of the Fifth Amendment to the U.S. CONSTITUTION that declares "nor shall private property be taken for public use, without just compensation." The takings clause requires the government to pay for the property it takes. In *Armstrong v. U.S.* (1960) Justice Black summarized the purpose of the takings clause as assuring that no individual is forced to bear the cost of government projects "which in all fairness and JUSTICE, should be borne by the public as a whole." Since the whole community benefits from public projects, it is only fair that the whole community (rather than the individual property owner) pay for them.

The government does not have to come into possession of an owner's property but must merely have deprived him of the ability to use it, in order to have effected a taking. This issue arose in the case *U.S. v. Causby* (1946). The Causby family ran a small chicken farm. When the air corps built a training field next to their house and began flying planes over their property, the Causbys became upset and had difficulty sleeping through the noisy flights. Many of the chickens died from fear, and the productivity of the others decreased, as a result of low flying aircraft. The government argued that it should not have to pay compensation because it had not physically occupied the farm. The Supreme Court disagreed, arguing that "it is the owner's loss, not the taker's gain, which is the measure of the property taken."

When the government does exercise the power of eminent domain, it is required to pay compensation equivalent to the fair market value of the property. Owners do not always accept that the price offered is sufficient to compensate them for their loss. In such cases, owners may seek arbitration or file suit seeking greater compensation. Owners may then refuse to surrender the property until some compromise has been reached. This can slow the progress of public projects, but it is considered necessary to protect property rights.

Eminent domain is supposed to be exercised for public purposes, not merely for the benefit of a private individual or group. In *Cole v. LaGrange* (1884) the Supreme Court held that property may not be taken "for any but a public object." Owners have objected to government projects that seem designed to benefit private parties. Even so, courts have recently tended to defer to legislative judgments about public purpose. For example, in *Hawaii Housing Authority v. Midkiff* (1984) the Court upheld a state program that transferred property from large landowners to a significant number of private people who had been leasing the land. The Court ruled that breaking up the oligopoly controlling most Hawaiian land was a sufficiently public purpose, even though private individuals would benefit.

Perhaps the most controversial recent decision regarding the use of eminent domain was *Kelo v. City of New London*, 545 U.S. 469 (2005). In that case, a closely divided Supreme Court ruled that the Fifth Amendment's public use stipulation permitted the taking of a private residential property and turning it over to another private party in order to promote economic development. The Court rejected arguments to declare promoting economic development was not a valid public purpose for the use of eminent domain. As a result of this case, many states passed legislation restricting or narrowing the conditions under which eminent domain might be used.

Overall, eminent domain remains a powerful tool for the national, state, and local governments to use in order to promote a variety of public purposes. The main restriction on its use is that just compensation must be paid to owners when their property is taken.

For more information

Epstein, Richard A. *Takings: Private Property and the Power of Eminent Domain.* Cambridge, Mass.: Harvard University Press, 1985.

Schultz, David. *Evicted! Property Rights and Eminent Domain in America.* Westport, Conn.: Praeger Press, 2009.

David Schultz
Hamline University

Employment Division, Department of Human Resources of Oregon v. Smith 494 U.S. 872 (1990) *Employment Division, Department of Human Resources of Oregon v. Smith* marked an abrupt shift away from nearly three decades of the Supreme Court's settled position on First Amendment free exercise law, prompting political debate over how government regulates individual religious freedom.

Two Native Americans, Alfred Smith and Galen Black, were members of the Native American Church, whose religious sacraments required ingesting peyote (a hallucinogen produced from cactus plants), a controlled substance in Oregon. Smith and Black were fired from their jobs with a private drug rehabilitation organization and applied for unemployment compensation, but Oregon's Employment Division denied them benefits based on work-related "misconduct." Bringing suit in state court, Smith and Black argued that states could not withhold unemployment benefits because of an individual's religious exercise. Oregon responded that the use of peyote was criminalized by a general statute that incidentally affected religious practices, not by a law enacted specifically to burden RELIGION. Oregon's Supreme Court ruled that the state law violated the First Amendment's free exercise clause, and Oregon APPEALED to the Supreme Court.

The Court held that Oregon could deny unemployment benefits to Smith and Black for their use of a controlled substance. Writing for the majority, Justice ANTONIN SCALIA ruled that their free exercise claim was invalid because Oregon's criminal law was not specifically intended to infringe upon religious free exercise. The statute was a "valid and neutral law of general applicability" that only incidentally had the effect of burdening free exercise.

Until *Smith,* the Court's settled standard for free exercise claims had been its most rigorous: Laws burdening a person's free exercise of religion must be narrowly tailored to further a "compelling governmental interest." In *Smith* the Court replaced this high threshold that a state had to meet if it burdened an individual's free exercise—the "compelling interest" standard—with a much lower threshold of "neutrality" and "general applicability" that the Court explicitly had abandoned years before.

As a result of this abrupt shift in the Court's interpretation of the free exercise clause, *Smith* catalyzed the mobilization of diverse interest groups concerned with protecting free expression and the free exercise of religious beliefs and practices. These groups lobbied for federal legislation incorporating the "compelling interest" standard for free exercise claims used by the Court prior to *Smith.* Congress listened, enacting the 1993 Religious Freedom Restoration Act (RFRA). The RFRA borrowed the Court's pre-*Smith* language, requiring that laws passed at the state or federal level that burdened an individual's religious exercise meet the "compelling interest" standard. Although the RFRA was intended to return to the pre-*Smith* standard, it gave rise to many more questions than it answered, particularly from states concerned that it unduly burdened the legislative process.

In *City of Boerne, Texas v. Flores,* 521 U.S. 507 (1997), the Supreme Court struck down the RFRA, holding that Congress had overstepped its legitimate lawmaking role by broadening constitutional rights that already had been interpreted by the Court. (A ruling of the Supreme Court can be explicitly overturned only by constitutional amendment.) The Court thus breathed new life into *Smith*'s guidelines for balancing the role of government against individuals' exercise of religious beliefs. However, the Court still has not fully resolved the appropriate standard for free exercise disputes, suggesting the inevitability of future political conflicts over the role of religion.

For more information

Choper, Jesse. *Securing Religious Liberty.* 1995.

Epps, Garrett. "To an Unknown God: The Hidden History of *Employment Division v. Smith.*" *Arizona State Law Journal* 30 (1998): 953.

Steven A. Light
University of North Dakota

employment law Employment law is the set of legal rules, other than LABOR LAW, that govern the workplace. Employment law differs from labor law in that it regulates the individual employer-employee relationship while labor law regulates the collective rights and obligations resulting from union representation.

Until the 1960s, the employment relationship largely was free from governmental regulation in the nonunion setting. The employment law of today, in contrast, consists of a complex web of federal and state regulation. With no single law governing the employment relationship, a major employment law issue concerns the need to accommodate the sometimes overlapping federal and state laws.

The at-will rule long has served as the principal legal foundation for the employment relationship. In the absence of some contractual understanding to the contrary, the at-will rule gives both employers and employees the right to terminate their relationship without cause or notice. Put another way, an employer may discharge an employee under the at-will rule for any or no reason.

While the at-will rule still survives, it is now subject to a number of exceptions. The principal limitation is provided by antidiscrimination statutes. Three federal statutes ban discrimination in employment based upon certain employee characteristics. Title VII of the 1964 Civil Rights Act prohibits discrimination in hiring or firing on the basis of race, color, religion, sex, or national origin. The Age Discrimination in Employment Act, adopted in 1967, protects employees over the age of 40 years from discrimination in hiring, discharge, and mandatory retirement. Finally, the AMERICANS WITH DISABILITIES ACT, enacted in 1990, prohibits employers from discriminating against an otherwise qualified disabled person who, with or without a reasonable accommodation, is capable of performing the essential functions of the job.

State courts also recognize certain common-law limitations on an employer's right to terminate an employee. Most states, for example, permit a discharged employee to recover TORT damages if he or she is discharged for a reason that offends notions of public policy, such as for refusing to commit an illegal act or for exercising a right conferred by statute. A smaller number of states recognize a covenant of good faith and fair dealing, which prohibits bad faith terminations that frustrate legitimate contractual expectations.

Beyond those laws limiting an employer's discharge right, a number of other federal employment laws regulate the terms and conditions of the employment relationship. These include the following:

Occupational Safety and Health (OSH) Act. The OSH Act authorizes the secretary of labor to adopt workplace health and safety standards. The secretary is empowered to enforce these standards through workplace inspections and by issuing citations for noncompliance.

Employee Retirement Income Security Act (ERISA). ERISA regulates pension and employee welfare benefit plans. It establishes procedural requirements with respect to the reporting, disclosure, and fiduciary responsibilities for such plans and broadly preempts state laws relating to employee benefits.

Worker Adjustment and Retraining Notification (WARN) Act. The WARN Act requires employers with 100 or more employees to provide at least 60 days advance written notice to employees who will suffer an employment loss by virtue of a plant closing or a mass layoff.

Family and Medical Leave Act (FMLA). The FMLA requires employers with 50 or more employees to permit employees to take up to 12 weeks each year of unpaid leave in order to care for a new child or a family member with a serious health condition. The FMLA's leave entitlement also extends to an employee who is incapacitated because of his or her own serious health condition.

Various state statutes provide further regulation of the employment relationship. These include the following:

Unemployment compensation statutes. Every state has a law providing for short-term benefit payments following an involuntary termination of employment that is not the result of misconduct. An employee generally must be actively seeking suitable reemployment in order to qualify for these benefits.

DRUG TESTING statutes. A number of states have statutes that specify the circumstances in which employers may test applicants and employees for the illegal use of drugs.

Whistleblowing statutes. Many states also protect employees from retaliatory acts if they report employer wrongdoing to governmental authorities.

The number of employment law claims has risen substantially over the past 20 years. Employment law disputes now make up approximately 20 percent of the cases on FEDERAL COURT dockets.

For more information

Befort, Stephen F., and Karen G. Schanfield. *Employment Law and Practice.* St. Paul, Minn.: West, 1995, 1999–2000 Supp.

Rothstein, Mark A., Charles B. Craver, Elinon P. Schroeder, and Elaine W. Shoben. *Employment Law.* 2nd ed. St. Paul, Minn.: West, 1999.

Stephen F. Befort
University of Minnesota Law School

Engel v. Vitale 370 U.S. 421 (1962) *Engel v. Vitale* prohibited public school–sponsored prayer. The case concerned a prayer that read, "Almighty God, we acknowledge our dependence upon Thee, and we beg Thy blessings upon us, our parents, our teachers and our Country." Engel sought to overturn a lower court ruling that found the prayer constitutional, arguing that any prayer supported by the state violated the ESTABLISHMENT CLAUSE of the First Amendment. Engel was represented by William J. Butler and supported by the AMERICAN CIVIL LIBERTIES UNION and a number of Jewish groups. Vitale sought to uphold the lower court, arguing that the statute was constitutional because it was not coercive and did not spend state funds. Vitale was represented by Wilford E. Neier and Porter R. Chandler and supported by the Board of Regents of the State of New York and 20 state ATTORNEYS GENERAL. The case was argued in the Supreme Court on April 3, 1962, and decided on June 25. In a 6-1 decision, Justice Black, writing for the Court, ruled in favor of Engel, finding the prayer unconstitutional. Justice Douglas concurred, Justice Stewart dissented, and Justices Frankfurter and White did not take part in the decision.

The constitutionality of the prayer considered in *Engel v. Vitale* depended on the justices' understanding of the establishment clause of the First Amendment, which reads, "Congress shall make no law considering an Establishment of religion." Two separate traditions make very different statements about the establishment clause. One tradition, drawing on the writings of Thomas Jefferson and James Madison, urges strict separation of church and state. The other tradition takes the clause to mean only that the state cannot establish an official RELIGION.

Justice Black's majority opinion finally embraced the tradition of separation. The footnotes in his decision include references to the writings of Jefferson and Madison. Black's opinion is long on history and perhaps a bit short on legal PRECEDENT. Black emphasizes the repression of religious minorities by majorities and the role that this fact played in the founding. Black rejects the claim that prohibitions on school prayer constitute a hostility to religion. He argues that the separation of church and state preserves the dignity of religion and the autonomy of religion from state interference.

Justice Stewart took a very different view of the establishment clause. He argued that the clause merely prohibited the state from establishing an official religion. In his dissent, he emphasizes that the prayer is not coercive and is nondenominational. Stewart dismisses Black's detailed historical inquiry as irrelevant and argues that the CONSTITUTION mentions no "wall of separation." He also argues that many government institutions, including the Supreme Court and Congress, open their days with prayer, and that the Pledge of Allegiance and National Anthem both mention God.

Engel v. Vitale set a strong precedent against the constitutionality of prayer in schools. Allowing the student to be excused at the request of the student or the student's parents did not constitute proof that the prayer was not coercive. The Court also established that even though prayer may be a part of the country's cultural heritage, it is also essentially spiritual. It is the first decision of many on the controversial issue of school prayer, which continues to be important as a political issue today, as schools seek to have prayers at football games and graduations. The Court reaffirmed the no coercion principle of *Engel* in 1992 in *Lee v. Weisman,* when it refused to permit prayer at graduation, and in 2000, in *Sante Fe Independent School District v. Doe,* in which it refused to allow a school board policy that authorized students to vote, first, whether to allow religious invocations at football games, and then to choose the person to deliver them. Thus, *Engel v. Vitale* has served as a foundation for many other cases, including school prayer, state support to religion, and accommodation of religious practices.

For more information

Fraser, James W. *Between Church and State: Religion and Public Education in a Multicultural America.* New York: St. Martin's Press, 1999.

Ravitch, Frank S. *School Prayer and Discrimination: The Civil Rights of Religious Minorities and Dissenters.* Boston: Northeastern University Press, 1999.

Ronald Kahn
Oberlin College

enterprise crime Enterprise crime is a crime committed by a set of individuals or groups.

An enterprise is a set of individuals, groups, or corporations that may or may not represent a legal entity. These may include corporations, unions, GANGS, organizations, or any other grouping of people. Criminal enterprises are highly organized, hierarchical, and focused on making large sums of money. Those at the top of the enterprise structure not only manage the affairs but are most handsomely rewarded and in the least threat of ARREST.

Syndicates are often formed between the larger enterprise crime organizations in order to best exploit the markets of interest and/or to otherwise provide mutual support to the interests of each. The similarities between enterprise crime and free enterprise are many. In fact, some would argue that the only difference between free enterprise and enterprise crime is that one is clearly engaged in illegal activities. While free enterprise works to maintain an air of legitimacy, enterprise crime carries no such burden.

Enterprise crime is at times referred to as ORGANIZED CRIME. Enterprise crime, however, is sometimes carried out in cooperation between legitimate business and organized crime. It is often difficult to ascertain whether the legitimate business is aware of its dealings with the criminal enterprise. It can be argued that these legitimate businesses know or should have known that they are dealing with criminals and, therefore, are also engaged in a form of criminal enterprise. For example, a bank that allows a wealthy customer to deposit large sums of cash, bypassing the federal regulations on reporting, should know that this money is ill-gotten and that the business favor granted is in fact a crime. The bank then is engaged in money laundering in exchange for large deposits whether they admit to knowing this or not.

Enterprise crime knows no borders and respects no ideologies. Although, historically, these groupings have at times developed along particular ethnic or national lines, these groups have shown a remarkable flexibility in their loyalties. The successful criminal enterprise tends to follow the most productive markets and use the most skilled operatives regardless of origin. Therefore, the globalization of markets has meant an expansion of criminal enterprises across the globe and an intensification of their presence in every market.

Illegal goods and services tend to be the bread and butter of criminal enterprises, and these are global markets. Drugs, guns, pornography, sex slavery, and other smuggling operations are central to the global criminal enterprise. The relationships between these operations and businesses considered legitimate as well as the political structures of every country in which production, transportation, and/or sales occur are necessary to the perpetuation of enterprise crime.

For more information

Morselli, Carlo. *Contacts, Opportunities, and Criminal Enterprise.* Toronto: University of Toronto Press, 2005.

Nordstrom, Carolyn. *Global Outlaws: Crime, Money, and Power in the Contemporary World.* Berkeley: University of California Press, 2007.

Loretta Capeheart
Northeastern Illinois University

entrapment Entrapment occurs when a person is led to commit a crime by law enforcement personnel that he or she would otherwise have no intention of perpetrating.

In cases where a defendant is accused of a crime, a critical issue is whether the person is ready and willing to commit a crime without suggestion or provocation from law enforcement officials. The term is usually invoked in relation to defense in criminal cases. Over time, two opposing standards have emerged for determining the validity of an entrapment defense: the objective and subjective tests.

The objective test is focused primarily on the conduct of the police officers who are party to the ARREST, whereas the subjective test attempts to grapple with the state of mind of the defendant at the time the crime was committed. This latter standard emerged from two drug-related cases decided in the 1970s. The first case was *United States vs. Russell,* 411 U.S. 423 (1973), in which the conviction was upheld, involved a known drug dealer who manufactured methamphetamine to sell from components that were partially supplied by government agents. The second was *Hampton vs. United States,* 425 U.S. 484 (1976), which affirmed the conviction of a drug dealer poised to sell drugs to a DEA agent upon seeing exposed track marks on the agent's arm. Both of these cases rested on the notion that the defendants were already strongly predisposed to engage in illegal drug activity and, therefore, the conduct of the agents was irrelevant. Many have balked at these findings, claiming they minimize government culpability, including several justices who have in dissent advocated an objective standard. This objective standard they are invoking rises out of earlier cases and is more in keeping with the notion that the government should not induce criminal conduct and that to do so cuts dangerously close to transgressing constitutional freedoms.

The first and most notable case in which an entrapment defense was allowed to stand was *Sorrells v. United States,* 287 U.S. 435 (1932), which lays bare what objective entrapment means. Sorrels, a recovering alcoholic, was repeatedly badgered and bated by a PROHIBITION officer, and, upon finally giving in, was charged with consumption of "intoxicating liquors" in violation of the Eighteenth Amendment. Clear inducement by government agents, coupled with Sorrells's previously affirmed sobriety, makes it clear that he was led to commit a crime he otherwise had no intention of committing. Thus, this case can be taken to define entrapment and illustrate the objective standard often advocated for by justices of the Court.

For more information

Lafave, Wayne R. *Criminal Law.* St. Paul, Minn.: Thomson-West, 2003.

Adam L. Kress
SUNY Albany

environmental law Environmental law is a complex collection of federal and state statutes and regulations, and common-law principles, which seek to control the impacts of human beings and their activities on the natural environment and natural resources. These laws seek to control the deterioration of the environment by (1) the overuse or depletion of natural resources, such as land, water, and biodiversity, and (2) pollution, such as air and water pollution, and waste production and disposal.

Prior to 1970, the vast majority of environmental litigation was based on common law. Injured parties utilized tort law causes of action, such as NUISANCE, trespass, strict liability, and negligence to halt environmental degradation and for compensation for environmental injuries. However, TORT-based environmental litigation was difficult to initiate because plaintiffs often had difficulty proving who caused their injuries. Even when injured parties could overcome these obstacles, courts were often reluctant to grant INJUNCTIONS to prevent future environmental harm.

The federal government responded to these common-law problems, and inadequate and inconsistent state and local government environmental laws and ordinances, in the 1970s. While common-law remedies are still available, and state and local government enactments serve an increasingly important role, the most important and effective environmental laws are federal statutes.

Federal environmental statutes usually begin as comprehensive laws designed to remedy an entire environmental problem. These enactments are often followed by a set of amendments that ultimately address manageable aspects of the problem. This pattern defines a key feature of federal environmental laws—complex layers of detailed statutes.

Federal environmental statutes can be grouped into three categories: broad policy statutes, ecological and natural resource conservation statutes, and public health statutes. The National Environmental Policy Act is the most famous broad policy statute. It requires the federal government to consider the environmental consequences of its actions when it plans major projects.

Ecological and natural resource conservation statutes conserve these resources on public and private lands. The Endangered Species Act requires the federal government to safeguard endangered and threatened species on its lands and requires private landowners to protect these species on their lands. The National Forest Management Act specifies how the U.S. Forest Service manages National Forests, and the Wilderness Act dictates the management of wilderness areas.

Congress has enacted scores of statutes to protect the public health, including the Clean Air Act (CAA), the Clean Water Act (CWA), the Resource Conservation and Recovery Act (RCRA), and the Comprehensive Environmental Response, Compensation, and Liability Act (CERCLA). The CAA and CWA use complex regulatory mechanisms to control air and water pollution. RCRA provides for the "cradle-to-grave" regulation of hazardous materials. CERCLA, also known as Superfund, is designed to clean up hazardous waste disposal sites.

While the complexity of environmental law often makes compliance costly, these laws have improved U.S. environmental quality. However, as scientists increasingly demonstrate that many environmental problems are global, rather than national, humanity needs international environmental laws that address these issues.

For more information

Chapman, Stephen. *Environmental Law and Policy.* Upper Saddle River, N.J.: Prentice Hall, 1998.

Kubasek, Nancy, and Gary Silverman. *Environmental Law.* 3rd ed. Upper Saddle River, N.J.: Prentice Hall, 2000.

Robert W. Malmsheimer
SUNY College of
Environmental Science and Forestry
Syracuse, New York

Environmental Protection Agency The Environmental Protection Agency is a federal independent regulatory agency responsible for the enforcement of numerous federal laws designed to protect the environment. Throughout the 1960s, Americans became increasingly concerned about harm to the quality of the natural environment. Private interest groups formed for the purpose of protecting the environment and began to pressure government to enact laws to do so. In 1970 Congress finally created the Environmental Protection Agency (EPA).

The act combined 15 different agencies and parts of agencies from throughout the federal government to consolidate a variety of research, monitoring, standard setting, and enforcement activities relating to pollution control and abatement. EPA's primary role is to establish and enforce standards for air, soil, and water quality, monitor and analyze the environment, conduct research, and support and coordinate research and antipollution activities carried out by state and local governments, private and public groups, individuals, and among other federal agencies with respect to the impact of their activities on the environment. The EPA is authorized to research possible and known environmental pollutants, adopt regulations limiting the levels of those pollutants, and enforce those regulations through monitoring, legal sanctions, and cleanup supervision.

The EPA at first was given authority only over air and water quality. However, throughout the 1970s and 1980s the EPA was given authority to enforce many more major federal environmental statutes. The EPA now has the primary responsibility for overseeing the implementation of major federal environmental laws such as the Clean Water Act; the Safe Drinking Water Act; the Clean Air Act; the Resource Conservation and Recovery Act; and the Comprehensive Environmental Response, Compensation, and Liability Act (Superfund). The agency now has more than 18,000 employees, and its annual budget is now more than $7 billion and is likely to steadily increase in future years.

The EPA has been responsible for numerous achievements during its relatively short life span. Among the major accomplishments have been a ban on the use of the toxic pesticide DDT, the elimination of lead from gasoline, improved automobile gas mileage efficiency while reducing automobile emissions, a ban on the use of chlorofluorocarbons (CFCs) responsible for ozone destruction, the cleanup of countless toxic waste dumps under the Superfund program, a ban on the dumping of sewage sludge into oceans and coastal waters, substantially improved water and air quality nationwide (especially in areas that were highly polluted beforehand), and the encouragement of widespread recycling programs.

Despite its history of successes, the EPA has been criticized, often severely, by both liberals and conservatives. Liberals argue that the agency is not doing enough to protect the environment, and that the EPA's focus on specific health risks from measurable pollution levels often ignores other equally or more important threats to the environment, such as ecosystem destruction. Liberals also charge the EPA with ignoring issues of environmental justice, such as the problem of hazardous waste sites often being located in poor or minority communities. Conservatives, on the other hand, accuse the EPA of imposing harsh and costly regulations on businesses, when the same goal of pollution reduction could be achieved by giving businesses flexibility in choosing the means by which pollution is decreased. Conservatives also attack the agency's calculations regarding unsafe levels of pollutants as being overly restrictive and not based on sound scientific evidence.

Regardless of whether criticisms from either end of the ideological spectrum are valid, public concern over the environment is likely going to remain high on the political agenda. Issues such as global warming, acid rain, depletion of the ozone layer, the destruction of rain forests and other ecosystems, and the extinction of endangered plant and animal species globally have all shown the need for regional and international solutions to environmental problems. Such problems cannot be solved merely by calculating, for example, the risk of cancer from exposure to a chemical and then restricting the use of that chemical to a safe level. Thus, public pressure will continue for Congress to enact additional environmental laws to address these problems more effectively. Given its tradition of having the primary enforcement responsibility for other major federal environmental laws, the EPA will most likely be involved with the implementation of these future environmental laws as well.

For more information

Landy, Marc K., Marc J. Roberts, and Stephen R. Thomas. *The Environmental Protection Agency: Asking the Wrong Questions*. New York: Oxford University Press, 1990.

Ortney, Paul R., Katherine N. Probst, and Adam M. Finkel. "The EPA at 'Thirtysomething,'" *Northwestern School of Law of Lewis and Clark College Journal of Environmental Law* 21, no. 1461 (1991).

Kristin L. Stewart
Attorney Rick Swanson, University of Louisiana, Lafayette

The Equal Pay Act The Equal Pay Act is a federal law aimed at eliminating pay discrimination based upon sex. Passed in 1963, it was the first major federal legal measure attempting to remedy the wage differential between men and women. The act requires that employers pay the same wage to men and women workers doing "equal" work. Essentially, equal work requires "equal skill, effort and responsibility, and which are performed under similar working conditions." The courts have interpreted this to mean that jobs should be "substantially identical," though they may have different titles, such as janitor and maid, or nurse's aide and orderly. The act provides employers with four defenses for wages that are not equal—seniority, merit, differences in quantity or quality of production, or any other factor not related to gender.

The act was intended to prevent paying women less than men in the same job classification, and it did confront the most blatant instances of sex discrimination in regard to pay. Still, a sizable wage gap prevails; in 1999 women continued to receive about 20 percent lower pay than men for comparable work. Economists have not been able to account for this gap, even after examining a wide range of productivity-related characteristics that determine wages (e.g., differences in education and training, job tenure, absenteeism, and hours of work). Much of that gap reflects the fact that women tend to work in female-dominated occupations that are lower paying. But even when these occupations involve the same skill, effort, responsibility, and working conditions as the male-dominated jobs, they tend to pay less than the male-dominated jobs.

Part of the problem may be that the act does not include differences in the rate of pay among different jobs, and this may create more subtle forms of wage discrimination in which changes in job description are used to mask sex discrimination and the resulting pay gap. This has given rise to policies of equal pay for work of equal value or "COMPARABLE WORTH." Comparable worth generally requires that male-dominated and female-dominated jobs within the same establishment receive equal pay for work of equal value. The value of a job is determined by gender-neutral, objective procedures like job evaluation.

The Equal Employment Opportunity Commission (EEOC), a federal agency, is charged with enforcing the act.

For more information

Lindgren, J. Ralph, and Nadine Taub. *The Law of Sex Discrimination.* 2nd ed. New York: West, 1993.

Ashlyn K. Kuersten
Western Michigan University

equal protection of the laws by state and local governments is guaranteed to all persons within the JURISDICTION of the United States by the Fourteenth Amendment. The federal government must also provide equal protection under the Fifth Amendment though that amendment does not explicitly say so, according to the Supreme Court decision in *BOLLING V. SHARPE,* 347 U.S. 497 (1954). The equal protection clause guarantees the right of "similarly situated" people to be treated the same by the law. For example, people who commit the same crimes should have similar PUNISHMENTS, and people who have the same qualifications should have an equal chance at government jobs. The equal protection clause also guarantees equal CITIZENSHIP rights, such as equal treatment in voting, running for office, serving on JURIES, and bringing cases to court.

The equal protection clause was added to the CONSTITUTION as one of the post–Civil War amendments. At first, the Supreme Court interpreted the equal protection clause primarily as a way to protect freed slaves from unfair state laws that did not allow African Americans to vote or serve on juries. The clause was used against state officials who refused legal protection when former slave owners tried to bind former slaves to oppressive employment or land CONTRACTS, or when KU KLUX KLANsmen and marauding bands threatened African-American lives and homes. In *PLESSY V. FERGUSON,* 163 U.S. 537 (1896), however, the Supreme Court took a step back from racial equality when it held that separate public accommodations, such as separate seating for black and white travelers, were constitutional so long as they were equal. Eroded by several court cases in the 1940s and early 1950s, this "SEPARATE BUT EQUAL" doctrine was finally overruled in *BROWN V. BOARD OF EDUCATION,* 349 U.S. 294 (1954), and the Civil Rights Act of 1965 eliminated other "separate but equal" public programs.

By the 1960s, the equal protection clause began to be applied more often to protect citizens against all arbitrary laws, not just those based on race. It has played an important role in outlawing racial and gender discrimination and providing limited protections for lawful aliens, the mentally disabled, gays and lesbians, and other groups. For example, Supreme Court rulings outlawing segregated schools and state practices that discouraged black people from voting, such as literacy requirements and a poll tax, are based on the equal protection clause. Similarly, laws that gave males better Social Security protection for their families, benefits in the armed services, and the right to support from their parents have been struck down as equal protection violations. Some fundamental rights have also been protected under the equal protection clause, such as the right of poor people to a lawyer to help in APPEALING a court decision, and to travel from state to state without losing welfare benefits.

In reviewing most laws under the equal protection clause, the Supreme Court only asks whether the legislation is rational, or whether it is arbitrary or invidious. Laws passed just because of legislators' desire to harm an unpopular group, such as homosexuals or "hippies," or laws that reflect fears that have no basis in fact violate this "rational basis" test. For laws classifying by race or national origin, and most state laws harming legal aliens, the Court has used the "STRICT SCRUTINY" test, which requires that the state show that its reason for the law is "compelling" and that it has "narrowly tailored" the law not to disadvantage any more people than necessary to meet its goals. Gender-based laws are viewed with "intermediate" scrutiny, which has been used to strike down laws that allowed females but not males to purchase 3.2 percent beer, that gave DIVORCING women but not men alimony, and that made spouses of working women but not men prove dependency in order to get Social Security benefits.

For more information

"Equal Protection." In *The Oxford Companion to the Supreme Court of the United States,* 257. New York: Oxford University Press, 1992.

Redlich, Norman, John Attanasio, and Joel K. Goldstein. *Understanding Constitutional Law.* New York: Matthew Bender, 1999, pp. 247–356.

Schultz, David, John R. Vile, and Michelle D. Deardorff. *Constitutional Law in Contemporary America,* vol. 2. New York: Oxford University Press, 2010.

Marie Failinger
Hamline University, School of Law

Equal Rights Amendment The Equal Rights Amendment was first introduced in Congress in 1923 and was reintroduced at every subsequent session of Congress but never passed. After passage of the Nineteenth Amendment (in 1920) that gave women the RIGHT TO VOTE, the Equal Rights Amendment (ERA) was an attempt to give women more equality in the workplace. The ERA read: *Men and women shall have equal rights throughout the U.S. and in every place subject to its* JURISDICTION. *Congress shall have power to enforce this article by appropriate legislation.*

An AMENDMENT TO THE U.S. CONSTITUTION may be proposed by two-thirds vote of both houses of Congress but must then be ratified by three-fourths of the state legislatures. Therefore, 38 states (three-fourths of 50) are required for ratification of any amendment. In 1972 the ERA passed both houses of Congress and was then sent to the states for ratification. Within a year, 30 states ratified it. Yet by the 10-year deadline set by Congress (1982) only 35 states had ratified.

Questions continue as to why the amendment stayed three states short of total ratification. A majority of those who supported giving women the right to vote opposed the ERA; they considered it a threat to the interests of poor mothers and full-time homemakers. Spearheaded by Phyllis Schlafly and her organization, Stop ERA, which benefited from the conservative backlash that gained momentum in the mid-1970s, supporters and opponents alike certainly did perpetuate this argument. Supporters tended to be professional career women with few or no children; opponents tended not to work outside the home and identified themselves as housewives. Nonetheless, despite its defeat, public support for the amendment never fell below 54 percent, and both political parties included it in their platforms until 1976.

For more information

Stetson, Dorothy McBride. *Women's Rights in the U.S.A.: Policy Debates and Gender Roles.* 2nd ed. New York: Garland, 1997.

Ashlyn K. Kuersten
Western Michigan University

equitable remedies are used by courts when an award of money damages will not sufficiently aid a plaintiff harmed by the legally wrongful conduct of a defendant. Also, equitable remedies are used in cases where the law does not allow successful plaintiffs to be compensated monetarily. In this sense, equitable remedies are a supplement to common-law remedies, providing relief to plaintiffs for whom financial compensation will not adequately offset the harm done by a plaintiff.

Our legal tradition embraces a preference for common-law remedies, i.e., awards of money damages, as a way of redressing private or civil wrongs. Plaintiffs that have suffered losses due to the tortious actions of another or as a result of a breach of CONTRACT typically seek an award of money as a way to "make themselves whole again." Common-law remedies include compensatory, punitive, nominal, and liquidated forms of money damages.

Compensatory damages are awarded to plaintiffs in order to offset financial losses caused by the defendant's breach of a duty or failure to perform contractual obligations. When creating a contract, parties may predetermine the sum of money to be paid in the event of a breach. Referred to as liquidated damages, this sum is paid to the non-breaching party if the other party fails to perform obligations created by the contractual agreement. Sometimes, when it is found that a defendant has knowingly or maliciously harmed the interests of the plaintiff, courts award PUNITIVE DAMAGES in addition to compensatory damages. Punitive damages are not awarded in cases of negligence but may be awarded in cases involving intentional TORTS. Nominal damages may be awarded to plaintiffs whose rights have been infringed but who are unable to demonstrate the existence of actual financial losses resulting from the defendant's behavior.

Before awarding common-law remedies, courts must identify the existence of a legal duty owed to the plaintiff, determine that the defendant has breached that duty, and then assign a dollar value to be paid to the plaintiff by the defendant in recognition of the violation of that duty. In the U.S. courts, JURIES often participate both in determining whether a legal duty has been violated and in the process of identifying the amount of money damages to be awarded to a successful plaintiff.

By contrast, equitable remedies are fashioned by courts only. Juries consider neither the facts nor the proper remedy to be applied in suits at equity; the law of equity is applied entirely by a JUDGE or magistrate. This method of EQUITY proceeding is rooted deep in the history of Anglo-American law. Although the English common-law system attained maturity in the 13th century, it was not until the 15th century that a structure of equity courts was fully in place. Equitable remedies were initially the prerogative of the chancellor, an official in the English clergy trained not in the legal rules that guided the common-law system but steeped in the law of the Roman Catholic Church. As an increasing number of disputes were referred to the chancellor, the Court of Chancery was developed. The masters in chancery, as they were called, resolved disputes by applying principles of morality and right. Whereas common-law remedies could be awarded only where the courts or Parliament had previously recognized the existence of a right, equitable remedies could be extended to plaintiffs in cases that were factually unique. Moreover, in deciding cases the early equity courts were not bound by PRECEDENT or the strict rules that guided the decisions of common-law courts. Thus, the law of equity provided remedies to plaintiffs for whom the rigidities of the common law precluded relief.

English settlement brought the common-law tradition and the doctrines of equity to North America. The tenets of English common law and equity influenced the development of judicial systems and legal practice in the early settlements. Although law and equity remained functionally distinct systems during much of the first 300 years of American history, by the early 20th century most states provided for one court system in which both common law and equity suits were resolved. In 1938 law and equity were fully merged in the FEDERAL COURTS. Today, U.S. courts routinely award combinations of common-law and equitable remedies in resolving a single dispute between litigants. Doing so requires that courts are able to employ the rules of procedure unique to equity at one moment, and, at another moment, observe the rules of common-law actions. Arguably, this procedural flexibility explains the durable nature of the legal system in the United States.

Today, various types of injunctions, the order of specific performance, and the remedies of reformation and rescission comprise the standard forms of equitable relief. INJUNCTIONS are court orders requiring a defendant to either stop or start taking some particular action. Specific performance, reformation, and rescission are equitable remedies used in disputes arising out of contractual relationships. When money damages are an unsuitable way of compensating a party harmed by another's breach of a contractual agreement, courts sitting in their equity jurisdiction may issue an order of specific performance—a demand that the breaching party perform the obligations that form the substance of the contract. Plaintiffs often seek the remedy of rescission when wishing to affect the cancellation of a contract because of FRAUD or deceit on the part of the defendant in making the contract. The remedy of rescission is also applicable in cases where a party entered into a contractual agreement under duress or after relying on another party's innocent, though false, misrepresentation of important facts. If a court grants a request for rescission, each party to the contract must return to the other anything of legal value that was exchanged in the partial or full performance of the agreement. A plaintiff may seek the remedy of reformation in instances where the terms of a contract do not express the exact nature of the agreement between the parties or when key provisions of a contract are written in ambiguous language. When ordering the reformation of a contract, courts redraft the terms of a contract to more accurately reflect the intentions of the parties.

A subtle feature of the relationship between the common law and equity is that the latter is sometimes employed to prevent a use of the common law that would be contrary to a sense of fairness. Litigants may seek an equitable remedy in order to prevent the use of the common law as a vehicle for achieving an unjust result. Herein lies the kernel of equity remedies; equitable remedies do not replace common-law remedies. but exist alongside the common law and, at times, are used to achieve just and fair applications of the common law.

For more information

Plucknett, Theodore F. *A Concise History of the Common Law.* Boston: Little, Brown, 1956.

Potter, Harold. *Historical Introduction to English Law and Its Institutions.* London: Sweet and Maxwell Ltd., 1958.

Bradley J. Best
Austin Peay State University

equity Equity deals with cases involving individuals and hardships that the law (common or statutory) is unable to remedy. It developed in England, after the Norman Conquest, to mitigate the rigidities of the common-law courts. In that day the king's courts of law had developed highly technical rules, forms, and procedures for bringing cases to court. If an aggrieved person's case did not fit the forms, they would very likely be denied their day in court. Consequently, appeals for justice (equity) made to the king were eventually heard in separate courts of chancery.

The CONSTITUTION OF THE UNITED STATES (Article III, section 2, clause 1) continued English practice saying, "The judicial power shall extend to all cases, in law and equity, arising under this Constitution. . . ." Alexander Hamilton, *Federalist Papers #80* (et al.), discussed extensively the power of the courts to decide cases of equity. He argued the right to decide cases of equity was needed because people unwittingly enter CONTRACTS, with no fraudulent INTENT, which if enforced upon the original terms would create an injustice.

In the 19th century most states had separate courts of chancery that dealt only with equitable relief. Other states provided some way for equity cases to be handled. Until 1938 federal district courts had two separate sides of "law" and "equity." Today, in U.S. law, it is almost the universal practice to have the same courts that can issue a legal remedy be able to prescribe an equitable one. Efficiency is an important advantage of this merger of the administration of law and equity.

Equity follows the law. It provides a special set of remedies and associated procedures which aim to establish substantive JUSTICE or fairness. Equitable relief from some harm is generally only available when a legal remedy is insufficient or inadequate in some way. For instance, an INJUNCTION might be issued to prevent an irreparable harm from taking place, such as the demolition of a home by a wrecking crew accidentally at the wrong address.

Other matters for which an individual might seek relief are accountings of money matters and rescission of documents. Remedies, besides an injunction, include specific performance, reformation, contribution, and estoppel. Specific performance is an order to parties to a contract to perform the specifics of a contract. Reformation is an action the court may take when a written agreement does not clearly express the real agreement between the parties. Contribution may be used to distribute loss in a situation. Estoppel is used in contracts to prevent one of the parties from denying certain facts. Trust law conflicts generate many cases of equity. Equity easily may be thought of as the conscience of the law.

For more information

Hill, Myron G., Howard M. Rosen, and Wilton S. Sogg. *Remedies: Equity—Damages—Restitution for Law School and Bar Examinations*. St. Paul, Minn.: West, 1974.

McClintock, Henry Lacy. *Handbook of the Principles of Equity*. St. Paul, Minn.: West, 1948.

Andrew J. Waskey
Dalton State College

ERISA ERISA, or the Employee Retirement Income Security Act of 1974, is the primary federal law concerning employee benefits.

Congress passed this legislation in 1974 in order to regulate management of retirement funds. Employers who engage in interstate commerce and provide defined benefit or welfare plans to employees must abide by ERISA requirements. ERISA covers every "employee pension benefit plan" and "employee welfare benefit plan." An employee pension benefit plan is any plan which provides for retirement income for employees. An employee welfare plan is any plan which provides for benefits such as medical, sickness, accident, vacation, and disability for employees and their dependents.

ERISA requires that employers with pension plans provide both the U.S. Labor Department and employees with detailed descriptions of benefits they are to receive once they become eligible. Regulations of the department outline which employees must receive a pension if they are so offered and requires that a percentage of the retirement benefits become vested in the employees after they have worked for a given number of years, reached a given age, or both. ERISA also requires that pension plans pay benefits to survivors of deceased employees. The legislation also requires employers to adequately fund their programs and establishes fiduciary responsibilities that must be followed. The Pension Benefit Guaranty Corporation insures defined benefit plans. Employers must pay premiums so that their plans are covered against insolvency by the PBGC. The Pension and Welfare Benefit Administration enforces fiduciary (decisions on claims), reporting, and disclosure requirements under ERISA. PWBA requires those who manage plans to meet certain standards of conduct and it is authorized to proceed in CIVIL ACTIONS to enforce requirements that retirement funds are protected and that eligible participants receive benefits. Congress has authorized tax breaks to employers who follow the guidelines under the Internal Revenue Code in order to encourage employers to follow pension plan regulations.

Regulations concerning employee welfare benefit plans are also extensive. For example, and importantly, ERISA requires that employees be provided summary plan documents of employee welfare benefit plans. Summary plan documents are intended to summarize the full plan document issued on behalf of the employer and be written in plain language that ordinary persons may understand.

ERISA preempts all state law that relates to employee welfare benefit plans, meaning that ERISA controls the plans, not separate state laws. As a result, ERISA controls the interpretation of funding of benefits such as daycare centers, scholarship funds, apprenticeship or training programs, even prepaid legal services. The purpose behind preemption is that multistate employers may depend upon a consistent interpretation and enforcement of the ERISA, rather than a potentially inconsistent approach among different states. ERISA does not preempt plans such as plans sponsored and funded by government agencies or churches. It also does not preempt workers' compensation or unemployment compensation laws. If an employee welfare benefit plan is an ERISA plan, the administrator may state in the summary plan document that it reserves the right to interpret the meaning of the plan and which beneficiaries are entitled to payment. Federal courts typically defer to the findings of the administrator in such situations. This deference provides considerable advantage to administrators of ERISA plans as opposed to insurers who are subject to actions under state law. While individual participants may file civil actions to seek enforcement of the policy, their chances for success are not high when the administrator is granted deference under the summary plan document. The deference given to administrators to deny or limit medical treatment is one of the many reasons why many consumer groups have advocated in the last several years that Congress pass a "patients' bill of rights."

Other provisions of ERISA include the continuation of employee welfare benefit plans after an employee ceases employment with the employer that provided the plan. Congress required under the consolidated Omnibus Budget and Reconciliation Act of 1986 that employers provide what is commonly known as "COBRA" coverage for a period of 18 months following the end of employment, though at cost to the employee. That legislation also eliminated the ability of employers to limit participation in their retirement plans for new employees who are close to retirement and the ability to freeze benefits for participants over age 65. In 1996 Congress required that such coverage be able to be transferred from one plan to another (essentially one employer to another) under the Health Insurance Portability and Accountability Act. Congress also amended ERISA to generally require that benefit levels for mental disorders be the same as that for physical disorders. It also recently increased the rights of women who seek medical treatment for breast cancer or who are pregnant.

In addition, self-funded ERISA plans (ones in which all operations are funded by employers rather than premiums paid to traditional insurance companies) may under certain circumstances be able to recover amounts paid for benefits when the beneficiary recovers from a third party, such as personal injury actions, workers' compensation claims, or similar actions.

For more information

29 U.S.C. Sections 1001 et seq. Employee Retirement Income Security Act of 1974.

29 CFR Parts 2500 et seq. Pension and Welfare Benefits Administration.

29 CFR Parts 4000 et seq. Pension Benefit Guaranty Corporation.

29 U.S.C. Sections 401 et seq. Tax Considerations.

Patrick J. Platter
Daniel, Clampett, Powell and Cunningham
Springfield, Missouri

Escobedo v. United States 378 U.S. 478 (1964) *Escobedo v. United States* was a Supreme Court decision that guaranteed accused criminals the right to have an attorney present when the police question them. Specifically, *Escobedo* involves the SIXTH AMENDMENT issue of the right to be represented by counsel, and it indirectly involves the Fifth Amendment privilege against SELF-INCRIMINATION.

Escobedo was accused of MURDERING his brother-in-law and was brought to the police station for questioning. His attorney arrived a short time later and requested that he be allowed to consult with Escobedo. However, the officers in charge, including the chief, did not allow him to do so. During the interrogation, Escobedo admitted to knowledge of the murder and also made statements to the police that implicated himself in the crime. Before, and during, the trial Escobedo tried to have the incriminating statements thrown out of court because he had made them without his attorney present. His requests were denied, and he was ultimately convicted of the murder. After losing in the Illinois Supreme Court, Escobedo APPEALED to the Supreme Court of the United States, asking that his statements be declared inadmissible at trial.

In a 5-4 decision the Supreme Court ruled that Escobedo's statements, made outside the presence of his attorney, should not be admissible in court. As a result, this case set the PRECEDENT that nobody accused of a crime may be interrogated without an attorney, if one has been requested. In making its decision, the Supreme Court made two key arguments about why the accused should have the RIGHT TO COUNSEL during police interrogations.

First, the Court noted that many confessions are obtained during police interrogations, which suggests that there is a critical need for legal advice at this stage of the process. If attorneys were only guaranteed at trial, and not before, the Court argued that they would be useless because most confessions would already be obtained. This would then make it virtually impossible for the defendant to win once the trial begins.

Second, the justices made a distinction between the investigation of an unsolved crime and the point at which a suspect is accused of committing the crime. That is, when the police focus on one suspect, when they interrogate that suspect, and when the suspect requests to see an attorney, it is a violation of that suspect's Sixth Amendment rights to be denied the right to meet with an attorney. The justices concluded that the CONSTITUTION guarantees the accused the right to be advised of his or her right against self-incrimination by an attorney prior to, and during, a police interrogation.

Escobedo is the precursor to another criminal rights case—*MIRANDA V. ARIZONA*, where the Court ruled that the police must advise the accused of the right to meet with an attorney during an interrogation. Together, these cases are two of the most important criminal rights cases decided by the Supreme Court. Indeed, *Escobedo* guarantees the right to have counsel present, and *Miranda* set out the framework for enforcing the previous decision.

For more information

Epstein, Lee, and Thomas Walker. *Constitutional Law for a Changing America: Rights, Liberties, and Justice.* Washington, D.C.: Congressional Quarterly Press, 1998.

Medalie, Richard J. *From Escobedo to Miranda.* Washington, D.C.: Lerner Law Books, 1966.

Timothy R. Johnson
University of Minnesota

establishment clause The establishment clause in the First Amendment to the CONSTITUTION, which was ratified by the states in 1791 as part of the BILL OF RIGHTS, the first 10 AMENDMENTS TO THE CONSTITUTION. The establishment clause reads, "Congress shall make no law respecting an establishment of RELIGION." The establishment clause was developed largely through the efforts of Thomas Jefferson and James Madison, and the philosophy of it is eloquently laid out in the latter's "Memorial and Remonstrance." The establishment clause was their response to the question of whether government should be permitted to establish an official state religion, such as was the case in England with regard to the Anglican Church. Supporters of the establishment clause had three arguments: the establishment of a church by the state corrupted religion, argued by Roger Williams; too much influence on the part of religion can be dangerous to the public interest, argued by Madison; and true religion needs no aid from the state, argued by Jefferson.

For most of the history of the United States, the establishment clause was not a vigorously enforced provision of the Constitution. Prior to the Fourteenth Amendment, the Bill of Rights had been held in *Barron v. Baltimore* (1833) to apply only to the federal government and not to the states. Furthermore, the Protestant religion was simply assumed to be a fact of life and an essential part of American public life. Several factors transformed the establishment clause into the highly contentious issue that it is today. First, the turbulent events in Germany in the 1930s and 1940s affected the whole world, and the United States Supreme Court was no exception. Justice Jackson's service at the Nuremberg trial of Nazi leaders, and Justice Frankfurter's Jewish heritage, among other things, helped bring recognition and increased sensitivity of the importance of pluralism and difference in American society. At the same time, with Justice Black taking the lead, the Court began INCORPORATING the Bill of Rights as part of the definition of liberty in the DUE PROCESS clause of the Fourteenth Amendment and applying it against intrusion in those liberties by the states.

In 1947 the Supreme Court first applied the establishment clause to the states in *EVERSON V. BOARD OF EDUCATION*. In that case, the Court ruled that parents of both public and Catholic schoolchildren could be reimbursed for the bus fare of students. More importantly, the Court ruled that any issues raised under the establishment clause would have to meet a high standard: The state cannot in any way aid religion, rather it must be neutral between religion and non-religion. In *Everson,* all members of the Court agreed to this high standard. The first statement of the originalist position that the establishment clause meant only that the state may not establish an official church, but could accommodate religion in other ways, came in Justice Potter Stewart's 1962 dissent in *ENGEL V. VITALE.*

The two most important areas of law under the establishment clause are school prayer and aid to religion. In the area of school prayer the Court has consistently held, from *Engel v. Vitale* to *Lee v. Weisman* (1992), that state-sponsored prayer violates the establishment clause. In the area of educational aid to religion, the Court's rulings are more ambiguous. In the area of released-time programs for religious education, the Court has struck down some, such as in *McCollum v. Board of Education* (1948), which allowed religious instruction in public school classrooms, and upheld others, as in *ZORACH V. CLAUSON* (1952), a program that provided released time in the public school day for students to attend religious classes conducted in non-school buildings. The Court also allowed reimbursement for bus fares for Catholic schoolchildren in *Everson v. Board of Education* in 1947. These indirect forms of aid have survived the courts because they give financial support to parents of schoolchildren directly, not money to schools for religious instruction. For example, in *Mueller v. Allen* (1983), the Supreme Court allowed a Minnesota law which permitted taxpayers to deduct from their gross income taxes the actual expenses for tuition, textbooks, and transportation costs of sending their children to both public and private schools, many of which were sectarian. Most direct aid to primary and secondary religious institutions is not allowed by the Supreme Court. However, in a recent 5-4 decision, *Agostini v. Felton* (1997), the Supreme Court allowed government support for remedial education, guidance, and job counseling by public employees within parochial school buildings to students who reside within the attendance boundaries of a public school located in a low-income area who are failing, or are at risk of failing.

The process of Supreme Court interpretation of the establishment clause, which began in the 1947 *Everson* ruling, culminated in 1971 in *LEMON V. KURTZMAN,* when the Supreme Court established the three-pronged *Lemon* test for determining the constitutionality of a law under the establishment clause: For a statute not to be in violation of the establishment clause it must have a secular legislative purpose, its principal or primary effect must be one that neither advances nor inhibits religion, and it must not foster an excessive entanglement of government with religion.

Two areas where the application of the *Lemon* test have been particularly difficult and controversial to apply are in school settings and in the public display of religious symbols. In addition to the decisions in *Engel* and *Lee,* the Supreme Court has also ruled in *WALLACE V. JAFFREE,* 472 U.S. 38 (1985), that a mandated moment of silence to begin a public school day had religious purposes and therefore violated the establishment clause. Additionally, in *Sante Fe Independent School District v. Doe,* 530 U.S. 290 (2000), the Court invalidated a practice that permitted a student to offer a prayer before all home football games. Again, the Court ruled that the practice violated the establishment clause. These decisions continue to reaffirm the Court's precedent that state-sponsored prayer in public schools is unconstitutional. Contrary to critics of these decisions, the Court has never ruled or banned students from privately praying on their own in public schools.

In addition to school prayer decisions, the Court in *Zelman v. Simmons Harris,* 536 U.S. 639 (2002), upheld a voucher program that allowed school children to attend private religious schools, and in *Zobrest v. Catalina Foothills School District,* 509 U.S. 1 (1993), the Court also upheld the use of public money to be used to pay for a sign language interpreter who attended a private religious school. In both of these cases, the Court ruled that the use of public money neither created an excessive entanglement under the *Lemon* test nor constituted a state endorsement of religion.

Displays of religious symbols on public property also are controversial. In *Lynch v. Donnelly,* 465 U.S. 668 (1984), the Court upheld the display of a religious crèche on public property. It ruled that because the crèche was near other secular symbols of the Christmas season, including a reindeer, it was not an establishment clause violation. Conversely, in *County of Allegheny v. ACLU,* 492 U.S. 573 (1983), the Court struck down the display of a crèche at a county courthouse because it was by itself while at the same time upheld the display of a menorah next to a Christmas tree. Finally, in *Van Orden v. Perry,* 543 U.S. 1135 (2005), the Court upheld the display of a monument inscribed with the Ten Commandments on the Texas state capitol grounds. But on the same day as this decision, the Court struck down the display of the Ten Commandments on walls in two Kentucky courthouses in *McCreary County v. ACLU,* 5435 U.S. 844 (2005). In the former case, the Court ruled that the display of the Ten Commandments was "passive" and did not endorse religion, whereas in the Kentucky case there appeared to be a clear religious endorsement.

Overall, efforts to use the *Lemon* test and distinguish between permitted and unconstitutional displays of religion are often controversial and difficult to apply.

For more information

Irons, Peter. *God on Trial: Dispatches from America's Religious Battlefields.* New York: Viking, 2007.

Kahn, Ronald. *The Supreme Court and Constitutional Theory, 1953–1993.* Lawrence: University Press of Kansas, 1994, chap. 4, "Constituting the Separation of Church and State," pp. 107–138.

Levy, Leonard W. *The Establishment Clause: Religion and the First Amendment.* New York: MacMillan, 1986.

Rosenblum, Nancy L., ed. *Obligations of Citizenship and Demands of Faith.* Princeton, N.J.: Princeton University Press, 2000.

Schultz, David, John R. Vile, and Michelle D. Deardorff. *Constitutional Law in Contemporary America*, vol. 1. New York: Oxford University Press, 2010.

Ronald Kahn
Oberlin College

Ethics in Government Act Ethics in Government Act is a federal law enacted in 1978 and significantly amended in 1989.

The Ethics in Government Acts of both 1978 and 1989 made major changes in the way in which the federal government regulates the ethical conduct of its elected and appointed officials and employees. The act consists of four main parts: public financial disclosure, conflicts of interest, honoraria and outside income and activities, and post-government employment restrictions.

The public financial disclosure provisions, which apply to certain defined individuals or positions in the executive, legislative, and judicial branches of the federal government, include instruction on what must be reported, how reporting is done, and what the review process is. For example, those covered by the act must report positions they hold as officers, directors, and trustees of certain organizations or institutions.

The conflict of interest laws include definitions of conflicts, such as knowingly and substantially participating in a matter in which the employee has a financial interest; instructions on how to divest oneself of holdings that give rise to a conflict; a process for recusing oneself from participation where a conflict exists; and rules for setting up blind trusts to eliminate the conflict. The restrictions and requirements connected to honoraria and outside income and activity establish specific dollar amounts one may receive, for example, for speaking engagements or as earned income apart from one's federal position.

Finally, there are restrictions on post-government employment of certain elected and appointed officials and employees. These limitations extend from lifetime bans to two-year bans, to a one-year cooling off period. During those periods of time the persons to whom the laws apply may not, for example, represent an organization on a matter in which that person had been substantially involved while working for the U.S. government.

Additionally, the Ethics in Government Act established a process for the appointment of independent counsel charged with investigating alleged criminal conduct by high-level executive branch officials and created the U.S. Office of Government Ethics. Initially located in the Office of Personnel, the Office of Government Ethics later became a federal agency whose responsibilities are to provide guidance, education, regulation, and enforcement.

For more information

Ethics in Government Act and Related Statutes, 5 U.S.C. 101–111; 18 U.S.C. 201–218.

President's Commission on Federal Ethics Law Reform. *To Serve with Honor: Report and Recommendations to the President*. Washington, D.C.: U.S. Government Printing Office, 1989.

Jane Calabria McPeak
Hamline University

Everson v. Board of Education 330 U.S. 1 (1947) *Everson v. Board of Education* first applied the RELIGION clauses of the First Amendment to the states.

The case involved a New Jersey law that allowed local school districts to create their own rules for the transportation of students attending any school, except for students attending private schools operated for profit. Under this law, the Board of Education of the Township of Ewing enacted a resolution that reimbursed parents of public and Catholic schoolchildren for the costs of transportation on the public bus systems. The appellant, Arch Everson, challenged the constitutionality of the resolution, claiming that any use of public funds that affected religion violated the clause of the First Amendment that said that government must not establish religion, known as the ESTABLISHMENT CLAUSE. Edward R. Burke and E. Hilton Jackson argued Everson's case, supported by the Seventh-Day Adventists, the AMERICAN CIVIL LIBERTIES UNION, and other groups. The Board of Education argued that the law treated religion and non-religion equally. William H. Speer represented the Ewing School Board, and it was supported by numerous states and some Catholic groups. The case was argued in the Supreme Court on November 20, 1946, and decided on February 10, 1947. In a 5-4 decision, Justice Black, writing for the Court, ruled in favor of the board, finding that the reimbursement of transportation costs for Catholic as well public school students did not violate the establishment clause. Justice Jackson, joined by Justice Frankfurter, and Justice Rutledge, joined by Justices Frankfurter, Jackson, and Burton, wrote dissenting opinions.

Although Justice Black ruled that the reimbursement did not violate the establishment clause, he set a high standard of judgment in cases involving the establishment clause that would ensure a separation of church and state in most cases. Black outlined the history and theory of the establishment clause from its roots in the thought of James Madison and Thomas Jefferson. He states that not only does the establishment clause prohibit the establishment of a state religion but it also prevents both the federal government and states from aiding religion, coercing worship, discriminating on the basis of creed, and using tax revenues to fund religious institutions. However, Black ruled in favor of the transportation reimbursements in question in *Everson* because, he argued, the state must neither favor nor disfavor religion. The case, he wrote, concerned a law that was neutral between religion and the public sector, treating them equally. Black was a strong advocate of the separation of church and state; *Everson* is one of the few cases in which Black voted to uphold a law favorable to religious institutions.

The dissent in *Everson* agreed with Black that a high standard of state neutrality to religion and non-religion must be established if a law that might conflict with the religion clauses of the First Amendment is to be valid. Like Black, the dissenters invoked the words of Madison and Jefferson. They did not agree with Black, however, that the law in question met that standard. In his dissent, Justice Rutledge argued that any allocation of tax dollars with an effect of promoting religion is unconstitutional. In his dissent, Justice Jackson emphasized that the New Jersey law only provided reimbursement to public and Catholic school students. He argued that by including reimbursement to parents of students attending schools of only one religion and excluding others, the law was impermissibly discriminatory in its effect. Beyond its specific and narrow ruling allowing transportation reimbursement for both public and Catholic schools, *Everson* is important and remains good law, because the case held for the first time that the establishment and free exercise clauses, that is the religion clauses of the First Amendment, are made applicable to the states by the Fourteenth Amendment and set the standard by which the religion clauses are to be interpreted. For most of the history of the country, the guarantees in the BILL OF RIGHTS have only been held by the courts to be limits on the federal government. Only in the 1940s did First Amendment guarantees come to be held applicable against actions of the states, and *Everson* is a crucial part of that change.

The *Everson* ruling began the process that would culminate in 1971 in the *LEMON V. KURTZMAN* standard: that state financial support for parochial schools violates the establishment clause of the First Amendment unless it can be shown to have a clear secular purpose, the primary effect is not to advance religion, and there is no excessive entanglement between church and state. The *Everson* reimbursement to parents, like later cases involving state reimbursements directly to parents of schoolchildren in all schools, had a secular purpose whose primary effect was not to advance religion but to aid safety, and because the direct payments to parents did not constitute excessive entanglement.

For more information

Fraser, James W. *Between Church and State: Religion and Public Education in a Multicultural America.* New York: St. Martin's Press, 1999.

Rosenblum, Nancy L., ed. *Obligations of Citizenship and Demands of Faith.* Princeton, N.J.: Princeton University Press, 2000.

Ronald Kahn
Oberlin College

evidence Evidence is information presented in court to a JUDGE OR JURY in order to prove or disprove a question at issue in a civil or criminal lawsuit.

Evidence comes in four general forms: TESTIMONIAL, physical, documentary, and demonstrative. Witness testimony under oath can be provided by either lay or EXPERT WITNESSES. Lay witness testimony is provided by individuals with personal knowledge of the facts of the case, either by something they saw, heard, or know, such as an EYEWITNESSES. An expert witness testifies about conclusions drawn based upon expertise in an area, such as a doctor or forensic specialist. Most evidence not testimonial is introduced in the form of an exhibit. Physical evidence is the first of these types and consists of tangible objects that are real and direct. They can include things such as a gun used to commit the crime, hair found at the CRIME SCENE, personal property recovered, handwriting, etc. Documentary exhibits document certain facts and can include such things as business records, letters, and sound or video recordings. Demonstrative exhibits, on the other hand, are created after the fact to illustrate or recreate certain facts, such as photographs, charts, or diagrams created for the case.

Evidence can also come in the form of a stipulation, which is an agreement between the parties of the truth of some fact, such that it need not be otherwise proven in court. Finally, evidence can be introduced through judicial notice, where the court accepts a fact as true without evidentiary proof because the fact is indisputable or is common knowledge, such as the locations of streets, buildings, or geographic areas. Unlike civil trials, in criminal trials the jury is not required to accept as conclusively proven such judicially noticed facts but may choose to do so.

Attorney statements, questions, and objections are not evidence and may not be considered as such by the jury. Rather, they constitute the attorney's effort to help the trier of fact (the jury or the judge) interpret the evidence. Any evidence that has been excluded or stricken by the court, or that which the jury was instructed to disregard, is likewise not evidence. Information obtained out of court by the judge or jurors may not be considered evidence in the case, and jury instructions given by the judge prior to deliberations are likewise not evidence.

All evidence is either direct or circumstantial, although the difference is not always easy to ascertain. Contrary to popular myth, circumstantial evidence is not necessarily weak, and a case that is primarily circumstantial in nature does not necessitate an ACQUITTAL. Circumstantial evidence is simply more indirect; it requires an inference of some sort in order to be useful to the case. Evidence that a defendant was seen standing over a corpse with a smoking gun in hand is circumstantial, as the actual event was not witnessed and an inference is required before concluding that the defendant was in fact the murderer. There is no rule prohibiting circumstantial evidence from being admitted in a case. Direct evidence is that for which no inference is required; the evidence speaks for itself. The most common types of direct evidence are eyewitness accounts of the events in question (which, although direct, can still be highly unreliable) and defendant confessions. For example, a witness who observed a defendant point a gun at someone and pull the trigger would constitute direct evidence, though it could still be rebutted if the witness was unreliable.

Not all evidence may be admitted in a trial. Rules of evidence exist to determine what evidence is admissible, and these rules are generally based on the reliability of the evidence and the risk of undue prejudice in the case. Until the 1970s, rules of evidence were generally determined by the common law (judicial PRECEDENT created by cases over time). During the 1970s, JURISDICTIONS began to move away from this framework and instead established statutory evidence codes. California was the first U.S. jurisdiction to do so in 1967.

In 1975, the FEDERAL RULES OF EVIDENCE (FRE) were formally adopted by the U.S. Congress to apply to all federal trials, and they have been amended several times since then. While each state is free to adopt its own evidence code, many states have incorporated the FRE into their own statutes in whole or in part. The advisory committee that wrote the FRE included comments on the rules, which provide historical context and explanations. According to FRE 102, the stated purpose of the rules was to create "fairness in administration, elimination of unjustifiable expense and delay, and promotion of growth and development of the law . . . to the end that the truth may be ascertained." Thus, while the rules are somewhat complex, their essential focus is that the evidence admitted in a lawsuit be relevant, efficient, reliable, and fair. Although the rules were written by a committee and adopted by Congress, the application and interpretation of the rules is still conducted by the courts. Trial judges generally have broad DISCRETION to determine the admissibility of evidence but are subject to review by appellate courts.

There are many important evidence rules under the FRE. Rules 401 and 402 deal with relevance, defining what makes evidence relevant and providing that irrelevant evidence should be excluded from trials. Rule 403 is important in that it declares that relevant evidence may be excluded if it would waste time or create unfair prejudice to the other side (not just any prejudice, for that is generally the purpose of all evidence). When a witness is impeached, her or his credibility is attacked by various methods, and the requirements for this procedure are addressed in rules 607–610 and 613. The use of character evidence in a case is strictly regulated by rules 404 and 405. This type of evidence is generally prohibited, unless it falls within certain specific exceptions; a defendant in a criminal case, for instance, is permitted to bring up evidence of her or his own good character. One of the most important and complex issues detailed in the FRE is that of HEARSAY. Hearsay is a statement made out of court that is introduced in a trial to prove the truth of what was claimed in the original statement made before trial. If the statement is introduced in the trial for some other reason, such as to show that the speaker was angry or insane, but not to show that what she or he said was actually true, it is not hearsay. While hearsay is generally inadmissible, there are enough exceptions to dwarf the rule. FRE 801–807 all deal with this issue.

The admissibility of evidence can also be a constitutional issue. The U.S. Supreme Court has held that evidence is not admissible at trial if it is obtained in violation of the FOURTH AMENDMENT's protection against unreasonable SEARCH AND SEIZURE, the Fifth Amendment's right against SELF-INCRIMINATION, or the SIXTH AMENDMENT's provisions allowing for the assistance of counsel and the right to confront one's accusers. While there are some exceptions to this inadmissibility principle, the general rule is believed to serve as an incentive for law enforcement to abide by the terms of the amendments.

For more information

Frisch, Benjamin H. *Evidence: Investigation, Rules, and Trials*. New York: Thomson Delmar, 2008.

Nemeth, Charles P. *Law & Evidence*. Upper Saddle River, N.J.: Prentice Hall, 2001.

Deborah Anthony
University of Illinois at Springfield

evolving standards of decency Evolving standards of decency is a concept used by the courts to evaluate the constitutionality of PUNISHMENTS. It is a vital and somewhat controversial principle used by the U.S. Supreme Court in its interpretation of the EIGHTH AMENDMENT to the UNITED STATES CONSTITUTION. The phrase, of course, does not come from the Constitution itself; rather, its genesis is found in a Supreme Court decision.

In the case of *Trop v. Dulles*, 356 U.S. 86 (1958), the Supreme Court ruled that the CRUEL AND UNUSUAL PUNISHMENT clause of the Eighth Amendment prohibits the government from revoking one's CITIZENSHIP on account of a previous court-martial. CHIEF JUSTICE EARL WARREN wrote the majority opinion for the Court. He argued that the words of the Eighth Amendment "are not precise, and that their scope is not static. The Amendment must draw its meaning from the evolving standards of decency that mark the progress of a maturing society."

In the years since the *Trop* ruling, and especially when dealing with the death penalty, the Court has relied heavily on the conclusion of Chief Justice Warren. Seldom has the Court been unanimous in deciding death penalty cases, and that lack of unanimity is clearly seen when the Court debates what is meant by "evolving standards of decency." In almost every death penalty case of the modern era, especially since *FURMAN V. GEORGIA*, 408 U.S. 238 (1972), the Court has struggled with what these standards are, and how one knows.

Consider the case of *Atkins v. Virginia*, 536 U.S. 304 (2002). Here the Supreme Court considered the question whether the cruel and unusual punishment clause of the Eighth Amendment allowed for the mentally retarded to be put to death for MURDER. The Court decided, by a vote of 6-3, that our nation's standards had evolved to the point where CAPITAL PUNISHMENT for those found to be mentally retarded violates the Constitution. In *Atkins*, the Court majority found evidence of evolving standards in states that had outlawed the death penalty completely, or outlawed for the mentally retarded, or had not carried out an execution of someone with limited mental capacity for decades.

Similarly, in *ROPER V. SIMMONS*, 543 U.S. 551 (2005), the Supreme Court found that the Constitution prohibits the execution of all juvenile defendants below the age of 18. In *Roper*, the Court again confronted "evolving standards of decency" and the necessary and proper sources of evidence for deciding what these standards do in fact prohibit or allow.

What the Court, at least a majority of its members over the last generation or so, has concluded is that, given the ambiguous language of the Eighth Amendment, it is appropriate to consider "evolving standards of decency" as a legitimate concept and principle of interpretation, especially with regard to the death penalty. Not all justices agree with this approach; Associate Justices ANTONIN SCALIA and CLARENCE THOMAS especially take strong and consistent exception to this part of the Court's Eighth Amendment/criminal justice jurisprudence.

For more information

Atwell, Mary W. *Evolving Standards of Decency.* New York: Peter Lang, 2004.

Walker, Thomas G. *Eligible for Execution: The Story of the Daryl Atkins Case.* Washington, D.C.: CQ Press, 2009.

Stephen K. Shaw
Northwest Nazarene University, Nampa, Idaho

exceptions to the exclusionary rule Exceptions to the exclusionary rule refer to situations in which law enforcement officials do not need a warrant to search or person or place. The exclusionary rule is a constitutional principle based in the FOURTH AMENDMENT, which generally requires a warrant to execute searches by the government.

The exclusionary rule is primarily based on U.S. constitutional protections guarding the individual against excessive government action. These protections include: the right against unreasonable SEARCHES AND SEIZURES (Fourth Amendment); the right to be free from compelled SELF-INCRIMINATION (Fifth Amendment); and the RIGHT TO LEGAL COUNSEL in a criminal proceeding, and confront witnesses (SIXTH AMENDMENT). The rule is, therefore, established to protect these rights by limiting EVIDENCE presented by an accuser during a criminal proceeding. The evidence that can be excluded under this rule includes the following categories: verbal (witness testimony at trial), and physical (documents or physical evidence such as a gun or knife submitted at trial).

The exclusionary rule is not absolute, and there are numerous categorical exceptions. For example, the exclusionary rule does not apply to evidence presented in a civil case. In addition, it does not apply in either GRAND JURY proceedings or PAROLE hearings. However, the rule does apply to criminal cases, but even here, there are numerous specific exceptions.

In *HUDSON V. MICHIGAN*, 547 U.S. 586 (2006), the U.S. Supreme Court reiterated a longstanding preference for the admission of incriminating evidence in criminal proceedings, thus suggesting exceptions to the exclusion of evidence should be favored when available. The rationale of the Court centered on a policy argument, suggesting the exclusionary rule results in significant social costs, sometimes allowing the guilty to go free. Thus, based on the PRECEDENT of *Hudson*, there seems to be a judicial preference favoring the inclusion of evidence, even evidence obtained in violation of constitutional protections.

As stated above, exceptions to the exclusionary rule can be categorized based on two general types of evidence offered in a criminal proceeding: verbal testimony and physical evidence.

Physical evidence, including instruments used in a crime, face potential exclusion from a trial primarily based on Fourth Amendment considerations, specifically whether the search (assuming the physical evidence was found through a search of some private premises) by the government was supported by sufficient PROBABLE CAUSE. In addition, the search itself must be reasonable in both its inception and scope. See *NEW JERSEY V. TLO*, 469 U.S. 325 (1985).

If a search is not supported by probable cause (for instance, a search warrant was not sought to search a private residence and there was sufficient time to seek a warrant), then the exclusionary rule generally prohibits this evidence at trial. An exception that might apply under this circumstance is inevitable discovery, which allows physical evidence that ultimately is discoverable to be admitted even though the government failed to actually secure probable cause prior to discovering the evidence in the present case. Since the evidence would likely have been constitutionally discovered at some point, it is excepted from exclusion. An example might include physical evidence that is discovered through an unlawful search but could just as well have been discovered through lawful means.

Another exception to the exclusionary rule for physical evidence is the independent source doctrine, which allows for the admission of physical evidence where the evidence was obtained both through an unconstitutional search (one not supported by probable cause), and a constitutional search (one supported by probable cause). The example often used is a search for incriminating documents. One search, unsupported by probable cause, turns up photocopies of the incriminating documents. Another search, supported by probable cause, turns up the originals of the documents. Although the photocopies are excluded because the search violated the Fourth Amendment, the originals are allowed because they were independently discovered with probable cause, thus meeting the Fourth Amendment requirements. Also, searches without warrants may be allowed if police have evidence being destroyed.

A final exception to the exclusion of physical evidence is the good faith exception to the exclusionary rule. This exception applies where there is an administrative error in the process of establishing probable cause. The example case is a police officer conducting a search based on a technically invalid warrant. The police officer believes the search is valid, because he or she has obtained a warrant from a government official (magistrate). However, the warrant is technically invalid because the government official has not followed proper procedures to meet Fourth Amendment requirements. The policy officer is unaware of this technical error and, therefore, acts in good faith, believing the search to be valid. Under such circumstances, the evidence is allowed. Additionally, if the police execute a search that was legal at the time but later the Supreme Court rules it was not, that evidence need not always be suppressed.

Verbal testimony is the other category of evidence that is potentially excludable during a criminal trial. Generally speaking, verbal evidence is excluded from a criminal proceeding if the evidence is not relevant, HEARSAY, or its probative value is outweighed by its prejudicial value.

Verbal testimony is admissible if it is relevant to the criminal proceedings. Hearsay testimony (an out-of-court statement offered to prove the truth of the matter asserted) is generally excluded from trial. However, exceptions to hearsay exclusion generally include using the hearsay testimony for purposes other than trying to prove the truth of the matter asserted (in other words, using the statement to prove something else during the trial). These types of hearsay exceptions are restricted or conditional exceptions. There are also unrestricted exceptions to the hearsay rule, even though they technically meet the definition of hearsay. The restricted or conditional exceptions to hearsay will be described immediately below; unrestricted exceptions will follow.

The first example of a conditional exception to hearsay exclusion is using the statement to impeach the witness. This can be done through prior inconsistent statements, where the hearsay statement is being introduced to show the witness in contradicting some prior statement. This is usually done on cross-examination, and is used to impeach the witness, or otherwise lessen the value of the witness's statement to the JURY.

Another conditional exception to hearsay exclusion is to use the hearsay statement to establish the state of mind of the person speaking the words. For instance, a witness might be called to provide testimony about a conversation between the witness and the accused. Although the testimony cannot be used to prove the truth of what was said in the conversation (for instance, if the accused stated he or she wanted to kill his or her spouse in the conversation, this statement cannot be used to prove that the accused actually killed the spouse), it can be used to establish the state of mind of the accused (discussing the killing of the spouse during the conversation).

Yet another conditional exception to the exclusion of hearsay rule is the use of character evidence to prove the accused may have committed a particular crime. Character evidence includes statements that go to the reputation of the accused, as well as statements of opinion and specific acts engaged in by the accused. In criminal cases, the character of the accused is generally excluded as evidence; however, it can be admissible as rebuttal evidence by the prosecution. This can occur when, for example, the defense offers direct testimony of the good character of the accused. Because the defense has placed character at issue by doing this, the prosecution can then introduce character evidence to rebut the implications of good character established on direct examination. Limitations exist on the use of character evidence in this manner. For instance, the character trait being proven through verbal testimony must be relevant to the charges being made against the accused. For example, if the accused is being charged with theft, then character evidence of the accused as an honest person is relevant.

Under the FEDERAL RULES OF EVIDENCE, crimes, wrongs, or prior bad acts are generally not admissible, and therefore excluded, to prove the likelihood that the accused committed the current crime. However, there are conditional exceptions to this general rule. For instance, although prior crimes, wrongs, or bad acts cannot be introduced to prove a current alleged crime, these acts can be admitted to prove the following: knowledge, identity, scheme, MOTIVE, opportunity, mistake, preparation, INTENT, and plan.

For example, a prior crime of CARJACKING cannot be introduced to show the accused committed carjacking in the current criminal proceeding, but it can be introduced to show the accused has knowledge on how to commit a carjacking. Similarly, a prior history of gambling debts cannot be used to prove the current crime, but it may be used as evidence of a motive to steal if stealing is a part of the current accusation.

As mentioned above, there are also unrestricted exceptions to the exclusion of hearsay evidence. These include: present sense impressions; excited utterances; then existing mental, emotional, or physical condition; statements for purpose of medical diagnosis; past recollection recorded; records of regularly conducted activity (also referred to as the business records exception); and public records and reports. The rationale behind allowing these forms of hearsay evidence is that they are generally reliable sources of information; and therefore, the probative value of the evidence outweighs its prejudicial value. In addition, because these forms of evidence have high degrees of reliability, they do not have to be proven through direct testimony (such as the inherent reliability of records kept in the normal course of business).

Present sense impressions are statements made immediately while the declarant is perceiving a particular event, or immediately thereafter. Thus, a witness statement describing a ROBBERY scene (say it is being recorded in a call to 911) is considered sufficiently reliable to be admissible as evidence, even though it technically meets the definition of hearsay. Similarly, a recorded admission of guilt of the accused may be admissible as an excited utterance, where the accused makes the utterance during an excited event, for instance, being confronted by a victim of the crime outside of court or custody (indicating, "yes I did it," or something to that effect).

Also included in categorical exceptions are statements made regarding a mental, emotional, or physical condition, including statements made for medical diagnosis purposes. The rationale is, again, that such statements contain inherent reliability because one is not assumed to make false statements regarding one's present medical condition, especially when answering questions for diagnosis purposes.

Finally, there are the business and public record exceptions, which memorialize the activities conducted in the regular course of business, or activities recorded pursuant to government regulation. Tax returns would be one example of a public record, while internal accounting summaries might be an example of a business record.

As a final point, it should be noted that under American law evidence that is otherwise admissible might yet be excluded based on procedural evidentiary requirements. For instance, all evidence submitted in a court of law, including admissible evidence, must be properly authenticated for admission. Authentication generally refers to documentary evidence but may also refer to verbal testimony. In essence, authentication requires sufficient evidence to support a finding that the matter in question is what it purports to be. For example, if a knife is being introduced as the MURDER weapon, then there must be sufficient evidence (foundational evidence, FINGERPRINTS of the accused, blood of the victim) to prove the knife being presented is actually the knife that may have committed the crime. Since authentication is a prerequisite to the admittance of evidence, it may be seen as a general exception to the exclusion of evidence (in other words, without proper authentication, all demonstrable evidence would be excluded in the U.S. CRIMINAL JUSTICE SYSTEM).

For more information

Henning, Anna Cir, and Kenneth R. Thomas, Coordinators. "Judge Sonia Sotomayor: Analysis of

Selected Opinions." *Congressional Research Service, Reports and Issue Briefs* (June 19, 2009): 28.

Lafarve, Wayne R. "The Smell of Herring: A Critique of the Supreme Court's Latest Assault on the Exclusionary Rule," *Journal of Criminal Law and Criminology* (Summer 2009): 757.

Savage, David G. "Who's Policing the Fourth Amendment? Tow Cases Push the Unevenly Enforced Exclusionary Rule Closer to Repeal *(Pearson v. Callahan)*," *ABA Journal* (April 2009): 19.

Chad J. McGuire
University of Massachusetts, Dartmouth

executive privilege Executive privilege is the idea that presidents have claimed to shield confidential communications from subordinates against demands by the other branches for its production. Although executive privilege has been often asserted, it has never had the firm constitutional position that its presidential advocates have claimed for it.

Executive privilege is an old doctrine, dating from the first major congressional investigation in 1792, when Congress attempted to investigate the reason for the Indian defeat of an expedition led by General St. Clair. A House committee asked President Washington for all papers and records related to the incident. Although Washington turned over the papers, his cabinet decided, in the words of Secretary of State Thomas Jefferson, that "the Executive ought to communicate such papers as the public good would permit, and ought to refuse those, the disclosure of which would injure the public." Jefferson would invoke executive privilege several years later when he refused to turn over documents that he claimed would show that his former vice president, Aaron Burr, had committed CONSPIRACY against the United States. A decision by CHIEF JUSTICE JOHN MARSHALL, sitting as a trial JUDGE in the Burr case, has framed judicial doctrine regarding executive privilege ever since. Marshall found that there is no absolute privilege in criminal cases for communications to which the president is a party and that a court may assess both the need for production of the information and the reasons against its disclosure in a closed examination. Marshall also stated that, if the president refuses to produce material relevant to a criminal case, the court hearing the case may draw inferences in favor of the accused or order that the prosecution be dismissed.

The modern controversy over executive privilege largely dates to early cold war years. President Harry Truman refused to provide documents to the HOUSE UN-AMERICAN ACTIVITIES COMMITTEE investigating allegations of communists in the State Department or to allow testimony by General Omar Bradley regarding their discussions over whether to remove General Douglas MacArthur from his command in Korea. President Dwight D. Eisenhower also invoked executive privilege in response to Senator Joseph McCarthy's investigations into the U.S. Army during the same period.

The most important modern judicial decision regarding executive privilege occurred during the Watergate crisis. In *U.S. v. NIXON* (1974), President Richard Nixon had refused to hand over to the special PROSECUTOR tapes of Oval Office meetings during which Nixon and his advisers had discussed covering up the BURGLARY of Democratic Party headquarters. Nixon's aides, who were facing criminal prosecution, had insisted that the tapes would show that their actions had been authorized by the president. The Supreme Court unanimously decided that the tapes had to be submitted to a judge who would balance the president's interest in confidentiality against his aides' fundamental right to a fair trial through an inspection in chambers.

For more information

Rozell, Mark J. *Executive Privilege: The Dilemma of Secrecy and Democratic Accountability.* Baltimore: Johns Hopkins University Press, 1994.

Daniel Levin
University of Utah

expert testimony Expert testimony is a crucial component of many criminal and civil trials. This testimony, just like a bloody knife and FINGERPRINTS, is considered EVIDENCE. Whether or not evidence is admitted at trial can make the difference between winning and losing the case. Both the federal and state courts have rules that determine the admissibility of evidence. Only evidence that assists the JURY is allowed to be seen or heard. JUDGES are responsible for excluding testimony that might confuse, mislead, or prejudice the jury.

One difference between expert and lay witnesses is that experts can testify as to their opinions while laypersons can testify to facts only. Expert witness testimony deals with specialized knowledge beyond the range of an average person's experience. For example, an expert might testify regarding DNA comparisons, economic projections, psychiatric evaluations, or disease causation. There has been an explosion of expert witness testimony in the last two decades due to the increased number of cases that rely on specialized knowledge as evidence. Two good examples are the use of DNA identification in criminal trials and the use of epidemiology and toxicology evidence in toxic TORT cases, a type of product liability case. Critics have argued that along with this increase in expert witnesses came a decrease in the standards for expert testimony and some even have accused experts of basing their testimony on so-called junk science.

In the case of *DAUBERT V. MERRELL DOW PHARMACEUTICALS, INC.*, 509 U.S. 579 (1993), the United States Supreme Court clarified the standard to be used in deciding admissibility where the expert witness is a scientist. The *Daubert* case was one of more than 1,000 lawsuits alleging that the antinausea drug Bendectin, taken by millions of pregnant women, caused a limb reduction birth defect. Before the *Daubert* ruling, there was inconsistency in the admissibility of expert evidence in the federal and state courts. Approximately two-thirds of American courts applied the older *Frye* test, *Frye v. United States,* 293 F. 1013 (D.C. Cir. 1923), which requires that "novel" scientific opinions offered as evidence must be "generally accepted" by scientists in the relevant field to be admissible. Other courts applied the more liberal FEDERAL RULE OF EVIDENCE 702, that "a witness qualified as an expert by knowledge, skill, experience, training, or education" may testify as to their opinion.

Under the *Frye* standard, the judge defers to the opinion of an expert scientific witness as long as the opinion is consistent with conventional scientific wisdom. In *Frye,* the defense wanted to introduce the results of a forerunner of the modern POLYGRAPH test that they believed demonstrated the defendant's veracity when he denied killing the victim. The Court disallowed the evidence on the basis that the theory and method of the test were not "generally" accepted" by scientists in the relevant fields of psychology and physiology. The introduction of Rule 702 in 1975 left undecided the question of whether *Frye* survived as the standard for specialized testimony. The landmark *Daubert* decision held that FEDERAL COURTS must apply Rule 702, not the *Frye* test, in determining admissibility of scientific evidence. The Supreme Court emphasized the judge's role as "gatekeeper" of scientific evidence testimony, ensuring that "not only relevant, but reliable" testimony be admitted. *Daubert* places the responsibility on the trial judge to determine whether the expert has used sound scientific methodology in arriving at her conclusions and offers guidelines to the judge in his gatekeeping role of excluding unreliable scientific testimony.

The United States Supreme Court decision in *Kumho Tire Co. v. Carmichael,* 119 S. Ct 1167 (1999), extended the *Daubert* holding beyond scientific testimony to include all expert witness testimony. *Daubert, Kumho,* and the *General Electric v. Joiner* opinion, 118 S. Ct. 512 (1997), which held that the trial judge has DISCRETION in deciding whether the studies relied upon by the expert witness are sufficient, form the trilogy of opinions that determine the admissibility of expert testimony in the federal courts. The state courts are free to adopt the federal rules, a modified version, or continue to use the *Frye* test in determining admissibility of expert witness testimony.

For more information

Faigman, David L. *Legal Alchemy: The Use and Misuse of Science in the Law.* New York: W. H. Freeman, 1999.

Foster, Kenneth R., and Peter W. Huber. *Judging Science: Scientific Knowledge and the Federal Courts.* Cambridge, Mass.: MIT Press, 1999.

Reference Manual on Scientific Evidence. Washington, D.C.: Federal Judicial Center, 2000. Available online. URL: *http://www.fjc.gov.*

Karen Gottlieb
BioLaw
Nederland, Colorado

expert witness Expert witness refers to an individual who testifies, whether in person or by affidavit, about an ultimate fact at issue or conclusions which can be drawn from other EVIDENCE. If scientific, technical, or other specialized knowledge will assist the JUDGE or JURY in understanding the evidence or in the determination of a fact, a witness qualified as an expert may testify by giving an opinion. In short, an expert is unlike other witnesses because she can and does give her opinion regarding some aspect of the dispute at hand. Other, nonexpert witnesses are limited to recounting what they have seen, heard, or otherwise experienced.

Experts may testify regarding exceedingly complex phenomena such as DNA EVIDENCE or the intellectual property rights to a computer program. Experts also may testify about less complex things such as the cost of used clothing at a yard sale or the price of a commodity on a certain date. Often experts testify regarding hypothetical situations that match or contrast with the issue in dispute. Experts could be engineers, economists, social or natural scientists, doctors, fire marshals, or anyone else with specific detailed knowledge about a discreet topic area. Knowledge, skill, training, or education could be the grounds for asserting that an individual qualifies as an expert.

While the judge must accept the proffered witness as an expert before testimony can be presented to the jury, qualifying as an expert is relatively easy. Often, the parties to litigation will stipulate that the opposing experts meet the "minimal qualifications" necessary to testify. Since experts are subject to cross-examination, few resist any individual being qualified as an expert because the less qualified the opposing expert, the easier the opinion is to impeach. Moreover, cases in which experts are used generally have experts on both sides of the litigation. In such cases, the judge or jury may be persuaded by the more credible expert, or two comparable experts may offset each other with a negligible impact on the proceeding. Importantly, because most experts are paid, usually on an hourly basis, the disclosure of that underlying economic incentive can impact the jury's assessment of the expert's credibility. Many states require disclosure of experts consulted but not retained to avoid litigants simply purchasing the most useful opinion.

In general, the expert may rely on any fact, belief, or premise in order to form an opinion. However, the expert must disclose when asked all that contributed to the formation of the opinion. For example, a doctor on the stand may express an opinion that a certain medical procedure was negligently performed. Whether that expert is a medical doctor or a sports physiologist may affect the credibility of the opinion. Whether the expert has reviewed all medical records in question or only those supplied by the attorney might impact the credibility of the opinion. Indeed, regardless of whether the expert consulted tarot cards, tea leaves, or a psychic hotline friend, any grounds for the opinion must be disclosed. In short, the opinion of the expert is only as good as the foundation upon which that opinion is based.

For more information

Consult Federal Rule of Evidence 702 and the following texts:

Matson, J. V. *Effective Expert Witnessing*. 3rd ed. New York: CRC Press, 1998.

Warren, R. A. *The Effective Expert Witness: Proven Strategies for Successful Court Testimony*. New York: Gaynor, 1996.

Charles Anthony Smith
University of California, San Diego

ex post facto is Latin for "after the fact"—an ex post facto law is a statute enacted after some previous act or conduct and tries to make it a crime. Ex post facto laws are excluded from the enumerated powers of Congress by Article I, section 9, and likewise explicitly prohibited for the state legislatures by Article I, section 10.

These twin clauses codify the ancient principle of the common law that it is fundamentally unfair to punish a person for having done an act that was not unlawful at the time it was done. They apply only to crimes. But the prohibition on criminal ex post facto laws manifests an underlying mistrust of any retroactive legislation—after-enacted statutes that change the law and then try to make the change apply to past conduct. The CONTRACT clause and the BILL OF ATTAINDER clauses in Article I, as well as the DUE PROCESS clauses in the Fifth and Fourteenth Amendments are analogous constitutional provisions on the noncriminal or civil side of the law. The ex post facto clauses apply only to statutes and do not apply to changes in the law affected by judicial decisions.

The ex post facto clauses also prohibit an after-enacted statute that would aggravate an offense and increase the PUNISHMENT for a crime already committed, beyond the punishment that was on the books at the time of the criminal act. Likewise, an after-enacted statute is unconstitutional if it would remove a defense that would have been available at the time the crime was committed or otherwise would so change the legal rules of EVIDENCE and procedure as to subvert the defendant's presumption of innocence.

The ex post facto clauses do not prohibit a legislature from changing the type of penalty within the same category. For example, a state could change the method of execution in a capital crime from electrocution to lethal injection. The clauses do allow a legislature to be more lenient, however, to give a criminal defendant the benefit of a reduction in the punishment after the crime was committed. It also is not a violation of the clauses to impose a punishment on a person who continues a course of unlawful conduct after a legislature enacts a statute to declare it a crime.

"The creation of crimes after the fact, or, in other words the subjecting of men to punishment for things which, when they were done, were breaches of no law," Alexander Hamilton observed in *Federalist Papers* number 84, has had a history of being one of "the favorite and most formidable instruments of tyranny." To our lasting benefit and protection, the framers of the CONSTITUTION stood against this brand of tyranny.

For more information

Calder v. Bull, 3 U.S. (3 Dall.) 386 (1798).

Goebel, Julius, Jr. *History of the Supreme Court*. Volume I: *Antecedents and Beginnings to 1801*. New York: Macmillan, 1971.

LaFave, Wayne R., and Austin W. Scott, Jr. *Criminal Law*. 2nd ed. St. Paul, Minn.: West, 1986.

Thomas E. Baker
University of Scranton

extortion Extortion is the criminal act of knowingly obtaining or attempting to obtain, by threat, property, or services of another. In some situations, extortion is commonly known as BLACKMAIL.

Many states have apportioned their extortion statute into differing levels or degrees. For example, extortion by force (see also ROB-

BERY) may be punished more severely and be characterized as a higher degree of offense than someone who extorts by use of threats (harassment); even less severely punished may be the person who threatens to falsely accuse another of a crime or provide false testimony (see also PERJURY), or some form of official action or withholding of official action in order to gain property or favor (intimidating a public servant or official misconduct). As is evident, extortion can take many forms and be combined with other criminal conduct. As a result, many PROSECUTORS use the extortion statute as a type of enhancement.

Extortion, without committing another separate offense, is possible though unusual. Therefore, most crimes that involve extortion also involve some other criminal conduct and statute. For example, the threat or use of force to obtain property of another is extortion but may also be robbery and ASSAULT. Blackmail, loan sharking, protection schemes, to name a few, are also forms of extortion that also have separate criminal statutes. Because of this, many prosecutors add extortion to other, more serious offenses to enhance or expand the available PUNISHMENT or to provide a PLEA BARGAIN opportunity. Some states have enacted "merger statutes," which combine sentences for like offenses into one sentence rather than consecutive sentences. However, even in those states with merger statutes, certain offenses, which have differing criminal elements, may not merge, resulting in additional sanctions for a single act.

While extortion reaches as far back as the 1200s with English kings obtaining travel expenses by extortion of Jews and the Chinese, and with other expanding nations exacting a tax to allow the recently concurred to stay in their homes, the modern extortion statutes seek to curb corruption and large-scale criminal enterprises, such as ORGANIZED CRIME. However, as criminal enterprises seek new opportunities, prosecution use of extortion statutes have also evolved. Federal prosecutors have used extortion statutes to prosecute the challenging and broad-reaching crimes that are committed over the INTERNET (computer trespass).

For more information

Wrage, Alexandra Addison. *Bribery and Extortion: Undermining Business, Governments, and Security.* Westport, Conn.: Praeger Press, 2007.

Mark McClain
Central Washington University

extradition Extradition, or interstate rendition, is the process through which one state surrenders a fugitive to another state for trial on outstanding criminal charges. It is a unique process in the CRIMINAL JUSTICE SYSTEM because the fugitive has few procedural rights. This is so because extradition is not a substantive criminal justice proceeding in which the fugitive's guilt is considered or the fugitive's constitutional rights may be vindicated. Instead, it is a matter of interstate relations, whereby a state receiving a demand for extradition, known as the ASYLUM state, has a duty to surrender the fugitive to the demanding state.

The CONSTITUTION OF THE UNITED STATES imposes an obligation upon the states to extradite fugitives from other states. This obligation is found in art. IV, sec. 2, clause 2, which is commonly called the rendition clause: "A person charged in any State with TREASON, FELONY, or other Crime who shall flee from JUSTICE and be found in another State, shall on demand of the executive Authority of the State from which he fled, be delivered up, to be removed to the State having JURISDICTION of the Crime."

To implement the rendition clause, the federal government adopted the rendition act, codified at 18 U.S.C. § 3181, to establish a very basic procedure. The federal statute is supplemented by an interstate compact known as the Uniform Criminal Extradition Act (UCEA), which establishes a more detailed procedure. In one form or another, the UCEA has been adopted by 48 states, the District of Columbia, Puerto Rico, and the Virgin Islands. As of 2009, the states of Mississippi and Louisiana have not adopted the uniform act. Nevertheless, those states remain obligated to surrender fugitives under the rendition clause and the federal statute. In *Puerto Rico v. Branstad,* 483 U.S. 219 (1987), the U.S. Supreme Court ruled that FEDERAL COURTS may force an asylum state to perform the "mandatory, ministerial act" of extradition to the demanding state when the asylum state violates its constitutional obligation.

The extradition process begins when a suspected criminal flees a state to avoid prosecution and is deemed to be a fugitive from JUSTICE. Local authorities issue an ARREST warrant and broadcast it to other states. Subsequently, when the fugitive is located in the asylum state, the fugitive is arrested on a fugitive warrant and the demanding state is notified. The fugitive may choose to waive extradition and agree to return to the demanding state voluntarily. If that happens, the asylum state will notify the demanding state that the fugitive will be surrendered. Then agents from the demanding state will travel to the asylum state, take the fugitive into custody, and return the fugitive to the demanding state to stand trial for the criminal charges.

However, if the fugitive does not waive extradition, the asylum state will notify the demanding state that a formal demand for extradition will be required. At that point, the local PROSECUTOR in the demanding state prepares and submits an application for extradition to the governor of the demanding state. This request generally must include the fugitive's name and physical description, the state and location where the fugitive may be found, a certified copy of the outstanding criminal charges, a summary of the circumstances of the crime, a certification that the ends of justice requires the extradition, and a designated agent to handle the transportation of the fugitive from the asylum state. If application is legally sufficient, the governor of the demanding state submits a requisition for extradition to the governor of the asylum state. Upon receipt of a legally sufficient demand, the governor in the asylum state issues a governor's warrant for the surrender of the fugitive to the appointed agent of the demanding state.

Although the governor in the asylum state may conduct a hearing to allow the fugitive to challenge the legality of the extradition, such hearings are exceptionally rare. The typical method for challenging an extradition is by filing a petition for writ of HABEAS CORPUS in a trial court in the asylum state. The habeas corpus proceeding is limited to considering whether the demand is supported by legally sufficient paperwork, confirming the identity of the fugitive, verifying that the fugitive is charged with a crime, and determining whether the individual is a fugitive from justice. The courts in the asylum state are prohibited from hearing any claims related to the underlying criminal charges, constitutional violations committed by the demanding state, or challenging the adequacy of the demanding state's justice system. If the demand for extradition fails the habeas corpus test, the fugitive will not be extradited to the demanding state as a consequence of the challenged demand. However, the fugitive will remain a fugitive from justice as long as the criminal charges remain unresolved in the demanding state. Thus, the fugitive may be subsequently ARRESTED and subjected to the extradition process once again. On the other hand, if the demand for extradition is vindicated in the habeas corpus proceeding, the fugitive will be surrendered to the demanding state.

For more information

Abramson, Leslie W. "Extradition in America: Of Uniform Acts and Governmental Discretion, *Baylor Law Review* 33 (1981): 793.

Murphy, John J. "Revising Domestic Extradition Law." *University of Pennsylvania Law Review* 131 (1983): 106.

Mark A. Fulks
Tennessee State University

eyewitness An eyewitness is anyone at a CRIME SCENE who viewed the event and then provides this information to the investigating agency. If the case goes to trial, the eyewitness may be called to testify in court as to what they witnessed.

There are several different types of witness. An eyewitness was at the scene of the crime and saw, a least, some portion of the crime. This might be the entire crime as it occurred or as little as the suspect running away from the crime scene. An ear witness is someone who heard something related to the crime but did not see anything. The witnesses involved in the O.J. SIMPSON MURDER case who heard the barking dog would be an example of this. An EXPERT WITNESS would be someone who after examining the case information, EVIDENCE, or the suspect would testify regarding his or her expert opinion. An expert witness was not at the crime scene when the incident occurred. Finally, there is the profession witness. In most cases, this refers to a law enforcement officer who testifies regarding the investigation.

Eyewitness testimony is very important in the investigation and conviction of criminals. However, eyewitnesses are also notoriously unreliable for several reasons. First is the basic unreliability of human memory. People do not store and record information in a precise or perfect manner. After time, they will process what they saw and due to many factors such as stress, emotions, and factors of one's life, will add to or alter their description of events to better fit what they believed they saw.

Second, people are open to suggestions. One of the key factors in any police investigation is to separate the eyewitnesses from one another as soon as possible and to avoid any leading questions (i.e., "Was the car red?"). Even the U.S. Supreme Court, with regard to wrongful convictions based on mistaken identification by eyewitnesses, has stated, "The vagaries of eyewitness identification are well known; the annals of criminal law are rife with instances of mistaken identification."

Because eyewitnesses may be required to testify in court the issues of competence and credibility becomes factors. Competence refers to the eyewitness's ability to function as a witness in court. Thus, is the eyewitness qualified, based on factors such as intelligence, relationship to individuals involved in the case (i.e., husband and wife, doctor and patient), mental state, and age to give testimony in court?

Credibility refers to believability. Issues of credibility include questions such as was the witness conscious at the time of the crime, was the witness drinking or using drugs, what was the witness doing at the crime scene, does the witness have any bias or prejudice relating to the victim or suspect in the case. Because of the issues of competence and credibility, law enforcement will need to check on many background issue regarding eyewitnesses prior to going to court. Even with the issues presented, eyewitnesses are an important part of any criminal investigation. JURIES place a great deal of weight in the testimony of an eyewitness when deciding guilt or innocence. However, as it has been pointed out, eyewitness identification and description is regarded as the most unreliable form of evidence and causes more miscarriages of JUSTICE than any other method of proof.

For more information

Donigan, R., et al. *The Evidence Handbook.* 4th ed. Evanston, Ill.: Traffic Institute, Northwestern University, 1980.

Loftur, E., and E. Green. "Eyewitness identification." In *The Encyclopedia of Police Science,* edited by W. G. Bailey, 183–185. New York: Garland, 1989.

National Institute for Justice. *Eyewitness Evidence: A Guide for Law Enforcement.* Washington, D.C.: Department of Justice: 1999.

Pozzulo, J. D., and J. L. Dempsey. "Witness Factors and Their Influences on Jurors' Perceptions and Verdicts," *Criminal Justice and Behavior* 36, no. 9 (2009): 923–934.

Swanson, C., C. Chamelin, and L. Territo. *Criminal Investigation.* 8th ed. New York: McGraw Hill, 2003.

Kenneth L. Mullen
Appalachian State University

F

Fair Housing Act The Fair Housing Act prohibits housing discrimination that occurs because the victim is a member of one of seven protected classes. The Fair Housing Act (FHA) was passed by Congress in 1968 in response to the CIVIL RIGHTS MOVEMENT, and its coverage was broadened to protect additional classes by amendments passed in both 1974 and 1988.

The seven classes currently protected under the federal act are race, color, national origin, sex, RELIGION, familial status, and disability. Moreover, some states and municipalities have broader fair housing acts that prohibit discrimination based on additional classes such as sexual orientation and source of income. Not only are rental and sales housing transactions covered by the act, but also lending, insurance, and advertising. In addition to prohibiting intentional acts of discrimination, the FHA also prohibits seemingly neutral actions which have a disparate impact on one of the protected classes. So, for example, along with prohibiting an ad that states "whites only," the act also prohibits ad campaigns for housing which use only white models because such ads are likely to create the feeling among minorities that they are not welcome as customers.

Some classic examples of housing discrimination include:

1. Providing false information about the availability of housing due to the applicant's race,
2. Changing rental terms and conditions depending on an applicant's sex,
3. Steering a minority family to properties located in a minority section of town,
4. Refusing to sell homeowner's insurance in certain areas due to high concentrations of minorities,
5. Convincing homeowners to sell their dwellings by creating a fear that members of a protected class will be moving in all around them, and
6. Harassing and intimidating members of the protected classes.

In addition to the above types of housing discrimination, which can affect members of any protected class, there are other types of discriminatory conduct that only affect persons with disabilities. In fact, it is often difficult for a disabled person to even enter a dwelling or to use a dwelling's essential portions, such as a bathroom. In order to combat such accessibility problems, the Fair Housing Act requires that apartment buildings that contain four or more units and an elevator and were built after March 13, 1991, be accessible to persons with disabilities. The act also requires that ground floor units in buildings with four or more units without elevators be accessible.

Along with establishing accessibility requirements for new multifamily housing, the Fair Housing Act also requires that reasonable accommodations in rules and services be granted to disabled individuals. So, if someone is disabled and needs a service dog, a landlord generally must allow the dog even if the complex has a "no pet" rule. Finally, the FHA requires all housing providers to allow tenants with disabilities to make reasonable structural modifications at their own expense, such as installing grab bars in a bathroom.

Because housing discrimination is more subtle today than it was before the passage of the FHA and other civil rights laws, it is often not obvious when discrimination is occurring. Accordingly, many fair housing organizations use volunteer testers in order to investigate housing discrimination. Testers can be used in controlled experiments in which the only significant variable is one of the protected classes. So, for example, if a white tester and a black tester visit the same complex on the same afternoon and the black tester is told nothing is available while the white tester is told there are three vacancies, housing discrimination may be occurring. In *Havens Realty Corp. v. Coleman* (1982) the Supreme Court ruled that testers have a right to truthful information even though the testers have no actual intention of buying or renting a home and may, in fact, expect to receive false information. The Court also held that both testers and fair housing organizations can be harmed by a housing provider's discriminatory conduct.

The federal agency responsible for enforcing the Fair Housing Act is the U.S. Department of Housing and Urban Development (HUD). Individuals who believe their fair housing rights have been violated can file a claim with HUD, an equivalent state or local agency, or in federal or state court.

For more information

Dubofsky, Jean Eberhart. "Fair Housing: A Legislative History and a Perspective," *Washburn Law Journal* 8, no. 1. (Winter 1969): 149.

Fair Housing Act, United States Code Title 42, sections 3601 et seq.

HUD Website. Available online. URL: http://www.hud.gov

National Fair Housing Advocate. Available online. URL: http://www.fairhousing.com

Martha M. Lafferty
Staff Attorney
Tennessee Fair Housing Council

false confessions A false confession is an inculpatory statement given by an individual not responsible for the crime to which he or she confessed.

While false confessions may be induced by coercion, and are usually given by children or mentally infirm suspects, rational and lucid suspects have also been known to confess falsely for a variety of reasons. For instance, some suspects confess falsely to end a particularly onerous interrogation, while others do so to divert police attention from other aspects of a crime or from other suspects (i.e., a mother confessing falsely to protect her child). Often, criminal defendants will confess to a crime they did not commit pursuant to a PLEA BARGAIN to avoid a harsher sentence. The most famous example of a false confession was the Central Park jogger case from 1989, when five teenagers confessed to a brutal rape they did not commit after 48 hours of interrogation.

Richard Ofshe and Richard Leo have created a four-part false confession typology:

1. **Stress-complaint false confessions:** the result of the "inherent stressors" in a normal

interrogation, which cause confusion, exhaustion, and emotional instability.

2. **Coerced-complaint false confessions**: confessions extracted from an innocent person through classically coercive police interrogation tactics such as the use of threats, promises of leniency, as well as other forms of physical and psychological manipulation.
3. **Coerced-persuaded**: persuaded false confessions occur when an interrogator persuades an innocent suspect that he committed the crime of which he is accused. Persuaded false confessions "are given after a person has become convinced that it is more likely than not that he committed the crime, despite possessing no memory of having done so." The noncoerced version results from a relatively normal police interrogation.
4. **Coerced-internalized false confessions**: another type of persuaded false confessions, where police coercion causes defendants to falsely believe they committed the crime. Coerced-internalized false confessions result from the same tactics used to procure a coerced-compliant false confession, namely threats and promises of leniency. Persuaded false confessions—whether they are coerced or noncoerced—are extremely rare and difficult to detect because they are usually unintended and unrecognized by the interrogators.

To aid in the detection of false confessions, false confession theorists describe a sequence of errors during routine police interrogations that can produce false confessions. First, investigators must misclassify an innocent suspect as guilty. Second, interrogators subject the innocent suspect to an aggressive and guilt-presumptive interrogation designed to extract a confession at all costs. Finally, after recognizing that the extracted confession may not conform with the forensic EVIDENCE, interrogators actively shape the suspect's post-admission narrative with public and nonpublic facts.

Although the U.S. Supreme Court has yet to rule on the admissibility of false confession EXPERT TESTIMONY, courts on the federal and state levels remain bitterly divided. Some courts admit expert testimony that discusses a particular defendant's mental condition at the time the confession was given as a way to discredit its reliability. Others admit the testimony but limit the discussion to a general description of the phenomenon, while some permit not only a general discussion of the phenomenon but also a particularized discussion of the elements present in the suspect's confession, stopping short of allowing the EXPERT WITNESS to pass judgment on the veracity of the confession. Finally, for each example of admission, there are equally powerful examples of courts at the state and federal levels excluding the testimony, whether or not it discusses a cognizable mental condition, the false confession phenomenon in general, or the false confession theory as applied to the specific contours of the investigation.

For more information

Cassel, Elaine. *The False Confessions in the Central Park Jogger Case: How They Happened and How to Stop Similar Injustices in the Future. CounterPunch*, (December 21, 2002). Available online. URL: http://www.counterpunch.org/cassel1221.html.

Leo, Richard A., and Richard J. Ofshe. "The Decision to Confess Falsely: Rational Choice and Irrational Action," *Denver University Law Review* 74 (1997): 979.

Leo, Richard. *Police Interrogation and American Justice*. Cambridge, Mass.: Harvard University Press, 2009.

Leo, Richard A., and Richard J. Ofshe. "The Decision to Confess Falsely: Rational Choice and Irrational Action," *Denver Law Review* 74 (1997): 979.

Perez, David A. "The (In)Admissibility of False Confession Expert Testimony," *Touro Law Review* (2009).

David Perez
Yale Law School

family Family evokes a mental picture of one man married to one woman with their 2.1 biological children. We call this grouping the traditional nuclear family. Although we are brought up to expect this kind of traditional family, it is a stereotype that is no longer the norm in most American households. The term is more than a descriptive noun; it has a legal definition also, which is being challenged.

Although we view the heterosexual married couple with biological children as the definition of family, more and more groups of people are seeking to classify themselves as families. These groups are not necessarily bound by age distribution (two adults and one or more minor children), or biology (all parties being related to one another by blood), or even legal ties (marriage). These are groups of people who have come together due to common lifestyle, kinship bond, or a basic need to belong to a group. A common lifestyle may be based on one's sexual orientation, one's profession (high-stress jobs like the stock market or .com), or one's interests (sports, music).

All of these configurations of peoples or families stay together due to this need to feel a part of a group. This group provides support—emotional and financial—and interdependence. One may borrow money from one's family. One may protect one's family with health and life insurance. Family will provide advice, wanted and unwanted, about life's decisions. Family may help make life and death decisions, including DNR orders or organ donations. Family provides this critical sense of belonging, a part of one's identification.

The law used to be clear in its definition of family. The traditional nuclear family was not only the norm, it was all we recognized. As this group has become less common other groups have demanded acknowledgment.

In 1989 the New York Court of Appeals held in *Braschi v. Stahl Associates Co.* that a homosexual partnership would be included in the definition of family. In that case the surviving partner of a 20-year relationship sued to maintain possession of a rent-controlled apartment in New York City. The court found that the long-term relationship established family inheritance rights between and for the partners. The highest court in the state of New York recognized this relationship as a family.

In Minnesota in the case of *In re Guardianship of Kowalski* an appellate court allowed a homosexual partner to act as legal guardian for her partner following a devastating accident. The injured woman's biological family sought to exclude the lesbian partner. The court appointed the partner as guardian of the accident victim over the challenges mounted by the traditional family. The court viewed the lesbian relationship as family.

Law and society are slowly moving to expand the term *family.* No longer is it constrained by legal and biological lines. Many employers are now offering domestic partnership insurance coverage. This benefit affords one the opportunity to include one's partner, heterosexual or homosexual, under one's health insurance coverage.

Co-parenting is gaining acceptance in American courts. Co-parents are unmarried adults in committed partnerships who are allowed to adopt minor children. Prior to the 1990s only heterosexual married couples and occasional single persons were allowed to adopt children. Several states have allowed heterosexual and homosexual couples to adopt without the prior requirement of a marriage license.

Family still includes heterosexual married couples with children, but recent Census Bureau data indicate that by the latter part of the first decade of 2000 this type of arrangement constitutes less than half of the households in America. Increasingly, many households, and therefore families, include single parent, gay, lesbian, or other types of relationships. As more states begin to recognize the rights of same-sex and unmarried couples to live together, or as extended families of adult children, grandchildren, and other relatives move in together, the traditional notion of family will continue to evolve and change.

For more information

Braschi v. Stahl Associates and Co., 544 N.Y.S. 2d 784, 543 N.E. 2d 49 (N.Y. 1989).

In re Guardianship of Kowalski, 478 N.W.2d 790 (Minn. App. 1991).

Margaret R. Ryniker
SUNY, Oswego

Family and Medical Leave Act The Family and Medical Leave Act extended the principles of the 1978 Pregnancy Discrimination Act (PDA), which specified that discrimination on the basis of pregnancy, childbirth, or related medical conditions constituted illegal sex discrimination under Title VII of the Civil Rights Act of 1964.

The act was signed into law on February 5, 1993, the first piece of legislation of the new Clinton administration. The heart of the PDA, section 701(k), stated that: "women affected by pregnancy . . . shall be treated the same for all employment-related purposes . . . as other persons not so affected but similar in their ability or inability to work."

The Family and Medical Leave Act (FMLA) was first proposed in Congress in 1985. Although a number of Republicans favored the measure, two earlier versions of the bill were vetoed by President George H. W. Bush in 1990 and 1992 at the urging of major business interests such as the U.S. Chamber of Commerce and the National Federation of Independent Business; groups such as these opposed it on the grounds that it mandated benefits that would be too burdensome for employers. Another business group, the National Retail Federation, reversed itself and ultimately supported the bill. With Democratic control of Congress and the White House, the likelihood of the bill's passage increased after the November 1992 election, especially since it was one of President Bill Clinton's chief campaign issues.

In signing the FMLA in a Rose Garden ceremony, President Clinton said, "now millions of our people will no longer have to choose between their jobs and their families." The law provides that workers in companies with 50 or more employees are entitled to take up to 12 weeks of unpaid leave during any 12-month period for the birth or adoption of a child; the illness of a child, spouse, or parent; or the worker's own serious illness. To be eligible, employees must work for the same employer for at least a year and for at least 1,250 hours during the year. The employer must continue to maintain health-care benefits for employees during the leave time; workers must be allowed to return to their former, or equivalent, jobs after their return. However, the bill also allows employers to deny leave to the highest paid 10 percent of their workforce if the worker's absence would cause "serious and grievous injury."

The purpose of the FMLA is to allow workers of both sexes to balance the needs of work and family. However, although it furthers the principle of equal opportunity for women in the workplace, because it provides only unpaid leave, the FMLA does not greatly advance the goal of easing the financial burden of childbirth or family illness on working women. Moreover, in spite of its gender-neutral language, it appears that many more women are taking family leave than are men, suggesting that the primary responsibility for family care remains with women. Thus, although it is an important step in achieving gender equity, for these reasons, the FMLA represents only the initial stages of the process of making the workplace truly egalitarian.

For more information

Selim, Michael. "The Limited Vision of the Family and Medical Leave Act," *Villanova Law Review* 44 (1999): 395–413.

Susan Gluck Mezey
Loyola University, Chicago

Fay v. Noia 372 U.S. 391 (1963) In *Fay v. Noia*, the U.S. Supreme Court ruled that an individual who had been falsely convicted of a crime was entitled to use habeas corpus to obtain his freedom. This case is important because it affirmed an important constitutional right of individuals to protect themselves against false imprisonment.

In 1942, Charles Noia, Santo Caminito, and Frank Bonino were convicted of FELONY MURDER and sentenced to life imprisonment by a county court in Kings County, New York. The convictions stemmed from an armed ROBBERY in which the victim had been shot and killed. The only EVIDENCE for the prosecution was a confession made and signed by each of the defendants. Noia did not APPEAL from the conviction. The other defendants did appeal, and although their direct appeals were unsuccessful, both eventually won their freedom by persuading courts that their confessions had been obtained unconstitutionally. Noia, who was still in prison, then sought a writ of habeas corpus from the U.S. District Court for the Southern District of New York.

Since 1867, federal law has permitted federal district courts to entertain habeas corpus petitions from state prisoners who allege that their incarceration violates provisions of the U.S. CONSTITUTION or federal statutes or treaties. However, the district court denied Noia's application on the ground that the habeas corpus statute barred relief in cases where petitioners had failed to exhaust their remedies in state court. In effect, the district court held that Noia's failure to seek a direct appeal of his conviction barred him from subsequent federal habeas corpus relief. The U.S. COURT OF APPEALS for the Second Circuit reversed the district court and held that exceptional circumstances justified Noia's application for federal habeas corpus relief. Edward Fay, the warden of the prison where Noia was incarcerated, asked the U.S. Supreme Court to review the case on CERTIORARI.

The Supreme Court agreed to review the case but upheld the court of appeals' decision by a vote of 6-3. In an opinion by Justice WILLIAM J. BRENNAN, the high court held that a state prisoner is not required to take a direct appeal to a state appellate court in order to seek federal habeas corpus relief. Nor is a prisoner barred from raising a constitutional issue in FEDERAL COURT merely because the issue had not been raised on direct appeal in the state courts. Justice Brennan observed that "no just and humane legal system can tolerate a result whereby a Caminito and a Bonino are at liberty because their confessions were found to have been coerced yet a Noia, whose confession was also coerced, remains in jail for life." *Fay v. Noia,* 372 U.S. 391, 441 (1963). In dissent, Justice JOHN M. HARLAN (joined by Justice Tom Clark and Justice Potter Stewart) recognized that "Noia's predicament may well be thought one that strongly calls for correction. But the proper course to that end lies with the New York Governor's powers of executive clemency, not with the federal courts."

Fay v. Noia was one of several WARREN COURT decisions broadening state prisoners' access to federal habeas corpus review. (See, e.g., *Townsend v. Sain,* 372 U.S. 293 (1963). These decisions represent a significant element of the Warren Court's expansion of the constitutional rights of the accused.

For more information

Federman, Cary. *The Body and the State: Habeas Corpus and American Jurisprudence.* Albany: SUNY Press, 2006.

John M. Scheb II
University of Tennessee, Knoxville

Federal Bureau of Investigation The Federal Bureau of Investigation or FBI is the principal investigative arm of the U.S. JUSTICE DEPARTMENT. It has been called "the greatest law enforcement body in the world." It was established in 1908 as the Bureau of Investigation and received its present name in 1935. At first it dealt with antitrust violations, BANKRUPTCY, and FRAUD. It evolved from a force of examiners at first hired by the ATTORNEY GENERAL from other departments. In 1910 its JURISDICTION was expanded to include organized PROSTITUTION (under the Mann

Act) and in World War I sabotage and espionage. (Note the Palmer Red Raids of 1920.) After the revelation of the scandals of the Harding administration, the agency was reorganized in 1924. J. EDGAR HOOVER headed the Bureau from 1924 under eight presidents until his death in 1972. In his 48 years Hoover turned an incompetent and corrupt investigative service into a professional police force. However, the record was tarnished by embarrassments and exposés (spying on political enemies, abusing the First Amendment, harassing organizations with disruptive techniques, BLACKMAILING politicians). In 1976 Congress placed a 10-year, single-term limit on the FBI director. Though no agent has been appointed directly to the post of director, Clarence Kelley and Louis J. Freeh had both been special agents at some point in their careers.

In the late 1920s the Bureau's mission increased to include ORGANIZED CRIME, racketeering, and bank ROBBERY. In the 1930s it began to investigate kidnappings and to monitor radical and extremist organizations and in World War II to do foreign counterintelligence. It also investigates attacks on the president or other federal officers. The FBI investigates the backgrounds of presidential nominees and oversees the loyalty-security investigation program for federal employees. In the 1960s CIVIL RIGHTS violations were added to its scrutiny (for example, the 1964 MURDER of three civil rights workers in Mississippi). More recently the Bureau has become concerned with offenses involving high technology. In recent years the Bureau's reputation has been harmed with allegations of flawed performance at RUBY RIDGE and Waco and in the work of its laboratory. The FBI investigates more than 200 kinds of federal crimes. Normally the FBI's jurisdiction does not extend to income and tax matters, narcotics, COUNTERFEITING, customs matters, postal laws, and the protection of the president.

The FBI has 59 field offices in the United States and a number of "legal attaché offices" outside the country (maintaining liaison with foreign police and intelligence services). The agency provides cooperative services for other criminal justice agencies (laboratory services, FINGERPRINT identification, police training, etc.) Currently there are about 10,000 special agents of which about 10 percent are women, 5 percent African American, and 5 percent Hispanic. The FBI also employs another 14,000 workers (laboratory technicians, clerks, and secretaries). It has almost a quarter of the employees of the Department of Justice. The FBI has its own merit system distinct from the regular civil service.

For more information

Balcavage, Dynise, and Arthur M. Schlesinger, Jr., eds. *The Federal Bureau of Investigation.* Broomall, Pa.: Chelsea House, 2000.

Jeffreys, Diarmuid. *The Bureau: Inside the Modern FBI.* Boston–New York: Houghton Mifflin, 1995.

Theoharis, Athan G., ed. *The FBI: A Comprehensive Reference Guide.* Phoenix, Ariz.: Oryx Press, 1999.

Martin Gruberg
University of Wisconsin, Oshkosh

FBI (Federal Bureau of Investigation) Uniform Crime Reports The Uniform Crime Reports (UCR) is one of the most cited and comprehensive sources of crime data in the United States.

Since the 1930s, the FBI has collected information regarding offenses known to police in a voluntary program in which city, county, state, federal, tribal, and college law enforcement agencies submit crime statistics. For select crimes, the UCR includes data regarding the total number of known offenses and the rate of offenses per 100,000 inhabitants. The UCR also publishes clearance rates. A crime is considered cleared for reporting purposes if a suspect has been ARRESTED and charged, or if exceptional circumstances—such as the death of a suspect—cease police involvement. The clearance rate is the number of cleared crimes as a percentage of the number of crimes known to police.

UCR crimes are divided into two major groups: Part I and Part II offenses. Part I offenses (often called Index Crimes) are generally considered to be more serious crimes by nature and/or volume and usually receive the most media attention.

The eight Part I offenses are further divided into two categories—VIOLENT CRIMES and PROPERTY CRIMES. Violent offenses are those directly against a person and include MURDER/non-negligent MANSLAUGHTER, forcible rape, ROBBERY, and aggravated ASSAULT. The national violent crime rate (reflecting the sum of these four offenses) peaked in 1991. Subsequent declines have brought the violent crime rate to levels similar to those of the mid-1970s. The murder rate has hovered around 5.6 per 100,000 since 2000, half of its high (10.2) posted in 1980.

Property offenses are more common, involve the illegal taking or damaging of property, and include BURGLARY, LARCENY-THEFT, motor vehicle theft, and ARSON. The national property crime rate in 2008 was about 40 percent lower than the record set in 1980. Larceny-theft is by far the most reported Part I offense, typically accounting for well over half of all reported Index Crimes.

In Part II, the UCR tracks the number of arrests made for 21 other lesser offenses. These include simple assault, LOITERING, sex offenses, VANDALISM, and drug offenses, among others.

UCR data should be used and interpreted with care. Intended to be an overview of crime, the UCR includes only offenses reported to or otherwise discovered by police. Unreported offenses—often termed the "dark figure of crime"—are not included.

Definitional concerns also exist. While some offenses like murder are easy to categorize, other acts might be classified differently by different officers (e.g., simple assault versus aggravated assault). Moreover, for UCR reporting purposes, the definition of rape includes only female victims. A rape of a male would not be included in the count, though such an act could still be prosecuted as rape in many JURISDICTIONS.

The UCR count also differs from crimes prosecuted because the UCR uses the hierarchy rule. This rule stipulates that when a criminal act involves the commission of more than one Part I offense, police are to count only the highest-ranking offense. If a person robs, then assaults and kills a victim, only the murder is counted for UCR purposes. This applies only to the reporting process. The accused would likely face multiple charges in court. The UCR does not collect information regarding decisions by PROSECUTORS, JUDGES, JURIES, or CORONERS.

For these and other reasons, many scholars use the UCR in conjunction with other data sources such as surveys of victims, including the NATIONAL CRIME VICTIMIZATION SURVEY, which estimate the number of unreported serious crimes by interviewing a national sample of residents. The UCR is available as an annual publication *(Crime in the United States)* and on the INTERNET.

For more information

Blumstein, Alfred, Jacqueline Cohen, and Richard Rosenfeld. "The UCR-NCS Relationship Revisited: A Reply to Menard," *Criminology* 30 (1992): 115–124.

Menard, Scott, and Herbert C. Covey. "UCR and NCS: Comparisons over Space and Time," *Journal of Criminal Justice* 16 (1988): 371–384.

Michael A. McCall
San Diego State University

federal court system The federal court system occupies a small but unique niche in the U.S. system of government. Most civil and criminal disputes are handled by state and local courts, not FEDERAL COURTS. It is the other two branches—the executive and legislative—that most often are in the news or the subject of teachers' lesson plans. Yet it is the federal courts that have resolved some of the most important disputes in the history of the nation. The origin of the federal courts is traced to the

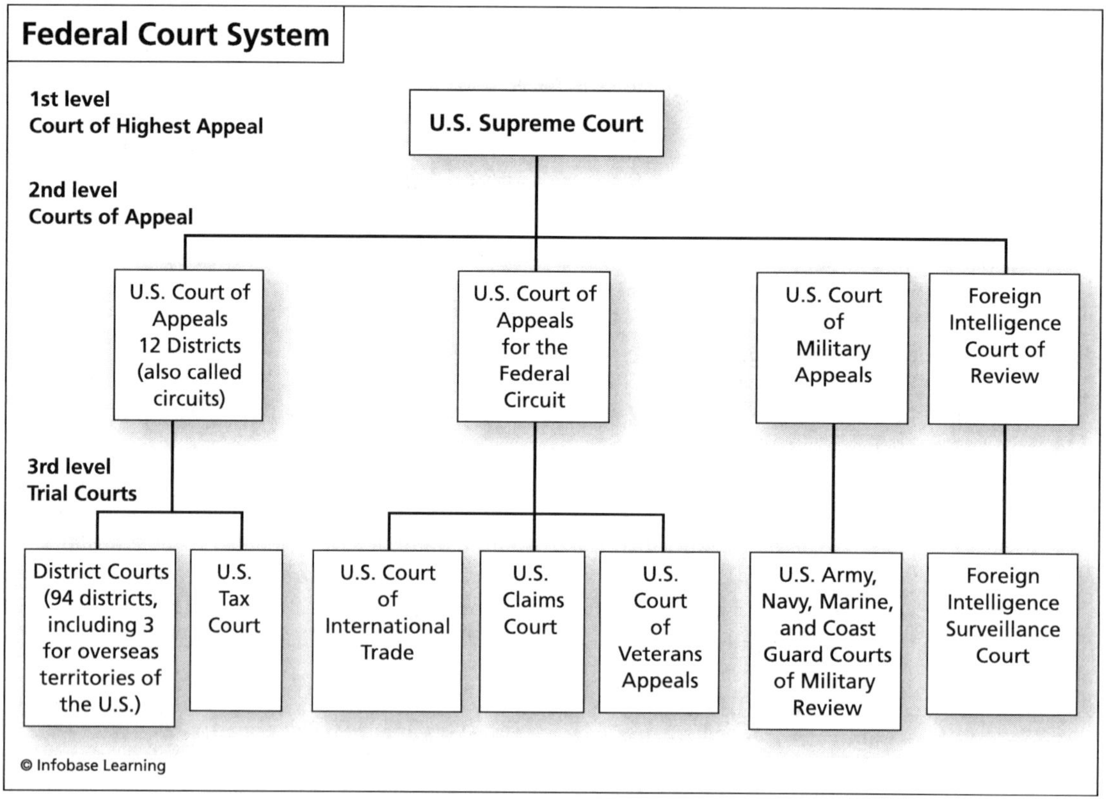

CONSTITUTION, which says little about the third branch of the government. The principles it enunciates, however, remain the keystone of the federal courts today.

Article III of the Constitution states that "The judicial power of the United States shall be vested in one supreme court and in such inferior courts as the Congress may from time to time ordain and establish." In other words, while the Constitution established the Supreme Court of the United States, it was Congress that later created courts of appeals and district courts.

JUDGES who serve on these courts are known as "Article III" judges. The Constitution protects the independence of these judges in two ways. First, judges hold their office during "good behavior." This means that they only can be removed from the bench through IMPEACHMENT for, in the words of the Constitution, "high crimes and MISDEMEANORS." The Constitution also states that a judge's compensation may not be reduced as long as he or she is a judge. Together these two provisions insulate judges so they can reach fair and impartial decisions free from political and societal pressures. They also protect the citizens because it is independent judges who serve as the guardians of the rights of the people. These two principles set federal judges apart from state and local judges and the judges of other nations.

The Constitution's treatment of the federal judiciary stems from the lessons the new United States learned in breaking away from England, where judges were subservient to the king. In addition to establishing the paramount importance of judicial independence, the drafters of the Constitution set up a delicate system of checks and balances, which continues to serve as the hallmark of our democratic system of government. While the number and types of cases have changed over the last 200 years—the drafters of the Constitution did not foresee the INTERNET—the function of today's federal courts remains virtually unchanged.

The federal judiciary is relatively small. In addition to the nine Supreme Court justices there are 179 court of appeals judges operating out of 13 regional circuits, and 654 district court judges working in 94 different districts. As stated in the Constitution, it is the job of the president to nominate and the Senate to confirm the judges who occupy these positions. While federal judicial nominees typically are highly respected lawyers, law professors, or state judges, the Constitution sets forth no criteria for judicial service. In fact judges need not be lawyers, although all recent nominees have come from the legal profession.

The district court, which is where trials are conducted, handles about 60,000 criminal cases and 260,000 civil cases a year. About 55,000 of these cases are APPEALED to one of the regional circuit court of appeals. From here, an appeal may be filed with the Supreme Court. The Supreme Court, however, has what is known as "discretionary JURISDICTION." This means that unlike the courts below it, it does not have to accept every appeal that is filed. In fact, it typically agrees to take only about 1 percent of the cases it is requested to hear—usually only serious constitutional issues or significant disputes among several lower courts.

Since few federal cases ever reach the Supreme Court, most disputes are resolved either by the district courts or courts of appeals. The subject of "jurisdiction," a court's authority to hear a case, is a complex one. The "docket" or case schedule of state courts involves most local crimes or civil disputes, such as disagreements over CONTRACTS, or car accidents. Federal courts, on the other hand, only may decide cases that involve the U.S. government, the Constitution, federal laws, or disputes between the states or the U.S. and foreign governments. For example, it is the responsibility of federal courts to hear most CIVIL RIGHTS cases, because the relevant laws are federal laws that were enacted by the U.S. Congress. Federal courts also would have authority to hear criminal cases that may have occurred in a national park, on a military base, or on other federal land.

For more information

Available online. URL: www.uscourts.gov.

David Sellers
Administrative Office of the U.S. Courts

federal courts Federal courts were established under Article III of the CONSTITUTION; however, the founders used vague language in describing the system. The Constitution requires that the president, with the advice and consent of the Senate, appoint JUDGES to the federal judiciary for life. Responsibility for constructing the rest of the system's specifics was left to Congress. The Judiciary Act of 1789 was passed by the first Congress and laid the foundation for the third branch of the federal government.

Today the federal court system is composed of three layers. The first layer is composed of the U.S. district courts. These 94 courts serve as the trial courts for the criminal and civil cases in the federal system. When a case is brought before this level of the court, one judge hears the case and with the help of a JURY makes a judgment on the facts of the case. The district courts do not overlap states. Each state has at least one district court that is unique to that state. Many states have several district courts, serving different geographic regions of the state. For example, the state of Alabama has three districts: the Northern District in Birmingham, the Middle District in Montgomery, and the Southern District in Mobile. Different districts have different numbers of authorized judgeships. Congress approves these judgeships as needed to handle the caseload in the district. In addition to these district courts, there are several specialty federal courts that hear trial-level cases on issues such as BANKRUPTCY, military issues, and international trade. Administrative agencies in the federal government also often have administrative law judges who hear cases regarding decisions made in a specific part of the bureaucracy.

The decisions made in the 94 district courts, the specialty courts, and the administrative agencies may be appealed to the second layer of the federal judiciary, the U.S. COURTS OF APPEALS. This layer is composed of 12 regional circuit courts and one federal circuit court. Cases coming before the U.S. Courts of Appeals are generally heard by a panel of three judges. These collegial courts make a consensus decision on each case based on findings of law. The appellate court does not decide whether the facts of the case are correct, rather they examine the accuracy with which the law was applied to the case. The panel is composed of three judges on the circuit. The number of judges in each circuit varies, as it does at the district court level. For example, the Seventh Circuit hears cases in the federal courthouse in Chicago, Illinois, from three states: Illinois, Indiana, and Wisconsin. While the Seventh Circuit has 11 judges, the much larger Ninth Circuit has 28 authorized judgeships. In some cases, litigants may request that the circuit court hear their case *en banc,* which means all of the judges in the circuit will make up one large panel to hear a case.

Litigants who choose to APPEAL their cases beyond the U.S. Courts of Appeals must appeal to the third, or top layer of the federal court system, the United States Supreme Court. The nine justices who serve on the Court have a great deal of control, as designated by Congress, over which cases they choose to hear. The cases may come from either state or federal courts, and they usually involve important questions involving either the Constitution or federal laws. The justices hear cases as a panel of nine and are again examining cases only for mistakes made in legal interpretation, not findings of facts.

For more information

An excellent map showing all of the geographic jurisdictions of the federal district and circuit courts is available at the Web site of the Administrative Office of the United States Courts. Available online. URL: www.uscourts.gov. For additional information on this topic see also the Federal Judicial Center at: www.fic.gov.

Nancy Winemiller Basinger
University of Georgia

Federal Rules of Criminal Procedure The Federal Rules of Criminal Procedure (the Rules) govern procedures for criminal proceedings in U.S. federal district courts, appeals courts, and the Supreme Court. The federal judiciary promulgates the rules pursuant to authority granted by the Rules Enabling Act, 28 U.S.C. §§ 2072, 2074.

The Rules procedurally guide all stages in the federal criminal trial process, including preliminary proceedings, GRAND JURIES, indictments, ARRAIGNMENTS, venue selection, trial, post-conviction proceedings, and other special or supplementary proceedings. The Rules also specify requirements as to warrants and ARRESTS. Standards for admission of evidence in criminal trials, however, are not contained in the Rules, as these standards are established pursuant to the FEDERAL RULES OF EVIDENCE. States promulgate their own criminal procedure rules, although they often adopt or closely mirror the Rules for proceedings in state courts.

Prior to adoption of the Rules, the FEDERAL COURT SYSTEM lacked uniform criminal procedure rules for much of its history. The Judiciary Act of 1789 instructed federal courts to apply the law of the state in which the court was located with respect to arrests, BAIL, and preliminary hearings. As to other proceedings, Congress enacted few procedural guidelines. Because the Supreme Court largely deferred to congressional authority to enact procedural rules pursuant to Article III of the U.S. CONSTITUTION, the legal guidelines for federal criminal proceedings remained disparate and incomplete.

The path toward more uniform and satisfactory procedural rules began in 1933, when Congress authorized the Supreme Court to promulgate criminal appellate procedures. Subsequently, Congress enacted the Sumners Courts Act in 1940, which authorized the federal judiciary to draft and promulgate all encompassing criminal procedures. Pursuant to this authority, the first Rules were submitted to Congress in 1944 and took effect in 1946. While the Sumners Courts Act initially granted the U.S. ATTORNEY GENERAL responsibility to transmit proposed amendments to Congress, a 1949 amendment transferred this responsibility to the CHIEF JUSTICE. In 1988, Congress incorporated under the Rules Enabling Act the current procedures for promulgating and amending the Rules.

As currently instituted, the Rules Enabling Act empowers the Advisory Committee of the Judicial Conference of the United States—comprising various JUDGES, lawyers, legal scholars, and DEPARTMENT OF JUSTICE representatives—to formulate drafts of any proposed amendments to the Rules. These drafts are then subjected to public comment and transmitted to the Standing Committee on Rules of Practice and Procedure, which may reject or modify the proposed amendments. If the Standing Committee's modifications implicate a substantial change, the proposed amendment may be returned to the Advisory Committee for further review. Following the Standing Committee stage, the Rules are transmitted to the Supreme Court for final recommendation of approval and, if approved, submitted to Congress no later than May 1 of the year in which they are to go into effect. Although the Congress retains the final power to reject or modify the proposed amendments, it regularly defers to the federal judiciary and rarely exercises its power to reject the amendments.

For more information

Levenson, Laurie L. *A Student's Guide to the Federal Rules of Criminal Procedure.* 2nd ed. St. Paul, Minn.: Thomson/West, 2003.

Wright, Charles Alan, et al. *Federal Practice and Procedure.* 4th ed. St. Paul, Minn.: West, 2009.

Phillip J. Wininger
University of Kentucky

Federal Rules of Evidence Federal Rules of Evidence are procedural trial rules by which a court determines what EVIDENCE is admissible at trial.

In the United States, the federal courts follow the Federal Rules of Evidence. State courts generally follow their own adopted rules of evidence, which are very closely modeled after the Federal Rules. There are 11 articles or sections under the Federal Rules of Evidence. Article I covers Rules 101 through 106. Rules 101–102 deal with general provisions such as the scope, purpose, and construction of the rules. Rule 103 states the effect of an erroneous ruling by a court as regards the admission of evidence, the rulings on evidence, and the manner in which a court may admit or consider evidence. Rule 104 addresses preliminary questions such as the qualification of a witness or existence of privilege. Limited admissibility is the subject of Rule 105. This rule recognizes that a court may admit evidence for a singular purpose, but that the same evidence may not be considered for other purposes.

Rule 106 is a rule of completeness and addresses misleading impressions that may be created by presenting only portions of statements or records or by taking matters out of context.

Article II contains one rule only, Rule 201, which deals with judicial notice of adjudicative facts. Adjudicative facts are the facts which are particular to a case such as who did what, when, how, and where. Normally, a JURY decides these types of matters. The court can take notice of adjudicative facts when the facts are such that there is no reasonable controversy (i.e., dogs are canines; men are humans; wounds sometimes bleed; 911 is an emergency call number).

Article III pertains to presumptions in civil trials. A presumption is an assumed fact. In order to invoke the presumption, the moving party must establish the basic facts giving rise to the presumption. The effect of invoking a presumption is that is causes the opposing party to bear the burden of proving nonexistence of the presumed fact. For example, a statute that makes railroads liable for any damages done, unless the railroad can show that reasonable care was exercised, creates a presumption against the railroad.

Article IV addresses relevancy. Rules 401 through 415 provide guidance as to the definition of legal relevance and discuss the test of whether relevance outweighs the prejudicial effect of the evidence on the jury. This section contains the rules pertaining to character and habit evidence, remedial measures, compromise, payment of expenses, admissibility of plea discussions, existence of liability insurance, and evidentiary limits regarding sexual assault cases.

Article V deals with the privilege of witnesses not to testify. The witness invokes the privilege when called upon to give testimony based on the witness's relationship with another person (i.e., lawyer-client, husband-wife, priest-confessor, trade secrets, psychotherapist-patient, identity of informant).

Article VI treats the matter of witnesses and is the most extensive section. Rules 601 through 706 address who is competent to testify, who may be a witness, administration of the oath, method and order of questioning, proper use of interpreters, matters of IMPEACHMENT, the effect of religious beliefs or opinions, how to treat witnesses who cannot recall the contents of a document, use of prior statements, when a court may call or exclude witnesses, opinion testimony, EXPERT TESTIMONY, and disclosure of facts underlying an expert's opinion.

Article VIII, Rules 801 through 806, addresses HEARSAY, non-hearsay, and the exceptions to hearsay. Hearsay is explained, in depth, within this publication.

Article IX contains Rules 901 through 903 and deals with authentication and identification as a condition precedent to admissibility. Authentication and identification mean sufficiently showing that the evidence is what the proponent says it is. For example, that the shoe is the shoe the defendant wore on the date in question; the voice is that of the victim; the document is not a FORGERY and was signed by the grantor.

Article X covers Rules 1001 through 1008 and provides guidance as to how evidentiary writings, recordings, and photographs should be treated. Also addressed are the admissibility of duplicates, public records, summaries of voluminous writings, recordings, or photos. Rule 1008 specifies the parameters of the court and jury.

Article XI contains the miscellaneous Rules 1101 through 1103. This section specifies when the rules apply and when they do not. The Federal Rules of Evidence do not apply at GRAND JURY proceedings, for preliminary questions of fact, EXTRADITION, criminal preliminary examinations, SENTENCINGS, BAIL hearings, or applications for warrants. The rules do apply to all U.S. district courts in criminal and civil proceedings.

For more information

Federal Rules of Evidence.

Imwinkelreid, Edward J., ed. *Evidentiary Foundations.* 4th ed. Charlottesville, Va.: Lexis Law, 1998.

Mauet, Thomas A., and Warren D. Wolfson, eds. *Trial Evidence.* New York: Aspen Law and Business, 1997.

Loretta M. Young
Family Court of State of Delaware

Federal Tort Claims Act The Federal Tort Claims Act is a federal statute enacted in 1946 that permits citizens to bring TORT claims (such as claims for personal injury and property damage) against the U.S. government.

Ordinarily, the United States and its agencies have IMMUNITY from suit for money damages, and thus, absent a federal statute waiving such sovereign immunity, citizens cannot bring suits for money damages against the federal government. The Federal Tort Claims Act waives the federal government's sovereign immunity with respect to tort claims, that is, claims such as those involving automobile accidents, products liability, medical malpractice, and negligence. Prior to the enactment of the Federal Tort Claims Act, Congress had to pass private bills awarding government compensation to particular citizens for injuries that resulted from the tortious conduct of the government or its employees.

The Federal Tort Claim Act makes the federal government liable for torts under the same standards that a private person would be liable for when committing a tort, with some exceptions. (The act does not waive the sovereign immunity possessed by states and is irrelevant to tort claims against state and local governmental entities.) Though the Federal Tort Claims Act does not establish a special substantive standard of liability for the government, it establishes special procedures for resolution of tort claims against the government. In particular, the act requires that potential claimants file their claims with the federal agency that harmed them before initiating litigation. The agency has six months to decide whether to offer the claimant compensation for his injuries. The act precludes citizens from suing federal employees personally, so long as the federal employee was acting within the scope of his employment at the time he injured the plaintiff. The act also limits that percentage of the plaintiff's award that the plaintiff's lawyer can take as compensation for his services (though this limitation is regularly disregarded). Perhaps most importantly, tort claims must by tried before a federal JUDGE sitting without a JURY, unlike tort cases against private defendants, which are generally tried before juries.

The Federal Tort Claims Act precludes citizens from recovering money damages against the government in several situations. The most important exemptions from the act's general waiver of sovereign immunity preclude recovery on claims arising out of military activities that occur during wartime; claims arising in a foreign country; claims involving ASSAULT, BATTERY, false imprisonment, false ARREST, or malicious prosecution (unless committed by a federal law enforcement officer); claims involving DEFAMATION and FRAUD; and claims involving allegedly tortious conduct that either was required by statute or qualifies as an exercise of DISCRETION.

Many suits are brought under the Federal Torts Claims Act. The suits are varied, involving a wide variety of claims against a wide variety of agencies. Some of the most common claims are for negligent operation of motor vehicles, failure to maintain safe premises, and medical malpractice.

For more information

Culp Davis, Kenneth, and Richard J. Pierce, Jr. *Administrative Law Treatise*. Vol. 3. 3rd ed. Boston: Little, Brown, 1994, pp. 229–252.

Dobbs, Dan B. *The Law of Torts*. St. Paul, Minn.: West, 2000, pp. 695–715.

Bernard W. Bell
Professor of Law
Rutgers Law School, Newark

federalism Federalism is one of the basic structural components of our system of government. Along with separation of powers, and checks and balances, federalism defines the relationship between various governmental actors.

Separation of powers and checks and balances describe and regulate the distribution of power within the national government or the state governments. Federalism regulates the relationships of power between the states and the national government. This division of power creates specific areas of government in which the states and the national government each have final decisional authority.

The authors of the CONSTITUTION realized, based on the failure of the ARTICLES OF CONFEDERATION, that there was a need to shift significant power to a new national government. At the same time, they feared creating a central government that was too strong and might tend toward tyranny. The balance that they struck was federalism, a system in which the new more powerful central government would be forced to share power with the states.

Federalism can be viewed as a flexible system that addresses the need for some level of national unity while simultaneously respecting and providing for divergent local needs and concerns. The powers that belong to the federal government are laid out in the Constitution—powers referred to as enumerated powers. Additionally the national government possesses implied powers that are based on the necessary and proper clause. The protection of the power of states can be found in the Tenth Amendment and the declaration of reserved powers.

While the system of federalism created by the framers has worked well, it has not been without its critics. From the beginning, the exact nature of the relationship between the two levels of government has been a source of considerable debate. Immediately after the ratification of the Constitution, Alexander Hamilton began to argue for national supremacy while Thomas Jefferson argued for the rights of states over the national government—rights which he believed included the power to nullify national laws.

The continuation of these debates led eventually to the Civil War. With the defeat of the Confederacy in the Civil War, states lost their power to nullify national laws as well as their power to secede from the Union. Expansion of federal power in the wake of the Civil War brought about changing ideas about the exact nature of federalism. The ongoing debate about federalism has caused the relationship between the two levels of government to evolve over time.

From the original intent of the framers, federalism has evolved through dual federalism, cooperative federalism, and creative federalism and toward the new federalism period of the latter half of the 20th century. Federalism is still an important feature of our government and still a matter of political debate. While the development of federalism in the history of our country has generally been toward increased national power at the expense of the states, recent efforts by conservative political forces have sought to reverse that trend.

Federalism as seen in the Constitution was an attempt to define the relationship of power between the national government and the states. Despite that document, the meaning of federalism and the nature of the relationship has remained politically defined and historically contingent.

Federalism and debates over states' rights continue to be debated into the 21st century. Some have argued that the passage of the Patient Protection and Affordable Care Act of 2010 by Congress, which extended health-care coverage to millions of Americans, exceeded the constitutional authority of the federal government and trampled on the rights of states. Similarly, disputes over gay marriage, such as the adoption of the DEFENSE OF MARRIAGE ACT by Congress, also raise federalism questions for some. Constitutionally, the battles often focus on the supremacy clause of the Constitution (art. 6), THE COMMERCE CLAUSE (art. 1, sec. 8), and the Fourteenth Amendment, which assert and support federal power versus the Tenth Amendment.

For more information

Bowman, Ann, and Richard Kearney. *State and Local Government*. New York: Houghton-Mifflin, 1999.

Nice, David, and Patricia Fredrickson. *The Politics of Intergovermental Relations*. Chicago: Nelson Hall, 1998.

David A. May
Eastern Washington University

felony Felonies are serious crimes that are punished with heavy fines, imprisonment, or death. Imprisonment is usually in a prison or a penitentiary for more than a year up to life imprisonment or death. Felony offenses include armed ROBBERY, ARSON, BURGLARY, drug trafficking, EMBEZZLEMENT, MANSLAUGHTER, MURDER, rape, and TREASON. A person (principal) convicted of a felony may be called a felon.

Felonies are usually contrasted with MISDEMEANORS, a wide range of minor offenses such as allowing a dog to run loose, jay walking, speeding, spitting in public, disturbing the peace, or any number of other offenses. Conviction of a misdemeanor can result in penalties that range from small fines to jail for less than a year and a day. The distinction is very historic and allows a great many minor offenses to be handled with lesser penalties.

The classification of a crime as a felony or a type of felony varies. Some states such as Massachusetts classify all crimes punishable by imprisonment as a felony. The federal government and many of the states distinguish between the severity of a crime by classifying offenses as A to E felonies or first- to fifth-degree felonies. The PUNISHMENT for conviction of a felony varies with its degree. Class A or first-degree felonies are the most severe, while Class E or fifth-degree felonies are punished with shorter prison terms or with much smaller fines. Felonies in the other classes or degrees range from more severe to less severe. Distinctions are important because what is a felony in one state may be a misdemeanor in another state.

Felonies are tried in federal district courts or in local state courts having general JURISDICTION. Most felony charges are handled in pretrial agreements. About 5 percent of all felony cases occur in FEDERAL COURT cases, and the remaining 95 percent in state cases. About half of those convicted are sent to prison. Only a few are put to death. The average prison term is about six years.

Principals are those who actually commit crimes. However, if a person AIDS OR ABETS a crime, then the person is a principal in the second degree rather than the first degree as are those who actually committed the crime(s). The punishment for conviction by a principal in the second degree is the same for first-degree principals. ACCESSORIES are persons who are never present at the commission of the crime. If an accessory incites, plans, counsels, or orders the commission of a felony, then the accessory is an accessory before the fact. If the accessory harbors or otherwise helps a principal felon, then this is an accessory after the fact. Both types of accessories are punishable as if they committed the crime. An exception is sometimes allowed for FAMILY members such as a wife or a child.

In some jurisdictions, repeated misdemeanor convictions for the same offense can be treated as a felony. In other jurisdictions, two or three felony convictions ("three strikes") can gain an automatic life imprisonment without PAROLE sentence. The Supreme Court has also ruled in *Sykes v. United States,* 564 U.S. __ (2011) that fleeing the police may constitute a felony.

Under the common law, felonies developed as crimes punishable by the total forfeiture of the felon's lands, goods, or both; however, the definition has changed to crimes punished by imprisonment, death, and/or heavy fines. Personal property or other property used during the commission of a felony may be seized. RICO forfeiture laws can be applied against those charged with racketeering offenses.

FELONY MURDER is a charge that arises when someone accidentally dies during the commission of a felony. For example, if a bank customer were to die of a heart attack due to fright during a bank robbery, then the robber(s) could be charged with felony murder. The prosecution would then only have to show that the death occurred; the defendant's state of mind would not matter as it would in a murder trial.

Convicted felons usually experience additional penalties, which vary widely between states. Conviction of a felony may be automatic grounds for DIVORCE, for denial of hunting and fishing licenses, voting rights, the right to own or possess firearms, the right to work certain professions, obtain a professional license, and many more penalties unless the felon's CIVIL RIGHTS are restored.

For more information

Livingston, Jay. *Crime and Criminology.* Upper Saddle River, N.J.: Prentice Hall, 1995.

Manza, Jeff, and Christopher Uggen. *Locked Out: Felon Disenfranchisement and American Democracy.* New York: Oxford University Press, 2006.

Zimring, Franklin E., Gordon Hawkins, and Sam Kamin. *Punishment and Democracy: Three Strikes and You're Out in California.* New York: Oxford University Press, 2001.

Andrew J. Waskey
Dalton State College

felony murder The felony murder rule refers to a common law practice codified in many states that makes it possible to convict individuals for first-degree MURDER while they are committing another FELONY, even if they did not intend to take the lives of any people.

In general, to convict individuals for first-degree murder, two elements must be proved. First, it must be shown that they performed a specific act (ACTUS REUS) or the taking of the life of another person and that they had the required state of mind (MENS REA) and intended to kill someone. Evolving out of British common law, the felony murder rule relaxes both of these requirements. What it states is that while in commission of another felony, such as armed ROBBERY, someone dies, the person committing the robbery can be charged with felony murder or first-degree murder, even if the person did not intend to kill someone. Normally, such an unintended death might be charged as negligent homicide or MANSLAUGHTER, but the commission of another felony elevates the death to felony or first-degree murder.

The rationale for treating this death as felony murder is the presumption that someone who commits a felony should have foreseen that the death of a third party could have occurred, or that the commission of a felony brings with it the possible intended consequence that someone might die. Supporters of the felony murder rule contend that the rule properly holds individuals responsible for deaths that occur as a result of certain crimes. Critics charge that the rule makes it too easy to convict individuals for crimes and that it bypasses the normal mens rea requirement.

Several states, including California, New York, and Texas have codified the felony murder rule. Generally, not all felonies qualify for the felony murder rule. It is generally limited to robbery, rape, ARSON, and felony prison escapes. If convicted of felony murder, individuals can be subject to the death penalty if they are a major participant to the crime.

For more information

Bonnie, Richard J. et al. *Criminal Law.* 2nd ed. New York: Foundation Press, 2004.

LaFave, Wayne, Jerold Israel, Nancy King, and Orin Kerr. *Criminal Procedure.* 5th ed. Eagan, Minn.: West, 2009.

David Schultz
Hamline University

feminist theories of crime Feminist theories of crime differ from traditional theories of crime in that they examine crime as an outgrowth of a culture's preference for, and promotion of, patterns of male dominance. In simple terms, feminist theories argue that all societies to some degree or another emphasize masculine traits such as power, subordination, and linear thinking over feminine traits such as community, equality, and symbiotic relationships (relationships that are linked together and mutually beneficial). Feminist theories of crime are usually classified as a set of theories that focus on critiquing and improving existing social structures. Like critical theory in general, feminist theories of crime fall into many different categories, including the liberal theory, Marxist theories, radical theories, and various forms of gender feminist theories. Each of these has different core assumptions about the degree to which society has been harmed by its emphasis on masculine virtues, but all of them claim that it is the imbalance in emphasis that has created the social harm feminists seek to redress.

ORIGINS OF FEMINIST THEORIES OF CRIME

The feminist movement has its origins very early in the American experience, although most scholars tend to divide its development into three distinct phases. The first phase, beginning at Seneca Falls, New York, in 1848, culminated in 1920 by gaining passage of the Nineteenth Amendment giving women the right to vote. However, the movement could not decide on a common direction after this victory and fell quiescent for many decades. The second phase of the women's movement, from 1960 to the late 1970s, is often called the women's liberation movement. This phase of feminism focused on equal pay, equal right to work, and social equality for women. During this phase, feminist social theories critical of American culture began to emerge. Feminist theories of crime emerged as part of the third wave of feminism in the late 1980s. During this period, feminist theory matured and developed theoretical depth. This phase of feminist theory focused analytical attention to the ways in which a patriarchical society used gender roles to subordinate women, children, and minority populations. Feminist theories of CRIMINOLOGY grew out of feminist social theories.

FEMINIST THEORIES OF CRIME

Feminist theorists approach crime from many different perspectives, but they all have three elements in common: They examine crime as a function of social dominance and subordination; They view crime as the result of patriarchy; they all claim that traditional criminal justice theories are essentially male crime studies generalized improperly to all groups. Feminist criminal justice seeks explanations for criminal behavior in an offender's broader cultural experience. Feminist criminal justice literature may be classified into three broad categories: explorations of the differences between male and female offenders, VICTIMIZATION theory, and social explanations for crime.

The earliest and most widely acknowledged strain of feminist research is the strain examining the difference between male and female offenders. This strain of research began with an analysis of the gender ratio problem in criminal justice studies. Studies of crime have always demonstrated that women were far less likely to commit crimes than were men; that women were even less likely to commit VIOLENT CRIMES; and when women committed crimes, they tended to do so less destructively. For example, female thieves tended to steal fewer items, and items of lesser value, than male offenders. Feminist theorists explained the relative lack of female criminals in terms of restrictive social roles. Women were wives, daughters, dating partners; all of these roles kept women in subordinate social roles and limited their opportunities to engage in criminal activities. Some feminist writers predicted that as the women's movement gained ground and women gained equality, society would see an increase in the number of female offenders. After the 1970s, there was indeed an increase in the number of females committing crimes, but scholars have attributed that increase not only to changing social roles but also to substantial changes in women's economic conditions.

A related line of feminist inquiry is the study of differing penalties male and female offenders receive. It has long been known that female offenders receive lighter sentences than their male counterparts, even for the same crime. Traditional criminal justice theory argues that this is due to a social belief that women should be protected, and consequently, male jurors are reluctant to sentence female defendants to harsh sentences. Feminist scholars accept this theory but also argue that in many cases women may receive harsher treatment once in prison because they are perceived to have violated the bounds of acceptable gender behavior.

Feminist scholars tend not to study WHITE-COLLAR CRIME, LARCENY or most INDEX CRIMES. Rather, they focus more narrowly on crimes against persons and on the root causes of such violence. Feminist scholars have broken new ground in explaining domestic and partner violence, rape, DATE RAPE, and spousal abuse and rape. Feminist scholars argue that rape and DOMESTIC ABUSE are so seldom reported or successfully prosecuted because women are still considered subordinate members of domestic relationships. Women remain easy victims of crime because society places them in unequal power relationships with men at all levels of society.

Feminist victimology argues that crimes against women are also evidence of unequal power relationships generally. Males are moved toward violent acts because they find themselves victims of superiors. This fosters a sense of powerlessness among males, which in turn feeds a fear of the future, which is in turn expressed as rage. Not all feminist scholars accept this model, however. Some feminist scholars argue that since this model portrays women as victims, it actually perpetuates female helplessness, rather than resolves it.

Feminist theorists argue that the best solution to crime does not solely involve PUNISHMENT for offenders. A comprehensive solution to crime requires scholars and criminal justice professionals to explore the culture of power and oppression that drives people to crime. Resolving these global issues should resolve the drive toward criminal conduct. These theories have led to many new experiments in criminal rehabilitation, and feminist theorists often find themselves working in conjunction with advocates of COMMUNITY POLICING and PROBLEM-ORIENTED POLICING.

For more information

Adler, Freda. *Sisters in Crime*. New York: McGraw-Hill, 1975.

Chamallas, Martha. *Introduction to Feminist Legal Theory*. 2nd ed. New York: Aspen Press, 2009.

Ford, Lynne E. *Women and Politics: The Pursuit of Equality*. 2nd ed. Boston: Houghton-Mifflin, 2006.

Millett, Kate. *Sexual Politics*. Bloomington: University of Indiana Press, 1970.

Michael P. Bobic
West Virginia Wesleyan College

fence (fencing of stolen goods) Fencing refers to the purchase and sale of stolen goods. Fencing is a crime, generally a FELONY.

The professional fence serves as a major criminal link to BURGLARY crimes. Burglars solicit the services of a professional fence because they purchase stolen property at approximately 10 to 20 percent of its value. Law enforcement officers understand that fencing operations feed the black market for stolen goods. Therefore, the logical follow-up to any burglary investigation includes determining the burglar's connection to pawnshops and the professional fence.

One sample scenario reveals a new professional fence in the neighborhood, and Jake "The Ace" is offering 30 percent of the stolen property's value. The word on the street is that he offers the best prices in the state. Burglars surface holding boxes of stolen electronic equipment, cameras, and other hot ticket items. A long line of professional thieves and drug addicts wait at the downstairs basement door. Satisfied customers smile when accepting ill-earned cash. There is only one problem: A strategically positioned police sting camera preserves the haughty criminals' images and words.

The criminal knowingly participated in the fencing operation, thereby, verbally admitting the original THEFT or burglary. The videotape is generally bursting with admissions that border on confessions. For example, a hijacking results in a truckload of electronics equipment. The offender looks at the bogus professional fence standing across the counter and unwittingly states, "How much cash will you give me for everything?"

The FBI and the Washington, D.C. Police Department conducted a similar operation: ROP-TIDE. Federal agents and local police teamed up and posed as sellers of stolen property. The success speaks for itself: 276 ARRESTS and the recovery of $8 million in stolen property. Similar fencing-sting operations have achieved success across the nation.

The investigative hand-to-hand transaction before a closed-circuit television camera is a very difficult case to beat in court. The real value of the investigation is an accurate reporting system and the return of stolen property. Undercover operations maximize the flow of criminal intelligence, expediting speedy removal of criminal offenders from the street.

A burglar without a professional fence does not have immediate access to illegal financial transactions. Any illegal property that accumulates at his or her residence is subject to police SEARCH AND SEIZURE. An abundance of suspicious property draws too much attention, a risk for arrest. The burglar may become desperate enough to engage in selling goods through classified ads and at garage sales and flea markets. Police officers may identify open sources of information and link intelligence that leads to the burglar's door.

The receivers of stolen property vary: professional, part-time, and amateur. Some individuals may not be aware that the property is unlawful. However, the three former receivers have knowledge about the property's illicit ownership and criminal consequences.

In conclusion, if the receiver has knowledge that the items were ill-gotten gain and illegal, the individual is culpable under the law in most states. It is difficult to prove knowledge; generally, proof comes from information collected from the circumstances. The receivers of stolen property are reluctant to talk, and they are difficult to prosecute in the CRIMINAL JUSTICE SYSTEM.

For more information

Swanson, Charles, R., Neil Chameleon, Leonard Territo, and Robert Taylor. *Criminal Investigation.* New York: McGraw-Hill, 2009.

Thomas E. Baker
University of Scranton

fingerprints Fingerprints refer to the unique patterns located on the fingers of all individuals. These patterns are used as EVIDENCE to identify individuals, oftentimes when they are accused of crimes.

Since the Sherlock Holmes novels of the last 19th century right up to the present day with the proliferation of CSI, the general public has been exposed to the concept of fingerprints within the CRIMINAL JUSTICE SYSTEM. In fact, this science is probably the best known of all the FORENSIC SCIENCES as a means of identifying a culprit (or excluding otherwise would be suspects).

According to Saferstein, one of the first detailed empirical studies of this science in an attempt to classify the anatomy of fingerprints was carried out by Francis Galton (1822–1911) in 1892; in addition, a Scottish physician, Henry Fauld (1843–1930), used skin-ridge patterns to examine a print left at the scene of a BURGLARY. When faced with the products of this new forensic science, the suspect confessed, no doubt to the relief of the man whom the police had in custody for the crime. Sadly, despite this success, when Fauld offered to set up a fingerprint bureau to continue this work (using his own funds), Scotland Yard declined his offer. However, in 1901, Scotland Yard did set up such a bureau, followed by New York City in 1903, and the state of Illinois in 1911 recorded the first conviction based on fingerprints in the United States.

Fingerprints are thought by many to be conclusive evidence of individual identification (i.e. did the subject create the print) with experts testifying in court with phrases such as "a perfect match" to the exclusion of all others. These sorts of statements by fingerprint examiners have recently come under scrutiny from many scholars who question the ability of these experts to definitively identify a CRIME SCENE print when compared to a fingerprint taken later under law enforcement observation, whether using an inked "ten-card" or a digital fingerprint scanner.

Fingerprints are created in three main ways. When an individual touches an object, he or she will leave grease or sweat on some surfaces (even human skin); if the fingerprint is covered in a substance such as dirt or blood, this may also leave a print; and finally, if a fingertip is placed on a plastic surface such as putty, a print can also be examined.

The identifying markers used, in general, by fingerprint examiners today are based on the typology set forth by Galton, who used various ridge characteristics to distinguish one print from another. These characteristics (or minutiae) include, ridge ending, ridge islands, ridge dots, bifurcations, and enclosures. Each print has and is widely considered unique to an individual to the exclusion of all others, as no two individuals have ever been discovered to possess identical fingerprints, even identical twins; however, it is important to note that there has been no scientific study that proves this assumption.

According to Stoney, there are four important factors that should be considered when assessing the veracity of a fingerprint match, including the extent of the print (area and number of minutiae), the clarity of the print, the presence or absence of dissimilarities, and the examiner's training, expertise, experience, and ethics.

The above potentially confounding factors has left the fingerprint community vulnerable to further examination by scientists who are unsure and concerned that there may be errors in the science not thought of previously, which may lead to the release of a guilty individual or the conviction of an innocent.

A recent high-profile case of fingerprint identification error was the case of Brandon Mayfield, a practicing attorney in Oregon who was ARRESTED and jailed for two weeks for the Madrid train bombing of 2004. The FBI declared a match with Mayfield from a print recovered at the scene; but the Spanish authorities on reviewing this finding stated they had concerns with the FBI's match. Upon further examination, the FBI declared that the so-called match was indeed erroneous and, after the filing of a civil lawsuit, the DEPARTMENT OF JUSTICE awarded Mayfield $2.5 million. This case should be a warning to all those (criminal justice professionals and laymen alike) before the science of fingerprinting is any longer accepted as infallible.

For more information

Fisher, B. *Techniques in Crime Scene Investigation.* New York: CRC Press, 2004.

Saferstein, R. *Criminalistics: An Introduction to Forensic Science.* Upper Saddle River, N.J.: Prentice Hall, 2008.

Available online. URL: http://science.howstuffworks.com/fingerprinting.htm

Available online. URL: http://www.fbi.gov/hq/cjisd/takingfps.html

Available online. URL: http://www.reachoutmichigan.org/funexperiments/agesubject/lessons/prints.html

Gavin Lee
University of California at Irvine

flag burning Flag burning is a constitutionally protected means of expressing opposition to policies and practices of the federal government that became the subject of a vigorous legal and political debate in the United States during the 1990s. The Supreme Court declared both a Texas law and a federal law that prohibited flag burning unconstitutional because they violated the FREEDOM OF SPEECH guaranteed by the First Amendment.

The First Amendment prohibits laws that restrict the freedom of speech. "Speech," as the Supreme Court has interpreted it, includes not only oral and written communication but "symbolic speech," such as wearing a black armband to protest the Vietnam War, or displaying an American flag upside down, with a peace symbol attached to it. Therefore, it is not surprising that the Court has held that burning the American flag in a statement of political protest is symbolic speech that the First Amendment protects. The Court has reached that conclusion twice, in *TEXAS V. JOHNSON*, 491 U.S. 397 (1989), which involved a Texas anti-flag-burning law, and in *United States v. Eichman,* 496 U.S. 310 (1990), which featured a federal law that prohibited flag burning.

Texas v. Johnson arose from a protest against the policies of the Reagan administration, which occurred in Dallas in 1984. Gregory Johnson, one of the protesters, unfurled an American flag, soaked it with kerosene, and set it on fire. Johnson was convicted of violating a Texas law that prohibited the desecration of "venerated objects," including the American flag. The law said that to "desecrate" was to "deface, damage, or otherwise physically mistreat in a way that the actor knows will seriously offend one or more persons likely to observe or discover his action." The Texas Court of Criminal Appeals reversed Johnson's conviction, and Texas APPEALED to the Supreme Court, where it argued that its interest in preserving the American flag as a symbol of national unity justified that conviction. The Supreme Court disagreed. Justice WILLIAM BRENNAN, writing for the majority, observed: "If there is a bedrock principle underlying the First Amendment, it is that the Government may not prohibit the expression of an idea simply because society finds the idea itself offensive or disagreeable." He added that government does not honor the flag by punishing those who burn it because to punish speech is to diminish the freedom that the flag represents.

Congress reacted to the Court's decision by passing the Flag Protection Act, which sought to survive First Amendment scrutiny by prohibiting flag burning merely to protect the physical integrity of the flag, not to punish the message associated with burning the flag. The act said: "Whoever knowingly mutilates, defaces, physically defiles, burns, maintains on the floor or ground, or tramples upon any flag of the United States shall be fined . . . or imprisoned for not more than one year, or both." The Supreme Court declared the Flag Protection Act unconstitutional in *United States v. Eichman.* The majority reasoned that although this law did not punish flag burning based on the message that flag burning conveyed, Congress's efforts to protect the physical integrity of the flag rested on a desire to preserve the flag against disrespectful treatment, which amounted to the suppression of symbolic speech, a violation of the First Amendment.

In the years since *Eichman,* Congress has tried several times to pass a constitutional amendment to prohibit flag burning, which would overturn the *Eichman* decision. Thus far, Congress has failed in that effort, and flag burning remains constitutionally protected speech.

For more information

Epstein, Lee, and Thomas G. Walker. *Constitutional Law for a Changing America: Rights, Liberties, and Justice.* 3rd ed. Washington, D.C.: CQ Press, 1998.

Fisher, Louis. *American Constitutional Law.* 3rd ed. Durham, N.C.: Carolina Academic Press, 1999.

Brian L. Porto
Vermont Law School

Fletcher v. Peck 10 U.S. (6 Cranch) 87 (1810) *Fletcher v. Peck* was an important and famous case to determine the scope of the CONTRACT clause in the U.S. CONSTITUTION. Decided in 1810, it involved judicial determination of the ownership of land fraudulently sold by the 1795 Georgia legislature. The major constitutional question pitted state claims of sovereignty over public land as opposed to constitutional contract clause provisions (Article 1, section 10). A main constitutional question was whether state impairment of obligation of contract applied to public as well as private contracts.

This case involved issues of wholesale bribery and FRAUD. In 1795 Georgia legislators passed a law under substantial bribery to sell about 35 million acres to four land companies, approximately the states of Mississippi and Alabama, for nearly $500,000. The 1796 Georgia legislature revoked the land grant. In the interim land companies sold some lands to land speculators and prospective settlers. Fletcher, as a good-faith purchaser, sued Peck to recover funds because the land title had been rescinded. The Supreme Court invalidated this portion of the land recision and said that Peck had a valid land title. Further, CHIEF JUSTICE Marshall ruled for a unanimous court that the vast majority of the land grant was rescinded because this grant, as a state contract, had been obtained through bribery and fraud, which invalidated the legislative act.

Marshall's broad reading of the contract clause argued that the 1795 legislative actions were unconstitutional because state actions violated the contract clause of the U.S. Constitution. The Georgia impairment of contracts meant that public contracts were within the scope of the contract clause. Previously, that clause had been assumed to apply only to private contracts between individuals. The national government could sanction state governments if they reneged upon their public contracts. This decision indicated constitutional and national protection for property rights against actual and potential state interference. In addition, this decision showed that FEDERALISM principles could restrict state regulatory powers. These two ideas were an important part of early U.S. constitutional doctrine concerning the scope of states' rights and individuals' legal protections.

For more information

Cardozo, Benjamin. *The Nature of the Judicial Process.* New Haven, Conn.: Yale University Press, 1931.

Fletcher v. Peck, 10 U.S. (6 Cranch) 87 (1810).

Magrath, C. Peter. *Yazoo: Law and Politics in the New Republic.* Providence, R.I.: Brown University Press, 1966.

White, G. Edward. *The Marshall Court and Cultural Change, 1815–1835.* New York: Macmillan, 1988.

Steven Puro
Saint Louis University

Food and Drug Administration The Food and Drug Administration or the FDA is an agency of the U.S. government located in the Department of Health and Human Services. With about 9,000 full-time employees and an annual budget of about $1 billion, it is the organization that has the major responsibility for insuring that the foods, cosmetics, drugs, medical devices, and color and food additives purchased by the American public are safe and not mislabeled.

The first major federal law regulating foods and drugs was passed in 1906. It was initially enforced by the Department of Agriculture's Bureau of Chemistry under the direction of Dr. Harvey Wiley, an outstanding civil servant whose crusading had led to its enactment. In 1927 the Food, Drug and Insecticide Administration was created to administer it. In 1930 the organization's name was changed to "Food and Drug Administration"; and in 1940 it was transferred to the predecessor of the Department of Health and Human Services.

The 1906 law prohibited the misbranding and adulteration of foods and drugs only. It was replaced in 1938 by the Food, Drug and Cosmetic Act (FDCA), which extended the FDA's JURISDICTION to cosmetics and increased its powers over the marketing of drugs. The agency still has no right to require that a food or cosmetic be proven safe before it can be sold. However, it inspects food and cosmetic manufacturing facilities for cleanliness. Moreover, if it finds that a food or cosmetic on the market is adulterated, is misbranded, or is making people ill, it will ask the manufacturer to recall it; and it will get a court order allowing its seizure if the manufacturer ignores its request. (The Food Safety and Inspection Service of the Department of Agriculture has jurisdiction over contaminated meat and poultry, while it is up to the Federal Trade Commission to take action against misleading advertisements of foods, drugs, cosmetics, and medical devices.)

Under the FDCA as amended, the FDA requires the makers of color and food additives to show that they are safe before they can be used in other products. Also, the agency will not allow certain medical devices and what the FDCA calls "new drugs" (which may be over-the-counter as well as prescription) to reach the market unless the manufacturer can demonstrate that they are both safe AND effective. The FDA insists that the manufacturer of a "new" drug conduct clinical tests that can take up to seven years. Once these are completed, the firm must apply for FDA review, accompanied by data from the tests. Once the application is filed, the agency is supposed within six months to okay or disallow the drug's sale, though in practice a decision takes on average about 15 months. (In a few cases, expedited development and review are possible.) Though most of the FDA's funding comes from Congress, since 1992 it has collected a user fee from drug companies applying for permission to market their products. These fees add $100 million annually to its coffers and enable it to hire more employees and thus to speed up its scrutiny of these applications. If a drug or medical device proves unsafe after it reaches the consumer, the FDA will recall it. Thus in March 2000 it ordered the diabetes drug Rezulin withdrawn from pharmacists' shelves because it had caused liver failure in 90 cases since 1997.

Under the FDCA's Delaney clause, any color or food additive that causes cancer in animals or humans, even a tiny number, must be banned. Ergo the FDA outlawed a color additive known as "Red #2" because its scientists had found that giving it to female rats at a high dosage caused a statistically significant increase in malignant tumors in these rodents.

Since FDA decisions can cost businesses a lot of money or expose consumers to serious health risks, it is not surprising that it receives a great deal of criticism. Tobacco companies were unhappy when it sought to regulate tobacco as a drug and ban its sale to people under 18. (The U.S. Supreme Court held in *FDA v. Brown and Williamson Tobacco Corp.*, 98–1152, March 2000, that the agency lacked authority to take this step.) It has been accused of delaying the approval of drugs for so long that patients suffering from certain diseases cannot get medication they desperately need. Some have charged it with approving dangerous food additives or not carrying out enough inspections of food-processing plants. Despite these attacks, the FDA or a bureau similar to it is likely to be around for many years, since the American public demands protection from dangerous foods, drugs, and cosmetics.

In 2009, Congress gave the FDA enhanced authority to regulate tobacco products, which included their advertising, marketing, and manufacturing. Similarly, in 2010, after a significant salmonella outbreak that led to the destruction of hundreds of millions of chicken eggs, Congress gave the FDA enhanced food safety authority to prevent future problems like this one.

For more information

"FDA Reform: Food and Drug Safety and Availability," *Congressional Digest*, February 1997, pp. 34–64.

Daniel C. Kramer
College of Staten Island, CUNY

Foreign Intelligence Surveillance Act (FISA)

The Foreign Intelligence Surveillance Act (FISA) is a law passed by Congress and signed by President Jimmy Carter in 1978. It established a legal framework for the executive branch to collect "foreign intelligence information" inside the United States through covert electronic surveillance, commonly referred to as WIRETAPPING (and later physical surveillance).

FISA does not apply to criminal investigations, although later amendments allowed for information collected through FISA-approved monitoring to be provided to criminal PROSECUTORS. Engaging in domestic electronic surveillance outside the provisions of FISA can bring civil and criminal penalties, including a fine of up to $10,000 and jail time up to five years. The target of the surveillance must be either a foreign power or agent of a foreign power as defined by the act. In most cases, FISA requires that the executive branch acquire a court order (called a FISA warrant) from a special judiciary body, the Foreign Intelligence Surveillance Court (FISC), prior to beginning domestic surveillance. Congress later amended FISA with the USA PATRIOT ACT of 2001, the Protect America Act of 2007, and the FISA Amendments Act of 2008. After the terrorist attacks against the United States on September 11, 2001, the law became a center of a controversy regarding domestic electronic spying by the National Security Agency (NSA) under the George W. Bush administration.

The motivation for enacting FISA grew out of revelations by the Senate's Church Committee of covert, warrantless wiretapping against U.S. citizens by the Nixon administration. President Nixon defended the actions by arguing that they were within his constitutional authority to assure the nation's security. Those revelations led many in Congress to see a clear need to balance legitimate, constitutional, foreign intelligence gathering by the president with the right of U.S. citizens and foreign residents to be free from unreasonable government searches banned by the FOURTH AMENDMENT. As previous court rulings had not clearly specified the limits of the president's authority to engage in domestic spying for national security purposes, FISA aimed to establish legal boundaries for the executive branch's foreign intelligence gathering by creating strict judicial and congressional oversight.

The chief administrator of FISA is the Foreign Intelligence Surveillance Court (FISC). It consists of 11 district court JUDGES chosen by the CHIEF JUSTICE of the Supreme Court and convenes in order to review FISA warrant requests from the ATTORNEY GENERAL. Issuance by the FISC of a warrant grants the government permission to engage in covert surveillance of specific persons or groups within the United States to collect foreign intelligence. To receive a warrant, the government must establish PROBABLE CAUSE that the target is likely a foreign power or agent of a foreign power and will likely be using the facilities to be surveilled. All court proceedings are conducted in secret, are not adversarial, and only involve the FISC and the JUSTICE DEPARTMENT. If the FISC denies a warrant, the government can APPEAL the decision to the Foreign Intelligence Surveillance Court of Review (FISCR). If this three-judge panel upholds the denial, the government can then appeal directly to the U.S. Supreme Court. Appeals have been infrequent because the FISC has rarely denied warrant requests.

In emergency circumstances, FISA also allows the executive branch to engage in domestic surveillance for up to a year without a FISA warrant. The attorney general must provide certification to the FISC that the operation targets strictly foreign powers or their agents and that there is little likelihood that a U.S. citizen's communications will be monitored.

In the years following the terrorist attacks on the United States in September, 2001, Congress passed several revisions to FISA. The USA Patriot Act of 2001 revised the statute to include the surveillance of international terrorists who cannot be linked to foreign powers. In 2004, a "lone wolf" amendment allowed for FISA-approved monitoring of individual non-U.S. citizens suspected of either plotting or having engaged in terrorist acts but with no demonstrable connection to either a foreign power or international terrorism.

At the request of the George W. Bush administration, Congress further revised FISA with the Protect America Act of 2006 and the FISA Amendments Act of 2008. These measures sanctioned a practice the Bush administration had been secretly pursuing since 2001: the warrantless monitoring by the National Security Agency (NSA) of telecommunications and e-mail transmissions within the United States so long as the communication originated or ended in a foreign country. The latter statute also provided IMMUNITY from privacy lawsuits to private telecommunications companies that had cooperated with the government in that warrantless surveillance program. Bush ended the practice in 2007.

In its campaign to monitor international terrorist activities, the Bush administration also employed the state secrets privilege, a judicial rule through which the government can petition to have lawsuits dismissed if the litigation would necessitate revealing EVIDENCE in court that could harm national security. This practice often precluded legal action by the targets of warrantless wiretapping. The incoming Barack Obama administration continued many Bush policies regarding foreign surveillance, including the application of the state secrets privilege to stop lawsuits against the government. In March 2010, however, the Northern District Court of California in *Al-Haramain Foundation v. Barack Obama* rejected a Justice Department request, based on the state secrets privilege, to dismiss a suit by an Islamic-based charity organization claiming two of its lawyers had been illegally wiretapped. The decision implied that the court was insisting that FISA warrant requirements preempt the government's right to invoke the state secrets privilege.

For more information

Engdahl, Sylvia, ed. *Domestic Wiretapping*. Farmington Hills, Mich.: Greenhaven Press, 2008.

Miller, Russell A. *US National Security, Intelligence and Democracy: Congressional Oversight and the War on Terror (Studies in Intelligence series)*. New York: Routledge, 2008.

John Kelly Damico
Georgia Perimeter College

forensic science Forensic science is an interdisciplinary enterprise that uses a wide range of tools and technologies in the criminal investigatory process.

Forensic science consists of analytical practices from many basic sciences such as anthropology, biology, chemistry, geology, genetics, medicine, meteorology, odontology, and physics. Forensic scientists are experts who serve and advise law enforcement and court professionals at several stages of the criminal justice process—from investigation to ARREST, prosecution, conviction, and even the exoneration of people wrongly convicted of crimes. The principles, protocols, and procedures of forensic science guide the collection and analyses of the physical or real EVIDENCE gathered at a CRIME SCENE.

Responding to the crime scene is the critical first step in the scientific investigation of a case. Unless the crime scene is handled with great care and precision, a criminal investigation can be severely compromised. As the key participants in forensic cases, crime scene investigators and specialists are responsible for identifying, securing, collecting, and preserving the crime scene evidence that is submitted to the crime laboratory for analysis. Physical evidence can provide the basic framework that helps crime scene investigators re-create the crime scene and establish the sequence of events and time line that occurred during the commission of a crime. Physical evidence also can corroborate statements from police officers, crime victims, witnesses, or suspects. If analyzed and interpreted properly, physical evidence is more reliable than TESTIMONIAL EVIDENCE, which is often fraught with ambiguities, inconsistencies, lapses, false reconstructions, and spotty recollections. In short, because the perception and memory of events are frequently incomplete or inaccurate, physical evidence, when documented, collected, and preserved properly, can supply the only definitive and reliable link between a suspect and a crime scene.

A forensic scientist's knowledge of the tools and techniques of crime scene investigation as well as the variety of methods used for the collection and processing of all types of real evidence is crucial. In addition, forensic scientists and crime scene investigators must often decide whether to obtain written consent or a search warrant in order to guarantee that the evidence collected will be admissible in court and not vulnerable to a motion to suppress. Real evidence refers to materials such as hairs, fibers, and latent FINGERPRINTS, and biological matter such as soil and vegetation. This evidence varies greatly in its composition and includes human secretions such as saliva, blood, and semen, and physical features, including hair, fingernails, and skin. Other real evidence with potential probative value includes paint chips, glass, footprints, fingerprints, tire tracks, tool marks, gunshot residue, bullets, shell casings, and blood splatter. Further, the body of a homicide victim can furnish a wealth of evidence for forensic scientists—through the autopsy process—that can be used to determine the cause (the physical process that led to death) and the manner (natural, accidental, homicidal) of death.

Forensic science specifies the strategies for collecting physical evidence in order to preserve its properties. Evidence that is compromised or contaminated cannot be used to help identify suspects and solve crimes. The preservation of the crime scene by cordoning it off and allowing only forensic experts (criminalists) to enter with protective gloves and shoe coverings is a mechanism for safeguarding the integrity of evidence for subsequent forensic analyses. Locard's Exchange Principle states that each time people enter an environment, they add or remove physical material from it. The notion that "every contact leaves a trace," applies to contact between individuals as well as between individuals and a physical environment. Crime scene investigators assume that physical evidence is always left behind; the nature, extent, and condition of the evidence gathered in the aftermath of a crime depend largely on the circumstances and location of the offense, as well as the training and experience of those who collect the evidence.

Forensic science has many highly specialized subfields. Experts can concentrate their knowledge and efforts in the examination of particular kinds of physical evidence. For example, forensic scientists are specialists in the analysis of hair and fiber, shoe prints, gunshot residue, blood, DNA, bones and bone fragments, and autopsy findings. The best-known case, which educated the public about the tremendous power, complexity, and limitations of forensic science, was the murder of Nicole Brown Simpson and Ronald Goldman. In that case, PROSECUTORS presented a wealth of evidence (hair, blood, fibers, DNA, footprints), all of which pointed overwhelmingly to the guilt of Nicole Brown Simpson's estranged husband, O.J. SIMPSON.

The defense in the O.J. Simpson case belabored the fact that the crime scene was contaminated (improperly preserved), and, therefore, the evidence it produced was tainted and could provide no real value in the search for the identity of the perpetrator of the double murder. The defense team also argued that the evidence was deliberately altered to inculpate O.J. Simpson as the murderer, and that the improper transfer of the evidence from the crime scene to the laboratory (chain-of-custody) rendered it useless to the JURY in its deliberations to decide the defendant's guilt.

As the preceding description suggests, the work of forensic scientists begins at the crime scene, continues with the preservation of the physical surroundings and the meticulous gathering and storage of the evidence, and proceeds to the laboratory, where highly expensive and technical equipment is used to analyze the physical evidence. The work of forensic scientists culminates in the courtroom, where they must without bias interpret, present, and explain complicated scientific results for consumption by the judge and jury. As an expert witness for the prosecution or defense, the forensic scientist represents the vehicle that translates for the court the meaningfulness and value of the real evidence in the context of the trial and in light of the defendant's alleged involvement in the case. In doing so, the forensic scientist must rely on the latest advances in the field, which are widely accepted and used by other experts. The forensic scientist must illuminate extremely arcane concepts, clarify the workings of scientific instrumentation, and describe complex mathematical formulations in a manner that can be understood by a general audience and applied to answer the question of guilt.

For more information

Gardner, Ross M. *Practical Crime Scene Processing and Investigation: Series in Practical Aspects of Criminal and Forensic Investigations.* New York: CRC Press, 2005.

Inman, Keith, and Norah Rudin. *Principles and Practices of Criminalistics.* New York: CRC Press, 2001.

Saferstein, Richard. *Criminalistics: An Introduction to Forensic Science.* Upper Saddle River, N.J.: Prentice Hall, 2008.

Arthur J. Lurigio
Loyola University Chicago

forgery Forgery is the making, altering, or completing of a false written instrument. In most states, one may also commit forgery by possessing or offering an instrument knowing it to be false. Generally, however, there is a requirement of the INTENT to injure or defraud that must accompany the forgery in order for the act to have criminal implications. While forgery statutes were initially adopted to address art recreations, these statutes were later expanded to protect the integrity of the financial system and individual wealth.

Initially adopted in the 16th century as a reaction to re-created paintings, forgery codes were adopted to ensure reliability and value of art. These codes remained relatively unchanged until the transition to paper currency and advancements in printing processes, which allowed the relatively easy reproduction of bank notes (currency). The ability to reproduce the commonly accepted, government-guaranteed notes required not only advancements in the manufacture of currency but also laws to combat the practice. Of additional concern was the ability to falsely reproduce other written instruments such as stock certificates and property deeds. However, it was not until the evolution of the personal check, and the forgery that followed, that the financial industry implemented widespread reform and legislative pressure to expand forgery statutes.

With the ease of reproduction, inability to quickly and accurately verify signatures, drafts, and amounts, as well as the common acceptance of the personal check, expanded legislation was enacted to prevent forgery. Statutes were broadened to authorize criminal sanctions for those who not only manufacture the instruments but also for those who alter the original documents. Statutes and law enforcement and prosecution response focused more closely on the individual forgery act rather than the printing reproduction. However, it was the financial industry's reaction that provided the greatest protection. Moving away from personal checks, financial institutions and merchants recommended credit and debit cards. However, the forger has adapted.

As a result of financial advancements in check production, which include watermarks, security strips, and electronic readers to verify signatures, forgers have adapted and now seek financial source data such as credit card and Social Security numbers. As a result, legislatures have further expanded forgery statutes to adapt.

For more information

Kersten, Jason. *The Art of Making Money: The Story of a Master Counterfeiter.* New York: Gotham Press, 2009.

Nickell, Joe. *Detecting Forgery: Forensic Investigation of Documents.* Lexington: University Press of Kentucky, 2005.

Mark McClain
Central Washington University

Fourth Amendment The Fourth Amendment to the UNITED STATES CONSTITUTION stipulates a general requirement that warrants are required when searches of persons and places are performed by the government. The Fourth Amendment was ratified as part of the BILL OF

Rights in 1791, just two years after the Constitution itself had come into effect. It states:

> The right of the people to be secure in their persons, houses, papers, and effects, against unreasonable searches and seizures, shall not be violated, and no Warrants shall issue, but upon probable cause, supported by Oath or affirmation, and particularly describing the place to be searched, and the persons or things to be seized.

As with many of the amendments in the Bill of Rights, the Fourth Amendment limits the power of the government. It forms, together with the Fifth, Sixth, and Eighth Amendments, the core of the procedural due process protections required of law enforcement, prosecutors, and the courts.

The Fourth Amendment was drafted following the model of Article XIV of the 1780 Massachusetts Constitution. The Fourth Amendment was included in the Bill of Rights in large part due to the experiences of the colonists with general warrants known as "writs of assistance." These writs allowed British customs officials to search any home or business for goods that had been smuggled to the colonies without required tax payments to the British Crown. The writs were frequently abused as they were permanent and nonspecific; British officials did not need to seek a new warrant each time they wanted to conduct a new search, nor did they have to identify the people or places to be searched. The use of these writs in the Massachusetts Colony in particular was a motivation for the Revolution, and later, the inclusion of the Fourth Amendment in the Bill of Rights.

Partly due to the founders' experiences with writs of assistance, all warrants were generally viewed with suspicion at the time of the drafting of the Bill of Rights (Amar, 1998). Notice is not given to the subject of the warrant, and he therefore cannot argue before a judge against the findings of the government. The proceedings are in secret, and no members of the community (such as jury members or spectators) are there to keep the proceedings honest. Thus, the founders did not want warrants issued unless they were supported by more than just a hunch—warrants must be supported by probable cause.

The Fourth Amendment prohibits the government from conducting unreasonable searches and seizures; searches conducted with warrants are presumed to be reasonable. A warrant is a judicial authorization for an arrest or search. In order to secure a warrant, a government official (usually a police officer or detective) must present an affidavit—a sworn statement—to a judge or magistrate, giving the facts known to the officer which suggest that a crime has been committed. If the officer seeks an arrest warrant, the affidavit must specifically name the person to be arrested, or else give a detailed description of the person to be arrested and where the person is to be found. If the officer seeks a search warrant, the affidavit must specifically list the items sought and the places to search. If the facts given in the affidavit amount to probable cause, the magistrate will sign the warrant, which authorizes the officer to effect the arrest or conduct the search. Because the police officer submits the affidavit under oath, he or she can be held liable for perjury if it is found that he or she intentionally misled the magistrate.

While any search conducted with a valid warrant is per se reasonable, the inverse is not necessarily true. In fact, there are a number of types of searches that are often considered reasonable despite being warrantless. The Supreme Court has declined to make blanket exceptions to the warrant requirement, but rather has held that warrantless searches are reasonable when the need to search outweighs the invasion of liberty and privacy rights of an individual, and there is some objective basis for the search, usually articulated as probable cause or reasonable suspicion.

Thus, police can stop (or "seize") a person on the street without a warrant if they have reasonable suspicion that the subject is involved in criminal activity, and they may further pat down the outer clothing of the subject for weapons if they have reasonable suspicion that the subject is armed. *Terry v. Ohio,* 392 U.S. 1 (1968). Police can arrest a person in public without a warrant when a MISDEMEANOR is being committed in their presence or if they have probable cause to believe that a FELONY is being or has been committed. *United States v. Watson,* 423 U.S. 411 (1976). To arrest a person in his or her home, however, the police must have a warrant. *Payton v. New York,* 445 U.S. 573 (1980).

There are numerous other exceptions to the warrant requirement. Searches conducted under exigent circumstances, or "hot pursuit," may not require a warrant. *Warden v. Hayden,* 387 U.S. 294 (1967). Limited searches incident to a lawful arrest do not require a warrant but cannot go beyond the area of immediate control of the suspect. *Chimel v. California,* 395 U.S. 752 (1969). In general, warrants are not required to search vehicles because of a reduced expectation of privacy in a vehicle and the mobility of vehicles; only probable cause is necessary to search a car, its contents, or the contents of containers therein. *Carroll v. United States,* 267 U.S. 132 (1925); *Wyoming v. Houghton,* 526 U.S. 295 (1999). If a suspect is arrested in a car, the car may only be SEARCHED INCIDENT TO ARREST if the suspect is within reaching distance of the passenger compartment of the car or the police have reason to believe that there is evidence of the offense of arrest in the car. *Arizona v. Gant,* 556 U.S. 332 (2009).

Some of the exceptions to the warrant requirement are not excepted because they are reasonable; rather, they are excepted because the Supreme Court does not view them as searches at all. In order to be considered a search under the Fourth Amendment, an individual must have (1) an actual or subjective expectation of privacy in the item or place to be searched, and (2) society is prepared to recognize that this expectation is reasonable. See *Katz v. United States,* 389 U.S. 347 (1967); *Smith v. Maryland,* 442 U.S. 735 (1979). "What a person knowingly exposes to the public, even in his own home or office, is not a subject of Fourth Amendment protection." *Katz v. U.S.,* 389 U.S. at 351. These nonsearches include PLAIN VIEW, open fields, and abandoned property.

What happens when the government conducts an unreasonable search in violation of the Fourth Amendment? The Supreme Court has held that any evidence that is collected in an unreasonable (and therefore illegal) search is excluded from evidence at trial. *Weeks v. United States,* 232 U.S. 383 (1914). Without such a rule, the Fourth Amendment would be nearly impossible to enforce against the government. Furthermore, the Supreme Court has held that when police use illegal evidence as the basis for discovering additional evidence, the new evidence must be excluded as the "fruit of the poisonous tree." *Silverthorne Lumber Co. v. United States,* 251 U.S. 385 (1920). If, however, police can find an independent source for the new evidence, they may do so without violating the Fourth Amendment.

The Fourth Amendment's provisions originally applied only to the actions of the federal government. It was not until 1961 that the Supreme Court INCORPORATED the Fourth Amendment against the states through the DUE PROCESS clause of the Fourteenth Amendment. In *Mapp v. Ohio,* 367 U.S. 643 (1961), the Court held not only that the requirements of the Fourth Amendment apply to the states but also that the prescribed remedy for violations of the Fourth Amendment—exclusion of evidence—applies as well. All states have constitutional provisions prohibiting unreasonable search and seizure, but the Fourth Amendment (as interpreted by the U.S. Supreme Court) sets the minimum standards for search and seizure law.

For more information

Amar, Akhil Reed. The Bill of Rights: Creation and Reconstruction. New Haven, Conn.: Yale University Press, 1998.

Clancy, Thomas. *The Fourth Amendment: Its History and Interpretation.* Durham, N. C.: Carolina Academic Press, 2008.

LaFave, Wayne, Jerold Isreal, Nancy King, and Orin Kerr. *Criminal Procedure.* 5th ed. Eagan, Minn.: West, 2009.

David I. Hull
St. Anselm College

Frankfurter, Felix (1882–1965) Supreme Court justice Felix Frankfurter was a justice of the United States Supreme Court from 1939 to 1962. He was appointed by President FRANKLIN DELANO ROOSEVELT.

He was born in Vienna, Austria, and emigrated to America with his family at the age of 12. He grew up in the Lower East Side ghetto in New York City, was educated at City College, and attended Harvard Law School. His top grades propelled him to the editorship of the *Harvard Law Review.* Upon graduating in 1906 he entered public service as an assistant U.S. attorney in New York under Henry L. Stimson, a leading Progressive. In 1911 Stimson became secretary of war and Frankfurter went to Washington as his assistant. In 1914 he was appointed to the Harvard Law School faculty, a position he retained until his appointment to the Court.

Not a secluded scholar, Frankfurter's public activities made him a nationally prominent liberal. During World War I, he served on President Wilson's labor mediation commission, where his report on the unfair trial of a labor radical caused a national stir. He attended the Paris Peace Conference after that war, representing Zionist interests. He was a founder of the AMERICAN CIVIL LIBERTIES UNION. He influenced liberal opinion as a frequent contributor to *The New Republic,* and his coauthored book, *The Labor Injunction,* attacked the FEDERAL COURTS for stifling the labor movement. He spoke out against the DUE PROCESS violations in the trials of convicted anarchists SACCO AND VANZETTI and did free legal work for the National Consumers' League. He appeared frequently before the Supreme Court on behalf of unions and other progressive causes.

At Harvard he developed a following among his students that combined a passion for academic excellence and a zeal for public service. He selected LAW CLERKS from his former students for Justices Holmes and Brandeis, with whom he had close rapport. During the New Deal, he became an important adviser to President Roosevelt and placed many of his former students in important administrative and policy-shaping positions, thus enhancing his influence.

Given his impeccable liberal credentials, it is a great irony that Frankfurter became a leading judicial conservative. This resulted from his judicial philosophy of *judicial restraint*—the belief that the courts should be passive on great public issues, leaving it to the legislature and administrative agencies to supply the popular will and expertise needed to run a complex modern state and resolve political conflicts. This philosophy was in tune with the beliefs of his fellow New Deal justices regarding economic issues, but as the Court, led by Justices HUGO BLACK and WILLIAM O. DOUGLAS, began to impose the CONSTITUTION on the states in CIVIL LIBERTIES cases, Frankfurter remained true to his original philosophy.

The first great rift occurred in public school flag salute cases during World War II. A majority of the Court eventually held that a law requiring a religious dissenter to salute the flag against his conscience violated the First Amendment. Frankfurter dissented on the basis of the need for national solidarity in time of war. This decision displayed his theory that legal rules are not based on constitutional absolutes but on the balanced reasoning that takes into account many factors.

Other major areas where Frankfurter led a conservative majority included several cases where the BILL OF RIGHTS was not applied to state and local criminal justice. In cases in the 1940s the Court denied that indigent state defendants were guaranteed the SIXTH AMENDMENT RIGHT TO COUNSEL, the Fifth Amendment rule against SELF-INCRIMINATION, or the FOURTH AMENDMENT

Justice Felix Frankfurter (Pach Brothers Studio, Collection of the Supreme Court of the United States)

(SEARCH AND SEIZURE) exclusionary rule. Frankfurter also led a split Court to rule that it had no JURISDICTION to hear an APPEAL challenging unequal legislative districts under the EQUAL PROTECTION clause of the Fourteenth Amendment because it was a *political question*. In these cases Frankfurter was powerfully opposed by Hugo Black, his main antagonist on the Court.

Black and Frankfurter had opposing judicial philosophies. Black tended to follow the Constitution and the Bill of Rights as literally as possible, while Frankfurter was comfortable in making rulings under the more elastic due process clause of the Fourteenth Amendment. Black, therefore, was guided by an absolutist belief that the text of the Constitution required the Court to extend the Bill of Rights in favor of the individual and against the interests of the state and to hold that disproportionate voting districts violated the equal protection of the laws.

Frankfurter's inherent liberalism would emerge where he felt unconstrained by judicial restraint and believed that Fourteenth Amendment due process could be interpreted to protect the rights of persons. Thus, in cases concerning confessions taken by local officers against the will of suspects, or in cases where local police officers engaged in particularly heavy-handed searches, he was willing to apply a somewhat subjective standard—whether the confession was voluntary or whether the search SHOCKED THE CONSCIENCE—to uphold the rights of the individual.

Frankfurter, the brilliant and irrepressible professor, tried to sway his colleagues on the Court with a steady stream of advice and blandishments. This often backfired, and some of the greatest justices of the era, including Black, Douglas, CHIEF JUSTICE Warren, and WILLIAM BRENNAN, turned against his often patronizing tutelage.

One of the high points of Frankfurter's judicial strategy and approach and cooperation with other justices came in the work surrounding *BROWN V. BOARD OF EDUCATION* (1954), the most important and the most sensitive case of the 20th century. Frankfurter understood that a case that would reverse school SEGREGATION would likely cause a social revolution and a massive negative reaction in the South. Because of this he worked to delay a decision at a time when it appeared that the Court might produce a split decision in the one case where unanimity was essential. When EARL WARREN became chief justice in 1953 Frankfurter was able to provide meaningful support, although the major credit to achieving unanimity goes to Warren for his personal leadership and his ability to draw Justices Robert Jackson and Stanley Reed into the majority.

When appointed, Frankfurter was seen potentially as being rated a great justice. In retrospect, most of his conservative decisions in the 1940s and 1950s were discarded by the Court in the 1960s. In that decade the Court ruled that disproportionate legislative districts violated the equal protection clause, that the

Fourth Amendment exclusionary rule applied to unconstitutional search and seizure by local officers, that the Sixth Amendment guaranteed the right to counsel in state courts, and that the privilege against self-incrimination applied to the states. Some of his liberal positions, especially on economic nationalism, are not congenial to the Court's present conservative majority, and his overlong, somewhat pedantic opinions have not stood the test as great examples of legal literature.

For more information

Burt, Robert. *Two Jewish Justices: Outcasts in the Promised Land.* Berkeley: University of California Press, 1988.

Hirsch, H. N. *The Enigma of Felix Frankfurter.* New York: Basic Books, 1981.

Parrish, Michael. *Felix Frankfurter and His Times.* New York: Free Press, 1982.

Marvin Zalman
Wayne State University

fraud Fraud is the deliberate misrepresentation of a material fact, made with the intention of inducing reliance in another person, that causes a loss of money or property. It can have both civil and criminal consequences.

Fraud forms the basis of the TORT of misrepresentation, a CIVIL ACTION sometimes called deceit. The victim is entitled to recover compensatory damages based on one or another of three measures. The most common is the "out of pocket" measure, which is the difference between the price paid and the actual value of the item received. A second, more generous measure is the "benefit of the bargain," being the difference between the value of the item as it was represented to be and its actual value. If the item can be made to correspond to the representation, a third measure used is the cost to do so, or "make good" damages.

Because it is a tort, fraud may also be the basis for PUNITIVE DAMAGES, which are awarded to punish and deter intentional wrongdoing. If the representation was merely reckless, rather than intentional, punitive damages would not be recoverable.

Fraud is also a basis for several forms of judicial relief in CONTRACT law. It may provide grounds for rescinding a contract, for recovering RESTITUTION of what was exchanged under a contract, or for reforming the terms of a contract to conform to representations made.

To rescind a contract is to "undo" it. If one party to a contract has been misled by the other party's fraud, a court can refuse to enforce the contract and order it rescinded. If a victim of the fraud has paid money or transferred property under the contract, a court can order its restoration to the victim, a remedy called restitution.

In the alternative, under certain circumstances a victim of fraud in the execution of a contract may ask for reformation. Reformation is an equitable remedy in which the court literally rewrites the contract language to make it conform to what was represented. Fraud may also be used in the writing of a will or trust.

Fraud can be the basis for criminal prosecutions under both state and federal law. Several closely related crimes exist in most states to deter fraudulent conduct. The crime of false pretenses occurs where a wrongdoer obtains title to property (which includes money) by intentionally defrauding a victim. Another crime predicated on fraud is LARCENY by trick, where a wrongdoer causes the victim to transfer possession of property, intending to steal it. Embezzlement is the fraudulent taking of property by one trusted with its possession. Such crimes generally are divided into degrees and punished more or less severely depending upon the value of the property taken.

A number of federal statutes punish fraudulent conduct, such as the False Claims Act, the Mail Fraud Act, and statutes aimed at preventing SECURITIES FRAUD. In addition, the Federal Trade Commission (FTC) has been given JURISDICTION to investigate and formulate rules against fraudulent practices that are aimed at consumers. Many states have passed "little FTC acts" that provide penalties such as treble damages for fraudulent business practices.

For more information

Dunn, Robert L. *Recovery of Damages for Fraud.* Westport, Conn.: Lawpress, 1995.

Freedman, Warren. *The Business Tort of Fraud and Misrepresentation.* Stoneham, Mass.: Butterworth, 1989.

Norman Otto Stockmeyer, Jr.
Thomas M. Cooley Law School

freedom of assembly and association Freedom of assembly and association is an essential part of the U.S. CONSTITUTION's First Amendment guarantees that restrict federal government regulation of a person's ability to present ideas or create organizations.

Freedom of assembly is directly mentioned while the right of association derives from a variety of First Amendment guarantees of speech and assembly. The assembly and association portions of the First Amendment protect democracy by enhancing discourse; moreover, they permit political advocacy and formation of interest groups as part of our fundamental freedoms. Interest groups are significant in national, state, and local political processes. Both freedom of assembly and association are subject to reasonable government regulations. These provisions do not allow assembly or association for unlawful purposes. Rights of association and assembly are often balanced against other societal interests, such as breach of peace or incitement to riot.

Individuals' ability to assemble and associate ranges from groups such as the Communist Party of the United States to Massachusetts Citizens for Life to labor unions. For example, in the 1930s and 1940s First Amendment rights to assemble and organize were essential for constitutional support of organized labor movements. The United States Supreme Court has often decided against government rules that would make political association ineffective; e.g., *NAACP v. Alabama ex rel. Patterson,* which prohibited Alabama from forcing the NAACP to disclose its membership lists. These lists were connected to individuals' rights of association. This part of the First Amendment also involves a freedom not to associate; see *Abood v. Detroit Board of Education,* which allows teachers not to associate with a union. In the 1980s the Supreme Court established connections between associational rules and discriminatory practices. Due to their public and business purposes both the Jaycees and Rotary International could not use freedom of association as the basis for discriminating against female members; see *Roberts v. United States Jaycees* and *Board of Directors of Rotary International v. Rotary Club.* However, in *Boy Scouts v. Dale,* 530 U.S. 640 (2000), the Supreme Court ruled that a local chapter of the Boy Scouts could revoke the membership of an individual who announced publicly that he was gay. The Court distinguished the case from its decision in *Rotary* by contending that gender was not relevant to membership in the former, but being "straight" was for the Boy Scouts. In both cases, the Court recognized that important freedom of association issues where implicated. Additionally, the Court has also stated that the right to freedom of association means not associating with those whom you do not want to be with. Thus, in *Hurley v. Irish-American Gay, Lesbian and Bisexual Group of Boston, Inc.,* 515 U.S. 557 (1995), the Court ruled that the sponsor of the Boston St. Patrick's Day Parade could bar gays and lesbians from marching in their parade, even though it took place on city streets.

Political, social, and economic interests' ability to associate and assemble to petition government are seen as essential to a regime based upon representation. James Madison in *Federalist Papers* number 10 asks whether the structure of government should thwart these political movements. Instead, he argues that freedom of assembly and association principles provide responsiveness to interests of different societal parts, which permit fragmentation of power concerning political and economic interests. These constitutional provisions permit advocacy of ideas, often controversial ideas, without government interference.

U.S. Supreme Court cases have considered rights of association of national and state political parties. Major political parties have maintained their rights to partisan primary elections. Some election laws have been ruled unconstitutional when imposing restrictions on the associational rights of minor political parties or supporters of an independent candidate.

For more information

Abood v. Detroit Board of Education, 431 U.S. 209 (1977).

Board of Directors of Rotary International v. Rotary Club of Duarte, 481 U.S. 537 (1987).

Horn, Robert A. *Groups and the Constitution.* Stanford, Calif.: Stanford University Press, 1956.

NAACP v. Alabama ex rel. Patterson, 357 U.S. 449 (1958).

Roberts v. United States Jaycees, 468 U.S. 609 (1984).

Schwartz, Bernard. *Super Chief: Earl Warren and His Supreme Court—A Judicial Biography.* New York: New York University Press, 1983.

Texas v. Johnson, 491 U.S. 397 (1989).

Steven Puro
Saint Louis University

freedom of conscience See *WEST VIRGINIA V. BARNETTE.*

Freedom of Information Act The Freedom of Information Act or FOIA is a federal law that provides for public access to records of the U.S. government. The act, which was passed by Congress in 1966, has increased government accountability and information availability. It established the presumption that documents of the federal government should be available to interested citizens and the press, rather than placing a burden on the requester to prove to the government that the information should be released. Indeed, prior to the passage of the FOIA, there were no statutory guidelines dealing with information release and no judicial remedies for those denied access. With the FOIA, the "need to know" standard has been replaced by a "right to know" doctrine. The government now has to justify the need to keep the information secret. The foundation of the act is the belief that the government is accountable for its actions and that the public possesses a right to obtain information about those actions. The act was further strengthened in 1974 following the Watergate scandal.

The FOIA exempts such records that are deemed crucial to foreign policy, national defense, confidential trade and financial information, and private personnel or medical files. If documents are requested that are partially exempt from FOIA disclosure, the agency is under no obligation to release the confidential parts merely because it must release the nonexempt material. Instead, it may edit or redact (usually, by literally blacking out) those portions that are exempt but must still produce those portions that are not exempt. Material obtained from such agencies as the Central Intelligence Agency or the FEDERAL BUREAU OF INVESTIGATION is often redacted to avoid disclosure of sensitive information or to avoid revealing the nature or identity of confidential sources.

The FOIA provides that each government agency publish descriptions of its operations and procedures. Each agency must also make available opinions, orders, and statements of policy that affect the public. Any person or organization can also obtain data from a government agency through a FOIA request. Agencies have 10 working days to comply with a request but may extend this deadline if the search requires them to collect records from field facilities, examine voluminous files, or consult with other agencies having a substantial interest in the matter under investigation.

Under FOIA, agencies may withhold nine categories of records, ranging from national defense information and matters under litigation to medical files. Agencies also may leave out identifying details to avoid unwarranted invasions of personal privacy. Federal courts, however, have JURISDICTION to block efforts to withhold records. The Office of Personnel Management also has the power to take disciplinary action against officials who withhold information contrary to the law.

Federal agencies annually spend more than $100 million to process these requests. FOIA's critics charge that the act diverts government personnel from their principal work and that those requesting files all too often use the information they receive at taxpayer expense for commercial purposes. Others charge that the process is too cumbersome, time consuming, and expensive to provide much practical benefit to average citizens. Indeed, although the original purpose of FOIA was to provide ordinary citizens with better access to information about the activities of their government, private companies seeking government records now account for as much as 75 percent of FOIA searches.

For more information

A Citizen's Guide on Using the Freedom of Information Act and the Privacy Act of 1974 to Request Government Records, 3rd report. Washington, D.C.: U.S. Government Printing Office, 1989.

Freedom of Information Act (5 U.S.C., section 552), July 4, 1967, as amended.

Montana, John. "The Freedom of Information Act," *Records Management Quarterly* (April 1998): v32 n2 p46(4).

Theoharis, Athan G. *A Culture of Secrecy: The Government Versus the People's Right to Know.* Lawrence: University Press of Kansas, 1998.

James H. Joyner, Jr.
Troy State University

freedom of speech Freedom of speech refers to one of the expressive rights contained in the First Amendment. This amendment prohibits Congress from "abridging the freedom of speech." Freedom of speech is considered important to the functioning of the American democracy, but the language of the First Amendment raises several questions regarding why speech is important and what types of communication are actually protected.

There are several arguments regarding the purpose of the free speech clause. Alexander Meiklejohn contended that the First Amendment's purpose is to protect the political speech of individuals. Steve Shiffrin argues that it is to protect the right to criticize, while Thomas Emerson asserted that its purpose is to promote self-expression. Lee Bollinger would argue that the First Amendment seeks to help promote toleration. Overall, as John Stuart Mill generally argued in *On Liberty,* freedom of speech and thought is essential to the discovery of truth that can only be found by promoting a marketplace of ideas that compete against one another. All of these different theories are important because they help inform or explain what type of communications are protected as speech.

A second question when seeking to interpret the freedom of speech clause is to ask exactly what it protects. Historically, WILLIAM BLACKSTONE, a famous 18th-century British jurist who was influential in early American law, contended in his *Commentaries on the Laws of England* that preventing prosecution of seditious LIBEL—criticism of the government—was the goal of free speech. The 1735 New York ACQUITTAL of the publisher JOHN PETER ZENGER in colonial America on charges of seditious libel against the British government reaffirmed this notion of what free speech protected. This core meaning was affirmed when Thomas Jefferson and James Madison published the Virginia and Kentucky Resolutions in 1798. These resolutions criticized the Sedition Act, a law adopted under President John Adams, which criminalized some criticism of the government. Repeal of the act and its disavowal by many cemented this core meaning regarding what the free speech clause protected. However, what speech is protected has evolved and broadened over time.

The *Schenck v. United States*, 249 U.S. 47 (1919), decision establishes more contemporary understandings of the free speech clause. While upholding the conviction of two individuals accused of violating the 1917 Espionage Act during World War I by seeking to disrupt military recruitment, Justice Oliver Wendell Holmes stated that speech was not protected under the First Amendment when it posed a "clear and present danger" that it would bring about the evils Congress intended to prevent. Thus, political speech that does not pose a clear and present danger would receive constitutional protection.

In *Masses Publishing Co. v. Patten*, 244 Fed. 535 (D.NY 1917), Judge Learned Hand adopted the "incitement" test to decide on the scope of free speech, arguing that if the speech stops just short of inciting or urging others to break the law, it is protected under the First Amendment. The incitement and clear and present danger tests get encapsulated into the "imminent lawless" test in *Brandenburg v. Ohio*, 395 U.S. 444 (1969), where the U.S. Supreme Court states that speech is protected until such time as it advocates imminent lawlessness or violence that is actually imminent. Mere advocacy of ideas or beliefs is protected by the First Amendment, regardless, it appears, of what those ideas advocate. The *Brandenberg* test remains the core test for what political speech is protected.

Another issue affecting interpretations of the free speech clause is whom it protects. Historically, the First Amendment only protected individual speech. However, the Supreme Court has also extended free speech protections to, for example, corporations, labor unions, and political parties, in some cases ruling that commercial speech or advertising is entitled to some First Amendment protection. Finally, in interpreting the First Amendment, the Supreme Court has had to address issues of how to regulate speech on public property, when it involves government employees, when speech and nonspeech activity are intertwined, and in the context of new technologies such as the Web and the Internet. In all these areas, complex rules have been fashioned to interpret what the First Amendment prohibits.

Another issue when interpreting the free speech clause is examining the different classes of speech protected. The Court has never said that all forms of communication are protected by the First Amendment. For example, blackmail, extortion, libel, and verbal harassment are speech, but they are not protected by the First Amendment. The Court has created numerous categories of speech. It has distinguished political speech of individuals from other types of communication such as symbolic speech and commercial speech.

Over time, the Supreme Court has examined numerous types of communication and found them to be protected speech. These include flag burning in *Texas v. Johnson*, 491 U.S. 397 (1987); cross burning and hate speech in *R.A.V. v. St Paul*, 505 U.S. 377 (1992); the use of offensive language in a court in *Cohen v. California*, 283 U.S. 359 (1971); sexually explicit materials in *Miller v. California*, 413 U.S. 15 (1973). Violent video games in *Brown v. Entertainment Merchants Association*, 564 U.S. __ (2011), and protests at military funerals in *Snyder v. Phelps*, 562 U.S. __ (2011). Conversely, the Court has stated that libel is not speech in *New York Times v. Sullivan*, 376 U.S. 254 (1964), and that obscene materials *(Miller v. California)* are also exempt from First Amendment protection. There is then a category of communications that may be speech but nonetheless is either entitled to some or very little First Amendment protection. Nude but nonobscene dancing is expressive, but it does not receive much constitutional protection. *Barnes v. Glen Theatre*, 501 U.S. 560 (1991). Money is not speech, but it may receive some First Amendment protections in the context of political contributions and expenditures. *Buckley v. Valeo*, 424 U.S. 1 (1976).

Finally, as new forms of communications emerge, so do debates regarding the scope of

First Amendment protections. The Internet and the Web are only the latest examples of this. Due to concern that children might be accessing sexually inappropriate materials, Congress has sought to regulate speech on it. The 1996 Communications Decency Act (CDA) sought to regulate the distribution of pornographic materials, but it was declared unconstitutional in *Reno v. ACLU,* 521 U.S. 844, (1997). Congress then passed the Child Online Protection Act, but again in *Ashcroft v. American Civil Liberties Union,* 542 U.S. 656, (2004), the Court again ruled that efforts to regulate nonobscene but sexually explicit material on the Web violated the First Amendment.

For more information

Bollinger, Lee C. *The Tolerant Society: Freedom of Speech and Extremist Speech in America.* New York: Oxford University Press, 1986.

Emerson, Thomas I. *Toward a General Theory of the First Amendment.* New York: Random House, 1966.

Kelvin, Harry, Jr. *A Worthy Tradition: Freedom of Speech in America.* New York: Harper and Row, 1988.

Meiklejohn, Alexander. *Free Speech and Its Relation to Self-Government.* New York: Harper and Row, 1948.

Shiffrin, Steven. *The First Amendment, Democracy, and Romance.* Cambridge, Mass.: Harvard University Press, 1990.

David Schultz
Hamline University

freedom of the press Freedom of the press is a subdivision of freedom of speech and generally refers to the protection given to the dissemination of speech expressing news, information, or opinion. The "press" includes such media as newspapers, television, radio, the INTERNET, and books. As with other clauses of the First Amendment, the purpose is to declare to the federal government what it may not do. Although the words of the CONSTITUTION are sparse, the courts, by way of their declared duty to interpret or discover the intent of the framers in placing such conditions on the Congress, determine what the Congress may or may not legislate. The courts have also ruled that the First Amendment applies to the states because of the adoption of the Fourteenth Amendment. Therefore, no state legislature or other governing body may enact a law contrary to the First Amendment

One of the most meaningful restrictions on the government is that it may not stop publication of a newspaper or book in advance of publication. This prohibition is called "PRIOR RESTRAINT." There are exceptions such as national security or public health and safety. An example of attempted prior restraint that failed was the "Pentagon Papers," in which the government attempted to enjoin the publication of documents detailing the various policies of the Vietnam War and its prosecution by the U.S. government. The Supreme Court unanimously refused to impose any restraint on what the justices determined to be political speech. This was not the case when a magazine called the *Progressive* sought to publish details of a working hydrogen bomb. In that instance, security and safety overrode the requirements of the First Amendment.

Broadcast media have special requirements because of the regulation of the broadcast spectrum. The restrictions are usually on the basis of time of broadcast. The arrangement that the government and broadcasters have entered into is a modification of the freedom available to print media. In exchange for use of the electronic spectrum, the broadcasters submit to licensing, agreements to air "public service announcements," and some content restrictions. An example of content restrictions is the case involving George Carlin, a comedian popular in the 1960s and 1970s who made a recording called "The Seven Dirty Words You Can't Say on Television." This routine was played over various radio stations and eventually the Supreme Court ruled that the routine could not be broadcast. Just to make sure that everyone knew what words could not be used, the Court thoughtfully appended a transcript of the routine to the written opinion.

Print media, and more recently the Internet, would not be subjected to content restrictions, and any attempt to impose such restrictions would be met with stiff resistance. The main restraint on the press is that neither print nor broadcast media may disseminate LIBEL. Libel consists of publication of false or injurious information about an individual or enterprise such that it damages that individual. If the individual is not a public figure, then the publication need only be negligent to cause the publisher liability and subject him or her to a claim for damages. If the individual is a public figure, then to show liability and damages, the person libeled must show that the publisher had actual MALICE in disseminating the falsehood.

In general, subject only to the constraints of libel, a publisher of news, information, or opinion may not be restrained from printing, broadcasting, or posting to the Internet what he or she wants.

For more information

Levy, Leonard W. *Emergence of a Free Press.* New York: Oxford University Press, 1985.

Stanley M. Morris
Attorney, Cortez, Colorado

Frontiero v. Richardson 411 U.S. 677 (1973) *Frontiero v. Richardson* was a Supreme Court decision that addressed the proper standard of review in cases of gender discrimination. A plurality of the Court held that classifications based on gender were inherently suspect and, therefore, should be subjected to a "STRICT SCRUTINY" analysis. However, this approach was not adopted by a majority of the Court in subsequent decisions.

The case came to the Court after Sharron Frontiero, a lieutenant in the air force, was denied additional housing and medical benefits available under federal law when, as required under the law, she was unable to demonstrate that her husband was dependent on her for over one-half of his support. The law awarded the additional spousal benefits to servicemen without evidence of dependent support. Frontiero filed suit, claiming that the difference in treatment was an unconstitutional gender discrimination violating the EQUAL PROTECTION component of the DUE PROCESS clause of the Fifth Amendment. A three-JUDGE district court upheld the constitutionality of the law, applying the less stringent "rational basis" analysis and finding that the saving of administrative costs that would be incurred if servicemen were required to prove dependency of their spouses justified the distinction, given that only a small percentage of their spouses would be ineligible.

In an 8-1 vote, the Court struck down the law as unconstitutional. While Justice Rehnquist was the lone dissenter, believing that the district court's decision should stand, a majority of the justices could not agree on the standard to apply in gender discrimination cases. Writing for the plurality of four justices, Justice Brennan argued that sex discrimination cases should be analyzed under a strict scrutiny analysis, requiring the government to show a compelling interest to justify the distinction. Justice Brennan believed the Court's most recent decision on gender discrimination, *Reed v. Reed,* 404 U.S. 71 (1971), supported the adoption of this more stringent analysis because that decision appeared to signal a departure from the then applicable and less stringent rational basis analysis. In addition, he asserted that a strict scrutiny analysis was justified to remedy the long history of sex discrimination and because gender discrimination imposed a legal burden unrelated to individual responsibility. Finally, he argued that the recent increased sensitivity of Congress to gender discrimination, in part evidenced by the proposal of the EQUAL RIGHTS AMENDMENT in 1972, justified the greater level of protection.

Justice Powell, joined by CHIEF JUSTICE Burger and Justice Blackmun, agreed that the statute was unconstitutional but rejected Justice Brennan's view that gender-based classifications should be inherently suspect and subjected to a strict scrutiny analysis. Justice Powell disagreed with Justice Brennan's reading of *Reed* and also believed it would damage both the Court and democratic institutions if the Court found that gender classifications were inherently suspect while the Equal Rights Amendment was being considered for ratification.

The level of review of classifications based on gender was later addressed in *Craig v. Boren,* 429 U.S.190 (1976), where the Court adopted a standard between the rational basis and strict scrutiny tests. Under this intermediate scrutiny approach, the gender classification "must serve important governmental objectives and must be substantially related to those objectives." The Court has followed this approach in more recent decisions, including *United States v. Virginia,* 518 U.S. 515 (1996).

For more information

Baer, Judith A. *Women in American Law: The Struggle toward Equality from the New Deal to the Present.* New York: Holmes and Meier, 1991.

Frontiero v. Richardson, 411 U.S. 677 (1973).

Goldstein, Leslie Friedman. *The Constitutional Rights of Women.* 2nd ed. Madison: University of Wisconsin Press, 1988.

James N. G. Cauthen
City University of New York

Fuller, Melville W. (1833–1910) chief justice of the United States Melville W. Fuller CHIEF JUSTICE of the United States between 1888 and 1910, was born in Augusta, Maine, in 1833 and educated at Bowdoin College. He received most of his legal education through law firm apprenticeship but also attended lectures at Harvard Law School. Fuller moved to Chicago and established a successful law practice focused on appellate advocacy. He often represented banks, railroads, and members of the Chicago business elite.

Reared in the Jacksonian political tradition emphasizing limited government, Fuller early became active in Democratic Party affairs. He developed a close relationship with President Grover Cleveland. In March of 1888 Cleveland nominated Fuller to replace the deceased MORRISON R. WAITE as chief justice. Fuller was not well known nationally, but after some delay he was confirmed by the Republican-controlled Senate.

Fuller was an outstanding judicial administrator. A genial man with an urbane sense of humor, he fostered a harmonious working relationship among the justices. Fuller wrote 840 majority opinions, speaking for the Court more often than any other justice during his period of service. He was also instrumental in reducing the huge backlog of APPEALS and in bringing about the creation of the circuit courts of appeals to ease the work burden of the Supreme Court.

As Chief Justice Fuller guided the Supreme Court to greater judicial solicitude for the rights of property owners against governmental incursions. The Fuller court established judicial review of railroad rate regulation, gave a new vitality to THE TAKINGS CLAUSE, strengthened the doctrine of SUBSTANTIVE DUE PROCESS, and vigorously expanded the reach of judicial authority. In *Pollock. v. Farmers' Loan and Trust Company* (1895), for example, Fuller struck down the 1894 income tax as an unconstitutional direct tax. In *United States v. E.C. Knight Company* (1895) Fuller distinguished between commerce and manufacturing and thus restricted application of the SHERMAN ANTITRUST ACT. The Supreme Court also ruled that just compensation for private property taken for public use was an essential element of due process as guaranteed by the Fourteenth Amendment. Fuller viewed property rights and individual liberty as closely related, and he sought to protect liberty by restraining government. Dedicated to economic liberty as a crucial constitutional value, Fuller and his colleagues were generally in accord with the prevailing public sentiment of the age. It should also be noted that the Fuller court upheld many regulations to protect the public safety and health.

Under Fuller the Supreme Court generally deferred to state control of race relations and criminal justice. Thus, in *PLESSY V. FERGUSON* (1896) the Court approved the emerging practice of racial SEGREGATION in the South. It likewise refused to apply the BILL OF RIGHTS to state criminal proceedings. With respect to federal criminal prosecutions, however, Fuller and his associates tended to give an expanded meaning to the procedural safeguards in the Bill of Rights.

Melville Fuller died in July of 1910. He had served as chief justice for 22 years during a pivotal era of American history.

For more information

Ely, James W., Jr. *The Chief Justiceship of Melville W. Fuller, 1888–1910.* Columbia: University of South Carolina Press, 1995.

Fiss, Owen M. *Troubled Beginnings of the Modern State.* New York: Macmillan Library Reference 1888–1910, 1993.

James W. Ely, Jr.
Vanderbilt University Law School

Furman v. Georgia 408 U.S. 238 (1972) In *Furman v. Georgia,* the U.S. Supreme Court ruled that, as then in operation in cases under review in Georgia and Texas, the death penalty constituted CRUEL AND UNUSUAL PUNISHMENT and thus violated the EIGHTH and Fourteenth AMENDMENTS of the U.S. CONSTITUTION. Justices WILLIAM O. DOUGLAS, WILLIAM J. BRENNAN, Potter Stewart, Byron White, and THURGOOD MARSHALL wrote separate opinions in support of this ruling. While the various opinions differed in terms of points emphasized and the legal reasoning employed, the five justices agreed that the imposition of the death penalty was unconstitutional when carried out under discriminatory circumstances.

The Court's logic in *Furman v. Georgia* is revealed, in part, in Justice Douglas's position that one can define "unusual"—as regards the concept of cruel and unusual—as that which is implemented "arbitrarily or discriminatorily." For example, as regards the latter, Douglas cited a study of capital cases in Texas during the period 1924 to 1968, in which it was empirically demonstrated that those who were young, African American, poor, or lacking in education were more likely to receive the death penalty than were their counterparts. In cases involving the same offense, Douglas pointed out, African-American defendants were more likely than white defendants to receive a death sentence, while white defendants were more likely than African Americans to receive a term of life sentence. How could this be interpreted in any manner other than "unusual," arbitrary, or discriminatory, Douglas reasoned.

Justice Stewart's opinion added that the imposition of a death sentence was cruel and unusual in much the same manner that "being struck by lightning is cruel and unusual." While many might be outdoors during a storm, it was the unfortunate few who were actually struck by lightning; similarly, while convicted felons who committed more reprehensible and VIOLENT CRIMES than those in the present case being reviewed by the Court might be given term sentences, the "capriciously selected random handful" were unfortunate enough to come before JURIES in states disposed to impose death sentences. Justice Marshall underscored the logic by adding that female offenders were less likely than male offenders to receive capital sentences for the same crimes; indeed, he pointed to empirical data suggesting that only 32 women had been executed between 1930 and 1972, while more than 3,000 men had been executed.

In his opinion, Justice White took the opportunity to point out that something could be cruel in what he called a "dictionary sense" without being cruel in a "constitutional sense." That is, if an act contributed to the promotion of constitutionally mandated ends it could withstand constitutional scrutiny even if, in lay terms, it appeared to be cruel. However, he added, unless one could find evidence that the death penalty more effectively deterred crime than did life terms, the death penalty would appear to have at best "marginal" justification, i.e., it would be "cruel" in constitutional terms. Thus, from a variety of perspectives—e.g., Douglas's use of empirical data from Texas, Marshall's citation of the gender imbalances—the Court found that, as practiced, the death penalty was unconstitutional.

For more information

Srikanth, Srinivasan. "Capital Sentencing Doctrine and the Weighing-Nonweighing Distinction," *Stanford Law Review* 47 (July 1995): 1,347–1,374.

Ellen Grigsby
University of New Mexico

G

Gacy, John Wayne (1942–1994) serial killer John Wayne Gacy, Jr., was a SERIAL KILLER and known in the media as the "clown killer."

He was born in Chicago and is believed to have suffered physical and psychological abuse from his alcoholic father, John Gacy, Sr. The abuse by his father led him to question his own masculinity, and he countered that by trying to look important to others. At the age of 11, an accident caused a blood clot to form in his head, which led to episodic blackouts. Although the blood clot was not removed until he was 16, there does not seem to be any claim in the literature that this head injury was the product of his later crimes. Throughout Gacy's life, he was known for thriving on attention and power. He enjoyed being viewed as important. He was a very social person who often lied about his life experiences.

He married his first wife in 1964. Four years later, he was ARRESTED on sodomy charges and subsequently sentenced to 10 years in prison. He was a model prisoner and received early release on PAROLE after serving 18 months of his 10-year sentence. It was shortly after his release that he claims he committed his first MURDER.

Gacy targeted victims who were young males ages 9 to 20. They were typically hitchhikers, but he would also bring young men to his home and attack them after showing them his act as Pongo the Clown. Gacy would show his victims a pair of handcuffs and trick them into being handcuffed behind their back. Without a means for escape, Gacy committed deviant sexual acts on his victims. He murdered them by strangling them with a rope or by putting a board on their throats.

Gacy dumped his victim's bodies in the crawl space under his home. Gacy was arrested after police went to his home to question him about the disappearance of Robert Piest, who was known to have been offered employment at Gacy's construction business. Gacy was finally captured because police, upon arriving to Gacy's home to question him about Robert Piest, smelled a rotting odor. This smell prompted police to investigate further. Upon examination, it was discovered that Gacy had buried multiple bodies in the dirt in the crawl space. Ultimately, Gacy was charged with the murders of 33 young men and boys. He was convicted for many of these deaths and was executed in 1994.

For more information

Newton, Michael. *The Encyclopedia of Serial Killers.* New York: Checkmark Books, 2000.

Riedel, Marc, and Wayne Welsh. *Criminal Violence: Patterns, Causes, and Prevention.* New York: Oxford University Press, 2008.

Michelle L. Foster
Kent State University

gangs The problem of gangs, usually considered to be criminal or quasi-criminal associations of male juveniles, is one that has persisted in American society since the beginnings of the nation's history. However, today's gangs are often multigenerational and have female members or auxiliaries. Additionally, gangs are an international problem as they control vice, crime, and drug traffic in many nations and across national boundaries. Some countries are so dominated by drug gangs and the chaos that they engender that they are sometimes called narco states. Wherever they are found, they are disruptive of order of the neighborhoods or regions from which they operate.

Gangs are often made up of men, and increasingly of women, of different age groups, however. The highly problematic gangs noted in the crime news of the late 1900s and early 21st century are generally multigenerational, that is, having members at a variety of age levels. Gangs are usually made up of lower-class, often immigrant, youth and have been of concern to CRIMINOLOGISTS and criminal justice professionals since the mid-1800s.

The first theories about juvenile delinquency and the dominant theories emerging from the 1950s concerned gang youth and their alienation from the "American Dream." This remains a preeminent theme in the research and various explanations for gang behavior. That is, lower-class boys run into problems while trying to compete with middle-class boys in middle-class-oriented schools and turn to gang peers for support, validation, and reinforcement. Alternatively, in a nonschool-oriented variation on this theme, lower-class boys cannot get ahead in middle-class society and turn to gangs for opportunity to fight for status and to make a living in the "rackets." In this sense, gangs also serve as resources for politicians: that is, as voters who also serve as political operatives sometimes used to get out the vote, or alternatively, to intimidate opposition voters and candidates.

Another notion that explains the attraction of gangs is simply that they are lower-class male social groups that are a normal outgrowth of lower-class culture. As such, gangs are not a reaction to the American Dream at all but a normal manifestation of lower-class culture and not properly a pathological development. Finally, classical gang theory (the Chicago School) suggests that gangs are the product of social disorganization and shabby neighborhoods. Immigrant parents and recent rural transplants from the South, for example, are so demoralized by poverty, work, mental illness, and oppressive work and social conditions, as well as being unsupported in the urban milieu, that their children are allowed to grow up on the streets. Gangs eventually evolve from spontaneous play groups and, unfettered by effective parenting and strong schools, and concern from police, church, and social agencies, grow into criminal organizations. This remains a convincing model given the preponderance of gangs in slums and among impoverished immigrant groups.

Gangs of young men were noted in East Coast cities in the United States of the early 1800s. As the apprenticeship system fell apart in that period, young men who had previously been under the strict supervision of a master craftsman, were forced into other forms of labor. Living in boardinghouses or on the street, they had time and financial resources that allowed them to drink and indulge in unregulated gambling, sexual adventures, and fighting. Taverns, barbershops, and firehouses (all viewed with strong disapproval by the Victorian mainstream), became their hangouts. In these places, they were sometimes recruited by politicians to act as shock troops or to populate political rallies, often in colorful, distinctive garb, very much like the colors adopted by modern gangbangers. Riotous Election Day violence erupted in New York City and more notoriously, Baltimore, particularly in the 1840s and 1850s. Gangs associated with political parties would kidnap unwary travelers and transients, confine them in "coops", ply them with alcohol, and then march the "voters" from poll to poll, often supplying changes of clothes to facilitate the FRAUD. Edgar Allan Poe's death in Baltimore, after being found insensible on Election Day, dressed in strange clothes in a polling place, was most probably due to having been a victim of cooping. Election Day violence by political gangs included direct obstruction of polls, threatening partisans of other political organizations with direct violence, and stabbing them with awls.

Sometimes gangs travelled to other cities to meet with allied gangs and to participate in Election Day violence in those municipalities. In one instance, U.S. Marines put down a gang riot caused by Baltimore gangs visiting in Washington, D.C., killing a number of Election Day spectators. Gangs were sometimes based in firehouses and were only brought under control when municipalities assumed control over the various volunteer companies that dotted the urban landscape. In Baltimore, known as Mob Town due to extreme violence and gunplay between factions, reform of the police department, insulating it somewhat from patronage, and the occupation of the city by Union troops during the Civil War helped to end gang conflict and hegemony in the city.

New Orleans also had political gangs in the pre–Civil War period, which seized the center of the city and engaged in urban warfare. Following the war, organized rebellions were fomented by various political gangs and political factions. Later MAFIA-oriented gangs gained control of the crime scene of that city and maintained organized crime dominance well into the 20th century.

Richmond, Virginia, had large numbers of rock-throwing "boy gangs" that engaged in pitched battles ranging over the hills of that city before, during, and after the Civil War that scarred the city. Those gangs lasted into the early 1900s and were a persistent feature of that city for 100 years but never evolved into criminal organizations. Gangs like this were common throughout the nation, but their activities were widely tolerated as normal lower-class juvenile behavior. The presence of these boy gangs in 1930s movie shorts such as *Our Gang* and *The Little Rascals* illustrates the nostalgia felt by many Americans and ambivalence evidenced by many of those who had left the slums and tenements behind in their pursuit of the American Dream.

Gangs became a serious concern in Chicago in the 1920s. PROSTITUTION, smuggling alcohol, and protection rackets gave ethnic-based gangs a strong foothold in that environment. Young men, some of whom were veterans of World War I, were recruited into these criminal associations or formed their own criminal bands. Such outlaws as JOHN DILLINGER and BONNIE AND CLYDE had small groups of associates, and these groupings could be called gangs. Although these bandits garnered much publicity and concern, they fall outside the purview of this discussion. However, criminal gangs of immigrant youth and second-generation mobsters were far more problematic and efficient. These gangs persisted into the 1960s in some cities, generally until their members made enough money to go "legit" and move into the suburbs. Their place was taken by gangs made up of newer immigrants. This law of ethnic succession has been applied uniformly throughout the American gang experience. Anglo-American gangs gave way to gangs of Irish, then Italian descent.

Presently, gangs of African-American, Hispanic, and Asian descent dominate the gang scene. Fearsome gangs such as the Crips and Bloods control entire lower-class neighborhoods in California and throughout the nation. Hispanic gangs such as Mara Salvatrucha and the

Mexican Mafia, originally from Central America, spread drugs and violence wherever Hispanics have settled in the United States and dominate the urban areas of Latin America. In some cities such as Boston and New York City, remnants of Italian-American and Irish-American gangs persist but are threatened by the growth of gangs from eastern Europe such as the Russian Mafiya. Gangs are now noted even in rural locales in the South, where large numbers of immigrants have settled, and in urban slums. These criminal organizations operate much as they do elsewhere in the nation, furnishing prostitutes, drugs, and, violence and prey almost exclusively on those from their own ethnic community. It is notable that American-style gangs are now found worldwide but are especially problematic in eastern Europe and Latin America.

It is extremely difficult to effectively police gangs, especially ethnically-based gangs, as they may enjoy considerable status and power within their communities. Recruiting police from those communities may be problematic, if not impossible, and the job of gang policing is beyond the abilities of the average officer. Special dedicated gang units patrol such areas, stopping, searching, and photographing suspected gang members, often focusing on their distinctive tattoos. Gang work is not the exclusive province of juvenile officers since gangs, many being multigenerational, may contain children and their grandparents. Gang task forces must involve officers from many areas of specialization, encompassing juvenile work, accounting, computer specialists, and drug and vice officers. Gangs remain a serious criminal justice issue for the foreseeable future.

For more information

Mays, G. Larry. *Gangs and Gang Behavior.* Chicago: Nelson-Hall, 1997.

Spergel, Irving A. *The Youth Gang Problem: A Community Approach.* Oxford: Oxford University Press, 1995.

Frederick Hawley
Western Carolina University

Gannett Co. v. Depasquale 443 U.S. 368 (1979) In *Gannett Co. v. Depasquale,* the U.S. Supreme Court ruled that the public (including news media) does not have an absolute right under the SIXTH AMENDMENT to the UNITED STATES CONSTITUTION to observe criminal pretrial suppression hearings. In this case, two defendants charged with MURDER had received negative press coverage by the time a pretrial suppression hearing was scheduled. Fearing more negative publicity that might bias potential jurors against them, the defendants asked that the press be excluded from the hearing. The trial JUDGE (Judge Depasquale) agreed, and a reporter from a newspaper owned by Gannett Company was excluded. Gannett Company argued that the public and press have a right under both the First and Sixth Amendments to the U.S. Constitution to observe such hearings. The trial judge ruled the defendant's right to a fair trial overrode any public right of access in this instance. The New York State Court of Appeals upheld the denial of public access, and Gannett Company appealed to the U.S. Supreme Court.

Writing for the Court, Justice Potter Stewart, joined by CHIEF JUSTICE WARREN E. BURGER, as well as Justices Lewis Powell, WILLIAM H. REHNQUIST, and JOHN PAUL STEVENS, upheld the courtroom exclusion. The Court first emphasized that negative pretrial press coverage within a community can bias potential jurors against the defendant, and so closing pretrial hearings to the public is an important method of protecting a defendant's right to a fair trial. Focusing on the Sixth Amendment's right to "public trial," the Court then declared that this right is personal to the defendant, not the public. Historically, secret trials were used for unjust persecution, so public trials help prevent prosecutorial or judicial abuse of the accused. The Court admitted the public does have its own interest in having open trials, such as inducing potential witnesses to come forward and causing trial participants to perform their duties more conscientiously, but these interests do not rise to the level of a Sixth Amendment right. If a defendant waives the Sixth Amendment right to a public trial, the public has no Sixth Amendment right to compel a public trial instead, just as the public has no right to compel a JURY trial or a speedy trial if the defendant waives those other Sixth Amendment rights. Also, although the old common law norm favored public trials, the writers and ratifiers of the Sixth Amendment did not intend to elevate this norm to a public right of access, and even if so, the old common law norm applied only to trials themselves, not to pretrial hearings. For all these reasons, there is no absolute right of public access to suppression hearings under the Sixth Amendment.

Finally, in a brief discussion, the Court also declared that it did not need to decide if the First Amendment provides a right of public access to pretrial suppression hearings. Even if there is such a First Amendment right, that right is outweighed by a defendant's right to a fair trial. Thus, in this case, the trial judge permissibly excluded Gannett Company from the suppression hearing in order to minimize the risk that additional negative pretrial publicity might bias potential jurors against the defendants.

In a later case, *RICHMOND NEWSPAPERS V. VIRGINIA*, 448 U.S. 555 (1980), the Supreme Court expressly ruled that the public, including the news media, does have a qualified right under the First Amendment to observe criminal trials, subject to the defendant's overriding right to a fair trial. Later Supreme Court cases applied either the First Amendment, the Sixth Amendment, or both, in extending this qualified right of the public to view the criminal justice process to include sexual assault to minors cases [*Globe Newspaper Co. v. Superior Court*, 457 U.S. 596 (1982)]; jury selection [*Press Enterprise Co. v. Superior Court*, 464 U.S. 501 (1984)]; pretrial suppression hearings [*Waller v. Georgia*, 467 U.S. 39 (1984)] (thus modifying the result of *Gannett Company v. Depasquale*); and preliminary hearings [*Press Enterprise Co. v. Superior Court II*, 478 U.S. 1 (1986)]; *El Vocero de Puerto Rico v. Puerto Rico*, 508 U.S. 147 (1993)].

For more information

Freedman, Warren. *Press and Media Access to the Criminal Courtroom*. New York: Quorum Books, 1988.

Lewis, Anthony. *Freedom for the Thought We Hate: A Biography of the First Amendment*. New York: Basic Books, 2010.

Rick Swanson
University of Louisiana, Lafayette

In re Gault 387 U.S. 1 (1967) *In re Gault* was a milestone U.S. Supreme Court case in JUVENILE JUSTICE.

The case began when 15-year-old Gerald Gault of Globe, Arizona, was charged with making lewd telephone calls to his neighbor. After he was found guilty in a hearing before a juvenile court JUDGE, Gault was committed to the Arizona Industrial School until he reached majority, that is, for six years. An adult convicted of the same offense would have been sentenced to a maximum of two months in jail or a fine of $5 to $50.

Gault's APPEAL claimed that he was denied constitutional rights stemming from the DUE PROCESS clause of the Fourteenth Amendment, including the right to an attorney and the privilege against SELF-INCRIMINATION. His appeal was denied by the Arizona state courts, including the state supreme court.

In an 8-1 opinion, the Supreme Court reversed the state supreme court and imposed new procedural requirements on juvenile courts throughout the nation. Speaking for the majority, Justice Abe Fortas began with the reminder that juvenile offenders are entitled to constitutional protections; he said, "neither the Fourteenth Amendment nor the BILL OF RIGHTS is for adults alone" (p. 13).

The Court recapitulated the history of juvenile courts, noting that the impetus behind their creation was to insulate juveniles from the harshness of the adult justice system. The relationship between the child and the state was intended to be non-adversarial, the Court pointed out, with the state conceiving its role as the child's parent, under the doctrine known as *parens patria*. Also, because the juvenile court's primary purpose was to rehabilitate the child, not ascertain guilt or innocence, it did not have to apply adult criminal procedures.

Although the theory is admirable, said Fortas, the practice is less so. Because juvenile court hearings are adversarial, children such as Gerald Gault are deprived of their liberty without the due process protections given to adult offenders. Acknowledging the advantages inherent in a separate juvenile court system with its special procedures, the Court held that the CONSTITUTION requires the state to provide procedural safeguards, largely stemming from the Fifth and SIXTH AMENDMENTS, to juvenile offenders. Under the rules announced in *Gault*, states must provide juveniles with specific notice of the charges against them and allow adequate time to prepare a defense; states must notify juveniles of the right to an attorney and provide one if the parents are unable to afford it; juveniles have a right against self-incrimination, and states cannot rely on confessions without showing that they are voluntary; and at trial, juveniles have the right to confront and cross-examine witnesses against them.

Applying these rules to Gerald Gault's case, the Court found that there was insufficient notice of the charges against him; he was not offered counsel; he was not told he did not have to make a statement, so his confession was not truly voluntary; and since the complainant was not called as a witness against him, he was deprived of his Sixth Amendment right to confront his accuser.

For more information

Manfredi, Christopher P. *The Supreme Court and Juvenile Justice*. Lawrence: University Press of Kansas, 1998.

Susan Gluck Mezey
Department of Political Science
Loyola University, Chicago

gay rights Gay rights refers to the political and social struggle of homosexuals, bisexuals, and trans-gender individuals to achieve the same legal rights as other Americans regardless of sexual orientation. Although recently debated in the context of gay marriage, gay rights extends to such issues as raising and adopting children, as well as the right to be free from bias in the workplace.

The birth of the modern gay rights movement is often traced to the raid and subsequent riot at the Stonewall Inn in Greenwich Village, a neighborhood in New York City. There in the summer of 1969 patrons of a local gay bar protested what they saw as police harassment. Although few knew about it at the time, the now famous "Stonewall Riot" has become symbolic of the political and social movement for equal rights by gays and lesbians over the last three decades.

The very expression "gay rights" is controversial—and not simply because Americans remain split in their acceptance of gay, lesbian, and trans-gender lifestyles. Rather, the term has come to mean two different concepts in popular culture, often dependent on individual views of homosexuality. To most gays, lesbians, and their supporters, gay rights means constitutional protection against discrimination on the basis of sexual orientation; to opponents, however, the term means "special rights" for homosexuals. This debate was highlighted in the United States Supreme Court case of *ROMER V. EVANS*, a 1996 challenge to a Colorado initiative prohibiting legal protection for gays and lesbians. Supporters of the law said that it merely put gays and lesbians on the same level as all other persons: just as red-haired people were not entitled to legal protection against discrimination, neither should gays and lesbians claim special rights. The Supreme Court ruled, however, that Colorado could not prohibit a class of people from ever seeking legal protection from discrimination. Noteworthy in the Court's decision was its conclusion that the law was "inexplicable by anything but animus toward the class that it affects."

Gay Pride March '77 (Library of Congress)

The *Evans* decision was a departure for the Supreme Court, which 10 years earlier had upheld a Georgia anti-sodomy law that punished two adult men for engaging in consensual sex in a private home. In that case, BOWERS V. HARDWICK, gay rights supporters had urged the Court to grant homosexuals the same constitutional protection it had given other minority groups with a history of exclusion and discrimination. But, rather than using the case to extend CIVIL RIGHTS protections to gays and lesbians, the Court narrowly interpreted the Georgia statute as being simply about sodomy. Since *Bowers* a few states have instituted antidiscrimination statutes that apply to gays and lesbians, and at least one state supreme court—Hawaii's—has created legal protection for homosexuals under state constitutional law. The vast majority of states, however, have not.

The battle for gay rights has taken place on several fronts. One was an effort to repeal the "Don't ask, don't tell" policy that Congress adopted in 1993. The law barred gays and lesbians from openly serving in the military. The law was repealed in 2010.

A second issue surrounds FAMILY issues. Gays and lesbians have generally been successful in securing rights to adopt and to devise property to others in their will. But another issue is gay marriage. The Massachusetts Supreme Court in *Goodridge v. Department of Public Health,* 440 Mass. 309 (2003), ruled that precluding same-sex couple from marrying violated its state constitution. As a result, same-sex couples have been able to marry in that state. Other states, including Iowa, Connecticut, and New York either by court decision or legislation, have also changed their laws to allow same-sex couples to marry.

As a result of the *Goodridge* decision, many states adopted their own DEFENSE OF MARRIAGE ACTS in 2004. As of 2010, 37 states have their own DOMAs. That law is currently facing challenges in the FEDERAL COURTS.

Finally, supporters of gay and lesbian rights have sought to generally fight discrimination. Many state and local governments have extended antidiscrimination to include sexual orientation. However in *Boy Scouts v. Dale,* 530 U.S. 640 (2000), the Supreme Court ruled that a local chapter of the Boy Scouts could revoke the membership of an individual who announced publicly that he was gay. In *Hurley v. Irish-American Gay, Lesbian and Bisexual Group of Boston, Inc.,* 515 U.S. 557 (1995), the Court ruled that the sponsor of the Boston St. Patrick's Day Parade could bar gays and lesbians from marching in their parade, even though it took place on city streets. Both of these cases indicate that gays and lesbians face discrimination in many areas of their life still.

For more information

Alsenas, Linas. *Gay America: Struggle for Equality.* New York: Amulet Books, 2008.

Marks, Robert B. *The Gay and Lesbian Movement: References and Resources.* New York: G. K. Hall, 1996.

Newton, David E. *Gay and Lesbian Rights: A Reference Handbook.* Santa Barbara, Calif.: ABC CLIO, 1994.

Jon Gould
George Mason University

gender and crime Gender influences every aspect of the CRIMINAL JUSTICE SYSTEM, from police investigation of crime through conviction and SENTENCING. At the investigatory stage, the standards governing police conduct are generally tailored to the objective reasonable person, meaning that they do not take into account differences that correlate strongly with gender. For example, the definition of a "seizure"—the point at which the FOURTH AMENDMENT is implicated—is defined as the point at which "a reasonable person would not be free to terminate the encounter or decline the police officer's requests." *Florida v. Bostick,* 501 U.S. 429, 435 (1991); *United States v. Drayton,* 536 U.S. 194, 197–98 (2002). If a reasonable person would feel at liberty to terminate an encounter, that person is not "seized" for purposes of the Fourth Amendment.

This standard does not take into account the fact that women may respond differently to situations involving law enforcement officers—that is, a woman may be more intimidated by a police officer and thus more likely to acquiesce to demands, even if an average person—the so-called reasonable person—would feel free to disregard those demands. Women are thus vulnerable to law enforcement intrusions that would not be deemed to violate the Fourth Amendment.

The same gendered vulnerability arises whenever the reasonable person standard is used in criminal law. For example, the police are required to cease questioning a suspect without her lawyer only after she invokes her *Miranda* rights. *Edwards v. Arizona,* 451 U.S. 477, 478–487 (1981). Such a standard does not necessarily take account of the possibility that women, on average, may be more intimidated by the custodial setting and less likely to unambiguously refuse to answer questions. Similarly, in the context of police interrogation, a suspect has been "interrogated" and therefore should have received her *Miranda* warnings when the police should have known that their words or actions are deemed "reasonably likely to evoke an incriminating response from a suspect." *RHODE ISLAND V. INNIS,* 446 U.S. 291, 296 (1980). In applying the standard, however, courts have not taken into consideration the likelihood that women may be more likely to acquiesce to police questioning.

Gender also plays a role in the criminal justice system with respect to the identities of both the victims and the alleged perpetrators of crime. In 2005, more than 87 percent of homicide perpetrators were male, and 75 percent of homicide victims were male. But the relationship between the victim and the offender differs for male and female victims: 30 percent of female homicide victims were murdered by a spouse or other intimate partner, while the same was true for only 5 percent of male homicide victims. Moreover, about two-thirds of women who are victims of VIOLENT CRIME are harmed by an acquaintance, intimate partner, or other FAMILY member. The same is true for only one-third of men. And about 20 percent of nonfatal violent crime against women is perpetrated by intimate partners, as compared with only about 3 percent of nonfatal violent crime against men. Unsurprisingly, the vast majority of victims of rape, sexual assault, and DOMESTIC VIOLENCE are women. Indeed, the UNIFORM CRIME REPORTING PROGRAM of the FBI defines rape specifically with respect to women, as "the carnal knowledge of a female forcibly and against her will." Men, however, are a small but increasingly visible minority of rape victims.

A study conducted in the mid-1990s found that nearly 25 percent of women had been raped or physically assaulted by a current or former spouse, cohabiting partner, or dating partner at some point in their lifetimes. In raw numbers, about 1.3 million women are assaulted by an intimate partner annually. Only about two-thirds of these incidents are reported to law enforcement. Domestic violence is costly from a financial perspective: One study found that about 15 percent of the total cost of crime is attributable to domestic violence incidents. Encouragingly, judicial remedies appear to be effective in many instances, with 84 percent of women reporting that the domestic violence ceased after they obtained a civil protection order.

The perpetration of many criminal activities is strongly correlated with gender. Overall, men are more likely to be ARRESTED for crimes. In 2004, 76.2 percent of people arrested for all offenses were men, while 82.1 percent of people arrested for violent crimes were also men. Women are arrested most frequently for offenses related to drug use, and a large percentage of arrests of women are for offenses secondarily related to drug use, such as PROSTITUTION and THEFT. Moreover, drug use is correlated with arrest for other crimes, with between 30 percent and 85 percent of women testing positive for an illegal narcotic substance at the time of arrest.

Gender may also play a role at the sentencing phase. Research conducted while the SENTENCING GUIDELINES were mandatory has found that women receive an average 5.51 fewer months in jail than their male counterparts when researchers controlled for offense level and type, criminal history, and JURISDICTION. This finding persisted even when researchers controlled for education,

Imprisonment Rate in the United States by Gender, 1925–2008

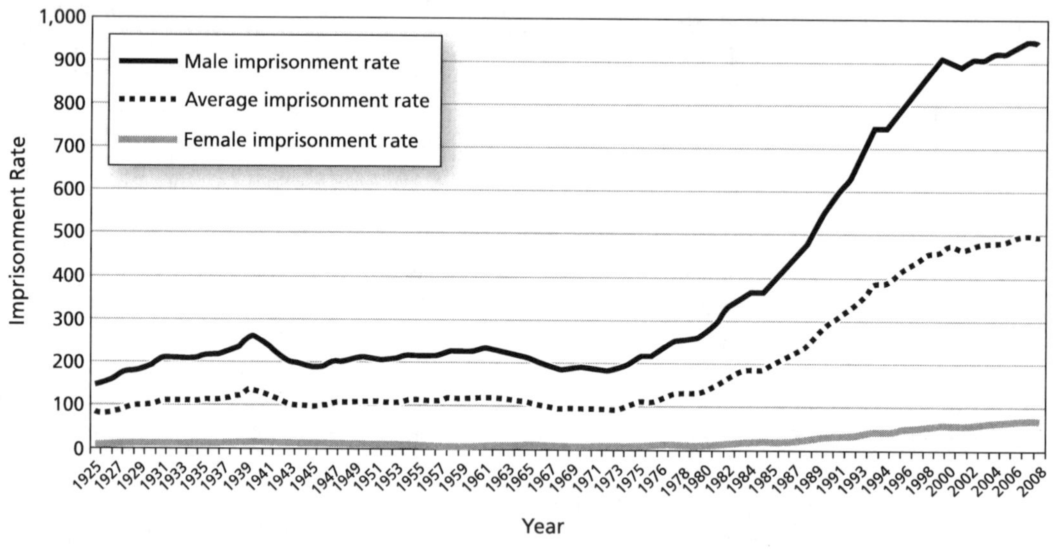

Note: Imprisonment rate is defined by the Bureau of Justice Statistics as the number of prisoners sentenced to more than one year under state or federal jurisdiction per 100,000 U.S. residents. It does not include jail inmates.

Source: Bureau of Justice Statistics

Gay Pride March '77 (Library of Congress)

income, CITIZENSHIP, age, and number of dependents. The reason underlying the finding, however, is complex. The explanation may involve factors including victim demographics, judicial ideology, accomplice status, and prosecutorial DISCRETION.

Finally, with respect to PUNISHMENT, men are much more likely to be incarcerated than women, with about eight times as many men currently imprisoned as women. Women, however, are the fastest-growing demographic in prisons in the United States. Although the number of both male and female prisoners has increased over the past 30 years, the rate of incarceration for women has increased at nearly double the rate for men since 1980. New drug policies have especially affected incarceration rates for women. Nearly one in three women in prison today is serving a sentence for a drug-related crime.

For more information

Heimer, Karen, and Candace Kruttschnitt, eds. *Gender and Crime: Patterns in Victimization and Offending.* New York: New York University Press, 2006.

Tjaden, Patricia, and Nancy Thoennes. *Prevalence, Incidence, and Consequences of Violence against Women: Findings from the National Violence against Women Survey.* Washington, D.C.: U.S. Department of Justice, National Institute of Justice, 1998.

Nancy Leong
William and Mary School of Law

Gibbons v. Ogden 22 U.S. 1 (1824) *Gibbons v. Ogden* is the case in which the Supreme Court held that the national government's power to legislate in the area of commerce is very broad.

Gibbons was the first case in which the Supreme Court attempted to interpret THE COMMERCE CLAUSE of the U.S. CONSTITUTION. The Court, in an opinion written by Justice Marshall, held that the monopoly granted by the New York legislature to Robert Fulton and Robert Livingston regarding steamboat navigation in the waters of New York violated Article I, section 8 of the Constitution, which gives Congress the "Power . . . To regulate Commerce . . . among the several States."

The case arose when Ogden, a successor to the monopoly rights held by Livingston and Fulton, filed suit in the New York courts seeking an INJUNCTION against Gibbons's operation of a steamboat that ran from New York City to Elizabethtown, New Jersey. The highest court in New York to hear the case upheld the request for an injunction, holding that the license granted to Gibbons by the U.S. government to navigate the waters of any particular state did not preempt the New York state legislature's grant of the monopoly. In his appeal to the United States Supreme Court, Gibbons argued that the state had no right to grant the monopoly because navigation is commerce among the states and therefore only Congress can legislate on that subject.

The case raised several important issues. First, what is interstate commerce; second, what is the extent of Congress's power to regulate interstate commerce; and third, what is the effect on the states as a result of the Constitution's express grant of power in this area to Congress? Marshall's opinion clearly resolves the first two questions, but it only hints at the answer to the third.

In answer to the first question, Marshall wrote that commerce is not just buying and selling, but that it comprehends "every species of commercial intercourse." Marshall went on to note that such an expansive definition of commerce encompasses navigation.

As to the second question, Marshall opined that Congress's power was "complete in itself, may be exercised to its utmost extent, and acknowledges no limitations other than are prescribed in the Constitution." In other words, Congress possessed the power "to prescribe the rule by which commerce is to be governed."

Marshall's answer to the third question is as hazy as the answers to the first questions are clear. Marshall wrote that the argument that the commerce power was exclusive, meaning that the states had no authority to regulate in the area of commerce, had "great force." However, he avoided answering the question definitively by finding that the New York legislature's grant of a monopoly was in conflict with the federal statute under which Gibbons operated his steamboats, and therefore the New York legislation violated the supremacy clause and was thus not enforceable.

By not providing a definitive answer to the third question, Marshall left open the possibility that some state legislation in the area of commerce would be tolerated, thus avoiding huge controversy for the Supreme Court. Marshall's opinion in *Gibbons* is widely viewed as a classic display of his foresight and keen political sense.

For more information

McCloskey, Robert G. (as revised by Sanford Levinson). *The American Supreme Court.* Chicago: University of Chicago Press, 1994.

White, G. Edward. *The Marshall Court and Cultural Change 1815–1835* (abridged edition). New York: Oxford University Press, 1991.

Michael H. Walsh
Senior Lecturer, Political Science Dept.
Loyola University, Chicago

Gideon v. Wainwright 372 U.S. 335 (1963)

In *Gideon v. Wainwright,* the U.S. Supreme Court held that an indigent defendant charged with a serious crime under state law has a Fourteenth Amendment right to be provided a government-appointed attorney.

The SIXTH AMENDMENT states, "In all criminal prosecutions, the accused shall enjoy the right . . . to have the Assistance of Counsel for his defence." Like other parts of the BILL OF RIGHTS, the Sixth Amendment does not protect a defendant accused of a crime under state law. The Sixth Amendment technically applies only to the federal government. *BARRON V. BALTIMORE,* 32 U.S. 243 (1833). Thus, the Supreme Court's decision in *Johnson V. Zerbst,* 304 U.S. 458 (1938), announcing a Sixth Amendment RIGHT TO COUNSEL for indigent defendants, did not affect state criminal procedure.

In a series of 20th-century decisions, however, the Supreme Court held that the DUE PROCESS clause of the Fourteenth Amendment limits state government power in ways similar to, if not exactly like, the Bill of Rights' limits on federal power. This phenomenon is referred to as the process of "INCORPORATION." Before *Gideon,* the Supreme Court wrestled with the question of whether and how the Sixth Amendment's assistance-of-counsel language applied to state criminal defendants through the Fourteenth Amendment. For example, the Supreme Court held that there was a due process right to appointment of counsel in specific state criminal cases that were seen as egregious miscarriages of justice. *POWELL V. ALABAMA,* 287 U.S. 45 (1932). Between 1932 and 1963, the Court also adopted a rule requiring assistance of counsel for indigent defendants in all state capital (i.e., death penalty) cases.

The major pre-*Gideon* PRECEDENT regarding assistance of counsel in state cases was *Betts v. Brady,* 316 U.S. 455 (1942). In *Betts,* the Supreme Court was asked to hold that the Fourteenth Amendment mirror the Sixth Amendment and require the appointment of counsel for indigent criminal defendants in all state cases. Instead, the *Betts* Court, based on a review of historical material, determined that appointment of counsel was not "essential for a fair trial" in every case. The question of whether denial of counsel violated due process was to be decided on a case-by-case basis, examining "the totality of facts in a given case." A defendant's due process rights were violated only if denial of counsel was "a denial of fundamental fairness, shocking to the universal sense of justice . . ."

The *Gideon* decision overruled *Betts,* replacing case-by-case analysis with a bright-line standard and making assistance-of-counsel doctrine consistent across federal and state criminal procedure. The Court reasoned that it is highly likely in all cases that a proper defense requires the sophisticated understanding of criminal law and procedure possessed by an attorney. Absent assistance of counsel, a person's legitimate defense may be obscured or lost in a procedural and substantive thicket. As stated by Justice Harlan in his concurring opinion, "The Court has come to recognize, in other words, that the mere existence of a serious criminal charge constituted in itself special circumstances requiring the services of counsel at trial."

Clarence Earl Gideon was accused of a FELONY, breaking and entering (a pool hall) with INTENT to commit a MISDEMEANOR. Denied his request for an attorney, Gideon conducted his own defense at trial. He was convicted and sentenced to five years in prison. After losing several APPEALS in the Florida court system, the U.S. Supreme Court accepted his case, always a rare event, and assigned Gideon an attorney to assist him. That attorney, Abe Fortas, later would become an associate justice of the Supreme Court.

The *Gideon* decision is one of the hallmarks of the WARREN COURT expansion of criminal procedure rights. It is notable, however, that the case largely tracked, rather than cut against, public opinion, at the time it was handed down. An indication of this is the fact that 22 states filed amici BRIEFS supporting Gideon's position, while only two states supported Florida's position. Furthermore, Gideon's story resonated culturally as a symbol of American determination and JUSTICE. It was immortalized by the contemporaneous publication of *Gideon's Trumpet*, Anthony Lewis's account of the case.

For more information

Lewis, Anthony. *Gideon's Trumpet*. New York: Random House, 1964.

Powe, Jr., Lucas A. *The Warren Court and American Politics*. Cambridge, Mass.: Belknap Press of Harvard University Press, 2000.

James Daniel Fisher
Edinboro University of Pennsylvania

Ginsburg, Ruth Bader (1933–) Supreme Court justice Ruth Bader Ginsburg is a leading legal advocate for women's rights and the second woman to be appointed to the Supreme Court.

Although Ginsburg graduated at the top of her 1959 class at Columbia Law School, Supreme Court Justice FELIX FRANKFURTER turned her down for a clerkship, considering a woman clerk unthinkable. No law firm in New York City would hire her either, but a federal district court JUDGE chose her as his clerk.

She subsequently taught at Rutgers Law School, where some of her students asked her to offer a course on women and the law. Surprised at how little had been written about the subject, she and two colleagues put together one of the nation's first casebooks on gender-based discrimination (1974).

At the same time, Ginsburg was helping to create and direct the ACLU Women's Rights Project. She argued six major Supreme Court gender equality cases for it between 1973 and 1979, winning five of them and remaking U.S. law in the process (*FRONTIERO V. RICHARDSON*, 1973; *Kahn v. Shevin*, 1974; *Edwards v. Healy*, 1975; *Weinberger v. Wiesenfeld*, 1975; *Califano v. Goldfarb*, 1977; *Duren v. Missouri*, 1979).

One of her goals was to persuade the Court to view gender-based legal distinctions as suspect on their face. It was a difficult task. "The response I got when I talked about sex-based discrimination," she recalls, "was 'What are you talking about? Women are treated ever so much better than men.'"

The pervasiveness of that assumption led Ginsburg to utilize a cautious and incremental approach with the Court. She selected a number of cases with male plaintiffs to show the justices that when working women were discriminated against, it was their FAMILIES, husbands included, who suffered. While the Court did not go as far as she would have liked, it did create a somewhat tighter standard for evaluating whether gender-based laws were constitutional.

Justice Ruth Bader Ginsburg (Hulton Archive)

President Jimmy Carter named Ginsburg to the D.C. Circuit Court of Appeals in 1981. She made a solid record there as a hardworking and nonideological "judge's judge," and when President Bill Clinton nominated her to the Supreme Court in 1993, she was confirmed by a Senate vote of 97-3.

Throughout her career she has concentrated on the real people involved in a case. As an advocate, she frequently began an argument before the Supreme Court by telling the story of the plaintiff and the discrimination he or she had suffered; her opinions from the bench emphasize the facts and human dimensions of a case as well as legal principles. As a judge she has tended to respect PRECEDENT and to support the government's power to regulate. She favors leaving policy matters to the president and legislature, although she has written that "when political avenues for redressing political problems become dead-end streets, some judicial intervention in the politics of the people may be essential in order to have any effective politics."

One of the crowning moments of Ginsburg's career came in 1996, when she wrote the Supreme Court's opinion ordering the Virginia Military Institute to admit women *(U.S. v. Virginia)*. In it, she drew on the precedents she had gotten the Court to set in her days as an advocate and took them further to establish a new and more stringent standard for the adjudication of gender discrimination cases.

During her tenure on the Supreme Court, Ginsburg has generally voted with the liberal bloc. She has taken a lead in supporting reproductive and GAY RIGHTS, opposing the death penalty, and supporting laws banning discrimination.

For more information

Merritt, Deborah Jones. "Hearing the Voices of Individual Women and Men: Justice Ruth Bader Ginsburg," *Hawaii Law Review* 20 (1998): 635.

Rosen, Jeffrey. "The New Look of Liberalism on the Court," *New York Times Magazine,* 5 October 1997.

Philippa Strum
City University of New York

Gitlow v. New York 268 U.S. 652 (1925) *Gitlow v. New York* was the first Supreme Court decision to hold that the BILL OF RIGHTS limited the states' power to regulate free speech and press.

Benjamin Gitlow was indicted for the FELONY of advocating criminal anarchy, defined by New York as "the doctrine that organized government should be overthrown by force or violence . . . . or by any unlawful means." Gitlow, a Socialist Party activist, arranged for the printing and distribution of the party's "Manifesto," which advocated "proletarian revolutionary struggle" and a "mass political strike" directed at "the overthrow of the political organization upon which capitalistic exploitation depends."

Gitlow's lawyers argued that the statute was unconstitutional. The Fourteenth Amendment to the CONSTITUTION prohibits states from denying anyone "life, liberty, or property without DUE PROCESS of law." One of the elements of the liberty protected, Gitlow contended, was liberty of speech and press, as it was referred to in the First Amendment ("Congress shall make no law . . . abridging the FREEDOM OF SPEECH, or of the press"). Speech was a right that could be restrained only when its exercise was likely to cause a substantive evil. As the statute did not require a showing of such a connection between speech and an illegal result, it was unconstitutional.

The argument was rejected by the courts of New York. The case reached a Supreme Court that had adopted Justice OLIVER WENDELL HOLMES's formulation in *SCHENCK V. UNITED STATES* (1919) that Congress could punish speech if it constituted a "clear and present danger." Justice Edward T. Sanford, writing for the Court, relied on that in rejecting Gitlow's APPEAL. It was up to the legislature to decide if the articulation of particular ideas constituted a clear and present danger, he declared, and by passing the statute, New York had declared speech like Gitlow's to be such a danger.

Justices Holmes and Brandeis dissented, saying there was no clear and present danger here. Rejecting Sanford's holding that the manifesto was an incitement rather than mere advocacy, Holmes wrote, "Every idea is an incitement," because it is offered in the hope that the listener will accept and act upon it. Holmes denied that the state could punish speech because of its content, for "the only meaning of free speech" as guaranteed by the Constitution was that Gitlow's speech had to be allowed in the absence of a "present danger of an attempt to overthrow the government by force."

While Gitlow went to prison, his case was important because the entire Supreme Court agreed in it that the Fourteenth Amendment's due process clause protects the rights of speech and press from state action. Until then, the law had been that the First Amendment limited the powers only of Congress, not the states. In subsequent years the new doctrine would be utilized to minimize state restrictions on speech. *Gitlow* would be heralded as the case that began the process of INCORPORATING most of the Bill of Rights into the Fourteenth Amendment's due process clause, thereby extending protection against CIVIL LIBERTIES violations by the states as well as the federal government.

For more information

Murphy, Paul L. *The Shaping of the First Amendment: 1791 to the Present.* New York: Oxford University Press, 1992.

Wermiel, Stephen J. "Rights in the Modern Era: Applying the Bill of Rights to the States," *William & Mary Bill of Rights Journal* 1 (1992): 121.

Philippa Strum
City University of New York

graffiti Graffiti includes unauthorized writing, marks, or images placed on buildings, vehicles, or other private or public structures. Graffiti is often associated with illegal activity, GANGS, or as a form of criminal communication to mark or tag territory. Many communities find graffiti a problem and seek to regulate it through the CRIMINAL JUSTICE SYSTEM.

Early examples of graffiti date to primeval times. Drawings of bison and deer found in caves are examples of graffiti left by prehistoric humans. This graffiti often depicted ceremonial or sacred locations. Other examples of early graffiti date to ancient Greece and the Roman Empire. In addition to ceremonial significance, graffiti from this time included politics, humor, and other characteristics associated with contemporary graffiti.

The Kilroy image American soldiers drew on the walls of the cities they occupied during World War II was an example of the "I was here" form of graffiti. Similarly, tags or throw-ups, the most common type of graffiti, may be limited to the signatures of graffiti writers intending to leave their mark. These tags are not intended to communicate territory or control. In contrast, gang graffiti can be used to mark territory. More intricate graffiti, including images or murals, may range from temporary statements to more permanent representations of community and cultural pride.

Graffiti has traditionally been used to make political statements, although this type of graffiti became much more common in the 1960s, perhaps as a result of social unrest. As a form of VANDALISM, or communication, graffiti is exercised by marginal groups who are denied legitimate outlets to communicate frustrations or disapproval with the status quo. Graffiti is also an important tool for cultural communication. Building on the political expressions of the 1960s, graffiti has more recently been associated with hip-hop culture. The mainstream public has been introduced to hip-hop graffiti through references in films, music, fashion, and other forms of communication. This exposure has provided opportunities for taggers to move from the underground world to museums. Graffiti has also moved from temporary to permanence as artists are recognized and commissioned to create "legitimate" forms of artistic expression.

Graffiti has also attracted increasing interest from the criminal justice system, perhaps as a result of the association with political and cultural communication. Local laws intended to restrict graffiti focus on vandalism rather than expression, often arguing that graffiti is detrimental to the safety and welfare of the public, reduces the value of private property, invites vandalism and additional graffiti, and encourages other criminal activities, eventually producing urban blight. Cities that have adopted a BROKEN WINDOWS approach to crime control argue that graffiti, along with other signs of vandalism, lead to increased lawlessness. This perspective has resulted in graffiti laws that are overbroad, vague, and an infringement on FREEDOM SPEECH. For example, in *Ecko Complex LLP v. Bloomberg,* 382 F.Supp.2d 627 (S.D.N.Y. 2005), the Court ruled that it is a violation of the First Amendment to refuse to issue a permit based on the fear that a legal display or graffiti could encourage others to paint graffiti.

Graffiti-control efforts also include architectural or environmental features such as graffiti-resistant finishes, monitoring, and other forms of target hardening. Police may also target areas where graffiti is common. Many communities have passed graffiti abatement ordinances that call for quick removal or covering of graffiti. Business owners also remove graffiti out of concerns about intimidating patrons or creating or allowing a hostile work environment. Laws may also restrict access to spray paint and other supplies. As the artistic merit of graffiti writers becomes accepted, communities have also created legal alternatives such as approved graffiti walls or other public spaces that highlight the work of graffiti writers.

For more information

Castleman, C. *Getting Up: Subway Graffiti in New York City.* Cambridge, Mass.: MIT Press, 1982.

Ferrell, J. *Crimes of Style: Urban Graffiti and the Politics of Criminality.* New York: Garland, 1993.

Ferrell, J. "Culture, Crime, and Cultural Criminology," *Journal of Criminal Justice and Popular Culture,* 3, no. 2 (1995).

Kurlansky, M., and N. Mailer. *The Faith of Graffiti.* Westport, Conn.: Praeger, 1974.

Kenneth Mentor
University of North Carolina at Pembroke

Graham v. Connor 490 U.S. 386 (1989) In *Graham v. Connor,* the Court ruled that the FOURTH AMENDMENT covers a claim that law enforcement personnel used excessive force in making an ARREST or stop. The case is important because in it the U.S. Supreme Court articulated the legal standard for determining when law enforcement officials have used excessive non-lethal force.

On November 12, 1984, Dethorne Graham, a diabetic, experienced an insulin reaction. He asked a friend, William Berry, to drive him to a convenience store so that he could purchase some orange juice to counter the reaction. Graham walked into the store, saw a long line, panicked, rushed out of the store, and asked Berry to drive him to a friend's house instead. Officer M.S. Connor of the Charlotte, North Carolina, Police Department saw Graham quickly enter and leave the convenience store. Suspicious of Graham's motives, Connor followed Berry's car and stopped it. Berry told Connor that Graham suffered from a medical condition. Connor ordered Berry and Graham to wait while he called for backup. Graham exited the car, ran around it twice, sat down on the curb, and briefly passed out. Another Charlotte police officer ignored Berry's request to get sugar for Graham and instead handcuffed Graham.

The police believed that Graham was drunk. Several officers then lifted Graham and placed him facedown on the hood of Berry's car. When Graham awoke and asked officers to check his wallet for a diabetic decal that he carried, the police told him to "shut up" and shoved his face against the hood. Four officers then grabbed Graham and threw him headfirst into the police car. When one of Graham's friends brought orange juice, the police refused to allow him to have it. When Connor learned that nothing had happened at the convenience store, the police drove Graham to his home and released him. After his encounter with the police, Graham had a broken foot, cuts on his wrists, a bruised forehead, and an injured shoulder as well as loud ringing in his ear.

Graham charged the police had used excessive force in violation of the Fourteenth Amendment. He lost at the district court level on the grounds that the officers had used an appropriate amount of force under the circumstances. A divided COURT OF APPEALS upheld the decision because the force applied was not constitutionally excessive. On May 15, 1989, CHIEF JUSTICE WILLIAM REHNQUIST delivered the opinion of the Supreme Court. Other courts had concluded that there is a generic right to be free from excessive force, but the Court rejected this notion. Rehnquist explained that all claims that law enforcement used excessive force should be analyzed under the Fourth Amendment and its reasonableness standard rather than a substantive DUE PROCESS approach. The Fourth Amendment explicitly protects against physically intrusive governmental conduct while the substantive due process provision is too generalized.

Specifically, the Court stated in *Graham* that nondeadly force is that which is neither likely nor intended to result in death or great bodily harm. In determining whether law enforcement officials used excessive nondeadly force, they declared that all claims would be examined under the Fourth Amendment. The legal standard is objective reasonableness to determine application of the Fourth Amendment. Objective reasonableness was determined by a fourfold standard based on the perspective of a reasonable officer with 20/20 hindsight. These factors consider: (1) Was the suspect an immediate threat to officers or others; (2) severity of the crime; (3) was the suspect actively resisting arrest; and (4) was the suspect attempting to escape. If in applying these four factors a court does not determine the use of nonlethal force was reasonable, it is a violation of the Fourth Amendment and the person administering the force may be personally liable.

Connor is an important case that seeks to draw lines between the use of excessive and permissible use of nondeadly force by law enforcement officials. While criticized by some as opening the police up to personal liability, it is also an important case to limit police DISCRETION and protect citizens.

For more information

Avery, Isaac T., III, and Mary Easley. *Legal Aspects of Police Supervision.* Incline Village, Nev.: Copperhouse, 1997.

Kappeler, Victor E. *Police Civil Liability: Supreme Court Cases and Materials.* Prospect Heights, Ill.: Waveland Press, 2007.

Caryn E. Neumann
Miami University of Ohio

grand jury A grand jury is a group of citizens, usually selected from lists of registered voters and drivers, whose task it is to decide whether a PROSECUTOR has presented enough EVIDENCE against a person accused of a crime to justify a trial on the charges presented. If the grand jury decides that there is sufficient evidence for a trial, it issues an "indictment" (a.k.a. a "true bill"), and the prosecution is permitted to go forward.

An indictment expresses no opinion on the guilt or innocence of the accused; it merely states the grand jury's conclusion that the prosecutor has presented sufficient evidence of criminal behavior to justify a trial. If a trial is held, a separate group of people, known as a "PETIT" JURY, will hear the evidence and render a verdict.

The term "grand jury" refers merely to the size of the accusatory body, which has historically been larger than the petit jury. Today, state grand juries can have as few as five and as many as 23 members, while federal grand juries have between 16 and 23 members. A grand jury's term can last from one month to one year, but a typical term lasts three months, during which time the grand jurors meet periodically to consider cases that the prosecutor presents to them, and to conduct other investigations. A court can extend a grand jury's term if the grand jury is conducting a major investigation, such as one of ORGANIZED CRIME or official corruption.

The grand jury's major task is to evaluate the evidence that the prosecutor presents to it in order to decide whether or not to issue an indictment. Toward that end, it can issue a reluctant witness a SUBPOENA, which requires the recipient to appear before the grand jury, and it can offer the witness IMMUNITY from prosecution in exchange for testimony. A witness who refuses to testify before the grand jury despite a grant of immunity is subject to a citation for "CONTEMPT of court," which can result in the witness being jailed until either the witness testifies or the grand jury's term ends. A grand jury proceeding is unlike a trial. There is no JUDGE present; only the prosecutors, the witness, and the grand jurors are present. The prosecutor directs the process, and the grand jurors hear only the prosecutor's version of the evidence, as no defendant(s), defense witnesses, or DEFENSE ATTORNEYS are present. This arrangement gives the prosecutor an enormous advantage in the search for an indictment, and, more than 95 percent of the time, it results in a decision by the grand jury to return an indictment. After the grand jurors consider the evidence presented, if a majority (e.g., twelve of twenty-three federal grand jurors) votes to indict, it issues a "true bill," which forms the basis for prosecution; if a majority votes not to indict, it issues a "no bill," which ends the case.

In the FEDERAL COURT SYSTEM, a grand jury is constitutionally required to indict an accused before a prosecution can proceed. That is not true in most states, though; indeed, most states do not use grand jury indictments to determine that there is sufficient evidence for a trial. In 30 states, most or all prosecutions begin by means of an "information," which is a document in which the prosecutor argues that there is enough evidence against the accused to warrant prosecution. A judge scrutinizes the information at a "preliminary hearing," where the judge must decide whether there is "PROBABLE CAUSE" to believe that a crime occurred and that the accused committed it. If the prosecutor's case satisfies the judge, the judge will approve the information, and the prosecution will go forward.

The current predominance of the information procedure reflects the controversial nature of grand juries, which do not live up to their promise. There are two traditional arguments in support of grand juries. One argument is that they check prosecutors who would otherwise harass innocent persons for political or personal reasons. Another argument is that they force prosecutors to gather enough evidence to justify holding a criminal trial. There is some truth to these arguments, but not as much as their supporters think there is. Moreover, there is substantial evidence that prosecutors so dominate the grand jury process that a grand jury's check on prosecutorial bad faith, laziness, or incompetence is likely to be minimal. Still, grand juries are an established institution in U.S. law and are likely to remain so indefinitely.

For more information

Neubauer, David W. *Judicial Process: Law, Courts, and Politics in the United States.* 2nd ed. Fort Worth, Tex.: Harcourt Brace College, 1997.

Schmalleger, Frank. *Criminal Justice Today: An Introductory Text for the Twenty-First Century.* 4th ed. Englewood Cliffs, N.J.: Prentice Hall, 1996.

Brian L. Porto
Vermont Law School

Green v. New Kent County School Board

391 U.S. 430 (1968) *Green v. New Kent County School Board* was the most important Supreme Court case dealing with school desegregation after BROWN V. BOARD OF EDUCATION in 1954.

In 1954 the Supreme Court declared racially segregated public schools unconstitutional under the Fourteen Amendment's EQUAL PROTECTION clause. A year later the Court sought to give courts and school boards guidance by requiring the dismantling of racially segregated schools "with all deliberate speed" (*Brown v. Board of Education* [II], 349 U.S. 294, at 301 [1955]). In *Green* the Court repudiated *Brown*'s 13-year-old strategy and moved from demanding an end to SEGREGATION to demanding the immediate integration of public schools.

New Kent was a lightly populated rural county in Virginia whose county school board participated in the South's resistance to court-ordered desegregation of its public schools. Threatened by the withdrawal of federal moneys for segregated public schools, the school board introduced a "freedom-of-choice plan" in 1965 allowing students to choose to attend either the formerly all-white New Kent School or the formerly all-black Watkins School. After three years no white student attended Watkins School and only 15 percent of the county's black students attended New Kent.

Justice Brennan, writing for a unanimous Court, held that "it is against this background" of resistance to *Brown* that school boards had an "affirmative duty to take whatever steps might be necessary to convert to a unitary system in which racial discrimination would be eliminated root and branch" (437–38). Brennan dismissed the "freedom-of-choice" plan as a mere token effort, impermissibly transferring the burden of dismantling the outlawed dual school system from the school board to the students (441–42). The school board must "fashion steps which promise realistically to convert promptly to a system without a 'white' school and a 'Negro' school, but just schools" (442).

The finding in *Green* was later expanded to include state action hindering desegregation even though there was no discriminatory motive or purpose (*Wright v. Council of the City of Emporia,* 407 U.S. 501 [1972]). *Green*'s emphasis on achieving racial balance eventually led the Court in SWANN V. CHARLOTTE-MECKLENBURG BOARD OF EDUCATION (402 U.S. 1 [1971]) to approve school busing.

Justice Rehnquist, dissenting in *Keyes v. Denver School District No. 1,* 413 U.S. 189, 254 (1973), challenged what he considered to be *Green*'s mandate for racial balance in public schools. While never winning a majority for his position, in 1991 the now CHIEF JUSTICE Rehnquist made the issue irrelevant when he wrote for a majority of the Court that once a school district eliminated "the vestiges of prior discrimination," it no longer had to maintain racial balance (OKLAHOMA CITY BOARD OF EDUCATION V. DOWELL, 498 U.S. 237, at 250 [1991]).

For more information

Kluger, Richard A. *Simple Justice: The History of* Brown v. Board of Education *and Black America's Struggle for Equality.* New York: Knopf, 1975.

Timothy J. O'Neill
Southwestern University

Gregg v. Georgia

428 U.S. 153 (1976) In *Gregg v. Georgia,* the U.S. Supreme Court upheld the constitutionality of CAPITAL PUNISHMENT when

implemented by states in a nonarbitrary and nondiscriminatory manner. That is, the Court ruled that capital punishment was not a violation of the EIGHTH or Fourteenth Amendments to the U.S. CONSTITUTION. The Gregg case is significant in upholding the power of states to implement capital punishment in the aftermath of *FURMAN V. GEORGIA*, 408 U.S. 238 (1972).

At issue in *Gregg v. Georgia* was a procedure through which an individual, Tony Gregg, was tried in a two-tier process: Gregg was charged and tried in the first tier to determine guilt and, upon being found guilty, he was tried in the second tier, to determine PUNISHMENT. Specifically, upon being found guilty of armed ROBBERY and MURDER (tier one), Gregg went before a JURY to determine whether he should be given life in prison or capital punishment. During the second tier proceedings, the jury was instructed to consider whether Mr. Gregg's case fit the criteria of "aggravating circumstances" when weighing the options of life imprisonment against the death penalty. Following these instructions, the jury found that Mr. Gregg had, indeed, committed "aggravating circumstances," and thus the jury handed down the sentence of death.

Justice Stewart wrote the opinion of the Court and affirmed the constitutionality of the death penalty in this case. One can discern four central points behind the Court's decision. First, the Court stated its preference for following PRECEDENT where possible; that is, the Court expressed its awareness that "history and precedent" upheld the legitimacy of capital punishment under various circumstances. Second, the Court expressed the view that legislatures were the appropriate organs of government for conveying public morality as regards capital punishment; considering that fact that 35 states had enacted death penalty statutes in recent years, the Court continued, it was clear that public norms were not violated by capital punishment.

Third, the Court expressed its disinclination to rule against capital punishment per se. Fourth, it remained only to consider whether Georgia, in the case under consideration, had successfully addressed the requirements set forth in the earlier *Furman* case—namely, the Court had to determine whether Georgia implemented capital punishment procedures in a manner that was neither arbitrary nor discriminatory. Insofar as Georgia had instituted such practices as the two-tier system and given jurors specific instructions on what constituted aggravating circumstances and had put in place automatic APPEALS in capital cases, the Court concluded that Georgia had taken steps to ensure fairness rather than randomness or discrimination in the implementation of capital punishment.

For more information

Bienen, Leigh B. "The Proportionality Review of Capital Cases by State High Courts after Gregg: Only 'the Appearance of Justice'?" *Journal of Criminal Law and Criminology* 87 (Autumn 1996): 130–314.

Bohm, Robert M. "Capital Punishment in Two Judicial Circuits in Georgia: A Description of the Key Actors and the Decision-Making Process," *Law and Human Behavior* 18 (June 1994): 319–338.

Ellen Grigsby
University of New Mexico

Griggs v. Duke Power Company 401 U.S. 424 (1971) *Griggs v. Duke Power Company* is a major early ruling holding that certain employment discrimination practices based on race violate Title VII of the Civil Rights Act of 1964.

Decided in 1971, in a unanimous decision written by CHIEF JUSTICE WARREN E. BURGER, the Supreme Court ruled for the black plaintiffs. It argued that consequences of employer practices is the key test of whether those practices fall within Equal Employment Opportunity Commission (EEOC) guidelines.

In this case, the employer used job tests that were not performance-related and had the effect of screening blacks from supervisory jobs. If employers use systematic employment discrimination practices, Title VII "required the removal of all barriers perpetuating the benefits that white employees obtain at the expense of blacks." In *Griggs* the Court held that invalid practices, however neutral in INTENT, caused a disparate impact upon a group protected by the act. The Griggs disparate impact concept was based on the court's analysis of section 702 (a) (2) of Title VII and required that tests used for hiring and promotion must be job related and validated under EEOC guidelines. In *Griggs* the Supreme Court held that the statutory standard should also be the constitutional standard. Under Title VII the EEOC exercises JURISDICTION on matters of employment discrimination and can initiate charges and enforce regulations. Often the EEOC reaches a settlement between the parties, thereby avoiding a lawsuit in FEDERAL COURT.

Following this case, lawyers became aware of Title VII as a potential remedy for claims based upon employment discrimination. The central constitutional question was whether an employer's employment practices or activities, such as preemployment tests, constituted a disparate impact or other impermissible forms of employment discrimination. These activities include those that have consequences of discrimination even if selection criteria did not intend to have discriminatory purposes.

Supreme Court decisions and congressional statutes have altered which party has the burden of proof in employment discrimination cases. *Griggs* placed that burden upon the employer and as of *Ward's Cove Packing Co.* (1989) the Court shifted that burden to the employee. Employees faced a difficult task to show EVIDENCE of racial discrimination. Congress has the authority to revise Supreme Court decisions that are based upon congressional statutory provisions. In the Civil Rights Act of 1991 Congress reversed the Court decision and required employers to sustain the burden of proof that their practices do not racially discriminate.

For more information

Griggs v. Duke Power Company, 401 U.S. 424 (1971).
Ward's Cove Packing Co. v. Antonio, 490 U.S. 642 (1989).

Steven Puro
Professor of Political Science
Saint Louis University

Griswold v. Connecticut 381 U.S. 479 (1965) *Griswold v. Connecticut* was a Supreme Court decision in which the Court recognized that the right of privacy was a fundamental constitutional right, even though it was not expressly set out in the CONSTITUTION. The Court did not address the scope of the right of privacy it its decision but did decide that the right protected married couples from governmental interference in their consensual sexual relations.

The case came to the Supreme Court after Estelle Griswold, executive director of the Planned Parenthood League of Connecticut, and Dr. C. Lee Buxton, the medical director at the League's center in New Haven, gave birth control advice and devices to married couples. Griswold and Buxton were convicted as ACCESSORIES in the violation of a Connecticut law that made it a crime to use any drug or medical device or instrument for the purposes of preventing conception. After the Connecticut appellate court upheld their convictions, they brought their case to the Supreme Court, asserting that the Connecticut law violated the Fourteenth Amendment.

In a 7-2 vote, the Supreme Court reversed the convictions and struck down the law as an unconstitutional intrusion into the right of privacy. While a majority of the Court recognized that such a right existed even though not expressly set out in the BILL OF RIGHTS, there was disagreement among the justices about the location of the right in the Constitution. In his majority opinion, Justice Douglas concluded that the right flowed from the "penumbras" of express rights provided in the First, Third, FOURTH, Fifth, and NINTH AMENDMENTS and applied to the states through the Fourteenth Amendment. These penumbras, Justice Douglas wrote, were "formed by emanations from those guarantees that help give them life and substance." They provided for a constitutionally protected zone of privacy, and the Connecticut law outlawing the use of contraceptive devices infringed on the marriage relationship that fell within the zone.

In his concurring opinion, Justice Goldberg, joined by CHIEF JUSTICE EARL WARREN and Justice WILLIAM BRENNAN, believed that the source of the right of privacy was the Ninth Amendment, because its language evidenced that fundamental rights existed although not expressly set out in the first eight amendments. By contrast, Justices Harlan and White, in their concurring opinions, believed that the Connecticut statute infringed on a right of privacy found in the DUE PROCESS clause of the Fourteenth Amendment, which protected basic values "implicit in the concept of ordered liberty."

Like the majority, the dissenters, Justice Black and Justice Stewart, were critical of the Connecticut law; however, they did not believe it infringed upon any fundamental right. They rejected the view that a right of privacy existed in the Constitution, whether under the penumbras of express rights, the Ninth Amendment, or under the Fourteenth Amendment's due process clause. To them, the recognition of a right not expressly set out in the Constitution was beyond the power of the courts.

The right of privacy recognized in *Griswold* was extended in subsequent Supreme Court decisions to other social relations, including a woman's right to choose to have an ABORTION (*ROE V. WADE*, 410 U.S. 113 [1973]). However, the status and scope of the right continue to be debated by legal scholars and among members of the Court.

For more information

Dionisopolous, P. Allan, and Craig Ducat. *The Right to Privacy: Essays and Cases*. St. Paul, Minn.: West, 1976.

Emerson, Thomas I. "Nine Justices in Search of a Doctrine," *Michigan Law Review* 64 (1965): 219–34.

Griswold v. Connecticut, 381 U.S. 479 (1965).

James N. G. Cauthen
City University of New York

group standing (also known as associational standing or third-party standing).

Group standing is a term describing the set of rules JUDGES use to decide whether a group can participate in a court case as a litigant. Sometimes a group of individuals with a similar claim against one individual or legal entity file a case and ask that it be made into a CLASS ACTION suit. This means that the characteristics the claimants have in common become the basis for a legal class. Anyone fitting those criteria specified in the definition of the class is entitled to join the suit. In other cases, groups that already exist seek to gain standing in the courts. These are usually interest groups like the NAACP (NATIONAL ASSOCIATION FOR THE ADVANCEMENT OF COLORED PEOPLE) or the Sierra Club. The members of these groups usually have something in common. That commonality may be their race, as is the case with the NAACP, or a love of the environment, like members of the Sierra Club. The groups are usually involved as litigants because they want the court to provide an interpretation of a law, or even to overturn a law. Generally we assume that the group wants this change in public policy because it would be beneficial to most of their members. Unlike the groups in class action suits, these groups exist with a membership base outside of the lawsuit. Their court involvement is only one area of the group's activities.

The term *STANDING* refers to a set of legal rules used to decide whether a particular litigant may present a specified case in court. These ground rules apply to every case filed in any court in the United States. The judicial system prefers to hear cases from people who have real disputes and not from groups who solely wish to change laws. The origin of modern standing PRECEDENT in FEDERAL COURTS comes from *Association of Data Processing Service Organizations v. Camp* (1970). Here the Supreme Court established a two-prong test for claimants who rely on the CONSTITUTION for standing. The plaintiff must (1) claim that they fall within the zone of interests protected or regulated by the relevant statute and (2) allege an injury-in-fact.

When the litigant is a group, the requirements for standing are even more stringent. The rules for third-party standing are complex. First, a group cannot gain standing by claiming that they are enforcing the rights of others. Therefore they cannot claim that they are enforcing the rights of a member of the group, rather, they must claim that the group itself has a constitutional or statutory right to be heard. In addition, group litigants have no right to prevent diffuse harms. Second, the group cannot claim that it is filing the case to prevent diffuse harms. For example, a group cannot file a case against the government alleging that they are filing to remedy infringements on the rights of all taxpayers. Finally, a group does not have a right to an undistorted market. In other words, the group cannot enter the courts simply because a change in public policy would benefit them. The access to the courts is limited to groups who are alleging that an actual injury, not simply an inequity, has resulted from the law.

The NAACP is one example of a group that has often been granted standing in the courts. The Legal Defense Fund of the NAACP gained standing as a group and fought the restrictive covenants neighborhoods put in place to block African Americans from buying houses in their area. In more recent times, a number of AIDS (acquired immunodeficiency syndrome) groups were granted standing as litigants in their efforts to expand the provisions of the AMERICANS WITH DISABILITIES ACT to include persons living with AIDS.

Groups are frequently involved in the courts. It is important to remember that before groups can participate as litigants, they must meet the stringent standing regulations discussed above.

For more information

Adler, Jonathan H. "Stand or Deliver: Citizen Suits, Standing, and Environmental Protection," *Duke Environmental Law and Policy Forum* 12 (Fall 2001): 39.

Stearns, Maxwell L. "From *Lujan* to *Laidlaw:* A Preliminary Model of Environmental Standing," *Duke Environmental Law and Policy Forum,* II (Spring 2001): 321.

Nancy Winemiller Basinger
University of Georgia

Guantánamo Bay Guantánamo Bay refers to a piece of U.S. property in Cuba that has been used as a detention facility for many individuals after the terrorist attacks in New York and Washington, D.C., on September 11, 2001. Its use generated significant legal controversy.

Guantánamo Bay, a 2.5-mile span on the southeastern corner of Cuba, is commonly used to refer to the United States operated Guantánamo Bay Detention Camp located on its shores (also referred to as Guantánamo or Gitmo). Following the Spanish-American War, American officials convinced the newly independent Cuba to include constitutional provisions for the lease of land to the United States government for a naval base, leading to the subsequent lease of 45 square miles in Guantánamo Bay. Early on, there were questions surrounding Cuban sovereignty and U.S. JURISDICTION in the area, and more recently the George W. Bush administration came under attack for its strategic use of the Guantánamo Bay facility as a means to avoid JUDICIAL REVIEW on the status of detainees.

Following Cuba's communist revolution and Fidel Castro's rise to power, diplomatic tensions regarding the base steadily increased. Originally, the station served as a strategic logistics base for the U.S. Navy; however, in 1991, their mission expanded as the facility took on 34,000 Haitian refugees following a violent coup. During operations related to the influx of refugees,

A detainee at Guantánamo Bay (GITMO) prison in Cuba (David P. Coleman/U.S. Department of Defense)

several camps were set up to house migrants, including Camp X-Ray, a camp that would later gain worldwide attention as a holding facility for al-Qaeda and Taliban detainees following the events of September 11, 2001, and subsequent executive orders that allowed the U.S. military to detain noncitizens involved in terrorist activities. Reportedly, detainees were moved to Guantánamo on a recommendation from the DEPARTMENT OF JUSTICE, which claimed that the facility was considered outside U.S. legal jurisdiction. The camp began receiving detainees in 2002, and almost immediately concerns of overcrowding and inhumane treatment plagued the temporary facility. Within the year, construction of the more permanent Camp Delta was approved for the purpose of detaining suspects relevant to the war on terror, and Camp X-Ray was closed. The interrogations and related operations are run by Joint Task Force Guantánamo (JTF-GTMO), and security is provided by U.S. Army Military Police. At least 520 prisoners are reported to be detained at Guantánamo, only a few of which have been charged.

Both the facilities and judicial proceedings at Guantánamo have recently come under public scrutiny as a result of some high-profile court cases. In *Al Odah v. United States*, 542 U.S. 46 (2004), which incorporated numerous HABEAS CORPUS petitions, the Court ruled that detainees do indeed have the right to challenge their captivity in civil courts despite legislative obstacles to doing so. The Bush administration's argument that detainees were not entitled to protections under the Geneva Conventions came under fire following a highly publicized 2006 Supreme Court ruling, *HAMDI v. RUMSFELD*, 542 U.S. 507 (2004), which confirmed the prisoner's minimal protections as set forth under Common Article 3 in the Geneva Conventions, which requires humane treatment and fair trial. In response to this ruling, the Bush administration initiated the Combatant Status Review Tribunal (CSRT), which sought to circumvent the requirements of the Geneva Conventions by classifying detainees as enemy combatants. Shortly afterward in *Boumediene v. Bush*, 553 U.S. 723 (2008), the Supreme Court ruled that prisoners being held at Guantánamo were entitled to protections as dictated by the U.S. CONSTITUTION and that the CSRT was inadequate for such purposes.

In January 2009, in response to an international outcry over Guantánamo Bay's legality and inhumane treatment of detainees, President Barack Obama signed an order that suspended the proceedings of the facility's military commission, ended the Central Intelligence Agency's secret interrogations, and set the stage for the detention facility to be closed within the year. On May 19, 2009, the Senate refused to appropriate the $80 million request from President Obama for the purpose of closing detention facilities at Guantánamo Bay. That move left the president's plan to close the camps by 2010 in limbo. The eventual fate of this facility remains uncertain.

For more information

Herszenhorn, David M. "Democrats in Senate Block Money to Close Guantánamo." *New York Times* (19 May 2009).

Margulies, Joseph. *Guantánamo and the Abuse of Presidential Power.* New York: Simon and Schuster, 2006.

Kathleen Searles
Washington State University

guardian ad litem Guardian ad litem is a special guardian for a minor child who is appointed by the court in connection with a particular litigation. The guardian ad litem is very different from a regular guardian. A guardian, or custodian, has physical custody of the child. The guardian makes decisions regarding where the child will live and go to school and provides all monetary support for the child. The guardian ad litem has a relationship with the child that is limited in scope and duration. He or she simply advises the court on what is in a child's best interests. The words *ad litem* mean "for the lawsuit."

The guardian ad litem is charged with performing assigned duties competently and should be prompt and diligent and give attention to detail in making recommendations to the court regarding the child's best interests and has great leeway in doing so. Guardians are entitled to receive copies of all pleadings, notices, discovery, and correspondence relating to the child (the same as any party to the litigation). They can independently conduct investigations on behalf of the child by interviewing specialists such as physicians, psychologists, counselors, or other treatment providers who were involved with the child. The guardian can review records, talk to the police or agency officials concerning the child, and should interview and have regular contact with the child. They may take information obtained during the investigation to experts or specialists in order to obtain further recommendations on what is best for the child. The guardian can also monitor agencies that were court ordered to provide services to the child to assure that orders of the court are being followed. They can act as a buffer, shielding the child from insensitive questioning and preventing the child from feeling that he or she is at the heart of the controversy. A guardian assures that the child's wishes are heard. In short, the guardian ad litem is the ears and eyes of the court in determining what is in the best interests of the child.

At the conclusion of the investigation and prior to trial, the guardian makes a written report to the court. The JUDGE is not bound to follow the recommendations of the guardian, but usually the court gives the report great consideration. The guardian makes his or her own decision about what is best for the child. They do not work in conjunction with any agencies or for the court.

The recommendation of the guardian to the court might not be exactly what the child wants. In some circumstances, the guardian may require independent representation. This is normally reserved for cases where the guardian and the child, who is of sufficient age and mental maturity, have a material conflict in position or interest. A guardian ad litem does not have to be a lawyer and does not perform this role for the child. If the guardian is not a lawyer, the court may also appoint counsel to represent the child's legal interests. Any person who possesses good judgment and common sense can be a guardian ad litem. In most states guardians must complete a training program and be certified before being permitted to act on behalf of a child. The court may waive the training qualification upon finding the guardian is qualified due to prior service or is otherwise qualified.

The guardian ad litem will be expected to continue their assigned duties until the litigation is concluded or until relieved by the court. Guardians may be removed from a case, upon proper motion to the court, if they are not acting in the child's best interest. The decision to remove would be made by a judge or other hearing officer assigned to the case.

Guardians may be volunteers, appointed by the court, or hired through private means. If the guardian is court-appointed, he or she will be awarded a reasonable fee for their services in an amount to be determined by the court and paid from public funds.

For more information

Alschuler, Jain N., et al. *The Guardian Ad Litem Handbook*. Madison, Wis.: ATS-CLE, State Bar of Wisconsin, 1987 (loose-leaf supplementation).

Heartz, Rebecca H. "Guardians Ad Litem in Child Abuse and Neglect Proceedings: Clarifying the Roles to Improve Effectiveness," *Family Law Quarterly* 27 (Fall 1993): 327–47.

Loretta M. Young
Family Court of State of Delaware

gun control *Gun control* is an umbrella term encompassing a wide variety of local, state, and federal laws aimed at the regulation of the manufacture, importation, sale, ownership, and use of firearms. Most of these laws are intended to reduce firearm-related crime by restricting the sale of dangerous weapons and keeping weapons away from people who have been designated as dangerous by the state.

The first major federal restrictions on firearms came in the 1934 National Firearms Act (26 United States Code §§5801–5872). The National Firearms Act (NFA) was originally written to regulate the dangerous firearms being used by PROHIBITION-era gangsters: machine guns and sawed-off shotguns. The NFA now also covers short-barreled rifles, silencers, and other "destructive devices," including grenades, mortars, and rocket launchers. The NFA does not outlaw these weapons per se, but rather requires the approval of the BUREAU OF ALCOHOL, TOBACCO, AND FIREARMS (ATF) for manufacture and transfer of any such weapon, and imposes heavy taxes on their importation, manufacture, and sale. In addition, the NFA requires that these dangerous weapons be registered with the federal government and have an engraved serial number.

The 1938 Federal Firearms Act (15 U.S.C. §§901–909, since superseded by the 1968 Gun Control Act, 18 U.S.C. §§921–931) set the stage for modern gun control legislation. The Federal Firearms Act (FFA) prohibited the shipment of a firearm through interstate commerce to those convicted or under indictment for a violent FELONY and fugitives from JUSTICE, among others. The FFA also established licensing and record-keeping requirements for importers, manufacturers, and retailers. These requirements were minimal, however, and resulted in many private citizens holding dealer licenses, which allowed them to transfer firearms through the mail (Zimring, 1975).

The Gun Control Act of 1968 (18 U.S.C. §§921–931) was passed in the context of rising crime rates and the assassinations of the CIVIL RIGHTS leader DR. MARTIN LUTHER KING, JR. and Senator Robert F. Kennedy. The Gun Control Act (GCA) and its amendments expanded on the 1938 FFA, requiring a more tightly regulated Federal Firearms License (FFL) to transfer firearms in interstate commerce, essentially eliminating private citizens from the interstate commerce in firearms. Further, the GCA prohibited the importation of firearms unless they were certified as being suitable for "sporting purposes." The GCA and its amendments also prohibited the sale of shotguns and rifles to anyone under age 18, the sale of handguns to anyone under age 21, and the transfer of firearms to a number of statutorily-defined groups, including: those convicted (or under indictment for) a felony; those convicted of a MISDEMEANOR crime of DOMESTIC VIOLENCE; those who have been "adjudicated as a mental defective" or have "been committed to any mental institution;" members of the armed forces who have received dishonorable discharges; those renouncing their U.S. CITIZENSHIP; those under a restraining order; fugitives from justice; drug users and drug addicts; and

ILLEGAL ALIENS. The GCA also made it a crime to purchase a firearm with the INTENT to transfer it to someone who was disqualified from purchasing a firearm under the Act (Zimring, 1975).

When purchasing a firearm, individuals are required to sign a statement to the effect that they are not a member of one of these prohibited groups. Prior to 1993, however, there was no federal requirement to actually document a gun buyer's eligibility. The 1993 Brady Handgun Violence Prevention Act, which amended the 1968 GCA, now requires that licensed dealers conduct a background check through the National Instant Criminal Background Check System (NICS), which is maintained by the FBI. More than 84 million background checks were conducted between 1998 and 2008, with nearly 1.8 percent (1,500,000) of those transfers denied (Bureau of Justice Statistics, 2009). Different states have different definitions of these categories, or provide differing amounts of information to the NICS, however. For instance, some states will only report a person to NICS as a "mental defective" if they have been involuntarily committed to a mental institution, while other states will give the classification if the person has been deemed by a court to be a danger to themselves or others.

No federal law requires a background check to be conducted on an *intra*state transfer of a firearm between two private citizens. This results in what is often called the gun show loophole, where all licensed dealers at a gun show must conduct NICS background checks on their customers, but a private seller at the next booth may sell his or her wares without such a background check. Some states require background checks for private transfers (National Research Council, 2005).

The federal government and nearly every state have enhanced sentences (or separate criminal statutes) for the use of firearms in crime. The federal government adds five years to a sentence for any crime of violence or drug trafficking if a person possesses a gun during the crime, seven years if the gun is "brandished," and 10 years if the gun is "discharged" (Title 18 U.S.C. §§924(c)(1)(a)(i)-(iii)). These sentences are on top of the penalties for the original crime and are meant to deter the use of guns in crime.

There are many state firearm regulations apart from the federal limitations on manufacture, purchase, importation, and sale. Some states have a requirement that individuals have a "permit to purchase," which often requires a safety class and a background check. Some states, such as Massachusetts, have different levels of permit for longguns and handguns. Most states, however, do not require a permit to purchase (Halbrook, 2009).

Many states have consumer protection rules that often require that firearms be made of a minimum quality steel and pass a "drop-test" without unintentional discharge. These regulations are meant to keep cheap, and often dangerous, "Saturday night special" handguns off the streets. A few states have instituted consumer protections that require firearms sold in their borders to have certain safety features, such as heavy trigger pulls or loaded chamber indicators. Some states also require firearms to be stored in a locked container or with a trigger- or action-locking device (Halbrook, 2009).

As part of the 1994 Violent Crime Control and Law Enforcement Act, the federal government banned the manufacture or sale of "assault weapons." This ban included particular weapons (e.g., Uzi, AR-15) and magazines that could hold more than 10 rounds of ammunition (18 USC §§922(v)-(w)). It also created a statutory definition of an "assault weapon," which was determined by a combination of characteristics of the gun such as a folding stock, pistol grip, or flash suppressor (18 U.S.C. §922(v)). The federal ban expired in September 2004, allowing these weapons and magazines back onto the market in most states. Some JURISDICTIONS, such as California, New York, Connecticut, Massachusetts, New Jersey, and Cook County, Illinois, have instituted their own assault-weapons and/or high-capacity magazine ban (Halbrook, 2009).

Nearly all states allow citizens to carry concealed weapons upon application for a permit. Most of these states have what are known as "shall-issue" laws; except for those people who are specifically excepted in the statute (e.g., felons, "mental defectives," etc.), the licensing authority must issue the license to carry. A minority of states, such as Massachusetts, New York, Maryland, and California, have "may-issue" statutes, which allow the local licensing authority—usually the municipal chief of police—the DISCRETION to grant or deny the license. Two states—Alaska and Vermont—do not require any license to carry a concealed firearm (Halbrook, 2009).

Those who hold a concealed carry license are still subject to restrictions. Civilians are almost never allowed into a courtroom or school with a gun. Title 39 Code of Federal Regulations §232(l) prohibits the carry of a weapon into a Post Office facility. Most states that allow concealed carry prohibit carrying weapons into bars, and most states recognize the right of individual business owners and churches to prohibit the carrying of guns onto their private property. Of course, in the states that require a license to carry, there are penalties for those who carry a concealed firearm without a license. Massachusetts, for example, has a minimum 18-month sentence for a first offense (M.G.L. c. 269 §10(a)).

The fate of many of these restrictions are in question as a result of two Supreme Court decisions. In *DISTRICT OF COLUMBIA V. HELLER*, 554 U.S. 570 (2008), the Supreme Court held that the Second Amendment protects an individual right to own guns, while in *McDonald v. City of Chicago*, 561 U.S. __ (2010), the Supreme Court ruled that the Second Amendment was INCORPORATED through the Fourteenth Amendment's DUE PROCESS clause to apply to the states, and therefore the city's law banning the possession of handguns was unconstitutional. How these rulings affect gun control will be determined by subsequent court cases and litigation.

For more information

Bureau of Justice Statistics. "Background Checks for Firearm Transfers, 2008." Available online. URL: http://bjs.ojp.usdoj.gov/index.cfm?ty=pbdetail&iid=1706.

Halbrook, Stephen P. *Firearms Law Deskbook*. Eagan, Minn.: West, 2009.

National Research Council. *Firearms and Violence: A Critical Review*. Washington, D.C.: National Academies Press, 2005.

Zimring, Franklin E. "Firearms and Federal Law: The Gun Control Act of 1968," *Journal of Legal Studies* 4 (1975): 133–198.

David I. Hull
St. Anselm College

H

habeas corpus and 9/11 Habeas corpus and 9/11 refer to the ability of those detained, especially in GUANTÁNAMO BAY, following the terrorist attacks on the United States on September 11, 2001, and associated with terrorist activity, to challenge their detention in court.

Following the unprecedented terrorist attacks of September 11, 2001, on the United States, many CIVIL LIBERTIES were restricted by the national government in the interest of national security, including the writ of habeas corpus. This is the right of a person who has been imprisoned to request a JUDGE to issue a writ that can result in the prisoner being brought before a court of law to determine whether his or her imprisonment is lawful (habeas corpus translates from the Latin "produce the body"). This fundamental right is provided for in the U.S. CONSTITUTION in art. 1, sec. 9, which states, "The Privilege of the Writ of Habeas Corpus shall not be suspended, unless when in Cases of Rebellion or Invasion the public Safety may require it." The Constitution specifically gives the power to suspend the writ of habeas corpus to Congress, presumably in a crisis context. However, prior to September 11th, there have been instances of presidential suspension of habeas corpus. President Lincoln during the Civil War suspended the writ, citing expanded executive power in an emergency.

In the immediate wake of the terrorist attacks on the World Trade Center and the Pentagon on September 11th, the government detained and questioned nearly 1,200 individuals, mostly males of Muslim descent. ATTORNEY GENERAL John Ashcroft of the George W. Bush administration declared these detainees to be of "special interest," and they were subsequently subject to immigration proceedings and in some instances eventual deportation. Many of these men were held for long periods of time by the government without being given access to an attorney or being formally charged with any crimes, a violation of habeas corpus. Though the USA PATRIOT ACT of October 2001 permitted such immigrants to be held without formal charges for a maximum of seven days, a later report by the JUSTICE DEPARTMENT revealed that some were held for as long as eight months, and only one such person received an actual conviction for "supporting" TERRORISM. These detentions were further supported by President Bush's military order of November 13, 2001, which asserted the military's right to detain those connected to terrorism and to try them through military commissions if the government decided to prosecute. Critics have asserted that not only was the president thus usurping Congress's constitutional power to suspend the writ of habeas corpus, he was also directly contradicting the specific time limits and provisions the legislative branch created for detentions in the USA PATRIOT Act.

The Bush administration, in pursuing the war on terror, also sought to prevent hundreds of men and boys it labeled enemy combatants and imprisoned in Guantánamo Bay or military brigs within the United States from having access to habeas corpus rights. Under the Third Geneva Convention, individuals who are captured on the battlefield are to be taken to a tribunal to determine whether they are lawful or unlawful combatants or merely innocent civilians. Instead, the Bush administration immediately classified all such detainees as enemy combatants and, thus, without access to basic civil liberties and DUE PROCESS rights. The administration did claim that detainees had some access to habeas corpus rights, but that no rebuttal by the detainee could be offered in response to the government's charges, and that officials only needed to provide some EVIDENCE to justify the detention. Furthermore, by placing detainees in Guantánamo Bay, a naval base in Cuba, the administration's legal advisers believed that domestic laws and U.S. courts' JURISDICTION would not reach to the area.

In 2004, several cases involving detainees challenging their denial of habeas corpus rights reached the Supreme Court, including *Rasul v. Bush* and *HAMDI V. RUMSFELD*. The government argued that the president as commander in chief constitutionally had the power to capture and detain enemy combatants for as long as hostilities in the war on terror continued, even if these individuals were American citizens. Additionally, the Bush administration claimed that Congress's authorization of the use of force in the conflict also legally covered the president's ability to capture and detain such individuals. However, in *Rasul v. Bush*, the Supreme Court contended that historically the writ of habeas corpus had always acted as a provision for reviewing the legitimacy of executive detentions, and that even when prisoners were held in Guantánamo Bay, the courts had a right to examine the president's actions. Further, in *Hamdi v. Rumsfeld*, the Court asserted that detainees had the right to challenge their categorization by the administration as an enemy combatant, to know the evidence and facts that led to this classification, and to be given an opportunity to answer those charges before an impartial body such as the courts.

The Bush administration's response was to obtain a provision in the Military Commission Act of 2006 that took away the jurisdiction of the federal courts to hear habeas corpus petitions from enemy combatants. In June 2008, in *Boumediene v. Bush*, the Court deemed this portion of the law unconstitutional, ruling 5-4 that all 250 detainees at Guantánamo Bay had the right to habeas corpus APPEALS to the courts. A flurry of such petitions inundated the courts, and speculation abounded as to whether the prison would remain open. Newly elected President Obama ordered all detainee cases to be reviewed in January 2009 and stipulated through executive order that Guantánamo Bay should be closed within the year.

For more information

Ball, Howard. *Bush, the Detainees, & the Constitution: The Battle over Presidential Power in the War on Terror.* Lawrence: University Press of Kansas, 2007.

Silkenat, James R., and Mark R. Shulman, eds. *The Imperial Presidency and the Consequences of 9/11: Lawyers React to the Global War on Terrorism,* vols. 1 and 2. Westport, Conn.: Praeger Security International, 2007.

Jennifer Hopper
CUNY Graduate Center

Hamdi v. Rumsfeld 542 U.S. 507 (2004) In *Hamdi v. Rumsfeld* (2004), the Supreme Court ruled that there are legal limits to the power of the president of the United States to suspend the rights of enemy combatants. The majority of the Court, in an opinion penned by Justice SANDRA DAY O'CONNOR, limited the authority of the Executive Branch to suspend habeas corpus and allowed detainees to challenge their classification in a court of law.

Following the terrorist attacks on the United States on September 11, 2001, Congress passed the Authorization for Use of Military Force, which gave President George W. Bush the authority to act to prevent future acts of TERRORISM against the United States. In response, President Bush ordered American forces into Afghanistan. While in armed conflict, 20-year-old Yasser Esam Hamdi was taken into custody by the American military as a member of the terrorist organization the Taliban. Hamdi was transferred to the American military detainee center at GUANTÁNAMO BAY, Cuba. Later, Hamdi was relocated to a military prison in Charleston, South Carolina. Hamdi, who was classified by the Bush administration as an enemy combatant, could be held indefinitely and not have access to an attorney. Hamdi, an American citizen, and his father sued Secretary of Defense Donald Rumsfeld for a habeas corpus petition for his son, arguing that Hamdi's Fifth Amendment Right to DUE PROCESS of law had been violated.

The Supreme Court, in a 5–4 decision, ruled that Hamdi could challenge his classification as an enemy combatant and could bring forth a habeas corpus petition. Justice O'Connor found that absent a suspension of habeas corpus, the right remained with every individual detained within the United States. The Court affirmed the right of a citizen to be free from involuntary confinement by the government without due process of law. Furthermore, the Court also ruled that a citizen-detainee seeking to challenge his or her classification as an enemy combatant must receive notice of the factual basis for this classification, as well as a fair opportunity to rebut the government's assertion of such classification before a neutral decision maker.

Justice ANTONIN SCALIA and Justice JOHN STEVENS, in a dissenting opinion, argued that Hamdi's right to habeas corpus and ability to challenge his enemy combatant status could be relaxed under the suspension clause of the CONSTITUTION. They argued that when the government accuses a citizen of waging war against it, barring a trial for TREASON, article 1, section 9, clause 2 of the Constitution allows Congress to ease the usual protections of those accused for a temporary period of time. The justices contended that the Authorization for Use of Military Force was an implementation of the suspension clause, and thus Hamdi's indefinite detention was constitutional. Justice CLARENCE THOMAS also dissented. Justice Thomas held that the detention of Hamdi falls squarely within the federal government's war powers, and the Court lacks the capacity and expertise to second-guess that decision.

This case was a victory for limiting the power of the federal government. As a result of *Hamdi v. Rumsfeld* (2004), persons being imprisoned as enemy combatants could petition for habeas corpus and had the authority to attack their classification as an enemy of the state before a military tribunal. Also, the case reflected the Supreme Court's shift away from the policies of President George W. Bush.

For more information

Epstein, Lee, and Thomas G. Walker. *Constitutional Law for a Changing America: Institutional Powers and Constraints.* 6th ed. Washington, D.C.: CQ Press, 2007.

Pious, Richard M. *The War on Terror and the Rule of Law.* Los Angeles: Roxbury, 2006.

Posner, Richard A. *Not a Suicide Pact: The Constitution in a Time of National Emergency.* New York: Oxford University Press, 2006.

Ryan Adoor and Tobias Gibson
Westminster College

Hammer v. Dagenhart 247 U.S. 251 (1918) *Hammer v. Dagenhart* was a U.S. Supreme Court decision invalidating a congressional law regulating the interstate shipment of goods produced by child labor.

Since 1937 the Supreme Court has liberally interpreted congressional exercises of power under the clause in Article I, section 8 of the U.S. CONSTITUTION, granting Congress power "to regulate Commerce . . . among the several States." From about 1890 to 1937, however, the Court often invalidated such laws for unduly interfering with state police powers. *Hammer v. Dagenhart* is such a decision.

Although children have long worked on houses and farms with their parents, the rise of mass production meant that children could work in factories without parental supervision and protection. Such labor could prove physically injurious and keep children out of school. State child labor laws varied from one state to another, giving industries incentives to locate in states with lax laws.

Congress accordingly adopted the Keating-Owen Bill in 1916. This law enacted a 30-day prohibition on the transportation of goods produced by companies employing children under the age of 14 or violating standards set for children from 14 to 16. Dagenhart, a father with two sons employed in a North Carolina cotton mill, sued a U.S. DISTRICT ATTORNEY named Hammer to prevent enforcement of the law.

Justice William Rufus Day authored a 5–4 decision in which the Supreme Court struck down the congressional law for impermissibly interfering with state police powers. Justice Day distinguished this case from others where the Court had upheld congressional laws regulating the interstate transportation of lottery tickets, impure food and drugs, prostitutes, intoxicating liquors, and other such goods. Justice Day ruled that, whereas these goods were in and of themselves harmful, the products of child labor were not. Justice Day further distinguished between the manufacturing of goods and subsequent control over the commerce of such items. Manufacturing, Day argued, was a local matter subject to state prerogatives, guaranteed by the Tenth Amendment of the Constitution.

Dissenting, Justice OLIVER WENDELL HOLMES, JR., argued that the congressional law was within the language of THE COMMERCE CLAUSE and should be upheld. Challenging the distinction between goods that were inherently harmful and those that were not, Holmes argued that civilized countries agreed on the evil of child labor.

Rebuffed in *Hammer*, Congress adopted an amendment to the Revenue Act of 1919 taxing goods produced by child labor. The Supreme Court voided this law in an 8–1 decision in *Bailey v. Drexel Furniture Company* (1922). Congress proposed a child labor amendment in 1924, but a sufficient number of states never ratified.

During the New Deal, Congress again incorporated child labor provisions into laws, including the Fair Labor Standards Act of 1938. The Supreme Court upheld this law and repudiated *Hammer* in *United States v. Darby* (1944). Although the Supreme Court has struck down provisions of the Gun-Free School Zones Act of 1990 and the VIOLENCE AGAINST WOMEN ACT in recent cases on the grounds that they exceed national authority under the commerce clause, current child labor laws appear more closely related to control over interstate commerce and do not appear to be in similar jeopardy.

For more information

Bittker, Boris I. *Bittker on the Regulation of Interstate and Foreign Commerce.* Gaithersburg, Md.: Aspen Law and Business, 1999.

John R. Vile
Middle Tennessee State University

Hand, Learned (1872–1961) Federal judge Learned Hand was a federal JUDGE who is widely regarded as one of the most important figures in the history of American law. He served on the federal bench for more than 50 years, beginning his tenure in 1909 when President WILLIAM HOWARD TAFT appointed him to the federal district court in New York. In 1924 Hand was tapped by President Calvin Coolidge to serve on the federal appeals court for the Second Circuit. He became chief judge of that court in 1939 and served until his formal retirement in 1951. He continued, however, as a federal judge in senior status and continued to decide cases until his death in 1961 at the age of 89.

Despite his stature as a distinguished jurist, politics, timing, and bad luck kept Hand from being selected for a seat on the U.S. Supreme Court. In the 1920s William Howard Taft kept Hand from getting a nomination largely due to Hand's support of Theodore Roosevelt in the election of 1912. When FRANKLIN ROOSEVELT had numerous opportunities to make High Court appointments, he passed over Hand partly because he was inundated with pleas to nominate Hand and partly because he wanted younger men. Even though he never advanced to the nation's highest tribunal, Hand was still able to leave a lasting legacy in the law.

Hand's judicial philosophy was not unlike that of Supreme Court Justice FELIX FRANKFURTER. Both studied under the same law professors at Harvard Law School and on the bench espoused a limited role for courts and judges. Like Frankfurter, Hand argued that judges ought to leave important decision up to the people through their elected branches of government. Though this philosophy of judicial restraint did not hold sway over more activist justices like HUGO BLACK and WILLIAM O. DOUGLAS, Hand has proved influential with a new generation of jurists like WILLIAM H. REHNQUIST and ANTONIN SCALIA.

Hand's greatest contribution as a judge came in the area of statutory interpretation where he saw his role as developing legal rules to interpret legislative aims. For example, he developed an influential formula used in TORT cases for analyzing negligence. As a lower court judge, Hand felt that he did not enjoy the freedom that his colleagues on the Supreme Court had to interpret the CONSTITUTION in new areas of the law. Despite his own judicial views, he saw his role as applying the PRECEDENTS handed down by the High Court. However, in one area of CONSTITUTIONAL INTERPRETATION, free speech, Hand played an important role in that doctrine's development.

Learned Hand (Library of Congress)

Hand viewed the First Amendment as a strong protection of free speech rights and in the case of *Masses Publishing Co. v. Patten,* 244 F. 535 (1917), he argued in a controversial opinion that all speech short of direct incitement to illegal action was permissible. Two years later, in *SCHENCK V. UNITED STATES,* 249 U.S. 47(1919), the Court used a less protectionist "clear and present danger" test articulated by Justice OLIVER WENDELL HOLMES. Though Hand was critical of the Holmes standard as too restrictive of speech, he set aside his personal views and applied the "clear and present" danger test in *UNITED STATES v. DENNIS*, 183 F.2d 201 (2d Cir. 1950) in upholding the conviction of Communist Party leaders for conspiring to overthrow the government. Eventually, in 1969, a more liberal Supreme Court moved away from its earlier cases and adopted the "incitement to imminent lawless action" standard in *BRANDENBURG V. OHIO*, 395 U.S. 444, which is generally viewed as virtually identical to the rule Hand had established over 50 years earlier in *Masses*.

For more information

Griffith, Kathryn. *Judge Learned Hand and the Role of the Federal Judiciary.* London: Jonathan Cape, 1973.

Gunther, Gerald. *Learned Hand: The Man and the Judge.* New York: Knopf, 1994.

Artemus Ward
California State University, Chico

Harlan, John Marshall (1833–1911) Supreme Court justice John Marshall Harlan was perhaps the most significant U.S. Supreme Court justice of the late 19th and early 20th centuries. Harlan's significance was in his advocacy of strong national power in regulating interstate commerce and in promoting expanded rights against individual state power, especially for African Americans after the Civil War. Because both positions went against the grain of U.S. legal thought and Supreme Court decisions of most of his 34-year tenure on the Court, Harlan's influence on development of CONSTITUTIONAL LAW was waged in hundreds of dissenting opinions.

Harlan, a unionist opposed to Kentucky's secession from the United States to the Confederacy, served as the state's ATTORNEY GENERAL during the war and unsuccessfully ran for governor twice after the war ended. President Rutherford B. Hayes appointed him to the Court in 1877.

On the Court Harlan advocated SUBSTANTIVE DUE PROCESS rights under the Fourteenth Amendment, one of the so-called Civil War amendments that guaranteed due process of law to citizens of the states. Harlan believed this amendment "INCORPORATED" the protections that citizens had against the national government under the BILL OF RIGHTS. He also was a strong proponent of ANTITRUST LAW passed by Congress, believing that concentrated power in trusts was destructive to a free market economy.

Harlan's most famous opinion was his dissent in *PLESSY V. FERGUSON*, 163 U.S. 537, 16 S.Ct. 1138, 41 L.Ed.256 (1896). The Supreme Court in *Plessy* upheld a Louisiana law that required separate passenger coaches on trains for whites and African Americans and made it a crime for someone of one race to enter a coach reserved for the other race. "[I]n view of the CONSTITUTION, in the eye of the law, there is in this country no superior, dominant, ruling class of citizens," he wrote. "There is no caste here. Our Constitution is color-blind, and neither knows nor tolerates classes among citizens."

A half-century later, the U.S. Supreme Court would strike down the rule in *Plessy* that state laws maintaining SEGREGATION of the races were constitutional if they assured "SEPARATE BUT EQUAL" opportunity for the races. Before that, in 1925, the Court began the first in a series of cases that held that protections under the Bill of Rights like the RIGHT TO A JURY TRIAL for a criminal offense applied to the states—under the Fourteenth Amendment. Harlan, one of the Court's greatest dissenters, had persuaded a majority in the end.

For more information

Beth, Loren. *John Marshall Harlan: The Last Whig Justice.* Lexington: University Press of Kentucky, 1992.

Wm. Osler McCarthy
Supreme Court of Texas
University of Texas Department of Journalism

Harmelin v. Michigan 501 U.S. 957 (1991) *Harmelin v. Michigan* involved a challenge to mandatory SENTENCING laws. The sharply divided

U.S. Supreme Court, with Justice ANTONIN SCALIA delivering the majority opinion, held that severe, mandatory penalties do not constitute CRUEL AND UNUSUAL PUNISHMENT. Therefore, mandatory prison sentences do not violate the EIGHTH AMENDMENT of the U.S. CONSTITUTION.

The case originated when Michigan police stopped Ronald Allen Harmelin after he ran a red light in 1986. They discovered 672.5 grams of pure cocaine (about 1 ½ lbs.), worth between $67,000 and $100,000 in his car. A 1978 Michigan law required that anyone convicted of possessing more than 650 grams of cocaine be sentenced to a mandatory term of life in prison without possibility of PAROLE. The law supposed that such an amount of drugs indicated INTENT to deal cocaine. Harmelin, an honorably discharged air force veteran who made a living as the night manager of a billiard parlor, had no prior ARRESTS. He did apparently have an addiction to cocaine, though, as well as the tools of a drug trafficker: a beeper, a coded address book, a gun, and $2,900 in cash. The state law did not permit the JUDGE to take into account mitigating circumstances, such as Harmelin's lack of an arrest record. Harmelin APPEALED his sentence on the grounds that it was cruel and unusual because it was significantly disproportionate to the crime that he committed and because the sentencing judge could not take into account the circumstances of the crime and of the criminal.

When Harmelin lost his appeal at the state level, he took his case to the U.S. Supreme Court. The Court, in a narrow 5–4 decision, ruled against the defendant. Scalia noted that the Eighth Amendment contains nothing about PROPORTIONALITY. He also observed that state legislatures have the prerogative to set penalties for crimes classified as FELONIES. The Court concluded that the Eighth Amendment bans certain types of PUNISHMENT, such as drawing and quartering. Meanwhile, the idea of FEDERALISM allows states to set penalties that take into account local needs, concerns, and social conditions. Accordingly, the Eighth Amendment forbids only extreme sentences that are far out of proportionality to the crime. CHIEF JUSTICE WILLIAM REHNQUIST and Justices SANDRA DAY O'CONNOR, David Souter, and ANTHONY KENNEDY concurred in the decision.

The dissenting justices, including Byron White, Harry Blackmun, JOHN PAUL STEVENS, and THURGOOD MARSHALL, argued that the Constitution prohibits excessive fines, thereby indicating some restraint on excessive sentences. White noted that prior Court decisions had construed the words of the Eighth Amendment to include a proportionality requirement. Accordingly, as Marshall wrote, Michigan's law mandating life sentences with no possibility of parole even for first-time drug possession offenders is unconstitutional.

For more information

Vincent, Barbara S. *The Consequences of Mandatory Minimum Prison Terms: A Summary of Recent Findings*. Washington, D.C.: Federal Judicial Center, 1994.

Caryn E. Neumann
Miami University of Ohio

hate crimes A hate crime is a traditional offense against a person, personal, or community property motivated by bias toward the group affiliation presumed of the victim or group, such as race, RELIGION, disability, ethnic origin, or sexual orientation.

Racial bias motivates about one half of hate crimes, and while hate crimes against persons account for well over half the total incidents, homes, places of worship, cemeteries, and community centers are frequent sites of hate crimes against property. The FBI's 2008 Hate Crime Statistics report indicated a total of 9,168 bias offenses that year. Today, 45 states and the District of Columbia have various statutes criminalizing bias crimes, alongside federal hate crimes laws. The categories of bias may overlap in any particular case, as they are not mutually exclusive, and the categories need not be regarded as static. Advocates for the homeless, for example, have suggested that since recently the number of VIOLENT CRIMES specifically targeting homeless people has been increasing, perhaps this category warrants inclusion as a hate crime.

Hate crimes do not criminalize hate but do acknowledge that MOTIVE is an important aspect of criminal prosecution and that the harm to society caused by crimes motivated by bias is greater than otherwise. Hate crimes tend to have a chilling effect on the victim's community as a whole, and those against some groups of persons tend to be more vicious than others because of the prejudice involved. In the unanimous decision in *Wisconsin v. Mitchell,* 508 U.S. 476 (1993), a case involving the 1989 severe beating of a white teenager that left him in a coma for four days, CHIEF JUSTICE WILLIAM REHNQUIST wrote that while "a defendant's abstract beliefs, however obnoxious to most people" are free expression and so protected, they do not remain abstract when they provide the motive for a crime, and a legislature can take "bigoted motivations" into consideration as providing a reason for an enhanced sentence due to the enhanced harm to the community reflected in the crime. If bias is established as an element in the crime, then it can be a factor to be considered during SENTENCING.

Trained law enforcement officials review factors known as bias crime indicators to determine whether a hate crime has occurred. These factors include racial, ethnic, or cultural differences between victim and perpetrator, as well as any comments or written statements by the perpetrator, gestures or GRAFFITI, membership in organized hate groups, and lack of clear other motives. These factors suggest that the crime was neither random nor a crime of opportunity, but that the victim was specifically targeted because of his or her ethnicity, religion, or sexual orientation, for example. Although a victim may allege a hate crime has occurred, or a PROSECUTOR may pursue a conviction for an alleged hate crime, this is by no means a guarantee that a JUDGE or JURY will be persuaded that what occurred was not simply an ordinary crime. The DEPARTMENT OF JUSTICE infrequently seeks a hate crime conviction because, among other reasons, the EVIDENCE warranting the enhanced crime and penalty may be deemed insufficient, or a lesser crime and penalty may be more likely successfully prosecuted.

What today are called hate crimes have been of concern to the FBI since the 1920s, when crimes of hatred and prejudice such as lynching and VANDALISM of synagogues were the focus of attention, especially as perpetrated by the KU KLUX KLAN in the South. Following the Civil Rights Act of 1964, when the federal government deemed the protection of CIVIL RIGHTS not merely a local function, the FBI has actively pursued crimes exacerbated by prejudice. The term *hate crime* itself entered legal parlance with the 1969 Federal Civil Rights Law, 18 U.S.C. § 245(b)(2), which provided a federal hate crime law that extended to crimes motivated by perceived race, color, religion, or national origin against a person while engaging in a federally protected activity such as voting or going to a public school.

The Hate Crimes Statistics Act, 28 U.S.C. 534, took effect in 1990, requiring local law enforcement officials to gather and maintain statistics on the incidence of hate crimes so as to ascertain their extent and whether to legislate further hate crimes laws. The Hate Crimes Sentencing Enhancement Act, 28 U.S.C. 994, took effect in 1994 and provides for perhaps the most controversial aspect of any hate crimes legislation, an enhanced penalty for convicted perpetrators of hate crimes. Detractors of hate crimes legislation have inferred from this that certain groups of Americans are more worthy, while other groups are less worthy, because the same crime committed against a group not enumerated in hate crimes legislation does not merit as severe a PUNISHMENT as when committed against a member of a protected group. For example, while Americans as a whole tend to react negatively at racial or religious prejudice, the inclusion of sexual orientation as a proscribed bias in hate crimes legislation has proved more challenging. The category sexual orientation is usually taken to mean homosexual, and the challenge has been to convince Americans that crimes motivated by animus toward homosexuality or gay and lesbian persons as a group merit condemnation just as do crimes motivated by racial or religious animus. A defender of hate crimes legislation might rely on *Wisconsin v. Mitchell* and reply that a crime motivated by hate is not the same crime, but a different one, warranting a different response from the CRIMINAL JUSTICE SYSTEM, including the possibility of a stiffer sentence.

The Local Law Enforcement Hate Crimes Prevention Act, introduced in 2000 as the Hate Crimes Prevention Act and also known as the Matthew Shephard and James Byrd, Jr. Hate Crime Prevention Act, eventually passed and was signed into law by President Barack Obama on October 28, 2009, added sexual orientation, gender, and disability, and brought some uniformity to the nation's hate crimes laws. It mandated federal prosecution should the hate crime have been violent, occurred on federal lands or hindered a person in the exercise of a civil right. Today, 28 states and the District of Columbia have hate crimes statutes that include sexual orientation, while 18 lack this category.

Hate crimes reinforce negative stereotypes about certain groups and imply that some groups are legitimate targets of criminal acts due principally or solely to their relative standing in society.

For more information

Bell, Jeanine. *Policing Hatred: Law Enforcement, Civil Rights, and Hate Crimes.* New York: New York University Press, 2002.

Perry, Barbara. *In the Name of Hate: Understanding Hate Crimes.* New York: Routledge, 2001.

U.S. Department of Justice—Federal Bureau of Investigation. *Uniform Crime Report, Hate Crime Statistics.* Available online. URL: www.fbi.gov/ucr/hc2009/index.html.

Gordon A. Babst
Chapman University

hearsay Hearsay is a concept in the law of EVIDENCE that refers to statements made out of court. It addresses questions of what statements made outside of court may be used to determine the guilt or innocence of an individual in a criminal setting.

Hearsay is generally defined as an out-of-court statement that is introduced in a hearing or trial in order to prove the truth of the matter asserted in that statement. It is a statement made sometime before trial, which is being repeated in a trial by a witness or document in order to prove that the assertion in the original statement was in fact true. If the statement is introduced in the trial for some other reason, such as indicating that the speaker was angry or insane but not to indicate that what she or he said was actually true, then it is not hearsay. If a witness in court testifies that she heard a man scream at his wife that she had ruined everything, the statement could be used in court to prove the truth of the matter asserted: that the wife in fact did something terrible. In that case, it is hearsay, as it is being used to prove the truth of the matter asserted in the husband's statement. However, it could also be used to prove something else entirely: that the husband was upset. This is not hearsay because the purpose of introducing the statement has nothing to do with the truth of the matter asserted in his statement—it only goes to show the husband's state of mind at the time he made the statement. Nonverbal conduct can also be considered a statement (and can therefore be hearsay) if it is intended as an assertion, such as one's pointing toward an alley when asked where a man went.

The FEDERAL RULES OF EVIDENCE (FRE) 801-807 and the evidence rules of most states generally prohibit the use of hearsay in a hearing or trial. Hearsay evidence is considered unreliable, and the purpose of the prohibition is to prevent the use of a person's assertion as equivalent to actual testimony of a fact when the person making the statement is not present in court to be questioned under oath and cross-examined.

While hearsay is generally inadmissible, there are many exemptions and exceptions that allow hearsay statements to be admitted. FRE 801(d) lists several exemptions where certain types of statements are by definition not hearsay, including a party's own admissions. Rules 803 and 804 list 29 exceptions to the hearsay rule. Rule 804 exceptions may be used only when the original declarant (the person who made the statement that is being introduced) is unavailable to testify at trial, and they include deathbed statements among others. Rule 803 provides exceptions that may be used whether the declarant is currently available to testify or not, including statements made while perceiving an event and statements describing a person's own state of mind or body.

Criminal defendants have additional protection when it comes to accusations against them admitted as hearsay evidence, according to *Crawford v. Washington,* 541 U.S. 36 (2004). When deliberate accusations are made, the defendant has the right to question in court the motives and perceptions of the accuser under the CONFRONTATION CLAUSE of the U.S. CONSTITUTION, and in these cases, hearsay rules will be more limited in their application. The hearsay rule applies only to actual trials; hearsay is admissible in other judicial proceedings, including GRAND JURY deliberations, PROBATION hearings, and administrative hearings.

For more information

Fenner, Michael G. *The Hearsay Rule.* Durham, N.C.: Carolina Academic Press, 2003.

Deborah Anthony
University of Illinois at Springfield

Hearst, Patty (1954–) heir Patricia (Patty) Hearst was a famous heiress kidnapped by the SYMBIONESE LIBERATION ARMY who eventually was convicted of participating in crimes with this organization. Her conviction was controversial and raised questions about whether she was brainwashed and a willing participant in these activities.

Patty Hearst was born in 1954 (now Patty Hearst Shaw), and is the granddaughter of William Randolph Hearst and daughter of Randolph Hearst, both wealthy newspaper magnates. In 1974, as a 19-year-old undergraduate at University of California at Berkeley, she was kidnapped from her apartment by a radical group calling itself the Symbionese Liberation Army. The group announced that they were serving an "ARREST warrant" on her and that rescue attempts would result in her death. They ended their message with the words "DEATH TO THE FASCIST INSECT THAT PREYS UPON THE LIFE OF THE PEOPLE." She was targeted because the Hearst family, prominent, rich, and conservative, was unpopular among the Berkeley left-wing counterculture. Not only did Patty's father control a vast media empire; her mother, Catherine, was the voice of conservatism on the University's Board of Regents.

Shortly thereafter, the group released tapes, including the voice of Miss Hearst, demanding that her father use several million dollars to buy food for the poor. He attempted to comply, but distribution efforts did not proceed smoothly, and he ultimately announced that he could not meet all the SLA demands.

Patty Hearst was kept bound in a closet for some weeks, during which time several tapes were released in which she said she was okay, criticized her father's failed food relief efforts, said her captors were good people, and ultimately claimed loyalty to the SLA. She took the revolutionary name of Tania, soon thereafter was seen on surveillance video participating in an SLA bank ROBBERY, and was placed on the FBI's most wanted list. In response to public speculation as to whether she was a willing participant, a tape was released in which she claimed to be just that. She later fired a round of bullets into a sporting goods store to aid in the getaway of two SLA members caught SHOPLIFTING.

She was arrested in San Francisco in September 1975. Upon her arrest, she gave her occupation as urban guerrilla and continued to pledge loyalty to the SLA. However, at her trial in federal district court in 1976, she claimed to have been brainwashed. She also invoked the Fifth Amendment numerous times, raising doubts for some about the veracity of her tale. She was represented at trial by the well-known attorney F. LEE BAILEY, whose approach, enlisting the aid of psychiatrists, was to depict her as brainwashed and as a victim of the Stockholm syndrome—i.e. one who through dependency on one's captors ultimately comes to sympathize with them. (Speculation was that he chose this strategy because it was the preference of her parents who had hired him.)

However, it was easy for the prosecution to find flaws in this approach. Moreover, federal law did not include brainwashing as a defense for bank robbery. The government also relied heavily on the testimony of psychiatrists, who depicted her as amoral, aimless, and an easy target for peddlers of any radical ideology. She was found guilty of armed bank robbery and received a seven-year prison sentence. President Jimmy Carter commuted her sentence, and she was freed after 22 months. Shortly after leaving prison, she married her prison bodyguard, Bernard Shaw. In 2001, President Bill Clinton included her among those he pardoned before leaving office.

For more information

Linder, Douglas O. "The Trial of Patty Hearst, 1976," Available online. URL: www.law.umkc.edu/faculty/projects/Ftrials/hearst/hearsthome/html.

McLellan, Vin, and Paul Avery. *The Voices of Guns.* New York: G. P. Putnam's Sons, 1977.

Jane G. Rainey
Eastern Kentucky University

Herrera v. Collins 506 U.S. 390 (1993) In *Herrera v. Collins,* the Court concluded that newly found EVIDENCE of innocence in a death penalty case does not require a conviction to be overturned. The decision was controversial because the Court held that a claim of "ACTUAL INNOCENCE" would not bar the execution of an individual otherwise lawfully convicted of MURDER.

In September 1981, the body of Texas Department of Public Safety Officer David Rucker was found on the highway outside of Los Fresnos, Texas, a few miles north of Brownsville. Rucker, lying beside his patrol car, had been shot in the head. Meanwhile, Los Fresnos Police Officer Enrique Carrisalez saw a car speeding along the highway heading away from the location of Rucker's death. Carrisalez, accompanied by Enrique Hernandez, turned on his flashing red lights and pursued the speeding car. The driver signaled that he would pull over and did so. As Carrisalez spoke with the driver, the man fired at least one shot at the officer. Struck in the chest, Carrisalez died nine days later. Leonel Torres Herrera, ARRESTED a few days after the shooting, was charged with the capital murder of both police officers. Hernandez identified Herrera as the shooter and the only person in the car, supporting Carrisalez's deathbed statement. Herrera had the keys to the car, which was registered to his live-in girlfriend and which he was known to drive. Additionally, Herrera's Social Security card had been found alongside Rucker's patrol car. Tried and found guilty of Carrisalez's murder in January 1982, Herrera pled guilty to Rucker's killing in July 1982. For killing Carrisalez, Herrera received a death sentence.

Herrera unsuccessfully challenged the Carrisalez and Rucker convictions in Texas state courts. In February 1992, Herrera proclaimed his innocence in a federal habeas petition supported by affidavits that accused his now-dead brother of the murders. He argued that the EIGHTH AMENDMENT's prohibition against CRUEL AND UNUSUAL PUNISHMENT and the Fourteenth Amendments's guarantee of the process of law forbid his execution. The Supreme Court ruled against Herrera.

CHIEF JUSTICE WILLIAM REHNQUIST delivered the opinion on January 25, 1993. Rehnquist concluded that Herrera should have offered evidence of his innocence at trial when the JURY could have considered issues of credibility. By waiting 10 years, Herrera fell far short of the evidence necessary to trigger a constitutional claim. Justice SANDRA DAY O'CONNOR agreed that Herrera was not innocent and therefore had no claim to the constitutional provisions against executing an innocent man. No JUDGE at any point in the judicial proceedings had expressed any doubt about Herrera's guilt. Accordingly, the Supreme Court was not permitting the execution of an innocent person. As Justices ANTONIN SCALIA and CLARENCE THOMAS concurred, the CONSTITUTION does not require the judicial system to consider newly discovered evidence of innocence after an individual has been convicted. Justices Harry Blackmun, JOHN PAUL STEVENS, and David Souter dissented on the grounds that there is a risk that an innocent person could be executed. They held that such an event would violate the norms of decency and, thus, the Eighth Amendment's protections as well as the DUE PROCESS clause of the Fourteenth Amendment.

For more information

Darmer, M. Katherine, and Robert M. Baird, eds. *Morality, Justice, and the Law: The Continuing Debate.* Amherst, N.Y.: Prometheus Books, 2007.

Caryn E. Neumann
Miami University of Ohio

Herring v. United States 555 U.S. 135 (2009) In *Herring v. United States,* the U.S. Supreme Court clarified the circumstances under which the exclusionary rule would prohibit the admission of illegally seized EVIDENCE. In particular, the Court held that the exclusionary rule did not apply when an illegal ARREST and search were the result of a record-keeping error attributed to a law enforcement agency.

The exclusionary rule was created by the Supreme Court as a means of safeguarding citizens' FOURTH AMENDMENT rights to be free from unreasonable SEARCHES AND SEIZURES. Generally, it prohibits the use of unlawfully seized evidence at trial. However, in *United States v. Leon,* 468 U.S. 897 (1984), the Supreme Court recognized that application of the exclusionary rule depended upon the nature of the police conduct that resulted in a violation of the Fourth Amendment. The Court explained that the rule applies when the conduct is deliberate and culpable. By analyzing these two factors, courts can determine if the police will be deterred from similar conduct in the future and if the costs imposed upon the justice system are justified. The linchpin of the analysis is the "objective reasonableness" of the illegal search or seizure. More particularly, the Court announced the following rule: When police rely on a search warrant that is subsequently invalidated for lack of PROBABLE CAUSE, the exclusionary rule does not apply if the reliance on the warrant was objectively reasonable. This is commonly called the good-faith EXCEPTION TO THE EXCLUSIONARY RULE.

In subsequent cases, the Supreme Court applied the good-faith exception in cases involving warrants invalidated due to clerical errors, searches conducted in reliance upon unconstitutional statutes, and warrants invalidated because of mistaken information in a court's database. However, the Court did not address whether the good-faith exception would apply to illegal searches and seizures that are attributed to mistaken information in a police database. The Court decided to review Herring's case because the lower courts were divided on that question.

The facts of the case were straightforward. The investigator Mark Anderson learned that Bennie Herring, a convicted felon well known to the police, was going to the sheriff's department to remove something from his impounded truck. Anderson asked his county's warrants clerk to check for any outstanding warrants against Herring, and he was told there were none. Then Anderson asked the clerk to check for outstanding warrants in a neighboring county. At that point, he was told that there was a warrant for

Herring's arrest. Anderson asked for a hard copy of the warrant to confirm the charges. But before confirmation was received, Anderson arrested Herring. During a SEARCH INCIDENT TO ARREST, Anderson found illegal drugs in Herring's pocket and a handgun in his pickup truck. Meanwhile, the warrant's clerk in the neighboring county sent word that the information in its database was incorrect and that the warrant against Herring had been recalled. However, by the time that information was given to Anderson, Herring had already been arrested and searched. Herring was charged with drug and weapons offenses.

Before trial, relying upon the exclusionary rule, Herring moved to suppress the evidence. He claimed that his arrest and search were unconstitutional because the warrant had been rescinded. The trial court denied the motion, the evidence was admitted at Herring's trial, and Herring was convicted. The intermediate court of appeals affirmed. Both of the lower courts concluded that the officers acted in good-faith reliance on the warrant and that exclusion of the evidence would not deter future mistakes.

The U.S. Supreme Court decided to hear the case because the lower courts were divided on the question of whether to suppress evidence that was illegally obtained as a result of a police department's clerical mistake. In deciding that the exclusionary rule did not apply in Herring's case, the Court focused on the purpose of the exclusionary rule. The Court explained that exclusion of evidence is a "last resort," not a "first impulse." The Court also identified two principles from its prior opinions, which were designed to limit application of the rule. According to the first principle, the exclusionary rule is not an individual right and applies only when it will deter illegal searches and seizures to a considerable degree. The second principle requires that the benefits of deterring future Fourth Amendment violations outweigh the social costs of excluding evidence. The social costs, the court explained, include the risks associated with letting guilty and potentially dangerous people escape accountability for their offenses, an outcome that is contrary to basic notions of JUSTICE and that undermines the truth-seeking function of the justice system. Therefore, the flagrancy of the misconduct is the critical factor. Additionally, the Court explained that the exclusion of evidence is not a necessary consequence of a Fourth Amendment violation because reasonable mistakes are acceptable.

In the end, the Court summarized the exclusionary rule as follows: "To trigger the exclusionary rule, police conduct must be sufficiently deliberate that exclusion can meaningfully deter it, and sufficiently culpable that such deterrence is worth the price paid by the justice system. As laid out in our cases, the exclusionary rule serves to deter deliberate, reckless, or grossly negligent conduct, or in some circumstances recurring or systematic negligence." In other words, mistakes that result from police negligence will not justify application of the exclusionary rule.

For more information

Signorelli, Walter P. *The Constable Has Blundered: The Exclusionary Rule, Crime, and Corruption.* Durham, N.C.: Carolina Academic Press, 2010.

Stephens, Otis H., and Glenn, Richard A. *Unreasonable Searches and Seizures: Rights and Liberties under the Law.* Santa Barbara, Calif.: ABC-CLIO, 2006.

Mark A. Fulks
Tennessee State University

high-speed vehicle chases High-speed vehicle chases refer to the pursuit of suspects by law enforcement officials at speeds in excess of what would otherwise be permitted by the law. While in many situations law enforcement officials are permitted to engage in high-speed chases, their use has decreased over time because of public safety as well as constitutional and personal liability concerns.

Police dramas and movies almost always feature high-speed chases to enhance drama. It also seemed unavoidable to police officers in earlier decades. Drivers who sped away from police cruisers threw down red flags, challenging police authority. The police culture and philosophy encouraged tracking them down; giving up pursuit was not an honorable alternative. Individuals who escape apprehension provoke anger and embarrassment for the officer in pursuit and police agency. Police executives purchase police high-performance cruisers to compete with muscle cars that cruise the streets.

Vehicle pursuits can result in low- and high-speed evasive maneuvers when an officer is attempting to stop a vehicle. Police officers in pursuit must evaluate the seriousness of the offense. Fleeing dangerous felons have the highest priority; minor traffic offenses do not produce the same sense of heightened urgency. However, police officers often navigate their surroundings, hampered by an information void. Multiple legal violations accumulate as the suspect moves through several JURISDICTIONS: reckless driving, drunk driving, or evading arrest.

FEDERAL BUREAU OF INVESTIGATION research revealed that accidents are the primary cause of police deaths. Their reporting system indicates that from 1987 to 2006 vehicle-related incidents were the most likely cause of police deaths. On-duty fatalities account for almost 37 percent. The fatality count: 968 law enforcement officers died as the result of automobile, motor cycle, or aircraft accidents.

The increased incentive is to save the lives of police officers, innocent drivers, passengers, and pedestrians. The National Highway Traffic Safety Administration (NHTSA) Fatality Analysis Reporting System (FARS) statistics indicate that there were more fatalities as the result of police pursuits in 2007 than in any other year preceding their reports. The death toll reached 424 deaths. Police pursuits are extremely dangerous. The number of pursuits continues to escalate, as do the related fatalities. The reporting system needs improvement. NHTSA captures less than one-half of the actual data regarding high-pursuit deaths.

The concerns about police harm and public safety have led to decreased reliance on the use of high-speed chases. But in addition, courts have ruled that high-speed chases must be evaluated under the CONSTITUTION, and law enforcement officials must have good reasons to engagement in pursuits. In general, when there is no emergency, police must obey normal traffic laws. However, in emergencies they may disobey them, but obey if reasonable. When engaging in high-speed chases, the courts will evaluate reasonableness based on several factors, including the nature of the crime, traffic and weather conditions, officer training, and whether there are clear procedures in place regulating the pursuit. Law enforcement officials who fail to exercise due care when making decisions to engage in a high-speed chase may not only violate the Constitution but face personal liability for their actions. However in *Scott v. Harris,* 550 U.S. 372 (2007), the Supreme Court ruled that a law enforcement official did not violate the FOURTH AMENDMENT when he engaged in a high-speed chase that resulted in the person being pursued becoming paralyzed after having his car run off the road by the sheriff. In this case, the Court said: A "police officer's attempt to terminate a dangerous high-speed car chase that threatens the lives of innocent bystanders does not violate the Fourth Amendment, even when it places the fleeing motorist at risk of serious injury or death." Similarly, in *Sykes v. United States,* 564 U.S. 1 (2011) the Supreme Court held that fleeing from the police in a car or vehicle is a felony justifying police pursuit.

As a result, law enforcement units have developed policy statements that attempt to provide officer guidance addressing high-speed vehicle chases. However, department policy and statements provide guidance only if officers read, understand, and follow the prescribed requirements. Central to the problem is insufficient training that mandates field application of policy. Classroom training is only a lead-up activity for officers that require pursuit-driving techniques. They need behind-the-wheel simulations to experience the pursuit reality.

More important, police officers must understand when to back off and not continue to pursue drivers in dangerous situations. Pursuit termination reduces the possibility for traffic accidents, fatalities, and injuries. The suspect's offense, weather, traffic conditions, and risk to innocent lives are significant factors to consider in the pursuit decision. In many cases, establishing the fleeing suspect's vehicle description and license plate leads to a successful follow-up and case closure.

In conclusion, pursuit driving is an important leadership issue; related policy and training represent law enforcement mandates. The opportunity for civil suits is abundant when inadequate training and negligence remain the standard. The sudden surge of adrenaline might affect officers, generating negative consequences for drivers when captured. This emotional and physical assault could lead to criminal charges against officers. While few high-speed pursuits are necessary, many produce an inherent risk that represents irresponsible and dangerous police practice. The financial risks for law enforcement agencies are considerable. CIVIL ACTIONS, insurance premiums, medical retirements, officer and civilian deaths merit definitive department policy and mandated police training.

For more information

Hicks, Wendy. *Police Vehicle Pursuits: Constitutionality, Liability, and Negligence.* Chicago: Charles C. Thomas, 2007.

Kappler, Victor E. *Critical Issues in Police Civil Liability.* Long Grove, Ill.: Waveland Press, 2006.

Thomas E. Baker
University of Scranton

history of policing Scholars often divide the history of American policing into four periods. Earliest efforts through much of the 1800s are commonly cast as an era of informal or transitional policing. Modern policing models became common by the end of the 1800s, marking the beginning of the political era. Policing in the 20th century underwent significant transformations, first during the reform/professional era, then during the COMMUNITY POLICING era.

Many early American communities drew upon social control methods practiced in England at the time, such as the watch system and the use of constables and sheriffs. Night watchmen walked the streets and alerted others to crimes and fires. Common complaints held that watchmen often slept on duty and did little when encountering serious offenses.

Constables served larger towns, served warrants and other official papers, and ARRESTED offenders. Victims usually paid a fee for a constable's assistance. Like the watchman, early American constables primarily took a reactive approach to law enforcement. A civic expectation often obligated property owners to take turns as a constable and/or watchman, though some paid others to serve in their place.

Charged with keeping the peace in counties, sheriffs also maintained jails, supervised elections, and collected taxes. Law enforcement was usually a relatively low priority. In the western frontier, relatively few federal marshals or local officers operated. Maintaining order was often left to citizen groups called vigilantes. Many southern cities instituted larger, more militaristic forces—often uniformed and heavily armed—specifically to quell slave uprisings and capture runaway slaves. It was commonly expected that all capable white men would rotate service in such patrols.

Sir Robert Peel developed the world's first modern police force in London (1829). Serious social problems related to health, poverty, and disorder mounted there as the Industrial Revolution generated phenomenal population growth. Riots over food, ethnic conflict over jobs, and bloody clashes between protesters and the military quickly revealed the inadequacies of a constable-watch system. Peel's model emphasized crime prevention. Rather than a watchman waiting to react to crime, publicly funded officers were to be proactive, walk city beats, and wear distinctive uniforms. These highly visible officers (nicknamed "peelers" and, later, "bobbies" after Robert Peel) were intended to be more accessible to residents and more likely to deter would-be criminals. Peel established a centralized, quasi-military system of command. Fearing resistance to what could have been perceived as an occupying military force, Peel chose uniforms that did not resemble military attire, and his officers were unarmed except for a small baton.

Using Peel's model as a blueprint, officials in New York City established the first unified, full-time, professional American police force in 1845. Most major American cities established a similar municipal police force by the end of that century, often prompted by tensions related to cultural heterogeneity and immigration, as well as growing concerns about crime.

But American cities modified the London model in important ways. By the late 1850s, New York cops carried revolvers, and officers elsewhere soon followed. American policing also was more decentralized with significant powers vested at the precinct level rather than in a central headquarters. The long American tradition of distrusting strong, centralized government pushed control of policing to the local level.

The decentralized nature of 19th-century American policing allowed political leaders in wards and neighborhoods to exert considerable power over police recruitment and practices in what became known as the POLITICAL ERA OF POLICING. Political machines—often formed along ethnic lines—ran many cities, controlled law enforcement, and doled out police jobs to groups in exchange for political support. One could purchase an appointment to the police force from some political machines. Turnover was high, and little job security existed; when a local political leader lost an election, the winning party or machine could fire all existing cops and replace them with their own supporters.

Crime control during this political era tended to be inefficient. Enforcing the law competed for officers' attention as many police departments also performed social welfare services, including providing overnight housing for the homeless, enforcing various business and housing codes, and helping locate lost children. Police activities emphasized maintaining order more than controlling crime.

POLICE CORRUPTION was widespread during the political era. Officers were encouraged to serve the interests of their sponsors by selectively enforcing laws and, at times, deterring certain voters from the ballot box. The taking of bribes from gambling and PROSTITUTION houses, as well as EXTORTING protection money from business owners also were pervasive.

In the ensuing reform era, numerous social, political, and technological innovations reshaped policing toward a more professional model. The Progressive Movement (1880–1910) depoliticized policing somewhat by centralizing power within departments away from local precincts. Reformers also heightened training and selection standards. The civil service system (Pendleton Act, 1883) weakened political patronage by requiring that many federal jobs be filled based on the merits rather than the political allegiances of the applicant. Cities soon placed many of their nonelected jobs, including policing, under civil service. Social welfare reforms moved some functions from police to other governmental agencies. These and other changes prompted a slow transition in policing from focusing on public order toward a crime-control model targeting more serious offenses.

Other reform efforts—led by AUGUST VOLLMER and his student, O.W. Wilson—focused on increasing police professionalism. Vollmer, police chief in Berkeley, California, during the early 1900s, emphasized the role of officers as crime fighters, helped establish an early university CRIMINOLOGY program, and was a pioneer in forensic investigations. He developed specialized departmental units and increasingly centralized command and record keeping to streamline investigations. Drawing upon technology to modernize policing, his department was among the first to: routinely conduct blood and fiber analyses (1907), institute a juvenile delinquency program (1919), use a lie detector (1921), rely on handwriting analysis (1921), develop a FINGERPRINT classification system (1924), be fully motorized (1917) and to have radio-equipped squad cars (1928). In 1931, Vollmer helped author the WICKERSHAM COMMISSION reports, the first comprehensive national study of crime and law enforcement, in which he strongly criticized police abuses. Among other remedies, Vollmer advocated stringent selection standards, including early calls for college-educated officers.

O.W. Wilson established police review boards, reorganized departments to emphasize efficiency rather than ward politics, and instituted merit systems, higher salaries, and other strategies to attract more qualified recruits and to reduce corruption. Wilson incorporated innovations into policing such as mobile radios, crime laboratories, and computerized record keeping. His methods, including the rotation of commanders and the elimination of most foot patrols to further reduce police corruption, were widely imitated. Building on Vollmer's strict rules of conduct, Wilson's 1928 code of ethics for police is the foundation for the standard used today by departments across the nation.

Although policing became more professional during the reform era, in many ways crime fighting became more reactive. While centralization, specialization, and technology allowed police to respond quickly to calls, car patrols distanced officers from the community.

During the 1950s and early 1960s, scholars increasingly characterized police-public relationships as antagonistic. Tensions worsened substantially during the CIVIL RIGHTS and anti–Vietnam War movements as police responses to protests, general disorder, and riots at times led to violent confrontations. Many watching televised clashes in which officers used water cannons, police dogs, and other harsh techniques on citizens came to see police as a symbol of an oppressive government. Public interest in policing also sharpened as crime rates more than doubled during the 1960s.

Unsatisfactory relationships between police and the communities they served encouraged many to advocate major changes in the recruitment, training, and deployment of officers. These and other forces prompted a slow shift in local law enforcement by the 1980s to community policing—the most widely used term for a loosely defined set of police strategies, tactics, and philosophies geared toward enhancing public trust, police-resident contact, and crime prevention; common alternative labels include community-oriented policing, PROBLEM-ORIENTED POLICING, and neighborhood-oriented policing.

At first, departments in some cities experimented with specialized units to perform more social service roles, partially in an attempt to improve community relations and to reduce perceived root causes of crime. Then the concept of team policing, popular briefly during the 1970s, decentralized some police operations and gave patrol officers more investigative responsibilities in particular, assigned neighborhoods. These and related efforts, however, often were short-lived; several departmental middle managers resisted what was seen as a threat to their power, and departments typically established such operations in relatively few neighborhoods in any given city.

Beginning in the 1980s, various aspects of these and other earlier experiments were broadened into the approach dominant today—community policing. In the last three decades, foot patrols have become a more central component of local law enforcement; crime prevention programs have attempted to increase community input (e.g., neighborhood watches, town meetings with police, citizen advisory boards); and permanent geographic assignment increasingly characterizes patrol deployment. Under the community policing approach, departments have embraced a broader mission that includes resolving conflicts, assisting victims, solving neighborhood problems, and reducing fear. Through this, it is believed that officers will benefit from a greater knowledge of and status within the community they serve, which will improve the officer's ability to reduce serious crime through prevention and detection. Despite early opposition from some officers who viewed such activities as something less than traditional crime fighting, the approach gained widespread support from police administrators and politicians at least at the conceptual level. Many scholars, however, assert that the theoretical assumptions of community policing are underdeveloped and that the variety of operations in different cities lumped together under the label of community policing makes it difficult to measure accurately the value of the approach.

For more information

Kelling, George, and M. H. Moore. "From Political to Reform to Community: The Evolving Strategy of the Police." In *Community Policing: Rhetoric or Reality,* edited by L. Greene and S. Mastrofski. New York: Praeger, 1998.

Monkkonen, Eric H. *Police in Urban America, 1860–1920.* Cambridge, Mass.: Cambridge Press, 1981.

Walker, Samuel, and C. M. Katz. *The Police in America: An Introduction.* New York: McGraw-Hill, 2002.

Michael A. McCall
San Diego State University

history of prisons Prisons are places where individuals are confined as PUNISHMENT for committing a crime. The history of prisons reveals different philosophies and approaches regarding how individuals are incarcerated and the purpose these institutions serve.

For most of history, prisons have been used for a number of purposes other than long-term confinement. Modeled upon England's use of prisons, the American colonies adopted prisons as a place to hold those who engaged in disorderly and/or petty offenses, awaiting punishment. Mainly due to lack of space and the value of publicly shaming those who transgressed the law, prisons did not serve to incapacitate, deter, or rehabilitate inmates for long periods of time. In light of the value placed on punishment, the colonial prisons were frequently used as temporary places to retain people awaiting public punishment or death due to criminal behavior; however, because prison conditions were so horrid, many people died from illness and disease before ever receiving their punishment. In fact, earlier accounts demonstrate that prisons were not used as a method of societal punishment as it is today. For example, the use of punishment was a widely accepted practice, where individuals accused of criminal behavior were often killed in gruesome, public ways to demonstrate intolerance for deviance.

In the late 18th century, the first American prison was established in Philadelphia as an outgrowth of the Walnut Street Jail—America's first jail in Pennsylvania. Shedding the old colonial punishment practices, the Quakers advocated for a new prison model that included contemporary views of punishment and confinement, such as reformation and repentance of inmates. Part of this reformation process included solitary confinement in individual cells and religious teachings to correct demoralization and provide for repentance. The typical architectural structure of prisons that still exists today was established in the Walnut Street Jail and consisted of a long corridor with separate cells to house inmates.

As an outgrowth of the Walnut Street Jail model, the Auburn model shortly followed in New York's Sing Sing prison. The main objective of this model was to organize and manage inmates under strict rules and regulations in an effort to reform inmates into law-abiding citizens. Other than solitary confinement and repentance, the Auburn model called for harsher administration and management of inmates, strict scheduling of activities, and prison labor in an effort to defray prison costs. Most of the prisons built in the 1800s and 1900s were prodigious edifices and offered only the most basic needs for the inmates incarcerated in them. Their idea of reform centered on breaking the spirits of the inmates and ensuring that they conformed. Critics of prisons considered many of the methods they used to be archaic and barbaric.

Until the late 1800s—when prisons were experiencing crowding and overall poor management and administration of services—the sole purpose of prisons was containment and repentance. However, a new penology movement was born and is referred to as the reformatory era. Under the direction and leadership of Zebulon Brockway of the Elmira Reformatory in New York (1876), reforms included the following: the classification of inmates organized by gender and offense type; the separation of adults from juveniles; the provision of individualized education and vocational training; the provision of moral and psychological counseling; and the provision of rewards for good behavior and PAROLE. Much emphasis was placed on INDETERMINATE SENTENCING whereby prison administrators could decide at their DISCRETION when an inmate made sufficient progress in education and could then be released. Although the idea of providing education and vocational training to inmates is extremely important, many problems arose from this system, including poorly trained staff and management and crowding and competition for services. In the 1900s, prisons continued work programs for inmates with the onset of industrialization. While the industry sector rapidly grew, inmates were needed to work in trades. Four main work arrangements grew out of this period: private companies contracting with prisons for inmate work; convict leasing; manufacturing of goods within prisons; and public systems work outside of prisons.

The National Prison Congress of 1870, paralleling the industrialization of work production and capitalism, laid the groundwork for the idea that prisons are an industry and should be operated as such. This new era of industrial prisons provided a more palpable platform for an array of privatization methods. Inmates produced goods while confined at meager wages, while prisons readily sold the goods to companies. The profits retained by these sales were used to finance and defray prison costs, while inmates received low wages. The concept of convict labor has been strongly opposed by manufacturers, employers, and labor leaders who argued that they could not compete with the low costs of goods produced by inmates, hence making competition even more difficult. The U.S. government institutionalized prison industries with the founding of the Federal Prison Industries (FPI) or UNICOR. UNICOR is a government-owned corporation established by Congress on June 23, 1934. FPI provides job skill training to inmates while reducing inmate idle time. In turn, goods produced by inmates confined in prisons are for sale to the federal government.

Today, jails and prisons function differently. The major difference is that jails are used to house inmates awaiting trial or those with sentences of one year or less, while prisons are used for confinement of individuals with long-term sentences of more than one year. In most states around the country, prisons are providing inmates with a range of services, including vocational, educational, work opportunities, and physical and mental health services. Many of these programs offer psychological counseling and group therapy, aggression and anger management, and other programs that target reentry and engaging in civil society. Despite varying degrees of what is offered in prisons, for the most part, inmates have opportunities to engage in various activities.

According to the latest numbers as of 2007, 1,595, 034 people are under state and federal JURISDICTION. State prisons hold 87.5 percent of prisoners, and the remaining 12.5 percent are under federal jurisdiction. Ninety-five percent of prisoners who are in state and federal custody received a sentence of more than one year. When one includes jail figures for 2007, 2.3 million prisoners were held in state, federal, and local jails. Of those held in jails and prisons, it is estimated that two-thirds (66 percent) of inmates are housed in prisons and a third (34 percent) are held in local jails. Currently, 118,239 prisoners are held in privately managed facilities. This accounts for a 5.4 percent increase from 2006, when the latest data were reported. Federal privatization increased by 12.1 percent from 2006 through today. Federal, jail, and juvenile privatization appear to be increasing in growth, while state prison privatization remains stagnant, and in some cases has declined. The custody count is derived from counting inmates under confinement in state or federal public prison facilities, privately operated facilities, and local jails. Inmates held in U.S. territories, military facilities, U.S. Immigration and Customs Enforcement facilities, jails in Indian areas, and juvenile facilities are not included in the custody count.

For more information

Carlson, Peter, and Judith Simon Garrett. *Prison and Jail Administration: Practice and Theory.* Sudbury, Mass.: Jones and Bartlett, 2006.

Pollack, Jocelyn M. *Prisons Today and Tomorrow.* 2nd ed. Sudbury, Mass.: Jones and Bartlett, 2006.

Sabol, William J., and Heather Couture. "Prison Inmates at Midyear 2007," *Bureau of Justice Statistics Bulletin,* June 2008.

Leila Sadeghi
Center for Executive Leadership in Government, Rutgers University, New Brunswick

Byron E. Price
Barbara Jordan Institute, Texas Southern University

Holmes, Oliver Wendell (1841–1935)

Supreme Court justice Oliver Wendell Holmes served as an associate justice of the Supreme Court from 1902 to 1932 and influenced the transition in jurisprudence from formalism to realism.

Holmes was born in 1841, the son of a prominent Boston physician and essayist. After completing studies at Harvard College, Holmes served in the Union army. When the Civil War ended, he studied law at Harvard, was admitted to the Massachusetts bar, entered private practice, and lectured part-time at his alma mater. Holmes wrote for legal periodicals and edited Kent's *Commentaries on American Law.* In 1880 he delivered a series of lectures that were published the following year as *The Common Law.* The work has been considered one of the most important pieces of U.S. legal scholarship. In it, Holmes argued that human experience, public institutions, moral and cultural beliefs, and judicial attitudes had a greater impact on the meaning of the law than pure logic. He advised the courts to do what he would later do as a jurist, to make legal determinations based on the public interest. For Holmes, the definition of the public interest would grow from an understanding of history, science, and the evolutionary process.

After the publication of *The Common Law,* Holmes was appointed to the Supreme Judicial Court of Massachusetts, where he served for 20 years, the last three as chief justice. In 1902 President Theodore Roosevelt nominated Holmes to the U.S. Supreme Court. He remained on the Court for 30 years, during which he wrote 873 opinions and served under four CHIEF JUSTICES. Although a number of his opinions seem anachronistic, Holmes is remembered most for his dissents, which often seemed to anticipate the majority rulings of future Courts.

Holmes believed in the principle of competition and in several cases he objected that the SHERMAN ANTITRUST ACT was an "imbecile statute." He also supported the application of human eugenics in *Buck v. Bell* (1927) where he wrote the 8–1 opinion upholding a Virginia law providing sterilization of the "feebleminded." Justice Holmes's reputation as a progressive comes more from his dissents in LOCHNER V. NEW YORK (1905) and *Adkins v. Children's Hospital* (1923). In both cases, Holmes argued for judicial deference to the will of elected legislatures. The Court majority in *Lochner,* he stated, would substitute their own beliefs in laissez-faire economics for the reasonable determination of the New York legislature that working hours were a public health concern and within the police powers of the state. Likewise, in *Adkins,* the justice upheld their definition of "freedom of CONTRACT" against Congress's reasonable effort to provide a minimum wage for women workers in the District of Columbia. Holmes again maintained that it was not the Court's job to strike down the reasonable acts of elected representatives.

On the question of FREEDOM OF SPEECH, Holmes was less willing to defer to the political process. Two cases arising out of World War I restrictions on free expression gave rise to several of Holmes's most quoted principles of free expression. In *SCHENCK V. UNITED STATES* (1919), he upheld Congress's power to prohibit speech that presents a "clear and present danger." The same year in *ABRAMS V. UNITED STATES* he dissented, claiming that in the absence of imminent danger, opinions must be allowed free expression to compete in the marketplace of ideas.

Holmes retired from the Supreme Court in 1932 and died in Washington, D.C., in 1935.

For more information

Frankfurter, Felix. *Mr. Justice Holmes and the Constitution.* 2nd ed. New York: Cambridge University Press, 1961.

Novick, Sheldon M. *Honorable Justice: The Life of Oliver Wendell Holmes.* Boston: Little, Brown, 1989.

Mary Welek Atwell
Radford University

homicide see MURDER.

Hoover, John Edgar (1895–1972) FBI director J. Edgar Hoover was the director of the FEDERAL BUREAU OF INVESTIGATION (FBI) from 1924 to 1972, turning a relatively obscure government agency into one of the top law enforcement organizations in the world. In his youth, Hoover applied himself to his schoolwork, being named valedictorian of his high school class. He graduated from the LAW SCHOOL at George Washington University and took a job in the U.S. DEPARTMENT OF JUSTICE in 1917. There he distinguished himself for his attention to detail and his ambitious career goals. During World War I, Hoover made his mark investigating opposition to the Wilson administration and its role in the war. In 1924 he was selected to head the Justice Department's Bureau of Investigation.

Though the agency was small, Hoover quickly set about establishing it as a well-respected national policing unit. He set up an academy to train future personnel, modernized criminal investigation techniques such as FINGERPRINTING and FORENSICS, and gained national attention in the ARRESTS of notorious gangsters. In 1935 the organization formally became known as the FBI. The Bureau's JURISDICTION was increased during FRANKLIN ROOSEVELT's administration and Hoover set out to uncover EVIDENCE of espionage. After World War II, Hoover became an outspoken anticommunist and his agency set about exposing American communist operatives and sympathizers. Hoover's most notorious method of keeping track of alleged misconduct and impropriety was by establishing a "file." The FBI kept track of the

J. Edgar Hoover (LBJ Library)

activities of many prominent individuals by the information obtained and placed into their files.

One such individual that Hoover was particularly preoccupied with was MARTIN LUTHER KING. Hoover engaged in such activities as bugging King's phones, following his movements, and even urging colleges not to award him honorary degrees, suggesting that he was affiliated with communists.

Under Hoover, the FBI's power began to wane following the 1960 election of JOHN F. KENNEDY as president. Kennedy appointed his brother Robert to head the Justice Department and it soon became clear that the Kennedys intended to scale back the power that Hoover had amassed over the years under far more receptive administrations. The press was also involved in efforts to demystify Hoover and the Bureau's activities.

Following Hoover's death in 1972 at the age of 77, the FBI continued to lose much of its power. Under the FREEDOM OF INFORMATION ACT, many of the controversial files that Hoover had amassed were made public. They reveal the great lengths, which some would say were unethical and even illegal, that the FBI went to in their zeal for uncovering sabotage and subversion. The files also reveal a government agency that was transformed from a small inept group of government bureaucrats into a respected, and even feared, professional organization.

For more information

Deloach, Cartha D. *Hoover's FBI: The Inside Story by Hoover's Trusted Lieutenant.* Washington, D.C.: Regnery, 1995.

Powers, Richard Gid. *Secrecy and Power: The Life of J. Edgar Hoover.* New York: Free Press, 1987.

Artemus Ward
California State University, Chico

hot pursuit Hot pursuit refers to one of the exceptions to the search warrant requirement of the FOURTH AMENDMENT. In some situations, law enforcement officials may be able to SEARCH AND SEIZE individuals and things as a result of a hot pursuit of a suspect.

To comprehend the legal meaning of hot pursuit, one must first have a basic understanding of the Fourth Amendment to the U.S. CONSTITUTION. This amendment guarantees U.S. citizens freedom from unreasonable searches and seizures, and to this end, prohibits law enforcement officers from searching a privately owned building without first obtaining a search warrant that is based on PROBABLE CAUSE and that describes the premises to be examined and the person or item(s) sought.

Although the Fourth Amendment is easily understandable and clearly defines the difference between legal and illegal searches, during the 200-plus years since the BILL OF RIGHTS (which includes amendments one through 10) was added to the Constitution, the U.S. Supreme Court has added layers of interpretation to the Fourth Amendment and has actually defined circumstances under which a law enforcement officer could conduct a WARRANTLESS SEARCH. The Court established this specific exception to freedom from unreasonable searches and seizures by allowing a warrantless search of private property if exigent circumstances exist that overcome the presumption of unreasonableness that attaches to all warrantless home entries.

An important factor to be considered when determining whether any exigency exists is the gravity of the underlying offense for which the ARREST is being made. The application of the exigent circumstances exception should be reserved for situations in which there is probable cause to believe that a serious crime, rather than a mere MISDEMEANOR, has been committed. In *WARDEN V. HAYDEN*, 387 U.S. 294 (1967), the Supreme Court explicitly stated that exigent circumstances, such as hot pursuit of a suspect, may constitute exceptions to the warrant requirements of the Fourth Amendment.

Hot pursuit of an individual suspected of committing a crime qualifies as one of these exigent circumstances, provided the officer in pursuit believes that delay or interruption of the pursuit would endanger the officer's life or the lives of others and aims to end the pursuit by either preventing the suspect's escape or by arresting him or her. Finally, in addition to the confusion inherent in the exceptions to the Fourth Amendment, courts cause further problems by using hot pursuit to refer to an emergency situation in which a law enforcement officer is chasing a suspect or escaped felon into a neighboring JURISDICTION and has had no time to alert law enforcement people in that area.

The exclusionary rule provides an additional safeguard against violations of the Fourth Amendment. This rule prohibits PROSECUTORS from presenting any evidence obtained in the course of an unconstitutional search and seizure. And since courts make the final determination of whether a warrantless search is permissible and reject misuses of the doctrine of hot pursuit, law enforcement officers are simply not permitted to ignore constitutional safeguards on POLICE POWER. Rather, hot pursuit is a strictly limited and intended to be used only when the need for practicality in everyday policing is carefully weighed against the necessity of compliance with the dictates of the U.S. Constitution.

For instance, a U.S. COURT OF APPEALS decided that officers were not in hot pursuit and could therefore not enter a suspect's home without a warrant when they had chased a suspect to his home, surrounded his residence, and remained there for six hours without seeking a search warrant. As a practical matter, the officers had ample time to obtain a warrant before storming into the suspect's home. The court held that since the suspect could not have fled the scene and the officers had no fear of destruction of evidence or threat to safety, there were no exigent circumstances that would authorize a warrantless search.

U.S. and state courts allow warrantless searches only in carefully limited situations that avoid, to as great a degree as possible, allowing exceptions to the Fourth Amendment's right against unreasonable searches and seizures. The hot pursuit doctrine embodies one such exception. Its use is allowed only when it would be extremely impractical to follow any other procedure.

For more information

LaFave, Wayne, Jerold Isreal, Nancy King, and Orin Kerr. *Criminal Procedure. 5th ed.* Eagan, Minn.: West, 2009.

Beth Simon Swartz
Attorney

"hot spot" policing "Hot spot" policing is a crime prevention strategy designed to identify areas of a community with a high propensity for criminal activity and to marshal police resources effectively to reduce crime and the number of citizen calls for assistance in that area. While use of police resources may involve traditional policing technique, or nontraditional community-based strategies, the goal is to reduce the propensity for crime in the targeted area while preventing displacement of criminal activity to new areas within a community.

"Hot spot" policing grew out of several large-scale studies of crime activity conducted in the 1970s and 1980s. Egon Bittner (1970), and David Weisburd and Lorraine Greene (1995), using early versions of statistical spreadsheets and map plotting software, discovered that a majority of small-scale crime is committed by a relatively small number of offenders, often confined to a small geographic area. For example, in some communities, as little as 3 percent of a city's intersections generated more than 50 percent of its citizen calls for assistance, or close to half of all ARRESTS (Weisburd, 5). Many police programs in the 1980s and 1990s began using this information to plan different ways to patrol their communities and to allocate resources. Changing patterns of patrolling based on allocating resources to community "hot spots" of crime represents one major reform in the way police have done their jobs over the last half-century.

"Hot spot" policing begins by discovering what areas in a community attract, or have the potential to attract, high rates of crime. Once a "hot spot" is located, police must then decide how to address that area. Police officers use several common methods to address a "hot spot," including increased patrols, pro-active arrests based on searches, BROKEN WINDOW policing (aggressive patrols in areas that first show signs of GANG tagging), and the use of NUISANCE ordinances to compel landlords and barkeepers to assist in identifying and controlling criminal or suspicious behavior.

"Hot spot" policing is effective, uses resources well, and seems to reduce crime without transporting it to other areas of a community. It is controversial, however, for three reasons. First, it is not what police departments have done traditionally. Second, because of its focus on place, rather than people, some argue that "hot spot" policing violates individual's CIVIL LIBERTIES. Finally, "hot spot" policing requires accurate data collection and management, expertise many departments lack. Despite these criticisms, most scholars believe "hot spot" policing will remain a viable tool for law enforcement.

For more information

Bittner, Egon. *The Functions of the Police in Modern Society.* New York: Aronson, 1970.

Braga, Anthony A. *Crime Prevention Research Review #2: Police Enforcement Strategies to Prevent Crime in Hot Spot Areas.* Washington D.C.: Department of Justice Office of Community Oriented Policing Services, 2008.

Weisburd, David. "Place-Based Policing," *Ideas in American Policing* 9: (January 2008).

Weisburd, David, and Lorraine Greene. "Policing Drug Hot Spots: The New Jersey DMA Experiment," *Justice Quarterly* 12 (1995): 711–736.

Michael P. Bobic
West Virginia Wesleyan College.

House Un-American Activities Committee

The House Un-American Activities Committee was an investigatory committee in the U.S. House of Representatives charged with discovering the extent of communist infiltration in the government, the labor movement, and various other areas of American life. The members of this committee used its investigations primarily to expose to the public persons suspected of belonging to or being affiliated with the Communist Party. The committee was created as a special or select committee in 1938, but it became a permanent committee of the House in 1945 and remained so until it was disbanded in 1975 (it was renamed the Internal Security Committee in 1969). From 1945 to 1957, the committee held at least 230 public hearings, at which more than 3,000 persons testified. During this period, 135 of these witnesses were cited for CONTEMPT of Congress, usually for refusing to answer all the committee's questions.

Thus the committee's investigations produced several U.S. Supreme Court decisions that helped to define the limits of Congress's investigatory powers. The first case was *Watkins v. United States,* 354 U.S. 178 (1957), which provided a sharp rebuke to Congress. Watkins was a regional officer of the Farm Equipment Workers Union. Appearing before the committee in 1954, Watkins answered fully the questions pertaining to his affiliation with the Communist Party. He also answered questions about people he knew to be current members of the party, but he refused to answer questions about individuals who had disassociated themselves from the party. In a 6–1 decision, the Supreme Court threw out Watkins's conviction for contempt of Congress. The ruling articulated broad constitutional limits on congressional investigatory powers by balancing the congressional need for particular information with the individual's interests in privacy. The Court also reaffirmed a previous holding that the questions asked by a congressional committee must be pertinent to the stated matter under inquiry, and the purpose of the hearing could not solely be to expose individuals who held unpopular political beliefs or associations.

J. Parnell Thomas, chairman of the House Un-American Activities Committee (right), and Robert E. Stripling, committee investigator, examine films to be shown to the committee investigating the degree of communist infiltration in the motion picture industry.

The second case regarding this committee was *Barenblatt v. United States,* 360 U.S. 109 (1959). Barenblatt, a former professor at the University of Michigan, refused to answer questions regarding communist infiltration into higher education. He APPEALED his conviction for contempt of Congress based on the *Watkins* precedent and based on his First Amendment rights. In a 5–4 decision, the Court's majority upheld his conviction, retreating from the broad limits on congressional investigations detailed in its earlier decision. The *Watkins* decision had produced concerted efforts in Congress to curb the Court's authority over congressional investigations. Although these efforts were not successful, the Court cited a need for self-preservation when it pulled back from its former defense of the rights of witnesses. Although this decision was never overturned, in later cases the Court did reverse the convictions of various uncooperative congressional witnesses.

For more information

Beck, Carl. *Contempt of Congress: A Study of the Prosecutions Initiated by the Committee on Un-American Activities, 1945–1957.* New Orleans: Hauser Press, 1959.

Bigel, Alan I. "The First Amendment and National Security: The Court Responds to Governmental Harassment of Alleged Communist Sympathizers," *Ohio Northern University Law Review* 19 (1993): 885.

Mark C. Miller
Clark University

Hudson v. McMillian 503 U.S. 1 (1992) In *Hudson v. McMillian,* the U.S. Supreme Court held that a malicious and sadistic use of force against a prison inmate may violate the EIGHTH AMENDMENT prohibition against CRUEL AND UNUSUAL PUNISHMENT even if the inmate did not suffer a significant injury.

Keith Hudson was an inmate at the Louisiana State Penitentiary when two corrections officers punched and kicked him while he was handcuffed and shackled. A supervisor observed the beating and told the officers "not to have too much fun." Hudson, who experienced facial bruising and swelling and loosened teeth, argued that he was entitled to compensation for his injuries because the officers violated the Eighth Amendment by their excessive use of force. The officers argued that Hudson should be required to prove that he suffered a significant injury in order to prevail.

Before *Hudson,* the Supreme Court held that when an inmate claims an Eighth Amendment violation based on excessive force, the inmate must show an "unnecessary and wanton infliction of pain." *Whitley v. Albers,* 475 U.S. 312, 89 L. Ed. 2d 251, 106 S. Ct. 1078 (1986). The Supreme Court arrived at this standard for determining excessive force by balancing the need to maintain order in prisons against the harm inmates might suffer from the use of force. This standard arose primarily from cases in which officers used force during prison disturbances or riots. *Hudson* involved neither, but the majority adopted the same standard for any use of force, finding that the same concerns arise whenever corrections officers use force. In order to prove an unnecessary and wanton infliction of pain, the inmate must show that the officer maliciously and sadistically used force for the purpose of causing harm. If force is applied in good faith for the purpose of maintaining order, it does not violate the Eighth Amendment.

Justice CLARENCE THOMAS authored the dissent. He argued that the Court's previous cases required that the inmate prove that the injury was objectively harmful enough to establish a constitutional violation. The majority rejected this argument, writing that the objective component of an Eighth Amendment claim changes depending on the nature of the alleged violation and also varies with contemporary standards of decency. In the excessive force context, the majority held that whenever officials use force maliciously and sadistically to cause harm, contemporary standards of decency are always violated, regardless of injury. Therefore, although the seriousness of the injury is a relevant factor to consider in determining whether the inmate proved his claim, it is not determinative.

Justices Stevens and Blackmun agreed with the result but argued that in situations not involving a riot or prison disturbance, inmates should only be required to prove an unnecessary and wanton infliction of pain rather than the heightened standard of "malicious and sadistic" infliction of pain. Justice Blackmun wrote separately to observe that "harm" under the Eighth Amendment is not limited to physical injury and that there are inflictions of psychological harm that might be cruel and unusual.

For more information

Nelson, Diana L. "*Hudson v. McMillian:* The Evolving Standard of Eighth Amendment Application to the Use of Excessive Force against Prison Inmates," *North Carolina Law Review* (1992): 1,811.

Palmer, John W. *Constitutional Rights of Prisoners.* 8th ed. Albany, N.Y.: Anderson, 2006.

Cassandra L. McKeown
University of South Dakota.

Hudson v. Michigan 547 U.S. 586 (2006) In *Hudson v. Michigan,* the Supreme Court decided a violation of the "knock-and-announce" rule did not require the suppression of all EVIDENCE found in the search. In doing so, the Court resolved the intersection of two lines of PRECEDENT.

A longstanding common law principle required law enforcement officers to announce their presence and provide residents an opportunity to open the door when officers arrive with a search warrant. In *Wilson v. Arkansas,* 514 U.S. 927 (1995), the Court held that this "knock-and-announce" rule was also a command of the FOURTH AMENDMENT. Even so, the Court recognized that there were exceptions to this rule, such as when officers feared a threat of physical violence or were concerned that evidence would be destroyed. None of the exceptions applied in this case.

In this case, the Detroit police officers announced their presence but waited only three to five seconds before entering the unlocked door, warrant in hand. They found crack cocaine and a loaded gun in the home. The Court recognized that the police officers violated the CONSTITUTION, but it faced the question of whether to exclude the evidence found in this search.

In *WEEKS V. UNITED STATES,* 232 U.S. 383 (1914), the Court held that evidence seized from a home without a warrant in violation of the Fourth Amendment must be excluded from court. The Court applied the same rule to the states in *MAPP V. OHIO,* 367 U.S. 643 (1961). In *Hudson,* the Court stated that "Suppression of evidence, however, has always been our last resort, not our first impulse." This is because the costs of the exclusionary rule "sometimes include setting the guilty free and the dangerous at large" (591).

The Court drew a distinction between the interests protected by the Fourth Amendment's warrant requirements and those protected by the knock-and-announce rule. Rather than shielding evidence from the government's eyes, the rule protects life and limb by preventing accidental violence against police officers by surprised residents. The rule also protects a homeowners' property rights by allowing them to open the door rather than have it broken down. Finally, the rule protects privacy and dignity by allowing residents to put clothes on and collect themselves before answering the door. The Court, however, found that the rule did not protect a person's interest in preventing the government from seizing evidence. Consequently, applying the exclusionary rule to that evidence was inappropriate.

The Court also balanced the benefits of deterring police misconduct against the substantial social costs of the exclusionary rule. Treating the issue as only "the right not to be intruded upon in one's nightclothes," and believing that professionalism in police forces would prevent most violations, the Court found that the social cost of excluding evidence outweighed that interest (597–600). Police officers are still required, in most circumstances, to knock and announce their presence before entering a home with a warrant. But if they fail to do so, the evidence they find will not be excluded solely because the officers violated the knock-and-announce rule.

For more information

Moran, David. "Waiting for the Other Shoe: Hudson and the Precarious State of Mapp," *Iowa Law Review* (2008) 1,725.

Tomkovicz, James J. "*Hudson v. Michigan* and the Future of Fourth Amendment Exclusion," *Iowa Law Review* (2008): 1,819.

Jason C. Miller
United States Court of Appeals for the Sixth Circuit

Hurtado v. People of California 110 U.S. 516 (1884) *Hurtado v. People of California* was one of the earliest cases heard by the Supreme Court of the United States that interpreted the meaning of the Fourteenth Amendment to the U.S. CONSTITUTION. In this 7-1 decision authored by Justice Matthews, the Supreme Court held that the words *DUE PROCESS of law* in the Fourteenth Amendment do not require an indictment by a GRAND JURY in a state prosecution for MURDER. Thus the Court's majority refused to apply to the states the federal grand jury requirements found in the Fifth Amendment.

This criminal case arose when the defendant was tried for murder in the California state courts and sentenced to death. A provision in the California constitution authorized prosecutions for FELONIES by "information," which means that the prosecutor presents the charges directly to a magistrate without ever presenting the charges to a grand jury. The Fifth Amendment, however, requires in federal capital cases that the charges be presented to a grand jury. The defendant argued that, after the passage of the Fourteenth Amendment, the Fifth Amendment provisions should also apply to the states. The defendant also argued that even if the Fifth Amendment did not apply to the states, the term *due process of law* in the Fourteenth Amendment would require the prosecutor to present the charges to a grand jury in a capital case. The Supreme Court majority disagreed with both of these arguments.

The defendant's Fifth Amendment arguments were based on what is known as the INCORPORATION doctrine. Before the adoption of the Fourteenth Amendment, the Supreme Court had ruled in *BARRON V. BALTIMORE*, 7 Pet. 243 (1833) that the guarantees of the BILL OF RIGHTS only restricted the actions of the federal government and did not apply to the states. After the passage of the Fourteenth Amendment, Justice Bradley, in his dissent in the *SLAUGHTERHOUSE CASES*, 16 Wall. 36 (1873), advanced the theory that the Fourteenth Amendment's due process clause fully incorporates all of the guarantees in the Bill of Rights, thus applying them to the states. The Supreme Court majority rejected this theory in both the *Slaughterhouse Cases* and in *Hurtado v. California*. In *Hurtado* the Court also stated that the meaning of "due process" in the pre-colonial common law did not require the use of grand juries in capital cases.

Although the Court has never accepted the total incorporation theory, in a variety of decisions mostly from the 1960s the Court has selectively incorporated many of the guarantees of the Bill of Rights, thus applying them to the states. The Court, however, has never overturned *Hurtado v. California*. Thus today state PROSECUTORS are still not required to use grand juries in capital cases, even though federal prosecutors must do so.

For more information

Fisher, Louis. *American Constitutional Law.* 3rd ed. Durham, N.C.: Carolina Academic Press, 1999.

Israel, Jerold H. "Selective Incorporation: Revisited," *Georgetown Law Journal* 71 (1982): 253.

Mark C. Miller
Clark University

I

ignorance of the law The saying "ignorance of the law is no excuse" is a legal maxim that states a defendant cannot expect to have a plea of ignorance of an existing law accepted by the court as justification for violating the law. This policy presumes that everyone knows the law. Without the policy, people would be encouraged to remain ignorant of the law.

As a policy, the prohibition of ignorance of the law as a defense has been upheld in numerous cases because to allow it would invite chaos. Anyone charged with a criminal offense or made subject of a civil suit could then simply plead ignorance. The policy has been one that encourages everyone to learn the law, especially the common law.

The maxim of "ignorance of the law" goes back at least to Roman law. It was stated in Latin as *Ignorantia juris non excusat* ("Ignorance of the law does not excuse"). In other places, it was stated as *Ignorantia legis neminem excusat* ("Ignorance of the law excuses no one"). The maxim entered English common law as "ignorance of the law is no excuse." It became a part of American law with the adoption of common law under the CONSTITUTION.

Modern courts have allowed limitations to the maxim of ignorance of the law. One is the willfulness of the defendant. With the growing complexity of law, violations were separated between the intentional and the unintentional. Legally, the willfulness of an action is stated as MENS REA ("guilty mind"), but this element may be missing in some cases and allowed by the courts as a proper defense.

Some courts have allowed ignorance of the law in complicated areas of law such as business, environmental, or other complex areas. In these cases of great legal complexity, the courts may allow an ignorance of the law defense because it may not be clear what the law is. To do otherwise would very likely lead to the convictions of persons simply engaged in innocent activities. Another possible limitation for allowing ignorance is if a defendant relied upon an interpretation of the law that was issued by a public official.

Ignorance of the law may not be an excuse, but ignorance of fact can be an excuse. If the misapprehension of fact is true, then in actions such as the innocent purchase or sale of stolen goods by a merchant or a private individual, ignorance can be used as a successful defense.

For more information

Bergman, Paul, and Sara J. Berman. *The Criminal Law Handbook: Know Your Rights, Survive the System.* 11th ed. Berkeley, Calif.: NOLO Press, 2009.

LaFave, Wayne R., and Austin W. Scott. *Handbook on Criminal Law.* Minneapolis, Minn.: West, 1986.

Morgan, J. Tom. *Ignorance Is No Defense: A Teenager's Guide to Georgia Law.* Atlanta, Ga.: GDG, 2007.

Walton, Douglas. *Arguments from Ignorance.* University Park: Pennsylvania State University Press, 1995.

Andrew J. Waskey
Dalton State College

illegal alien Illegal alien refers to a foreign-born person not a citizen or national of the United States who is physically present within the United States unlawfully. An alien may lack legal immigration status because he or she entered the United States illegally, or because he or she remains here illegally after having entered legally.

Immigration status is governed by federal law. Currently, lawful forms of admission include, but are not limited to, (1) admission for permanent residence; (2) admission for a temporary stay for authorized purposes, such as diplomacy, business, pleasure, education, cultural and artistic activities, athletics, and certain employment; (3) admission as a refugee or ASYLUM seeker; and (4) temporary PAROLE into the United States for urgent humanitarian reasons or for reasons in the public interest. Once an illegal alien is present within the United States, that individual may be eligible for an adjustment of status to that of a legal resident.

Admission into the United States may be denied or restricted on a variety of grounds, including, but not limited to, (1) numerical limitations based on worldwide levels of immigration, country of origin, familial status, employment status, immigration status, and other factors; (2) health-related grounds, such as a physical or mental disorder that may pose a threat to the safety, welfare, or property of the alien or the public; (3) criminal grounds, such as conviction for crimes of moral turpitude, crimes relating to controlled substances, PROSTITUTION, or commercialized vice; (4) security grounds, related to espionage, sabotage, TERRORISM, violent overthrow of the government, membership in the Communist Party, participation in genocide, or other proscribed activity; (5) the likelihood that the alien will become a "public charge," based on factors such as age, health, family status, financial resources, education, and skills; (5) the alien seeks to enter the United States to perform skilled or unskilled labor, where the performance of such labor may adversely affect workers in the United States, or the alien lacks prescribed professional credentials and qualifications, or certain conditions imposed upon the prospective employer of the alien have not been met; (6) the alien lacks proper documentation, such as a valid immigrant or nonimmigrant visa issued by the United States, or a valid passport or similar document; (7) the alien has violated certain provisions of the immigration laws relating to admission into the United States; (8) the alien has committed some other specified offense(s), such as draft evasion, polygamy, or child abduction.

Illegal aliens who are physically present in the United States, and thus within its territorial JURISDICTION, are bound to obey the law, and they also are entitled to the protection of the law. Although the CIVIL RIGHTS enjoyed by illegal aliens are not necessarily coextensive with those afforded citizens and legal residents, illegal aliens are entitled to protection under the U.S. CONSTITUTION. For example, illegal aliens enjoy FREEDOM OF SPEECH and of the press under the First Amendment, and freedom from unreasonable SEARCHES AND SEIZURES (with notable limitations relating to entry and deportation) under the FOURTH AMENDMENT. Illegal aliens may not be deprived of life, liberty, or property without DUE PROCESS of law under the Fifth and the Fourteenth Amendments. The SIXTH AMENDMENT's provisions securing certain rights to the accused in criminal proceedings apply to illegal aliens, as do the EIGHTH AMEND-

MENT's prohibitions against excessive BAIL and CRUEL AND UNUSUAL PUNISHMENT. Illegal aliens are entitled to EQUAL PROTECTION of the law under the Fourteenth Amendment. Illegal aliens may sue to enforce their civil rights under federal civil rights statutes.

Despite enjoying these and other legal rights under federal and state law, illegal aliens also face significant legal disabilities and penalties. Illegal entry into the United States is a crime punishable by fines, imprisonment, and civil penalties. Illegal aliens who are apprehended are subject to detention and may be ordered removed from the country unless eligible for a waiver or for an adjustment of immigration status. Illegal aliens (like all noncitizens) do not have the RIGHT TO VOTE. Unless granted employment authorization, an illegal alien may not lawfully be employed. Illegal aliens may be disqualified from receiving some public welfare benefits.

In general, illegal aliens do not possess too many rights under the Constitution. However, in *PLYLER v. DOE*, 457 U.S. 202 (1982), the Supreme Court ruled that the children of undocumented or illegal aliens do enjoy many rights. Specifically, in this case the Court struck down as unconstitutional a state law that would deny children of illegal aliens from receiving a public education.

Moreover, concerns about illegal aliens entering the United States have prompted numerous responses. One has been the effort to build a high wall or border fence between the United States and Mexico. Second, while regulation of ALIENAGE and immigration is generally a federal and not a state issue, several states have sought to address these issues. In 2010, the state of Arizona passed a law granting police broad authority to stop and question individuals whom they suspect are illegal aliens. Critics claimed the law is discriminatory or constitutes RACIAL PROFILING. Others claim that the law is preempted by the 1986 Federal Immigration Reform and Control Act. In July 2010, several portions of that law were enjoined by a federal JUDGE. Additionally, an Arizona law imposing tough new sanctions on employers who hire illegal aliens was also challenged and awaiting Supreme Court review.

A fence that runs along part of the border of the United States and Mexico (Getty Images)

Finally, in 2010 and 2011, many advocated denying CITIZENSHIP to the children of illegal immigrants born in the United States. This would require amending the Constitution. Advocates of this proposal say that granting citizenship to the children of illegal aliens creates incentives to enter the United States illegally. Critics of the law argue its adoption would create a two-track level of citizenship in the United States.

For more information

8 U.S.C., sections 1101 *et seq.* 3A–3C.

Aliens and Citizens. St. Paul, Minn.: West, 1998.

Victoria S. Shabanian
Office of Andrew J. Wistrich,
Magistrate Judge
U.S. District Court, Central District of California

Illinois v. Gates 462 U.S. 213 (1983) In *Illinois v. Gates*, the Supreme Court announced a "totality-of-the-circumstances" test when deciding the constitutionality of a JUDGE-issued search warrant based on an anonymous tip. The majority of the Court, in an opinion penned by Justice WILLIAM REHNQUIST, made it easier for police to obtain search warrants.

The Bloomingdale (Illinois) Police Department received an anonymous letter that described in detail how Lance and Sue Gates would transport marijuana from Florida to Illinois. The informant included the date the couple would transport the drugs, the street value of drugs in their basement, and that the couple bragged about never having to work. The Bloomingdale Police Department took several actions toward surveilling the suspects, eventually searching their car, which held 350 pounds of marijuana. At trial, the defendants' attorney argued that the EVIDENCE from the car search should be withheld because the police department lacked PROBABLE CAUSE, because the letter failed to explain how the information provided was gathered, thereby violating the existing test used to determine admissibility of evidence based on anonymous tips. Both the trial judge and the Supreme Court of Illinois agreed with the Gates's attorney. The Supreme Court of Illinois understood previously court decisions as requiring an anonymous letter to satisfy both independent requirements before the letter could be relied on.

The Supreme Court, in a 7-2 decision, held that the affidavit was unjustified but did not agree that the "two-pronged test" should be applied so rigidly to every case. Justice Rehnquist, in the opinion of the Court, found that the elements do not have to be understood as entirely separate and independent. Rather than using the Supreme Court of Illinois implications of the "two-pronged test," Rehnquist emphasized that the "two-pronged test" should be used to illuminate the practical question of whether there is "probable cause" to believe that evidence is located in a particular location. In addition, the Court found that if every case used the "two-pronged test" as rigidly as the Illinois Supreme Court, then anonymous informant tips would not be valued police work.

Justice Rehnquist found that a "totality of circumstances" approach is more consistent with how probable cause is treated, in comparison to a rigid test that has to be satisfied by "every informant's tip." The Court found that the "two-pronged test" should be used as a relevant consideration for the "totality of circumstances" because a "deficiency in one may be compensated for, in determining the overall reliability of a tip, by a strong showing as to the other, or by some other indicia of reliability." The majority found that the "totality of circumstances" better achieves the accommodation of public and private interests required by the FOURTH AMENDMENT than the existing test.

Justice WILLIAM BRENNAN, in a dissenting opinion, argued that the affidavit was invalid under the newly decided "totality of circumstances" test. He also dissented in the Court's rejection of the two-pronged test, arguing that "the Court gives virtually no consideration" to assuring that information given a judge to procure a search warrant "has been obtained in a reliable way by an honest or credible person . . ."

This case is a landmark for the Fourth Amendment's probable cause and search warrants clause because the Court overrules the *Spinelli-Aguilar* "two-pronged test" and replaces it with the "totality of circumstances" criteria. This case made it easier for police to obtain a search warrant from a judge. This does not mean, however, that police are without standards in their searches. Only the areas specified in a warrant may be searched; only items specified in the warrant may be seized, unless possession of the item is illegal; and the warrant must be executed in a orderly and timely fashion. *Gates* is also important because, like many other BURGER COURT opinions, it signals a retraction of individual protections initiated by the prior, and more liberal, WARREN COURT.

For more information

McCall, Madhavi M., and Michael A. McCall. "Chief Justice William Rehnquist: His Law-and-Order Legacy and Impact on Criminal Justice." *Akron Law Review* 39 (2006): 323–372.

Olivia Kathleen Leonard
Monmouth College

Tobias Gibson
Westminster College

Illinois v. Wardlow 528 U.S. 119 (2000) In *Illinois v. Wardlow,* the U.S. Supreme Court ruled that unprovoked "headlong flight" is a "pertinent factor" in establishing whether police have "reasonable suspicion" to stop a person for questioning.

The case began around noon on September 9, 1995, when four, two-officer patrol cars were called to a Chicago neighborhood that was notorious for trafficking illegal narcotics. William "Sam" Wardlow was standing in front of a building at 4035 West Van Buren Street when the patrol cars passed. Suddenly, Wardlow began running away from the patrol cars. Wardlow's actions drew the attention of Officers Harvey and Nolan in the last squad car. The two officers quickly broke from the caravan and began pursuing Wardlow. The officers further noticed Wardlow cradling a white opaque bag as he scurried down a gangway and an alley. When the police finally cornered the fleeing Wardlow, they immediately commenced a *Terry* pat-down search (see *TERRY V. OHIO*, 392 U.S. 1 [1968]). Officer Nolan then squeezed Wardlow's opaque bag and discovered a .38 caliber handgun with five live rounds of ammunition. Wardlow was ARRESTED and subsequently charged with unlawful possession of a weapon by a former felon.

At his trial, Wardlow made a motion to suppress the EVIDENCE, asserting the officers lacked reasonable suspicion to initiate the stop and frisk. The motion was denied, and Wardlow was found guilty. On appeal, the Illinois Appellate Court reversed and the Illinois Supreme Court affirmed, citing the U.S. Supreme Court's ruling in *Florida v. Royer,* 460 U.S. 491 (1983). In *Royer,* the Court ruled, "although police have the right to approach individuals and ask questions, the individual has no obligation to respond . . . and [may] go his or her way." However, on APPEAL, a badly split U.S. Supreme Court reversed, again upholding Wardlow's conviction.

Writing for the five-member majority, CHIEF JUSTICE WILLIAM REHNQUIST (joined by Associate Justices SANDRA DAY O'CONNOR, ANTONIN SCALIA, ANTHONY KENNEDY, and CLARENCE THOMAS) ruled that, given the circumstances, the Chicago police were justified in stopping and frisking Wardlow. The fact that Wardlow was in an area known for drug trafficking and aroused suspicion when he suddenly began running were pertinent factors to consider in determining the constitutionality of an investigative stop. Citing *United States v. Brignoni-Ponce,* 422 U.S. 873 (1875), Rehnquist underscored that, "nervous, evasive behavior is a pertinent factor in determining reasonable suspicion." He concluded that, "Headlong flight—wherever it occurs—is the consummate act of evasion."

A dissenting opinion was offered by Associate Justice JOHN PAUL STEVENS (joined by Justices David Souter, RUTH BADER GINSBURG and STEPHEN BREYER). "I am not persuaded," Stevens wrote, "that the mere fact that someone standing on a sidewalk looked in the direction of a passing car before starting to run is sufficient to justify a forcible stop and frisk." Here Stevens believed the prosecution did not articulate sufficient facts to support an argument for reasonable suspicion. For example, the testimony did not indicate whether the squad car was marked or whether the two arresting officers were in uniform. Stevens also believed there may be many reasons an innocent pedestrian might take flight, such as a minority living in a high-crime area who fears that cooperating with police might endanger one's life.

For more information

Bender, Jonathan. "*Illinois v. Wardlow:* The Supreme Court Dodges the Race Bullet in the Fourth Amendment Terry Stops," *Denver University Law Review,* 78, no. 1 (2000): 125–148.

Greenhouse, Linda. "Supreme Court Roundup; Flight Can Justify Search by Police, High Court Rules." *New York Times* (13 January 2000).

Jarret, Joseph G. "To Flee or Not to Flee: The Implications of *Illinois v. Wardlow* on the Practice of Criminal Law in Florida," *Florida Bar Journal* (June 1, 2000).

Johnson-Liu, M. Emily. "Running from the Law in the Wrong Part of Town: *Illinois v. Wardlow,*" *American Journal of Criminal Law* 27 (October 1, 1999): 129.

Patel, Shan. "Per Se Reasonable Suspicion: Police Authority to Stop Those Who Flee from Road Checkpoints," *Duke Law Journal* 56 (2007): 1,621–1,651.

Richardson, Pamela. "*Illinois v. Wardlow:* The Empowerment of Police, the Weakening of the Fourth Amendment," *Court Review: The Journal of the American Judges Association* 38, no. 4 (Winter 2002): 36–40.

Richard J. Hardy
Western Illinois University

Immigration and Naturalization Service

The Immigration and Naturalization Service or INS deals with the admission, naturalization, and deportation of aliens. It also patrols the Canadian and Mexican borders to prevent illegal entry of aliens. In addition it monitors immigrants living in the United States as resident aliens. The INS issues permits ("green cards") that allow nonresidents legally to obtain employment in the United States.

The first immigration office in the federal government was created in 1864. There was a commissioner of immigration within the State Department. (At the time each state had officials responsible for immigration.) The commissioner's office was abolished four years later. In 1891 Congress established complete and definite national control over immigration and the INS was created. At first it was housed in the Treasury Department. In 1903 it was transferred to the Department of Commerce and Labor. Its JURISDICTION was expanded in 1933 to include naturalization functions. In 1940 it was moved to the DEPARTMENT OF JUSTICE. The INS includes immigration examiners, patrol agents, and deportation officers. The U.S. Border Patrol is a part of the INS. The INS is headed by a commissioner appointed by the president. The INS became part of the DEPARTMENT OF HOMELAND SECURITY in 2002.

INS operations are divided between two major program categories: enforcement and examinations. The former prevents aliens from entering the country illegally. It finds and removes them. The latter deals with evaluating applications of foreign nationals who wish to come to the United States temporarily or permanently and with resident aliens who want to become U.S. citizens. The INS also works with the Department of State, the UN, and the Department of Health and Human Services in the admission and resettlement of refugees. It enforces provisions of the Immigration Reform and Control Act of 1986 relative to sanctions against employers who knowingly hire aliens not authorized to work in the United States.

The 1996 Illegal Immigration Reform and Immigrant Responsibility Act called for a doubling of border patrol agents over three years and allowed for cooperation between local police and the INS. Congress made it harder for ASYLUM seekers to enter the United States and stripped the courts of their power to review arbitrary decisions by immigration officers and mandated the deportation of legal immigrants for even minor criminal offenses committed decades ago. (Immigrants whose countries refused to take them back are now locked up indefinitely in federal detention.) The INS has long been accused of being notorious for arbitrary action. While there is public concern about protecting our porous borders, the agency has been accused of overzealousness through ethnic profiling. The INS has a mediocre record of defending its actions in FEDERAL COURTS, a success rate of 56 percent (cf. the FTC's record of 91 percent, the NLRB's of 75 percent, and the IRS's of 73 percent).

Each year 800,000 legal immigrants arrive. The booming economy and concomitant labor shortages resulted in 2000 in proposed legislation to provide some form of amnesty for up to one million undocumented aliens. The pendulum was swinging away from the anti-immigrant fervor of a few years before. Even labor unions, historically wary of immigrants as a cheap-labor threat, supported the proposed Latino and Immigrant Farmers Act. They saw immigrants as a new source of stable union membership and energy and noted that when immigrant workers whose legal status was in doubt tried to unionize, employers sometimes called in the Immigration and Naturalization Service to haul away the troublemakers.

For more information

Gimpel, James G., and James R. Edwards, Jr. *The Congressional Politics of Immigration Reform.* Boston: Allyn and Bacon, 1999.

Juffras, Jason. *Impact of the Immigration Reform and Control Act on the Immigration and Naturalization Service.* Santa Monica, Calif.: The RAND Corporation and the Urban Institute, 1991.

Martin Gruberg
University of Wisconsin at Oshkosh

immigration law Immigration law controls which persons are allowed to enter the United States. It has evolved from an open-door policy during the country's first century to a highly regulated system today. States do not regulate immigration; it is a power retained by the federal government. Congress makes the law and the FEDERAL COURTS exercise limited review. The executive branch enforces immigration law with the assistance of five major departments, the Departments of State, Justice, Labor, Health and Human Services, and the U.S. Information Agency. Immigration law is extremely complicated and the subject of constant political debate and changing legislation.

The early immigration laws were designed to exclude certain persons, including, for example, convicts, prostitutes, and persons likely to become public charges. Another early exclusionary law, the Chinese Exclusionary Act of 1882, discriminated against persons from China. This law was not repealed until 1943.

The goals of the current immigration law are promotion of FAMILY unity, strengthening of the U.S. workforce, and protection of the national interest and borders. Immigration laws regulate travel to the United States by nonimmigrants and immigrants. Nonimmigrants come to the United States for a limited period of time and purpose, immigrants intend to reside in the country permanently.

Nonimmigrants generally apply for visas at U.S. embassies in their home countries for permission to come to the United States. There are 18 nonimmigrant categories, including ambassadors, members of foreign press, students, fiancées, religious workers, scholars, persons of extraordinary ability and national acclaim, and certain workers coming to the United States to perform temporary labor in jobs for which workers cannot otherwise be found. Nonimmigrants must prove their financial ability to support themselves in the United States and demonstrate the ties to their homeland that make it certain that they will return home after their temporary visa.

Immigrants come to rejoin family members, engage in skilled jobs for which there are inadequate U.S. workers, or as a result of winning a lottery designed to promote diversity and immigration from countries that have been adversely effected by U.S. immigration policies. Congress sets worldwide limits on the number of persons who may come to the United States each year in each of these categories. In addition, there are per country limits.

Spouses and children under 21 of U.S. citizens and parents of U.S. citizens who are over 21 are considered immediate relatives and may immigrate to the United States without being subject to a waiting period. Four other categories of relatives may immigrate to the United States including:

1. unmarried sons and daughters of citizens,
2. spouses, children, and unmarried sons and daughters of permanent resident aliens,
3. married sons and daughters of citizens, and
4. siblings of citizens.

Due to demand for visas and INS limits there are substantial waiting periods in some of these categories. For example, the waiting period for sibling visas is more than 10 years.

Petitions for family members are filed at INS offices in the United States. Before the relative may immigrate to the United States the sponsor must sign an affidavit of support. A recent immigration law change made these affidavits legally enforceable CONTRACTS.

For humanitarian reasons refugees can be admitted to the United States each year. The president in consultation with Congress sets the numerical limit. Refugees are persons outside their country of nationality who are unwilling or unable to return due to well-founded fear of persecution on account of race, RELIGION, nationality, membership in a particular social group, or political opinion. Similarly, persons who meet the same definition and are present in the United States may file for ASYLUM.

Immigration law has significant intersections with other areas of law such as family, employment, public benefits, and criminal law. For example, employers who fail to properly document a worker's permission to work in the United States face potential civil and criminal liability. Criminal defense lawyers need to be familiar with immigration law so that they can properly advise clients who are not citizens of the immigration consequences of PLEA BARGAINS or convictions. Recent immigration law changes make a large number of crimes deportable offenses.

For more information

Ira Kurzban. *Immigration Law Sourcebook.* Washington, D.C.: American Immigration Law Foundation, 1998.

Weissbrodt, David. *Immigration Law and Procedure in a Nut Shell.* St. Paul, Minn.: West, 1998.

8 U.S.C. sections 1101–1537 (2000).

Angela McCaffrey
Hamline University School of Law

immunity Legal immunity refers to the act of relieving a person or institution of liability from damages or crimes they have or potentially may commit. Immunity grants persons a full PARDON for an illegal act they have committed. Generally, immunity may be granted to governmental units as a whole (sovereign immunity) or to individuals carrying out government functions (official immunity). Another form of immunity may be granted for those offering EVIDENCE in criminal trials. Sovereign immunity is the most comprehensive form of immunity and generally involves immunity for governmental units. The doctrine, stemming from the British legal system, assumes that the sovereign will perform in the best interest of the aggregated population and, as the highest authority, can legally do no wrong. Government entities granted sovereign immunity are free from civil suits or criminal prosecution. Government units with sovereign immunity may be tried only if they choose to waive their right to immunity or otherwise consent to be sued.

Several types of immunity protect individuals acting in their official capacities as government officials. For example, DIPLOMATIC IMMUNITY is reserved for government representatives serving in foreign states, such as ambassadors. Under diplomatic immunity, diplomats cannot be sued or criminally tried for crimes under the host country's laws while serving their duties in that country. The goal of this type of immunity is to ensure the continued diplomatic relations between governments and ensure that diplomats cannot be wrongly punished for an unpopular statute or treaty. Diplomats who are found to have committed a crime in another country are typically deported back to the home country while remaining immune from legal prosecution.

Executive and legislative immunity exists for a government's elected officials, eliminating the fear of prosecution to persuade or punish legislative members for their votes and protecting certain executive positions from being held liable for carrying out government policy. Nonelected government employees may also possess official immunity, particularly those that are given the ability to use DISCRETION in their job duties. Although officials have immunity from prosecution and civil liability, such protections may be deemed as merely qualified immunity, indicating possible liability when an official acts with MALICE or unreasonably violates established laws or rights. JUDGES also are protected by official immunity, meaning they are protected from liability for acts they commit while carrying out their judicial duties. This immunity helps to ensure that judges will make rulings within the proper legal framework rather than out of fear of a legal prosecution.

Also within the realm of the court system is the application of immunity to testifying witnesses, known as immunity from prosecution. A prosecutor will grant immunity to a witness's crimes in exchange for testimonial evidence about a defendant on trial. At times during testimony, a witnesses may in fact be forced to incriminate themselves by parts of given testimony, contradicting the Fifth Amendment of the CONSTITUTION. To solve this problem, immunity may be granted to witnesses when they may implicate themselves in criminal actions through their testimony about others.

For more information

Cooper, Phillip J. *Public Law and Public Administration.* Belmont, Calif.: Thomson-Wadsworth, 2007.

Emily Greenelsh and Todd Collins
Western Carolina University

impeachment Impeachment is a concept in the law of EVIDENCE that involves attacking the credibility of a witness who is testifying in a hearing or trial.

There are a number of permissible methods of impeachment, many of which are outlined by FEDERAL RULES OF EVIDENCE (FRE) 607–615. While historically under the common law a party could not attack his or her own witness, the FRE now allow either party to impeach a witness.

Evidence of a witness's character may be admissible to impeach the person under the FRE as well as state evidence rules. Only character for truthfulness is allowed, however; other character evidence regarding issues such as violence or drug use may not be admitted. Furthermore, evidence of a witness's truthful character is allowed only after the person's credibility has been attacked. This requirement is devised to save time from voluminous testimony about one's good character when there has been no suggestion otherwise. The JUDGE or JURY may not use character evidence to draw conclusions about the actual conduct of the witness; they may only infer a lack of credibility. A witness may testify, for example, that another witness is a well-known scam artist, for which the jury may conclude that he is dishonest and his current testimony should be questioned.

Impeachment of a witness may also be achieved by demonstrating that the witness has reason to be biased for or against a party

Sketch showing the U.S. Senate as a court of impeachment for the trial of Andrew Johnson (Library of Congress)

or have a personal interest in the case. It may be brought out, for example, that a witness for the prosecution is awaiting SENTENCING in his or her own criminal case and has been given better treatment as a result of her cooperation. A party may also expose a witness's prior statements that conflict with his or her current testimony in order to impeach credibility, or may elicit two contradictory statements in the trial itself.

If a witness has been convicted of a crime, this also potentially opens the door for impeachment. A FELONY conviction is admissible to cast doubt on the credibility of the witness, as long as it does not create unfair prejudice in the case, and that standard is more strict when the witness is also the defendant in the same criminal case. It is assumed that a lack of respect for the law comports with a general lack of trustworthiness. If the crime involved dishonesty or false statement, such as PERJURY or FORGERY, then it is admissible even if it was a MISDEMEANOR, and with no judicial DISCRETION for prejudice. However, if the crime is more than 10 years old, its probative value in the case must be quite high for it to be admitted.

It may also be demonstrated that a witness had inaccurate perceptions and was therefore unable to witness what he or she claimed. A witness who claimed to have seen an ASSAULT may be impeached with evidence of very poor vision, for example. While historically the common law would exclude incompetent witnesses, the FRE and modern law permits the testimony, charging the jury with determining their credibility.

When the credibility of a witness is attacked, it may then be bolstered or rehabilitated by the other side. Generally, a party is limited in rehabilitation to the areas for which the witness was attacked; an attack on perception must be met with a response to that issue and no other. If the impeachment was accomplished with a prior inconsistent statement, then a prior consistent statement may be admitted to bolster the testimony.

For more information

Best, Arthur. *Evidence.* New York: Wolters Kluwer, 2009.

Nemeth, Charles P. *Law & Evidence.* Upper Saddle River, N.J.: Prentice Hall, 2001.

Deborah Anthony
University of Illinois at Springfield

In Cold Blood *In Cold Blood* (1965) is a nonfiction novel written by Truman Capote. It tells of the brutal November 1959 murders of the Clutter family in Holcomb, Kansas, by two assailants.

The book is precisely researched and written and is noted for its clarity of style. Truman Capote developed the book for nearly six years. He took thousands of pages of notes during his research. In this research process, Capote was aided by Nelle Harper Lee, author of *To Kill a Mockingbird* and a childhood friend. The book was dedicated to Ms. Lee and Capote's life partner, Jack Dunphy.

In Cold Blood was particularly notable for capturing the essence of the life of the Clutters. Parents Herbert and Bonnie Clutter, as well as teens Nancy and Kenyon Clutter, were vividly understandable and developed as "characters" in the book. All had been stalwarts of their hometown and active in the nearby Garden City First Methodist Church. Friends and neighbors painted pictures of the Clutter family through Capote's writing.

More shocking was the at least equally vivid depiction of the killers, Richard "Dick" Hickock and Perry Smith. Capote spent many hours interviewing the killers and was able to get into their psyches. Richard Hickock had been a popular student athlete in high school. Perry Smith had an unusual interest in cultural and literary pursuits despite his poor formal education and criminal activity. Smith had an unusual vocabulary and interest in words. Capote and Smith developed some sort of friendship, but the true nature of Capote's attachment for Smith cannot be fully established. Certainly modern notions of journalistic ethics may have been crossed by Capote, despite the fact that Capote and *In Cold Blood* were at the vanguard of the New Journalism movement, a genre combining journalistic and literary characteristics especially popular in the 1960s and 1970s.

Two particularly notable films have resulted from *In Cold Blood.* This first is also titled *In Cold Blood* (1967). It starred Robert Blake and was nominated for four Academy Awards; Richard Brooks directed and wrote the screenplay. More recently, the film *Capote* (2005) starred Philip Seymour Hoffman, who won an Academy Award for his performance as best actor. This film, produced many years after Capote's 1984 death, was a depiction of the grueling process that Capote endured to write *In Cold Blood.* It provided much background information for the writing of the book. The biography *Capote* by Gerald Clark was the inspiration for the film.

In Cold Blood is a staple on many college and law school reading lists to this day. It intermingles the human story of a case of criminal law with aspects of criminal procedure.

For more information

Capote, Truman. *In Cold Blood.* New York: Random House, 1965.

Clark, Gerald. *Capote: A Biography.* New York: Carroll and Graf, 1988.

Maria Collins McGregor
University of North Carolina at Wilmington

***in forma pauperis* petitions** *In forma pauperis* petitions are filed at the United States Supreme Court by persons unable to afford an attorney yet seeking review of a lower federal court or state supreme court decision. *In forma pauperis* petitions comprise a large percentage of the applications for review received each year by the Supreme Court. Of the nearly 8,000 cases that arrive at the Court during each term, more than one-half are placed on the "miscellaneous" docket of *in forma pauperis* ("in the form of a pauper") filings.

Seeking to avoid the expense of hiring an attorney, litigants proceeding *in forma pauperis* also request a waiver of filing fees required by Supreme Court rules. Most *in forma pauperis* petitions are filed by prisoners held in state or federal correctional institutions. Typically, these applications for review deviate from Supreme Court rules concerning the format of incoming petitions. In fact, many *in forma pauperis* petitions arrive at the Court in handwritten form. Although Supreme Court rules are relaxed when handling these petitions, persons who wish to proceed *in forma pauperis* must comply with several guidelines.

Supreme Court Rule 39 requires that persons may proceed *in forma pauperis* only when granted permission to do so by the Supreme Court. Permission may not be obtained until the party files 10 copies of a motion requesting the privilege of proceeding *in forma pauperis* along with a document supporting the party's claim of indigent status. Also, parties wishing to proceed in this manner must file with the Supreme Court clerk an original draft plus 10 copies of their petition for issuance of the writ of certiorari.

Less stringent guidelines are applied to *in forma pauperis* petitions filed by state and federal prisoners. Prisoners are allowed to provide to the Court only one draft of a petition for CERTIORARI. Should the Supreme Court decide to grant the writ of certiorari, indigent petitioners are provided at public expense an attorney to both assist in the preparation of an APPELLATE BRIEF and represent the petitioner should the Court schedule the case for oral argument.

Most requests for Supreme Court review are denied. During the early years of the 20th century, the writ of certiorari was granted in fewer than 20 percent of cases placed on the "paid" docket—the group of petitions filed under standard Supreme Court rules and procedures. Since the late 1970s, the justices have granted review to fewer than 10 percent of "paid" cases filings. In recent years the justices have agreed to hear an even smaller percentage of requests for review. For example, in the 1997 term, the justices granted review to only 75 (3.1%) of the 2,432 cases placed on the "paid" docket.

Petitions filed *in forma pauperis* are even less likely to be granted review. All but a few petitions placed on the "miscellaneous" docket are denied or dismissed without comment by the justices. During the 1990s, less than one percent of all petitions filed *in forma pauperis* were placed on the Court's docket of cases decided with written opinions.

Although only a small percentage of indigent cases are accepted for review, some of the most significant decisions in Supreme Court history involved appellants proceeding *in forma pauperis*. The most prominent of these decisions is that which resulted from the case brought by Clarence Earl Gideon. Accused of a FELONY, denied counsel at his trial, and unable to secure a hearing from the Florida Supreme Court, Gideon filed a petition with the U.S. Supreme Court and asked to proceed *in forma pauperis*. Granting his petition, a unanimous Court handed down a landmark decision, ruling for the first time that persons tried for felonies in state courts are guaranteed a RIGHT TO COUNSEL under the SIXTH and Fourteenth Amendments of the CONSTITUTION. Moreover, the decision in *GIDEON V. WAINWRIGHT* (1963) expanded the scope of constitutional protections enjoyed by indigent defendants in all criminal courts and fueled a growth in *in forma pauperis* filings that continues today.

For more information

Hazard, Geoffrey C., Jr., and Michele Taruffo. *American Civil Procedure: An Introduction*. New Haven, Conn.: Yale University Press, 1993.

Silberman, Linda J., and Allan R. Stein. *Civil Procedure: Theory and Practice.* Gaithersburg, Md.: Aspen Law and Business, 2001.

Bradley J. Best
Austin Peay State University

in loco parentis In loco parentis is a legal doctrine describing a relationship whereby an adult, who is not the natural parent of a minor, elects to temporarily undertake the care and control of that child, acting in the place of the minor's natural parents.

This doctrine of substitution of parental guidance and supervision surfaces in many different situations. When a school or university set curfews for residents, establishes guidelines for "appropriate behavior," or bans alcohol from the campus, this is acting in the stead of a parent. The university is substituting for the guidance that a prudent parent might exercise. This doctrine imposes a duty upon schools to maintain a safe environment for students and is the legal rationale behind permitting WARRANTLESS SEARCHES of school lockers or book bags.

Caregivers in a day care setting have the delegated authority to act as a careful and prudent parent would. They are expected to exercise adequate supervision, keep the child safe from obvious dangers, give appropriate advice and guidance, and recognize when medical attention is needed. The responsibilities of a careful parent are not legally defined, but it can be expected that there is a duty to exercise adequate supervision given the age, ability, needs, and experience of the child.

The doctrine of in loco parentis can also be an element in certain custody, visitation, and adoption cases. In cases where there is no allegation that the biological or current custodial parent is unfit, the individual who is seeking a custody or visitation order must initially show that they have more than a bond by mere blood or affection. The plaintiff must show that they have been a "psychological parent." That is, they acted as a parent over some period of time, and the child, in return, recognizes and depends on that control and guidance.

Existing case law in the area of custody, visitation, and adoption indicate that in determining whether the individual stepped into the parents' shoes, the following factors be considered: (1) the age of the child; (2) percentage of financial support contributed to the child's maintenance requirements; (3) whether the relationship between the person and child was one of a continuous nature and whether the parties' expectation was one of permanence; (4) whether the scope and nature of the decision making has been broad and has concerned major issues in the child's life.

While a finding that a person or group has acted in loco parentis may bestow many rights, entitlements, and privileges, it should be noted that this may also impose expansive and continuing duties and might be a basis for liability should the party fail to act appropriately.

Litigation has ensued over a school's duty to protect and provide a safe environment for students based on the doctrine of in loco parentis. In both cases, the school failed to implement reasonable security measures and was sued when other students or outsiders on the school grounds injured students.

In another case, a claim for negligent failure to control a minor child was based on the doctrine of in loco parentis. Under the facts, the defendant was sued when his girlfriend's minor son inflicted serious injury on a neighbor child who came to play for the afternoon. The complaint alleged that the defendant stood in loco parentis by assuming custody and control, that he knew of the child's violent nature, and that he failed to use ordinary care to control the child so as to prevent him from intentionally harming others.

In nearly all instances, a person who acts as stepparent to his spouse's minor children does not incur an ongoing obligation to the children if the marriage terminates. However, some courts have opined that where that person has actually stood in loco parentis, they cannot unilaterally terminate that status.

For more information

In re Custody of D.M.M., 404 N.W.2d 530 (1987). Court considered whether the word *parent* also meant a person in loco parentis.

In Interest of L.L. v. Circuit Ct. of Washington County, 280 N.W.2d 343 (Ct. App. 1979). Court described state's authority to supervise children during school hours in loco parentis.

In re Montell v. Dept. of Soc. And Health Servs., 775 P2d 976, 978 (Wash. App. 1989).

Lipscomb v. Lipscomb, 660 So.2d 986, 986 (Ala. Civ. App. 1993).

Loretta M. Young
Family Court of State of Delaware

incarceration theory Incarceration theory refers to the rationales or justifications for imprisoning those citizens who violate legal mandates.

Generally, theories of incarceration include incapacitation, REHABILITATION, DETERRENCE, and retribution. Throughout the evolution of the American CRIMINAL JUSTICE SYSTEM, various theories of incarceration have served as a basis for constructing and maintaining a prison system that is the largest in the world. The fluid character of the U.S. prison system and its underlying rationales reflect continued attempts by policy makers to eliminate criminality through imprisonment in the face of harsh criticisms levied by prison reformers, who allege that incarceration is far from an optimal method for reducing crime.

The birth of the modern prison and the practice of incarceration largely resulted from American settlers' desires to distance the colonies from English penal practices they perceived as excessively harsh. In particular, colonists recoiled against the death penalty, viewing CAPITAL PUNISHMENT as a key element of tyrannical rule by claiming that its imposition necessarily objectified citizens. Hence, the colonial rule of law largely rejected execution, opting instead for what early Americans concluded was a more enlightened form of PUNISHMENT—incarceration.

At the outset, Americans predominately justified incarceration as a general and specific deterrent to criminal behavior. General deterrence theory holds that incarcerating an individual offender sets an example that will deter other potential offenders from committing criminal acts. Specific deterrence theory proposes that imprisonment will prevent and discourage individual offenders from behaving criminally in the future. Arguing that crime is the product of conscious and rational choice, both general and specific deterrence theorists uniformly contend that to be effective deterrents, punishments must be certain and swift. Early proponents of the American prison, advocates of the deterrence theory of incarceration, believed that the proper use of incarceration could curtail a society's criminality. Thus, American penology originally focused almost entirely on the form of the prison sentence, virtually ignoring the organization and management of the structures in which they kept those who violated recognized law. The earliest American prisons were little more than local jails. For example, in 1790, Pennsylvania opened the United States's first prison by simply rededicating the Philadelphia Jail at Walnut Street. As a result, prisons of the time were increasingly overcrowded, replete with violence, and, as critical observers noted, ill-equipped to curb crime rates.

In the early 1800s, prison reformers sought to change the way Americans conceived of crime and, in turn, incarceration. Troubled by an apparent threat posed by widespread criminal activity and a perceived lack of social organization, reformers argued that the rehabilitative efforts ought to replace the deterrence theory of incarceration. The rehabilitative ideal, reformers contended, would serve to structure society by teaching offenders discipline and order prior to their release back into the community. To this end, New York and Pennsylvania developed two similar prison models, the Congregate Plan and

Incarcerated Americans, 1920–2006

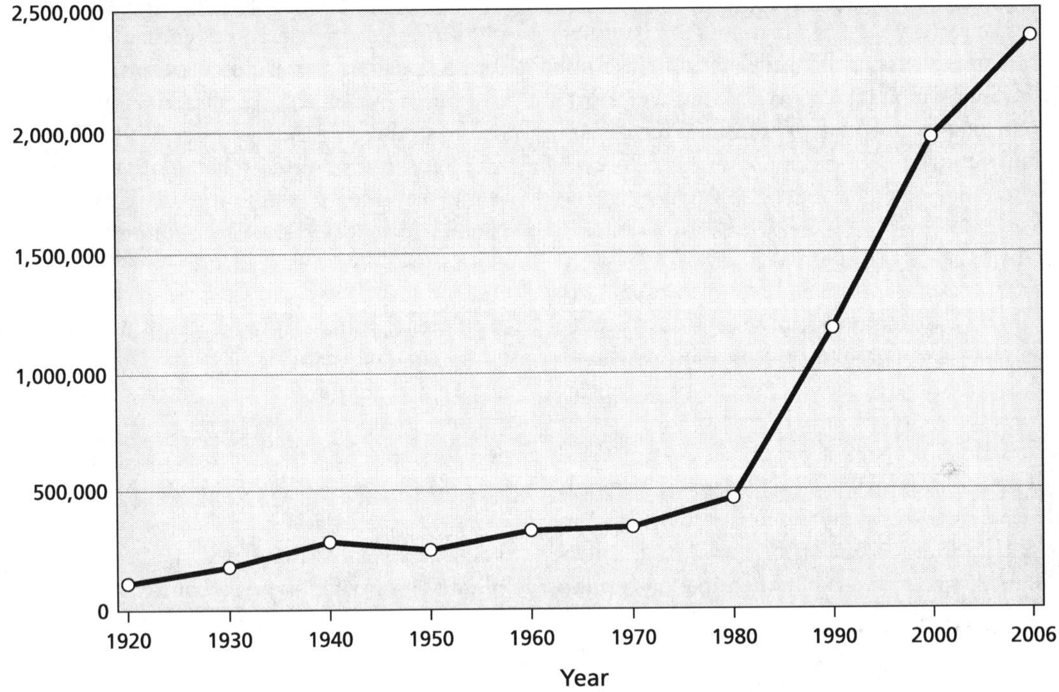

Sources: Justice Policy Institute Report: The Punishing Decade, and U.S. Bureau of Justice Statistics Bulletin NCJ 219416-Prisoners in 2006.

the Separate System. Adopted by many states, the two models stressed prisoner isolation, regimented schedules, and intense prison labor. Moreover, such institutions operated in complete silence, maintained by a constant threat of brutal forms of CORPORAL PUNISHMENT handed down by prison personnel organized as a paramilitary unit.

But in 1867, concerned that the prison system in the United States was failing, the New York Prison Association conducted a nationwide study of the institutions that housed criminal offenders. The results of the study done by Enoch Cobb Wines and Theodore Dwight indicated that severe overcrowding, inadequate staff training, lack of state oversight, and reliance on corporal punishment all defeated the rehabilitative goals of the American prison. Specifically, they noted that prison administrators found it difficult, if not impossible, to adhere to the principles of rehabilitation. The structure of the institutions that dotted the nation's landscape was simply inadequate. Many prisons were too small to maintain single-cell isolation, and operating in silence was no longer possible. Nevertheless, because many of the nation's prisons were relatively young and represented significant investments, the Wines and Dwight report did not prompt prison management to discard the rehabilitative theory of incarceration. Instead, the report elicited reforms that included state-administered prison oversight, a reinvigorated dedication to inmate education, and the institution of PAROLE and other merit-based incentives through which prisoners could earn early release.

In the early 1900s, again amid a concern that the American prison did little to control crime or prepare inmates for release, another reform movement aimed at enhancing the effectiveness of incarceration. Associated with the Progressives' political agenda, this prison reform movement supported the psychotherapeutic model of prisons. The psychotherapeutic model hypothesizes that crime intimately relates to psychiatry and that incarceration ideally serves to treat or rehabilitate an inmate in preparation for release. In short, the psychotherapeutic model of incarceration is another form of rehabilitation that emphasizes the "sickness" of the inmate and proposes individualized treatment for criminal behavior. Accordingly, reformers of this era ushered in the concept of the Big House, a self-contained prison that functioned like a hospital, where professionals classified inmates based on the level of treatment they required and then administered healing protocols. Also part of the psychotherapeutic model of prison management was the repopularizing of INDETERMINATE SENTENCES, parole, PROBATION, and alternatives to incarceration.

Yet, the Big House proved incompatible with the psychotherapeutic model for prison management. For example, San Quentin in California and Sing Sing in New York, famous examples of the Big House, each housed well over 2,500 inmates. Accordingly, they were ill-equipped to accommodate an individualized approach to treatment. Because of their size, penal administrators struggled with the practical impossibility of attending to the specific needs of correctional clients. Thus, prisons veered from the particularized approach the psychotherapeutic model called for, and management transformed correctional institutions into mechanized assembly lines where staff superficially treated inmates for general maladies. Still, the prosperity of the 1950s and early 1960s brought a reinvigorated call for the United States to place a greater emphasis on the rehabilitative function of prisons. Additionally, a series of judicial opinions published around that time contained language that urged the vindication of prisoner rights and the enforcement of prison administrators' responsibilities. Thus, well into the 20th century, proponents of the rehabilitative ideal clung to versions of rehabilitation, dedicated to the general idea that those who commit crime can change and eventually live as law-abiding citizens.

RECIDIVISM rates, however, continued to climb in the late 1960s and early 1970s. Moreover, critics of the rehabilitative ideal and the psychotherapeutic theory of incarceration gained ground. For example, in 1974, the sociologist Robert Martinson published *What Works? Questions and Answers about Prison Reform,* an article in which he declared that "nothing works" to rehabilitate those who have committed crime. Soon thereafter, politicians and prison administrators, frustrated with crime rates and prison violence, began to alter the goals of incarceration, discarding rehabilitation in favor of incapacitation and retribution. Thus, the prison became a place where staff merely held and punished an offender, allegedly protecting society but ignoring treatment altogether.

Throughout the 1980s and 1990s, America continued to endorse a more punitive approach to crime and incarceration. Mandatory minimum sentences replaced alternative to incarceration, and truth-in-sentencing schemes won out over indeterminate sentences and parole. Some scholars argue that this New Penology, though still rhetorically devoted to rehabilitation, is practically concerned only with incapacitation and retribution. As support for this proposition, still others characterize the modern American prison as a warehouse, operating only to store and punish deviants. Such observers note that a drastic increase in prison populations nationally has led to the construction of a plethora of new facilities, not increased efforts to treat those behind bars.

They also point out that the form of these new facilities (e.g., underground supermax prisons, higher-capacity solitary confinement units, and windowless cells) increasingly reflects the goals of incapacitation and retribution.

For more information

Feeley, M. and J. Simon. "The New Penology: Notes on the Emerging Strategy of Corrections and Its Implications," *Criminology* 30 (1992): 449–474.

Martinson, R. *What Works? Questions and Answers about Prison Reform.* 35 Public Interest 22–54 (1974).

Morris, N., and D. J. Rothman. *The Oxford History of the Prison: The Practice of Punishment in Western Society.* New York: Oxford University Press, 1995.

Robertson, J. "Houses of the Dead: Warehouse Prisons, Paradigm Change, and the Supreme Court," *Houston Law Review* 34 (1997): 1,003–1,063.

James M. Binnall
University of California at Irvine

incorporation doctrine Incorporation doctrine refers to the belief that the DUE PROCESS clause of the Fourteenth Amendment makes the provisions of the BILL OF RIGHTS applicable to the states. Adherents to the incorporation doctrine hold that the first eight amendments to the U.S. CONSTITUTION (which contain the substantive guarantees of the Bill of Rights) apply to the states exactly as they do to the federal government. This is to say that whatever is forbidden to the federal government by the Bill of Rights is likewise forbidden to the states by the due process clause of the Fourteenth Amendment, which incorporates the Bill of Rights and makes it applicable to the states.

Adherents to the doctrine of incorporation differ among themselves as to whether the due process clause of the Fourteenth Amendment incorporates all the provisions of the first eight amendments to the Constitution, or only some of those provisions. Some justices, most notably HUGO BLACK, held that the first eight amendments are incorporated in their entirety. Others, such as former CHIEF JUSTICE EARL WARREN, held that only those provisions of the Bill of Rights which the Supreme Court has found to be fundamental principles of liberty and JUSTICE are incorporated into the due process clause and made applicable to the states. Other provisions, deemed by the Court not to be fundamental, are not made applicable to the states.

Advocates of the first view are known as full or total incorporationists. Advocates of the second view are known as selective incorporationists. At no time in the Court's history was there a majority of justices who believed in the total incorporation of the Bill of Rights. Indeed, until the 1950s, a majority of justices held to a different doctrine, known as ordered liberty. According to this doctrine, the meaning of the due process clause is independent of the Bill of Rights. It is thus the responsibility of the Court to determine on a case-by-case basis whether a state procedure is consistent with "due process of law." Justice FELIX FRANKFURTER was one of the foremost advocates of this view that "due process of law is a summarized constitutional guarantee of respect for those personal immunities which, . . . are 'so rooted in the traditions and conscience of our people as to be ranked as fundamental,' . . . or are 'implicit in the concept of ordered liberty,'" *Rochin v. California* (342 U.S. 165).

From the 1950s through the 1970s a coalition of both full and selective incorporationists nationalized the Bill of Rights by incorporating most of its provisions one at a time. By the 1960s the doctrine of selective incorporation had become the dominant view on the Court. Since the mid-1970s, selective incorporation has been the unchallenged doctrine of the Supreme Court.

Although the process of incorporating provisions of the Bill of Rights has not necessarily ended, no additional provisions of the Bill of Rights have been incorporated since the 1970s. More importantly, no provision of the Bill of Rights has been unincorporated. At this point, most of the Bill of Rights has been incorporated, including all of the First, SECOND, FOURTH, and SIXTH AMENDMENTS, most of the Fifth (except for the requirement that indictments be by GRAND JURY), and that portion of the EIGHTH AMENDMENT which prohibits "CRUEL AND UNUSUAL PUNISHMENT." The Third and Seventh Amendments have not been incorporated. Other rights, such as the right to privacy, have also been protected by the due process clause of the Fourteenth Amendment. However, despite Justice Douglas's efforts in *GRISWOLD V. CONNECTICUT*, 381 U.S. 479 (1965) to read a right to privacy into the penumbras of the emanations of the Bill of Rights, the better view is that protection for the right to privacy lies outside the doctrine of incorporation.

For more information

Abraham, Henry, and Barbara A. Perry. *Freedom and the Court: Civil Rights and Liberties in the United States*. 7th ed. London: Oxford University Press, 1998.

Auerbach, Bruce E. "Incorporation and the Bill of Rights." In *Law and Politics: Unanswered Questions*, edited by David Schultz. New York: Peter Lang, 1994.

Schultz, David, John R. Vile, and Michelle D. Deardorff. *Constitutional Law in Contemporary America*, vol. 2. New York: Oxford University Press, 2010.

Bruce E. Auerbach
Albright College

indeterminate sentencing Indeterminate sentencing is a system of PUNISHMENT created by legislatures that establish statutory minimum and maximum sentences for particular criminal violations and vest JUDGES with wide DISCRETION to determine an appropriate term of incarceration. The sentence meted out by the judge, however, is unlikely to be completed by the offender whose final release date from prison will be determined by an arm of the corrections department, usually a PAROLE board. Additionally, inmates may receive a sentence reduction for good behavior while behind bars, often referred to as good-time credits.

Generally, individuals incarcerated under indeterminate sentencing laws are required to complete a minimum of one-third of the original sentence before conditional release may be granted. After discharge from prison, offenders are frequently subject to continued supervision by authorities for a set period of time. During the time of supervised release, violation of the terms of parole or conviction for a new crime may result in a return to prison for the remaining term of incarceration for the original offense.

Indeterminate sentences have been employed since the advent of the modern prison. However, the practice gained a significant number of adherents in the United States after the National Congress of Penitentiary and Reformatory Discipline convened in Cincinnati in 1870. Advocates of this approach to sentencing argued that the central purpose of incarceration should be reformation of the criminal through individualized sentences for every offender. Tailoring the length of imprisonment would allow for the application of specific rehabilitative programs and techniques that would restore the character of the criminal and return the offender to the community as a contributing member of society. Popular rehabilitative efforts included vocational training, educational classes, psychological therapy, addiction treatment, and religious programs. Nearly a dozen states adopted this model by the end of the 19th century, and by 1970, every state, the District of Columbia, and the federal government used some form of indeterminate sentencing.

Despite the universal implementation of this approach to sentencing, the method has not been without its critics. Opponents from diverse political camps argue that indeterminate sentencing has failed to deliver on its promise of rehabilitation. Conservatives contend that RECIDIVISM rates remain high as many individuals who have been released or paroled go on to commit additional crimes and return to prison. Challengers of indeterminate sentencing also claim that limited funding and poor quality limit the effectiveness of remedial programs that were meant to address the underlying criminal behavior. Additionally, advocates of retribution who promote longer and more complete sentences rail against the early release of offenders, especially those who committed serious crimes.

These sentiments are echoed by the public, which finds the process often subverts the will of the community through arbitrary decisions of parole boards that too often put the safety and welfare of the public in jeopardy. Liberals, too, criticize indeterminate sentencing, but for different reasons. The fault with the approach, they claim, is that it creates wide disparities in the length of incarceration for individuals who committed the same or similar offenses. Opponents suggest that biases for or against particular racial, ethnic, and socioeconomic groups produce wildly different sentencing outcomes that undermine the fairness of the system.

Among the most outspoken critics of the approach was U.S. district court judge Marvin Frankel, who published a book-length condemnation of indeterminate sentencing in 1972 entitled *Criminal Sentences: Law without Order.* He characterized the entire process of sentencing under the indeterminate paradigm as cruel and unjust. Frankel found fault with judges for meting out sentences in a wholly inconsistent fashion, resulting in evident biases based upon race, ethnicity, and gender. He maintained that the quality and success of rehabilitation programs touted as remedies for criminal behavior could not be adequately measured. Frankel also targeted the parole boards empowered to determine release, claiming they were staffed with unqualified members who were endowed with too much power and subject to too little supervision. His prescription was the replacement of indeterminacy with legislatively created sentencing standards whose purpose was punishment rather than healing.

These objections led to a reform movement in the early 1970s that helped to dismantle indeterminate sentencing in many states and at the federal level. The restructuring of sentencing systems generally accommodated the concerns of both liberals and conservatives who sought a fairer but tougher approach to determining appropriate criminal sanctions. The resulting changes included a number of policy innovations, including SENTENCING GUIDELINES systems, two- and three-strike provisions, and MANDATORY MINIMUM SENTENCES. Despite the dissatisfaction with indeterminate sentencing systems, nearly three-quarters of the states retained the basic contours of the approach, modifying their processes to address the most egregious problems while preserving the basic model of rehabilitation.

For more information

Tonry, Michael. *Sentencing Matters.* New York: Oxford University Press, 1996.

Walker, Samuel. *Popular Justice: A History of American Criminal Justice.* New York: Oxford University Press, 1980.

Charles F. Jacobs
St. Norbert College

index crime Index crime refers to those crimes reported by state law enforcement agencies to the FEDERAL BUREAU OF INVESTIGATION (FBI) and included in the UNIFORM CRIME REPORTS (UCR). Originally, crimes were reported in two classes, crimes against persons and crimes against property, but in the 1980s, the system was redesigned to include less often reported offenses. The index crime system remains the basis for measuring changes in crime in the United States. UCR data are collated and reported each year in the FBI's *Crime in the United States,* available at www.fbi.gov.

The index crime system was the result of efforts by the International Association of Chiefs of Police (IACP) in the 1920s. The IACP formed the Committee on Uniform Crime Records in 1927 to propose an improved, uniform system for gathering and disseminating crime information to replace the many different state methods for collecting crime data. In 1929, the IACP published the first set of guidelines for gathering information on index crimes, a handbook called *Uniform Crime Reporting.* By 1930, it had persuaded Congress to pass 28 USC §534, authorizing the ATTORNEY GENERAL to collect and analyze crime data from all 48 (now 50) states. In 1935, the FBI became the agency responsible for collecting, analyzing, and reporting crime data.

Index crimes used to fall into two categories, Crimes against property (ARSON, BURGLARY, LARCENY under $50.00, and vehicle THEFT) and crimes against persons (rape, MURDER, ASSAULT and ROBBERY). In the 1980s, the UCR divided crimes into two categories; Part I is the old set of eight index crimes, and Part II includes crimes such as simple assault, curfew violations, EMBEZZLEMENT and FORGERY. The new classification arose because many critics argued that the index system did not adequately quantify so-called WHITE-COLLAR CRIME.

Critics of the UCR argue that it fails to account for white-collar crime (increasingly important in a technological society) and ORGANIZED CRIME. These criticism have led the FBI to create the National Incident-Based Reporting System (NIBRS), which claims to capture criminal activity with greater precision. However, the NIBRS is still in development, so the UCR will remain the standard measure of crime in the United States for the immediate future.

For more information

Federal Bureau of Investigation. *Crime in the United States, 2000.* Washington, D.C.: Department of Justice. Available online. URL: www.fbi.gov/ucr/cius_00/conttents.pdf.

James, Nathan, and Logan Rishard Council. *CRS Report for Congress: How Crime in the United States Is Measured.* Washington, D.C.: Congressional Research Service, 2008.

Michael P. Bobic
West Virginia Wesleyan College

Indian rights Indian rights are rooted not in race but in sovereignty: They derive from the inherent sovereign powers of the tribes as preexisting political entities. Rights belonging to Native Americans and tribes largely are determined according to a few general principles of federal Indian law: First, Native-American tribes are sovereign nations with inherent powers of self-government; second, tribal sovereignty is subject to Congress's power to regulate the tribes; third, Congress, rather than the states, has the power to regulate the tribes; and fourth, the federal government serves as a guardian to the tribes.

Both federal regulation and tribal sovereignty stem from the historical context of America's colonization. As the "New World" was colonized, settlers sought lands belonging to the tribes. Recognizing that the vast frontier prevented effective defense against "hostile" tribes, the newly formed federal government negotiated massive land cessions (transfers of lands) with the tribes through treaties and agreements, with certain rights promised in return. Necessary to the treaty-making process was the treatment of tribes as sovereign nations—political entities with valid rights to the lands they occupied. These treaties remain in force, providing the basis for current protection of Indian lands and reserved rights relating to hunting, fishing, gathering, and water usage.

By the time the CONSTITUTION was ratified, a long tradition of dealing with the tribes as sovereign nations was in place. In the "Indian Commerce Clause," found in Article I, section 8, the Constitution expressly confers to Congress power "to regulate Commerce . . . with the Indian Tribes."

The Supreme Court further defined the relationship of the federal government and Native-American tribes through a series of decisions. First, in *Johnson v. M'Intosh,* 21 U.S. (8 Wheat) 543 (1823), the Court held that although tribes retained the right to occupy their lands, ownership belonged to the United States under the doctrine of discovery, which gave "discover-

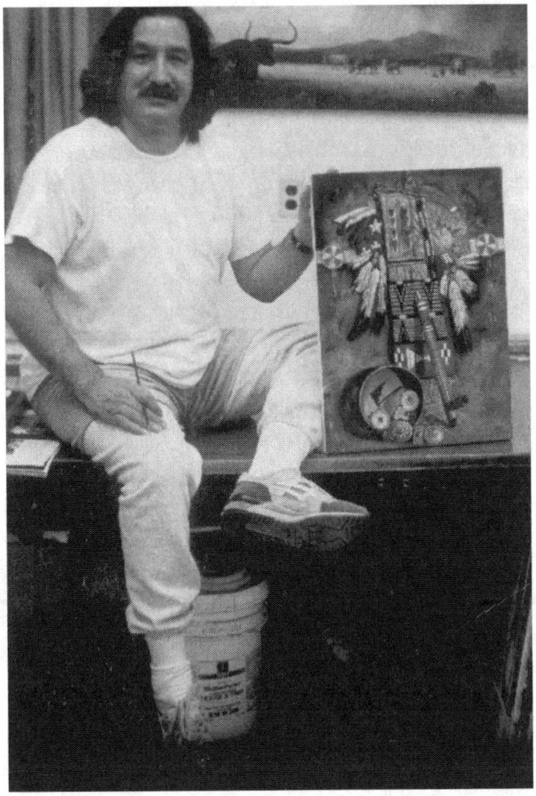

American Indian Movement (AIM) activist Leonard Peltier, who was convicted in 1976 for the murder of two FBI agents, ca. 1985 (Hulton Archive)

ers" rights over aboriginal peoples. In *Cherokee Nation v. Georgia,* 30 U.S. (5 Pet.) 1 (1831), the Court recognized that tribes were self-governing and distinct political entities but held that tribes were not foreign nations. Instead, tribes were "domestic dependent nations" existing as wards to the federal government's guardianship. In *Worcester v. Georgia,* 31 U.S. (6 Pet.) 515 (1832), the Court explained that tribal sovereignty necessarily was limited by the federal government's status as the "protector" of tribes, so that they were subject to federal law. Taken together, these cases hold that Native-American tribes are not entitled to sovereignty in the traditional sense of the word (as a foreign country would be) but are afforded only limited sovereignty as domestic dependent nations subject to limitations set by the federal government.

The federal government's relationship with the tribes has varied with federal interests and political climate. In the mid-1800s, the federal government forcibly removed Native Americans from their land, culminating in the Trail of Tears and the death of more than 4,000 Native Americans. At the turn of the 20th century, the federal government transferred title of Indian lands from tribes to individual Native Americans in an effort to weaken tribal governments and to require assimilation.

In the 1930s the federal government attempted to encourage, rather than force, assimilation of Native Americans, but in 1953 Congress adopted a resolution calling for the termination of the tribes' special status as wards of the federal government. Under this policy, Native Americans were treated simply as citizens of the United States, without any recognition of tribal sovereignty. Although not all tribes were terminated under the policy, forced assimilation was widespread.

The Civil Rights movement influenced federal Indian policy, leading to the protection of individual rights through the 1968 Indian Civil Rights Act. President Nixon called for the end of the termination era and urged Congress to return control of federal Indian programs to the tribes. In 1978 Congress passed the Indian Child Welfare Act, intended to protect tribal interests in custody decisions affecting Native-American children. Most recently, the federal government has encouraged tribes to undertake economic development as a means of strengthening tribal sovereignty.

Native-American tribes are either federally recognized or nonfederally recognized. Federal law sets out mandatory criteria that a tribe must meet before it is recognized by the federal government and thus entitled to federal benefits and rights. There are 557 federally recognized Native American tribes in the United States. Many tribes have their own governments, laws, and court systems that are separate from their state or federal counterparts. Whether tribal, state, or federal law will apply usually depends on whether the people involved in a dispute or crime are Native American, and whether the events at issue took place within "Indian country"—within a reservation or on other Indian land.

For more information

Cohen, Felix S. *Handbook of Federal Indian Law,* updated ed. Washington, D.C.: U.S. Government Printing Office, 1982.

Wilkinson, Charles F., ed. *American Indians, Time and the Law.* Buffalo, N.Y.: William S. Hein, 1988.

Kathryn R. L. Rand
University of North Dakota School of Law

ineffective assistance of counsel Ineffective assistance of counsel refers to a legal standard fashioned by the U.S. Supreme Court in *Strickland v. Washington,* 466 U.S. 668 (1984), under the SIXTH AMENDMENT to determine if a defendant facing criminal charges had adequate legal representation.

The Sixth Amendment guarantees criminal defendants the RIGHT TO COUNSEL—that is, the right to be represented by an attorney during the state's prosecution. However, this right would be hollow if the legal assistance rendered by the defendant's attorney were deficient or ineffective. A defendant is not just entitled to assistance of counsel, but rather *effective* assistance of counsel. Ineffective assistance of counsel deprives a criminal defendant of the right to an attorney.

Although the "historical background suggests that the core purpose of the counsel guarantee was to assure 'Assistance' at trial," over time the Court has recognized that this assistance "would be less meaningful if it were limited to the formal trial itself." *United States v. Ash,* 413 U.S. 300, 309–10 (1973). As a result, the Supreme Court has consistently held that the right to effective counsel attaches during all critical stages of the prosecution. In particular, the Court in *POWELL V. ALABAMA,* 287 U.S. 45, 57 (1932), concluded that pretrial arrangements could be "perhaps the most critical period of the proceedings." According to the Court in *Santobello v. New York,* 404 U.S. 257, 260 (1971), since PLEA-BARGAINING is an "essential component of the administration of JUSTICE," a defendant's counsel has a duty to provide effective assistance during this process. This ensures that "the ultimate authority remains with the defendant 'to make certain fundamental decisions regarding the case, as to whether to plead guilty, waive a jury, testify in his or her own behalf, or take an appeal.'" *Nunes v. Mueller,* 350 F.3d 1045, 1053 (9th Cir. 2003). In this way, the right to counsel protects more than simply a fair trial, for it also serves to protect the reliability of the entire trial process.

When considering claims of ineffective assistance of counsel, state and federal courts must adhere to the standards set forth in *Strickland v. Washington,* 466 U.S. 668, 688 (1984). The *Strickland* test has two prongs. First, the defendant must demonstrate that defense counsel's performance was objectively and unreasonably deficient—effectively not performing as a lawyer. After demonstrating that defense counsel's advice was deficient, a defendant must then show that the deficient performance was prejudicial such that but for the performance the verdict would have gone the other way (ACQUITTAL).

It is often easy, especially in hindsight, to point out trial counsel's errors, in both strategy and delivery. Attorneys are human and invariably will make mistakes; but the Court in *Strickland* made clear that errors, "even if professionally unreasonable," do not warrant setting aside a judgment if the error had no effect on the disposition of the case. Even constitutional deficiencies must be prejudicial in order to constitute ineffective assistance of counsel under the Sixth Amendment. To determine prejudice, a court asks whether confidence in the outcome is at all undermined by the counsel's deficient conduct. If there is a reasonable probability that but for counsel's unprofessional errors the result of the proceeding would have been different, the deficiency is prejudicial. In this way, considering a claim of ineffective assistance of counsel is invariably a mixed question of law and fact.

After determining that a defendant suffered from constitutionally deficient counsel, a court must then craft a remedy. Remedies for the deprivation of the right to counsel "should be tailored to the injury suffered from the constitutional violation and should not unnecessarily infringe on competing interests," according to *United States v. Morrison,* 449 U.S. 361, 364 (1981). Usually, trial errors that lead to a conviction can only be remedied by granting the defendant a new trial.

For more information

Bibas, Stephanos. "The Psychology of Hindsight and After-the-Fact Review of Ineffective Assistance of Counsel." *Utah Law Review* (2004): 1.

Fatino, John F. "Ineffective Assistance of Counsel: Identifying the Standards and Litigating the Issues," *South Dakota Law Review* 49 (2003): 31.

Primus, Eve Brensike. "Structural Reform in Criminal Defense: Relocating Ineffective Assistance of Counsel Claims," *Cornell Law Review* 92 (2007): 679.

David Perez
Yale Law School

injunction An injunction is an order a court issues prohibiting someone or some entity from doing a specified act or commanding that some action be reversed.

A court issues an injunction only when necessary to protect against substantial interference with a right and not over trivial matters where the injury is small or technical. The applicant for the injunction must show two essential elements to justify a court issuing one. The applicant must first show that real or personal property or some other legal right is subject to irreparable harm, and next that there is no adequate remedy at law. Generally, "irreparable harm" means an injured party cannot be readily, adequately, and completely compensated with money. The term "adequate remedy at law" means that a later suit for damages will not adequately compensate the applicant for the threatened injury or that the applicant would be faced with multiple lawsuits.

Typically, there are three possible stages in an injunction proceeding: (1) temporary restraining order granted against defendant with or without notice or hearing; (2) preliminary injunction granted after notice and brief hearing; and (3) permanent injunction granted after a full hearing of the evidence.

A judge typically issues a temporary RESTRAINING ORDER, without notice to or hearing the defendant, primarily as a means for stopping a defendant's act. Usually, a temporary restraining order is effective for only 10 days unless the JUDGE for good cause extends the time or the defendant agrees to a longer period.

An injunction may be preliminary or permanent. A judge may issue a preliminary injunction only after notice to the defendant. The judge may hear brief argument and conduct limited hearing of EVIDENCE, or join the hearing on the preliminary injunction with the hearing on the permanent injunction.

A permanent injunction is the final order the judge issues after a complete hearing of the evidence on the issues determined by the pleadings. Since an injunction often stops a defendant from conducting his business, the court will, in most cases, not grant an injunction without proof that the applicant is likely to suffer irreparable injury if the defendant is not stopped.

For more information

Federal Rule of Civil Procedure 65.

"Injunction." In *Black's Law Dictionary.* 7th ed., 1999, p. 788.

Paul D. Link
Daniel, Clampett, Powell and Cunningham
Springfield, Missouri

Innocence Project Barry C. Scheck and Peter J. Neufeld, professors of law at the Benjamin N. Cardozo School of Law in New York City, founded the Innocence Project in 1992 to assist prisoners who were wrongly convicted. The project seeks to exonerate wrongly convicted prisoners through DNA TESTING, and to systematically reform the CRIMINAL JUSTICE SYSTEM. As of 2009, the project has exonerated 244 prisoners. A breakdown of the 244 exonerations reveals common trends:

1. Seventeen of those prisoners were on death row awaiting execution;
2. 70 percent of those exonerated were ethnic minorities;
3. Almost all the cases involved some sort of sexual assault;
4. About 25 percent of the convictions involved MURDER;
5. The prisoners served an average sentence of 12 years before exoneration;
6. In 40 percent of the cases, the real perpetrator was later identified using DNA EVIDENCE.

One aspect of the Innocence Project's research is to understand why people are falsely convicted in the first place. The primary causes of wrongful convictions include: mistaken EYEWITNESS identification, inaccurate forensic data, FALSE CONFESSIONS, snitches and jailhouse informants, INEFFECTIVE ASSISTANCE OF COUNSEL, prosecutorial misconduct, and police misconduct. Mistaken eyewitness identification is the leading cause of wrongful conviction, affecting more than 70 percent of all cases. Improper handling of forensic EVIDENCE, either on the crime scene or in the laboratory, is the second-leading contributor to wrongful convictions, affecting more than 50 percent of all cases of DNA exonerations, while false confessions implicate about 25 percent of all cases.

In addition to its criminal defense work, the Innocence Project also advocates the creation of Innocence Commissions, which investigate the causes of wrongful convictions. The project urges state and local governments to create these commissions so that they may understand the circumstances that lead to miscarriages of JUSTICE and reform their system accordingly. Once formed, these commissions can recommend changes to police investigations, police conduct during interrogations, quality control within forensic laboratories, and prosecutorial DISCRETION. These commissions may also investigate defense misconduct and set minimum levels of attorney competence during certain criminal proceedings. The North Carolina Actual Innocence Commission is considered a model for the rest of the nation to follow. Pennsylvania created one such commission in 2006 after nine prisoners were exonerated through DNA evidence. Responding to the recommendations of a special commission created in Illinois, in 2003, the Illinois State Legislature passed 85 reforms to safeguard against wrongful convictions and wrongful executions. Other commissions have also been created in California, Connecticut, and Wisconsin.

Although the Innocence Project became a nonprofit organization in 2003, it retains strong ties to the Cardozo Law School. The organization employs staff attorneys, legal interns, as well as clinical students at Cardozo.

For more information

Scheck, Barry, Peter Neufeld, and Jim Dwyer. *Actual Innocence: When Justice Goes Wrong and How to Make It Right.* New York: NAL Trade, 2003.

David Perez
Yale Law School

insanity defense Insanity is an affirmative criminal defense by which defendants argue that they should not be held criminally liable for breaking the law because they were legally insane at the time of an alleged crime. The legal definition of *insane* is quite different from the medical definition of *mental illness*. Indeed, insanity is a legal rather than a psychiatric concept. By itself, the presence of a mental disorder is insufficient justification, from a legal standpoint, to exonerate a defendant from responsibility for committing an illegal act.

Although the elements of proof vary by JURISDICTION, for the insanity defense to persuade the court, the defense must prove that the defendant committed the crime explicitly because of a mental disorder. Defendants who invoke the insanity defense are required to undergo a thorough psychiatric history and mental status examination. The EVIDENCE must demonstrate that the mental disorder interfered with the defendant's ability to distinguish right from wrong at the time the offense was committed; that is, the defendant lacked the mental capacity to realize that a wrongful act was committed or to appreciate that the act was wrongful.

Several states allow insanity defendants to argue that they understood their behavior was criminal but were unable to control it, which is called the irresistible impulse defense. This defense permits JUDGES and JURIES to decide that defendants are not "criminally responsible" for their actions even though their acts would be a crime under different circumstances; that is, in the absence of a mental disorder that compelled them to commit the act. Diminished responsibility (or diminished capacity) can be employed as a mitigating factor in cases other than those that proffer the insanity defense. For example, jurisdictions may accept inebriation or drug intoxication as a mitigating factor, whereas such conditions alone are insufficient as an insanity defense. A defendant proffering the insanity defense is said to be pleading not guilty by reason of insanity (NGRI).

A trial in which the insanity defense is invoked generally involves the testimony of forensic psychiatrists or psychologists who present opinions on the defendant's state of mind at the time of the offense. However, mental health practitioners are restrained from offering direct opinions on the issue of whether a defendant is actually insane or not, which is known as the "ultimate issue" prohibition. If a defendant is willing to plead guilty or is proven guilty in a trial, numerous jurisdictions have an alternative to the NGRI defense, which is referred to as either a guilty but mentally ill (GBMI) or a guilty but insane (GBI) verdict.

The insanity defense has prompted a vociferous debate among lawyers, clinicians, and the public. Most people believe that defendants abuse the insanity defense as a legal loophole to escape serious criminal charges. They also believe that defendants use the insanity defense more often than they actually do, probably because insanity defense cases often are accorded a high profile in the media. In fact, the insanity plea is used in less than 1 percent of all criminal cases and is successful in only 26 percent of those; 90 percent of insanity defendants have been diagnosed previously with a serious mental illness.

Rarely do people ACQUITTED under an insanity defense walk free. In almost all cases, a verdict of NGRI leads judges to commit defendants to lengthy terms in treatment centers until mental health officials determine that the defendants pose no further danger to others. For some, that could be tantamount to a life sentence. A successful NGRI defense typically results in an indeterminate commitment to a psychiatric facility.

The court can apply a number of different legal rules in making a determination of insanity. The oldest, the M'Naghten Rule, states that a person may be "insane" if ". . . at the time of the committing of the act, the party accused was laboring under such a defect of reason, arising from a disease of the mind, as not to know the nature and quality of the act he was doing, or, if he did know it, that he did not know what he was doing was wrong."

During the mid-20th century, the M'Naghten Rule was gradually replaced in most jurisdictions by other tests, such as the American Law Institute's MODEL PENAL CODE, which states that people suffering from a mental disease or defect are not responsible for their actions if they lack the substantial capacity to appreciate the criminality of their conduct or to conform their conduct to the law, which includes both the cognitive and volitional aspects of insanity. Hence, proof of insanity requires that defendants suffer from a mental defect such that they either lacked substantial capacity to appreciate the criminality of their actions or to conform their conduct to the requirements of the law.

The Durham Rule or "product test" was prescribed by the United States Court of Appeals for the District of Columbia Circuit in 1954 and states that ". . . an accused is not criminally responsible if his unlawful act was the product of mental disease or defect." Since the 1970s, jurisdictions have generally rejected this argument because it is somewhat ambiguous, overly emphasizes "mental disease or defect," and places undue weight on the testimony of psychiatrists and psychologists.

The Brawner Rule set aside Durham by arguing that the ruling's requirement that a crime must be a "product of mental disease or defect" placed the question of guilt on expert witnesses and diminished the jury's role in determining guilt. Under Brawner, juries are allowed to decide the "insanity question" as they see fit. Basing its ruling on the American Law Institute's Model Penal Code, the court declared that for a defendant to be found NGRI, the defendant must, "lack substantial capacity to appreciate that his conduct is wrongful or lack substantial capacity to conform his conduct to the law." This case was decided by the United States Court of Appeals for the District of Columbia Circuit and not the United States Supreme Court. Hence, the case did not establish a national precedent, nor was it based on constitutional arguments. It was superseded by Congress with the Insanity Defense Reform Act of 1984.

Widespread public outcry ensued after John Hinckley, Jr.'s successful use of the insanity defense in his trial for the attempted assassination of President Ronald Reagan. The Insanity Defense Reform Act, enacted by Congress in 1984 in response to the verdict in the Hinckley trial and codified at 18 U.S.C. § 17, states that a person accused of a crime can be judged NGRI if "the defendant, as a result of a severe mental disease or defect, was unable to appreciate the nature and quality or the wrongfulness of his acts."

After the Hinckley ruling, Congress and several states passed laws designed to toughen standards in insanity defenses. Instead of requiring PROSECUTORS to prove a defendant's sanity, DEFENSE ATTORNEYS now carry the burden of persuading a judge or jury that their clients are insane. The Insanity Defense Reform Act mirrors the M'Naughten Rule, except that it requires that the defendant suffer from a severe mental defect, and it places the burden on the defendant to prove this by offering clear and convincing evidence (higher than the PREPONDERANCE OF EVIDENCE standard required of the defendant by most states following the M'Naughten Rule).

Any defendant can invoke the insanity defense. Lee Boyd Malvo and Andrea Yates are examples of high-profile, highly dramatic, and media-worthy cases that have used the insanity defense. Lorena Bobbitt argued that she was temporarily insane when she severed her husband's penis with a kitchen knife. A Virginia jury agreed, and she was released after three months of psychiatric evaluation. A jury rejected Jack Ruby's claim of insanity and sent him to prison for shooting Lee Harvey Oswald, the assassin of President JOHN F. KENNEDY. Almost 20 years later and also in front of television cameras, John Hinckley, Jr. shot President Ronald Reagan but was declared NGRI and sent to a mental institution.

The court rejected the insanity defense of David Berkowitz, New York's SON OF SAM murderer, who claimed that he was commanded to kill by a demon that possessed his neighbor's dog. A Pennsylvania jury found millionaire John DuPont GBMI in the MURDER of a wrestling coach. Lawyers for the unabomber Theodore Kaczynski argued that he was insane, but Kaczynski resisted such a defense and pleaded guilty. Jeffrey Dahmer dismembered and ate his victims, but a jury failed to find him insane.

For more information

Ahn-Redding, Heather. *The Insanity Defense the World Over.* Lanham, Md.: Lexington, 2008.

Fersch, Ellsworth L. *Thinking about the Insanity Defense: Answers to Frequently Asked Questions with Case Examples.* Lincoln, Nebr.: iUniverse, 2005.

Arthur J. Lurigio
Loyola University Chicago

insider trading Inside trading is a securities law violation making it illegal for individuals to trade stock on private information about their companies before that information is made available to the public. Insider trading is illegal because of concerns that it allows for stock manipulation, gives unfair advantages to some, and undermines public confidence in the securities market.

The Securities and Exchange Act of 1934 began the development of proscribing insider trading. Prior to that time, federal regulation was nonexistent or covered by common law theories of FRAUD or left to state security laws. At the time the act was adopted it did not specifically define insider trading, which is now defined as trading in the stock market by persons who have material information unavailable to the trading public. In other words, it is illegal in the United States for individuals to buy or sell stock if they have information affecting the stock's price that the general public does not yet have. The use of such knowledge hinders the fair and orderly concept of markets by making insider trading profits the fruits of fraudulent transactions. If allowed to occur, the integrity of free markets would be damaged if not soon destroyed. The Securities and Exchange Act is in effect a consumer protection act because companies must file information in registration statements that reveal the good, the bad, and the ugly about every material fact that can affect the values of a company's securities.

Insider trading during the great bull market of the 1920s provoked the Securities and Exchange Act of 1934. Insider trading market manipulations such as spread false rumors or investment pools that colluded to bidding up the price of a stock to draw in naïve investors to buy at the artificially higher prices. Section 10 of the act makes it a crime to use such practices to deceive outsiders.

At first, the act focused on traders who owned 10 percent or more of the stock of a company. A report to the SECURITIES AND EXCHANGE COMMISSION (SEC) was and still is required at the end of any month in which shares are sold or more shares are purchased. Officers and later others are forbidden from using information that affects the price of shares for six months prior to its publication. In subsequent development of the law, it has become unlawful for traders to provide tips or for others to use the tips.

In the 1980s, there was a spate of insider trading cases. Starting in August 1984, the SEC authorized agents to seek not only the return of profits from insider traders but penalties amounting to three times their profits from their insider trading. However, it is permissible for insiders to trade if their trades are reported (SEC Forms 3, 4, 5 and 144) along with information about their holdings and other pertinent information.

For more information

Macey, Jonathan R. *Insider Trading: Economics, Politics, Policy.* Washington, D.C.: American Enterprise Institute for Public Policy Research, 1991.

Wang, William K. S., and Marc I. Steinberg. *Insider Trading.* New York: Oxford University Press, 2010.

Andrew J. Waskey
Dalton State College

intent Intent refers to a purpose, aim, or determination to act; a mental attitude to use particular means to effect a certain result.

The term implies a willing consent to engage in a course of action—a free will to do the act. Of course, it is often difficult or impossible to prove a person's subjective intent. For this reason, courts generally hold that intent may be proved by logical deductions made from the person's acts, declarations, and the surrounding circumstances. As one court has explained, a person intends "whatever he voluntarily does."

The civil law of TORTS recognizes both intentional and unintentional wrongs. Intentional torts include such actions as ASSAULT, BATTERY, and false imprisonment. To be liable for an intentional tort, the defendant need not intend to actually injure the plaintiff, so long as the defendant intends to do the act that causes the injury. For example, if I shove another person in jest but without his consent, I have committed a battery. If the other person falls and sustains an injury as a result of my shove, I will be liable for his injury even though I did not intend to inflict any harm. The law presumes that a person intends the natural and probable consequences of his acts. In contrast, if I shove another person because I accidentally trip while walking down the sidewalk, I have not committed a battery. I am not liable for the injuries sustained by the other person (assuming I was not negligent) because I had no intent to do the act. An accident is an act done without any purpose or state of mind to effect the result.

Criminal law is also concerned with the mental state of the defendant. Generally, a person commits a crime only if the person engages in prohibited conduct *and* possesses a culpable mental state, or "MENS REA." In criminal law, the term *intent* is an elastic one that describes a variety of these culpable mental states, such as purpose, knowledge, recklessness, or negligence.

The mere commission of an act, even though harmful, is generally insufficient to warrant criminal punishment in the absence of an intent to do the act. For this reason, a person incapable of forming the requisite intent due to mental incapacitation generally may not be found guilty of the offense. However, a person need not intend to commit a "crime," or even be aware that his conduct is illegal, to be guilty of committing an offense. It is normally sufficient if the state proves that the defendant engaged in a prohibited act with the intent to do so.

Some crimes require more than just a general intent to commit the offense. For example, the crime of BURGLARY is defined under many statutes as the breaking or entering into a building *with the intent to commit a FELONY inside.* For this offense, the state must prove not only that the defendant intended to enter the building, but also that the defendant specifically intended to commit a felony once inside the building. As with tort law, this intent may be proved by circumstantial EVIDENCE.

Intent should be distinguished from ATTEMPT. Intent is the mental state of planning to achieve a goal, while attempt is an actual effort to achieve the goal. Thus, an attempt to commit a crime requires some action on the part of the defendant. Intent should also be distinguished from MOTIVE. Motive refers to the underlying reasons that explain a person's act, rather than the will to do the act itself. Proof of motive is generally unnecessary in a criminal case.

For more information

Kadish, Sanford H., et al. *Words and Phrases,* "Intent," vol. 22, Perm. ed. St. Paul, Minn.: West, 1994.

Kadish, Sanford H., and Stephen J. Scholhofer. *Criminal Law and Its Processes.* 4th ed. New York: Aspen, 1983.

Nathanael Causey
United States Military Academy, West Point, New York

international law International law is the compilation of rules and principles that nation-states regard as binding upon them and that they are expected to observe in their relations with one another. International law is that whole body of law impacting the international community.

Modern international law stems from three main sources: treaties and international conventions, customs and customary usage, and the generally accepted principles of law and EQUITY. Additionally, judicial decisions made by international and domestic courts are important to the overall lawmaking process of the international community. Furthermore, United Nations resolutions also impact the growing body of what is known as customary international law.

International law today is based on the concept of sovereign states. Thus, it is within each country's discretion whether they wish to participate in the negotiation of, or to sign or ratify, any international treaty. Similarly, each member state of an international agency, such as the United Nations, is free to ratify any convention adopted by that agency.

Treaties and conventions were, at first, restricted in application only to those countries that ratified them. Nevertheless, regulations and procedures contained in treaties and conventions have frequently developed from "particular" international law into general customary usage; that is, they have come to be considered binding on even those countries that did not sign or ratify them. Customs otherwise may become part of international law because of continued acceptance by the great majority of nations, even if they are not part of a written treaty instrument.

International conferences have played an important role in the development of international law since the 19th century. For example, the Congress of Vienna reorganized Europe after the defeat of Napoleon and contributed greatly to the body of international law by establishing rules for diplomatic procedure and the treatment of diplomatic representatives.

The League of Nations was established at the end of World War I by the covenant signed in 1919 as part of the Treaty of Versailles. As a result of this covenant, the Permanent Court of International Justice was established in 1921. The League of Nations was created as a permanent organization of independent nations for the purpose of maintaining peace and preventing war. However, membership in the League of Nations was not universal, and unstable relations led to World War II. Nonetheless, in 1945, after the end of the war, the United Nations Charter created a new organization with a highly structured system for solving disputes among countries and for further development of international law.

Since World War II, international law has become increasingly concerned with issues ranging from trade, finance, and business to the protection of human rights, the global environment and ecosystems, and indigenous peoples issues. Continually emerging global issues call for new international responses. Examples include the conventions against acts of TERRORISM and the distribution of drugs. With the development of modern multilateral treaties, customary international law maintains a central role in the legal system of the international community.

For more information

International Law and Its Relation to United States Law, Restatement of Foreign Relations Law of the United States, 3rd. ed., section 101. Washington, D.C.: American Law Institute, 1986.

Kristin L. Stewart
Attorney

Internet and World Wide Web The Internet and World Wide Web are a decentralized transnational telecommunications medium and their development and use raise important legal issues, including taxation, free speech, and copyright law.

Originating in a Department of Defense network but largely under civilian control today, the Internet enables wired and wireless e-mail, file transfers, the graphical World Wide Web, chat, telephony, fax, video, and cybercash. The Internet is transforming law and governance.

Spurred by an expanding Internet, the Telecommunications Act of 1996 overhauled federal telecommunications law for the first time since the 1930s. The act's expansive goal is to let anyone enter any communications business and to compete in any market against any firm. This statute has left open or created several legal issues.

For example, if e-commerce remains a tax-free haven, will state and municipal governments feel forced to hike non-sales taxes since states can't force out-of-state businesses to serve as their tax collectors? To answer these questions, an Advisory Commission on Electronic Commerce was set up in 1998 to examine the issue of e-commerce taxation and to make recommendations to Congress on tough questions like price-setting cases where government assistance to platform products and encouragement of monopolies is hurtful to peripherals.

If "trespass theory" prevails in the short run, restricted information access and speech may inhibit general portals, search engines, and other aggregators of information. The Patent and Trademark Office issued 399 Internet-related business method patents in 1999, more than doubling the previous year's total. However, uploading and downloading of compact discs can become LARCENY, as charged in *Napster v. Recording Industry Association of America* (2000). Under *U.S. Code* Title 47, Sec. 227(b) (1) (C), broadcasting unsolicited commercial e-mail ("spamming") can be illegal.

Under the "fair use" portions of the 1976 Copyright Act, unauthorized use of "crucial" excerpts of a work invites remedial litigation. By exposing an author's work to all of cyberspace, the Internet raises the stakes, giving copyright holders greater incentive to sue college teachers for infringement.

Computer and Internet crime of all types doubled between 1998 and 2000. During the same period, the SECURITIES AND EXCHANGE COMMISSION and FEDERAL BUREAU OF INVESTIGATION utilized the Internet to crack an INSIDER TRADING ring.

But the rise of the Web and Internet as a new communications tool has raised new questions about CENSORSHIP. Specifically, the concern is access or exposure of minors to sexually suggestive materials. The 1996 Communications Decency Act (CDA) sought to regulate the distribution of pornographic materials, but it was declared unconstitutional in *Reno v. ACLU*, 521 U.S. 844 (1997). Congress then passed the Child Online Protection Act, but again in *Ashcroft v. American Civil Liberties Union*, 542 U.S. 656 (2004), the Court again ruled that efforts to regulate nonobscene but sexually explicit material on the Web violated the First Amendment.

Finally, in December 2010, the Federal Communications Commission issued rules promoting "net neutrality." These rules were meant to ensure that cable and DSL internet service providers do not deny access to some content providers. The rules would not apply to wireless Internet service providers. The rule was defended as a way to maintain open access for all content on the Web. However, many criticized the rule as either inadequate to achieve net neutrality or as too much regulation of the Web.

Will citizen resistance to state intrusiveness survive antiterrorism campaigns? Will FOURTH AMENDMENT privacy rights erode in the face of supervisors reading employees' e-mail, "Carnivore" FBI surveillance, anti-encryption statutes, and online entrapment? Long-term effects of Internet socialization on civic life also remain uncertain.

For more information

The Berkman Center for Internet and Society, Harvard Law School. The Filter. Available online. URL: http://cyber.law.harvard.edu/.

Lemley, Mark A., Peter S. Mennel, Robert P. Merges and Pamela Samuelson. *Software and Internet Law.* New York: Aspen, 2000.

Vincent Kelly Pollard
University of Hawaii at Manoa

Interstate Commerce Commission The Interstate Commerce Commission or ICC was established in 1887 as the first independent regulatory agency in response to demands to create order in the railroad industry. From then until its demise in 1995, the ICC had authority over all commercial traffic that crossed state boundaries, whether by rail, truck, bus, or boat. The ICC's duties began to diminish in the late 1970s and 1980s during a period of intense deregulation under the Carter and Reagan administrations. It was finally abolished by Congress in 1995, and its few remaining functions were transferred to other agencies.

The ICC was historic as the first independent regulatory agency. Like its successors, such as the Federal Communication Commission (FCC), Federal Trade Commission (FTC), the SECURITIES AND EXCHANGE COMMISSION (SEC), and the Occupational Safety and Health Administration (OSHA), the ICC was not subordinate to a cabinet agency and was largely autonomous even of the president. These agencies were created with the idea of being apolitical, professional regulators of key sectors of the national economy. Independent regulatory agencies are in a sense minigovernments, having some measure of legislative (rule-making), executive (enforcement and administration), and judicial (hearings and appeals) authority over the narrow sectors under their purview.

The ICC was created in response to a chaotic environment in interstate commerce brought on by rapid westward expansion and the proliferation of railroads. While regulation of interstate commerce had always been a federal function, enshrined in Article I, section 8, clause 5 of the CONSTITUTION, it was a relatively minor power in an era dominated by subsistence agriculture and before the creation of a national transportation infrastructure. The issue came to a head in 1886, when the Supreme Court ruled in *Wabash, St. Louis and Pacific Railroad v. Illinois* that the states had virtually no authority to regulate interstate commerce, declaring it an exclusive power of the central government. The ICC was created the very next year after demand by both industry and consumer groups, who all argued that a national economy required some standardization and central management. This included some rather fundamental regulations, such as setting a uniform gauge for railroad tracks and allowing for uniform pricing for commercial shipping by limiting price gouging.

The power of the ICC expanded rapidly in the first decades of the 20th century. The agency aggressively managed the railroad industry, forcing the consolidation of several smaller networks into a few large ones and even gaining the authority to regulate prices. By the middle of the century, its power had grown to include all types of surface transportation and most shipping. Eventually, however, the emergence of cheap air travel and the completion of the interstate highway system proved too much for the now-antiquated rail system to compete with. Efforts to reduce rates and introduce greater efficiencies came too late. The portion of the economy under the regulation of the ICC fell precipitously during the 1950s and 1960s and diminished even further with the deregulatory fever that emerged in the 1970s. By the time Congress passed the ICC Sunset Act in 1995, the commission had shrunk to a fraction of its former size. Its few remaining functions were transferred to other agencies, including the new Surface Transportation Board in the Department of Transportation created by that legislation.

For more information

Hoogenboom, Ari, and Olive Hoogenboom. *A History of the ICC: From Panacea to Palliative.* New York: W. W. Norton, 1976.

Interstate Commerce Act (24 Stat. 379), February 4, 1887.

James H. Joyner, Jr.
Troy State University

interstate inmate transfers Interstate inmate transfer refers to the American penal practice of transferring local, state, and federal prison and jail inmates from one state to another.

For more than 30 years, federal and state-level prison administrators have used interstate inmate transfers (IITs) to manage their institutions. Currently, IITs are used by 46 states and are implemented by correctional managers situated at multiple levels within state correctional bureaucracies. Jurisdictionally speaking, these transfers are facilitated (and constrained) by correctional policy and unique interstate agreements, by state and federal law, by the territorial boundaries of the United States, and by the availability of receptive correctional facilities. IITs may also be used to transfer inmates to (or from) local jails or from jails or state-level correctional institutions to other state and federal correctional facilities.

IITs are, in many ways, a familiar policy manifestation closely associated with traditional notions of federalism, interstate compact law, and the accepted notion that states may (and should) form agreements with one another in order to solve problems. Although it is currently impossible to document every variation on the three main types of interstate corrections compacts and bed rental agreements (and their variable relationship to one another), it is informative to document and describe the three main types of interstate corrections compacts (ICCs).

One interstate corrections compact is national in scope, and two are regional arrangements between geographically proximal states, and all of them specify a general, administrative intent. The National Interstate Compact for Corrections "Provides for uniform procedures and treatment of prisoners who are transferred from the supervisory agency of one state to that of another." The intent of this compact, as stated, is to "provide for the mutual development and execution of programs of cooperation for the confinement, treatment, and rehabilitation of offenders with the most economical use of human and material resources." As of July 1, 2005, 40 states were party to this compact.

The Western Corrections Compact has 11 signatory states and "provides for the joint use of corrections facilities in the West." As is the case with the national agreement, the intent is the same. Party states are: Alaska, Arizona, California, Colorado, Hawaii, Idaho, Montana, Nebraska, Nevada, New Mexico, Oregon, Utah, Washington, and Wyoming.

The New England Corrections Compact provides for cooperation in the confinement, treatment, and rehabilitation of offenders. Six northeastern states have adopted this compact: Maine, New Hampshire, Vermont, Massachusetts, Connecticut, and Rhode Island.

All of these agreements also specify constraints on behavior and include a number of variations within each state-to-state agreement.

Interstate inmate transfers are an extraordinarily complex phenomenon, and the use of IITs, though widespread, has become somewhat controversial in recent years. However, one can get some sense of the IIT phenomenon through previous legal rulings, in particular, the U.S. Supreme Court case *Olim v. Wakinekona,* 461 U.S. 238 (1983), in which the case itself, and especially THURGOOD MARSHALL's dissent, highlight some of the legal problems and controversies associated with long-distance inmate transfers.

The debates surrounding the use of IITs typically focus on the administrative intent of IITs and manifest as normative assessments derived from critical theory, personal opinion, and/or media portrayals of anomalous incidents. Although the debates over IITs may differ in a variety of ways, two positions emerge most often.

Supporters of IITs—typically correctional managers themselves—argue that in addition to serving the management needs of correctional institutions, IITs may also serve to help inmates reenter society, remain physically safe while incarcerated, remain close to family and friends, and have access to appropriate correctional programming and treatment. On the other hand, critics of IITs argue that they are much more than a correctional management tool. Rather, IITs are evidence of an informally emerging new penology in American corrections that—due to the increasingly problematic conditions of confinement encountered by correctional managers (e.g., overcrowding)—emphasize a shift in focus away from what is good for the individual inmate to what is good for managing the correctional system as a whole.

Based upon an understanding of the relevant literature regarding correctional management, the legal intricacies and problems surrounding interstate inmate transfers, and the multiple theoretical problems inherent in a "new penology" approach, it seems apparent that neither side in this debate is completely accurate. Rather, it is clear that there are significant problems *and* benefits associated with the use of interstate inmate transfers. However, it is only through the implementation of additional much-needed research that interstate inmate transfers can be more fully understood and, thus, be used more effectively.

For more information

Feeley, M. M., and J. Simon. "The New Penology: Notes on the Emerging Strategy of Corrections and Its Implications," *Criminology* 30, no. 4 (1992) 449–474.

Shichor, D., and D. K. Sechrest. "Privatization and Flexibility: Legal and Practical Aspects of Interjurisdictional Transfer of Prisoners," *Prison Journal* 82, no. 3 (2002): 386–407.

Talvi, S. J. A. "No Room in Prison? Ship 'em Off," *Prison Legal News* (September 2006): 28–29.

United States Department of Justice, National Institute of Corrections, February 2006. Biasca, D. "Interstate transfer of prison inmates in the United States." In *Special Issues in Corrections,* edited by C. Clem. Washington, D.C. Available online. URL: http://www.nicic.org/library/021242.

Robert Swan
University of South Dakota

inventory searches An inventory search is a WARRANTLESS SEARCH of a person's personal effects conducted when a person is booked into jail. Inventory searches also include AUTOMOBILE SEARCHES of impounded vehicles for the purpose of compiling a list of all of its contents.

The FOURTH AMENDMENT of the UNITED STATES CONSTITUTION protects citizens from unreasonable SEARCHES AND SEIZURES. Under most circumstances, the reasonableness requirement of the Fourth Amendment requires searches to be conducted based on PROBABLE CAUSE and with the authority of a warrant. The U.S. Supreme Court held in *Illinois v. Lafayette,* 462 U.S. 640 (1983), that inventory searches, however, are reasonable and constitutionally permissible in the absence of the probable cause and search warrant requirements. The rationale for the inventory search exception differs slightly in the contexts of personal effects and automobiles.

In order for the police to conduct a warrantless inventory search of a person's effects, that person must have been subject to a valid ARREST, be facing prospective incarceration, and the DISCRETION of the searching police officer must be properly channeled through standard operating procedures. In justifying the warrantless search of the personal items of someone being booked into jail, the Supreme Court balanced the interests of the police against the privacy interest of the individual.

When someone is being placed in jail, the police have an interest in searching and creating an inventory of personal items to prevent weapons and drugs from being introduced into the jail population. Additionally, creating an inventory of the items prevents things from being lost or stolen, may help identify the person, and protects the police from any false claims that a person may make about what they had, or did not have, in their possession. The Supreme Court has held that these interests outweigh the privacy interest individuals have in their personal effects. While the privacy interest may be high in a vacuum, once persons have been placed under a valid arrest, much of their privacy interest is extinguished.

For a warrantless inventory search at a police station to be valid, standard operating procedures of the police department must be in place, and they must be followed. While no specific procedures detailing the process have to be in writing, there must be some established practices that prevent rogue officers from conducting general crime fighting searches under the guise of the justifications for inventory searches.

Following a valid arrest, the police may at times choose to impound the vehicle the person under arrest was driving. It is constitutionally permissible for police to conduct a warrantless inventory search of a lawfully impounded vehicle when standard operating procedures limiting the discretion of the searching officer are followed. When the vehicle is taken to a secure facility, many of the jailhouse justifications for inventory searches of personal effects are not present. Nonetheless, the Supreme Court held in *Colorado v. Bertine,* 479 U.S. 367 (1987), that the interest of the police in making a complete list of all of the items of an impounded vehicle still outweighs the privacy interest of the individual.

For more information

Buffaloe, J. Y. "Special Needs and the Fourth Amendment: An Exception Poised to Swallow the Warrant Preference Rule," *Harvard Civil Rights-Civil Liberties Law Review* 32 (1997): 529.

Eric McAdamis and Ryan C. Black
Michigan State University

Iran-contra affair The Iran-contra affair refers to a 1987 political and constitutional scandal involving the illegal sale of military arms to Iran by members of President Reagan's administration in order to finance military aid to the Nicaraguan Contras.

The Iran-contra affair, falling between the Watergate "crisis" of 1974–75 and the Clinton IMPEACHMENT of 1998, provides a fascinating example of postmodern constitutional politics. Despite a lengthy congressional inquiry and Herculean efforts by a special PROSECUTOR, Iran-contra seems destined to fade, as a distinct event with consequences of its own, from both popular memory and constitutional history. Any attempt to narrate definitively Iran-contra or to assess its constitutional significance initially founders on the shadowy nature of the events and the contested meanings that can be attributed to them.

Most accounts begin in 1985 with a secret arrangement by certain members of President Ronald Reagan's National Security Council (NSC)—particularly Robert McFarlane, John Poindexter, and Lieutenant Colonel Oliver North—to sell U.S. military arms to Iran. The hope, it appears, was that these sales might help, albeit indirectly, to secure the release of American hostages being held by various groups throughout the Middle East. Here, the NSC apparently worked with a vaguely defined collection of international arms merchants and with officials from several Middle East nations, including Israel. Later, Colonel North diverted money from the Iranian sales to the right-wing forces, the *contras,* who were working with the Reagan administration to overthrow the left-leaning Sandinista government in Nicaragua. This global effort, which clearly clashed with the professed aims of the Reagan administration and seemingly violated U.S. law, apparently was known to the president, Vice President George Bush, and other high-ranking American officials. Opponents of the administration and much of the media dubbed the affair "Iran-Contragate," likening it to the Watergate episode of the Nixon years. This analogy, however, never effectively signified this Reagan-era controversy that increasingly seemed more of a made-for-TV spectacle than a constitutional crisis.

Iran-contra became public knowledge in a curious, circuitous, and ultimately incomplete manner. During the fall of 1986, an obscure periodical in Lebanon exposed the Iranian part of the plan. The Reagan administration, after a brief delay, confirmed the Lebanese paper's story and also announced the hitherto secret relationship of the Iranian deal to the effort to aid the contras. Congress immediately launched an inquiry, and a special prosecutor, Lawrence Walsh, eventually began a criminal investigation. Congressional hearings, which began during the spring of 1987, featured the televised testimony of Colonel North. Capitalizing on his military bearing, his quick wit, and his timely destruction of relevant documents, "Ollie" North decisively won his showdown with the committee and emerged as an antibureaucratic hero in the mold of John Wayne and Clint Eastwood's "Dirty Harry." Unable to untangle labyrinthine machinations of North and his cohorts, the congressional inquiry failed to produce an authoritative chronicle of events and, consequently, to establish convincingly that Iran-contra involved constitutional misdeeds on the scale of Watergate. In contrast to the Watergate hearings, for example, there was no John Dean to answer questions such as "what did the president know, and when did he know it?"

Lawrence Walsh's lengthy investigation, as he himself bitterly conceded, could not break through the conflicting, vague, and perhaps even PERJURED testimony offered by participants such as North. President Reagan acknowledged that "mistakes had been made," but both he and Bush successfully maintained that they could not recall having known about the Iran-contra arrangement. Walsh did secure convictions against Poindexter and North, but appellate courts overturned these, in part because of IMMUNITY provisions that had covered their congressional testimony. Although several others, including McFarlane and Eliot Abrams, were convicted of lying to Congress, President George H. W. Bush PARDONED them, and several others who were awaiting trial, before leaving office in 1993.

A decade later, the Iran-contra episode seemed to blend into a series of trials and hearings—such as the Supreme Court confirmation hearings of ROBERT BORK and CLARENCE THOMAS, the O. J. SIMPSON trial, the RODNEY KING case, the Clinton impeachment, and the Elián González dispute—that lay somewhere on the border between constitutional law, partisan politics, popular drama, and postmodern spectacle.

For more information

Lynch, Michael, and David Bogen. *The Spectacle of History: Speech, Text, and Memory at the Iran-Contra Hearings.* Durham, N.C.: Duke University Press, 1996.

Walsh, Lawrence E. *Firewall: The Iran-Contra Conspiracy and Cover-Up.* New York: W. W. Norton, 1998.

Norman L. Rosenberg
Macalester College